The Study of Spirituality

The Study of Spirituality

Edited by
Cheslyn Jones, Geoffrey Wainwright
Edward Yarnold, SJ

First published in Great Britain 1986
SPCK
Holy Trinity Church
Marylebone Road
London NW1 4DU

Acknowledgement
The extract by Owen Chadwick from *Christian Spirituality: essays in honour of Gordon Rupp*, ed. P. Brookes, is reprinted by permission of SCM Press.

British Library Cataloguing in Publication Data

The Study of spirituality.
1. Spirituality
I. Jones, C.   II. Wainwright, G.
III. Yarnold, Edward
248.4   BV4501.2

ISBN 0-281-04150-4 (paper)
ISBN 0-281-04241-2 (cased)

Printed in Great Britain by the
University Press, Cambridge

CONTENTS

ILLUSTRATIONS

As in *The Study of Liturgy* we have been encouraged to provide illustrations. But here the two subjects are not comparable, for liturgy lends itself to illustration, while the real core of spirituality is inherently invisible. So one tends to be forced back on reproductions of faces and places, which we have done to a limited extent. But we must remember that the spiritual writers themselves have not been able to get very far without the use of imagery, usually visual imagery; this is often apparent in their titles, such as *The Cloud of Unknowing* or *The Living Flame of Love*. But some have gone further: St Hildegard of Bingen not only caused her revelations to be written down, but also herself directed their illustration (see plate 4); Nicholas of Cusa sent Roger van der Weyden's 'omnivoyant' self-portrait to the monks of Tegernsee with the gift of his *De Visione Dei* (see plate 8); St John of the Cross roughed out sketches of Mount Carmel and its ascent (see plate 10).

Religious art, however much or little it may be depictive or descriptive, must also be *suggestive*, hinting at the invisible dimension, as we hope our cover illustration demonstrates. Rouault's *Christ and the High Priest* shows Christ in severe tranquillity, despite the High Priest's accusations; between the two there is a coloured space, which at first sight seems meaningless, but which to sensitive eyes gradually reveals a shadow or outline or hint of a Hand and a Flame, suggestive of the Father and the Spirit with whom the accused is in perpetual and all-sufficing communion.

We are grateful to those of our contributors who have suggested, or have in other ways helped us with these illustrations, as well as to the Revd Urs von Arx, Hellikon, Switzerland, and P. Werner Rörig, OMI, Mainz.

PLATES

2 The Ladder to Heaven icon, St Catharine's Monastery, Sinai.

By courtesy of Ronald Sheridan's Photo-Library

3 A hesychast at prayer. Miniature from a MS of John Climacus, *The Ladder of Divine Ascent*, 12th century, Vatican Gr 1754. Compare the description of Elijah at prayer in 1 Kings 18.42.

By courtesy of St Vladimir's Seminary Press

4 St Hildegard of Bingen (see p. 290) not only wrote *Scivias* but also supervised its illustration in colour. Here is the first illustration (attached to the Preface) depicting the saint in her cell in the course of inspiration (the five-pronged flame of the Holy Spirit); she makes notes on a wax tablet, while the monk Volmar eavesdrops to facilitate his task of making a full transcription on parchment. The illustrated volume was completed about 1165; it was in the State Library at Wiesbaden until 1945, when it disappeared.

By courtesy of Otto Muller Verlag, Salzburg

5 The ten-stringed psaltery, according to the vision of Joachim of Fiore (see p. 292) and his interpretation of it. This diagram, which is from Oxford MS CCC 254a, is judged by its style to be from a monastery in south Italy, quite possibly Joachim's own, perhaps under his direction.

With acknowledgement to the President and Fellows of Corpus Christi College, Oxford

6 St Francis by Cimabue (fl.1272), in the lower church of St Francis of Assisi, is one of the earliest portraits of the saint; it is faithful to the description of him by Thomas of Celano in 1229, and brings out his poverty and simplicity.

By courtesy of the Mansell Collection

7 Dante, as portrayed by Nardo di Cione (fl.1380), among the blessed, in a fresco depicting the universal judgement in the Strozzi Capella in the church of S. Maria Novella, Florence.

Photograph by Alinari, Florence

8 Detail from the tapestry based on a picture by Roger van der Weyden (ob.1464) now lost, which once hung in the Hôtel de Ville, Brussels, where it was seen by Nicholas of Cusa. The artist has included in the scene a portrait of himself with an omnivoyant eye. It was a copy of this picture that Nicholas sent to the monks of Tegernsee with his gift of *De Visione Dei* (see p. 327).

By courtesy of Historisches Museum, Bern

9 Part of one of the many surviving letters of St Teresa of Avila (including her signature); E. Allison Peers gives a total of 458 letters in his 2-volume edition and translation of *The Letters of Saint Teresa of Jesus* (London, Burns, Oates & Washbourne, 1951). This one is translated as no. 308 (II, pp.723–4), sent to M. María de Jesús from Malagon in February 1580. Though preserved in the Teresan Museum in Rome, it is the property of the Carmelite Convent in Darlington; we are grateful to the Sisters for this reproduction.

10 The original sketch of *Mount Carmel*. St John of the Cross used to draw plans of the way to perfection, as taught in *The Ascent of Mount Carmel* and other works, first in a rudimentary form for the nuns of Beas ('for each of our breviaries'), later more elaborately and comprehensively, as here reproduced. This is not the saint's autograph, but a certified exact copy, now MS 6,296 in the Biblioteca Nacional, Madrid (see E. Allison Peers, *The Complete Works of St John of the Cross* (London, Burns, Oates & Washbourne, 1943[1], 1953[2]) I, pp. xxxii–iii).

For the simplified anglicized version printed in the text (p. 367) we are indebted to E. W. Trueman Dicken and the Sisters of the Love of God, Fairacres, Oxford.

11 These illustrations are taken from *La Vie Symbolique du Bienheureux François de Sales, comprise sous le voile de 52 Emblèmes*, by A. Gambart (Paris 1664), a chaplain at a Paris Visitation convent. Religious emblems were starting points for prayer and intended to affect mind and heart at a deeper level, which was also the aim of François' imagery in his writings. These symbolical pictures were summarized in a terse, memorable motto in Latin and often also, as here, in a rhymed caption in the vernacular. The ship steered by a star across stormy waters and between towering rocks towards the church symbolizes François' capacity to guide souls, discreetly holding a middle course; while the sunflower, *tourne-sol* in French, illustrates perfect conformity to God's will.

12 The illustration is of the title page of the *New Whole Duty of Man* (1743), the official successor to the original (1657). The books are quite different, while covering much the same ground. Yet they share the Caroline anti-Puritan outlook. Here the giver of the law is depicted as in opposition to Christ the giver of grace: has Moses got horns?

13/14 Two faces of Methodism:
(a) The 'Holy Club', from a painting by Marshall Claxton (1813–81).
By courtesy of A. R. George, Bristol; photograph by C. Momber

(b) 'Primitive Methodists', by H. Y. Titcomb (1858–1930).

By courtesy of the Dudley Art Gallery

15 This drawing by Gerda Ploug Sarp (1881–1968) portrays Søren Kier-kegaard standing at his wooden desk in front of the picture of his dreaded father, Michael, who in the same study had drilled Søren in the classics. Søren Kierkegaard used to write standing up at the same desk.

By courtesy of the Royal Library, Copenhagen

16/17 Paul Couturier (1881–1953), from a photograph in the House of SS Gregory and Macrina, Oxford. His widely known apostolate of prayer for Christian unity is described on pp. 541–44.

In contrast and complement, the work of Josef Höfer (1896–1976) was mainly diplomatic and off the stage. From the Paderborn circle (p. 545) he was sent to Rome in 1954 to be Ecclesiastical Counsellor to the West German Embassy to the Vatican. With his many contacts there and in Germany and with a wide circle of non-Roman friends, he probably did more than any other individual towards bringing about the revolution in Roman Catholic ecumenism connected with Vatican II.

Drawing by courtesy of Frau M. Nieggemeier, Paderborn

18 The Monastery of Simon Peter, Mount Athos, as it is today.

By courtesy of Ronald Sheridan's Photo-Library

19 Charismatic Movement (p. 550). Some of the 6000 members of the Pentecostal Church in Chile assembled for the last day of their week-long 30th Assembly in Curico, Chile, in April 1977.

By courtesy of Photo Oikoumene, WCC, Geneva

20 A variety of positions illustrating how the spirit of prayer may express itself through the body. 'The highest function of the body in prayer is to provide a language.'

From Le Corps et la Prière *by H. Caffarel, Editions du Feu Nouveau, 1971*

CONTRIBUTORS

A. M. Allchin, Canon of Canterbury Cathedral, Warden of the Sisters of the Love of God.

John Barton, Fellow and Chaplain of St Cross College, University Lecturer in Old Testament Theology, Oxford.

Sebastian Brock, Fellow of Wolfson College, University Lecturer in Aramaic and Syriac, Oxford.

Christopher Bryant SSJE, before his death Editor of *New Fire*.

W. O. Chadwick, formerly Master of Selwyn College and Regius Professor of Modern History, Cambridge.

James Cone, Charles A. Briggs Professor of Theology at the Union Theological Seminary, New York.

John Coulson, Reader in Theology, University of Bristol.

A. O. Davies, Research student of Wolfson College, Oxford.

C. M. Dent, Vicar of Hollingbourne, Maidstone, Kent.

J. D. M. Derrett, formerly Professor of Indian Law, School of African and Oriental Studies, University of London.

E. W. T. Dicken, formerly Warden of Lenten Hall and Senior Lecturer in Theology, University of Nottingham.

Elfrieda Dubois, formerly Reader in French at the University of Newcastle upon Tyne.

Milton McC. Gatch, Academic Dean and Professor of Church History at the Union Theological Seminary, New York.

Raymond George, Warden of John Wesley's Chapel, Bristol, and formerly Principal of Wesley College, Leeds.

Mark Gibbard SSJE, St Deiniol's Library, Hawarden, N. Wales.

W. J. Grisbrooke, formerly Professor of Liturgical Studies, St Mary's College, University of Birmingham.

John Gunstone, Ecumenical Officer of the Greater Manchester Council.

Sergei Hackel, Reader in Russian Studies at the University of Sussex, and Vicar-General of the Russian Orthodox (Patriarchal) Church in the British Isles.

Robert Handy, Henry Sloane Coffin Professor of Church History at the Union Theological Seminary, New York.

D. A. Hart, Chaplain of Shrewsbury School.

M. M. Hennell, Canon Emeritus of Manchester Cathedral and formerly Principal of Ridley Hall, Cambridge.

W. J. Hollenweger, Professor of Mission at the University of Birmingham.

Michael Ivens SJ, Director of Jesuit Tertians at St Beuno's Spiritual Exercises Centre, N. Wales, and elsewhere, and formerly assistant editor of *The Way*.

Louis Jacobs, Lecturer at Leo Baeck College, London.

C. P. M. Jones, formerly Principal of Pusey House, Oxford, and of Chichester Theological College.

Raymond Klibanksy, Extraordinary Fellow of Wolfson College, Oxford, and formerly Professor at McGill University, Montreal.

Kosuke Koyama, Professor of Ecumenics and World Christianity at the Union Theological Seminary, New York.

Kenneth Leech, Race Relations Field Officer of the Board for Social Responsibility, General Synod of the Church of England.

David Lotz, Washburn Professor of Church History at the Union Theological Seminary, New York.

Andrew Louth, Senior Lecturer and Head of the Department of Religion, Goldsmiths' College, University of London.

John Macquarrie, formerly Lady Margaret Professor of Divinity and Canon of Christ Church, Oxford.

James McConica, President of the University of St Michael's College, Toronto.

Edward Malatesta SJ, Director of the Institute for Chinese–Western Cultural History, University of San Francisco.

John Mbiti, formerly Director of the Ecumenical Institute, University of Geneva.

Anthony Meredith SJ, Tutor in Theology at Campion Hall, Oxford.

J. R. H. Moorman, formerly Principal of Chichester Theological College and Bishop of Ripon.

Diarmuid O'Laoghaire SJ, Lecturer at Milltown Institute of Theology and Philosophy, Dublin.

A. M. Priddis, Vicar of St John the Evangelist, High Wycombe.

Marjorie Reeves, FRHS, formerly Vice-Principal of St Anne's College, Oxford.

Philip Rousseau, Senior Lecturer in History, University of Auckland.

Anthony Russell, Director of the Arthur Rank Centre (National Agricultural Centre), and Canon Theologian of Coventry Cathedral.

Max Saint, formerly a missionary schoolmaster, hospital chaplain and parish priest.

John Saward, Lecturer in Theology at Ushaw College, University of Durham.

Alexander Schmemann, before his death Professor of Liturgical Theology and Dean of St Vladimir's Seminary, New York.

Cyprian Smith OSB, monk of Ampleforth Abbey, Yorkshire.

Placid Spearritt OSB, monk of Ampleforth Abbey, Yorkshire.

Elisabeth Stopp, Fellow of Girton College, and formerly University Lecturer in Modern and Medieval Languages, Cambridge.

Dale Stover, Professor of Religious Studies at the University of Nebraska.

Martin Thornton, formerly Chancellor of Truro Cathedral.

E. J. Townroe, Fellow of King's College, London.

Ralph Townsend, assistant master, Eton College.

David Tripp, Ecumenical Lecturer, Lincoln Theological College.

Simon Tugwell OP, Regent of Studies, Blackfriars, Oxford.

Ann Ulanov, Professor of Psychiatry and Religion at the Union Theological Seminary, New York.

Barry Ulanov, Professor of English and Chairman of the Program for the Arts, Barnard College, New York.

Geoffrey Wainwright, Professor of Systematic Theology at Duke University.

G. S. Wakefield, Principal of Queen's College, Birmingham.

Benedicta Ward SLG, Centre for Medieval and Renaissance Studies, Oxford.

Kallistos Ware, Fellow of Pembroke College, and Spalding Lecturer in Eastern Orthodox Studies, Oxford; Bishop of Diokleia.

Clifton Wolters, formerly Provost of Newcastle Cathedral.

E. J. Yarnold SJ, Tutor in Theology, and formerly Master, at Campion Hall, Oxford.

F. W. Zimmermann, Fellow of St Cross College, and University Lecturer in Islamic Philosophy, Oxford.

PREFACE

The editors of *The Study of Liturgy* now put before the public this introduction to *The Study of Spirituality*. They do this partly to satisfy their own consciences, lest they should have given the impression that liturgy is the single peak of Christian devotion, and partly to meet a felt need. The former symposium aimed at providing the theological and historical background of the current reforms of liturgy through most Christian churches, at least in the West; this present book aims at supplying a framework, also theological and historical, for the widespread and sporadic search by Christian individuals and groups for deeper and more personal prayer and intercourse with God, or for a richer or starker 'spirituality', to move, in T. S. Eliot's words, 'into another intensity, for a further union, a deeper communion',[1] and for a corresponding life-style. In doing this we incidentally hope to provide a fuller background for the *Classics of Western Spirituality* series which is being published jointly by the Paulist Press in USA and SPCK in England.

Both *The Study of Liturgy* and *The Study of Spirituality* are designed as introductions for students, professional or amateur, of the subject. Both follow the same general pattern: a theological introduction and a practical conclusion flank the historical exposition, which forms the largest part of the work. In both, the historical section has been divided between panels or groups of specialists; in liturgy, the division followed the main rites under consideration; in spirituality, the divisions have been determined by the main 'schools' and teachers of prayer and spiritual life, sometimes on a geographical or chronological basis, sometimes on grounds of theological or spiritual affinity. It is clear that spirituality provides a far wider variety than liturgy, just as individuals are more numerous than churches. Consequently we have had to be more selective; and no subject has been treated exhaustively. To make up for this, in both books we have aimed at providing adequate bibliographies in each section to guide further reading; they are a most important part of the present book and integral to its purpose. In addition, the three-volume study (ET) *A History of Christian Spirituality* (L. Bouyer *et al.*) covers much of our historical ground, but in greater detail; while *A Dictionary of*

---

[1] 'East Coker' in *Four Quartets* (London, Faber; New York, Harcourt Brace Jovanovich, 1943, 1971).

Christian Spirituality, edited by G. S. Wakefield, provides a useful work of reference throughout.

'Spirituality', we confess, is a vague word, often used with no clear meaning, or with a wide and vague significance;[1] but we can think of no better single word to describe our subject. We are concerned with the individual prayer and communion with God, both of the 'ordinary Christian' and of those with special spiritual gifts, and with the outer life which supports and flows from this devotion; in other words with mystical theology and with such parts of moral and ascetical theology as relate to it. These technical terms might clarify our purpose, but do not provide an adequate title for a work of wide-ranging interest.

Liturgy is by definition a public activity which easily lends itself to historical treatment; spirituality is personal, intimate and temperamental, and many may wonder whether it is properly purveyed and studied in a similar way. The individual seeker is confused by so many varied and sometimes contradictory approaches. Our justification is twofold:[2]

1. the individual's search for his or her own spirituality need not be, often cannot be, a purely internal quest; through reading other spiritual writers he or she can chance on a 'glove which fits', the external eliciting or corroborating the internal; or by trial and error many guides may contribute to the individual's unique development. Most lay Christians are unaware of the richness and depth of the Christian spiritual traditions and of the immense possibilities that are open to them for growth under the guidance of the Holy Spirit using the writings of earlier pilgrims in the way;

2. spiritual counsellors above all need to be aware of, and have knowledge of, other spiritualities than their own in order to detect and guide the needs of the countless differing individuals who consult them. For them a full working knowledge of diversities of spirituality is a professional necessity.

The Study of Liturgy was compiled for students in the English-speaking world, and so mainly of the Western Christian traditions; the Eastern Orthodox tradition was presented for the sake of completeness, but briefly and rather as a sideline. In this book we hope to have done full justice to the Orthodox traditions of spirituality. Liturgy is a mainly Christian phenomenon; but 'spirituality' can have wider ramifications and affin-

[1] See the note appended to this Preface.
[2] These two points briefly anticipate items in the final section of this book.

ities. Although we are primarily concerned with the Christian traditions, we have included brief accounts of the spirituality of other religions, and their similarities, contrasts and possible cross-fertilization with Christianity. *The Classics of Western Spirituality* series includes under the title 'Western Spirituality' all that stems from Hebrew roots and so includes representatives not only of all Christian traditions of East and West, but also of Judaism and Islam. We have gone further in including some representations of the purely oriental traditions of Hinduism and Buddhism, as well as the native traditions of Africa and America.

We are aware that many today are searching for 'spirituality', often understood as a technique of meditation, outside the penumbra of the Christian Church, and that some have even travelled as far as India in this quest, often because they are unaware that the Christian tradition, at least in its Anglo-Saxon pattern, contains anything like what they are looking for. Let us hope that this volume will help them to seek and find their quarry nearer home.

Even so, we hope that we are not encouraging a tendency or a reaction which gives individual communion a disproportionate place in the total Christian life in which prayer, even mystical prayer, must be balanced with the service of God and concern for our neighbour. Love must be expressed in obedience, if prayer is to avoid self-indulgence. In the Sermon on the Mount we are warned of the danger of the empty cry, 'Lord, Lord' (Matt. 7.21,22), and are assured that the vision of God is granted only to the pure in heart (5.8).

Under various names and guises our subject has recently been introduced into some University syllabuses. We hope this book will be useful to students of the subject; at the same time we hope that, by its avoidance alike of sentimentality and indifference, it may go some way towards assuring sceptics that Spirituality, at least in its historical manifestations, is capable of study on an academic level, along with all other sciences of human experience.

We have not tried to impose upon contributors any rigid uniformity in style or treatment, let alone theology. There will be found among the contributions different levels of academic intensity; and we have encouraged this variety, so that students may gain some understanding of the range of scholarship that is possible in this field.

The editors would like to thank the editorial staff and their colleagues at SPCK for their co-operation and patience; Robert Cathey and Carl Leth for their help in making the bibliographies appropriate to both sides of the Atlantic; David Cunningham for preparing the indexes; and Kallistos Ware, Simon Tugwell, Raymond George and Gordon Wakefield for co-ordinating individual sections of this book. They are also deeply indebted to Dr R. D. Williams, Dr R. Klibansky, Dr. A. Krailsheimer and the late Fr Kenelm Foster OP for suggestions and help in various ways. The editors also, and one in particular, wish to apologize to their patient contributors and publishers for the long delay in completing the work, and especially regret that death should have deprived Fr Christopher Bryant and Fr A. Schmemann of seeing the completed volume.

CHESLYN JONES   GEOFFREY WAINWRIGHT   EDWARD YARNOLD
October 1985

NOTE ON 'SPIRITUALITY'

The word *spirituality* is recent in its meanings. In its original English use it meant the clergy, as in Philip Stubbes's *Anatomie of Abuses* (1583), the 'corruptions and abuses of the spirituality'; or the ecclesiastical office as distinct from the secular office, so that a man, instituted to a living, was given by one authority the temporalities and by another the spiritualities. Thence it came, in various associations, to describe things of the spirit as distinct from things of matter, such as an immaterial essence, a spirit, a ghost, a soul. The meaning of devotion or piety came still later, chiefly through Catholic writers like Challoner. Yet in 1755 Dr Samuel Johnson defined, among the meanings, 'acts independent of the body; pure acts of the soul; mental refinement'.

In French the meaning came earlier. It appears first to have gained its special association with mystical or ascetical devotion as a term of reproach against the Quietist writers of the later seventeenth century. In the mystical doctrines propagated by Molinos or his successors the critics found an absence of free Christian attitudes to matter, an excess of striving after the purely immaterial; and they were inclined to blame 'la nouvelle spiritualité de Madame Guyon'. The usage was established by the later seventeenth century. In the course of the eighteenth, but more and more frequently in the nineteenth, the word became no longer a term of reproach but simply a description of ways of prayerful piety, with a hint, perhaps, of a link with the ideas of ascetics or mystics. Other French phrases, for example, 'the Inner Life' or 'the Interior Life', show how French models influenced and formed the language of English writers of the early twentieth century. There is a well-known French periodical called *La Vie Spirituelle*. We cannot yet conceive an English periodical with its exact equivalent in name. Though Ignatius Loyola's *Spiritual Exercises* were used by English Protestants during the later nineteenth century, this was not a natural taste for English books of devotion, which were more likely to be called *The Rule and Exercise of Holy Living*, or *The Practice of Piety*, or *The Whole Duty of Man*, *The Practice of True Devo-*

tion, or *A Practical Treatise upon Christian Perfection*. H. P. Liddon was one of the first to use the new type of language in his title *The Priest in his Inner Life*, 1856–7. F. P. Harton was one of the first to use the word *spiritual* in the French sense, in the title of a book, *The Elements of the Spiritual Life*, 1932. The meaningful description of a man as 'a spiritual writer', in the way of a category, entered the English language between the first edition of the *Catholic Encyclopaedia* and the second.[1]

According to P. Pourrat, spirituality or spiritual theology covers what was traditionally known as ascetic theology and mystical theology, with their basis in dogmatic and moral theology.[2] The great *Dictionnaire de la Spiritualité* was launched on the same basis in 1932, using exclusively Roman Catholic resources, though even then a side-glance at the spirituality of non-Catholics and non-Christians was permitted. In opening his *History of Christian Spirituality*, Louis Bouyer saw his subject as the psychological or experiential counterpart of dogma, both dogma and spirituality having a central, unchanging core as well as a genuine history.[3]

But there came a wind of change, beginning in Protestant Christendom. In an odd parallel with the late Victorian era,[4] the advance of biblical criticism, the limitations of the 'biblical theology' movement, and widespread scepticism on matters of faith (stimulated by, for example, *Honest to God* in Britain and 'the death of God' and other fashions in the USA), led pious people again to look for religious practice (*lex orandi*) that would be autonomous and independent of the vicissitudes of the *lex credendi*. 'Spirituality' somehow seemed to express what was sought. A turning-point was perhaps a conference in Durham in August 1967, whose papers and discussions were published under the title *Spirituality for Today*.[5] Though the participants were mainly British, a leading part was played by J. B. Coburn, then Dean of the Anglican seminary at Cambridge, Mass. Though the word 'spirituality' bounces round these pages, there is no systematic attempt to define it, except through off-the-cuff paraphrases, not all coherent: 'the forms and structures of the life of prayer'; 'the spiritual life *is* life' (pp. 16, 19); 'some kind of wholeness'; 'spirituality means a search for meaning and significance by contemplation and reflection on the totality of human experiences in relation to

---

[1] Owen Chadwick, writing in *Christian Spirituality: essays in honour of Gordon Rupp*, ed. Peter Brooks (London, SCM, 1975), pp. 205–6.
[2] *Christian Spirituality*, ET (London, Burns, Oates and Washbourne, 1922), p.v.
[3] ET 1968, vol. I, pp. ix–xi; the original was written in 1960.
[4] See p. 18 and p. 465 below.
[5] Ed. Eric James, London, SCM, 1968.

the whole world which is experienced and also to the life which is lived and may mature as that search proceeds' (p. 61).

Things have stabilized somewhat since then; writing in 1983, Gordon Wakefield adds: 'And spirituality concerns the way in which prayer influences conduct, our behaviour and manner of life, our attitudes to other people.'[1] Or take this:

> What then is spirituality . . .? It is by no means to be confused with theology, which is chiefly an elaboration of concepts. It is a life. All human existence has a spiritual aspect . . . Although the notion of spirituality is definitely a Christian notion, it by no means limits its attention to the Catholic world or even the Christian world. To exhibit the spirituality of human reality is to embrace this reality to its full extent, and such a quest does not just interest a few specialists.'

What provoked that? The tenth volume of the *Dictionnaire de la Spiritualité*![2]

CPMJ

[1] *A Dictionary of Christian Spirituality* (London, SCM, 1983), p.v.
[2] Jacques Madaule in *Le Monde*, Paris, 28 October 1980, as circulated by the publishers.

ABBREVIATIONS

AAS   *Acta Apostolicae Sedis*. Città del Vaticano, Typis Polyglottis Vaticanis, 1909—.

ACW   Ancient Christian Writers: The Works of the Fathers in Translation. Westminster, Md., Newman Press; London, Longmans Green; Ramsey, N.J., Paulist Press, 1946—.

Altaner   Altaner, B. and Stuiber, A., *Patrologie: Leben, Schriften und Lehre der Kirchenväter*. Freiburg, Herder, 1950, and latest edn, 1978; (ET) *Patrology*, New York, Herder and Herder, 1960.

Armstrong   Armstrong, A. H., ed., *The Cambridge History of Later Greek and Early Medieval Philosophy*. 2nd edn, CUP, 1970.

AS   *Acta Sanctorum*. Antwerp, Venice, Paris, 1643—.

BAC   Biblioteca de Autores Cristianos. Madrid, 1947—.

CCCM   Corpus Christianorum: Continuatio Medievalis. Turnhout, Brepols, 1971—.

CCSL   Corpus Christianorum: Series Latina. Turnhout, Brepols, 1953—.

comp.   compiled by

CSCO   Corpus Scriptorum Christianorum Orientalium. Louvain, Rome, etc., 1903—.

CSEL   Corpus Scriptorum Ecclesiasticorum Latinorum. Vienna, 1866—.

CUP   Cambridge University Press, Cambridge and London.

CWS   Classics of Western Spirituality. New York and Ramsey, N.J., Paulist Press, and London, SPCK.

DCS   *Dictionary of Christian Spirituality* ed. Wakefield, G. London, SCM, 1984.

DHGE   *Dictionnaire d'histoire et de géographie ecclésiastiques*, ed. Baudrillart, A., *et al*. Paris, 1912—.

Dict. Sp.   *Dictionnaire de spiritualité, ascétique et mystique*, ed. Guibert, Joseph de, *et al*. Paris, 1932—.

d   died.

DLT   Darton, Longman & Todd.

DS	Denzinger, H. and Schönmetzer, A., *Enchiridion Symbolorum, Definitionum et Declarationum de Rebus Fidei et Morum.* Barcelona, New York etc, Herder, 33rd edn, 1965; (ET) *The Church Teaches,* St Louis, Mo., Herder, 1955.
ECR	*Eastern Churches Review.* Oxford, Clarendon Press, 1973-8.
ET	English translation.
FC	Fathers of the Church, Washington DC., Catholic University, 1947.
HCS	Bouyer, L., *et al.,* (ET) *A History of Christian Spirituality,* 3 vols. London, Burns & Oates, 1963-8; New York, Seabury Press, 1963-9.
JTS	*Journal of Theological Studies,* vols. 1-50; new series, vol. 1—, OUP; New York, Macmillan Co., 1900—.
LACT	Library of Anglo-Catholic Theology. Oxford, 1841-63.
LCC	Library of Christian Classics. Philadephia, Westminster; London, SCM, 1953-66.
LCP	Latinitas Christianorum Primaeva. Nijmegen, Dekker and Van de Vegt, 1936—.
LF	A Library of Fathers of the Holy Catholic Church. Oxford, John Henry Parker, etc., 1838-81.
NT	New Testament
NTS	*New Testament Studies.* Cambridge, 1954-.
OCA	*Orientalia Christiana Analecta.* Rome, 1935—.
OCP	*Orientalia Christiana Periodica.* Rome, 1935—.
ODCC	Cross, F.L. and Livingstone, E.A. ed., *Oxford Dictionary of the Christian Church.* London, New York, OUP, 2nd edn, 1974; rev. 1983.
OECT	Chadwick, Henry, ed., Oxford Early Christian Texts. Oxford, Clarendon Press, 1970—.
OT	Old Testament.
OUP	Oxford University Press (Oxford and London, unless New York is cited).
PG	Patrologia Graeca, comp. Migne, J-P. Paris, 1857-66, 161 vols.
PL	Patrologia Latina, comp. Migne, J-P. Paris, 1844-80, 221 vols.
PO	Patrologia Orientalis. Paris, etc., 1907-49, 26 vols.

Quasten   Quasten, Johannes, *Patrology*. Westminster, Md, Newman Press, 1950–60, 3 vols; Westminster, Christian Classics, 1983.

RAM   *Revue d'ascétique et de mystique*, Toulouse.

RGG   *Die Religion in Geschichte und Gegenwart*, ed. Galling, Kurt, *et al.* Tübingen, J. C. B. Mohr (Paul Siebeck), 1957–65, 7 vols.

RRM   *The Russian Religious Mind*, Fedotov, G.P. Cambridge, Mass., Harvard University Press, 1946–66, 2 vols.

SC   Sources chrétiennes. Paris, 1942—.

SCM   Student Christian Movement.

SL   *The Study of Liturgy*, ed. Jones, C., Wainwright, G., Yarnold, E. London, SPCK; New York, OUP, 1978.

SLG   Society of the Love of God.

SPCK   Society for Promoting Christian Knowledge.

ST   Aquinas, St Thomas, *Summa Theologiae*.

s.v.   under the word.

TRS   *A Treasury of Russian Spirituality*, ed. Fedotov, G.P. New York, Sheed & Ward, 1948; London, Sheed & Ward, 1950.

VT   *Vetus Testamentum*. Leiden.

VTS   *Vetus Testamentum, Supplementum*. Leiden.

vol.   volume

WCC   World Council of Churches.

PART ONE

The Theology of Spirituality

1 Liturgy and Personal Devotion

C.P.M. JONES

We may reach a clearer understanding of what we mean by Christian spirituality by contrasting the theological principles which underlie our practice of liturgy or common prayer and each Christian individual's personal or private devotion. Both practices rest on different aspects of Christian faith and truth, which will be seen to be complementary. This is not often realized, to the impoverishment of both. It can lead to a complete dichotomy: some reduce the practice of religion entirely to 'going to church'; others regard it as a purely private and interior matter. It can issue in wrong or inappropriate ways of participating in, and of assessing, both types of practice. Many people look on public worship as an encouraging occasion for saying their private prayers, or judge it as a performance by purely personal religious, or even aesthetic, standards. Equally, many Christians who wish to take their prayer seriously are not happy without a set routine, a sort of 'service', to follow as though in church, with no regard for the wide liberty of the spirit which is open to them. Let us look more closely at these principles of worship, differing but complementary, as they are drawn from the leading features of our Christian faith.

1 GOD OUR CREATOR

In our common worship we confess our belief in and allegiance to 'one God, the Father almighty, maker of heaven and earth and of *all* things visible and invisible', the words of the ecumenical creed. The God we worship is the creator and source of the *whole* universe. In this universe the human race has been created in a special way 'in God's image', with mind and will; and so is capable of discerning and adoring the glory of God and of voicing praise and thanksgiving. And we can do this not solely on our own account but also as the representatives and mouthpieces of our fellow creatures who belong to the dumb orders of creation. This is magnificently articulated in the Song of the Three Children, in the apocryphal addition to the book of Daniel, in which we call on the whole range of creation to 'bless the Lord; praise and magnify him above all for ever'; sun, moon and stars, rain, lightning, clouds, snow and frost, mountains and greenery, beasts, bird and fish, are all spoken for, along with *all* humankind, Israel and God's special servants. We are the priests of the lower creation. Moreover in our worship we are raised to join with the higher creation; 'with angels and archangels and with all the company of heaven' we sing 'Holy, holy, holy' (cf. also Rev. 5.11–13). In our intercessions we are invited to pray 'for the *whole* state of Christ's Church' or 'for the *whole* church of God in Christ Jesus and for *all* men according to their needs'.

But when we come to pray individually, we think on a smaller and more intimate scale. God the creator of the universe has made *me* in his own image by no process of mass production; I am a specially designed reproduction of his image. So there is a special place in his providence that only I can fill. I have a unique responsibility before him which cannot be delegated to any other being. Moreover, I have a capability of understanding him and loving him which is in principle unique. He has made me for this, and he desires to elicit this from me. Accepting and entering into this unique and unshareable relationship is first the embarrassment and then the joy of my aspirations and movements towards personal communion with God.

2   JESUS CHRIST OUR REDEEMER

We confess in the creed that the Son of God became incarnate 'for *us* men and for *our* salvation'; 'he was crucified for *us* under Pontius Pilate'. His saving work is for the whole human race; the whole seed of Adam is included in his death and resurrection (cf. Rom. 6.4–6). As St Paul says (2 Cor. 5.18), 'God was in Christ reconciling the *cosmos*, the whole world, to himself'. In St John's Gospel, the Baptist greets Jesus as 'the lamb of God that takes away the sin [*sic*, singular; the total sin rather than the sum of sins] of the *world*'. Jesus himself asserts that in his 'lifting up' he will draw (lit. drag) *all* to himself (1.29; 12.32). In the eucharistic prayer we hear of Christ's sacrifice 'for the sins of the whole world'; we plead before the Father Christ's offering on behalf of all humankind. All the Church's intercessions are offered 'through Jesus Christ our Lord'.

All humankind was included in Christ's death and resurrection, including each single person. In words ascribed to St Paul (1 Tim. 1.15), 'Christ Jesus came into the world to save sinners, of whom I am the first'. The universal salvation has to be appropriated by each individual convert, and not only by way of forgiveness. St Paul gives this experience primitive and classical expression: 'I am crucified together with Christ; it is no longer I that live, but Christ lives in me; the life I now live in the flesh, I live in faith of the Son of God who loved me and handed himself over for me' (Gal. 2.19, 20). Here is the first expression of 'Christ-mysticism', Christ dwelling by faith in the heart (Eph. 3.17), which comes to its fullest expression in the New Testament in the last discourse in St John's Gospel: 'abide in me, and I in you'. The corporate worship of the Eucharist reaches its climax in the communion of each individual; the Lord's universal commission of the task of reconciliation to his apostles (John 20.21–3) reaches its fulfilment in the baptism of the individual convert and in the absolution of the individual penitent.

3   THE HOLY SPIRIT

In the liturgy we come to God as members of the Christian community, of the body of Christ, the image to which St Paul gave classical expression in ch. 12 of his first letter to Corinth. 'In the one Spirit we were all baptized into one body . . . and we were all made to drink of the one Spirit' (v. 13). The Holy Spirit distributes his gifts to every member of the body and co-ordinates and harmonizes their exercise (vv. 4–11). So the co-operation of each member is required and enabled for the concerted activity of the whole. All are mutually interdependent, whether their functions are humble or glorious, hidden or conspicuous (vv. 14–26). This is not unbridled democratic chaos, but concerted order (vv. 24, 25) including an elementary principle of hierarchy (v. 28).

We have travelled a long way from St Paul and the turbulent assembly at Corinth (see 1 Cor. 14). As far back as 1 Clement (chaps. 40, 41) and Ignatius (*Magn.* 6, 7, 13; *Trall.* 3, 7; *Smyrn.* 8) at the liturgical assembly the church is 'on parade' with all ranks assembled together. This is so now on important liturgical occasions, such as an episcopal Eucharist with ordination, when the bishop, his presbyters and deacons and a large number of lay assistants, some with specific functions and some without, assemble to co-opt new presbyters and deacons into the ministry. As in Corinth, the liturgy shows forth both the fullness and the unity of the Church.

We come to liturgy as members of the whole Church, and each time we do not invent it anew; we come as members of a world-wide body with its own historic inheritance. The Old Testament readings and psalms come from before Christ; and Christ's own actions and their adaptation in apostolic times are the core of this heritage. The basic patterns of the eucharistic liturgy as a whole (readings, sermon, intercessions, Eucharist) and of the eucharistic action itself (offertory, anaphora, fraction, communion) were already fixed by the middle of the second century and have been universally preserved. Differing traditions of music, ceremonial and ethos prevail in different historical periods and different geographical areas. In short, in liturgy various external standards apply, over and above the passing whims of particular congregations. It is a co-ordinated corporate activity, for which there must be 'rules of the game'.

But the Holy Spirit, equally and complementarily, indwells each individual. If the Christian community is God's temple (1 Cor. 3.16, 17), each Christian must see his or her own body as a temple of the Holy Spirit (ibid. 6.19). The Holy Spirit develops and perfects in each individual his or her distinctive character made in the image of God, and the unique reproduction of the sonship of Jesus. He bestows and disciplines the special gifts with which each member of Christ's body is endowed. He is the source and sustainer of distinctive vocations within the total body with their varying degrees of self-sacrifice and heroism. In some he can arouse and support original and dynamic insights into the being of God or the character of Jesus, such as set going new beginnings in the Church, whether of innovation or renovation.

Moreover, the Holy Spirit is the source and sustainer of many patterns of sanctity and of 'spirituality', ways of direct approach to God and from God; in other words, of the great men and women of prayer, particularly of those who have been enabled to commit to writing their experience and its lessons and so have been able to act as guides to other individuals, and even to whole 'schools'. In looking for guidance from them and through them, each individual seeker after God must rely on the leadership of the Holy Spirit to discern what should be accepted and assimilated, or put aside and rejected, in the path towards consolidation in that distinctive and authentic personal love of God for which he or she was made and in which he or she can alone find progress and peace. If we are right in this, liturgy and spirituality are here contrasted; in spirituality, there are ultimately no 'rules of the game', even those laid down by the saints, but only 'tips of the trade', freely offered to be freely available, to those who need them, sometimes permanently and sometimes in a passing stage of development.

4   OUR FINAL HOPE

As a last consideration of the differing perspectives of liturgy and spirituality, let us consider the doctrine of the End, the last things, the future hope, all that is contained under the technical term 'eschatology'. Christianity was from the first, and always should be, highly eschatological, orientated towards the future. In the New Testament this is described as 'the coming (*parousia*) of our Lord Jesus Christ and our gathering together to him' (2 Thess. 2.1), and is set out classically in dramatic form in our Lord's final discourse on the future in Mark 13; which chapter also provides the framework for the drama elaborated in fuller detail in the Revelation of St John the Divine. The drama is set out in cosmic terms, including all nature, all history, all humankind, and above all the people of God; it finds its consummation in the vision of the new Jerusalem, the city of God, the bride of Christ, which contains not only the fulfilment of all human happiness (Rev. 21.4) but also the perfection of all human achievement (21.22–4). This is essentially a corporate goal; it is indeed the end of liturgy (cf. Heb. 12.22–4; Rev. 21.22, 23). And the Eucharist from the earliest days had this eschatological reference (1 Cor. 11.26; Mark 14.25). One of the earliest liturgical acclamations was *Maranatha*, Come, Lord (1 Cor. 16.22; cf. Rev. 22.20). The Eucharist today remains not only a remembrance (*anamnesis*) of the Lord's passion and resurrection, but also an anticipation of the messianic banquet and the consummation; the Church directs herself to her goal in the new Jerusalem, of which she already enjoys an anticipated fulfilment.

But within the total and corporate pattern there is an infinite number of individual eschatologies, in fact as many as there are human consciences, to face judgement. 'We must all appear before the judgement seat of Christ, so that each may receive his reward for what he has done in the body whether good or bad' (2 Cor. 5.10). Examination and judgement of self can forestall universal condemnation (1 Cor. 11.31, 32). Characteristics of the victorious Christ and of the new Jerusalem his bride are promised to the victorious individual Christian (Rev. 2.7, 11, 17, 28; 3.5, 12, 21).

To the Eucharist as the corporate anticipation of the messianic banquet corresponds the presence of Christ and the operation of the Holy Spirit in the individual soul, a present and incomplete possession leading to the desire for fuller and complete union and communion. This is the quest often called mystical, leading to the higher levels of prayer and sacrifice in this life; as with the pilgrim in Walter Hilton's *Ladder of Perfection*,[1] whose constant protection and encouragement is the simple aspiration: 'I am nothing, I have nothing, I desire nothing but the love of Jesus in Jerusalem'. And the highest level has been frequently described in nuptial imagery; in the spiritual betrothal and marriage of selected souls with Christ the final consummation of the Church is anticipated and realized.

We have given these four illustrations of the theological principles behind common prayer and private prayer, liturgy and spirituality, in the hope of making clearer the area covered by the word 'spirituality'. These principles have been contrasted absolutely for the sake of clarity. But they are complementary and seldom does either exist in pure form; in fact they not only coexist, they interpenetrate each other. When as an individual Christian one goes to the liturgy, one does not go just because one is an individual but because one is a member of the Church; when one gets there, one does not leave one's individuality at the door and put on the

[1] See pp. 334–5.

7

impersonal cloak and role of a pure 'churchman'. One goes in as one is, and puts one's own contribution of prayer and praise, of offering and petition, into the common pool of the community's worship. The total offering of the Church is enriched, not distorted, by the individual contributions of her members. Similarly, the isolated Christian, separated from others by illness, accident or design, never prays as a purely solitary individual. Such a one always prays as one of a countless number of invisible witnesses; and, wonder of wonders, their prayer is being expressed through that person.

Finally, to exhaust and dismiss the subject of liturgy, it remains to say that liturgy itself can be a form of spirituality. And this in two ways.

1. The corporate recitation of the Divine Office, above all the Psalms, over an extended period of time, cannot fail to reproduce in the participants the spiritual outlook and piety of the Psalmists, and that both at a conscious and at an unconscious level; particularly in those who follow St Benedict's precept that 'the mind should move in harmony with the voice' (*Rule*, ch. 19).[1]

2. In relation to the eucharistic liturgy we sometimes find a phenomenon which might be styled 'liturgical mysticism'. By this we do not mean the use of the liturgy for purposes other than corporate worship, which has characterized periods of liturgical degeneration, such as the use of the liturgy as a framework for purely musical composition, or as an occasion for reciting the rosary, or for mental prayer whether under the guidance of meditations on the life of Christ or on the incidents of his passion as in medieval manuals of devotion for layfolk or by the use of their more sophisticated modern equivalents.[2] The liturgical mystic is rather one who in some way distances himself from the corporate action in order to concentrate on its inner or deeper meaning. Some clear examples of this can be traced in an earlier phase of the current recovery of the liturgy.[3]

> Gestures turn inwards, words become silent, chants listen, colours set forth the soul's seasons, incense bears her prayer aloft, the whole of matter offers the depths of its being to be the tabernacle of the Spirit. Creation is seen from within, transparent in the living unity of love. The light of the world shines in the flame of a candle, its heart beats in the mystery of the flickering lamp. In

---

[1] See pp. 148–56.
[2] See Aloysius Roche's magnificent *Mysteries of the Mass in Reasoned Prayers* (London, Longmans, 1916).
[3] See for instance Maurice Zundel, (ET) *The Splendour of the Liturgy* (London, Sheed & Ward, 1939), p. 8.

this state of contemplation the universe has become one immense sacrament . . .

Escaping from, or soaring above, the common action, such sentiments are far removed from liturgy; rather they are evidence of a rarified and specialized mysticism occasioned by the liturgy or by the contemplation of its scenery.

2 The Theology of Christian Spirituality

EDWARD YARNOLD

Baker, J. A., *The Foolishness of God*. London, DLT, 1970, Collins, 1975; Atlanta, John Knox Press, 1975.

von Balthasar, H. U., (ET) *Prayer*. London, Chapman, 1961, SPCK, 1973; New York, Paulist Press, 1967.

de Guibert, J., (ET) *The Theology of the Spiritual Life*. New York, Sheed & Ward, 1953; London, Sheed & Ward, 1954.

Pannenberg, W., *Christian Spirituality and Sacramental Community*. Philadelphia, Westminster, 1983; London, DLT, 1984.

Rahner, K., (ET) *Nature and Grace*. London, Sheed & Ward, 1963, 1976.

Rahner, K., (ET) *The Trinity*. London, Burns & Oates; New York, Herder, 1970.

Taylor, J. V., *The Go-Between God: the Holy Spirit and the Christian Mission*. London, SCM, 1972; Philadelphia, Fortress, 1973.

Underhill, E., *Mysticism*. London, Methuen; New York, Dutton, 1911.

Underhill, E., *Man and the Supernatural*. London, Methuen, 1927; New York, Dutton, 1928.

Vanstone, W. H., *Love's Endeavour, Love's Expense*. London, DLT, 1977 = *The Risk of Love*, New York, OUP, 1978.

Wainwright, G., *Doxology*. London, Epworth; New York, OUP, 1980.

Yarnold, E. J., *The Second Gift: a Study of Grace*. Slough, St Paul Publications, 1974.

Each Church, and probably each theologian within each Church, would produce a different theology of spirituality. This essay, therefore, cannot be expected to satisfy all. But I hope that most Christians will be able to find in it some ideas with which they feel at home. In any event the bibliography points the reader to other treatments of the subject based on different Christian traditions.

I shall take as my starting point Geoffrey Wainwright's definition of spirituality as the 'combination of praying and living'.[1] It is this embodi-

[1] Below, p. 592.

9

ment of prayer in life that the NT writers describe in such phrases as 'a living sacrifice', 'spiritual worship' (Rom. 12.1), and 'a sacrifice of praise to God, that is, the fruit of lips that acknowledge his name' (Heb. 13.15). Christians are to be 'a holy priesthood, to offer spiritual sacrifices acceptable to God through Jesus Christ' (1 Pet. 2.5; cf. 2.9). In the search for understanding of this priesthood we shall consider the nature of the God who called us to it, the human nature which God designed for the fulfilment of this priesthood, and the sin and grace which respectively frustrate this priesthood and make it possible.

GOD THE CREATOR

God made us because it is his nature to create; not out of need, as if he would be bored or unfulfilled without creatures to interest him, or impotent without creatures to serve him, for then God would be reduced to our own level. God creates because his nature is to love (cf. 1 John 4.8, 16). Nothing could exist unless there were such a God whose being is loving. Descartes proposed the one basic, indisputable truth: 'I think, therefore I am.' Perhaps we can formulate a second, even more basic truth: 'I am, therefore there exists a God whose nature is to love.'

Human love, despite the mystic confusion of Wagner's Tristan and Isolde who wanted to become totally one in annihilation, respects the otherness of the loved one and wishes to be united with that other in their otherness. The same is true of God's love. In John Macquarrie's evocative phrase, derived from the first chapter of Genesis, God 'lets us be' in the double sense of bringing us into existence and respecting our otherness.[1] But he also enables us in our otherness to be united with himself. There are accordingly three coefficients in God's love: he is the source of being, he gives rise to beings outside himself, and he unites those beings with himself. Christian tradition, following the NT, has identified these three coefficients as the Father who is the source of being, the Son or Word through whom all things are made, and the Holy Spirit who unites personal beings with God as his sons and daughters (cf. Rom. 8.15–16).

What has been said so far contains a paradox. It is God's *nature* to create, but he does not *need* to create. The explanation of the paradox is found in the doctrine of the Trinity. The threefold movement by which the one who is self-sufficient being gives existence to another and is united with that other in love, which we saw in God's relation with ourselves, is found primarily and wholly fulfilled within the unchanging

[1] *Principles of Christian Theology* (London, SCM; New York, Scribners, 2nd edn, 1977), ch. 5.

and indivisible nature of God. From all eternity, independently of creation, God is satisfied love, that is to say, he is Father, Son and Holy Spirit. But his nature as love is such that freely, without necessity or need, it is also expressed outside himself in time when he creates other beings who can love him in return. The doctrine of the Trinity is the doctrine of the altruism of God. [1]

HUMAN NATURE

God did not create because he wanted toys to play with. It would be unworthy of him to create except for the sake of entering into a relationship of mutual love with his creatures. Therefore the existence of *personal* creatures, who are capable of loving, must be the reason for the existence of impersonal creatures too; [2] the impersonal exist in order to help the personal to attain and express that love. It is by providing this opportunity for personal beings that material objects fulfil what Pierre Teilhard de Chardin called their 'spiritual power'. [3]

Yet *of themselves* not even personal beings are capable of entering into a relationship of love with God: to believe otherwise would be to bring God down to our own level. For this reason Catholic tradition has called this relationship 'supernatural', meaning by that term that such a relationship with God is utterly beyond the powers of any created beings. God's love is creative and transforms his creatures, and becomes a principle of new life in them, so that they become capable of loving him. This creative power of God's love is often called 'grace'; sometimes it is called 'sanctifying' or 'habitual' grace, terms which imply that it is not just a momentary help, but a permanent, vital source of holiness. The NT writers express the same idea in other terms: for St Paul Christians '*in* Christ' become a 'new creation', so that Christ is their life; 2 Peter speaks of Christians becoming 'partakers of the divine nature'. Grace is the presence of the Holy Spirit, who makes us God's sons and daughters. [4] Eastern Orthodox writers have often applied to this transforming power of God's love the startling description of 'deification'.

God designed human nature specifically so that we might undergo this creative transformation. Here we are brought up against a second para-

[1] St Augustine, according to the basic analogy which he proposes in *de Trinitate*, viii.14, describes the threeness in God as that of lover, beloved and love. J. Macquarrie speaks of primordial, expressive and unitive being (op. cit., ch. 9). For another treatment of the subject see K. Rahner, *The Trinity*, pp. 34–8; 80–120.

[2] I prefer not to enter into the question whether human beings are the only personal creatures, or whether angels and horses and Martians should be included.

[3] *Le Milieu Divin*, (ET). London, Collins; New York, Harper & Row, 1960.

[4] Gal. 3.27–8; 2 Cor. 5.17; 2 Pet. 1.4; Rom. 8.14–17.

dox. God's transforming grace is *super*natural; yet it could not transform us unless God had already set in our natures an affinity to himself. To express this affinity many writers have borrowed from the first chapter of Genesis the phrase 'the image of God'. Thomas Aquinas, who spoke of the fundamental urge in each being's nature as its 'natural desire', believed that the natural desire of human beings was for God.[1] St Augustine was making the same point when he wrote: 'You have made us for yourself, and our heart knows no rest until it finds rest in you.'[2] God could not enable a doll to become his daughter, because to do so it would have to cease to be a doll, because there is in a doll no affinity to God. But because there is in human nature the image of God and the natural desire for him, he can make us a new creation so that, *while remaining ourselves*, we are able to become his daughters and sons.

I have elsewhere[3] referred to grace as God's 'second gift', the first gift being his creation of humanity in his own image. However, such terms as the supernatural and the second gift do not imply that God could ever leave human beings without the offer of grace. It seems incompatible with God's goodness to make us capable of receiving his transforming love and to deprive that receptivity of its fulfilment. But grace *is* a second gift. It is one thing to make us capable of receiving his transforming love, and another actually to transform us; it is one thing to make us capable of receiving his Spirit, and another actually to give us his Spirit.

The life of the person who has become a new creation in Christ and the son or daughter of God is a relationship based on knowledge and love of him. 'This is eternal life, that they know thee, the only true God, and Jesus Christ whom thou has sent' (John 17.3). 'God's love has been poured out into our hearts through the Holy Spirit who has been given to us' (Rom. 5.5). Therefore, to return to the question we raised at the beginning of this chapter, the nature which God must give to a being he has created to exercise a spiritual priesthood must involve a capacity, not yet to know and love God, but to be transformed by his love into a creature who can know and love him. If the doctrine of the Trinity is about the altruistic God, the doctrine of human nature is about the restlessness for God in the human heart.

Several attempts have been made to define that aspect in our nature which makes us capable of being transformed by God's grace.[4] Perhaps one can recognize it in two human capacities. The first is our ability to

---

[1] *Contra Gentes*, iii. 50–1.
[2] *Confessions*, i.1.
[3] *The Second Gift*. Slough, St Paul Publications, 1974.
[4] ibid., pp. 73–4. K. Rahner, (ET) *Foundations of the Christian Faith* (London, DLT; New York, Seabury, 1978), vi.3, 'Transcendental Christology'.

make moral choices; in such decisions, when we reach for the highest good we know, God is leading us on to himself, whether we recognize the fact or not. The second is our ability to know and love other human beings. God does not allow our love to stop there, but enables it to reach through the other human being to himself. This is one way in which the second great commandment, to love our neighbour, is 'like' the first commandment, to love God (Matt. 22.37–9). Whenever we act as responsible, loving persons, we are in the field of grace, and exercising our spiritual priesthood.

SIN

Sadly, however, the gulf between God and man which grace has to bridge is not just that between the infinite and the finite: it is also the gap between the All-holy and the sinner. 'All have sinned and fall short of the glory of God' (Rom. 3.23). Nor can we find security in the thought that we used to be sinners, but by the grace of God are sinners no longer. We should take seriously the confession of *present* sinfulness that is often found in the lives of saints, and is typified by this remark of St Bruno's, addressed to the members of the Carthusian order which he founded: 'I rejoice indeed, as is right, for the growth of the fruits of your virtues, but I lament and am ashamed that I lie inert and torpid in the filth of my sins.'[1] Therefore God's love and his grace always need to be forgiving.

The Catholic tradition maintains that, even though the gift of grace, which is the presence of the Holy Spirit, becomes part of our own being, making us essentially holy and pleasing to God, we will often fail to reflect that essential holiness in our everyday choices. Human beings in this life are never perfectly integrated. The doctrine of venial sin expresses this gap between the two levels of our being. It implies that ordinary Christians at the deepest level of their being will have made a choice of values which can be described as a 'fundamental option' for God, while repeatedly failing to express that option fully in their everyday choices.[2] Thus St Paul bewailed the discrepancy between his ideals and the reality of his life: 'I do not do the good I want, but the evil I do not want is what I do' (Rom. 7.19). Paul Tillich, adapting scholastic terminology, spoke of this disharmony as the distinction between essence and existence.[3]

The gap, then, which separates human beings from God is both

---

[1] *Letter to his Carthusian Sons* (SC 88.82).
[2] See L. Monden, (ET) *Sin, Liberty and Law* (London, Chapman; New York, Sheed and Ward, 1965), pp. 30–3.
[3] P. Tillich, *Systematic Theology* (University of Chicago, 1951; London, SCM, 1958), vol. I, pt. ii, IC10.

ontological and moral. Accordingly we have a double need for God's grace: so that we may share in his nature, and so that our sins may be forgiven and healed. The Catholic and Orthodox traditions on the one hand, and the Protestant tradition on the other, have tended to emphasize different aspects of this double action of God's grace. The former stress the need human beings would have for grace even if there were no sin; the second stresses the fact that in practice everybody is a sinner requiring forgiveness. Hans Küng's first, and perhaps his best, book, *Justification*, and the pioneering ecumenical work by Charles Moeller and Gérard Philips on grace suggest that the Catholic and Protestant viewpoints need not be incompatible.[1]

THE GRACE OF CHRIST

The highest and unique instance of God's self-giving is his entry into the world in the person of Jesus Christ. The highest and unique fulfilment of the human capacity for God is found in the life of Jesus Christ. But the incarnate divinity and the God-filled humanity of Jesus are not only for himself; they are 'for us and for our salvation'. In other words the grace which we have been discussing as the vital principle of all spirituality is the grace of Christ. This means not only that Christ won this grace for us by his death and resurrection, but also that it is a share in the life of the God-man himself. Accordingly St Paul could describe the life of the spirit by saying equally that we are in Christ and that Christ is in us. In him is the life which is the light of humanity (cf. John 1.4). Consequently the imitation of Christ, which has been a theme of spiritual writers from the time of the NT, is not just the copying of Jesus as a model, nor just the acceptance of Christ's values: it means that we share Christ's own life organically, as the scriptural images of the vine and the body imply, so that we grow from within into the likeness of Christ, unless by sin we distort our development.[2]

The life of Christ that we share is the life of the risen Christ, who still in the resurrection bears the marks of the passion (cf. Rev. 5.6). According to the Fourth Gospel, the passion is identical with the glory of Christ (cf. John 17.1). One interpretation of the great christological hymn in Philippians 2 is that Jesus Christ's divinity is expressed in self-emptying and humiliation, and not concealed by them.

[1] H. Küng, (ET) *Justification*, London, Burns & Oates; New York, Nelson, 1964. C. Moeller and G. Philips, (ET) *The Theology of Grace and the Ecumenical Movement*, London, Mowbray, 1961; Paterson, NJ, St Anthony Guild Press, 1969. G. Philips, *L'union personnelle avec le Dieu vivant*. Gembloux, Duculot, 1974.

[2] Cf. E. J. Tinsley, *The Image of God in Christ*, London, SCM, 1960; J. A. T. Robinson, *The Body* (London, SCM, 1952; Philadelphia, Westminster, 1977), pp. 47, 63.

The same truth seems to underlie such sayings as that it was 'necessary' that the Christ should suffer before entering his glory (Luke 24.26; for Luke the passion precedes the glory and is not identical with it), and that it was 'fitting' that the Saviour should be made 'perfect through suffering' (Heb. 2.10). It was necessary because the Father willed it. But that answer gets nowhere near the heart of the matter, for why did the Father will it? If we say it was because the Saviour had to conform to the pattern of all human nature, which must achieve fulfilment through self-emptying like the grain of wheat which must die if it is to be fruitful (John 12.24), then the question still remains why God made human nature so that it must follow the law of the grain of wheat. May one suggest that the answer is that human nature is made in God's own image? The law of the grain of wheat reflects God's own nature: the glory of God himself lies in self-giving.

The members of Christ's body, then, share the life of the Head, who bears a crown of glory which is still a crown of thorns. If both are seen in their full significance, there is no distinction between a spirituality of the cross and a spirituality of the resurrection.

MYSTICAL PRAYER

It follows from what has been said so far that all prayer, and therefore all spirituality, is the fruit of God's grace. It is the Holy Spirit who makes it possible for us to pray 'Abba, Father' (Rom. 8.15–16), just as he makes it possible for us to make an act of faith in the lordship of Jesus (1 Cor. 12.3). All prayer, then, is supernatural. Nevertheless, some writers, including one no less authoritative than St Teresa of Avila, reserve the term 'supernatural' for the higher stages of prayer, such as St John of the Cross describes as 'infused contemplation', and which are commonly referred to as 'mystical prayer'.[1]

The point at issue is not whether prayer is possible without grace: none of the great Christian writers on prayer has suggested this. In its dependence upon grace, all prayer is supernatural. The truth underlying St Teresa's confusing terminology is that the higher stages of prayer are a grace which God does not seem to offer to everybody. Some writers, like A. Poulain, make the difference between ordinary and mystical prayer a difference of kind, so that ordinary prayer does not contain 'the least germ of the mystic state'.[2] Others seem to make the distinction rather one of

---

[1] Teresa, Relation V, *Complete Works,* trans. and ed. E. Allison Peers, vol. i, p. 327. John, *The Dark Night of the Soul,* I.x.6; II.v.3. See below pp. 372–3.

[2] A. Poulain, (ET) *The Graces of Interior Prayer* (St Louis, B. Herder, 1912; London, Routledge & Kegan Paul, 1950), p. 213.

degree, like Hans Urs von Balthasar, when he writes that all forms of prayer depend fundamentally on 'grace as election, calling, justification by God the Father'.[1] David Knowles, while making the difference one of kind as well as degree, concurs with von Balthasar's description of the mystical life as 'a full expansion of the Christian life of grace'.[2] So too for Friedrich von Hügel mysticism is one of the essential elements of religion.[3]

THE DARK NIGHT

Many of the great writers on spirituality have spoken of mystical prayer in terms of darkness. Sometimes writers, such as Gregory of Nyssa, have used the metaphor of darkness to state that human concepts are inadequate to express God's nature, for God is 'separated on all sides by incomprehensibility as by a darkness' (*Life of Moses*, ii. 163. See pp. 166–7). More often, however, the image of darkness is applied, not to human thinking about God, but to prayer itself. Thus in the fourteenth century the author of the *Cloud of Unknowing* spoke of a cloud which 'hindereth thee, so that thou mayest neither see him clearly by light of understanding in thy reason, nor feel him in sweetness of love in thine affection'.[4] All that we may be aware of is a 'naked intent unto God'. St John of the Cross provided the classical discussion of this experience in the *Dark Night of the Soul*.[5] The experience serves to purify the intention, stripping the will of all unworthy motives for praying and leaving

[1] H. U. von Balthasar, *Prayer* (London, SPCK, 1961), p. 42.

[2] M. D. Knowles, *What is Mysticism?* (London, Burns & Oates, 1967), pp. 44–5 = *The Nature of Mysticism* (New York, Hawthorn, 1966).

[3] F. von Hügel, *The Mystical Element of Religion as studied in St Catherine of Genoa and her Friends*. 2 vols. London, Dent, 1908; New York, Dutton, 1923. The difference between religious and secular mysticism was analysed by R. C. Zaehner, especially in *Mysticism, Sacred and Profane: an Inquiry into some Varieties of Praeter-natural Experience* (Oxford, Clarendon; New York, OUP, 1957). It is the misunderstanding of Christian mysticism as a cultivation of religious experience that leads some Protestants to condemn mysticism as 'unChristian', because 'in the humanity of Jesus, we have struck upon a fact which is of incomparably richer content than are the feelings that arise within our own selves' (W. Hermann, *Der Verkehr des Christen mit Gott* (Stuttgart, 1892), vol. ii, p. 332, my trans. The work exists in ET: *The Communion of the Christian with God* (Philadelphia, Fortress, 1971; London, SCM, 1972).) A useful summary of controversies connected with mysticism is contained in Dom E. Cuthbert Butler, *Western Mysticism: the Teaching of St Augustine, Gregory and Bernard on Contemplation and the Contemplative Life*, (3rd edn, London, Constable, 1967; New York, Barnes & Noble, 1968), pp. ix–lviii, 'Afterthoughts', by David Knowles. See below, pp. 17–24.

[4] *The Cloud of Unknowing*, ed. J. McCann (5th edn, London, Burns, Oates & Washbourne, 1947; Westminster, Md., Newman Press, 1952), ch. 3. See below, pp. 332–4.

[5] See below, pp. 371–3.

only the desire of God for his own sake. Most writers agree that the dark night is often felt as an inability to pray, but the inability is only apparent. The spiritual darkness is really a light, which 'the soul which is not enlightened and purged' is unable to recognize, because it 'darkens' the act of the 'natural intelligence'.[1]

In other words, such darkness is not inability to pray but pure prayer. Often when we pray we use words or are aware of religious affections. But the essence of prayer is not words or feelings, but the movement of our wills to God in response to grace. In the prayer of darkness this movement of our wills is 'naked', stripped of words, ideas and feelings. People who are experiencing this form of prayer, and perhaps have been experiencing it for a long time, may have great difficulty in recognizing it, even though they have read all about it, and frequently despair of their ability to pray.[2] The spiritual director will need to help them to recognize genuine prayer of darkness, not for their own self-esteem, but to prevent them from discouragement or even from giving up serious prayer altogether.

At the beginning of this chapter we recalled St Paul's description of the Christian life as a living sacrifice. This insight into the connection between life and worship is expressed in the well-known saying *laborare est orare* (to work is to pray). But the principle is open to abuse. Work will be prayer only if there is also prayer which is not work. We cannot expect our whole life to become a continuous act of worship unless there are regular times when we lay aside our worldly occupations and raise up our mind and heart to God in prayer.

3 Mysticism, Human and Divine

C. P. M. JONES

Happold, F. C., *Mysticism, a Study and an Anthology*. Harmondsworth and New York, Penguin, 1963.

Heiler, F., (ET) *Prayer*. London and New York, OUP, 1932 (trans. and abridgement of the 5th [1921] edn of *Das Gebet*).

Hügel, F. von, *The Mystical Element of Religion*. 2 vols, London, Dent, 1908; New York, Dutton, 1923.

---

[1] John of the Cross, *The Dark Night of the Soul*, 11.v.3.

[2] The dark night is often experienced, not as something exalted, but as boredom, frustration and a sense of futility. Cf. Ruth Burrows, *Guidelines for Mystical Prayer* (London, Sheed & Ward, 1976).

Inge, W. R., *Christian Mysticism* (1899 Bampton Lectures). London, Methuen; New York, Scribner, 1899.

James, W., *The Varieties of Religious Experience*. London and New York, Longmans, 1902.

Katz, S. T., (ed.), *Mysticism and Philosophical Analysis*. London, Sheldon, 1978.

Knowles, M. D., *The Nature of Mysticism*. New York, Hawthorn Books, 1966; publ. in U.K. as *What is Mysticism?* London, Burns & Oates, 1967.

Otto, R., (ET) *The Idea of the Holy*. London and New York, OUP, 1932.

Toynbee, P., *Towards the Holy Spirit*. London, SCM, 1982.

Underhill, E., *Mysticism*. London, Methuen; New York, Dutton, 1911; rev. edn 1930.

Zaehner, R. C., *Mysticism, Sacred and Profane*. Oxford, Clarendon; New York, OUP, 1957.

The resurgence of a serious interest in mysticism in the Anglo-Saxon world at the turn of the century received considerable impetus from the publication of the books of William James, W. R. Inge and Friedrich von Hügel, and later from the more popular works of Evelyn Underhill. Protestant Christendom was predisposed to favourable reception in view of the uncertainties consequent upon biblical criticism, the prevalence of idealist, post-Hegelian philosophy, and the rise of 'comparative religion', often presupposing or seeking an inner core common to all religions. These authors approached the subject from different angles. W. James' approach was empirical, pioneering by including 'religious' experience, normal and paranormal, along with other experience in the general investigation of human psychology. Inge's interest in Christian mystics seems to have arisen from his own personal needs, though his study is presented historically, rooted in the New Testament. Von Hügel, a Roman Catholic by birth, was a deep student of philosophy and theology who, in the course of prolonged investigation of the spirituality of St Catherine of Genoa, concluded that the mystical and experiential element, along with the institutional and corporate, and the intellectual and critical, is a vital constituent of true religion. Evelyn Underhill, under his guidance, was led from theosophy to full Anglican faith and practice, and developed a remarkable personal ministry as a counsellor and retreat conductor.[1]

But what do we mean by 'mysticism', or who is a 'mystic'? Leaving aside the popular and promiscuous uses of the word, it is exceedingly difficult to define, like the word 'religion'. This can be shown negatively, in that attempted definitions always need qualification. Dom David Knowles begins by restricting the term to its use in traditional Catholic

[1] See C. J. R. Armstrong, *Evelyn Underhill (1875–1941)*, London, Mowbray, 1975.

orthodoxy, that is to the highest peak of supernatural prayer, practised by contemplatives in the 'unitive' way; but in the end he has to find an independent place for 'nature' mysticism. Friedrich Heiler, in his endeavour to establish a radical distinction between 'prophetic' and 'mystical' prayer, defines mysticism as 'that form of intercourse with God in which the world and the self are absolutely denied, in which human personality is dissolved and is absorbed in the infinite unity of the Godhead' (op. cit., p. 136), language clearly of oriental inspiration, which leads to great difficulty in considering Christian mystical writers, from the New Testament onwards. Similarly when Bertrand Russell understands mysticism as an intuitive apprehension of a timeless unity which transcends the distinction of good and evil,[1] he is in effect summarizing the tendencies of prevalent Hegelian idealism. Even R. C. Zaehner, who with much deeper knowledge of religions limited mysticism to three distinct categories (nature, monist and theist: op. cit., p. 158), has not escaped criticism.[2]

It is virtually impossible to establish categories which determine who is a mystic, as the full extent of the phenomenon is not known. Von Hügel conceived mysticism as 'existing, in some form and degree, in every mind'.[3] We do not realize that we have been, and probably always will be, completely dependent on those mystics who have had an additional, possibly adventitious, gift of the power to express their experience in writing, as well as a suitable occasion or call to do this.[4] There is, as yet, no way of tapping the hidden aspirations of the commuter on the Clapham omnibus.

Once the limitations of this proviso are accepted, it may nevertheless be possible to make some general statements. In the first place there seem to be *four constants* in mystical experience:

1. the mystic is in touch with an 'object' which is invisible, intangible and inaccessible, beyond sensual contact;

2. this 'object' is inexhaustible, infinite, and incomprehensible (in the purest sense, cannot be captured or surrounded), and therefore is also inexpressible, beyond full description;

3. the contact is intuitive and 'immediate' (un-mediated) and direct, even if after introduction by a third party or book;

---

[1] See *Mysticism and Logic* (London, Longmans, 1918), pp. 8–11.
[2] See the Katz symposium, pp. 30–2.
[3] *Selected Letters*, ed. B. Holland (London, Dent; New York, Dutton, 1927), p. 84; cf. also D. Cupitt, *Taking Leave of God* (London, SCM, 1980), p. 31.
[4] Including those who responded to invitations from the Religious Experience Research Unit at Manchester College, Oxford, founded by the late Sir Alister Hardy.

4. even so there is an inward affinity between the 'object' and the person, an attraction or fascination,[1] even leading to mutual interpenetration or communion.

Along with these constants there is room for almost infinite *variety*, and a wide range of *contrasts* is conceivable, and often actually met in the literature: for instance,

1. the 'object' can be 'immanent' (within the subject) or 'transcendent' (above and beyond);

2. the 'object' can be actually 'possessed' or perpetually sought, or both, alternately or simultaneously;

3. the 'object' can be experienced as personal, open to inter-personal communion, or impersonal, outside personal categories, or even super- or trans-personal, above personal categories but perhaps subsuming them;

4. the occasion can be a special experience, enthusiasm (n.b. derivation: 'full of a god') or ecstasy, of glory or of horror, or it can lack any notable experience, and consist mainly of quiet, passivity and peace (when fully developed, 'quietism');

5. equally it can take place definitely in time, even at a definite time (as in many of W. James' examples), or lead out of time or beyond time, with a hint or intuition of eternity;

6. the activity can be rational, involving the intellect and in continuity with its activity (as in St Augustine's classic experience recorded in his *Confessions* IX.10), or entirely non-rational, even irrational, either pure will (cf. the *Cloud*: 'God can be gotten by love, but never by thought'), or sheer emotion;

7. the activity can have physical concomitants or side-effects (levitation, stigmata), or be entirely non-physical;

8. it may be prepared for, or induced, by meditation, fasting, or even drugs, or it may be completely unprepared and adventitious, 'out of the blue', 'amazing grace',[2] and it can be a combination or alternation of these;

9. the experience can be open, capable of being shared or communicated (e.g. highly personal poems used as hymns), or essentially private and individual, and even incommunicable;[3]

---

[1] cf. R. Otto, op. cit., who defines the 'numinous' as *mysterium tremendum et fascinans.*

[2] See Kenneth Clark, *The Other Half, a Self-Portrait* (London, Murray, 1977), p. 108.

[3] e.g. the private letter of Bertrand Russell, printed in his *Autobiography*, II (London, Allen & Unwin; Boston, Atlantic Monthly Press, 1968), p. 90, quoted by R. C. Zaehner, *Our Savage God* (London, Collins, 1974), pp. 211–12.

10. the experience may appear as a detached occasion or series of detached occasions, or as a continuous factor throughout life;

11. it may appear as incidental to, or on the circumference of, one's life purpose, or as an essential, or *the* essential, constituent of one's life purpose, the centre rather than the circumference;

12. similar experiences, it seems, can arise in communal contexts, groups, crowds, tribes and nations, both on occasions and apart from occasion.

Readers may think of other possibilities, but these should suffice to suggest an infinite variety of contexts for mystical experience, and to reinforce the likelihood that most such experiences go unrecorded, and may well be unrecordable.

So, if we would go further, we are left with those who have considered these matters and have written of them. Even so, the way is not clear. First there are those who, after much consideration, conclude that silence is the only justifiable course on matters strictly beyond rational analysis and comprehension.[1] Others point out the inadequacy of verbal communication; words inevitably distort the intended meaning, are a crude approximation,

> a raid on the inarticulate
> With shabby equipment always deteriorating
> In the general mess of imprecision of feeling
> (T. S. Eliot, 'East Coker' V)

George Steiner sees this point graphically illustrated by Schoenberg's unfinished opera *Moses und Aron*: Moses has the authentic revelation of God, but cannot articulate and communicate it; this task is given to Aaron who transforms the ineffable vision into an effective national cult, culminating in the golden calf.[2] St Augustine and Dante say that we speak only to avoid silence, though our words are quite inadequate; Rowan Williams has drawn attention to St Augustine's commendation of wordless 'jubilation' in praise of God.[3]

We now go on to suggest that mystical experience in some form can penetrate into a wide range of human activities, though this has to be done in a hasty and cursory way. We can only indicate some of the areas where this has occurred, and so is possible; we do not have to show that all

[1] See George Steiner, *Language and Silence* (New York, Atheneum, 1977), p. 21, referring to L. Wittgenstein; see also St John of the Cross, *Dark Night*, II. xvii.3; *Spiritual Canticle* (B), St.VII 9, 10 (ET Allison Peers, I, 249 and II, 217–18).

[2] op. cit., pp. 127–39.

[3] *The Wound of Knowledge* (London, DLT, 1979), p. 87, quoting St Augustine on Ps. 32.8; Dante, *Paradiso*, canto 33, ll. 52ff.

musicians or all lovers have been mystics, but that some have been.

The contemplation of *Nature* is an obvious starting point, including wonder at nature, communion with nature, and communion with what is beyond nature through nature. Here many names spring to mind, from the poets Goethe and Wordsworth to the scientist Teilhard de Chardin and the first astronauts. It is voiced from prison by Oscar Wilde,[1] but most articulately by the nineteenth-century rustic Richard Jefferies.[2] Nature mysticism can be extended to include *humanist* revelling in the glories of human nature, as in Goethe.

From Nature to *Art*. Some creative artists have been conscious of being a channel of inspiration, and some have said so. William Blake says he wrote a poem 'from immediate dictation';[3] the composer Gustav Mahler is equally explicit; 'Creative activity and the genesis of a work are mystical from start to finish, since one acts unconsciously, as if prompted from outside, and then one can hardly conceive how the result has come into being'.[4] On a different plane, Rudyard Kipling told Rider Haggard, 'we are telephone wires'. On the performing side it is not difficult to imagine an inner identification between the actor or player and the drama or music. James Galway the flautist has already placed on record his ambition that people should feel that 'in some odd inexplicable way they have at some time heard the voice of the Infinite through me'.[5] The same factor can be detected in the appreciation of artistic work. Poetry has been described as 'private experience at its greatest intensity becoming universal' (T. S. Eliot, *A Note on War Poetry*, 1942). It was said of Mahler: 'Here the world finds its sounding board'.[6] There is also an aesthetic, even mystical, aspect in some branches of mathematics and science;[7] sometimes this is an instance of nature mysticism, sometimes of artistic, but it may also be *sui generis*.

A further large category may be designated *inter-personal* mysticism, i.e. arising within the association of human beings, both in groups and

---

[1] *De Profundis* (1897) in *De Profundis and Other Writings* (Harmondsworth, Penguin, 1973; New York, Penguin, 1976), p. 207.

[2] See F. C. Happold, op. cit., pp. 384-93.

[3] *Writings* II, ed. G. E. Bentley, jr (Oxford, Clarendon, 1978), p. 1572.

[4] *Mahler, A Documentary Study*, ed. Kurt Blaukopf, ET (London, Thames & Hudson, 1976), p. 196.

[5] *An Autobiography* (London, Hodder & Stoughton, 1978), p. 203.

[6] Alma Mahler, *Gustav Mahler, Memories and Letters*, ed. Donald Mitchell (London, John Murray, 3rd edn 1973), p. 90.

[7] I am indebted to Dr Lane Hughston, Fellow of Lincoln College, Oxford, for drawing attention to a paper by Dr R. Penrose, FRS, of the Oxford Mathematical Institute, entitled 'The Rôle of Aesthetics in Pure and Applied Mathematical Research' (*Bulletin of the Institute of Mathematics and its Applications*, vol. 10 (1974), pp. 266-71).

between individuals. Groupings rise from the family unit to the nation and beyond, wherever there is 'fellow-feeling' due to common membership. This is more powerful in some families than others, and in some African tribes than others; it could also apply to 'class' customs and caste systems. In nations it can take different forms at different times, ranging from the supine and routine performance of a national anthem to nostalgic fervour in the British singing of 'Rule, Britannia' or 'Land of Hope and Glory', or to the morbid enthusiasm of Hitler's rhetoric and the crowd's response. It can also be seen in the cameraderie of a football team and the mass response of the spectators.[1]

Between individuals we are really concerned with a dimension of the relationships loosely classed together as 'love', and this on various levels. On the physical level D. H. Lawrence describes sexual union as a kind of mystical experience, in his novel *Lady Chatterley's Lover*. Plato, in his *Phaedrus* and *Symposium*, portrays Socrates as guiding his followers through human physical beauty to beauty of character and on to heavenly beauty, as we also find in the letters and poems of Michelangelo Buonarroti.[2] On the pastoral level, an extraordinary capacity for 'empathy' with individuals is revealed in the letters of Forbes Robinson.[3] And many know that, when friends are separated, the friendship can still flourish at a deep level, through invisible co-operation and interior companionship; there can be a real, even if unexpressed, interpenetration of personalities. And such unions, it seems, need not be separated by death.[4]

This brief and hasty survey suggests that the capacity for mystical experience of some kind is widespread and not limited to any particular activity, in other words, a general capacity of the human spirit. It is not confined to 'religion'. But what of religious mysticism? It naturally finds its place alongside all the other evidence we have mentioned; the mystical genius can be drawn into a deeper appreciation and inner understanding of his or her religious tradition. So all traditions have their mystics, just as they have their pedants or their reformers.

But the religious traditions that spring from the Old Testament, i.e. Judaism, Christianity and Islam, all share the same personal monotheism

---

[1] Bertrand Russell, in the letter referred to in note 3 on p. 20 above: 'at times I have been very near it in crowds when I have been feeling strongly what they were feeling'.
[2] Conveniently summarized in A. Blunt, *Artistic Theory in Italy 1450–1600* (Oxford, Clarendon, 1940), pp. 58–81. I owe this reference, as much else in this essay, to Dr K. J. Garlick, Fellow of Balliol College, Oxford.
[3] M. R. J. Manktelow, *Forbes Robinson, Disciple of Love*. London, SPCK, 1961.
[4] See William Blake, op. cit., p. 1533, on his brother; K. E. Kirk, on his wife (see E. W. Kemp, *The Life and Letters of Kenneth Escott Kirk, Bishop of Oxford, 1937–1954* [London, Hodder & Stoughton, 1959], p. 205).

and believe that God is living and active, thus opening the possibility of a relationship of personal communion. And this possibility is more precisely crystallized in Christianity, when the gracious but invisible Father sends his Son to invite such fellowship, and his Spirit to move the human heart to co-operate with the invitation.

4 Prayer and Personality: Prayer as Primary Speech

ANN AND BARRY ULANOV

Personal prayer exists right at the centre of any spirituality. In it we search, both individually and in groups, for deeper, more personal intercourse with God – moving into an ever greater intensity, union, and communion that will radically alter the way we live our lives. Here the truths of faith come home, or find no home. Here God speaks to the specific person who is made in the divine image, to the one who opens to that image or closes up against it. Here God calls us to be one with each other – and we listen and hear or fall deaf. Here we respond, or turn away, as the fallen Adam did. Here we accept grace and are transformed or we stonily refuse it.

Prayer above all else is conversation with God. It is the primary speech of the true self to the true God. It reaches far below words into the affects and images and instincts living in us unconsciously – into what depth psychologists call primary-process thinking. Prayer makes use of all we know verbally and emotionally – our conscious secondary-process thinking – forming words and wishes sent in urgent pleas or in quiet meditations to our Lord. We speak in prayer from our most hidden heart to the hiddenness of God, in whose astonishing image we were fashioned and find our true faces.

In prayer we speak to and of ourselves, of what lies heavy on our minds, of what rumbles in fear at the pit of our stomachs, of the grudges and resentments we hold behind our eyes below the surfaces of our outward being. We speak what we have to say, whatever that is, and however we are moved to say it. The saints give us tremendous help in outlining patterns of prayer, teaching us by example and by instruction how to move from verbal prayer, spoken with our lips out loud, to the mental prayer we say in our minds silently. We move from meditations where we methodically examine aspects of the divine mysteries, to prayers of simple union where we lift our hearts spontaneously to God in bursts of affect. [1] Sufficiently tutored and graced, we may move to prayers of quiet, an even deeper union, where our words and feelings fall ever more still, and God's moving in us becomes ever more dominant. But the saints also tell us repeatedly not to expect these remarkable experiences to come right away and not to be disappointed when they do not. We must begin where we are. We must not chain ourselves to expectations or to methods. The advice given in *The Cloud of Unknowing* sums it up very well: God wants us to pray and will tell us how to begin where we are. [2] The Holy Spirit, God's presence within us, moves us to want to pray and to pray as we must, leading us to the things of Christ. Thus what begins as our desire to pray, as our seeking after God, may turn out to be God stirring in us, opening us to grace. Methodological prayer and our hope for rich experiences can help then, but they are not the main thing. The main thing is God touching the self, bringing it into conversation.

God touches the self, the self touches God – it is all but impossible in prayer to say where the movement originates. To speak of religious experience as the basis for the confidence that leads to prayer is to miss the fact that very often it is prayer that leads to religious experience. We could say that 'we believe in prayer because our own prayers have been answered.' John Baillie thinks it 'truer to say . . . that only through faith, only by believing in a God who answers prayer, can we have experience of our own prayers being answered'. [3] The question is not central, except perhaps to those system-centred theologians to whom orders of precedence really do matter. But it does point to something of great importance, the psychological conditions of prayer. The way one is prepared or prepares oneself for prayer is what this question raises. For what one brings to prayer is either the true self or the lying self. One prays, if

---

[1] Father Juan Arintero's discussion of the stages of prayer and the spiritual life is notably clear and succinct, and though with no indicated awareness of modern depth psychology, remarkably astute in its reading of the psyche of the praying person. See his *Stages in Prayer*, ET Kathleen Pond (London, Blackfriars; St Louis, Herder, 1957), especially ch. 2.

[2] All of *The Cloud of Unknowing* is instructive in this sense, taking us as we are and where we are into the life of prayer, giving us confidence that even in our 'wretchedness' we can choose 'to be meeked under the wonderful height and the worthiness of God', as the appropriately unknown fourteenth-century writer of *The Cloud* puts it in his or her eloquent way. See *The Cloud of Unknowing*, ed. Dom Justin McCann (London, Burns Oates & Washbourne, 1924; 6th edn, Westminster, Md., Newman Press, 1952), p. 67. The modern translation by Clifton Wolters (Harmondsworth and New York, Penguin, 1961) is a very useful one, perhaps more intelligible to the late twentieth-century reader than the McCann, which makes only minimal changes in the original text, but it is not so engaging to read as the slightly amended medieval English. See pp. 332–4.

[3] See John Baillie, *The Sense of the Presence of God* (London, OUP; New York, Scribner's, 1962), p. 64.

one prays in all honesty, with as much knowledge of oneself as one can muster for the occasion and with as much charity. As St Augustine says, if one asks for forgiveness, one must oneself be prepared to forgive. If one seeks favourable answers, one must be prepared to give favourable answers. Under every circumstance, one must be honest with oneself. That is the special scourging that is in prayer. That is what really comes first in prayer. That is what makes it the special mode that we call primary speech.

Augustine's warnings are blunt: 'He that lies in his prayers, loses the benefit he seeks: he that lies in his prayers, both loses his cause and finds his punishment. And if any one lies to the emperor, he is convicted of his lie at his coming: but when thou liest in prayer, thou by thy very prayer art convicted.' In truth, God, 'He who dictated the prayers to thee', is our Advocate. In lies, God is a witness against us. If we do not change ourselves, he becomes our Judge. Out of this reasoning Augustine constructs a moral theology in what he himself calls 'a brief summary': 'So then thou wishest to receive, give; thou wishest to be forgiven, forgive.'[1]

The doctrine receives striking witness in R. G. Collingwood's exploration of the relation of imagination to consciousness as the basis of that 'generative act' which produces art. 'A true consciousness is the confession to ourselves of our feelings; a false consciousness would be disowning them, i.e. thinking about one of them, "That feeling is not mine."' When an artist says what he feels he must say in a particular work, as a result of an act of consciousness, such a speaking is 'necessarily an attempt to state the truth'. Collingwood goes to some lengths to make clear that consciousness is not intellect and 'therefore art as such, not being intellect, does not and cannot argue'. The truth of art is not the truth of arguments, arrived at through the processes of the reason. It is a truth of consciousness, of facts gathered by consciousness, producing a knowledge about which questions may be raised and arguments pursued – and oh, how they are! It is exactly the same with prayer. The artist and the praying consciousness speak out of what they know of themselves. What they know of their worlds is not separated from what they know of themselves. All things are 'steeped in the emotion with which [one] contemplates them: they are the language in which that emotion utters itself to [one's] consciousness'.[2] That is the way we talk to ourselves and of ourselves and through ourselves to God in the art of prayer. This is speech at its truest. This is primary speech, speech at its most elemental.

Prayer remains this elemental speech with God throughout the ages; that is constant. But times change and the ways we are moved into such

---

[1] Sermon 64.5: ET R. G. Macmullen in the LF, vol. 16, pp. 474–5.
[2] See R. G. Collingwood, *The Principles of Art* (Oxford, Clarendon, 1955; New York, OUP, 1958 [1938]), pp. 216, 287, 291.

speech are marked differently in different ages. The saints tell us and show us that again and again. One of the major marks of our age is our awareness of the place of the self in coming to God. The saints emphasize the denial of self as the way to God. But that, we must recognize, must be reinterpreted for our time or simply be put aside. For we today cannot accept as holy the repression or denial of our human stuff, the rejection of the substance of our being. Maiming results from such asceticism, and frustration of all access to God. People are put off religion, seeing it only as that ancient burdensome yoke that Christ actually enjoins us to discard so that we may take his lighter one instead.

For our age prayer must be the bringing of the full self to God: all the sexual and aggressive fantasies, the fears and mediocrity, the petty faults and the major turnings away, the grandiose wishes and secret longings, the laziness, the angers, the buried hopes and desires to give and serve, the caring for other people, the hatred of enemies, the pain of the suffering and unfairness in our world, the bounding into praise and the falling-away into sleep in mid-prayer. All this human stuff – ordered, unordered, disordered – is what we must bring in a big sack and dump out and sort through and talk over with God.

The Russian traditions of prayer encourage such a complete turning to God. Vladimir Lossky declares it as *the* dogma of prayer, and with ample witness from the Fathers of Orthodoxy, such as Macarius of Egypt, Evagrius, and Isaac the Syrian, asserts that there is no cure for man, unless he comes 'towards God of his own free will and with all his longing . . .' Nothing must be held back, though one must be careful not to make of the tears and contrition with which prayer often begins a passionate end in itself. One must look with equal fervour towards active verbal prayer and wordless contemplation. Every opening of self to the essence of Self is appropriate, for seen this way prayer 'is the motive power behind all human efforts' and 'every presence of man before the face of God is a prayer . . .' To ensure that presence, it 'must become a constant and conscious attitude – prayer must become perpetual, as uninterrupted as breathing or the beating of the heart'.[1]

---

[1] Vladimir Lossky, *The Mystical Theology of the Eastern Church* (London, James Clarke, 1957), pp. 206, 209. For the Orthodox tradition, see below, pp. 176–83. The great example of prayer that becomes perpetual is the so-called Jesus Prayer of Eastern Orthodoxy – 'O Lord Jesus Christ, Son of God, have mercy on me a sinner.' As Lossky says, 'This prayer, continually repeated at each drawing of breath, becomes to a monk as it were second nature. Not mechanical, it frees the interior life, makes it contemplative, by driving away . . . all contagion of sin, and every external thought or image . . .' (pp. 210–11). Readers of J. D. Salinger, a large number in the 1960s, were fascinated with the Jesus Prayer because of the fixation on it of Franny in the *Franny and Zooey* stories (J. D. Salinger, *Franny and Zooey* [Boston and Toronto, Little, Brown, 1961]).

This is the human soul God wants, the heart which prays, not just the lips which mouth the proper words.[1] God wants the glad soul who really speaks, saying what is really on the mind and in the heart, not a dull recital of those only too-familiar formalities, the set speeches laid down by the 'authorities', confident that they know exactly what God wants to hear. Have pity on the divine ears – all those dull prayers, those boring hymns, those dry sermons filled with unctuous phrases!

In this full speech, this primary speech – meaning a speech that is of first importance and absolutely basic to our humanity – we find a sufficient asceticism.[2] For what we find are the modern versions of the saints' scourgings. When we bring into conversation with God all that really happens in us and around us and to us, when we translate into the terms of our own lives the grandeur of our inherited petitionary, intercessory, confessional, and adoring prayers, we find soon enough that we are being scourged, stripped, opened up to make room for new growth. We are radically rearranged. Our psyches are struck hard. For the conversation of prayer moves two ways, into us as well as out of us, from God as well as towards God, full of deep silence as well as noisy acclamation.

The defensive uses of prayer soon fall by the way if prayer really consists of honest conversation that proceeds from true consciousness. Hectoring, guilt-making, fantasizing, narcissistic wool-gathering just do not hold up day after day against the silences that invade prayer. They fall into their own silences. The silences swallow them up.

In a prayer of true consciousness, we know the beginnings of what the saints call the prayer of purgation, the first of the three stages that end in union with the divine.[3] Here there occurs that first stripping away of the false, of mere appearance, of cover-ups and counterfeit poses which seal us off from our true selves and from God. Whatever hounds us that we despise, or fear, or despair over, will turn up in these moments for

---

[1] The fixing of the heart in prayer is the special consideration of the great gathering of Eastern Orthodox texts in *Writings from the Philokalia on Prayer of the Heart*, ET E. Kadloubovsky and G. E. H. (or Kadleigh) Palmer (London, Faber, 1973). It is also the burden of much of the writing of the German mystic Jacob Boehme (cf. below pp. 450–1). See his *The Way to Christ*, ET Peter Erb (CWS, 1978), especially the opening pages of the Third Treatise on Holy Prayer, pp. 71ff. 'If we wish to pray properly,' says this Renaissance psychologist of prayer, 'we must look in the first place at ourselves and consider well whether our heart has formed itself in another creature . . .'

[2] See Ann and Barry Ulanov, *Primary Speech: A Psychology of Prayer* (Atlanta, John Knox, 1982), especially chaps 1 and 2.

[3] The classical locus for a discussion of the triple way of the prayer of affects, the sequence of the stages of purgation or purification, illumination, and union, is St Bonaventure's *De Triplici Via*. A good modern translation is in (ET) *The Works of Bonaventure* (Paterson, St Anthony Guild Press, 1960–70), vol. i, *Mystical Opuscula*.

prayerful consideration with God. Here we are scoured, stripped bare of the myriad deceits, large and small, that infiltrate our being. Painfully, our values, even our best – our esteem of justice, love, health, peace for ourselves and our world – are often exposed as values held with such possessive force that they have built a wall in us against the force of God's will.

The earnest conversation of such prayer leads to our offering of what we have, indeed of all that we have, and all that we are, as we are drawn further and further into the mysterious passion of God displayed in Christ. This is a modern renunciation, the equivalent for us of the offerings of the saints. God moves us to this point, ploughing us up and down to make room for new seeds to grow.

Purging in prayer becomes a refurbishing of the whole instrumentality of our being. We no longer concentrate on this or that little part of ourselves, no matter how important or how troubling. We see our total being in prayer, as William of St Thierry, writing on *The Nature of the Body and the Soul*, sees our intellectual nature, as 'not in any one part but in the whole. It is not located within, in the cavities of the body, nor is it forced out when one gets fat, or anything like that. For its purposes it uses the whole body as if it were a musical instrument.' Age or rot may damage the instrument. But the player of the instrument always has the art of playing it at his or her disposal. Purgation is, in a sense, a return of the skills of the art to the artist, no matter in what shape he may find his instrument.[1]

Purgation really surprises us. It turns things around in both psyche and soul. It is not just castigation. And it may be more difficult to take than any mere chastening, for it requires accepting ourselves and some-times accepting that what superficially looks like a fault or a limitation, even a sin, may turn out to be a major part of our identity, even an opening through which God reaches right into us. There, in our own special way, no matter how lowly, we can become part of the sodden earth in which Christ appears. Thus a deep wound to the formation of an ego, that centre of personal identity, that might leave us forever fragile, anxious, boarded up against others, may instead become the aperture, the very point of sure accessibility through which God touches the soul and moves it to give all its needs and hopes into God's care.

If prayer works, the human personality always increases. It never diminishes. The self that emerges this way comes forth unshackled, scoured, clean, uncovered because anchored in God. Yoked to a true

[1] See William of St Thierry, (ET) *The Nature of the Body and Soul*, in *Three Treatises on Man: A Cistercian Anthology*, ed. Bernard McGinn (Kalamazoo, Cistercian Publications, 1977), pp. 130–1.

centre, one finds everything personal rearranged. This is the leaving of the world that the saints did literally in their retirement to the wilderness or a remote hermitage, which those who pray sincerely today do symbolically. The inner movement, however, remains what it always was – detachment from peripheral concerns as one is drawn toward the heart of things. We seek, now, first things above all else, seeing the goal of life as praising and glorifying God in numerous ways, thoughts, words, deeds, some open and obvious, some subtle, even sly. This is what is meant by loving God with all our heart, strength, mind, and soul. This is a love so full it spills over to change all our dealings with each other, with our neighbours, with our own selves, as the spirit invades psyche and soul and enlists us in its service.

The 'service of the spirit', as Rudolf Otto points out in a memorable essay on 'The Battle between Flesh and Spirit', is one in which the flesh – another way of saying 'the world' – is not turned away from or forbidden, but rather 'itself becomes spiritual'. To cultivate a readiness of spirit, to be available to serve 'the holy "Thou shalt" we must be strongly self-possessed, we need a firm and determined self-will, we must train and look after ourselves; indeed a lively appreciation of life becomes a necessary condition for a wholesome and vigorous state of the soul without which a will, strong in the service of the "Thou shalt", is not possible.'[1]

Thus the prayerful life never produces withdrawal from self or from other into some cheery, cosy haven of private chats with the divine. Prayer exposes, strips bare, and yet brings us ever more consciously and constantly into the world's life, into the deep wounded heart of the world. This life of a true prayerful consciousness is not an easy one. We are left with less and less protection against the assaults of meanness, inexcusable suffering, and avoidable misery we inflict upon each other. Reading in the newspaper of a mother beating her son to death can no longer be easily blotted out and forgotten by us if we are involved in praying. We feel the boy's fear, his horror that the one who is his support has been transmogrified into his crazed killer. We feel the mother's madness that has transmuted her dependent child into the target of her obsession. By the time we learn the story, the child is dead, but we must pray nonetheless – for his last hours of terror, for her waking to the horror of what she has done, for all the evil in the world and those who in any way suffer it, as cause or effect.

Suffering such as this, and all the myriad sufferings it symbolizes, we can never digest. Not even anger can burn it away. Programmes of mental health will help, but they will not cure all the madness in the world, let

---

[1] See Rudolf Otto, (ET) *Religious Essays: A Supplement to 'The Idea of the Holy'* (London, OUP, 1931), p. 11.

alone the suffering that springs from hate-fed discrimination, bad law, inconscient waste, indifferent schooling. Only the prayer that carries us into the deep river of God's compassion, flowing beneath and through our lives, can enable us to bear the pain and go on living by giving us the toughness of psyche to permit our soul to carry its burden. For then we no longer have to carry it alone, or solve it, or explain it. We can consent to being finite, which means we can do all we can and know it will not be enough. We can offer the pain and suffering to the heart of God's suffering, there to find redemption. In all pain we pray for God's good will to work in that situation like yeast in the heavy, inert lump of our sin.

Nothing is so daunting to the human spirit as the extremes of suffering, experienced directly, as in the Nazi concentration camps or the Russian gulags, or indirectly, as we come to know about those extremes of human tyranny. At the very least, we can add our prayers of remembrance to the litanies of those who sustain their compassion for such suffering in such additions as those to the Jewish Passover service that invoke the memory of the victims of Hitler. We can look in our prayers for some understanding of such suffering, even if we cannot verbalize it as Emil Fackenheim does at the end of his arresting set of lectures on *God's Presence in History*. There is a model for such prayer in the words that follow his repetition of the end of the song of the Warsaw Ghetto Jewish Underground, *Wir zeinen do* (We are here):

> We are here, exist, survive, endure, witnesses to God and man even if abandoned by God and man. Jews after Auschwitz will never understand the longing, defiance, endurance of the Jews at Auschwitz. But so far as is humanly possible they must make them their own as they carry the whole Jewish past forward into a future yet unknown.[1]

Prayer draws us into the world: we feel others' pain and joy more acutely. Our defences, our ability to withdraw, our numbness, our retreat into self-preoccupation dilute, thin out, prove less effective. Prayer opens our eyes, ears, our very pores, to the complete interdependence of ourselves with others and others with ourselves. Not the least of the openings is in the psyche, which has become the active collaborator of the spirit. In liturgical worship, for example, we feel keenly our dependence on all the other worshippers gone before us, those who fashioned the rituals, the worship-forms, the set prayers. All those in the past support our personal prayers in the present. And our prayers in their turn feed back into the liturgy, imbuing it with a personal immediacy and quickening life, a constant psychological presence. Our private devotions flow

[1] See Emil C. Fackenheim, *God's Presence in History* (New York, Harper Torchbooks, 1972), pp. 97–8.

into the public and the public worship reaches us in our most personal identities.

The Church as the Body of Christ takes on vivid reality as a living organism of God's presence in the world. There we find peace for all the stutterings of our speech, all our unformed energies, individual and collective, personal and social. There, in prayer both private and liturgical, we find a space for aggressions, hatreds, discouragements, chaotic urges, and undirected longings to be experienced, brought into conversation with God. Slowly they take on shape to be used in our shared life. When ignored, these unharnessed energies are acted out by us against our neighbours and ourselves. The anger we do not understand whips out at our defenceless child. The love that is undirected and unreceived turns to hate.

In the interior space that prayer opens up in us, we can make good use of the undirected energies that so often take the form of a hate-filled acting-out or an equally destructive angry love. Our psyche provides the necessary distance in which to see what is happening to us, good or bad. Our soul provides the necessary container in which to carry what is happening in us, good or bad. The terrible extremes of the human condition are acceptable now as the necessary polarities and paradoxes of freedom. We can say anything, dare anything, in prayer. We can follow Dante, for example, when he puts such startling words in the mouth of Bernard of Clairvaux praying to the Mother of Jesus at the end of *The Divine Comedy*:

> Vergine madre, figlia del tuo figlio,
> umile e alta più che creatura . . .

> Virgin Mother, daughter of thy son,
> lowly and yet higher than any other creature . . .[1]

We can see what it means for us to say with him, in our own words, or in his, that human nature was so ennobled in her that its maker did not disdain to be made in its making. We can dare to follow Julian of Norwich in her reading of the persons of the Trinity, not simply with a modern determination to remedy the injustices of sexism, but with a much older practice of prayer than most people know about. We can see and say with Lady Julian that 'God almighty is our kindly Father: and God all-wisdom is our kindly Mother', and seeing that 'of God's making we are double: that is to say, substantial and sensual', say that Jesus is 'our

---

[1] See the opening lines of Canto 33 of the *Paradiso* of Dante's *Commedia*. For Bernard and Dante, see below pp. 287–8 and 309–11 respectively.

Mother of mercy in taking our sensuality', and look to 'our precious Mother Jesus' to 'feed us with himself'.[1]

Nothing is too daring for the life of prayer. Nothing is too difficult, at least to contemplate in ourself and in God and converse about with ourself and with God. We are not made perfect in such contemplation or conversation nor is our world. But neither are we daunted by our imperfection or our world's. We know that in prayer the centre of Christian truth is made accessible to us, the lowly brought to the heights, the creature joined to the Creator, God made open to us as Mother and Father, everything to the fullest possible living together of God and man.

5 Sociology and the Study of Spirituality

ANTHONY RUSSELL

An Orthodox monk and an Anglican layman who shared a room at an ecumenical congress were each equally puzzled by the practices of the other. The Anglican awoke early to spend time in private prayer and meditation, but the monk did not appear to pray at all. When they came to discuss this matter, the Anglican layman spoke of the significance of private prayer and a personal spirituality, whilst the monk explained that he belonged to a community which prayed eight times a day. Initially, it might be thought that such differences in spirituality and the practice of prayer might be accounted for entirely by reference to history and theological tradition. However, as this chapter seeks to examine, the perspectives of sociology can contribute to an analytical study of spirituality.[2]

At one level, it might be suggested that spirituality is a general, widely distributed phenomenon which is subjected to a particular discipline by the churches. At another level, it might be regarded as a peculiar and distinctive experience vouchsafed to only exceptional individuals. In this latter context, the term 'mysticism' is sometimes used to denote *virtuoso* religious experience.[3] In part the difference may lie in the extent to which spirituality can be institutionalized, in so far as there can be routinized and ritualized procedures for its attainment (as in the case of the Orthodox monk). The existence of spiritual exercises and acknowledged

---

[1] See (ET) *The Revelations of Divine Love of Julian of Norwich* (London, Burns Oates; New York, Harper, 1961), pp. 158, 159, 160, 164. See below, pp. 335-7.

[2] I am indebted to many people for their help in the preparation of this chapter and in particular to Dr Bryan Wilson and Canon Leslie Houlden.

[3] See F. C. Happold, *Mysticism* (Harmondsworth, Penguin, 1963), pp. 15-21.

33

procedures carries the implication that spirituality is something that can be attained by diligent and conscientious effort along properly conducted lines. By contrast, the concept of mysticism suggests a different understanding (although of course, we know that physical deprivation can induce mystical experience) and it may be that mysticism is essentially an individual experience in which there is much less direct control and consequently less predictable results.

The intellectual life of Western society is largely based on the capacity to distinguish between knowledge, as that which can be apprehended and verified by individuals for themselves, and mere belief and opinion. The writings of saints and mystics are not concerned with 'knowledge' in the sense of empirically verifiable facts, but rather with 'an awareness of God' in the sense of private or communal experiences of the encounter with God. Spirituality has its source in that which is the raw material of all religion, namely, a consciousness of a beyond, a something which, though it is interwoven with this world, is essentially external to the material phenomena of the world. Indeed, spirituality may be considered as the essence of the religious phenomenon for it is concerned with the nature and content of the relationship between an individual and God. Like all relationships, spirituality is principally a matter of the heart rather than the intellect; as the unknown author of *The Cloud of Unknowing* wrote: 'By love can God be gotten and holden, by thought and understanding never.'[1]

The principal characteristics of the spiritual experience are its subjectivity and its inwardness: it is an intensely personal experience. Many of the leading texts of spirituality are predominantly autobiographical. Otherwordly orientation is frequently a distinctive feature of spiritual writing, some of which expresses a longing to escape from the world and worldliness. Influenced by Neoplatonist and gnostic thought (see pp. 93–9), it is concerned with the soul's developing detachment from the world and its flight to God. This configuration of subjectivity, inwardness and otherworldliness makes it possible for much spiritual literature to be regarded as 'purely devotional' and to exist in a realm beyond philosophical arguments and theological controversies. Like music or poetry it can be appreciated quite independently of critical analysis and of knowledge of its background or context. Most of the books on the Christian spiritual tradition are written essentially as guides to the faithful and as devotional reading.

Often such books tend to portray the saints and mystics of the Church as lonely and isolated figures wrestling with their vision of God and their

[1] Anon., *The Cloud of Unknowing* (CWS 1981), ch. 6. See below, pp. 332–4.

developing understanding of his ways. However, they may also be seen as speaking for a community whose thought-patterns and language they use, and which in turn interprets, and seeks to understand and apply the spiritual knowledge that has been gained. In a sense, there is no such thing as the isolated religious visionary or the solitary experience of the mystic, for mystical experience as described closely interrelates with the religious and cultural tradition from which it comes. Such experiences have to be understood and interpreted within the context of the corporate belief of that church, and of the society of which that church is a part.[1] Just as Durkheim demonstrated the social constraints on such an apparently random, irrational and personal act as suicide, so the perspective of sociology is able to show that the mystical experience is closely related to the social and religious context in which it occurs.

Although early sociologists tended to regard religion as a naive and pre-sociological theory of society, the influence of the sociological perspective can now be discerned in many areas of theological studies, and particularly in the study of the organizational aspects of religion and religious literature. Analysis of the functions and role of the writings in the New Testament, together with an account of their interrelationship with the social and cultural context in which they were written, have opened up a new understanding and approach to the study of the New Testament.[2] The beginnings of a similar approach may be discerned in the study of spirituality.[3] It has been shown for instance how external factors, particularly persecution, have given rise to particular forms of spirituality, whether in the second or twentieth centuries. There are many accounts of a remarkable flowering of mysticism in the fourteenth century, and particularly in England, and these accounts relate this occurrence to the social and economic conditions of the period.[4] The studies of witchcraft in the sixteenth and seventeenth centuries have demonstrated the complexity of the interrelationships between belief,

[1] See David Edwards, *Religion and Change* (New York, Harper & Row, 1969; London, Hodder & Stoughton, 1974), pp. 45f.

[2] See R. Scroggs, 'The Sociological Interpretation of the New Testament: the present state of research', *NTS* 26 (1980), pp. 164–79; and Stephen Barton, 'Paul and the Cross: a sociological approach', *Theology* 85 (Jan. 1982), pp. 13–19.

[3] See Rowan Williams, *The Wound of Knowledge* (London, DLT, 1979); US edn, *Christian Spirituality: a Theological History from the New Testament to Luther and St John of the Cross* (Atlanta, John Knox Press, 1980); Peter Brown, *The Cult of the Saints* (London, Faber; Chicago, University of Chicago Press, 1981); and D. Weinstein and R. M. Bell, *Saints and Society: the Two Worlds of Western Christendom 1000–1700* (University of Chicago Press, 1982).

[4] For instance, David Knowles, *The English Mystical Tradition* (London, Burns Oates; New York, Harper, 1961), p. 39.

culture and social constraints.[1]

So far there is no entirely satisfactory typology of spirituality, but it may be possible to distinguish between two forms – 'ecclesial' spirituality and 'privatized' spirituality. Clearly, such a distinction is not easy to maintain, for both social and personal dimensions are closely interwoven and held together in the Christian understanding. However, in traditional, pre-industrial society, religious belief and practice belonged essentially to the public realm of activity and drew upon images, thought-patterns and language which belonged to the public realm of religious affirmation. By the same token, the belief pattern and the practice of spirituality were closely held together and interrelated.

Medieval spirituality (in so far as generalizations are possible) was essentially public, communal and 'ecclesial' in nature and focused in the liturgy of the Church, the Bible and the cult of the saints. The effect of the Reformation, and its challenge to the divine authority of human institutions and traditions, was to give considerable impetus to a movement towards a more privatized and internalized spirituality. Clearly, this had its antecedents in the practices of the early medieval period, particularly the growth of a more privatized understanding of sin and penitence (and the development of personal sacramental confession). In the post-Reformation period, both in the Catholicism of the Counter-Reformation and in Protestantism, there developed forms of spirituality which were characterized by a greater personal and internalized orientation and this is reflected in the spiritual writing of the period. Protestants declared that God spoke to them personally through Scripture and also in the intimacy and secrecy of their own consciences. Such changes in spirituality can be related to wider changes in society as the old constraints of traditional, agrarian, *Gemeinschaft* patterns were increasingly broken down under the impact of social change.[2]

Since the sixteenth century, several developments may be noted which have served to accentuate further the tendency to more private styles of spirituality. The direct appeal to the individual conscience and to the private and internalized 'experience' of God found in the language of personal conversion in Methodism, in the Evangelical Movement in England and in the Awakenings in America, came to characterize the privatized spirituality of an increasingly *gesellschaftlich* society. Luther's criticism of the Church as a human rather than divine institution gath-

[1] See Keith Thomas, *Religion and the Decline of Magic* (London, Weidenfeld and Nicolson; New York, Scribner, 1971).
[2] The distinction between *Gemeinschaft* (community) and *Gesellschaft* (association) was made by Ferdinand Toennies in his book with that title (1887; (ET) *Community and Society*, New York, Harper & Row, 1963).

ered momentum. Later, when historical criticism showed the extent to which the Bible itself was a product of human literary creation, religious people affected by this tended to turn in upon their own personal relationship with God. Both the spirituality of Kierkegaard and the lonely mysticism of Dag Hammarskjöld provide striking examples of the movement away from the 'ecclesial' spirituality of pre-industrial society. Of course, any neat periodization is impossible but the interrelationship between changes in society and in spirituality can be discerned.

One of the dominant perspectives of sociology is that of functionalism, for it offers the student of religion a means of understanding, within the social context, phenomena that seem arbitrary, non-rational and random. It may be that salvation and the provision of appropriate guidance for its attainment are the manifest functions of spirituality. In traditional societies, salvation may be seen as essentially communal in its orientation, in that those seeking salvation are regarded as a body (the pilgrim band) and that salvation itself is seen in corporate terms (the city of God). In advanced societies, the dominant orientation shifts to a privatized conception of salvation and the appropriate guidance becomes increasingly personal and internalized, and concerned increasingly with individual techniques and methods. In advanced societies, the tradition of the Church ceases to be a public reference for society but becomes the private possession of individuals who speak predominantly of their personal spirituality and their private spiritual quest.[1] In all periods of Christian history both 'ecclesial' and 'privatized' orientations have coexisted but the dominance of privatized understanding in contemporary Western society can be seen as related to the context in which those understandings arise, and, in advanced urban societies, the process of change has encouraged developments in spirituality which have a close relationship to the secular psychotherapeutic movements of contemporary society. There has also been a growing interest in the meditation techniques of Hinduism and in the Buddhist faith (historically the most privatized of the world religions) even within the Christian churches.[2]

A further, though related, classification of spirituality may be attempted by observing the difference between two traditions in spirituality which might be termed 'the clerical-priestly tradition' and the 'lay-popularist tradition'. Many of the masters of Christian spirituality have not been members of the clergy, and women have played a more signifi-

[1] Concern for the increasing privatization of religion can be seen in the report of the Doctrine Commission of the Church of England, *Believing in the Church* (London, SPCK, 1981; Wilton, Ct., Morehouse-Barlow, 1982).

[2] See Bede Griffiths, *Return to the Centre* (London, Fount, 1978; Springfield, Ill., Templegate, 1982); and Herbert Slade, *Exploration into Contemplative Prayer* (London, DLT; New York, Paulist, 1975).

cant part in this dimension of church life than in other areas. The dichotomy between the two traditions has existed throughout the history of the Church. In all ages, the attitude of the 'lay tradition' has tended to be more privatized, more localized, and more mystical in its orientation. Its roots lie in the personal experience of spiritual realities and in mystical contemplation of the natural world and God. It finds expression in the cult of the holy place, in the nature-mysticism of much 'folk spirituality' and in such diverse writings as those of William Wordsworth, Thomas Traherne, Richard Jefferies, Emily Dickinson, Simone Weil, Evelyn Underhill and Teilhard de Chardin. The Catholic Church's attitude to the writings of Teilhard de Chardin (though he was a Jesuit) may be regarded as symptomatic of the suspicion in which the mysticism and theological imprecision of the 'lay tradition' is regarded. By contrast, the 'clerical tradition' is essentially sacramental and biblical in its orientation and concerned with the public and communal dimension of spirituality.

It is possible to see in the progress of the Tractarian Movement in the nineteenth century the development of a more clericalist spirituality (allied to a more sacerdotal and professional understanding of the nature of the priesthood) which in large measure supplanted the essentially lay spirituality of eighteenth-century Anglicanism. The lay tradition in spirituality finds expression principally in popular devotion and in hymns. Perhaps the history of popular devotion should play a larger part in the study of spirituality, which has so far been concerned almost exclusively with the leaders of spirituality (the 'athletes of the Spirit' as they are sometimes referred to in devotional literature).[1]

In the study of liturgy and doctrine the place of the sociological perspective does not have to be argued, and this tentative essay has sought to indicate some of the areas in which it could widen and enhance the study of spirituality (and have helped the Orthodox monk and the Anglican layman mentioned above, to understand one another's spirituality). It is clear that contemporary interest in the spiritual tradition of the Church is increasing, not only for its own sake, but because Christian identity can be discovered precisely in humanity's religious sense and spiritual experiences. But spirituality is not 'pure devotion'; like other aspects of church life, it is a cultural phenomenon and it needs to be studied within the context of its interrelationship with the society in which it is found.

[1] For exemplary studies in lay spirituality, see L. F. Church, *The Early Methodist People* (London, Epworth, 1948; New York, Philosophical Library, 1948); and *More about the Early Methodist People* (London, Epworth, 1949).

6 Media of Spirituality

EDWARD YARNOLD

To study the spirituality of a person or a community, you would look at what they read and what they wrote. But spirituality is expressed in many ways apart from treatises explicitly dealing with the subject. The purpose of this chapter is to consider some of them.

I LITURGY

The principle *lex orandi, lex credendi*, asserting as it does the mutual interaction of prayer and belief,[1] implies a similar interaction of liturgy and spirituality. No one's spirituality is entirely individual. Spirituality is shaped by public worship; and conversely forms and styles of public worship are conditioned by the spirituality of the worshipping community.

The movement from spirituality to liturgical forms is easier to demonstrate than the reverse. A staple diet of hymns, long and perhaps improvised prayers, and an extended sermon expresses a different spirituality from that which is embodied almost exclusively in the celebration of the Eucharist. And, within the sacramental tradition, a liturgy which encourages the people to participate in the action and to express their fellowship by the sign of peace expresses a different spirituality from a Mass celebrated inaudibly in Latin, by a celebrant facing away from the people, who are engrossed in private devotions.[2]

The movement from liturgy to spirituality is harder to establish. In the Church of England a spirituality emphasizing social commitment has been nourished both by Anglo-Catholic ritualism and by evangelical worship in which the word dominates. One cannot even show that active Christian engagement in the world is impossible without the nourishment of a liturgy in which the sense of community is strongly expressed. Among Roman Catholics charitable and apostolic organizations like the Society of St Vincent de Paul and the Legion of Mary have flourished in parishes where the people's liturgical participation was near zero. Perhaps the sense of sharing with fellow Christians in the service of others provided a substitute for the experience of community in public worship. Christian discipleship is a tough creature, and can survive much liturgical maltreatment.

Nevertheless a liturgical celebration contains a number of elements

[1] See G. Wainwright, *Doxology*, and C. P. M. Jones's article above, pp. 3–9.
[2] See G. Wainwright, 'The Periods of Liturgical History', *SL* 33–8.

which express, and can be expected to foster, a particular form of spirituality in the participants.

(*a*) *Place*.   A celebration held in the home can arouse the sense of God's presence in the family; and, if neighbours are invited, there can be a strong feeling that the families concerned form a community, with corresponding privileges and obligations. Sunday worship held in a hall for lack of a church can foster in the congregation the sense that they form an underprivileged group within the local community; it might also arouse the feeling of apathy and indifference. On the other hand, a simple wooden church can symbolize a community's sense of identity, which the people might be afraid of losing if they joined a group worshipping in a larger, more worthy building.

(*b*) *Architecture*.   When worship is conducted in a church building, the architecture can affect the people's spirituality in many ways.[1] A church can be constructed like a meeting hall, so as to provide ideal conditions for a congregation to hear a sermon; the building itself proclaims a faith in the paramountcy of the word. It can be constructed so that the focus of attention is the altar; and even this can be done in several ways. The altar can be set within a raised sanctuary, symbolizing the people's role as prayerful observers at the eucharistic sacrifice conducted by the priest; it can be hidden behind an icon-screen, as is the Orthodox custom, so as to arouse a sense of mystery and awe; it can be set in the middle of the people, emphasizing their share in the sacred action. Architects have devised means of expressing visually the link between baptism (the font), the Eucharist (the altar) and the word (the lectern, ambo or pulpit).

(*c*) *Apparel*.[2]   The dress of the celebrants can be chosen to express an other-worldly solemnity, as do the vestments of the Orthodox priest. It can be decorated with motifs expressing certain aspects of the celebration, such as the bread and the cup, or a dove and fire at Pentecost. Among Roman Catholics baroque vestments might be chosen to express a rejection of what are seen as modern desacralizing trends. A conservative evangelical Anglican might choose surplice, scarf and bands, so as to proclaim his adhesion to the principles of the Reformation.

(*d*) *Sacred art*.   Unlike architecture, the purpose of church art is contemplation rather than use. Sacred art is an expression of faith, and

---

[1] See A. Biéler, (ET) *Architecture in Worship* (London, Oliver and Boyd; Philadelphia, Westminster, 1965); P. G. Cobb, 'The Architectural Setting of the Liturgy', *SL* 473–87.
[2] See W. J. Grisbrooke, 'Vestments', *SL* 488–92.

therefore of spirituality. In secular life art is one of the non-verbal forms by which we express a personal relationship; we exchange, and lovingly regard, photographs of those who are dear to us. So too faith, which is a personal relationship with God, finds expression in visual forms. Theology is capable of more precision as an expression of faith; but, unless it is theological poetry like that of Dante or G. M. Hopkins or T. S. Eliot, it does not engage the affective level of the personality as art does. William Purdy, in his illuminating little book on this theme, speaks of the 'shared function of theology and art' in articulating the basic personal relationship with Christ in faith.[1] Art is no mere visual aid illustrating the theologian's work; it is an expression of faith and spirituality in a different medium from theology, appealing to a different level of the human psyche. No one who has looked at the enormous stern features of Christ the *Pantocrator* which dominate the apses of so many Byzantine churches can doubt that art can express and foster a spirituality more powerfully than theological treatises can.

(*e*) *Ceremonies.* Anthropologists like Mary Douglas and sociologists like David Martin[2] have studied the way in which rites give the worshipper a sense of identity within a society and a tradition. Both writers have castigated the ignorant iconoclastic spirit with which liturgical reform has sometimes been implemented. Examples of ceremonies which embody spiritualities are easy to find: the sign of peace expressing fellowship in Christ, and avoided by those whose idea of public worship is that of a gathering of people directed individually towards God; genuflection before the reserved sacrament, expressing adoration and respect for Christ present in the Eucharist, and discarded not only by those who have no belief in the continuing eucharistic presence, but also by those who see the Eucharist as essentially an *action*, in which worshippers are one in and with Christ, but which terminates at the end of the celebration.

(*f*) *Music.* Liturgical music can express a spirituality of sober restraint (German chorales), a sweet sentimentality, an otherworldly peace (Gregorian chant), or contact with the secular (liturgical folk music). The choice of instrument – organ or guitar? – can likewise represent a choice of spiritualities (see below, p. 599).

---

[1] W. A. Purdy, *Seeing and Believing: the Theology of Art* (Cork, Mercier Press; Butler, Wisc., Clergy Book Services, 1976), p. 115.

[2] D. A. Martin, *The Breaking of the Image: a Sociology of Christian Theory and Practice.* Oxford, Blackwell; New York, St Martin's Press, 1980. Mary Douglas, *Natural Symbols: Explorations in Cosmology.* Harmondsworth, Penguin, 1973; New York, Pantheon Books, 1970.

2 THE BIBLE

All genuine Christian spirituality is built on a scriptural foundation. This is so not only for the 'Bible-believing' Protestant, but also for the Roman Catholic; Paul VI reminded his Church that devotion to Mary must be based on Scripture.[1] But this foundation will always be the Bible *as interpreted according to a living tradition*; even the fundamentalist reads and applies the sacred text in the light of the traditions of his or her community.

The Bible can be used in many ways for the nourishment of the spiritual life. The most formal setting is the word of God read in a worshipping assembly, so that it is manifestly proclaimed and interpreted within the community. But there is also a long tradition of individual, prayerful study of the Scriptures: the eunuch whom Philip baptized (Acts 9) was reading Isaiah. Medieval monasticism described this private meditative reading of the Bible as *lectio divina*.

3 NON-LITURGICAL PRAYER

It is probable that nowadays less importance is attached to regular private prayer on rising and retiring. If so, the change is indicative of a loss of faith not so much in the value of prayer as in the value of discipline for all areas of life. But the change may also illustrate a triumph of secular over religious values: ordinary Christians are less prone to see themselves as different from their non-Christian peers, and are often even less inclined to wish to appear so. On the other hand, in the Roman Catholic Church, the morning and evening offices of the revised Liturgy of the Hours have been adopted by many people who have no obligation to recite them. The old-fashioned prayer-books, like *The Garden of the Soul*, of Bishop Richard Challoner (see below, pp. 424–5), have been replaced by more liturgical books, or collections of prayers expressing social commitment, like those of Michel Quoist.[2] Prayer-groups, including those of the charismatic variety, flourish in many Christian traditions (see p. 571).

Non-Christians, or former Christians, or half-Christians are more likely to seek techniques of prayer in the non-Christian East, or in systems like Transcendental Meditation, rather than in the Christian mystical tradition. The search seems sometimes to be for a new experience to relieve boredom, for peace of mind, or for contemplation without sacrifice or faith – like Franny's disastrous experiments with the Jesus Prayer (see p. 176) in J. D. Salinger's story, *Franny and Zooey*.[3]

[1] *Marialis Cultus* (1974), n. 30.
[2] e.g. (ET) *Prayers*. London and New York, Sheed and Ward, 1963.
[3] Boston and Toronto, Little, Brown, 1961.

Nevertheless there is a flourishing market in books on Christian prayer, and a demand even among laypeople for retreats lasting as much as six, eight or even thirty days. It is however odd that, at a time when there is an interest in techniques of contemplation involving the repetition of words or syllables, there has been a decline in the praying of the Rosary, with its repeated Our Fathers, Hail Marys and Glory Bes, which are intended to hold the mind in the presence of an episode in Christ's life.

4 WAYS OF LIFE

In many Christian Churches there are communities whose whole life is dedicated to the following of Christ according to a definite rule. The clearest examples are the religious orders, whose members usually take the three vows of poverty, chastity and obedience. These communities embody the spirituality not only of their members but also of the Churches which regard them as an authentic form of Christian life. The decrees of Vatican II, however, insist that the search for holiness which motivates such people is not something additional to the call of every Christian to follow Christ, but is a particular form of obeying that call without reserve.[1] It is not only in the Roman Catholic and Orthodox Churches that the religious life is to be found. The Anglican Communion contains many religious congregations, some of them long established; and the Taizé community shows that the ideal is also practised in the Reformed tradition (see pp. 573–5).

5 THE CULT OF THE SAINTS

Devotion to the Blessed Virgin Mary and the saints, expressed by statues, pictures, shrines, lights, pilgrimages, prayers and hymns, can of course deflect the Christian's heart from the love of Christ, which should be its focus, though many who observe such practices find on the contrary that they are brought closer to Christ.[2] Such devotions can express a joy and confidence in the way in which God works through human inter-mediaries; they depend upon the doctrine of the communion of saints, which asserts the interdependence of all Christians, living and dead. These practices, at their best, harness human emotions and created beauty to the service of God, and often lead to a gentler, more tolerant spirituality than the austerer devotions of a strict Calvinist.

---

[1] Decree on the Church, *Lumen Gentium*, ch. 6.
[2] See *Marialis Cultus*, e.g. n. 25.

6   IMAGINATIVE WRITING

In addition to explicitly devotional works, like *The Imitation of Christ* of Thomas à Kempis (see p. 324), the *Introduction to the Devout Life* of St Francis de Sales (see p. 380), and, in the Anglican tradition, William Law's *Serious Call* (see p. 453), spirituality can often be more movingly expressed in the form of poems and works of fiction. Sometimes the theme is explicitly devotional, as in the poems of G. M. Hopkins and George Herbert (see p. 433) or Newman's *Dream of Gerontius* (see p. 426); sometimes the religious message is cast in the form of parable or allegory, as in most of C. S. Lewis's stories (d. 1963); sometimes, as in J. R. R. Tolkien's *Lord of the Rings* (d. 1973), the values expressed are human, though the religious sense is present as an all-pervasive concern with goodness and dignity. At the time of writing there is a fashion for films about visitors from other worlds (e.g. *Close Encounters of the Third Kind* and *E.T.*). Many of these films are dangerously confused, as they seem designed to evoke religious feelings directed not towards a deity but towards a lovable and utterly benevolent space-invader.

PART TWO

The History of Spirituality

I

INTRODUCTION

A BIBLICAL ROOTS

1 The Old Testament

JOHN BARTON

Albertz, R., *Persönliche Frömmigkeit und offizielle Religion: Religionsinterner Pluralismus in Israel und Babylon*. Stuttgart, 1978.

Anderson, G. W., '"Sicut Cervus": Evidence in the Psalter of Private Devotion in Ancient Israel'. *VT*, 30 (1980), pp. 388–97.

Balentine, S. E., *The Hidden God: The Hiding of the Face of God in the Old Testament*. Oxford and New York, OUP, 1982.

Barr, J., 'Theophany and Anthropomorphism in the Old Testament'. *VTS*, 7 (1959), pp. 31–8.

Bradshaw, P. F., *Daily Prayer in the Early Church. A Study of the Origin and Early Development of the Divine Office* (Alcuin Club, no. 63). London, SPCK, 1981.

Childs, B. S., *Exodus. A Commentary* (Philadelphia, Westminster Press; London, SCM, 1974), pp. 553–600.

Eichrodt, W., (ET) *Theology of the Old Testament*, vol. ii (Philadelphia, Westminster; London, SCM, 1967), pp. 268–315.

Johnson, A. R., *The Cultic Prophet in Ancient Israel*. 2nd edn, Cardiff, University of Wales, 1962.

Johnson, A. R., *The Cultic Prophet and Israel's Psalmody*. Cardiff, University of Wales, 1979.

Kaufmann, U. M., 'Expostulation with the Divine', in *Twentieth Century Interpretations of the Book of Job*, ed. P. S. Sanders (Englewood Cliffs, N. J., Prentice-Hall, 1968), pp. 66–77 (= *Interpretation*, 18 (1964), pp. 171–82).

Kraus, H.-J., (ET) *Worship in Israel*. Oxford, Blackwell; Richmond, Va., John Knox Press, 1966.

Mowinckel, S., (ET) *The Psalms in Israel's Worship* (2 vols.). Oxford, Blackwell; New York, Abingdon, 1962.

Perlitt, L., 'Die Verborgenheit Gottes', in *Probleme biblischer Theologie* (Gerhard von Rad zum 70. Geburtstag), ed. H. W. Wolff (Munich 1971), pp. 367–82.

Rad, G. von., *Wisdom in Israel* (London, SCM; Nashville, Abingdon, 1972), pp. 144–76.

Saggs, H. W. F., *The Encounter with the Divine in Mesopotamia and Israel*. London, Athlone Press; Atlantic Heights, N.J., Humanities Press, 1978.

Silberman, L. H., 'The Human Deed in a Time of Despair: the Ethics of

Apocalyptic', in *Essays in Old Testament Ethics*, ed. J. L. Crenshaw and J. T. Willis. New York, Ktav Publishing House, 1974.

Terrien, S., *The Elusive Presence*. San Francisco, Harper & Row, 1978.

de Vaux, R., (ET) *Ancient Israel. Its Life and Institutions* (New York, McGraw-Hill, 1961; 2nd edn, London, DLT, 1965), pp. 457–66.

Viviano, B.T., *Study as Worship. Aboth and the New Testament* (Studies in Judaism in Late Antiquity 26). Leiden 1978.

Vorländer, H., *Mein Gott. Die Vorstellung vom persönlichen Gott im Alten Orient und im Alten Testament*. Neukirchen 1975.

Wilson, R. R., *Prophecy and Society in Ancient Israel*. Philadelphia, Fortress, 1980.

The theme of 'Old Testament spirituality' may be addressed in two ways. It may be taken as 'the spirituality of Old Testament times', a subject for which the Old Testament happens to provide nearly all our evidence: in this sense, to study Old Testament spirituality is to study the *ancestry* of Jewish and Christian spirituality. But for Jews and Christians alike the Old Testament is not merely a collection of historical evidence. It is also a text that continues to form part of Scripture, and from which therefore the modern believer expects to be able to derive spiritual nourishment. And so 'Old Testament spirituality' can also mean a spirituality nourished by the Old Testament – by the Old Testament *as we now have it*, rather than by the stages through which Israelite religion may have passed on its way to the final synthesis that the finished Old Testament expresses.

Of course these two things, the Old Testament as evidence for ancient Israel and the Old Testament as a document of the believing community, are not opposed to each other. On the contrary, in many ways the finished Old Testament is the natural outcome of the long and winding course of the religious beliefs and practices of ancient Israel. Nevertheless we shall gain a clearer picture of our subject if we try to hold them apart in our exposition.

1 SPIRITUALITY IN ANCIENT ISRAEL

CORPORATE OR INDIVIDUAL?

If it is agreed that by 'spirituality' we are to understand the spiritual life of individuals, rather than those corporate expressions of religious conviction that are better classified as 'liturgy', then it must be said that our evidence for spirituality in ancient Israel is extremely limited. In the first place, a great many psalms and prayers are plainly corporate in character: see, for example, Pss. 20, 21, 33, 44, 46–48, 60, 65, 67, 74, 79, 80, 115, 124–127, 137, where the speaker, in the first person plural, must be the congregation at worship. This is often the case even where the psalm is ostensibly individual but, in the opinion of most scholars, this individual is a personification of the community. A clear example of this would be the Song of Moses (Exod. 15.1–18); very probably the same is true of the poems that make up Lamentations; and many of the psalms make much better sense if understood as 'cultic' or liturgical poetry, in which the 'I' who speaks is the voice of the congregation (even if a single singer was charged with the actual recitation), than if they are treated as religious lyrics for use in private prayer. Thus the purpose of Ps. 118 is surely to give thanks for victory in battle, and the 'I' who was 'surrounded' (vv. 10–11), who 'called on the LORD' (v. 5), and who 'will not die, but live, and recount the deeds of the LORD' (v. 17), is the nation as summed up in its spokesman (perhaps the king?), rather than an individual. Form-critical study of the Psalms generally assumes as a starting-point that most psalms have a liturgical, rather than a private, origin. Although there is no doubt that all of the psalms came in the course of time to have an individual use, comparatively few seem to have begun life with this function. Genuinely personal psalms do exist, and will be discussed later; but for now we must recognize that the liturgical origin of many biblical prayers and hymns makes them less promising than might be thought as evidence for the spirituality of ancient Israelites.

EXCEPTIONAL INDIVIDUALS

But even where we do possess what purport to be the prayers of individuals, our problems are not over. In very many cases the individuals in question are clearly treated by the biblical writers as wholly exceptional. Moses, Jeremiah, Job or Abraham are hardly presented as examples to be imitated in the matter of prayer; they are men who had a privileged access to God, and who could speak to him with a freedom and directness that ordinary worshippers would not dare to claim for themselves. We might say, though, that the prayers attributed to such people must have represented a type of spirituality that was *thinkable* for an ancient Israelite, and the God they presupposed as the object of prayer must have been recognizable to ordinary Israelites as the God to whom they also prayed, however much more circumspectly they would need to approach him themselves. Four aspects of the prayer of the famous heroes of Israel's past are important here.

(a) *Intercession*

Not everyone associates intercession with 'spirituality'; in some traditions it does not belong to the higher reaches of the spiritual life, where the soul enjoys communion with God, and prayers of 'asking' are left behind. This does not seem to have been so for the earliest Christian communities whose prayer-life we can reconstruct, nor for first-century Judaism, and the Old Testament certainly does not lead one to think that prayer devoid of intercession had ever existed in Israel. Indeed it may well be that the further advanced people were in the 'spiritual life' (a term which sounds anachronistic in Old Testament study), the greater the part intercession played in their prayer. Whoever was thought, in different periods and by different groups, to count as a 'prophet', it seems clear that this term was understood to imply peculiar closeness to God, and that this closeness could be seen most clearly in the prophet's powers of *mediation* between God and his people – in bringing them messages from God, certainly, but also in interceding for them with God (Gen. 20.7; Amos 7.1–6; and Jer. 7.16 and 15.1, which presumably imply that prophets were normally expected to intercede, and that their intercession was efficacious). Moses in particular spends much time in praying for his people, and sometimes succeeds in changing God's mind even when it seemed quite made up (Exod. 32.7–14; Num. 14.13–25). The God to whom people prayed in Israel was evidently not an implacable God, even though in practice there might not always be anyone like Moses available to assuage his anger. To stand before God in prayer for the needs of the nation, and to ask that its sins might be pardoned, was the highest of spiritual vocations.

(b) *Arguing with God*

We have just seen that in intercession God might be asked, in a straight-forwardly anthropomorphic way, to change his mind. But this is not, in the prayers of prophetic figures, a matter of making polite requests; and the saving clause 'nevertheless, not my will but thine be done' is conspicuously lacking from the cases we are looking at. It is rather a matter of using all possible arguments in order to persuade God of the justice of one's cause, and of the benefit to himself of acceding to one's request. Abraham asks him, 'Shall not the Judge of all the earth do right?' (Gen. 18.25) – i.e., Will God show himself less just than human judges? Moses argues that God will get a bad name as a distinctly second-rate divinity if he allows his own people to perish (Exod. 32.11–12). Jeremiah demands that he act to avoid the suspicion that the moral order has got out of control (Jer. 18.20; cf. 15.15–18). Job, better known than these three for his quarrel with God, uses every type of argument he can think of to compel God to appear and justify his own conduct. These confrontations with God are by no means always successful, indeed most often they produce no more than a compromise (Exod. 32.33–4; Amos 7.1–9); but they are a proper part of the calling of heroes of the faith. To submit to

God's will without a struggle would not be an improvement.

(c) *The vision of God*

In pre-exilic times the Israelites seem to have spoken rather freely of 'seeing God', meaning by this apparently little more than 'standing before' him in prayer, especially at the major festivals (see, for example, Ps. 42.2; 84.7; and cf. Ps. 27.8–9). But in later times (and this is reflected in the Hebrew text we have received) such references were understood to mean that *God* saw the worshipper – in other words, the verb 'see' was changed into a passive. This development is of a piece with the tendency in post-exilic texts (e.g. Ezekiel) to avoid any suggestion that people might see God, and to suggest that if they did, they would die. It is important to notice, however, that this development makes sense only on the supposition that God was held to be *inherently* visible. Sin (Isa. 6.5) or perhaps finitude (Exod. 33.20) makes it *dangerous* for a human being to see God; but it is not *impossible*, as it is in a philosophical theology where God is not physical. Consequently it is possible throughout the Old Testament period to hold that the vision of God, in a literal sense, had been granted to a few chosen individuals, and among these Moses is of course the prime example. Despite Exod. 33.20 just cited, where even Moses cannot see the face of God, though he is allowed to see his back, a strong tradition held that God talked to Moses 'face to face, as a man speaks with his friend' (Exod. 33.11). It is possible to 'spiritualize' this experience and to see Moses as a type of Jewish or even Christian mystical experience; but it does not seem that Israelites took that way of interpretation during Old Testament times. On the contrary, the vision of God is seen as a reward for exceptional gifts of obedience and leadership, as something which is experienced literally, and as a goal that ought not to be aimed at at all by the ordinary person. Ordinary Israelites, it is said, could not bear to look even at Moses after he had seen God (Exod. 34.29–35); how much less should they seek to see God himself!

(d) *The absence of God*

There are many passages in the Old Testament that stress God's continual presence with his people; but the prayers we are considering at the moment are more notable for speaking of his absence. Job is the most obvious example of this: Job's complaints can be summed up by saying that he is acutely aware of God's absence, and calls on God to *appear*, to become present, to make himself known. But Moses also confronts the possibility that God's presence is not with his people any longer (Exod. 33.12–16); and the prophets (especially Jeremiah) are presented as fearful that the divine presence may have departed from them. (Contrast Jonah, the deliberate parody of a prophet, who cannot bear the fact that God is present, and tries to flee from him.) Here, it seems, we have a real point of contact between the great heroes of Israelite tradition and the ordinary worshipper, for the absence of God is also an important theme in the Psalms. In his anxiety that God might not be present, Moses is no longer an exceptional case, but is reassuringly like both the Israelite nation ('Why sleepest thou, O Lord? Awake! do not cast us off for ever! Why dost thou hide thy face?', Ps. 44.23–4) and the individual worshipper ('Thou didst hide thy face, I was dismayed', Ps. 30.7). It may not be safe to look at God's face, yet for him to turn it away spells desolation (the sun, perhaps, is the model for this). We can certainly speak of a spirituality of the absence of God in ancient Israel, where the experience that God has veiled his face is accompanied by redoubled prayers and entreaties which make out a case for him to return and again reveal it: Psalm 80 is the best example.

ORDINARY INDIVIDUALS

With this we can appropriately turn to what evidence there is of the themes and modes of individual spirituality in Israel. Some at least of the psalms make better sense as the prayers of individuals than as corporate acts of worship. Although we cannot tie them to *particular* individuals – since they are formulaic, all-purpose prayers for use on many similar occasions – nevertheless they clearly belong to occasions in the lives of individuals and their families, rather than of the nation. Form-critical studies try to classify the psalms under various categories, and even if there is no complete agreement about these categories, we can certainly say that the individual psalms deal with a very small range of basic situations. Everyone agrees that there are 'individual laments' – by which is meant not just texts like Ps. 55, lamenting personal distress, but all psalms in which the worshipper is asking God to grant a petition or to act to change some situation in which he finds himself. And everyone agrees, too, that there are 'individual thanksgivings', such as Ps. 30, where the psalmist gives thanks, in effect, that an 'individual lament' has been heard. We should also note, however we classify them, psalms which make confession of sin and ask for forgiveness, and psalms in which the psalmist simply praises God for his actions in creation and redemption, without mentioning any circumstances peculiar to himself (Ps. 147), though it is not clear whether any psalms in this latter category are strictly speaking individual. What this amounts to is that the repertoire of psalmody available to the individual worshipper in Israel made it possible to express praise, thanksgiving, intercession, petition, and penitence – a conclusion that will hardly seem surprising to anyone used to the devotional or liturgical traditions of Judaism and Christianity! The apparent banality of the fact is actually quite important, for it helps to bring out the continuity between ancient Israel and its spiritual descendants down to this day; and, more importantly, to emphasize that the God these Israelites worshipped was conceived, for all his differences from later Jewish or Christian ideas, essentially after the same model. He is a God who is concerned for the needs of the individual as well as the group; powerful enough to grant their requests; angry with sin yet willing to forgive it; amenable to reasoned argument; glorious yet terrible, deserving of praise but dangerous to behold; reliable, yet not predictable; merciful but just; above all a person, even if a larger-than-life person, whose absence is acutely painful even if his presence can be far from comfortable. The God of personal devotion seems to be one with the God of public liturgy, except perhaps that liturgy made more mention of God's historical deeds on behalf of Israel as a nation, as one might expect. If this description of the God the Israelites worshipped sounds lacking in distinctiveness, that is only because he is the kind of God we are used to. No doubt a very similar picture of the God of personal devotion could be extracted from the religious literature of other Semitic peoples in the ancient world – though without the same assurance that the personal God is one with the great gods who created the world, for Israel's monotheism makes a crucial difference. But the difference from other ancient religions, say those of the Far East, should be plain enough.

LITURGICAL SPIRITUALITY

Before concluding this historical section we ought to probe more deeply the contrast between liturgical and private prayer that is a central idea of this volume. Though (as we have seen) the contrast is evidently of some value for the Old Testament, it can easily be exaggerated. 'Liturgy' in Israel hardly consisted of 'services' in our sense: a festival was something nearer a carnival, a holy time during which all actions could be hallowed. Not all prayers made during a festival need thereby have been 'liturgical' prayers. The scanty evidence that we have of how festivals were observed in early Israel suggests that individual worshippers might come into the temple during the festival (not necessarily during a liturgical performance) and offer prayers (1 Sam. 1). Such prayer is obviously 'private' or 'individual', yet it is also 'public' or 'corporate' in that the worshipper is at the sanctuary chiefly because he is taking part in a national festival. It may be because of this blurred distinction between private and public prayer that so many psalms and other prayers in the Old Testament seem to move back and forth between the individual's needs and aspirations and the great themes of the national faith of Israel. Thus in Ps. 77 the worshipper sets at rest his troubled thoughts about God's care for him, and his fears that God may have abandoned him, with a reflection on the miracle at the Red Sea. This integrates his own religious questionings within the framework of 'official' religion; indeed, we could almost say that it represents an appropriation by the individual of the faith of his community. There is no reason to think that this psalm was intended for use at one of the great festivals at which the crossing of the Red Sea was publicly commemorated, but undoubtedly it would make good sense in such a context.

Whatever may be true of the psalms, other Old Testament prayers quite clearly show private prayer being poured into a mould formed by public faith, or – and it is impossible to tell which way round the process actually worked – themes of public worship being adapted to individual needs. When, in the celebration of a festival, the worshipper asserts his or her identity with those who first experienced the events being celebrated, we have a style of 'liturgical piety' still very familiar to Jews and Christians. Thus in Deut. 26.1–11 the worshipper brings his harvest-offering and explains why he is offering it by recounting how God rescued his forefathers from Egypt:

> then *we* cried to the LORD the God of our fathers, and the LORD heard our voice . . . and the LORD brought us out of Egypt . . . And behold, now *I* bring the first of the fruit of the ground which thou, O LORD, hast given me.

The prayers from post-exilic Judaism which the Old Testament preserves seem to indicate that this tendency increased somewhat after the 'official' traditions of Israelite history were fixed in writing. Prayers designed (apparently) for quite specific occasions often make little allusion to the particular needs they were designed to express, but instead use largely stereotyped formulae and refer to a rather small range of historical events – those, in fact, for which there were already liturgical observances. The lengthy prayer of Ezra in Nehemiah 9 may serve as an illustration of this. It begins, in the manner of most later Jewish prayers, with an ascription of praise to God (vv. 6–17), which describes the creation, the guidance of the patriarchs, the Exodus, the giving of the law, and the provision of manna. There follows (vv. 16–31) an account of the subsequent history of Israel as a history of disobedience (cf. Ps. 78; 106), stressing the rebelliousness of Israel and the long-suffering mercy of God. Only then does the prayer turn to the immediate need of the community (vv. 32–7) for forgiveness and deliverance from the foreign yoke; and even here the style is formulaic, as can be seen by a comparison with the prayer of Daniel (Dan. 9) and the Prayer of Manasses. Other passages do record the prayers of individuals in a way that suggests they might have been composed for specific situations (see, for example, Esther 14 and Judith 9), but the tendency to set private petitions within a framework defined by sacred history – by typical events from the past rather than by concrete contemporary concerns – is a very marked feature of Judaism from the exile onwards. Such a blending of private and public prayers is a familiar feature of both the religions that descend from ancient Israel, down to this day.

2 SPIRITUALITY NOURISHED BY THE OLD TESTAMENT

What kind of spirituality will be characteristic of a person who tries to feed on the traditions of prayer and spiritual life which the Old Testament enshrines? There is no way of avoiding the fact that no one in the modern world receives the Old Testament in a 'pure' form. Jews and Christians alike can only assimilate its insights through their own interpretative traditions, and they will read it through Mishnaic-Talmudic, or New Testament/patristic/Reformation spectacles. Nevertheless we might ask, very tentatively, what are the ideas in the Old Testament that remain of importance for the spiritual life, and which would risk being lost if these Scriptures were no longer to claim authority over the heirs to the faith of Israel. Here are some suggestions that might repay more detailed study.

(a) *The presence of God*

As we have seen, the religion of the psalmists seems to hinge on the notion of God's presence with his people. Hymns are sung and prayers offered 'before Yahweh', a metaphor drawn perhaps from the language of the royal court. Sacrifices, cultic worship, and choral singing take place 'in the presence of God' in the manner of a Royal Command Performance; and by analogy the prayers of the individual are offered on the assumption that the worshipper is in the presence of God and so can be assured of a hearing. For this reason the worst thing that can happen, as a number of psalms make clear (e.g. Ps. 51.11), is for God to remove his presence and leave the worshipper in the dark.

One effect of this belief is the growth within the Psalter of the idea that God's presence is so essential that no merely earthly good can compare with it: to be 'with God' is better than riches, and no amount of material well-being can be worth having if God's presence is withdrawn (see especially Ps. 73.23–6). It is clear that for the psalmists themselves this was not a question of setting one's hopes on 'heaven': the sense of the presence of God operates on a wholly this-worldly level. But the idea that to live in the presence of God is better than literally *any* kind of earthly prosperity undoubtedly tends in a 'spiritual' direction, and has been a fruitful theme not only for Christian but also for Jewish mysticism. Even without such developments, however, we can say that the presence of God is one of the central themes of the Old Testament. The Torah sets out the terms on which God will be with his people; the histories show from concrete examples how his presence can be forfeited, and how gracious must be the God who never lets his absence from an unworthy people become permanent; the prophets look forward to the day when God will never be or even seem absent again; and the psalms reflect on all these aspects of presence and absence as they affect both the worshipping community and the individual at prayer. Many psalms speak of a sense of God's temporary absence, and of a hope for his reappearance; and by the most natural of images this is made parallel with the darkness of night and the new light of dawn, the daily pledge that God's mercies are 'new every morning' (Lam. 3.23). Consequently we may say that 'waiting for God' is a persistent theme, nowhere better expressed than in the psalm that encompasses almost every major theme of the Psalter, Ps. 62:

> For God alone my soul waits in silence, for my hope is from him. He only is my rock and my salvation, my fortress; I shall not be shaken. On God rests my deliverance and my honour; my mighty rock, my refuge is God.   (vv. 5–7).

(b) *The hiddenness of God*

There are a few passages in the Old Testament where the presence of God is experienced not as a blessing, but as a threat, where God is actually besought to *hide* his face (Ps. 51.9). Ps. 139 seems to reflect the awareness that God is all too oppressively present everywhere, that it is impossible to escape him; Ps 39.13 asks God to 'look away', not to take such an obsessive interest in his worshipper, to give him a little space in which to be himself for a while. In other places, of course, God's hiddenness is experienced as a punishment; the righteous can live in his presence, but sinners cannot bear the full force of it (Ps. 5.4–6) and have to suffer its withdrawal. The paradoxes here have many parallels in Old Testament talk about God. Because God is a person who is alive and active and who has, we might say, an extremely powerful personality, friendship with him is a great privilege yet also a demanding burden; it is difficult to live with him, even if it is impossible to live without him.

As we have seen, the *theoretical* problems about 'seeing' God which the Western philosophical tradition has raised within both Christianity and Judaism do not arise in the Old Testament world, where God is not literally invisible or lacking in physical substance; but the *practical* problems attaching to his vast scale and terrifying power are seen all too clearly. If even Moses could see only God's back, there was small hope that anyone else could see his face and live! For practical purposes, therefore, the God of the Old Testament is a hidden God, hidden not through any weakness or inadequacy, but because of his very glory and the unworthiness of his human creatures. Yet the God who is hidden from sight in the cloud of his own glory can be *known* by the person who does not seek to *see* him, but rather to obey his will: 'Thus says the high and lofty one who inhabits eternity, whose name is holy: "I dwell in the high and holy place, with him also who is of a contrite heart and humble spirit"' (Isa. 57.15).

(c) *'Torah-mysticism'*

This belief that God is present not with those who seek to see him, but with those who obey him, lies at the root of a style of spirituality that probably arrived in Judaism some time after the Exile, but which has coloured the whole Old Testament record by its influence on the minds of the biblical compilers. Its classic expression is Ps. 119. Here the Law – the system of detailed regulations that were believed in post-exilic Judaism to sum up God's will for Israel – becomes almost an object of veneration, to such an extent that some have spoken of God's being 'incarnate' in the Law for Judaism. This is not a way of putting the matter that would commend itself to most Jews, but it does capture, for the benefit of Christians, the extreme respect with which the Law is regarded. It is the one normative expression of the mind of God and of his intentions for humankind, and by observing all its detailed provisions the worshipper knows God as far as that is either possible or desirable. Furthermore, it is spiritually beneficial not only to *keep* the Law – though it is assumed that that will be done – but also to *meditate* on the Law, in other words to recite it prayerfully to oneself in the presence of God, and to *study* it, poring lovingly over every word, even over every letter. This approach has been described as 'Torah-mysticism'. Though it is a late arrival in the Old Testament, it builds on much earlier material, for Deuteronomy seems deeply imbued with the same desire to see the Law filling the minds and hearts of its readers (see Deut. 11.18–25). It might be said to be the Old Testament's answer to the question of how mankind is to arrive at the 'practice of the presence of God'.

2 The New Testament

C. P. M. JONES

GENERAL

George, A. R., *Communion with God in the NT*. London, Epworth, 1953.

Hamman, A., *La Prière, I. Le Nouveau Testament*. Tournai, 1959. (ET) *Prayer: The NT*. Chicago, Franciscan Herald Press, 1971.

Hoskyns, E. C. and Davey, F. N., *Crucifixion, Resurrection*, ed. G. S. Wakefield. London, SPCK, 1981.

Inge, W. R., *Christian Mysticism*. Bampton Lectures, 1899. London, Methuen, 1899, ch. 2.

Kirk, K. E., *The Vision of God*. London and New York, Longmans, 1931.

Schweizer, E., (ET) *Jesus*. London, SCM, 1971.

Underhill, E., *The Mystic Way: A Psychological Study in Christian Origins*. London, Dent, 1913.

THE SYNOPTIC GOSPELS

(a) General

Barrett, C. K., *Jesus and the Gospel Tradition*. London, SPCK, 1967; Philadelphia, Fortress, 1968.

Bell, G. K. A. and Deissman, A., *Mysterium Christi* (London and New York, Longmans, 1930). Essays by E. C. Hoskyns and C. H. Dodd.

Cadbury, H. J., *The Peril of Modernizing Jesus*. New York, Macmillan, 1937; London, SPCK, 1962.

Cadbury, H. J., *Jesus: What Manner of Man*. New York, Macmillan, 1947; London, SPCK, 1962.

Gerhardsson, B., (ET) *The Origins of the Gospel Traditions*. London, SCM; Philadelphia, Fortress, 1979.

Jeremias, J., (ET) *The Prayers of Jesus*. London, SCM, 1967; = *The Lord's Prayer*. Philadelphia, Fortress (Facet Books), 1964.

Manson, T. W., *The Teaching of Jesus*. CUP, 1931, 1963.

Manson, T. W., *The Sayings of Jesus*. London, SCM, 1949.

Schnackenburg, R., (ET) *God's Rule and Kingdom*. London, Burns & Oates; New York, Herder, 1963.

(b) with Jewish Background

Derrett, J. D. M., *Jesus' Audience*. London, DLT, 1973.

Neusner, J., *Judaism in the beginning of Christianity*. Philadelphia, Fortress; London, SPCK, 1984.

Sanders, E. P., *Jesus and Judaism*. London, SCM, 1985.

Vermes, G., *Jesus the Jew*. London, Collins, 1973.

Vermes, G., *Jesus and the World of Judaism* (London, SCM, 1983), esp. the Riddell Lectures, pp. 15–57.

(c) with 'Form-critical' Background

Bornkamm, G., (ET) *Jesus of Nazareth*. London, Hodder, 1960; New York, Harper, 1961.

Bultmann, R., (ET) *Jesus and the Word*. New York, Scribners, 1934; London, Collins, 1958.

Bultmann, R., (ET) *The Theology of the New Testament*, vol. i (New York, Scribners, 1951; London, SCM, 1952), pp. 3–26.

Conzelmann, H., (ET) *Jesus*. Philadelphia, Fortress, 1973 (=RGG vol. 3, cols. 619–53).

Dibelius, M., (ET) *Jesus* (1939). Philadelphia, Westminster Press, 1949; London, SCM, 1963.

Perrin, N., *Rediscovering the Teaching of Jesus*. London, SCM; New York, Harper, 1967.

(d) Additional

Farrer, A. M., *The Triple Victory*. London, Faith Press; New York, Moorhouse Barlow, 1965.

Goulder, M. D., *Midrash and Lection in Matthew*. London, SPCK, 1974.

Harvey, A. E., *Jesus and the Constraints of History*. Bampton Lectures 1980. London, Duckworth, 1982.

Hengel, M., (ET) *The Charismatic Leader and his Followers*. Edinburgh, T. & T. Clark, 1981.

THE LORD'S PRAYER

Boff, L., (ET) *The Lord's Prayer: The Prayer of Integral Liberation*. Maryknoll, Orbis, 1983.

Brown, R. E., 'The *Pater Noster* as an Eschatological Prayer', in *New Testament Essays* (Garden City, Doubleday, 1968; London, G. Chapman, 1965), pp. 275–320.

Evans, C. F., *The Lord's Prayer*. London, SPCK, 1963.

Goulder, M. D., 'The Composition of the Lord's Prayer', in *JTS*, 14 (1963).

Hamman, A., *La Prière* (Tournai, 1959), pp. 94–134.

Jeremias, J., (ET) *The Prayers of Jesus*, pp. 82–107.

Lampe, G. W. H., '"Our Father" in the Fathers', in *Christian Spirituality: Essays in Honour of Gordon Rupp*, ed. P. Brooks (London, SCM, 1975).

Lohmeyer, E., (ET) *The Lord's Prayer*. London, Collins, 1965 = *'Our Father': An Introduction to the Lord's Prayer*. New York, Harper & Row, 1966.

Robinson, J. A. T., *Twelve More New Testament Studies* (London, SCM, 1984), ch. 4 (excellent introduction).

Schürmann, H., *Das Gebet des Herrn*. 4th edn., Freiburg, Herder, 1981. (ET) *Praying with Christ*. New York, Herder, 1964.

ST PAUL

Beker, J., *Paul the Apostle*. Philadelphia, Fortress, 1980.

Bornkamm, G., (ET) *Paul*. New York, Harper & Row; London, Hodder & Stoughton, 1971.

Cerfaux, L., *Le Christ dans la théologie de S Paul*. Paris, Cerf, 1954. (ET) *Christ in the Theology of St Paul*. New York, Herder; Edinburgh, Nelson, 1959.
Cerfaux, L., *Le chrétien dans la théologie paulinienne*. Paris, Cerf, 1962.
Cerfaux, L., 'L'apôtre en présence de Dieu', in *Recueil Lucien Cerfaux* (Gembloux, Duculot, 1954), vol. ii, pp. 469–81.
Sanders, E. P., *Paul and Palestinian Judaism*. London, SCM, 1977.
Schweitzer, A., (ET) *The Mysticism of Paul the Apostle*. London, Black, 1931; New York, Henry Holt, 1931.

St John

Barrett, C. K., *Essays on John*. London, SPCK, 1982.
Brown, R. E., *The Gospel According to John*, 2 vols. Garden City, N.Y., Doubleday (Anchor Bible, vols. 29 and 29A), 1966 and 1970.
Brown, R. E., *The Community of the Beloved Disciple*. New York, Paulist Press, 1979.
Bultmann, R., (ET) *Theology of the NT*, vol. ii (1955), pp. 3–92.
Howard, W. F., *Christianity According to St John*. London, Duckworth, 1943; Philadelphia, Westminster, 1946.
Inge, W. R., 'The Theology of the Fourth Gospel', in *Essays on Some Biblical Questions of the Day*, ed. H. B. Swete (London, Macmillan, 1909), pp. 251–88.
Martyn, J. L., *History and Theology in the Fourth Gospel*. New York, Harper & Row, 1968.
Mollat, D., *Saint Jean, Maître spirituel*. Paris, Beauchesne, 1976 (based on *Dict. Sp.*, vol. 8, cols. 192–247).
Mollat, D., *Études johanniques*. Paris, Seuil, 1979.
von Hügel, F., 'John, Gospel of St', in *Encyclopaedia Britannica*, 11th edn. (CUP 1910–11), 15. 452–8.

In a forthcoming book from SPCK, the author of this chapter will develop many of the points which have been treated here only briefly.

INTRODUCTION

The historical and critical study of the Bible is a relatively new feature in Christian history, even when the Bible was sought as sole authority for doctrine; and it certainly raises problems, particularly of presentation. For critical study increasingly shows up the wide *diversity* of the contents of the NT. We have had to pass through a phase which sought to identify '*the* theology *of* the NT' behind all the writings, to recognize a plurality of theologies within the NT. Less attention has hitherto been paid in detail to 'spirituality', except in so far as it is implicit in 'theology'; but it is equally clear that we can no longer expect to extract *the* spirituality of the NT, but have every chance of detecting many.

How has this been done in the past? There seem to have been two types of approach.

1. This may be caricatured as Purple Passages, selected because each has clear and obvious spiritual reference and appeal. This is a useful procedure for those who want a quick anthology of quotations;[1] but it should not satisfy the serious student, as it suggests that the spiritual insights in the isolated quotations are either peripheral to the author's main theme or flash revelations that come from a different source to his normal aridity, neither of which should be assumed in advance.

2. This might be styled 'doctrinaire', that is to say that the modern author approaches the NT authors with some preoccupation, problem or prejudice, in reaction to which each is assessed and judged. So Evelyn Underhill in *The Mystic Way*, in relation to a preconceived pattern of the mystic's progress; K. E. Kirk in *The Vision of God*, in relation to asceticism and humanism; A. R. George in *Communion with God*, in relation to F. Heiler's violent contrast between prophetic and mystical religion. Such arguments may provide contributions to contemporary debate, and sometimes bring to light features otherwise undetected; but they do not help us to read and assess each author in his own light. There is really no alternative to approaching each author or school of authors separately and sympathetically to see what each can yield.

But here we necessarily have to be selective, and can deal at length only with the Synoptic Gospels, St Paul and St John. This is not an entirely arbitrary choice, but it leaves out of account both 'Luke-Acts' and the Epistle to the Hebrews, which could each be treated at similar length. On the Revelation of St John, see p.7 above.

THE SYNOPTIC GOSPELS

Here the reader may expect to encounter the character and teaching of Jesus of Nazareth in its purest form. These writings, later called 'Gospels' and attributed to St Matthew, St Mark and St Luke, were styled 'synoptic' in the early days of criticism, because they looked at the central figure from the same angle or viewpoint, particularly in contrast to the fourth, attributed to St John; but for many years it has been clear that each one has its own plan and dominant purpose, even 'theology'.

These Gospels are, of course, subtly interconnected, though absolute

[1] e.g. 1 Tim. 6.16; Jas. 1.17, 18; 4.8; 1 Pet. 1.8; 4.19; 2 Pet. 1.4; 1 John 1.5; 2.17; 3.1–3; 4.7, 12, 18.

unanimity on their interrelation has eluded scholars. There is however a widespread consensus that Mark antedates the other two, that its author may well have pioneered the gospel form, and that it was used by the other two. It is also clear that there is much material common to Matthew and Luke, mainly, but not exclusively, consisting of teaching material (designated as 'Q' for short); and that Matthew and Luke have combined this with Mark and their own individual material, each in his own way. Of the literary correspondences there can be no doubt, and for many years critics went further to infer that Q was in documentary form. But it has never been rediscovered, and there was no agreement as to its form and contents, or as to whether it was one document or more. More recently the suggestion has circulated that the hypothesis of a Q document can be dispensed with as superfluous; that Matthew enlarged Mark and that Luke used them both. M. D. Goulder has gone further in a well-argued effort to show that Matthew's additions need not come from an existing written or oral source, but are extensions by way of *midrash* (extended comment or illustration) of the text of Mark.

But first we must face some very fundamental difficulties. The Gospels are entirely *Christian* documents; they are not the work of neutral observers, but of those who are already committed to Jesus as the Christ and Son of God, and above all to his resurrection. They are post-Easter documents, though they record pre-Easter occurrences. And they are written, not for a purely historical purpose, but for the edification and instruction of fellow-believers. This undoubtable fact was republished by the 'form-critics', along with other hypotheses that are more questionable; for, in brief, some went on to maintain that the Christian faith as we know it owes its existence entirely to the post-Easter Church, and that even if some details of the life and teaching of Jesus can be salvaged (e.g. as in Bultmann's *Jesus and the Word*), they are irrelevant to the Christian gospel.

More recently there has been a reaction led by students of Judaism and those steeped in rabbinic literature. If the relation between Jesus and the early faith is as form-critics suppose, how did it come about that the Gospels arose in the form of biography? Can a risen Christ be effectively preached on the basis of ignorance of or apathy towards the actual, historical Jesus? The pressing needs of later churches could hardly account for the many similarities between Jesus and other Jewish religious figures, and for the many historical and typographical details to be found in the Gospels. They have given new realism to the picture of Jesus by portraying him as a Jewish holy man or itinerant charismatic; but, like the form-critics, have completely dissociated him from subsequent Christianity.

Our aim must be to give some account of Jesus and his teaching which will take seriously his Jewish roots and character, and yet also explain his position at the centre of the Christian cult and preaching, leaving room for a certain originality or distinctiveness in Jesus himself. This we will attempt under the guidance of our earliest written source, Mark, amplified by Q passages from Matthew and Luke.[1]

Mark offers us 'the beginning of the gospel of Jesus Christ' (1.1), and makes clear that this is founded on the OT prophets (1.2–3), coming to a head in John with his preaching and baptism of repentance to all Judea and Jerusalem, in the guise of Elijah (1.4–6). Jesus appears from Nazareth and associates himself with the great throng by being baptized (1.9); but his own ministry does not begin until John's has been cut short by imprisonment (1.14), suggesting that he regards himself as John's successor as well as fulfilment (cf. 1.7–8, 10). He comes into Galilee proclaiming 'the gospel of God', which Mark (1.15) summarizes:

1. The time is fulfilled.
2. The Kingdom of God has drawn near.
3. Repent.
4. Believe in the gospel.

1. Immediately this must refer to the event foretold by John (1.7–8), remotely to a future era of salvation variously portrayed in OT prophecy and apocalypse. NT writers see themselves as living in an age of special visitation and privilege (cf. Matthew 13.17‖Luke 10.24; and Gal. 4.4; 2 Cor. 6.2, quoting Isa. 49.8).

2. Clarifies 1 and rephrases it in terms of the *Kingdom of God*, a concept widely held to be dominant in Jesus' teaching, though its definition is none too clear. At least it is agreed that the word usually translated 'kingdom' is better understood as Kingship, reign or rule, the substantive form of 'Yahweh is king' (Ps. 93.1; 97.1; 99.1), God's immediate, direct or effective rule. This must be explored further.

3. The broadcast call to general repentance links Jesus' message with the Baptist's initial call to the nation, but surprisingly it is not followed through later. Jesus takes up John's call, and takes it for granted.[2]

---

[1] References in this section are to Mark unless otherwise specified. For a succinct summary of the teaching in Mark, reference to A. M. Farrer, *St Matthew and St Mark* (London, Black; New York, Macmillan, 2nd edn, 1966), p. 8, is strongly recommended.
[2] There are Q passages, Matt. 11.21–4‖Luke 10.13–15 and Matt. 12.38–42‖Luke 11.29–32 (also Luke 13.1–5), which might refer to national repentance.

4. Repent, negative; positive, believe in, adhere to, the gospel, the good news of divine salvation (cf. Isa. 40.9; 52.7), whatever that may turn out to be.

To return to 2, the word translated *has drawn near* has been controversial since C. H. Dodd claimed it for 'realized eschatology', translating it *has arrived*, in the light of Q (Matt. 12.28‖Luke 11.20); but in the light of 9.1 and the prayer of Matt. 6.10‖Luke 11.2, this cannot be accepted in an absolute sense. 'Inaugurated eschatology' is safer: in Jesus' active ministry the great day is beginning to dawn, throwing out in advance its rays of light. God's sovereignty is being reasserted in Jesus' authoritative teaching (1.22, 27) and his cures and exorcisms. Have we any other hint of what this approximation of the reign of God might mean, at least to St Mark? If *not far* is equivalent to *near*, we may get such a hint in 12.34, where Jesus assures the sympathetic scribe, 'You are not far from the Kingdom of God.' We had better examine this passage (12.28–34; not to be confused with supposed parallels in Matt. 22.34–40 and Luke 10.25–8).

The scribe has asked Jesus a legitimate rabbinic question, 'Which commandment is first of all?' Jesus gives a suitable rabbinic answer in quoting the opening section of the *Shema'*, a full version of Deut. 6.4, 5.[1] That comes first; he also, though unasked, adds a second, 'You shall love your neighbour as yourself', plucked from its context in Lev. 19.18. The scribe affirms the truth of this reply and adds that these two precepts are vastly superior to all sacrifices. At this Jesus pronounces him not far from the Kingdom of God. This has many corollaries.

Jesus reaffirms the core of OT religion, and so of contemporary Judaism. In quoting Deuteronomy *verbatim*, and not just the commandment, he reasserts the divine voice or initiative ('Hear, O Israel'); not only the unity and uniqueness of God, but also his activity and vitality as the living God, the God of the burning bush, to whom all souls live (12.26–7; cf. Luke 20.38). Moreover his generosity and providence anticipate the prayer of faith (11.22–4). Therefore anxiety about temporal welfare is treachery for those seeking God's Kingdom and righteousness (Matt. 6.25–34‖Luke 12.23–31), and his providence is unmediated and universal, down to the smallest bird and the hairs of the human head (Matt. 10.29–31‖Luke 12.6–7). Against this background the command to love God with all one's capacity takes on the character of an invitation as well as an injunction. In the original context this love would be understood

---

[1] The *Shema'* is a catena made up of Deut. 6.4–8; 11.13–21; Num. 15.37–41, whose twice daily recitation may already have been customary in Jesus' time (J. Jeremias, op. cit., pp. 67–72).

primarily as undivided allegiance and unquestioning loyalty to the God of Israel in the face of polytheism and idolatry; but the text is capable of increasingly deep and inward understanding, including the 'your heavenly Father' (11.25), accessible to praying disciples and reaching to the undescribed intimacy of Jesus' own nocturnal prayer (1.35; 6.46), articulated in Gethsemane as 'Abba, Father' (14.36; cf. 1.11; 9.7).

In this context everything comes from God and is owed to God. So there is irony and ambiguity in weighing up the relative claims of Caesar and God (12.17); he can claim only what he has stamped. Attachment to wealth is a disqualification for the Kingdom of God, and equally ridiculous (10.23–7); and the widow's farthing, representing her whole livelihood, is worth more than the larger contributions of the rich (12.41–4).

Total devotion to the one God must entail simplicity and singleness of aim. The simplicity is well illustrated by Jesus' reception of the children (10.13–16), with their commendable docility, receptivity and trust, and possibly also their untarnished sense of wonder. One contrast with simplicity is multiplicity, as is well illustrated in Luke's story of Martha and Mary (Luke 10.38–42; possibly expounding the first commandment as the story of the prodigal son expounds the second, cf. Luke 10.25–37). Here the contrast is not between the active life and the contemplative but between the *many* cares of Martha and the *one* preoccupation of Mary. The singleness of heart which enables and follows from total devotion does not come readily to the human heart, which is the source of all wickedness (7.14–23) and darkness, and so of duplicity. You cannot serve God and mammon, or two masters at once (Matt. 6.4‖Luke 16.13); therefore the single eye, the pure intention, is required (Matt. 6.22–3‖Luke 11.34–5 and Matt. 5.8). Those who perform customary acts of devotion, fasting, prayer and almsgiving, for reward, human as well as divine, receive their human reward but forfeit the divine; indeed, are actors, hypocrites (Matt. 6.1–18). Sometimes amputation might prove salutary (9.43–7).

The 'love' enjoined and elicited is nothing emotional or self-indulgent; total devotion entails the active will expressed in obedience to the will of God. Willingness to hear and carry out the will of God creates a fellowship with Jesus and others likeminded which transcends the natural family (3.31–5). Only those who adhere to God's will can be reckoned as good fruit, reliable prophets, or stable houses (Matt. 7.15–27). But how is the will of God known? When questioned on the way to 'eternal life', Jesus catechizes the enquirer in the ethical precepts (the second table) of the decalogue; when told that he has acted on them all his responsible life, Jesus looked on him and *loved* him (10.17–21, unique in the Synoptists). Even if that is not the end of the story, it says much.

If we are to love and serve God with our whole heart etc. and his will is made known in the decalogue, then we cannot be content with merely external or formal observance. So Matthew expects Christian righteousness to exceed that of the scribes and Pharisees by understanding each prohibition in the light of the fundamental vice at its root, by avoiding not only acts of murder or adultery but also anger, hatred and lust (Matt. 5.20–30). In Mark Jesus is a biblical reformer, going back to the text of Scripture where it conflicts with customary oral tradition (7.1–13); Matthew seems to accept both (Matt. 23.2).

To the first commandment Jesus gratuitously adds the second, 'Love your neighbour as yourself.' The second commandment raises our fellow human beings above the level of other creatures, such as food and clothing, on which we are not to spend much thought; human beings are not to be used, but enjoyed and loved, and so served. The two commandments are subtly linked, but not inseparable, as if the first can only be fulfilled in the second.[1] God cannot forgive, or hear the prayer, of those who approach him with unforgiving hearts (11.25, taken up in Matt. 6.12, 14–15 and illustrated in Matt. 18.21–35). The implications of the second commandment are considerably amplified in the Q tradition (Matt. 6.38–48)‖Luke 6.27–36; Matt. 7.1–5‖Luke 6.37–8, 41–2), as well as in Matt. 25.31–46 (sheep and goats)[2] and Luke 10.30–7 (the good Samaritan).

But both commandments impose infinite and undefinable obligations, incapable of distinct and precise fulfilment; in fact they are aspirations as well as commandments, aiming at a perfection in love and mercy comparable only to that of God himself (Matt. 5.48; Luke 6.36). We must be left 'unprofitable servants' (Luke 17.10). And the later evangelists, if not Jesus himself, caricature their Jewish counterparts for their complacency (Matt. 23; Luke 12.15–21; 18.9–14); only the lowly and humble can be acceptable to God (Matt. 5.3, 5, 7; Luke 1.51–3; 14.11; 18.14). There is no divine reward for those who perform acts of piety as self-exhibition, for they have got what they were looking for, human praise (Matt. 6.1–2, 5, 16). This infinite element in the two commandments is responsible for what H. J. Cadbury has called 'the principle of the second mile',[3] of going beyond what is strictly obligatory, in the teaching of Jesus. It also provides a starting point for what seems exceptional, if not unique, in his teaching, which hitherto has been seen as a variant of, or within, Judaism. Undoubtedly Jesus lived and taught as a Jew; what more is there to say?

[1] Conzelmann, op. cit., p. 63, as against Bultmann, *Jesus and the Word*, pp. 83–5.

[2] It is not clear whether the 'least' of vv. 40 and 45 refer to fellow-Christians or fellow human beings; in the light of Mark 9.37, 41–2 they would seem to be believers.

[3] *Jesus*, p. 30: see the whole passage, pp. 23–31.

Jesus looked on the law-abiding enquirer and *loved* him. We might expect that love to issue in a commendation with encouragement to continue; in fact we get a surprise, for the loving look penetrates beneath the correct observance to the heart (10.21). 'One thing you are missing: go and sell what you have and give to the poor, and you will have treasure in heaven; and come, follow me' (some MSS add: 'taking up the cross'). Sadly he cannot accept this diagnosis and prescription, and departs. Mark's drama is spoilt by Luke and Matthew; Luke 18.18 makes the man a ruler at the outset; Matt. 19.21 adds the challenge as a 'counsel of perfection', 'if you wish to be perfect' (cf. Matt. 5.48), a voluntary invitation to a higher style of life, mendicant poverty. In Mark the challenge is personal, based on a discernment of the man concerned, his inner attachment to his property, a condition which Jesus can then discourse on more widely (10.23ff.). The challenge reminds us of two other passages, the call of the earliest disciples, and the teaching which follows the first prediction of the passion (8.34ff.).

Immediately after the first proclamation of 'the gospel' (1.14–15) we are told of the imperious and inconsiderate call of the first two pairs of followers to follow behind Jesus and become the nucleus of his entourage and recruit others ('fish for men'). The same happens to Levi (2.14) despite his trade; indeed Jesus' social intercourse with disreputable types is not only to heal but also to 'call' (2.15–18),[1] to invite them to join him in his itinerant mission, which is a completely new venture, though of limited duration (2.18–22). At the heart of the movement is a personal call issuing in personal allegiance, even when the nucleus is fixed at twelve and so put on a national and 'eschatological' basis (3.13ff., cf. Matt. 19.28; Luke 22.30). It is a call to share a nomadic and unsettled life, without domestic stability (Matt. 8.19–22‖Luke 9.57–62).[2] The enquirer of 10.17–22 is invited to join them.

But by then there has been a change. Peter has been led to state that they think Jesus to be the Christ (Messiah); on this point silence is enjoined (8.29–30). 'He then began to teach them openly that it is necessary that the Son of Man should suffer . . .', to Peter's indignation, which is violently rejected: 'Get behind me, Satan; you are not God-minded but man-minded.' The divine road leads necessarily to the cross; from now on the journey, to which the enquirer is later invited, has a clearer objective. The whole section (8.27—10.45) is marked by this and two further predictions of the passion (9.30–2; 10.32–4), and the character of Jesus' teaching changes accordingly. For although Jesus starts by

---

[1] Contrast Luke's moralized version (Luke 5.32), where the call is to repentance.
[2] Though we are told in retrospect that they had been surrounded by a band of ladies in attendance (15.40–1); see also Luke 8.2–3.

speaking of his own future, he goes on to generalize and draw out its implications for his followers: 'If anyone wishes to follow after me, let such a one deny himself and take up his or her cross[1] and follow me' (8.34), primarily in this journey. But why? 'Whoever wishes to preserve his (her) life (soul) will lose it; and whoever will lose his (her) life (soul) for the sake of myself and the gospel will preserve it. What advantage is there in gaining the whole world and forfeiting one's soul? What can be given in exchange for one's soul?' (8.35–7). And he holds out the prospect of glory (8.38; 9.1).

Here I suggest we have a glimpse of the originality of Jesus in teaching without precedent in Judaism or Hellenism. It is amplified as the section continues. The disciples' sacrifice 'for the sake of myself and the gospel' will be rewarded, but *with persecutions* and the prospect of eternal life (10.28–31). James and John cannot be assured of privileged places in glory; Jesus can only offer them his cup and his baptism (10.35–40). The master must be the servant, even the slave (10.41–4). Stoics taught that the wise man should take the rough with the smooth, deprivation and surfeit, with equal detachment; the Jews had come to see that prophets inevitably suffer for their message, that the deaths of patriotic martyrs like the Maccabees could be seen retrospectively as efficacious, and that the persecuted righteous would eventually be vindicated. Jesus turns self-denial and selfless service into an internal and positive principle, in the first instance of active discipleship, but also of salvation.

Mark's narrative is marked by opposition and conflict from 2.1, and Jesus' death is hinted at as early as 2.20 and 3.6. The prophecies of the passion in their present detailed form may well be shaped by the events; but Jesus could well have foreseen a premature and violent death, if he pursued his vocation with fidelity.[2] He not only accepted this passively as a divine imposition, and transformed it into an active interior principle; he also went further to see his own passion and death as a vicarious sacrifice 'for many', as in 10.45 and in the words over bread and cup in 14.23–4 (cf. 1 Cor. 11.24–5), words of interpretation, not so much of the Eucharist as of his impending death. He designates his blood, shortly to be shed, as that required for the sealing of a (new) covenant between his Father and his people, presumably that already foreseen by Jeremiah (31.31–4), which includes an amnesty from the curse of sin. Here is not only originality but continuity, not only with the past but also with the future. The kernel of the Christian gospel was early defined, as St Paul witnesses (1. Cor. 1.1–3), that 'Christ died for our sins according to the

---

[1] Luke 9.23 adds 'daily', reducing it to normal Christian asceticism.

[2] See the full treatment by J. Jeremias, (ET) *New Testament Theology*, Part I (London, SCM; New York, Scribner, 1971), pp. 276–99.

scriptures', etc. This is not an early Christian imposition upon the passive execution of Jesus, but the outcome of his active intention.

The predictions of the passion all include the resurrection, even more suspect to the critics; even if we leave them aside, Jesus remains serenely confident of his vindication. The transfiguration story not only provides corroboration of the harmony of both covenants, but also a hint of eternal glory, which must not be divulged until the Son of Man is risen from the dead; indeed it is a hint of the risen glory. At the farewell supper, after committing himself by sign to a vicarious death, Jesus looks forward to speedy vindication and the perpetual novelty of the messianic banquet (14.25). So much without explicitly apocalyptic passages. This vindication is not based on merit, nor is it arbitrary; it is the effect of the normal and just working of God in response to selfless and singleminded devotion and obedience. 'With God all things are possible' (10.27; cf. 14.36). This vindication is not only for Jesus, but is also possible for his followers, and so is offered to the enquirer (10.21); it can be figured as the hidden treasure, the priceless pearl, obtainable only by the disposal of everything else (Matt. 13.44–6), the Kingdom of God or of heaven in the heart; 'a condition of complete simplicity (costing not less than everything)'.[1]

Thus Jesus' self-renunciation, faithfully pursued to the end (15.34 = Ps. 22.1, q.v.), and his blind filial confidence in his Father's faithfulness, provide the human context for the disciples' understanding of his cross and resurrection as saving acts of God, to be enshrined in the heart of their 'gospel' from the beginning (1 Cor. 15.1ff.).

It is clear that Jesus did not think his purpose, or God's, would be achieved in his own lifespan. This can be said without considering the 'eschatological' chapter (Mark 13), which some scholars persist in regarding as an extraneous intrusion both into Mark's Gospel and into Jesus' teaching, despite the fact that it has been shown to be integrally related to the passion narrative, and that its teaching is clearly re-echoed in the earliest Christian writings, the letters to the Thessalonians.[2] We are given a long-term prophecy which includes much suffering and treachery for the Church and the world, the universal gospel and the co-operation of the Holy Spirit, before a period of unparalleled suffering and final deliverance when the Son of Man appears to gather together his elect. No date can be set for the last stages, they are entirely in the Father's hands. What Jesus says to the four he repeats to us all, 'Watch'. The abominable

[1] T. S. Eliot, 'Little Gidding'.
[2] See R. H. Lightfoot, *The Gospel Message of St Mark* (Oxford, Clarendon, 1950), pp. 48ff; A. M. Farrer, *A Study in St Mark* (London, Dacre, 1951), pp. 133–41; C. P. M. Jones, in *Studies in the Gospels*, ed. D. E. Nineham (Oxford, Blackwell, 1955), pp. 129ff.

suffering and the divine rescue presage the crucifixion and resurrection, which in turn provide a stamp for impressing on future crises, above all on the trials of the saints. But Jesus has planted seed (4.3ff.) which will have a varying harvest (4.8), growing largely without human control (4.26ff.), and quite out of proportion to the seed (4.31–2). What is hidden and secret will be revealed in full daylight (4.22).

What then can we say of Jesus himself? The Christian church claims that Jesus is the 'Son of God' in a unique sense, the only Son, the Beloved, and this is not against the earliest evidence. Fatherhood is a recognized image for God as creator in many religions, and is often used in the OT for his relationship with Israel (e.g. Deut. 32.18–20; Hos. 11.1; Ps. 103.8–13), and in a special way for his adoption of the Davidic King (2 Sam. 7.14; Ps. 89.26–7; 2.7). Jesus took this image very seriously and developed it to include a profundity and intimacy that may have been original and even unique. Jeremias has seen the external sign of this in his use of *Abba* (14.36), the child's word for its father;[1] some versed in Jewish literature have questioned Jeremias' claim for the rarity and intimacy of this usage; yet Jesus' use of the word so impressed his followers that the Aramaic word was treasured and preserved in gentile churches (along with *Maranatha* (1 Cor. 16.22) and *Halleluia* (Rev. 19.1–8)) as a sign that by the power of the Spirit they too could cry 'Abba, Father', truly adopted into the Sonship of Jesus (Gal. 4.6; Rom. 8.15). The Q saying of Matt. 11.27‖Luke 10.22 supports the intimate and exclusive nature of the relationship between Jesus and God as between father and son, and the earlier Mark (13.32) can refer to Jesus as 'the Son'. The stories of the baptism and transfiguration, with the divine voice, tell in the same direction. So Jesus was not so concerned with titles, or with 'fulfilling a role', as with following through a vocation, with hints from the OT. And in doing that he was being true to his own being, his innermost nature, his true self.[2]

APPENDIX: THE LORD'S PRAYER

This prayer is used so often by Christians, in public worship, in groups and individually, that without doubt it is frequently used without reflection, and certainly without curiosity as to what originally it was or meant. And this is a difficult question. It appears in Matthew and Luke in different versions and contexts, which are hard to harmonize. The Matthaean version seems to have prevailed, as is first witnessed by the

---

[1] op. cit., pp. 54–65.
[2] See J. A. T. Robinson, *Twelve More New Testament Studies* (London, SCM, 1984), ch. 11, pp. 155ff., on the 'Self-consciousness of Jesus'.

Didache (ch. 8, see p. 105), undateable but perhaps first century, in a Syrian milieu, perhaps not far from Matthew's own church. If the prayer in either version was originally taught and dictated by Jesus, it is the only instance of such a procedure on his part; and if he did so it is surprising that his followers should have felt free to adapt it, either by embellishment (Matthew) or abbreviation (Luke). In Matthew it occurs in the sermon (on the mountain), in the section commenting on the religious duties of almsgiving, prayer and fasting (6.1–18), appended to the treatment of prayer, unbalancing the three otherwise carefully balanced paragraphs. His followers are not to pray in public places, and must not use frequent and empty repetitions. Not entirely congruously this stereotyped prayer[1] is added, in the first person plural, not immediately appropriate to the private closet. In Luke the context is different, in a detached episode (11.1–13) in the course of the rambling central section of the Gospel (though immediately following the episode with Martha and Mary at Bethany, 10.38–42). Jesus is praying (as Luke constantly mentions on important occasions, 3.21; 6.12; 9.18, 28–9); when he has finished, a disciple asks him to teach them to pray, as the Baptist had done for his disciples. This is best understood as a group or sect prayer, after the manner of a nineteenth-century guild or sodality. Then follows the prayer (11.2–4), with further teaching (11.5–13‖Matt. 7.7–11) on persistent petitionary prayer.

MATT 6.9–13	LUKE 11.2–4
1. Our Father in heaven,	Father
2. hallowed be thy name;	hallowed be thy name;
3. thy kingdom come;	thy kingdom come.
4. thy will be done, as in heaven, so on earth.	
5. Give us today our 'daily' bread;	Continually give us day by day our 'daily' bread;
6. and forgive us our debts, as we also have forgiven our debtors;	and forgive us our sins, for we ourselves also forgive everyone who is indebted to us;
7. and lead us not into temptation;	and lead us not into temptation.
8. but deliver us from evil.	

---

[1] The Greek word for 'in this way' (6.9) may mean 'exactly like this' or 'roughly like this'.

(1) Luke's Father is identical with his version of Jesus' address in Gethsemane (22.42), dropping Mark's *Abba* (14.36), and with his final prayers (23.34, 46) (cf. 15.12, 18, 21). Matthew's longer phrase is not only Matthew's, being found already in Mark 11.25. Although this address can be seen as an invitation to Christians to enter into Jesus' own intimacy with his Father, some Jewish scholars deny that it is unprecedented.

In what follows both versions divide clearly into two parts, the first addressed to God about himself, the second bringing in our needs. In Matthew's version there are three God-ward clauses, each beginning with the verb; then three us-ward clauses, each linked by 'and'.

(2) 'may your Name be sanctified', recognized as 'holy', God's Name being no less than God himself. By whom should he be recognized or proclaimed as holy, as by the seraphim in Isaiah's vision (6.3)? Israel can, or should, proclaim his holiness before the nations, and even partake of it: be holy, for I am holy (Lev. 19.2 etc.). But God himself can proclaim and vindicate his own holiness, over the head of their corruption (Ezek. 36.22ff).

The first two clauses concisely juxtapose and unite intimacy and awe, affinity and distance (see Evans, op. cit., p. 29). (2) and (3) may be linked by echoes of the Aramaic prayer the *Kaddish*, which may have been introduced into the synagogue by this time (see Jeremias, op. cit., p. 98; Robinson, op. cit. p. 55, for text).

(3) an urgent prayer to God to bring in his direct rule. All these imperàtives are aorist, demanding, almost peremptorily, definite action, fulfilling immediately the final eschatological hope. The prayer places the one praying on the brink of eternity; for it is a prayer of 'the last days'.[1]

(4) is an extension of (3); God's reign consists of the revelation of, acquiescence in, and co-operation with, his will. Literally the main clause is universal and fatalist, but the qualifying clause brings it, and (3), down to earth: may God's will be done on earth, therefore among humankind, and by humans as well as over them. Thus we have a clear link with the teaching of Jesus, and equally with his prayer and example in Gethsemane (which is closely related to this prayer), where he prays the Father to take away 'this cup' (of the imminent passion), 'nevertheless, not what I will, but you will'. Heaven too, as the God-centred court and society, is not a remote, but an immediate, model of human obedience and co-operation, as the 'heavenly' Father is not remote, and his angels are always active (Matt. 18.10).

(5) seems the simplest clause, but it is in fact the most obscure,

---

[1] For the sake of completeness, one should add that in a very few early versions, going back to Marcion, (3) runs 'May thy holy spirit come upon us and cleanse us', perhaps adapted for baptismal use or influenced by Luke 11.13.

entirely because of the word usually translated 'daily'. It is unlikely in this terse and economic prayer that it means 'daily', 'for this day', as that would double up with 'today'; and the meaning must be compatible with Matt. 6.25ff. (‖Luke 12.22ff.), where Jesus rebukes anxiety over food and clothing for the morrow. So the adjective, if referring to the present, may mean 'what belongs to our sustenance', 'what pertains to existence', 'sufficient' or 'necessary' (cf. Prov. 30.8; Jas. 2.15). Or it may mean 'for the morrow', even 'for the future age'; that would be the heavenly bread. In either case it is likely that the imagery of the divinely supplied ration of manna (Exod. 16) lies behind the clause, linking it with (4); or it could be a *double entendre*, with double sense, linking the heavenly with the subsequent down-to-earth petitions. Luke's version, by using the present indicative (iterative) and 'day by day' has robbed the petition of its urgency and immediacy, and is clearly an adaptation. Schürmann (op. cit., pp. 84ff.) reminds us that if the first recipients were disciples of Jesus, they may also have been his apostles or emissaries, who would be sent out without provision (Mark 6.8; Matt. 10.8ff.; Luke 9.2ff.; 10.3ff.); he sees it as an ideal prayer for a mendicant evangelist.

(6) builds on the image, current in Aramaic, of sin as *debt*, and remission of sin, or forgiveness, as releasing from or cancelling debt. This is consistent in Matthew (as also in Matt. 18.21–end); Luke prefers to make the meaning clearer by decoding the image and asking directly for forgiveness of our sins. But in the qualifying clause he reverts to debts, again revealing his dependence. Moreover, the qualifying clause is phrased to take it as a commonplace, daily fact of life (present tense) that we do in fact cancel our debtors' debts, or pardon their offences; why then the heavy injunctions of Luke 6.27–36? Matthew's qualifying clause is also difficult, as it makes God's forgiveness of us dependent on our *prior* (note perfect tense) forgiveness of others, making God's free grace and mercy dependent on our 'works'. But Matthew's text is entirely faithful to Jesus' teaching in Mark 11.25, which he takes over and amplifies (Matt. 6.14–15). Perhaps our own forgiving disposition is also the work of God's prevenient grace in us.

(7) and (8) go together, (8) being the positive version of (7). 'Temptation' is also 'testing'. As with Jesus (Mark 1.13; Matt. 4.1–11; Luke 4.1–13), so with Christians, God allows such testing by temptation, though not above their capacity (1 Cor. 10.13). The best commentary is Jas. 1.2–16; our liability to temptation is based not simply on weakness, but more specifically on duplicity, doublemindedness. We are fittingly enjoined to pray that God will preserve us from situations beyond our capacity.

In view of the high eschatological urgency of the first part of the prayer, some scholars have seen in (7) a reference to the ultimate catastrophe, the final trial before the end (cf. Mark 13.14–25; 2 Thess. 2.3–5); but the absence of the definite article before 'temptation' militates against this interpretation. Gethsemane is once again in the background; Jesus warns the three disciples in the same words (Mark 14.38). The test will be to hold fast in the face of the temptation to apostasy, in this case desertion and denial. In Jesus' own prayer he may regard 'this cup' as the testing from which he flinches, and prays for its withdrawal. Apostasy is only infidelity writ large.

In (8) we only need to mention that 'evil' has the definite article, but we have no means of deciding whether it is masculine or neuter, the evil One or the evil thing.

So it is not easy to see whether and in what form the prayer was Jesus' invention; it may owe its present form to St Matthew, as Goulder maintains; but he made it largely out of existing ingredients (Mark 11.22–5; 14.36, 38): Jesus' own teaching and example. In that sense it is still the Lord's Prayer.

The Lord's Prayer in Christian Tradition (by the Editors)

Many classical expositors treat the Lord's Prayer as a compendium of the whole gospel concerning God, humankind and salvation. Thus: Tertullian (E. Evans, *Tertullian's Tract on the Prayer*, London, SPCK, 1953); Cyprian (E. Bonin, *The Lord's Prayer: A Commentary by St Cyprian of Carthage*, Westminster (Md.), Christian Classics, 1983); Origen (E. G. Jay, *Origen's Treatise on Prayer*, London SPCK, 1954); Cyril of Jerusalem (Myst. Cat. 5, ET in LF vol. 64, 1970); Gregory of Nyssa (five sermons on *The Lord's Prayer*, ET in ACW vol. 18, 1954); John Chrysostom (the nineteenth homily on 'The Gospel of St Matthew', ET in LF, 1876); Augustine (in Sermons 56–9, ET in LF, 1844; and in his 'Commentary on The Sermon on the Mount', II.4.15–12.39, ET in ACW vol.5, 1951); Thomas Aquinas (ET by L. Shapcote, *The Three Greatest Prayers: Commentaries on the Our Father, the Hail Mary and the Apostles' Creed by St Thomas Aquinas*, Westminster (Md.), Newman, 1956); Luther (in the Large and Little Catechisms and in *A Simple Way to Pray*, written for his barber in 1535); Calvin (*Institutes of the Christian Religion*, III.20.34–49; and in *A Harmony of the Gospels: Matthew, Mark and Luke*, ET by A. W. Morrison, Edinburgh, St Andrew Press, and Grand Rapids, Eerdmans, 1972); Teresa of Avila ('The Way of Perfection', 25–42, ET in *The Collected Works of St Teresa of Avila*, vol. 2, Washington, D.C., Institute of Carmelite Studies, 1980); John Wesley (among his Standard Sermons, the sixth discourse on the Sermon on the Mount); Karl Barth (in a fragment of the 'Church Dogmatics' IV/4, (ET *The Christian Life*, Grand Rapids, Eerdman, 1981).

ST PAUL

We deal here with St Paul as he makes himself known in his letters, not as presented later in the Acts of the Apostles. Known through his letters, he is the most, even the only, distinctive individual character in the NT; he is also our earliest writing witness to the Christian religion and its origins, antedating the Gospels by a decade or more. The letters fall into three groups in probable chronological order, focusing attention on different facets of a faith which retains its basic identity throughout: (a) the Thessalonian letters, focused on the *parousia*, or expected coming, of the Lord; (b) the 'major epistles', those to Corinth, Rome and Galatia, developing the significance of his death and resurrection; (c) the 'captivity' epistles, Philippians and Colossians (with Philemon) and (possibly) Ephesians,[1] stressing the present, glorified Christ.

Before dealing with Paul's distinctive, and as far as we can tell original, insights, we must affirm that he was not entirely idiosyncratic; despite his later conversion, and his original vocation to pioneer the gentile mission, he was an apostle with the other apostles (1 Cor. 15.1–11), and sought to work in fellowship with those at Jerusalem (Gal. 1.18–2.10). He was not antinomian; despite his virulent rejection of the Law when regarded or used as a ladder of self-justification, he asserts its moral precepts and Jesus' summary of them (Gal. 5.14; Rom. 13.8–10). C. H. Dodd thinks it likely that the 'sermon on the mount' and other synoptic material lies behind the ethical teaching of Rom. 12—13.[1] He was not ignorant of, or indifferent to, the 'historical Jesus' (despite 2 Cor. 5.16; see 1 Cor. 7.10; 9.14; 11.23ff. (perhaps 1 Thess. 4.15); Rom. 1.3; 9.5; Phil. 2.7–8). He also encourages respectable Greek virtues in the Philippians (4.5, 8); and in the latest letters he gives domestic instruction (Col. 3.18—4.1; Eph. 5.22—6.9).

We aim to show that St Paul's deepest spiritual teaching flows from, and is of a piece with, his fundamental theology; but even on the surface his letters are patently spiritual documents, from their opening greeting 'from God our Father and our Lord Jesus Christ', to their final commendation (see especially 2 Cor. 13.13). The letters not only exhort to continual (even continuous, 1 Thess. 5.17) prayer and thanksgiving, but contain his own spontaneous prayers and thanksgivings, and are punctuated with acts of praise (e.g. 2 Cor. 11.31; Gal. 1.5; Rom. 1.25; 9.5; not to mention 11.33–6).

[1] We are not taking the 'pastoral' epistles, to Timothy and Titus, as by Paul, though they may contain authentic fragments. Our '2 Cor.' may not be a single letter. Ephesians is much debated, both contentions being succinctly set out in *Studies in Ephesians*, ed. F. L. Cross (SPCK, 1956), pp. 9–35. 2 Thess. and Col. have also been queried.

[2] *New Testament Essays*, Manchester UP, 1953, ch. on 'Matthew and Paul'.

But when we go on to claim that his spirituality flows from his theology, we run into deep waters; for the letters are not theological treatises (except perhaps Rom. 1.16—8.39), but pastoral letters dominated by the topics and situations of his correspondents. Some scholars claim that there is no coherent theology, merely an opportunist adaptation to the occasion. There is flexibility, certainly, and great variety in imagery; and there may still be coherent theology, underneath if not on the surface.

Where can we start digging? St Paul refers to his own conversion and apostolic commission on two occasions,[1] and in differing contexts and language (1 Cor. 15.8ff.; Gal. 1.15–16), presumably alternative ways in which he looked on his way in. Let us explore each in turn.

1. 1 Cor. 15.8ff. St Paul is about to expound the resurrection, but begins with a recapitulation of the kernel of the 'gospel', which continues into a list of the resurrection appearances of Christ, beginning with Peter and ending with himself, which include the 'apostles', emissaries or ambassadors, whose work is itself a necessary part of the 'gospel' (see above p. 67). His conversion is the last resurrection appearance of Christ, traumatic and violent though it was, which adds him to the limited number of apostles (cf. 1 Cor. 9.1; Rom. 16.7). Now the kernel is not that 'Jesus of Nazareth was crucified and resuscitated and seen again'; it is already codified and stereotyped: viz. 'that Christ died for our sins according to the scriptures, and that he was buried, and that he was raised on the third day according to the scriptures, and that he was seen . . .' (vv. 3–5). If in the case of Jesus' death 'according to the scriptures' has been rightly interpreted as 'in accord with scriptural type' (covenant blood, see above pp. 68–9), what of his resurrection? St Paul goes on to expound it (vv. 20ff.): 'as in Adam all die (inherit mortality), so in Christ all will be made alive', he is the first fruits of a new harvest. 'Adam' is an inclusive image of the whole human race; in his disobedience, sin and alienation, the whole race is included; so Christ in his resurrection includes potentially ('*shall be* made alive') the whole human race. Christ's role is both parallel and antithetical to Adam's (Rom. 5.12–21), with the added burden that the proclivities inherited from Adam are aggravated and crystallized by the Law (Rom. 5.20; 7.7ff.). The Adam image is not purely mythical or representative, but inclusive; in a late Jewish phrase, 'each one of us is his own Adam'.[2] So Christ's death is also inclusive: 'our old man (the old man of each one of us) was crucified together with him'

---

[1] 2 Cor. 12.1–5 is not being taken into consideration, because of St Paul's own diffidence and embarrassment about the experience related; he mentions it almost anonymously.

[2] Syriac Apocalypse of Baruch, 54.19, in *The Apocryphal Old Testament*, ed. H. F. D. Sparks (Oxford and New York, Clarendon, 1984), p. 875.

(Rom. 6.6). He took up Adam's role and identified himself with our race in its state of alienation, condemnation and curse (Rom. 8.3; 2 Cor. 5.21; Gal. 3.13); by his voluntary self-emptying (*kenōsis*) and humiliation to the limit of the cross, he became a point of reconciliation (*hilastērion*, lit. 'mercy-seat', Rom. 3.25). His resurrection was a direct act of God, of acceptance, vindication and glorification (Phil. 2.9–11), and like his death was also on our behalf (2 Cor. 5.21). In one concise verse (Rom. 4.25), 'he was handed over (to death) for our transgressions, and he was raised for our "justification"'; Christ's death and resurrection effect the 'justification' of the whole human race, the death atoning for sin, and the resurrection providing a source of new, divine life; not the one or the other, but one after the other and both together. St Paul's 'justification' words are used comprehensively, sometimes on the negative side (e.g. Rom. 3.24; 5.9–10), sometimes on the positive (e.g. Rom. 4.25; 2 Cor. 5.21), sometimes for both together (Rom. 5.1; 8.30; 1 Cor. 6.11). This is the kernel of the message of the salvation God has effected, and God also provides the messengers; when God also opens the ears of their hearers to receive message and messenger, the apostle reaches his goal (1 Thess. 2.1–13), Christ the foundation stone has been laid in Corinth (1 Cor. 3.10, 11), Christians have been begotten (4.15). Another word for such positive reception is 'faith' after the pattern of Abraham (Rom. 4), who accepted God's impossible promise, with no attempt to strike a bargain (4.14–16; cf. Gal. 3.15–18), but simply trusting in God's creative and recreative power (4.17–21); but with this difference, that whereas Abraham's faith had been entirely in a future possibility, Christian faith (in God's willingness to deal with the universal disobedience and alienation elaborated in 1.18—3.20) is focused on and through what God has already done (4.23–5; cf. 5.8).

This once-for-all act of redemption and revivification is not the end of the matter; it has to be preached and accepted, and each individual so touched must make his own transition, from the old to the new, by baptism, for which St Paul uses a number of images, the most dramatic of which is the identification with Christ in his burial and resurrection (Rom. 6.1–11; Col. 2.11ff.), or discarding old clothes and putting on new (Col. 3.9–11; Eph. 4.22–4). See also Rom. 6.12–8.11.

In a famous autobiographical passage (Phil. 3.3ff.), St Paul not only contrasts his former Jewish life of *faultless* legal correctitude with his new-found life in Christ, as between a 'righteousness of my own based on legal prescription' and 'the righteousness that comes through the faith of Christ, the righteousness that is from God on the basis of faith'; he also goes on to describe this righteousness as 'knowing Christ and the power of his resurrection and the sharing of his sufferings, being conformed to the pattern of his death, if I may somehow attain to the resurrection from the dead'. In other words there is no incompatibility between the language of 'justification by faith' and that of incorporation into Christ's death and resurrection.

This principle of incorporation into the double act of salvation Paul applies to wide areas of Christian life, sometimes both together, sometimes one before the other. He can apply it widely: 'one died for all, therefore all died; and he died for all so that those who live should no longer live for themselves but for him who died and was raised for them' (2 Cor. 5.14–15; cf. Rom. 14.7–9; 1 Thess. 5.9–10). He can apply it narrowly, to himself personally, with great conviction (Gal. 2.19–20, quoted p. 4; also 6.14, 17), and with utter realism, e.g. 2 Cor. 1.3–12; 11.16—12.10.

St Paul's vocation and work as an apostle readily ally him with the redemptive suffering and 'doing to death' (*necrōsis*, mortification, 2 Cor. 4.10) of Christ; but we should note that he does not have to engineer or contrive it. God who is the author and initiator of this plan of salvation is constantly at work, seeing it through; he provides the occasions of crucifixion as also of resurrection. The apostle has to see them in this light and detect the divine plan. There is discipline, but not elaborate self-mortification; that is superfluous. He applies the same principle to his converts, especially to the 'strong', or those who have arrived at deeper insight (*gnōsis*, inner knowledge; cf. 1 Cor. 8.1ff.). The 'gnostic', who has come to see that all meat is clean and edible, even if associated with pagan sacrifice, should not scandalize or cause offence to a weaker brother, who has been trained to wean himself from idolatry, for he is 'the brother for whom Christ died' (1 Cor. 8.9–13). The strong should bear with the weak, and not please themselves, following the pattern of Christ in his passion (Rom. 15.1–3).

So far the emphasis seems to have been on union with Christ's death; but that is not always so. To return to the autobiographical passage already cited (Phil. 3.3ff.): in the passage quoted we note that in knowing Christ 'the power of his resurrection' oddly precedes 'the sharing of his suffering, being conformed to the pattern of his death [which we have just amplified] if I may somehow attain to the resurrection of the dead', since identification with the death is a necessary condition for the hope of resurrection. But it is this aspect of resurrection that he goes on to elaborate, as a factor not limited to the past resurrection of Christ or to the final resurrection of Christians (as in 1 Cor. 15.20ff.). In the great baptismal passage (Rom. 6.3–11) past tenses are applied to death and sin, in Christ and in the baptized, as well as to Christ's resurrection, but future tenses to the resurrection of Christians (6.4–5, 8); even so, he concludes that they must 'regard themselves as corpses as far as sin is concerned, but living to God in Christ Jesus' (8.11). Here in Phil. 3.12–14 we get a fuller picture of the present phase of resurrection life. 'Not that I have already received it or am already fully initiated into it (or made perfect), but I pursue it, in the hope that I may myself grasp that for which Christ has already grasped me. I do not reckon myself to have grasped it; I simply do *one thing*, forgetting what is behind and stretching out to what is ahead, I press on towards the goal leading to the prize of the upward calling of God in Christ Jesus.' The resurrection life reproduces itself in him as a never flagging aspiration towards invisible and inexhaustible perfection. It would be too pedantic to call it 'spiritual progress'.

Paul's pastoral teaching to the newly founded church at Colossae also begins from the resurrection (Col. 2.11—3.17). As with the Phil. 3 passage, however, there is no mention of the Holy Spirit, intimately connected with the risen Christ in Rom. 1.4; and yet, 'the law' of the spirit of life in Christ Jesus has liberated me from the 'law' of sin and death' (Rom. 8.2). The relation of the living presence of the risen Christ and that of the living, ever present and ever active Spirit, is given in a few key texts: Rom. 4.17; 1 Cor. 15.44–7; Rom. 8.9–11.

2. In the other account of his conversion/commission (Gal. 1.15–16), St Paul uses different language: 'when it pleased God, who separated me from my mother's womb (cf. Isa. 49.1; Jer. 1.5) and called me by his grace, to reveal his Son in (to) me . . .'. Here the divine act is seen as the revelation, the uncovering of the truth, that the Jesus whose cult he is engaged in persecuting, is in a special sense God's Son. No wonder he flees human contact, seeking space and time to think out the aweful implications; something must have gone radically wrong if the crucified focus of the Christian movement is actually the Son of the God of Israel in whose name he is persecuting it. Henceforward the distinctive Christian innovation is to add to, and so complete, Judaism, with the news of this Son (Rom. 1.9). He can describe the Thessalonians' conversion from paganism in two stages: first, they were converted to the service of the living and true God (i.e. the full faith of the OT) and then 'to wait for his Son . . .' (1 Thess. 1.9–10). In the opening section of Romans Paul describes 'the gospel of God, which he promised in advance through his prophets in holy writings, concerning his Son', of whom he says two things, (a) 'who was born of the seed of David according to the flesh', and (b) 'who was defined as Son of God in power according to the spirit of holiness as the result of the resurrection of the dead . . .'. In this condensed and complicated sentence, often claimed to be an elaboration of

an existing formula, the Son has a two-stage career, flesh and spirit; flesh being used in the non-pejorative sense of ordinary frail created humanity (cf. Isa. 31.3; John 3.6–8; 6.63; Phil. 3.3ff.; Gal. 4.29; 2 Cor. 10.3–5), as constrasted with the inexhaustible dynamism of God. The time of the flesh is seen as a period of humiliation and limitation, culminating in the cross, as in Phil. 2.5–8, where it is cited as a model for mutual humility and respect (cf. 2 Cor. 8.9; Rom. 8.3).

But it is through resurrection that the Son becomes effective ('in power'), not just on behalf of, but in us: 'in the fulness of time God sent forth his Son, (to be) born of a woman, born subject to the law, in order to redeem (by death and resurrection) those under the law, (and) in order that we might receive adoption. And because you are sons, God has sent forth the Spirit of his Son into our hearts, crying Abba, Father. So you are no longer a slave but a son . . .' (Gal. 4.4–7). The mission of the Son is completed by the mission of his Spirit. So again in Rom. 8.14ff. It is God's original and ultimate plan that all he has called shall become 'conformed to the image of his Son, so that he (the Son) may be the firstborn among many brothers and sisters' (8.29), adopted into God's own family. This adoption is effected in baptism: 'all who have been baptized into Christ have put on Christ', all human divisions of culture, status or sex are abolished, 'for you are all *one man* in Christ Jesus. And if you are Christ's, then you are the progeny of Abraham, heirs as promised' (Gal. 3.26–9).

The human nature of 'the Son' qualifies the human race for adoption into the sonship of the Son by the power of the Spirit, reproducing in each, and uniting each to, the authentic prayer of the Son, Abba, Father. It would seem that already, by St Paul's time, the sonship of Jesus was understood to be intrinsic and inherent in him, and not in any way fortuitous, conditional or merited; there is no hint of adoptionism, just as there is not yet a clear doctrine of incarnation, though this is implied.[1]

For it is now clear that both paths lead in the same direction; for the Spirit of adoption and the resurrection Spirit are identical. Moreover, within the general plan, the Spirit has a relative independence (cf. 2 Cor. 3.17). We can now go on to unravel 1 Cor. 1.18—2.16, a passage which may well be seen to contain the roots both of Christian theology and of Christian spirituality. St Paul's message to Corinth was focused on Christ's cross (1.17) exclusively (2.2, perhaps a rhetorical exaggeration, cf. 15.1–5). This message goes against the current wisdoms, being utter nonsense to Greeks and topsy-turvy to Jews schooled in the God of battles. And yet to

---

[1] This must be affirmed, despite attempts to show that incarnation is pioneereed by St John (e.g. J. D. G. Dunn, *Christology in the Making*, London, SCM, 1980).

believers the cross of Christ exhibits the wisdom and the power of God (1.24–5). The folly of the message is matched by the rhetorical incompetence of the evangelist (2.1–5) and by the undistinguished character of those who accept the message (1.26–9). So no human being can boast of human achievement before God, 'as the result of whose initiative you are in Christ Jesus, who has become for us from God wisdom, righteousness and holiness' (1.30; cf. 2 Cor. 5.21; Col. 2.9); so that whoever is in Christ can boast *in* the Lord, in what the Lord, God in Christ, has done, and is, in him. This verse (1.30) contains the germ of the positive section that follows (2.6–16). We can talk of wisdom among those fully initiated, not wordly wisdom based on human intelligence and inference from worldly data, but divine wisdom, elusive to us and hidden in the divine mind, God's own plan for bringing us to glory (which was unknown to worldly authorities or they would not have unintentionally helped it on its way by engineering the crucifixion), a glory above and beyond any human intuition or intimation. A glimpse of this wisdom and glory has been revealed to us by the Spirit, who enables us to understand what God has graciously done for us, in other words to enter into the mind from which redemption in Christ issued.

Similarly the Spirit comes internally to help us in our inadequate and inarticulate prayer, intervening with undecipherable aspirations (quite beyond the articulate Abba) but discernible to the searcher of hearts (Rom. 8.26–7). He alone can precipitate the basic confession, 'Jesus is Lord' (1 Cor. 12.3), the criterion of genuine inspiration. There is a diversity of 'charisms' or spiritual gifts which he distributes and co-ordinates among the various members of Christ's Body; yet there is a hierarchy of gifts, and individuals are exhorted to covet and cultivate the higher ones, preferring any that lead to 'edification', to the building up of the whole by the strengthening of the weak (1 Cor. 12 and 14, cf. p. 5 above; Rom. 14.17–19), which requires restraint from the more impressive and spectacular. The community as a whole is a temple of the Spirit (1 Cor. 3.16–17); so equally is each individual (1 Cor. 6.19), which has special implications for chastity (1 Thess. 4.3–8). The body itself is not evil; God can be glorified in it (1 Cor. 6.13–20).

It is otherwise with the *flesh*, our human nature in its frailty, duplicity and rebelliousness. Here the warfare between the old Adam and the new is fought out in each individual between the flesh and the Spirit (Gal. 5.16–26). The 'works of the flesh', clearly enumerated in 19–21, meriting the condemnation of the Law, are contrasted with the fruit of the Spirit (vv. 22–3); they are all divisive, whereas the *fruit* (NB not 'fruits') of the Spirit, though capable of enumeration, beginning with love, joy and peace, is all unifying, forming one cluster. The 'works of the flesh' are not to be dealt with by prolonged discipline and careful self-control, but by the now familiar but radical remedy of crucifixion; 'those who are Christ's have crucified the flesh with its passions and desires' (v. 24), in the once-for-all acceptance of faith and baptism. Henceforth they must offer their bodies as a living sacrifice, acceptable to God as the homage of a rational creature; but this must be part of a total renewal and reorientation (Rom. 12.1–2).

The Spirit not only issues from the positive side of 'justification'; it also anticipates a further stage, 'glorification' (cf. Rom. 8.30). The Spirit inspires and aggravates our groans and aspirations towards complete redemption and liberation (Rom. 8.23) and is described as 'firstfruit', the first flowering of a harvest already ripening, i.e. of future glory; and elsewhere as a first deposit or pledge of full future payment, in 2 Cor. 1.21–2, where our anointing and sealing by God with the Spirit is seen as a pledge for the complete fulfilment of all his promises to us, and 2 Cor. 5.5, where the Spirit is seen as a pledge for our complete clothing in immortality, with our resurrection body. We have seen that God's original and ultimate design is 'for our glory' and that we should inherit blessings beyond experience or imagination (1 Cor. 2.7, 9). The earliest Christians believed fervently in the coming (*parousia*) of Christ, to complete his former work by gathering together his elect, even if already dead (1 Thess. 4. 13–17, 2 Thess. 2.1), and transforming them into his likeness (Phil. 3.20–21). The Thessalonian letters are dominated by this hope, and it persists to the end (Col. 3.4, our hidden life with Christ in God will be made manifest in glory). What should strike the modern reader is that this fulfilment is passionately desired by St Paul and the Thessalonian Christians, and the virtue of *hope* predominates; moreover, it is a uniting passion, as he and they will not be separated by individual judgement but will be permanently reunited, with the converts embedded in the apostles' crown (1 Thess. 2.19–20). It is generally held nowadays that this was an erroneous belief, to be discarded as primitive dross, rather than inwardly transmuted. Towards this inner understanding St Paul himself gives several hints, even to the Thessalonians. They are to progress in love towards each other and to all (3.12–13); though ever vigilant, they are already children of light (5.1–11); they must not be restless or neurotic, but calm and industrious (4.11–12; 2 Thess. 3.6–15). Christians should realize the transient nature of the things and relationships of this world and so should not be overattached to them (1 Cor. 7.29–31). Outward affliction can affect only the outside of us, though meanwhile renewal is going on within, infinitely more weighty and precious, being eternal rather than temporal, indeed the chrysalis of our future glory (2 Cor. 4.16 onwards). So Christians can not only aspire towards the ultimate goal, but practise for it, even practise it in advance.

Christians may have different gifts of the Spirit, but they can aspire to the greater ones (1 Cor. 12.31); and there is an even better way, as St Paul goes on to expound in his great panegyric on love (1 Cor. 13). Love is in the heart of God: the Father's love lies behind our redemption in Christ (Rom. 5.8; 8.32); and God's love has been poured into our hearts by the Holy Spirit given to us (Rom. 5.5). The overflowing of the love of God enables the human heart to beat in harmony with the divine. Not yet perhaps the clarity and simplicity of the First Epistle of John; but the substance is the same.

Many think St Paul far from Jesus; perhaps the Paul of their imagination from the Jesus of their imagination. But St Paul was a convert and apostle of the risen Christ, not of his earthly ministry. Jesus' concept of the Kingdom of God is not alien to Paul (cf. 1 Cor. 6.10; Rom. 14.17); but he sees the reign of God as effective ('with power') in the resurrection of Jesus, as Jesus may himself have hinted (Mark 9.1, 9; Rom. 1.4). His God-given function is to bring about subordination to (2 Cor. 10.5) and union with Christ; so far Albert Schweitzer rightly claims that he stands for 'Christ-mysticism' rather than 'God-mysticism'. But that is not the whole story; St Paul's christocentricity has a theocentric background. It is God's wisdom that lies behind Christ's coming and is available to us through it; it is God's creative power that is operative in his resurrection and diffused in his Spirit; when all alien forces are overcome and subjected to Christ as viceroy, he will deliver up his Kingdom to his Father, that God may be all in all (1 Cor. 15.28).

ST JOHN

'The Gospel of St John . . . is the charter of Christian Mysticism', claimed W. R. Inge,[1] striking a note which was to re-echo widely. Some twenty years earlier Benjamin Jowett had written: 'something like this is what the better mind of the age is seeking – a religion independent of the accidents of time and space',[2] i.e. immune from the varying fortunes of historical criticism and scientific discovery. Inge himself was in search of a Christianity independent alike of infallible Bible or Church, based on direct experience. This idea became widely accepted among scholars as a clue to the peculiar characteristics of the Gospel.[3]

---

[1] Christian Mysticism, p. 44.
[2] *Life and Letters*, ii, p. 77.
[3] e.g. F. C. Burkitt, *The Gospel History and its Transmission* (Edinburgh, T. & T. Clark, 3rd edn 1911), ch. 7; and B. H. Streeter, *The Four Gospels* (London and New York, Macmillan, 1924), pp. 363–92.

'Mysticism' is a plastic word, used in a variety of senses. At one level it can mean mysterious, enigmatic, paradoxical. In this sense the Fourth Gospel is undoubtedly 'mystical'; of all commentators R. H. Lightfoot continually points to the presence of *double entendre*, paradox and deeper allusion.[1] Jesus' crossing of the sea (6.22–5) is clearly mysterious, as are his subsequent references to his 'coming and going' (7.33–6; 8.21–3). The Samaritaness' five husbands (4.18) and the 153 fish (21.11) seem so concrete at first sight, and yet have symbolic overtones.[2] Siloam (9.7) is interpreted as 'sent'. There is the enigmatic use of 'lift up' or 'exalt' (*hupsoun*) both for the glorification of Jesus and for his crucifixion, the actual mention of cross being dramatically suspended until 19.6 (cf. 12.33; 18.32). Clement of Alexandria described the work as a *pneumatic* or spiritual (as opposed to fleshly) Gospel, concerned with retailing spiritual truth, even if under the cloak of factual error.[3]

'Mystical' teaching might be said to differ from ordinary, matter-of-fact, discourse in being 'deeper', more profound; so, at first look, is the Fourth Gospel in comparison with the Synoptists. The feeding of the five thousand (6.1–13) heads a long dialogue and discourse, in the course of which the feeding is compared and contrasted with the divine provision of manna (6.31), and Jesus expounds himself as the bread of life, the living bread (6.32ff.). The cure of the man blind from birth (9.1) has features in common with Mark 8.22ff. and 10.46ff., but is used by John to illustrate Jesus' statement, 'I am the light of the world' (8.12), and his purpose in reversing the roles of the seeing and the blind (9.39–41). Lazarus' death, like Jairus' daughter's, is described in terms of sleep (11.11–13; cf. Mark 5.39); but he is called after four days in the tomb by Jesus, who thus reveals himself as the resurrection and the life in action (11.25, 26; cf. 5.25–7). Here is 'profundification'; though it might be more accurately described as meditative exposition.

Religious language is so fluid that what is in one context described as *deep* or *profound*, may elsewhere be called *lofty, exalted*, even *celestial*. Here also John does not disappoint us. In reply to Nicodemus' ignorance, agnosticism or incredulity, Jesus says: 'If I have told you earthly things and you do not believe, how will you believe if I tell you of heavenly things?' (3.9–12). Despite Nicodemus' attitude, he goes on to talk of the descent of the Son of Man from heaven and of his exaltation (3.13–15). Indeed the Gospel does not begin with the Baptist's preaching (as Mark)

---

[1] *The Gospel of St John*, ed. C. F. Evans (Oxford, Clarendon, 1956), esp. p. 349.
[2] For 4.18, cf. 2 Kings 17.24ff.; for 21.11, see E. C. Hoskyns and F. N. Davey, *The Fourth Gospel* (London, Faber, 1940), p. 664; and A. M. Farrer, *The Rebirth of Images* (London, Dacre, 1949), pp. 253–5.
[3] In Eusebius, *Eccl. Hist.*, VI, 14, 7.

or birth (as Luke) or with Jesus' genealogy (as Matthew), but in heaven with the unity and duality of God and his Word (*Logos*). The Word has become flesh (1.14), after which Logos is used no more and is replaced by Son (1.18). Whether as a meditation and extension of the 'Q' saying (Matt. 11.27‖Luke 10.23), or from another source, or of his own inspiration, one of the main themes of the Gospel, repeated and progressively developed, is this unity-in-duality of the Father and the Son (see *inter alia* 3.30–6; 5.17–29; 6.57; 14.6–11; 17.1–5, 20–6); it lies behind both the words and the 'works' of Jesus. The Father and the Son will together come to dwell in the observant believer (14.23) and, conversely, the ultimate consummation of Jesus' work and prayer is that the believers should come to share the heavenly glory and mutual love which the Father and Son have shared from eternity.

Some critics have sensed an atmosphere of unreality, a pious haze, hovering over the Gospel, particularly in contrast to the concreteness of the Synoptists, and the author has been accused of 'docetism'.[1] But if it is a mystical treatise the author has included a large number of concrete details, and in particular almost goes out of his way to stress the reality of Jesus' human nature (4.6, 7; 11.5, 35–6; 19.17).

Von Hügel noted 'an intellectualist, static, abstractive trend', again in contrast to the Synoptists. In particular the imagery of the Kingdom of God is hardly found; instead we find the more abstract categories of Life, Light, Love, Spirit. It is true that we have to go to the closely related First Epistle to find 'God is Light' (1.5) and 'God is Love' (4.16), but the same categories dominate the Gospel; where we also find 'God is Spirit' (4.24), invisible activity, and the key references to Light (1.4, 5, 9). These are of course biblical concepts (cf. esp. Ps. 36.9); but they are more than that, as they can be understood without being tied to their Jewish roots, and can be seen as terms with a wider and more universal appeal,[2] and considered as a mystical treatise.

St John's Gospel continues to mystify scholars, though in a different sense. Most nowadays would give more weight to the biblical and Jewish background; following the lead of C. H. Dodd,[3] they see the Gospel as dependent on an independent source for topographical details of Judaea and Jerusalem; and many prefer his dating of the crucifixion. And all can agree that the study of the Gospel need not wait upon the resolution of these questions.

It is clear that the Fourth Gospel can only be called 'mystical' in a loose

[1] See especially E. Käsemann, (ET) *The Testament of Jesus*, London, SCM, 1968.
[2] On the vocabulary, see W. R. Inge in *Cambridge Biblical Essays*, ch. 9; and C. H. Dodd, *The Interpretation of the Fourth Gospel*, Cambridge and NY, CUP, 1953, part II.
[3] *Historical Tradition in the Fourth Gospel*, Cambridge and New York, CUP, 1963.

sense, and many definitions of mysticism would rule it out.[1] Accordingly some have asserted that John is anti-mystical,[2] because he offers no direct and immediate communion with God, but a communion mediated by a historical person, similar to the 'Christ-mysticism' ascribed to St Paul by Schweitzer, and so a variant of 'inter-personal mysticism'.[3]

Nor is it correct to describe the work as a static document or treatise. It is presented as a 'Gospel' after the pattern pioneered by St Mark, that is, a story of a divine action focused on the life, death and resurrection of Jesus. And like Mark, and the others in their various ways, it has a *dramatic* structure, though by no means Mark's structure, nor his plot.

To understand the drama of the Gospel, and so its message, we must take into account its clearly devised structure. According to all commentators, it clearly divides between ch. 12 and ch. 13; this is the clearest division in the book. It is also clear that ch. 21 is an appendix of some kind, even if it be by the same hand as the rest and part of the original conception. 1.1–18 seems to be a preface; but it is not clear whether the preface continues to 1.51 or 2.11 or even 2.25; it might be a preface to the whole work, though it leads naturally into the first part. Dodd styles the two parts the Book of Signs and the Book of the Passion, but these designations are not exhaustive. The author himself twice epitomizes the distinction: (1) in the preface (the Logos) 'came to his own (place, people), and his own people did not receive him; but to as many as received him he gave the right to become sons of God . . .' (1.11–13); (2) towards the end of the last discourse, in a climactic sentence (cf. 16.25–7 with 16.29–30), Jesus states: 'I came forth from (the side of) the Father and have come into the world; again I leave the world and go to the Father' (16.28).

According to (1), the distinction is between Jesus' rejection by the Jews and his acceptance by believers; according to (2), the distinction is between Jesus' witness to the world and his return home. Moreover, the first part has its own conclusion in the author's verdict (12.36a–43) and Jesus' final summary speech (12.44–50); while the supper scene has an elaborate beginning (13.1–3), introducing the key themes of the second part, Jesus' return and his love for 'his own'. And some of the key concepts change, *light* and *judgement* being prominent in the first part, *love*, *abide*, and *glory* in the second part, while *life* and *witness* are found in both alike, as is *spirit* in differing senses. The chief contrasts are articulated in the two texts cited.

---

[1] e.g. the definition of F. Heiler, cited on p. 19.

[2] e.g. Hoskyns and Davey, pp. xliii, 9.

[3] See pp. 22, 23 above, and p. 89; like St Paul's, St John's 'Christ-mysticism' is qualified by its ultimate theocentricity.

(2) above gives us the overall divine plan, (1) the human response; clearly the initiative is with the divine (1.1 ff.). God, through his Word, is the creator of all things, and the giver of life, and the human race is enlightened by the divine light. But the light shines up against darkness, in other words there is already a sphere of darkness or alienation. The Word 'became flesh' and revealed the glory of a unique reproduction of God, the only begotten of the Father; and the first part of the Gospel is a progressive manifestation of the characteristics of this glory in action, as new wine (2.1–11), new temple (2.21; 4.21–4), life restored (4.46–54; 5.1–9), living bread (6), sight for the blind (9) and life from the dead (11.1–45). And all this because 'God so loved the world that he gave his only begotten Son' (3.16) to be a source of eternal life to believers. God in himself, the Father, is utterly and inherently invisible (1.18; 5.37), but reveals himself, in word and action ('sign'), in his Word or Son (1.1–4, 18; 14.8–11), even in the OT (5.46; 8.56; and above all 12.41 = Isa. 6.1ff.), and now in the Word made flesh. The cripple is cured by Jesus, yet behind his action is the working of the Father (5.17), the source of his life and his life-giving action. Jesus is God's manna, gift of bread, but living bread and life-giving bread (6.35, 48–51b); and the living bread gives itself for the life of the world (6.51c) as flesh and blood (6.53ff.).

But this generosity is divisive; it provokes rejection and acceptance, and the first part is concerned with both, and in that order. The cripple's cure provokes persecution and the threat of death (5.16, 18). The life-giving manna provokes not only 'murmuring' (6.41) but the defection of many potential disciples, apparently all but the twelve (6.60–8). The blind man receives his sight but is excommunicated from the synagogue (9.24–34). Lazarus returns to life, but precariously (12.10), while the restorer of life has inevitably put his neck into the noose (11.7–16, 47ff., 57). But why so?

The answer is given in a number of images. Jesus has not come to judge, but to save, the world; but judgement is inevitable and immediate because light is rejected by those who prefer darkness and its deeds, and only accepted by those already open to God (3.17–21). He has come to bring light, as to the cured blind man; the Pharisees, who think they are right in rejecting the cured man, are shown up as blind: 'but you say We see; therefore your sin remains' (9.39–41). In other words, there is the world of the flesh, of nature and natural causality, and the world of the spirit, of God's free creative activity (3.6–8; 4.24), the world below and the world above (8.15, 23). The world below, the flesh, should be open to divine action; in fact the 'world', personified here by 'the Jews', prefers to remain closed and self-sufficient, and so destined to damnation (8.24, 31–3). So it must try to explain all Jesus' sayings and movements in terms of natural causality, on the plane of nature (6.42; 7.35; 8.22). Its enclosure on this level is a form of bondage (8.32ff.); they can seek glory only from among themselves (5.44; 7.18; 12.42); and in so far as they are aggressive, they are not only suicidal but homicidal and satanic (8.37–44).

But there is also acceptance. This seems to begin in Jesus' offering himself as the answer to a felt need: to John's disciples' curiosity (1.35–40), to the Samaritaness' thirst (4.10–15), to the nobleman's plea for his son (4.47), to the paralytic's complaint (5.7), to the request for manna (6.34), to the blind man's plight (9.1ff.) and then to his need for careful shepherding (9.35–8; 10.11ff.), to the sisters' importunity over Lazarus. The gift is offered in the most acceptable form, and when accepted, apparently freely accepted. And yet there is an invisible power working behind the offer and the acceptance (cf. 6.37ff.; 44–6, 63–5). In whatever guise it is offered, it is a gift of life, not just the restoration or prolongation of life, but 'eternal life', a share in the ongoing life of God (5.26; 6.57), the life which the Son has from the Father and shares with the Father, and so a more abundant form of life (10.10). This life is offered to, and is available to, those who accept Jesus and his offer, adhere to him, believe on him, and are divinely enabled to do so. The cost of this gift to Jesus is the giving of his life in and through death (6.51c, 53–4; 10.15; 17–18; 12.23–5), and until then the gift is not fully available (7.37–9); and it is hinted that the cost of acceptance is similar (12.26).

It is this strand in the first part which is elaborated in the second part of the Gospel, particularly in the supper scene (chaps. 13–17), where the intimacy between Jesus and his disciples, already hinted in the image of the shepherd and the sheep (10.14–16), becomes expressed in the language of love. The foot-washing is a kind of initiation into this deeper relationship (13.8–11); Judas has no place in this love-feast, and leaves for the darkness outside (13.11, 30). It is an example of mutual service (13.12–17), to be the hallmark of all his disciples (13.34–5).

He speaks openly of his departure and of his return (14.3, 28); in fact the discussion ranges widely over the future (like Mark 13), and Jesus speaks from both sides of death. The union between him and his disciples is further illustrated by the image of the vine and its shoots (15.1ff.), so close is the union: 'abide in me, and I in you'. That is the condition of fruitfulness, in mutual love, even to death (15.13; cf. 13.1), in joy (15.11), in obedience (15.14) and in apostolic work (15.16). So will they be able to accept and overcome, as he has done, the hostility of the world, even to martyrdom (15.18–16.4).

In his departure they cannot follow him (13.33, 36). He goes to prepare a place for them in his Father's house (14.1–3). He is the way there, as well as the truth and the life (14.6), the living image of the Father

(14.7–11); he will open up a new era of intimacy with the Father in intercession (14.12–14; 16.23–4). They will not be left orphans by his departure, which is no occasion for sadness, as it is entirely in their interest (16.5–7), so that they can receive a new and permanent, though invisible, companion, advocate and guide (*Paraclete*), whom the Father will send at his intercession (14.16), whom indeed he himself will send (16.7), the Spirit of truth, to teach them and remind them of all Jesus has said (14.26), and to make it plain (16.14). He will help them bear witness in the face of opposition (15.26), and enable them to convict the world by referring to Jesus' rejection as the touchstone for sin, righteousness and judgement (16.8–11).

But he will only be *another* Advocate alongside Jesus (cf. 1 John 2.1–2). He too will return, victorious over death, and share with them his life (14.19), joy and peace (14.27), and the obedient disciple will become the dwelling place of the Father and himself (14.23). There will be an interval, 'a little while' (16.16ff.), of bereavement and pain; but the subsequent reunion will show that the travail was fruitful, as in childbirth (16.20–2). Incidentally, most of the blessings promised in chaps. 14–16 are conferred in the brief resurrection-reunion scene in 20.19–23: peace, joy, mission, Spirit. Meanwhile, the disciples are to be scattered and Jesus will be left alone: 'in the world you will have oppression; but take courage, I have overcome the world'. This condensed summary cannot do justice to the rambling, ruminating discourse; it should be followed at its own pace.

The section concludes with the long prayer of Jesus to his Father, looking forward to his return to heavenly glory and beyond that to the witness and temptations of the disciples, and of *their* disciples, that they may all come to share in the primal and final unity of love and glory which the Son shares with the Father, and which the Son wishes to share with them by indwelling (17.20–6). We are taken virtually to heaven.

Thus we see that the first part of the Gospel covers the way of purgation and the beginnings of illumination; the second completes that and opens us to the way of union. Whether so conceived or intended, it can well be used as 'a mystic's charter'; its discourses provide powerful reinforcement for the life that 'is hid with Christ in God', the 'eternal life' of this Gospel. And under the guidance of 16.28 we see that it is neither 'world-affirming' nor 'world-denying', but both: God so loves the world, and so does his Son, that he lives and dies in it and for it, and to raise it to the higher level where the Son is eternally at home with the Father.

'The hour is coming, and is here now, when the true worshippers will worship the Father in spirit and in truth'; this is an austere hope, but not impossible, 'for the Father is actively seeking such worshippers' and drawing them.

B PHILOSOPHICAL ROOTS

1 Greek Philosophy, Wisdom Literature and Gnosis

ANTHONY MEREDITH

Armstrong, A. H. (ed.), *The Cambridge History of Greek and Early Medieval Philosophy*. 2nd edn, CUP 1970.

PLATO

Hare, R. M., *Plato*, in the series Past Masters. OUP 1982.
The Dialogues of Plato. Greek text and ET in the Loeb Classical Library.

ARISTOTLE

Barnes, J., *Aristotle*, in the series Past Masters. OUP 1982.
The works of Aristotle are also available in the Loeb series.

STOICISM

Rist, J. M., *Stoic Philosophy*. CUP 1969.
Sandbach, F. H., *The Stoics*. London, Chatto & Windus, 1975.
The Meditations of Marcus Aurelius. Loeb, 1916, rep. 1970.

GNOSTICISM

Hennecke, E., and Schneemelcher, W., *Neutestamentliche Apokryphen*. 2 vols. 3rd edn, Tübingen, Mohr, 1959–64.
James, M. R., *The Apocryphal New Testament*. Oxford, Clarendon, 1924.
Jonas, H., *The Gnostic Religion*. 2nd edn, Boston, Beacon Press, 1972.
Puech, H. C., Quispel, G., van Unnick, W. C., (ET) *The Jung Codex*, ET and ed. F. L. Cross. London, Mowbray; New York, Morehouse-Gorham, 1955.
Robinson, J. R., ed., *The Nag Hammadi Library in English*. Leiden, Brill, 1977.

GREEK PHILOSOPHY

PLATO (428/7–348/7)

Plato was at one with his great teacher Socrates in rejecting the intellectual scepticism and moral relativism of his day which found expression in the phrase attributed by Plato to the Sophist Protagoras, 'man the measure of all things' (*Theaetetus* 152C). The whole philosophical endeavour of Plato can be viewed as an attempt to find a remedy for the moral anarchy which he believed resulted from this axiom. His system can be summarized as follows. Right action, which is the most important thing in the world, cannot exist apart from knowledge. Virtue, indeed, is knowledge and vice is ignorance (*Protagoras* 352C). But knowledge is neither sense-perception, nor even right opinion of which one can give an account (*Theaetetus* 210A). A definition, which for Plato is clear and fixed, cannot apply to the shifting world of senses. His insistence on the distinction between knowledge and right opinion leads to the conclusion that the source of knowledge cannot be the visible universe, but derives instead from the world of unchanging reality, which he calls the world of forms. Such truth as is occasioned by sense-perception derives its certainty from the forms, which are known by 'reminiscence' (*Meno* 98A; *Phaedo* 72E). This leads Plato to conclude that the condition of the possibility of knowledge, and therefore of morality, is the pre-existence of the soul, from which he infers its immortality. These twin beliefs in the existence of the ideas and the immortality of the soul are the basis of Plato's asceticism.

In *Republic* vii (517B ff) Plato uses a famous image with which to describe the upward journey of the soul to the light of the sun by means of a gradual emancipation from the land of shadows in which we habitually dwell. He considers human beings to be languishing as prisoners in a cave where they ignorantly suppose that reality consists of the shadows cast by the light of the fire on to the back wall of the cave. The soul has to be gradually turned round and led up into the light of the sun, to whose brilliant rays it is gradually accustomed. The sun in the allegory stands for the supreme idea, the idea of the Good, the source of reality and value to the rest of the universe.

This picture must be complemented by the picture presented in the *Phaedrus* (245 ff) and the *Symposium* (210 ff), where the supreme form is that of beauty and not of goodness. (Neither Plato nor his great follower Plotinus supposed that beauty and goodness were identical.) The ascent to beauty is less a matter of being led upwards from shadows to reality, than of following the natural attraction each of us has for beauty and sublimating it, so that we pass from the love of beautiful physical objects, to love of beautiful actions and thence to love of absolute beauty. The contemplation of absolute beauty is the most perfect life for man (*Symp.* 211D). It is impossible to exaggerate the influence of such language on all the Christian mystical tradition from Origen onwards.

ARISTOTLE (384–322)

Though a disciple of Plato, Aristotle differed from his master in several important respects. Unlike Plato he does not seem to have been interested in mathematics. On the contrary, his greatest contributions to the history of thought lie in the areas of physics, biology and logic, the empirical sciences. This means that he was unwilling to restrict the area of knowledge to the objects of the mind in the unseen world of forms. In fact he questioned and ultimately rejected the actual existence and the theoretical value of the forms (cf. esp. *Nicomachean Ethics* book 1.v ff.) In another important respect, also, he differs from Plato. Plato subordinated the quest of knowledge to the living of the good life and in one passage he insisted that the philosopher must come back into the cave for the benefit of his fellow citizens (*Rep.* 520C). For Aristotle, however, the moral life is a preparation for and essentially subordinate to the life of contemplation, what he calls the *bios theorētikos*. This separation between practical and theoretical wisdom is made clearly at the beginning of the *Ethics* (1103Aff). In that passage Aristotle makes a sharp distinction between the moral virtues of liberality and temperance and the intellectual virtues of wisdom and intelligence. The suggestion is that life is to be viewed as existing on two separate levels or as comprising two stages, the life of moral virtue and the life of contemplation (cf. esp. *Ethics* 10.vii). In the second stage, by which Aristotle seems to have meant the study of natural science and theology, our inbuilt dynamism, or *entelechy* (cf. *Metaphysics* Θ.3; 8) is realized. Contemplation issues in, or is identical with, the truly blessed life and makes us like God, primarily because for Aristotle God is essentially engaged in self-contemplation (*Met.* Λ.9). To be truly human, therefore, means becoming something more than human.

STOICISM

The word derives from the Greek word '*stoa*' or porch, where Zeno of Citium (*c*. 336–264) used to conduct his school. Unlike Plato, who in his distinction of sense and intellect was a dualist, Zeno and his followers were all materialist monists. But it was by their ethical teaching rather than their metaphysics that they exerted influence. For them the end of life was happiness and this was to be achieved by 'life according to nature'. This entailed acceptance of whatever happened and a severe restriction of desire to what lies within our power, our moral choice. The suppression of desire – *apatheia* – becomes in their hands a necessary means for the gaining of true happiness. Under such a system the realm of moral intention is more important than that of action. Philo and Clement (see pp. 94–6 and 112–15) believed that *apatheia* was a necessary stage in the acquisition of contemplation, the ultimate end of life.

WISDOM LITERATURE

The title *Wisdom Books* is traditionally applied to the following OT writings: Job, Psalms, Proverbs, Ecclesiastes or Qoheleth, the Song of

Songs, Wisdom, Ecclesiasticus or Sirach. The genre was traditional and goes back to the collections of maxims of the wise, primarily concerned with the way this life is to be lived. The unsystematic origins of these collections is particularly clear in Proverbs and Sirach, where frequently enough there is nothing apart from a catchword to link one saying with the next.

While Proverbs and Sirach seem largely explicable in terms of traditional moral saws and maxims, perhaps of Egyptian provenance, Ecclesiastes' attitude to reality in its weary acceptance of a desacralized cosmos has affinities with the writing of Epicurus; and the book of Wisdom has both Platonic and Stoic overtones, though the actual extent of these is much disputed. 'Wisdom will not enter a deceitful soul, nor dwell in a body enslaved to sin' (1.4) undoubtedly suggests both the need for moral purification and a distinction of soul and body. A similar attitude to the body and soul is implied at 9.15: 'For a perishable body weighs down the soul and this earthy tent burdens the thoughtful mind', language reminiscent of *Phaedo* 81C. The fruits of wisdom are listed at 7.16: 'unerring knowledge of what exists, the structure of the world and the activity of the elements', and these are not unlike the fruits promised to the contemplative life by Aristotle in the *Ethics* Bk. x.

The permanent place of Wisdom Literature in the history of Christian spirituality is illustrated in the climax of the book of Wisdom (chs. 7–9), with its teaching concerning the kinship of divine and human wisdom; as Solomon prays, 'Give me wisdom that sits by thy throne . . . that she may be with me . . . and she will guide me wisely in my actions' (9.4–11).

GNOSTICISM

Opinions divide as to whether Gnosticism is a pre-Christian movement which subsequently infiltrated Christianity or basically a Christian phenomenon. Again, it is not clear if it ought to be regarded as an oriental/Jewish system or as 'acute Hellenizing' of the gospel. Finally, whereas H. Jonas thinks there was a 'gnostic syndrome' in which he includes not only the official systems of Valentinus and Basilides but also Origen and Plotinus, Armstrong is much more restrictive in his application of the term. Among writings definitely to be thought of as gnostic the following should be mentioned: *The Gospel of Truth* by Valentinus (*c.* 140 AD), part of the Nag Hammadi find and edited in the *Jung Codex*; *The Song of the Pearl* (*c.* 150 AD) from the *Acts of Thomas*, translated by James in *The Apocryphal New Testament*, pp. 411ff.; *The Gospel of Thomas* (*c.* 150 AD) surviving only in Coptic and printed in German, Latin and English in Aland's *Synopsis Quattuor Evangeliorum* (Stuttgart 1963), pp.

517–30. The systems of Valentinus, Basilides and Marcion are all described with a high degree of accuracy by Irenaeus in book 1 of *Adversus Haereses.*

Despite different stresses among the above mentioned writings, Jonas seems correct in isolating the cardinal feature of gnostic thought as the radical dualism governing the relation of God and the world (op. cit., p. 42): 'the world is the work of lower or evil powers and the aim of life is escape from it through the revelation offered.' Similarly H. Chadwick writes: 'Gnosticism . . . consists essentially in a radical rejection of this world as being at best a disastrous accident and at worst a malevolent plot' (Armstrong, p. 166). No importance is attached to the physical universe, to the body (*Gospel of Thomas*, 87), to sex (*Gospel of Thomas*, 114), to history or to morality. The *parousia* is ignored and Christ's life is barely mentioned. But although the central message could never be fully accepted into orthodox Christianity, certain elements were less hostile, and among them the following should be mentioned: first, an appeal from above; second, an invitation to wake up and discover one's true but forgotten identity – this above all in *The Song of the Pearl* and the *Gospel of Thomas*, 3; third, a conversion to self and to God and a flight from the world of illusion and body; fourth, the belief that evil is ignorance and is destroyed by knowledge, the communication of which, as the very word Gnosticism suggests, is the purpose of all the systems.

2 Philo

ANTHONY MEREDITH

Philo of Alexandria, *The Contemplative Life, etc.*, tr. David Winston. CWS 1981.
Chadwick, H., 'Philo', in Armstrong, ch. 8.
Daniélou, J., *Philon d'Alexandrie*. Paris, 1958.
Wolfson, H. A., *Philo*. 2 vols. Cambridge, Mass., Harvard University Press, 1947.
For further bibliography cf. *ODCC* s.v.

Philo was an Alexandrian Jew, born *c.* 20 BC and dead sometime after 41 AD. As such he stands in a discernible tradition going back to the translators of the Septuagint, to Aristeas, and to Aristobulus, the first known Jewish allegorizer of the Bible. All these writers share with Philo the desire to express, whether for the benefit of fellow Jews or, less likely, for that of outsiders, their religion in the language and, more importantly, in the ideas of their Greek contemporaries. Philo's work consists, with the exception of several occasional pieces, of an extended commentary on the first five books of the Old Testament, in the course of which he manages to combine the greatest possible reverence for the text with the greatest possible freedom in interpreting it. This he achieved by the method of allegory, which he arguably learnt from the Greeks (cf. the *Allegories of Homer* by the Pseudo-Heraclitus). The method assumes that the sacred text, Homer or the Bible, is the one vast cryptogram concealing, under cover of the narrative, information about the natural and moral order.

The influence of Philo, though greatly exaggerated by Wolfson, was nevertheless very considerable, above all among the Christian Platonists of Alexandria, Clement and Origen; and through them it passed to Gregory of Nyssa. The so-called Alexandrian school of exegesis, there-fore, can look upon Philo as its founder; indeed in later years Philo was disowned by the synagogue and was sometimes thought of as a Christian bishop. But great though the influence of Philo undoubtedly was, it would be unfair to attribute to him a coherent philosophical vision. He is emphatically eclectic; and this feature, too, he shares with the culture of his own day. In him we can find the influence of Plato in his transcendent conception of God and belief in the immortality of the soul. From the Stoa he derives a strong sense of the ordering of the cosmos, the occa-sional description of God as the active cause of the world, and the exaltation of *apatheia* as the height of moral excellence. Finally his description of the monastic type community on the shores of lake Mareotis has links with the Neopythagoreanism of his day.

The spiritual ideal that Philo outlines is an amalgam of Stoicism and Platonism, a fusion of the active or virtuous life and the contemplative life of study and prayer. The nature of the active life is described in some detail in the treatise *Quod Omnis Probus Liber Sit*. In sections 76–91 he describes a community of Essenes living on the shores of the Dead Sea and usually identified with the Qumran sect. The basic aim of the Essenes was inner freedom, an ideal which has close similarities with that preached by Epictetus (cf. esp. *Diss*.iv.1) and one which was to be achieved by overcoming the tyranny of the passions. So Philo writes in section 18: 'Freedom sets the mind at liberty from the domination of the passions . . . above all desire, fear, pleasure and grief.' These four pas-sions are the same as those enumerated by Diogenes Laertius in his account of the Stoics in *Vitae* vii.110. The firm establishment of inner freedom is the main aim of these 'athletes of virtue' and once gained it seems to be incapable of being lost (cf. section 88).

The second part of Philo's ideal is described in his *De Vita Contemplat-iva*. If the tone of the Essenes was decidedly Stoic, that of the Therapeutae, their Egyptian counterparts, is Platonic. Their primary aim is 'the worship of the Self-existent, who is better than the Good, purer than the One, and more primordial than the Monad' (section 2). In one sentence Philo shows also his own belief that God takes over and transcends at the same time the conceptions of Plato (the Good and the One) and the Pythagoreans (the Monad). Doubtless in his description of God as the Self-existent Philo has Exodus 3.14 at the back of his mind, but his expression of this in the neuter and not in the masculine may indicate the at times excessive lengths he was prepared to go to in expressing biblical insights in philosophical language.

The communal life of the Therapeutae is described in some detail. Apart from morning prayer for heavenly daylight and evening prayer for relief from the tyranny of the senses, 'the interval between early morning and evening is spent entirely in spiritual exercise' (28). This exercise itself consisted largely on the allegorical interpretation of the Bible, in order to discover its hidden 'mind'. But the end of this intellectual activity does not seem to have been simply a deeper understanding of the sacred text. It was instead some sort of ecstasy. This Philo describes, taking language from the *Ion* and *Phaedrus* of Plato, as 'sober intoxication'. This striking, if traditional, language is Philo's way of suggesting the state of high spiritual exaltation, in the course of which the normal processes of reason are temporarily suspended and a kind of ecstasy takes place. In this respect Philonic ecstasy differs markedly and importantly from that of Plotinus (see E. R. Dodds, *Pagan and Christian in an Age of Anxiety* [CUP, 1965], pp. 70–2). For Philo, ecstasy seems to mean that for its duration one's natural faculties recede before God and are replaced by him. For Plotinus, on the other hand (cf. *Ennead*, vi.9.11), ecstasy means the raising of one's natural faculties, which are divine anyway, to their most exalted and at the same time to their truest state. It is not altogether clear if this systematic and important difference is reflected in the psychological awareness of the Philonic and Plotinian visionary.

3 Plotinus

ANTHONY MEREDITH

Armstrong, A. H., 'Plotinus', in *Cambridge History* . . ., chaps. 12–16.
Armstrong, A. H., *The Architecture of the Intelligible Universe in the Philosophy of Plotinus*. CUP, 1940.
Arnou, R., *Le désir de Dieu dans la philosophie de Plotin*. 2nd edn, Rome, 1967.
MacKenna, S., *Plotinus* (ET of *Enneads*). 4th edn rev. B. S. Page. London, Faber, 1969.

Wallis, R. T., *Neoplatonism*. London, Duckworth, 1972.

Plotinus was born in Egypt *c*. 205 AD, went to Rome *c*. 244 and died there in 270. His life was written by one of his most distinguished pupils, Porphyry, who tells us that the decisive influence on Plotinus was the philosopher Ammonius Saccas, under whom he studied for about ten years in Alexandria prior to his departure for his abortive visit in the entourage of the emperor Gordian to Persia in 242. After his death his writings were gathered together by Porphyry and edited in six *Enneads*, each Ennead containing nine treatises. The organization is by topic, not chronological. In the East his effect on pagan philosophers was considerable, though he was not simply repeated uncritically even by his immediate follower and pupil Porphyry. The largely rationalist tone of his writing, which led him to set small store either by prayer or by worship of the gods, was rejected by Iamblichus; and Proclus modified the simple lines of his system considerably. Even so, largely through the mediation of Proclus, the Plotinian vision exercised an enormous influence on Christian spirituality. In the West, on the other hand, it was mainly through Christian influence that Plotinus spread from the very beginning. Marius Victorinus (*c*. 300–80) translated some of the *Enneads* into Latin and through these translations St Augustine became acquainted with Plotinian metaphysics. The immense influence exercised by these latter upon the thought of Augustine is seen especially in the stress both laid on the importance of introversion (cf. for example *Ennead* iii.8.6.40 and *Confessions* x.28.38).

Plotinus regarded himself as a follower of Plato and had sharp words for any, especially the Gnostics of his time, who made innovations in received teaching (*Enn.*ii.9.6.11). Plato is cited as authority for his own views (*Enn.*v.1.8.1ff) and, although he departs at times from the common teaching of other followers of Plato, he always works within the questions and most of the presuppositions of the school (cf. iv.8.8.1ff). Even so, he was himself by no means an uncritical repeater of the whole Platonic corpus. To begin with, there were areas in Plato's thought that were of no interest to Plotinus. For example, he shows no interest in politics. Again, Plato in the *Timaeus*, while asserting the existence of three principles, had in no clear way established a relation among them; Plotinus organized them in a descending triad of the One, Mind or Spirit, and Soul. Further, for Plato the supreme reality was conceived statically as forms, unchangeable patterns of reality; for Plotinus the supreme reality, the One, was conceived of as formless and infinite (*Enn.*v.5.6); the second reality, Mind, far from being thought of as static, is described as 'no corpse and full of life' (*Enn.*v.4.2.43).

97

It follows from what has been said that the two central features of the Plotinian universe are that it is a layered universe; and that it is dynamic. The first point can be seen as an effort to organize the insights of Plato; in asserting as he does at *Enn*.ii.9.1. that the universe is composed of three primary principles, Plotinus is simply following in the footsteps of his Middle Platonist predecessors Albinus and Numenius. The most striking element in his system is the One. This reality on the one hand transcends both the world of sense and that of form and intellect. It is also beyond being (cf. Plato, *Republic* 509B – a passage of great importance for Plotinus, cf. *Enn*.v.3.11.28; 12.47; 13.2: 17.13). It may not be named, even as 'one', though it is absolutely simple (*Enn*.v.5.6.26). On the other hand the One is also the cause of all that is outside it, life, intelligence and motion, all in fact that Plotinus includes under the general rubric of Mind (*Enn*.v.5.10.10). If it be asked how Mind comes from the One, the answer is by a process of emanation. The One can no more not produce some sort of offspring than the sun can fail to produce light or the fountain water (*Enn*.v.2.1.8); yet in the process of emanation the One itself is not in any way itself lessened (*Enn*.ii.9.3.8; iii.8.10.1–5). In these last two passages two of the cardinal principles are to be found: the necessary productivity of the One; and the principle of undiminished giving.

Everything derives from the One and everything is intended to return to the One. Conversion, however, is never so complete as to result in the total reabsorption of the All in the One. However close be the connection between the Soul and Mind and between Mind and the One, the three hypostases are and remain eternally distinct from each other. Yet despite this distinctness (cf. *Enn*.ii.9.1.) reality is also a continuum, and for Plotinus there are no sharp lines drawn across the map of the universe. The clearest illustration of this fundamental difficulty is the doctrine that the soul is never totally fallen, but always remains in the realm of Mind above it (*Enn*. iv.1.12; iv.8.8.1–3). In other words the language of return which Plotinus uses is not incompatible with one of never having fallen. Something of the puzzle of this condition is conveyed by Plotinus' own question at *Enn*.iii. 6.5.1ff: 'If the soul is in no way tarnished, then why does it need to purify itself?' For him it seems to be paradoxically the case that the condition of the possibility of return is the actual possession of that to which we do return.

It is possible to schematize the programme of return or ascent in five stages, not sharply distinct from each other. (i) We must be aware of the baseness of the things we honour, especially in comparison with the true nobility of our soul (*Enn*. v.1.1.25–8). (ii) Then follows the process of purification, which for Plotinus is the same as the acquisition of virtues; this leads to a likeness to or identity with God (*Enn*. i.2.5.1–5). (iii) At this point a process characteristic of the *Enneads* occurs, introversion. The return is not achieved by a spatial transference or by searching outside but by turning inwards (*Enn.* iii.8.6.40; i.6.8, 9; v.8.2.32). (iv) Introversion leads not only to the self, conceived as soul, but also to Mind. This follows from what has already been said, and from the principle of the immanence of the effect in the cause. Introversion issues in the contemplation of the Beautiful or Mind. This is a disturbing and exhilarating process (*Enn.* v.5.12; and for the centrality of contemplation cf. esp. *Enn.* iii.8). (v) The final stage brings one into direct relation with the One in ecstasy, the flight of the alone to the Alone (*Enn.* vi.9.11.51). Its character can best be guessed from E. R. Dodds' translation of *Ennead* vi.9.11.22–25: 'An *ecstasis*, a simplification and surrender of the self, an aspiration towards contact, which is at once stillness and a mental effort of adaptation.' It was a state which, according to his biographer Porphyry, Plotinus achieved four times in his life (*Vita Plotini*, 23.16).

4 Proclus

ANTHONY MEREDITH

Blumenthal, H. J., ed., *Neoplatonism and Early Christian Thought: Essays in Honour of A. H. Armstrong*. London, Variorum, 1981.

Lloyd, A. C., 'Athenian and Alexandrian Neoplatonism', in Armstrong, ch. 19.

Proclus, (ET) *The Elements of Theology*, trans. and ed. E. R. Dodds. 2nd edn, Oxford, Clarendon Press, 1963.

Rosan, L. J., *The Philosophy of Proclus*. New York, Cosmos, 1949.

Wallis, R. T., *Neoplatonism*. London, Duckworth, 1972.

Proclus (412–85) belonged to the school of Athenian Neoplatonists, and was the pupil of Syrianus, whom he succeeded as scholarch, or president of the Academy at Athens. It was to Syrianus, in all probability, that Proclus owed those modifications in Plotinian Neoplatonism that give his system its distinctive character. E. R. Dodds in his masterly edition of the *Elements* sees in Proclus an unoriginal scholastic mind that lost sight of the rational genius of Plotinus, but, as H. J. Blumenthal has suggested in his essay on Proclus in *Neoplatonism and Early Christian Thought* (London, 1981), such a view does less than justice to Proclus, partly because it overestimates the 'rationalism' of Plotinus, partly because it exaggerates the irrationalism of Proclus; moreover, it fails to take into account the considerable influence exercised by him on posterity. As J. Stiglmayr pointed out in 1895, the writings of the Pseudo-Dionysius (see pp. 184–9) become intelligible when it is realized that they show the marked influence of Proclus. And through Dionysius Proclus helped to mould the whole mystic tradition, in the East through Maximus the Confessor, in the West through Eriugena, the St Victor School, the Rhineland Mystics and finally St John of the Cross.

TEACHING

The most satisfactory way into his system is through his criticism of Plotinus. Though agreeing with him on the central doctrines of return and union, he differs on three important issues: (i) the Henads, (ii) the fall of the soul, (iii) the nature and origin of evil. On (i) it seems that Proclus, in common with the rest of the later Neoplatonists, starting from Iamblichus, deeply though they respected Plotinus, was dissatisfied with his failure, as they saw it, to elaborate a fuller system within the intellectual world. Plotinus at *Ennead* ii.9.1 and elsewhere had insisted that there were three and only three hypostases, One, Mind and Soul. Iamblichus, Syrianus and Proclus, not understanding the dynamic aspect of the Plotinian system, felt that it failed to bridge the yawning gulf which it seemed to leave between the utterly transcendent One and the rest of reality. It was the desire to fill the void which seems to have prompted them to people it with a multitude of intermediaries, called by Syrianus Henads. (ii) Plotinus is emphatic that the whole soul does not fall; in fact he denies that a member of the active intellectual world is capable of falling. In this, as he himself admits at *Ennead* iv.8.8.1, he deliberately departs from the traditional position held within the Platonic school. Against this innovation of Plotinus, Proclus himself consciously reacts, insisting in the last proposition (211) of the *Elements* on the total descent of the whole soul into the world of time and change. (iii) In *Ennead* i.8 Plotinus offers two connected but not quite identical theories for the origin of evil: (a) matter itself is intrinsically evil; (b) evil is caused by a combination of the negativity of matter and the movement towards it of soul. Proclus, however, in *De Malorum Subsistentia* 37.5–7 denies that matter can be evil, or that there can be any such thing as self-subsistent evil. Evil at its worst is moral evil, and consists, as St Augustine also held in *De Libero Arbitrio* iii, in turning away from a higher good. Clearly this view of Proclus is a corollary of (ii), because it entails a true downward movement or declension on the part of the soul.

'The whole of our life is a struggle towards vision' (*Commentary on the Parmenides*, col. 1015 38–40). So Rosan (op. cit.) characterizes the central thrust of the Proclan system. Elsewhere Proclus speaks of union as the end product; and at the end of *On Providence and Fate* the final result is described as 'divinization, as far as possible'. As with Plotinus before him and Dionysius after, advance towards this goal is marked by a series of withdrawals, first from involvement in civil society, then from the tyranny of sense, and finally through a process of introversion and self-knowledge to the knowledge of the supreme being. Philosophy is the chosen medium through which this combined withdrawal and journey upwards is achieved, and Proclus terms it 'the author of salvation'. Further, increase in purification makes the soul more and more like the object of its desire; *Elements* 32 states that 'all reversion is accomplished through the likeness of the reverting terms to the goal of reversion'. But as on his own principles soul is fallen and the One is absolutely above being, Proclus has to postulate as a principle of similarity within us a faculty in the soul which is higher than it, which he terms 'the flower of the mind' (*In Alcib.* iii). The expression has a history and seems to occur for the first time in the second-century AD collection *The Chaldean Oracles*, i (cf. Des Places *ad loc.* in the Budé edition). This is the unitary faculty, which not only enables the soul to have the vision of the One at which it aims, but also is the instrument of ecstasy within it. In other words, Proclus seems to believe both in the total descent of the soul and its complete detachment from the source of its being, while at the same time admitting through the 'flower of the mind' the possibility of vision.

II

THE EARLY FATHERS

1 The Apostolic Fathers and Irenaeus

SIMON TUGWELL

Texts and Translations

The Apostolic Fathers, ed. and tr. J. B. Lightfoot. London and New York, Macmillan, 1885–1901 (contains *Diognetus*).
The Apostolic Fathers, ed. and tr. Kirsopp Lake (Loeb Classical Library, 1912–13) (contains *Diognetus*).
Die apostolischen Väter, ed. F. X. Funk, K. Bihlmeyer and W. Schneemelcher. Tübingen, 1970 (useful bibliography).
Sources Chrétiennes contains useful editions, with French translation, introduction, notes and bibliography, of: 1 Clement, Ignatius, Polycarp, *Didache*, Barnabas, Hermas, *Diognetus*, Irenaeus *Against the Heresies* (vols. 167, 10, 248, 172, 53, 33, 263–4, 293–4, 210–11, 100, 152–3).
The Ante-Nicene Fathers contains a translation of Irenaeus *Against the Heresies*; reprint Grand Rapids, Eerdmans.
Irenaeus, *Proof of the Apostolic Preaching*, tr. J. P. Smith. ACW, 1952.

Studies

Barnard, L. W., *Studies in the Apostolic Fathers*. Oxford, Blackwell; New York, Schocken, 1967.
Cross, F. L., *The Early Christian Fathers*. London, Duckworth, 1961.
Daniélou, J., (ET) *The Theology of Jewish Christianity*. London, DLT; Chicago, Regnery, 1964.
Daniélou, J., (ET) *Gospel Message and Hellenistic Culture*. London, DLT; Philadelphia, Westminster, 1973.
Tugwell, S., *Ways of Imperfection* (London, DLT, 1984), pp. 1–12.
Tugwell, S., 'Irenaeus and the Gnostic Challenge', in *Clergy Review*, 66 (1981), pp. 127–30, 135–7.

THE APOSTOLIC FATHERS

The 'Apostolic Fathers'[1] reveal a Church still groping towards self-understanding and exposed to internal problems as well as to external

---

[1] The *Didache*, the Letter of Barnabas, the Letter of Clement, the *Shepherd* of Hermas, the Letters of Ignatius, the Letter of Polycarp and 2 Clement (a mid-2nd-century homily of unknown provenance having no connection with Clement). Ignatius, Bishop of Antioch, wrote his letters on the way to his martyrdom in Rome *c.* 110. Polycarp,

opposition. Where church structures were well developed, some people found them frustrating; they were discontented with 'the provisions Christ gives for the journey' (1 Clem. 2.1), wanting more scope for their intellectual, charismatic and moral powers (48.5)[2], or they found the Church insufficiently 'spiritual' (Ign., *Eph.* 8.2; *Trall.* 5.1f). Where structures were less developed, people supplemented Christianity with Judaizing practices (*Did.* 8; Barn.) or turned to soothsayers for advice (Herm., *Mand.* 11).[3] The crucial task, then, was to reaffirm the value of basic faith and of the Church, with all the disappointments and unanswered questions involved.

1 CLEMENT, IGNATIUS

Clement of Rome's letter was prompted by a schism in Corinth. It emphasizes church unity and submission to the official leaders, whose authority derives ultimately, by apostolic succession, from Christ (42). Clement likens rebellion against them to various disastrous Old Testament attempts to by-pass the official priesthood (4.12; 41.2f). All spirituality is based on obedience to God's will; we must trust that it is his commandments which lead to life and knowledge of God (35f). Presuming on our own wisdom, knowledge, purity or even faith, is folly, because we have nothing except what God gives us. We are justified by faith, not works; our works have value only if they come from obedience (32.3; 39.1; 48.5). It is dangerous to be too 'knowing', especially if it leads to 'funny ideas about God's gifts' (23.2; 41.4). We must be patient, like Abraham, when we see no immediate results: the Lord *will* fulfil his promises for those who obey him (10; 23.3ff), but he will punish those who deviate from 'the rule of our tradition' (7.2; 11.1). Instead of priding ourselves on our achievements, we must confess our faults and accept God's forgiveness (51f).

God's whole purpose is peace, as the harmony of the cosmos shows (19f), and the Church's hierarchical order exists to maintain and express

---

Bishop of Smyrna (martyred *c.* 156), wrote his letter soon after Ignatius' death. A strong case for dating the other writings to the first century is argued in J. A. T. Robinson, *Redating the New Testament* (London, SCM; Philadelphia, Westminster, 1976), pp. 312–35. The *Didache* is a compilation, consisting of an ethical catechesis, a rudimentary church order and a fragmentary apocalypse. The Letter of Barnabas is of unknown authorship; it is essentially an exercise in Christian exegesis of the Old Testament against Judaizers. Both the *Didache* and Barnabas could come from Palestine, Syria or Egypt. Clement was Bishop of Rome in the late first century. Hermas also wrote in Rome, though his date is uncertain.

[2] cf. H. von Campenhausen, (ET) *Ecclesiastical Authority and Spiritual Power in the Church of the first three Centuries* (London, Black; Stanford, Stanford University Press, 1969), pp. 86ff.

[3] cf. J. Reiling, *Hermas and Christian Prophecy* (Leiden 1973), esp. pp. 58–96.

peace; this is a more important value than the fulfilment of personal religious ambitions. Mutual charity, forbearance and hospitality are prime objectives (50.1). It is better to be 'in the fold', however ingloriously, than to excel on our own and be 'pitched out from hope' (57.2).

Ignatius hints at a rather more mystical doctrine of unity. For him the Church's hierarchical structure symbolizes heavenly realities, the bishop representing the Father, the deacons Christ, the presbyters the apostles (*Mag.* 6.2; *Trall.* 2f). A church structured like this *is* the 'type and teaching of immortality'; to be within it is to be protected against error (*Mag.* 6.2; *Trall.* 7). Only there can we eat 'the bread of God' which gives us life (*Eph.* 5.2).

Ignatius is 'a man made for unity' (*Phil.* 8.1), and what he celebrates in the churches is the threefold unity of Christ's flesh and spirit, of faith and charity, and, most importantly, of Jesus and the Father (*Mag.* 1.2). Jesus is the Word proceeding from the silence, the One from the one Father, who did nothing apart from the Father; his deeds and words are rooted in the silence of God, and this conjunction of inner and outer makes him 'the perfect man' (*Mag.* 7f; *Eph.* 15.1, *Smyrn.* 4.2). To deny his flesh through an over-spiritualized squeamishness or to fail to hear the silence within the manifestation is to miss perfection. 'Nothing that appears is good': Ignatius applies this slogan to Christ, who 'being with the Father' (no longer seen in the world) 'appears all the more' (*Rom.* 3.3). If we accept both the outwardness of Christ's flesh and the inwardness of his being with the Father, we too become perfect, having our own silence and our own words and deeds (*Eph.* 15.2). This is the conjunction of faith and charity which 'is God' (*Eph.* 14.1). Christ is our life; apart from him we are mere ghosts (*Phil.* 6.1; *Trall.* 10: *Smyrn.* 2). To share in his life involves flesh and spirit, faith in Christ, as God and man, and charity, including practical charity (*Smyrn.* 6.2). In this way Ignatius gives an orthodox meaning to the claim that spiritual people cannot do fleshly things: 'Everything that you do even in the flesh is spiritual, because you do it in Christ Jesus' (*Eph.* 8.2).[1]

'What God promises is unity, which he himself is' (*Trall.* 11.2). There is no attaining to God without unity. And the relative unimpressiveness of the Church and its leaders actually plays a part in the process. We attain to God through 'the passion of my God' (*Rom.* 6.3), which we must all volunteer to share (*Mag.* 5.2). Ignatius reckons that it is when he is no longer visible to this world that he will become a true disciple, a true human being; then he will be 'a word of God' not just 'a noise' (*Rom.* 2.1; 4.2; 6.2). He sees himself as a scapegoat, carrying the churches' filth, as he

[1] For Ignatius, doing things 'in Christ' meant doing things in submission to the bishop: *Trall.* 2.1; *Pol.* 5.2.

bids bishop Polycarp 'carry everyone' (*Eph.* 8.1; *Pol.* 1.2). He is unworthy to be counted among the Christians of Antioch, whose bishop he was (*Mag.* 14.1; *Trall.* 13.1). Paradoxically the bishop, who is a 'type of the Father', must be all the more reverenced when he is silent and unimpressive (*Eph.* 8.2), because the silence of God is particularly present in the humiliated silence of the passion, of martyrdom, of unimpressiveness. Heretics may 'talk big' (*Eph.* 10.2), but in the Church, for all its dullness, we find true life, the conjunction of word and silence.

THE *DIDACHE*, BARNABAS

For the Didachist and Barnabas, as for Clement, what matters is that Christians follow the path revealed by God. But whereas Clement and Ignatius are clear about what this means and disapprove of those who seek new doctrines, the Didachist and Barnabas see it as necessary to seek out the will of God and are sympathetic to teachers who supply 'extra righteousness and knowledge' (*Did.* 11.2). God has shown us 'the way of life', but this life must be guarded, and the best defence is for Christians to meet regularly to 'seek out what is good for your souls' (*Did.* 9.3; 16.1f; *Barn.* 2.1, 9; 4.10; 21.6). We are constantly threatened by 'the ruler of this age of lawlessness', who seeks to 'slip in some deception' and 'sling us out of life' (*Barn.* 2.10; 18.2).

For Barnabas, and perhaps for the Didachist, the typical error is Judaizing. The Didachist tells Christians not to fast or pray with the 'hypocrites' (8). Barnabas develops his objections more fully. In his view, Jewish religious observance was radically misconceived; the Jews were misled by a wicked angel at the outset and rejected God's covenant (4.7f; 9.4). As a result they took literally precepts which were intended spiritually, like circumcision and the dietary laws (9ff), and tried to apply immediately precepts which were intended for the future. The sabbath must be celebrated 'with a pure heart', and only at the end of the world shall we have a pure heart (15). We are not yet justified, and if we suppose we are, we shall simply 'go to sleep over our sins'. The Judaizing temptation is that of premature perfectionism (4.10ff). Christianity does not yet give us perfection, but it does set us on the right path, with a true understanding of where we are. We must be content to be as holy as we can (19.8), doing good works to atone for our sins (19.10) and putting our hope in Jesus (11.10). One work which Barnabas recommends is 'toiling with words' for each other's good; he himself derives confidence of salvation from the success of his preaching (1.3; 19.10).

The Didachist is less obviously anti-perfectionist and actually implies that perfection is required in the last days (16.2), but the conclusion to his ethical instruction is suggestive: 'If you can carry the whole yoke of the

Lord, you will be perfect; if not, do what you can' (6.2),[1] and his eucharistic prayer treats perfection as eschatological (10.5).[2]

HERMAS

The problem of perfectionism is central for Hermas. Some people in Rome were teaching that Christians who sin cannot repent again (*Mand.* 4.3.1). Hermas believed he was supernaturally commissioned to refute this doctrine. As a result of his message, many people regained hope and the Church was rejuvenated like a poor invalid receiving a large inheritance (*Vis.* 3.12.2f). Hermas saw that the real problem was that some people find it subjectively almost impossible to repent. Whole-hearted believers, who hope in God, associate themselves with the Church and do not blaspheme against Christ, stand a good chance of salvation and their sins will not do much harm. But people who become enmeshed in worldly attachments or are hard-hearted towards their fellow-Christians are less likely to repent. Deliberate apostasy is very difficult to undo (*Sim.* 8.6ff; 9.19ff; 31.2f).

Hermas has a strong doctrine of the influence of 'spirits'. Even the most determined sinner will be a bit virtuous if a good spirit gets hold of him, and even the most virtuous man will 'sin a bit' if an evil spirit gets hold of him. What matters, then, is not achievement but loyalty. We must trust the good spirit (*Mand.* 6.2), and since he is 'delicate', we must avoid offending him with things he dislikes, especially bitterness, and we must cultivate the things he does like, such as truthfulness, whole-heartedness, trust, joy and generosity. If he abandons us, our plight will be irremediable (*Mand.* 3.5, 9f).

POLYCARP, 2 CLEMENT

Polycarp's letter is disappointingly banal. He urges obedience to God's commandments, emphasizing the values of the Sermon on the Mount, faith ('the mother of us all'), hope and charity (2f).

The contemporary account of his martyrdom is more interesting. When the police arrive to arrest him, he gives them food and drink and asks permission to pray for an hour. It is two hours before he finishes praying for everyone he has ever met and for the whole Church. When the proconsul tells him to revile Christ, he replies, 'I have served him for eighty six years and he has done me no wrong; how can I blaspheme against my King who saved me?' (9.3).

---

[1] Commentators have devised ingenious ways round the plain sense of the text, but they are unnecessary; cf. S. Tugwell, *The Way of the Preacher* (London, DLT; Springfield, Ill., Templegate, 1979), pp. 136–9.

[2] For a powerful argument in favour of the eucharistic nature of the *Did.* prayer, see A. Vööbus, *Liturgical Traditions in the Didache* (Stockholm 1968), pp. 63–83.

2 Clement exhorts us to be appreciative of our redemption and to show it in our lives. We must not treat the flesh as unimportant: we were saved in it and we shall be judged in it (9). In fact, the coming together of the inner and the outer is one of the harbingers of the Kingdom (12). The heavenly reality of the Church was manifested in the flesh of Christ; unless we cherish it in the flesh, we shall lose the spiritual substance too. 'Keep the flesh, so that you may receive the Spirit' (14). In expectation of the judgement, we must repent wholeheartedly and practise prayer, fasting and almsgiving, especially the last, since 'charity covers a multitude of sins' (16f).

IRENAEUS

Irenaeus was born in Smyrna, where he was a disciple of Polycarp. He later moved to Gaul, where he became Bishop of Lyons in 177. His church was being infiltrated by Valentinian Gnosticism, and his major work, *Against the Heresies*, is a detailed, perceptive exposure of Gnosticism and a presentation of Catholicism, designed to show that the latter has a better answer to the very problems raised by the Gnostics, and that it forms a more coherent whole. Against Gnostic dismembering of Scripture, he affirms the integrity of 'the body of truth' (I.9.4). The later *Proof of the Apostolic Preaching* is a catechetical summary of Christian belief.

Irenaeus tries to do justice to the gnostic sense that we are meant for a more spiritual existence than is here possible, and that Christ frees us from a chaotic and alien world and an unsatisfactory law. But he rejects the gnostic interpretation of this situation as unconvincing. If this material world is not due to God's will, it must have come about either without his knowledge or contrary to his will, either of which destroys his claim to omnipotence (II.2). And if man's destiny is purely spiritual, why must he be formed for it, as the Valentinians alleged (I.5.6—6.1), by doing time in the body (II.19.4–6)?

Irenaeus agrees that our destiny is spiritual, but we are to be united with God as spiritual *human beings*, which involves the body as well as the spirit (V.8.2). 'Man alive' is God's most remarkable achievement precisely because human life requires a blending of flesh and Spirit (IV.20.7; V.4.1; 6.1; 9.1). God's power is shown in the weakness of flesh (V.2.3; 3.2f). The salvation of the flesh is the goal of creation and redemption (III.22.3; IV.Prol.).[1]

But flesh cannot attain to union with God without passing through many stages (IV.9.3; 38.3). Unlike other creatures, we do not come into

[1] cf. A. Orbe, *Antropología de San Ireneo* (Madrid 1969), pp. 486, 492.

being perfect: we are made, not defective, but immature (*Proof*, 12, 14).[1] It is intrinsic to being the kind of creature that we are that our perfection should be gradual (IV.38). Even after the end of this world, we shall need the millennium before we can enter the Kingdom of the Father (V.32–6).

The tragedy of the fall is that Adam and Eve would not wait (IV.38), and so snarled up the process of human growth. Christ unsnarled it again (III.18.22.4; V.19.1), by passing through all the stages of human life (II.22.4; III.22.3; IV.38.2). He becomes what Adam was meant to be, humanity in the image and likeness of God (*Proof*, 32). And this means a proper conjunction of flesh, in which the image of God resides, and the Spirit, who imparts likeness to God (V.6.1).

But sin is not a total disaster. God wanted humanity to be appreciative of its creator (IV.37.6), and by coming to know evil as well as good, human beings do become more appreciative of the good and of the God from whom it comes (III.20.1f; IV.39.1). The suffering which results from sin is educative, in that it trains human freedom (V.3.1; 29.1).

We must accept the leisurely way God works. All of history is only the one day in which humanity is created (V.29.1). All that God does is 'the making of human-kind' (V.15.2). God shapes humanity out of frail matter with his two 'hands', the Word and the Spirit (IV. Prol.), which have been at work on humanity from the beginning and are still engaged in bringing it gradually to perfection (V.16.1).

The final perfection is that we should see God. Seeing God is our life (IV.20.7). But we must begin with a feeble life and an indirect vision; we only gradually become capable of the more intense life of eternity (IV.6.6f; 26.1; V.3.3).

In this whole process Christ plays a crucial part. In him the invisible God becomes visible, without losing his mysteriousness (IV.6.6; 20.7). Only so can we receive the vision of God which makes us immortal (IV.20.2; *Proof*, 31). In Christ the union between flesh and Spirit, humanity and God, is effected, in him the two parties become, as it were, acclimatized to each other (III.18.7; 20.2; V.1.1). This is why any denial of the humanity or the Godhead of Christ is disastrous (V.1.2f). Unless God and humanity are united in him, we have no hope (III.19.1). We are drawn into this union through baptism and the Eucharist (III.17.2; IV.18.5; V.2.3), which build up our frail flesh so that it can carry the weight of divine life.

Irenaeus stresses human freedom, insisting that sin is due to the wrong use of freedom (IV.4.3; *Proof*, 11f) – though Adam's sin is 'without malice' and the real original sin is that of the angels (IV.40.3) – and that our service of God must be voluntary (IV.37.1). But we cannot achieve

[1] Orbe, op. cit., p. 19.

perfection simply by the exercise of free will. It is our part to 'be made', while 'making' belongs to God (IV.11.2). We must not try to take ourselves out of the hands of our Creator (IV.39.2f). It is wrong to suppose that immortality is ours by right (III.20.1; V.2.3). If we think we are already a finished product, we shall remain stunted for ever (IV.38.4; 39.2f). It is silly to want to be divine before we are even human (IV.39.2). The grateful acknowledgement of our Creator is the proper exercise of our freedom (IV.13.31; 37.1).

2 Tertullian and Cyprian

EDWARD YARNOLD

TERTULLIAN

Barnes, T. D., *Tertullian: a Historical and Literary Study*. Oxford, Clarendon, 1971.
Musurillo, H., ed., *The Acts of the Christian Martyrs*. OECT 1972.
O'Malley, T. P., *Tertullian and the Bible*. LCP 21, 1967.

CYPRIAN

Cyprian, (ET) *The Lord's Prayer*. Westminster, Maryland, Christian Classics, 1983.
Hinchcliff, P., *Cyprian of Carthage and the Unity of the Christian Church*. London, Chapman, 1974.

Cyprian's letters are quoted according to the numeration in the CSEL, Budé and the 1844 LF editions. Other editions may give slightly different numbers.

Further bibliography in Altaner and *ODCC*.

TERTULLIAN

Considering the influence which Tertullian exerted on the development of the theology of both East and West, few facts concerning his life have come down to us. A native of the Roman province of Africa, he left Carthage for Rome. His writings, which can mostly be dated to the first two decades of the third century, bear the stamp of a teacher and practitioner of rhetoric.

We have already noted the tendency to regard the Church on earth as a society of the perfect (cf. p. 106), and to emphasize the gulf between Christianity and the world. Tertullian's concern for the purity of the Church made him increasingly susceptible to the influence of Montanism, so that he finally broke with the Catholic Church and joined that sect. This pentecostal and rigoristic movement had originated in Phrygia in Asia Minor, but soon spread to other parts of the Roman Empire. Its adherents believed that they alone had received the Spirit and constituted the true Church. Stern asceticism was practised, second marriages were forbidden, as was any attempt to escape martyrdom. Yet their doctrine seems to have been mainly orthodox, and their liturgy does not seem to have differed much from that of the universal Church. Thus, although, as a Montanist, Tertullian's writings exhibit a growing harshness, much of his understanding of the spiritual life remains unchanged.

Though himself much influenced by pagan philosophy, particularly that of the Stoics, Tertullian insisted even in the earliest period of his writings that Christians must separate themselves from the values of this world. St Paul had learnt at Athens how human wisdom corrupts the truth which it claims: 'What then has Athens to do with Jerusalem?' (*De Praescriptione*, 7).

Sex and marriage Tertullian viewed austerely, even in his work *Ad Uxorem*, written in his Catholic period. The union of a man and a woman is 'permitted' and 'blessed by God' for the propagation of the human race, but abstinence is a greater good, as St Paul taught (i.2–3). The practice of married people who, once baptized, observe continence is to be commended: continence is an 'instrument of eternity', a 'testimony of faith' (i.6–7). It is better for widows and widowers not to remarry (i.5). He praises the marriage of two Christians:

> How can we describe the happiness of a marriage which the Church joins together, the Eucharist confirms, the blessing seals, the angels witness and the Father ratifies? (ii.9)

But it must be admitted that sex seems to play little part in his ideal of Christian marriage. In another work of the same period he describes the consecrated virgin as married to Christ (*de Oratione*, 22). As a Montanist he took a severer view of marriage, seeing the difference between marriage and fornication as a mere matter of law, both being based on concupiscence (*De Exhortatione Castitatis*, 9).

The belief that the martyrs provided the authentic example of Christian living was by no means confined to the Montanists. The tendency was particularly strong in North Africa, which was the source of such works as the *Acts of the Scillitan Martyrs* and the *Acts of Perpetua*. For Tertullian martyrdom is a 'second washing . . . of blood', which 'counts for [baptismal] washing not yet received and restores it if it has been lost' (*De Baptismo*, 16). Flight from martyrdom is resistance of God's will (*Scorpiace*, 4–5).

Many of the early schismatical movements such as Donatism (cf. p. 135) were so concerned with the moral purity of the Church that they denied the possibility of pardon for sins committed after baptism. Tertullian at first admitted the possibility of a 'second penance . . . but now only once' (*De Paenitentia*, 7; cf. Hermas, *Mand.* iv.3); but severe penance was required as 'satisfaction' to 'appease' (*mitigare*) God (*De Paen.* 9). As a Montanist, however, he denied the Church's right to forgive post-baptismal sin, finding particular fault with the practice of a 'pontifex maximus' – perhaps Pope Zephyrinus (d. 217) or Callistus (d. 222) – who was willing to absolve sins of adultery (*De Pudicitia*, 1, 5).

Tertullian's spirituality was not totally repressive. Both before and after he left the Catholic Church, the Holy Spirit was at the centre of his thinking. In his early work *De Oratione*, which is the first known commentary on the Lord's Prayer, he explains that the movement of prayer, being sent forth from the Holy Spirit, ought to be free from anger and perturbation of mind, because 'a defiled spirit cannot be acknowledged by the Holy Spirit, nor a sad spirit by the joyful, nor a burdened spirit by the free' (12). Modesty is the 'sacristan and high priest' of those whom the presence of the Holy Spirit makes into God's temples (*De Cultu Feminarum*, 2.1).

The *De Oratione* contains a general treatise on prayer. The hands should be modestly raised and spread out in imitation of the Lord's passion (14–17). Even the sound of the voice should be subdued (17) – a reminder that the ancients both read and prayed aloud. The customary times for prayers are the third, sixth and ninth hours of the day, as well as daybreak and nightfall (25).

CYPRIAN

In the life of Cyprian we see recurring many of the problems that a generation earlier had faced his fellow North African Tertullian, whom he used to describe as 'the Master'. Cyprian became Bishop of Carthage about 250 at a time of fierce persecution. Like Tertullian, he regarded martyrdom as the authentic example of Christian living, and wrote several works encouraging Christians to prepare themselves for it. He himself twice withdrew before the threat of martyrdom, and felt obliged to justify his decision in his letters (e.g. *Ep.* 81). His eventual martyrdom in 258 is recorded in the *Proconsular Acts of Cyprian*.

In the lull after the Decian persecution of 250–1, many of the Christians who had compromised themselves to escape torture and death sought reconciliation with the Church. Cyprian was caught up in the controversy about the proper treatment which should be accorded them (cf. *Ep.* 11 and 12). He set out his position in two works: the *De Lapsis*, in which he explained the ways in which the different degrees of lapsing should be treated; and the *De Unitate*, in which he discussed the unity of the Church and the evil of schism. These works express a spirituality founded on a deep conviction of the importance of the visible Church, held together by the unity of the bishops, and united with Christ as the water is mixed with the wine in the Eucharist (*Ep.* 63.13). He it was who coined the historic maxim, *salus extra ecclesiam non est* (no salvation outside the Church: *Ep.* 73.21).

In his treatise on the dress of virgins (*De Habitu Virginum*) Cyprian writes of consecrated virginity in more positive terms than his 'Master'. But he is much indebted to Tertullian in his treatise on the Lord's Prayer (*De Oratione Dominica*).

3 Clement of Alexandria

ANTHONY MEREDITH

Bigg, C., *The Christian Platonists of Alexandria*. 2nd edn, Oxford, Clarendon, 1913; New York, AMS Press, 1970.
Chadwick, H., 'Clement of Alexandria', in Armstrong.
Lilla, S. R. C., *Clement of Alexandria*. OUP, 1971.
Louth, A., *The Origins of the Christian Mystical Tradition*. Oxford, Clarendon; New York, OUP, 1981.

For further bibliography, see *ODCC* s.v.

Born towards the middle of the second century AD, Clement received his education principally from Pantaenus, probably head of the catechetical school at Alexandria, where he may have become his successor until his flight thence in *c.* 202 to Palestine during the persecution of Septimius Severus. He died there *c.* 215.

His earliest extant work is his *Protrepticus*, a persuasive appeal on behalf of the faith, full of pagan learning and showing a particular reverence for Plato, whose vision of the divine nature exercised a distinct influence on him. His other two main surviving writings, *Paedagogus* (the Tutor) and *Stromateis* (Miscellanies), offer a wide variety of instruction on ethical and theological subjects. The main discernible influences on Clement apart from the Bible are Philo, whom he quotes extensively verbatim, the Stoics, above all Musonius Rufus, who flourished in Rome towards the close of the previous century, and Plato, whose contemplative ideal is perceptible in *Str.* vii, and whose transcendentalism is reflected at *Str.* ii.16.

Clement believed that the Platonic ideal of 'assimilation to God as much as possible' (*Theaetetus* 176B) and the Christian notion, 'Be therefore imitators of me as I am of Christ' (1 Cor. 11.1), were in basic harmony. *Str.* ii.22 is devoted to showing the agreement between the scriptural and the Platonic visions.

Clement envisages the life of perfection as beginning with faith and ending with knowledge, the intervening stage being made up of growth in moral excellence, which itself contains two elements, *apatheia* and charity. To the first term, which is in origin a Stoic term, it is hard to give a precise sense. It means mastery of all disordered feelings and passions, and sometimes refers in particular to the destruction of the four main passions – anger, desire, fear and pleasure (cf. Diogenes Laertius, vii.110). The Stoic emperor and near contemporary of Clement, Marcus Aurelius (emperor 161–80), regarded imperviousness to all passion as an ideal to be striven for (*Med.* i.9.3).

The Christian life begins with faith, which is seen as the basis and origin of all knowledge (cf. esp. *Str.* ii. 2 and 4). By 'faith' Clement has in mind 'the conviction of things not seen' of Hebrews 11.1 rather than the more fiducial conception of Romans and Galatians. With the foundations provided by faith, itself indemonstrable, the house of knowledge may be erected (*Str.* ii.4.13).

But before the perfection of knowledge can be arrived at, the 'gnostic', that is the perfect Christian, must achieve moral excellence. He must learn to 'abstain from errors in speech, thought and sensation . . . reflecting that "Blessed are the pure of heart for they shall see God" (Matt. 5.8)' (*Str.* ii.11.50.2). This Matthaean text is used on several occasions to enforce the need for moral purification (e.g. *Str.* iv.6.39; vii.3.13), and in the latter passage it is linked with the Stoic ideal of *apatheia* as constituting part of that likeness to God without which it is impossible to see him. Here Clement seems to be consciously linking together the passionlessness of the Stoics with the Platonic principle of 'likeness to God' in the service of a Christian idealism. At *Str.* vii.3.14, for example, he quotes 2 Cor. 10.5 ('We take every thought captive to Christ') and Eph. 4.24 ('Put on the new nature created after the likeness of God') in support of the view that Paul, Plato and the Stoics are at one in their moral vision.

In *Str.* vi.9 the true gnostic is exhorted to practise passionlessness not as some sort of abstract or even rationally defensible ideal, but because 'the Saviour himself was entirely passionless, inaccessible to any movement of feeling either of pleasure or pain' (*Str.* vi.9.71.2). Christ has become a Stoic hero, free not only from anger, fear and lust but also from 'such movements of feeling as seem good, courage, zeal, joy, desire, through a steady condition of mind without changing at all'. To such a chilling condition he invites his followers. As the Word of God is completely in control in the person of Christ, and this is the source of his superhuman self-mastery, so we too, who possess the image of this Word in our reason, are invited to a similar self-mastery. Strangely enough, Clement does not think that this ideal excludes the possibility of love, though the love he admits seems to be one devoid of desire. 'For love is not desire on the part of him who loves; but it is a relation of affection, restoring the gnostic to the unity of faith' (*Str.* vi.9.73.3). This sole exception to the general inhibition on passion may itself be Stoic, and may be paralleled in the above-mentioned passage in Marcus Aurelius: 'To be at the same time utterly impervious to all passions and full of natural affection'. As Gataker, an early commentator on Marcus, notes, such a condition is nearly miraculous. This affection, strange and frail though it is, is the only exception admitted by either Clement or Marcus to the austere ideal which admits no room for affections 'commonly celebrated as good, gladness ... dejection ... and caution' (*Str.* vi.9.74.1–2).

A few words must here be said about the treatment given to the Christian virtue of charity, as distinct from the passionless affection just discussed. If by charity is meant altruistic love for one's neighbour in pursuance of Christ's command at Matt. 22.39 and parallels, it must be admitted that Clement has very little to say, nothing that seriously modifies the pursuit of self-perfection which marks the rest of his writing. Whereas, as we have seen, the commands to purity of heart and perfection, based on Matt. 5.8, 48, are frequently (e.g. *Str.* vi.12; 140) discussed and interpreted in a Stoic/Platonist direction, the Matthaean text and its Lucan parallel (Luke 10.27) are dealt with fairly summarily and not fully discussed at *Paed.* iii.11.82.3 and *Str.* ii.15.71.1; iv.3.10.3. At *Str.* iv.18 Clement does use 1 Cor. 13 in his discussion of love of neighbour, but even here the context is the pursuit of happiness, and we miss any reference to the parable of the good Samaritan. This omission, though regrettable, is scarcely surprising, for even if we do not take the step of confining Christian love to Nygren's concept of *agape*, that is, totally unselfregarding love, nevertheless altruistic love has no place in Stoicism or Platonism; and it was with those models in mind that Clement largely operated.

The principal thing in his whole system is *gnosis* (*Str.* vi.10.80) and the majority of *Str.* vii is devoted to discussing it. The description of prayer given there is as follows: 'He [the gnostic] holds converse with God by knowledge, life and thanksgiving; he is closely allied with God; he is the truly kingly man; he is the sacred high priest of God . . . He is able to pray properly, knowing as he does the divinity rightly, and having the moral excellence suitable to him' (cf. *Str.* vii.7.35.3, 6, 7).

In a further passage (*Str.* vii.7.39.6) Clement seems to dispense with the need both for vocal and religious prayer 'for God continually hears all the inward converse'. And although weaker souls may find definite hours 'as, for example, the third, sixth and ninth . . . yet the gnostic prays all through his life; and having reached this, he leaves behind all that is of no service' (*Str.* vii.7.40.3). This rarified conception of prayer has little obvious similarity with the New Testament. Above all there is an absence of any invitation to petitionary prayer or to the sacraments; indeed with Clement's suggestion that the gnostic is the priest, the importance of sacraments is diminished. Although Clement insists that petition is not superfluous, it is difficult to fit it into such statements as the following: 'For God knows who are and who are not worthy of good things, and he gives to each what is suitable. Wherefore to those who are unworthy, though they ask often he will not give; but he will give to those who are worthy' (*Str.* vii.7.41.5). The end of all the gnostic's striving is continual recollection. 'In every place, therefore, but not ostensibly and visibly to the multitude, he will pray' (*Str.* vii.7.49.6). The personal note apart, there is little in Clement's conception of perfect prayer to distinguish it from the private intellectual contemplation outlined by Plato in the *Republic* and Aristotle in the tenth book of the *Nicomachean Ethics*.

4 Origen

ANTHONY MEREDITH

Origen, *An Exhortation to Martyrdom, etc.*, tr. Rowan A. Greer. CWS 1979.
Bigg, C., *The Christian Platonists of Alexandria*.
Chadwick, H., 'Origen', in Armstrong, ch. 11.
Daniélou, J., (ET) *Origen*. London and New York, Sheed & Ward, 1955.
Louth, A., *The Origins of the Christian Mystical Tradition*.
de Lubac, H., *Histoire et Esprit: L'intelligence des Ecritures d'après Origène*. Paris, 1950.

Further bibliography in *ODCC* s.v.

Our main source for the life of Origen is Eusebius in Book 6 of his *Ecclesiastical History*. He was born AD *c.* 185 of Christian parents. His father Leonidas was martyred in 202 in the persecution of Septimius Severus, and Origen himself wished to follow his example. In time he became head of the catechetical school at Alexandria, reputedly founded by Pantaenus, and he remained there until 231/2 when, as a result of a disagreement with his bishop Demetrius, he removed to Caesarea in Palestine where he remained till his death in 254. His death was in part the result of sufferings endured during the persecution of Decius.

The majority of his voluminous literary output is concerned with the exposition of the Bible either by homily or commentary. He commented on most of the books of the OT, all the Gospels except Mark, and most of the epistles of St Paul. He compiled for the benefit of discussions with the Jews his *Hexapla*, a six-column edition of the OT, setting Greek versions in parallel with the Hebrew. Origen also produced the last great patristic work of apologetics in the *Contra Celsum*, and the first *Summa Theologiae*, entitled *De Principiis*, in which he tries to provide a philosophical substructure for the creed of the Church. A treatise *On Prayer* and the *Exhortation to Martyrdom* complete the list of his principal writings. It should be noted that though he wrote or dictated (Eusebius says that at Caesarea he used a stenographer) in Greek, the vast bulk of his surviving writings are in Latin. The translations come largely from the hand of Rufinus, who, arguably, modified some of Origen's more daring speculations in the direction of orthodoxy. Origen's influence was considerable, above all on the Cappadocian Fathers, Basil, Gregory of Nazianzus and Gregory of Nyssa, the first two of whom made an anthology of his writings, the *Philokalia*, for the benefit of those who wished to see how faith and philosophy might be harmonized. His influence is also markedly discernible in the work of Evagrius Ponticus, and it was probably in the form that Evagrius gave to the thought of Origen that the latter was condemned in 543. Through Evagrius he passed in the East to Maximus the Confessor and in the West through Cassian to the monastic movement.

The final end Origen envisages for humanity is the corporate, loving contemplation of God in heaven, after the resurrection of the body, though, as will be seen, this last quality does not easily lend itself to his overall pattern. For him the end repeats the beginning; we shall all in the end become what we once were in the beginning. Perfection, therefore, for him is a process of return to origins. The primeval condition of humanity is outlined in *De Principiis* ii.8.3. There we learn that initially there existed a single unity of minds, caught up in the knowledge and love of God, possessing complete likeness to him, as well as the image that they derived from the fact of their intellectual constitution. From this primitive stage of loving contemplation, of being, that is, in the image and likeness of God, the minds fell and in the process of falling became souls, losing the likeness but not the image of God. The cause for this fall away from union with God by knowledge and love is described as boredom or satiety. The idea seems to be that the minds became sick of the riches of contemplating God or became bored through lack of anything further to discover about him, God not being thought of by Origen as infinite. Two things should be noted about the fall in this system. First, it was a fall into a body and into the physical order. This suggests that the physical order was to some extent an afterthought and not part of God's original intention; but it does not lead to the conclusion that the visible order of the universe is evil. Rather does Origen wish us to think of it as a place of correction and education for fallen souls on their way back to their fatherland. Secondly, despite his teaching that minds become souls and lose their wings and the likeness to God as they cool in their affection for him, it is doubtful if Origen believed in any serious sense in a corruption of the soul resulting from its desertion of God. Even after the fall, human beings retain the natural image of God within them, after which they were created in the first place; and as God is defined at *De Princ.* i.1.6 as 'a simple intellectual nature', so the central feature of human beings for Origen is their intellectuality, which, though perfectly realized in the contemplation of God, yet remains with them in the body. If humanity does not lose its capacity of intelligence as a result of the fall, neither does it lose its power to love. At the opening of the second of his *Homilies on the Song of Songs*, Origen writes that 'the God who made the whole world created all the motions of the soul for good'. In other words, the doctrine of the image of God in humanity remains so strong in Origen that one might reasonably ask if he took the doctrine of the fall in its Pauline understanding sufficiently seriously. It is certainly true that he did not come across this doctrine till he met the practice of infant baptism at Caesarea, till then unknown at Alexandria. Also he did not take so sombre a view of the human condition as St Paul in Romans ch. 7 or as St Augustine in the Pelagian controversy; but it is not clear that these facts by themselves constitute a denial of original sin.

In fragment 80 of his *Commentary on St John*, Origen contrasts the active and contemplative lives on the basis of the comparison between Martha and Mary found at Luke 10.38–42. He was the first to treat the two women in this way, though he was not the first to distinguish between the two lives. In this he was following Philo and Clement and, more remotely, Aristotle, Plato and the Stoics. But it is not only two lives that Origen so contrasts. It is also two stages in the same life. Although it is not quite clear whether Origen thought the two stages followed one another or went along *pari passu*, what does emerge from his writing is that return to one's former condition was an impossibility unless accompanied by a programme of ascetic self-mastery. Without the training of moral discipline the good natural instincts of love and knowledge are capable of perversion (cf. Prol. in *Comm. on Canticle*). Punishment, which for

Origen is entirely corrective, plays a similar role in helping the soul back to its lost paradise. 'Those who have fallen away . . . must be remoulded by salutary principles and discipline . . . and so be restored to their condition of happiness' (*De Princ.*, i.6.2).

One of the most hotly disputed questions concerning Origen is that of the respective influence of his two main sources of inspiration, the Bible and Plato. There can be no doubt that both exercised a major control over his thought and expression. He was a great biblicist; the vast majority of his surviving works are commentaries on the Bible, and his work is soaked in biblical imagery and quotation. On the other hand, it is impossible to ignore the fact that his doctrine of pre-existence and fall has more in common with Plato's myth in the *Phaedrus* 245ff than with the book of Genesis, or that his picture of God both in *De Princ.* i.1.6 and *Contra Celsum*, vii.42, with its stress on the intellectual, unchanging nature of God, has more in common with the contemporary Middle Platonists Albinus and Numenius than with the God of Abraham, Isaac and Jacob. Finally, his view of God as supremely beautiful and his intellectualist, disembodied view of the origin and end of humanity begin at times to look more like the *Symposium* and *Phaedo* of Plato than St Paul and the gospel. Something of this tension, perhaps more evident to us than it was to Origen, will be clear from the following account.

The return of the soul to its former state is described by way of a journey, and for it Origen utilizes the biblical journey of the children of Israel from Egypt to the Promised Land. Although his *Homilies on Exodus* outline the individual and corporate return of humanity to its home, it is in the celebrated Homily 27 on Numbers that a full account of the spiritual journey of human nature is uncovered through the biblical narrative of the wanderings of Israel in the wilderness. Origen was not the first to do this – Philo has preceded him in his *Life of Moses* – nor was he the last – Gregory of Nyssa did the same in his work of the same name. With them he shared the conviction that it was by devout meditation on the text of Scripture that understanding of God and his purposes would be revealed. This is important, because, though it looks at times, as for example in *On Prayer* ix, as if Origen has replaced a Christian doctrine of prayer with Platonic contemplation, by and large he is, as de Lubac has pointed out, more christocentric in his exegesis of Scripture than some of his commentators have been willing to believe. For him the Bible was not a cryptogram, as it had been for Philo, by means of which certain physical and moral truths were conveyed, but rather a way of entering deeply into the mind of Christ, in whom the whole Bible found its meaning.

Even so, the treasures of Scripture were to be unlocked primarily through the action of the mind upon them; and in the fourth book of *De*

Principiis Origen outlines the three main senses of Scripture: literal, moral and spiritual. One of the main purposes behind this move on his part was to defend the use of the Old Testament in particular against Marcion and his followers, who held that because the picture of God offered by the OT was unworthy of him, it could not be about the true God who was Father of Christ; this position led them to reject the OT on account of its unworthy notions. Origen's defence of the OT is intimately bound up with his use of the allegorical method. But he also used it to provide activity for the mind in the study of Scripture. It is the mind that makes us like God and by the action of the mind that we become once again fully godlike. God is 'Mind'; human beings are essentially 'minds'. As a consequence there is no place for ecstasy in his picture of the end of man. If by mysticism is meant going beyond the natural powers of the mind in some sublime moment of self-transcendence, then Origen is not a mystic. Nor does he know of any dark night of the soul or seeing that we cannot see. His account of the journey of the Israelites in the wilderness significantly omits what for Philo (*De Posteritate Caini*, 15; 169) and Gregory of Nyssa (*Life of Moses*, ii.230ff) was the climax of Moses' experience, the vision of God in darkness described at Exod. 33.17–23.

5 The Desert Fathers, Antony and Pachomius

PHILIP ROUSSEAU

Major dictionaries will contain most necessary information, under the headings 'Antony', '*Apophthegmata Patrum*' (= *Sayings of the Fathers*), and 'Pachomius'. Indispensable is Derwas J. Chitty, *The Desert a City* (Oxford, Blackwell, 1966; Crestwood, N.Y., St Vladimir's Seminary Press, 1966 and 1977).

Festugière, A.-J., French trans. of Rufinus' *Historia Monachorum* (Greek version), in his *Les Moines d'Orient*, iv/1. Paris, 1964.

Gregg, R. C., ET of *The Life of Antony* (CWS XVI).

Lefort, L. Th., French trans. of Coptic *Lives* and other material, in his *Les Vies coptes de saint Pachôme*, Louvain 1943; and *Oeuvres de saint Pachôme*, Louvain 1956.

Meyer, R. T., (ET) *The Life of Antony*. Westminster, Md., Newman Press, 1950.

Meyer, R. T., (ET) Palladius' *Lausiac History*. Westminster, Md., Newman Press, 1965.

Veilleux, A., ET of all Pachomian material, in *Pachomian Koinonia*, 3 vols. Kalamazoo, Cistercian Publications, 1980–1982.

Waddell, H., *The Desert Fathers: Translations from the Latin*. London, Constable, 1936; New York, Sheed & Ward, 1942.
Ward, Benedicta, *The Desert Christian. Sayings of the Desert Fathers: the Alphabetical Collection*. Oxford, Mowbrays; New York, Macmillan, 1975.

To speak of 'the spirituality of the desert fathers' would be misleading. No such coherent corpus of ideas or recommendations ever existed. Against a rich religious background in the third and previous centuries, experiment and competition were inevitably the order of the day; and immense diversity of practice is revealed by the sources.[1] Yet there lies their value. These men may have laid the foundations of medieval monasticism; but they also explored avenues, subsequently rejected or forgotten, that offer as much to our needs today.

Two historical points must be made. First, social forms demand attention. It was an alternative to village order that these men sought. Some ascetics (although least in Egypt) embraced a wild and solitary life, without shelter, clothes, food cooked or even cultivated; but the majority were intent upon creating a new society. Their spirituality reflected that aim, catering for relationships as well as personal goals.

Second, they aroused enormous interest in their own day. At first highly localized, they had gained, by the end of the fourth century, an international reputation. Rumour, travel, and biography provided literate enthusiasts with the inspiration and the models that would help them to embark upon a monastic life as far afield as Spain and Gaul. That wider popularity presents the modern historian with a danger. Many of the texts upon which we rely originated outside the desert. Athanasius' *Life of Antony*, Rufinus' *Historia Monachorum*, Palladius' *Lausiac History*: all were by men who had visited the desert, but retained connections with a distant world, and wrote for a foreign audience. The same may be true of some of the *Lives* of Pachomius. The *Sayings of the Fathers*, as we now have them in Greek, close in their roots to the great pioneers, were designed even so for use over a wide area. We enjoy an outsider's view of the desert. It is possible with care to identify ancient elements; but we have to be content with an account often later than we

---

[1] For details on background reading, see the Bibliography. Much of what I say here is explained and defended more fully in my *Ascetics, Authority and the Church* (OUP, 1978), and in my *Pachomius* (Berkeley, Univ. of California Press, 1985), both of which contain extensive references. Sources are abbreviated here as follows: Arsenius, 9 and similar = anecdotes in the *Sayings of the Fathers*; simple numbers in the section on Antony = chapters from his *Life*; G^1, S^1, Bo and similar = the various Greek, Sahidic, and Bohairic *Lives* of Pachomius; Dion. = the Latin trans. of a *Life* of Pachomius by Dionysius Exiguus; *HM* = Rufinus' *Historia Monachorum*; *HL* = Palladius' *Lausiac History*; *DF* = Helen Waddell, *The Desert Fathers*, a collection of translations.

might wish, written for an audience the desert fathers never dreamed of.

What do the texts reveal? Concentrating for the moment on the *Sayings*, we find disciples approaching masters, asking for words of advice. That in itself reflects a spirituality. There was at first no programme of reading, no timetable: at the heart of the formative process was a meeting between the novice and the experienced ascetic. Both believed that the older man had the gift of wisdom to recognize an immediate need or state of soul, and to respond accordingly. We note, of course, the insight and trust displayed; but we must acknowledge also that this was a hand-to-mouth spirituality: men felt their way, growing with each consultation.

Neither young nor old maintained this primitive posture. The questioning novice would often arrive from somewhere else; and elsewhere he returned. The word of the master gained full effect only when pondered at home. Hence the exhortation, 'Sit in your cell', where the full meaning of what you had heard would slowly dawn on you. Indeed, the cell itself, its silence and protection against distraction, would be your teacher (Moses, 6; *DF* VII. xxvii).

We discover at once the social dimension of this spirituality. Ascetics would visit famous speakers of the word; but equally important was the opportunity to reflect in a setting apart. And the elders had a life of their own. They discussed spiritual problems among themselves, and prepared for confrontation with those who sought advice. Many armed themselves with reading and meditation (Sisoes, 17). A man as holy as Paul the Simple might see into people's hearts; but others had to pray hard to discern the individual's needs (Paul the Simple, 1; *DF* V. xix). Even the greatest acknowledged they were dealing with 'hidden matters'. It was not always clear what effect their words might have, and they hoped for the best by advising others as they would advise themselves (Joseph of Panephysis, 3; Poemen, S 2, Nau 184).[1]

Such periods of withdrawal enabled both parties to measure the inadequacies of their situation. That in turn heralded a new stage in the general understanding of spiritual direction. Perception and eloquence began, it was thought, to decline (Isaac of the Cells, 7; Macarius, 5; Felix, 1). The elders were seen more as intercessors: they would pray for your spiritual progress, rather than provide it. They were also a link with the true but remoter pioneers, faithfully recounting the teaching of a previous generation (Amoun of Nitria, 2; Pistus, 1). Disciples, for their part, began to find the process of consultation frustratingly obscure and

---

[1] F. Nau published a series of anonymous sayings in Greek in the *Revue de l'orient chrétien*, 1908–13. Although not all are available in translation (some, slightly altered, are in Helen Waddell), I have had to make some reference to the collection.

inconclusive. Instead of welcoming the pregnant phrase, the brief exegesis, designed to feed their minds over a period of time, they sought for greater clarity, for more general rules of progress, for full and immediate explanation (Peter the Pionite, 2; *DF* V. xxxii; Nau, 216, 223).

These painful developments betokened growth in community, dependence on less prompt or startling recommendations, something closer to formula and custom. The formative relationship came to be one's contact with authentic tradition and with ascetic colleagues. It was a process set in motion by the fathers themselves. They threw the disciple back upon his own resources, so that he might become 'self-sufficient in all things' (Agathon, 10). Knowledge and mastery of self were the two ideals: judgement and watchfulness. Salvation lay in one's own hands, even after the word or prayer of the elder (John the Dwarf, 2; Pambo, 8; Psenthaisius, 1; Nau, 175, 226).

This process is best described as meditative self-reliance in the loosely structured company of fellow devotees. It explains why the first major contribution of the desert fathers to the history of spirituality was their exhortation, not simply to sit in a cell, but to cultivate there the fear of God, and purify the heart. 'Humility and the fear of God are above all virtues', said John the Dwarf (22). They were for Poemen as vital as the air we breathe. He was particularly subtle in interweaving these elements: the words of God, he said, would wear away the hardest of hearts, and bring it to fear (Poemen, 49, 183).

Like Antony and Pachomius, the desert fathers thought of this fear in positive, even joyful terms. Some may have displayed an inclination to sorrow or morbidity (Arsenius, 41; Poemen, 50, 72); but sombre caution was rarely an end in itself, more often the soil in which the spirit would bear fruit, a lamp that gave light to a darkened heart. Even the fear of death was a salve and protection (Arsenius, 40; Evagrius, 4; James, 3; John the Dwarf, 10; Macarius, 34; Poemen, 50). More important still, links were forged between that inner virtue and the emerging society newly embraced by the earliest ascetics. Acceptable fear was associated with humility and poverty; but it involved also a refusal to judge others, and the fear and humility of the master himself was what led a disciple to hear his word and act upon it (Poemen, 70; *DF* I. xix; Nau, 315).

We need to hold fast to this connection. Partly because of an indiscriminate use of texts from different periods, the desert fathers have acquired a reputation for bizarre extremism; but equally apparent in the sources are constant shifts towards inner perception and community experience.

Take, for example, the matter of demons. They occur in the earliest texts; but they were more part of the environment than of a monk's mind, a hazard of existence you kept your eye open for (Macarius, 36; Poemen, 67). Associated most closely with vestiges of the pagan cults, open conflict between demons and spirits subject to the true God was carried on irrespective of a monk's own troubles (Moses, 1). Most important, a clear distinction was made between demons and 'thoughts'. Although a demon might wish to drag a monk back to sensuality and error, he had the most limited access to mind, and in particular to any spiritual mechanism of resistance based on prayer and reflection (Isidore of Scetis, 2; Macarius, 3).

Or look at sex, undoubtedly a preoccupation. Poemen had sound advice for a brother rebuffed with horror by another elder: 'Abba Ibiston's deeds', he said, 'are in heaven with the angels and he does not realize that you and I remain in fornication. If a monk controls his belly and his tongue and if he lives like an exile, be confident, he will not die' (Poemen, 62). A whole range of texts recounts how monks would escape into town, sleep with prostitutes and others, even knowingly sire children, and yet be received again in their communities. The power of repentance was more highly regarded than the danger of lust (*DF* V. xxvii, xxviii; Nau, 176, 179, 187).

What we see created here is a shared arena of self-possession, where heart and community were model and support for one another. Essential to that achievement was a persistent move towards moderation. Tough these upcountry Egyptian peasants undoubtedly were (Ares, 1: Zeno, 6; the 'Abba of Rome', 1); but text after text declares that endurance and deprivation were not the major aims. The most exalted programme of ascesis had to be, in a phrase of Evagrius, 'harnessed together with love' (Evagrius, 6). Striking self-denial was pointless if it gave offence; and consideration for the brethren was an immediate excuse for the relaxation of custom (Poemen, 17; Silvanus, 1; *DF* VIII. xxii). A visitor apologizes, 'Forgive me, father, for distracting you from your rule'; and the hermit replies, 'My rule is to put your mind at rest, and send you away in peace' (*DF* XIII. vii). By contrast, a brother on his travels contented himself with a single pea while dining in the company of pilgrims. The host took him aside, rebuked him for his ostentation, and suggested that if that was the type of life he desired, he should sit in his cell and never come out of it. The story concludes, driving home the point, that the monk became instead a follower of community life (*DF* VIII, xxii; see *HM* xxi).

Not that we need imagine the fathers attached no value to vigour. At their best they saw themselves as workers, and had a deep suspicion of religiosity that did not display itself in practical achievement. Quietness of spirit was not an alternative to labour, but its best setting and support (John the Dwarf, 34; Sisoes, 13). Could we expect anything less, when the question so often addressed to masters was, 'What shall I do?' The unfolding of inner thoughts was central to the primitive ascetic dialogue; but the ultimate aim was to force mind into action (Poemen, 20).[1] Only then could the cycle repeat itself, and practical achievement form the basis of advice to others (Theodore of Pherme, 9; Cassian, 5; Nau, 240).

Here we discover the second great contribution of the desert fathers to the history of spirituality: their desire to interrelate as clearly as possible the life of labour and the life of the heart. It was not a simple task. Agathon felt that inner watchfulness mattered more than bodily ascesis: it was the fruit of the spiritual life, while labour was the foliage that offered protective covering and pleasure to the eye (Agathon, 8). Another elder put matters almost in reverse, so that teaching and reflection became the foliage, while action was the fruit (Nau, 252). Neither text, however, concerns itself with mere sequence, as if to suggest that one achievement grew from the other: both were grafted upon something deeper, the man himself. Arsenius added another interesting inversion. 'As far as you are able, strive to make your inner life a work in accord with God, and then you will overcome the passions that afflict us from without' (Arsenius, 9).[2] Clearly there were few set prejudices as to what constituted the inner and the outer dimensions of a monk's life. Rather, a complex interweaving of attitude and endeavour characterized the asceticism of the desert (John the Dwarf, 34).

We have stressed all along that developing spirituality prompted openness to communal patterns of life. The value attached to consultation, admiration, charity, caution, humility, active service, and concern, all made a gradual engagement with others the natural outcome of ascetic practice. The group of disciples remained socially most characteristic of the desert life. Simply to be close to a virtuous man was a key to spiritual growth, distracting you from a sterile estimation of yourself (Theodore of Pherme, 2; Joseph of Thebes, 1; Poemen, 65, 73). Large groups would travel about, conscious of their bonds and their separateness from others (Agathon, 11; Nisterus, 1; Poemen, 26). These were, in a sense, protomonasteries. They engaged in painful debate as to whether they should live more settled lives together (Agathon, 6; Arsenius, 21, 25). The division between group and outside world was jealously guarded. 'Tourists' were rejected, even with silence or insults, and as much for the instruction of disciples as for the humiliation of the visitor (Arsenius, 7, 8; Theophilus, 2; Moses, 8; Poemen, 3, 5; *HL* xvi. 3f). Yet this new society encouraged also tenderness and affection. Disciples cared for sick and

---

[1] A translation should run, 'If we do not do anything about [our thoughts] *bodily* [in other words, in practice] 'then they will "disappear", and we lose our chance to harness them.'

[2] Ward, omitting 'work', avoids the contrast required by the Greek.

aged fathers over many years, often until death (Ammoes, 3; John the Theban, 1; Nau, 151, 156). They teased them, and ordered them around (John the Dwarf, 10; Silvanus, 4). They could even protect them from the mistaken kindness of strangers (Macarius, 10). The beauty of such relationships shines clearly in an anecdote about John the Dwarf, faced with a remarkably persistent inquirer, an elderly and most absent-minded ascetic. He consulted John frequently; always, on returning to his own cell, forgot the father's words; and returned constantly for reminders, until even he became embarrassed by the endless questioning. 'Abba John said to him, "Go and light a lamp." He lit it. He said to him, "Bring some more lamps, and light them from the first." He did so. Then Abba John said to the old man, "Has that lamp suffered any loss from the fact that other lamps have been lit from it?" He said, "No." The old man continued, "So it is with John; even if the whole of Scetis came to see me, they would not separate me from the love of Christ. Consequently, whenever you want to, come to me without hesitation"' (John the Dwarf, 18; see Arsenius, 32).

When we turn from the *Sayings of the Fathers* to the *Lives* of Antony (*c.* 251–356) and Pachomius (*c.* 290–346), we discover a recognizably similar world, if with a greater degree of literary sophistication. Like other ascetics he admired, consulted and imitated, Antony stayed at first in the vicinity of villages, gaining something of a reputation among the rural population along the river (*Life*, 2f). Then he withdrew beyond the fertile districts to the top of the escarpment above the valley, shutting himself in a deserted fort (8f). Even here he was visited by would-be disciples and admirers; and when he emerged, after nearly twenty years, he found an audience ready to accept his guidance and instruction (13f). His opening address to his new followers stressed their need 'to encourage each other in the faith'. 'Bring to your father what you know and tell it, while I, being your senior, share with you my knowledge and my experience' (16). Later he decided, under pressure of attention and inquiry, to withdraw even further to much wilder country, though still watered. Yet he continued to visit ascetic communities closer to the river, and was host in his turn to many who called upon his help (48f, 54; see *HL* xxi. 8f).

So his departure from society was neither sudden nor dramatic; and he never lost touch with the task of encouraging and instructing others on the basis of his own 'experience and truth' (39). The same attitude enlivened exchanges between all desert masters and their pupils; and Antony's *Life* recounts a 'dictum' here, 'stories' there, of precisely the sort we find in the *Sayings* (7, 54, 65).

Where the *Life* differs markedly from other early texts is in its emphasis on demons. It may seem hard to take seriously the bizarre accounts that so richly inspired the imagination of Hieronymus Bosch and others; but they deserve attention still.

His first encounter appears to contradict a point that emerged from the *Sayings*. The devil 'raised up in his mind a great dust cloud of arguments, intending to make him abandon his set purpose'. Such access to the interior is alarming; but the sequel makes it clear how one was to rectify the situation. Antony 'filled his thoughts with Christ . . . and thus quenched the glowing coal of temptation'. The devil 'saw himself thrust out of his heart': from now on he was condemned to taunt Antony from well beyond the limits of his inner person. Antony for his part was 'all the more alert in spirit', and 'his mind was master of the situation' (5f, 9).

He corroborated the teaching in his later address to disciples. Their first temptations would take the form of 'evil thoughts'. Then, when the demons could not 'deceive the heart by manifestly unclean pleasure', they would 'devise apparitions in order to frighten it, transforming themselves and mimicking women, beasts, reptiles' (23). Antony recalled his own initial vulnerability. Demons could do little more than augment an existing frame of mind; and their defeat was assured if a man took care to adopt an inner posture at odds with their intent, 'rejoicing in the Lord, meditating on the good things to come and contemplating the things that are the Lord's' (42).

So it is not so much the imagery as the mechanics that we must attend to. The ascetic was bent upon reclaiming his conscious life from memories of error, weakness, and indulgence. This he did by fixing his attention on a range of concepts and of texts or dicta that could not but exclude those other 'thoughts'. In this way he built up a psychic wall against his past, both cultural and personal.

But once the arena of thought had been recaptured, temptation could still take the form of apparitions. What was their true status? Antony attached little importance to these visible signs of demonic frustration (13); but the description of visions raises interesting points. After his struggles in the deserted fort, 'he looked up and saw as it were the roof opening and a beam of light coming down to him'. The sequel reveals that this was not a fresh event, but a deeper insight into the experience just passed. 'Where were you? Why did you not appear at the beginning to stop my pains?' 'Antony, I was right here, but I wanted to see you in action' (10). Other visions demanded subsequent reflection to be given sense. One is scarcely cynical in suggesting that they must have been at best ambiguous. The full narrative is often completed by phrases such as, 'he was astonished', 'he remembered', 'his understanding opened up and he realized', 'the wonder of it all absorbed him' (65f). We are dealing with interpretation, rather than vision pure and simple; the images are not alternatives to reason, but describe a different level of understanding.

Antony supported this distinction in his advice on discernment. He was far more impressed by a monk's reaction than by the visual content of his experience. 'A vision of the holy ones . . . comes so quietly and gently that instantly joy and gladness and courage arise in the soul . . . and the thoughts of the soul remain untroubled and unruffled, so that in its own bright transparency it is able to behold those who appear . . . On the other hand the attack and appearance of the evil ones . . . at once begets terror in the soul, disturbance and confusion of thoughts' (35f).

'In its own bright transparency' offers the clue to Antony's thinking here. The powers of the soul were heightened rather than displaced. Man's own nature lay at the root of all religious experience and achievement. Joy, gladness, and courage were natural to a soul redeemed from fear and error (20). Here again, Antony taught on the basis of his own experience. After his long incarceration in the fort, onlookers were surprised at how normal he looked; but in this he only reflected an inner balance. 'The state of his soul was pure, for it was neither contracted by grief, nor dissipated by pleasure nor pervaded by jollity or dejection.' He was a man 'guided by reason and steadfast in that which accords with nature' (14; see 67, 93). That purity led to true insight. 'I feel confident', Antony said, 'that if the soul is pure through and through and is in its natural state, it becomes clear-sighted and sees more and farther than the demons' (34; see 59f). Such was Antony's specific contribution to the desert doctrine on the inner life; and it becomes clear to us only through his preoccupation with demons and visions.

There was a relation between restoration of this natural inner balance and the visible practices of the ascetic life. Inner achievements were themselves visible. 'It was not his stature or figure', Athanasius explained, 'that made him stand out from the rest, but his settled character and the purity of his soul. For his soul was unperturbed, and so his outward appearance was calm' (67). This harmony of attitude and manner, coupled with great openness of spirit, was Antony's greatest achievement, and sprang most from an unwillingness to recoil from the world. Far from brooding on his state of soul, he was immensely industrious. He worked to support himself, and to give to the poor (3). Even in his ultimate retreat he sought out fertile soil to grow his grain, and made baskets to exchange for food from visitors (50, 53). Practicality extended further. His reported dialogues with 'pagan philosophers' championed above all a 'faith through love that works for Christ' (80). He espoused a wisdom that would devote itself unhesitatingly to the person of Jesus, and not wait upon the pressure of a cautious logic (72f). Immediacy was the aim: in matters of wisdom and insight ('often you [the "philosophers"] cannot even express what we [the monks] perceive!'), but also in relations with others. Such was the generosity and courage behind his ability to meet people full face, with understanding, humour, and advice. He never found it hard to correlate his daily task with this inner availability. A man of perseverance, wedded to the notion that ascetics lived for one day at a time (7, 16, 19), he retained also, precisely through that severe regime, a deep sense of loyalty, the 'devotion to Christ' he had admired in his first exemplars, and recommended to others (4, 30). 'Antony gained renown not for his writings, nor for worldly wisdom, nor for any art, but solely for his service of God' (93).

Pachomius should not be divided from this world: he too was a desert father! Antony may appear more primitive, while Pachomius, pioneer of corporate asceticism on the grand scale, seems to have broken away from the eremitic tradition. In truth both men grew in the spiritual life in similar circumstances, and shared to the end to a surprising degree their conviction and practice. Immediately following his baptism, Pachomius pursued a life of perfection in a village community, perhaps for as much as three years (Bo 8f). For several more he lived virtually the life of a hermit (G^1 6f). He was joined for a while by his brother: not a wholly successful experiment (G^1 14). Then he began to encourage the adherence of other followers: local villagers at first, and later, in more formal terms, disciples from further afield (S^1, G^1 23). All this recalls much in Antony's early experience. Although Pachomius went on to espouse a formality that Antony had eschewed, the monasteries he founded at Tabennesi and elsewhere represented not a break with earlier ascetic traditions but cautious development on the basis of what had been at some stages quite a solitary experience.

What impelled the eventual divergence that led Pachomius to structure and rule, where Antony preferred withdrawal, albeit available to others? For both it remained a matter of service, Pachomius faithful to his first promise to God, 'I will serve your will all the days of my life and, loving all people, I will be their servant according to your command' (G^1 5). Everything followed from that. Most important, at the core of all his associations with other ascetics lay a solemn pledge, which stressed in one way or another the enduring theme of mutual support (G^1 12, 20, 23f, Bo 20). The chief purpose of community was this sharing of responsibility for material welfare and spiritual growth, which explains why Pachomius adopted above all the guise of a servant among his followers.

---

[1] Our chief source here are the *Rules*, in a later Latin translation by Jerome. 'Rules' is a misleading word, since they were divided into overlapping and even contradictory

But what made even the earliest Pachomian communities most strikingly different was the pattern of liturgy and manual work.[1] Both were communal. The chief liturgical celebration of the monastery, apart from the Eucharist, was the *synaxis*, which consisted of readings from Scripture, interspersed by periods of silent reflection and corporate recitation of the 'Our Father'. An evening session in smaller groups involved a greater degree of discussion. Work was conducted in teams, directed mainly at first towards agriculture. The third great communal act of each day, the meal, completed a regime marked most, therefore, to the external eye, by collaboration and intimacy.

So there was a clear context for whatever spirituality Pachomius might wish to encourage. The daily round of prayer, work, refreshment, and sleep enclosed, but nourished also, an inner life peculiar to each monk. Paramount among the safeguards and stimuli thus promoted was the virtue of obedience. The pathway to success was chosen for you, and shared with hundreds, even thousands of fellow ascetics. Deep theological conviction lay behind these controlling practicalities. As Jesus obeyed the Father, so the monk should obey Pachomius, through whom the Father spoke once more (G^1 69). 'Even if a commandment is about a very small matter it is important . . . If that commandment were not profitable for their souls we would not have given it' (G^1 89).

Profit for the soul was the primary consideration. We need to be reminded that such motives predated rules, which did no more than provide a secure framework within which the power of obedience might go to work. Its impact would have been predominantly personal and interior. This brings us close to the inner emphasis of other desert fathers. The aim of guidance and command was, for Pachomius, to induce in others 'a great awakening and a sudden change of heart' (G^1 42).

So within the order, the discipline, the sheer crowdedness of a Pachomian community, we have to discern the inner achievements aimed at, above all by Pachomius himself. Even the *Rules* reveal an inner dimension. He hoped that his monks would not be 'fuddled with passion of any kind, but maintain a balance in accord with the truth' (*Praecepta et Instituta*, preface). Steadiness is perhaps the best word, with a note of perseverance included. This Pachomius himself achieved. 'He had received from the Lord the gift of being always the same . . . and he kept his soul carefully schooled' (Dion., 37; see G^1 28, 51f; G^2 39; *Life of Antony*, 14). The immediate fruit of such balance was an inner freedom, the 'life of complete liberty' as Palladius called it (*HL* xxxii. 7), and a freedom enjoyed not least in the growing awareness of the presence of

---

sections, clearly built up over a half-century. The many obscurities are discussed in the literature.

God (Catechesis in Lefort, *Oeuvres*, p. 10; *Praecepta et Instituta*, preface; *Praecepta ac Leges*, 8).

If we go back to the roots of Pachomius' experience, we find that, as with so many of his contemporaries, it was the behaviour of demons that provoked his interest and insight. A process of self-examination led him to think of the seat of virtue as a series of inner chambers, to be methodically occupied and guarded against intruders. As with Antony, it was a question of repossessing one's property; and the best safeguard of occupancy was to have God as fellow tenant, 'the King of Kings . . . seated as upon a throne in his heart' (G^1 75). An anecdote reflects the process. A demon had appeared, claiming to be Christ. Pachomius reflected carefully. 'When the apparition is of spirits that are holy, the thoughts of the man who sees it vanish completely, and they consider nothing but the sanctity of the apparition. Now here I am, seeing this and conscious and reasoning. It is clear that he deceives me; he is not among the spirits that are holy' (G^1 87; see *Life of Antony*, 35f). This achievement of self-possession in the presence of God (which was how Pachomius viewed 'purity of heart') is summed up in a famous phrase from the Greek *Life*: 'and because of the purity of his heart he was, as it were, seeing the invisible God as in a mirror' (G^1 22). But there was always that characteristic realism and concern for others – modulated differently from Antony, yet closely associated with inner perception: 'what is greater than such a vision, to see the invisible God in a visible man, his temple?' (G^1 48).

By placing Antony and Pachomius against the background of the desert as a whole, we avoid a suggestion that biographies, rules, and monasteries monopolized the future of ascetic history. The spirituality shared by these two with so many other great ascetics of their century had an equally lasting impact: the survival, expansion, and popularity of the *Sayings of the Fathers* is testimony to that. Unless we retain the sense of wide variety, we are likely to overestimate how sudden and original was the work of Evagrius and Cassian. Without their genius for presenting a systematic account of the inner life, no institutions could have survived; but they owed at the same time an enormous amount to the great 'abbots' of Egypt.

I wrote this chapter while holding a Fellowship at Dumbarton Oaks, and am most grateful for the facilities and stimulation thus provided. I would like to thank in particular Marie Taylor Davis and Brian Daley for their criticism and encouragement.

III

THE LATIN FATHERS

1 Ambrose

EDWARD YARNOLD

Dudden, F. Homes, *The Life and Times of St Ambrose*. 2 vols. Oxford, Clarendon, 1935.

Malden, R. H., 'St Ambrose as an Interpreter of Holy Scripture', in *JTS* 16 (1915), pp. 509–22.

Paredi, A., (ET) *Saint Ambrose, his Life and Times*. University of Notre Dame Press, 1964.

Roberti, M. Mirabella, 'Contributi della ricerca archeologica all'architettura ambrosiana milanese', in *Ambrosius Episcopus*, ed. G. Lazzati (Milan, 1976), pp. 335–62.

Ambrose, after a training in rhetoric and law, became governor of the Roman province of Aemilia-Liguria, with his residence in Milan. Though not yet baptized, he was elected Bishop of that city in *c*. 374. He learnt his theology largely from the writings of the Greek Fathers and the Neoplatonists, and helped to popularize their ideas in the West. He was fearless in standing up for Christian morality and the rights of the Church against the imperial family, refusing communion to the Emperor Theodosius until the latter had done penance for ordering a massacre in Thessalonica. His influence on the development of Christian thought was great, not least through his part in the conversion of St Augustine, whom he baptized in 387. He died ten years later.

Probably his greatest contribution to the development of spirituality lay in his writings on virginity. His first and fullest writing on the subject was his *De Virginibus*, which he addressed in 377 to his sister, who had taken the virgin's veil while continuing according to local custom to live at home. Though never married himself, he taught that marriage was in itself holy; nevertheless he attributed Jesus' virginal birth to the need to avoid the impurities (*vitia*) of conception (*Apologia Prophetae David*, I.ii.56; *De Paenitentia*, I.iii.13). Virginity was a higher good than marriage (*De Virginibus*, i.24). Virgins live like angels on earth (*Exhortatio Virginitatis*, 19). Christ is both the spouse and the model of virgins (*De Virginibus*, i.22, 36, 37).

The Blessed Virgin Mary was another model for virgins. Ambrose helped to develop the Church's theological understanding of her. She was a virgin 'not only in body but also in mind' (*De Virginibus*, ii.7). She is thus the model of the Church, which is itself a virgin (*Expositio Ev. Luc.* ii.7; *De Virginibus*, i.12).

Ambrose also laid down guidelines for other orders in the Church – widows (*De Viduis*), and clergy (*De Officiis*, modelled on Cicero's work of the same title) – and for Christian practices like fasting (*De Helia et Ieiunio*).

He was a man of keen sensibility: there is a marked sensuous imagery in his writing, for example in his use of the Song of Songs. He constantly bases his teaching on Scripture, which he interprets in the moral and mystical senses as well as the literal (cf. *Explan. Psalm.*, 36.1–2; *PL* 14.965–7). Ambrose's allegorical exegesis is apparent in the following prose poem which occurs in a commentary on Ps 22.5 (Vulgate): 'Your cup that inebriates, how splendid it is!':

> Drink Christ, for his is the vine. Drink Christ, for he is the rock from which water gushed. Drink Christ, for he is the fountain of life. Drink Christ, for he is the river whose current brings joy to the city of God. Drink Christ, for he is peace. Drink Christ, for streams of living water flow from his body. Drink Christ, and drink the blood by which you were redeemed. Drink Christ and drink his words (*Explan. Psalm.*, 1.33; *PL* 14.940).

It was perhaps from Cyril of Jerusalem that Ambrose discovered how to exploit the communicative power of the liturgy. His baptismal homilies, the *De Sacramentis* (and the treatise *De Mysteriis* based on them) show how he endeavoured to make baptism a deeply-felt experience of illumination and conversion. Himself a writer of tautly and vividly-worded hymns, he made innovations in the liturgical use of psalms. He is sometimes credited with the authorship of the *Exultet*, the hymn in honour of the paschal candle. He also inaugurated a programme of church-building in Milan, perhaps being the first to construct octagonal baptisteries and cruciform churches. Poems expressing the symbolic meaning of both architectural forms are attributed to him. He promoted the cult of martyrs, such as Saint Gervase and Saint Protase, and enjoyed remarkable success in finding their relics.

2 Jerome

EDWARD YARNOLD

St Jerome, *Letters*. ACW 33 etc., 1963 etc.

St Jerome, *Letters, Lives, Adversus Jovinianum*, etc. Nicene and Post-Nicene Fathers 6. Oxford, James Parker; New York, Christian Literature Co., 1893; repr. Grand Rapids, Eerdmans, 1979.

Burke, E. P., 'St Jerome as a Spiritual Director', in F. X. Murphy, ed., *A Monument to St Jerome* (New York, Sheed & Ward, 1952), pp. 143–69.

Kelly, J. N. D., *Jerome: his Life, Writings and Controversies*. London, Duckworth; New York, Harper & Row, 1975.

Rousseau, P., *Ascetics, Authority and the Church in the Age of Jerome and Cassian*. OUP, 1978.

Jerome was born in the 340s at Stridon on the border of Dalmatia. After studies in Rome, he embarked on a series of experiments in monasticism, trying successively life in an ascetic community of friends at Aquileia, in the Syrian desert as a hermit, and in a monastic community of his own founding at Bethlehem. He was the patron of various communities of high-born Roman ladies in Rome and Palestine, following the example of his friend, and later opponent, Rufinus.

He was influential in familiarizing the Western Church with the ascetic ideals and practices of the East. His *Letters* and three *Lives* of Saints have been described as 'the most significant corpus of ascetic literature in the West' of his time (Rousseau, *Ascetics*, p. 99). The letters reveal him as a sensitive spiritual director, and contain interesting ideas about the education of young Christians. Several of his writings express his understanding of the superiority of the celibate to the married life, especially his treatise *Adversus Jovinianum* and his *Letter* 22. Unfortunately even his ascetic works, as well as his polemical writings, contain much which is of an aggressive and satirical temper. He died in Palestine in 419 or 420.

It has been observed that, though Jerome wrote much on asceticism, he had little to say about contemplation. Nevertheless he saw that the study of the Bible played a vital role in the ascetic life: 'to be ignorant of Scripture is to be ignorant of Christ' (*Commentary on Isaiah*, prol. 1; *PL* 24. 17). His translation of the Bible into Latin from the Hebrew and Greek, undertaken at the request of Pope Damasus (d. 384), provided the West with its standard scriptural text until the Reformation, and beyond. The 'Clementine' edition of 1592 provided the official edition ordered by the Council of Trent. J. Wordsworth and H. J. White published a monumental critical edition between 1889 and 1954. In his many commentaries on the books of the Bible Jerome explored the spiritual as well as the literal sense of the text (see p. 119).

3 Augustine

ANDREW LOUTH

Abbreviations of Augustine's works cited

P = *Enarrationes in Psalmos*; C = *Confessions*; S = *Soliloquies*; M = *De Magistro*; AdS = *Ad Simplicianum*; Q = *De Quantitate Animae*; L = *De Libero Arbitrio*; DC = *De Doctrina Christiana*; EpJ = *Homilies on 1 John*; Serm. = Sermon; CG = *De Correptione et Gratia*; T = *De Trinitate*; Ep = *Epistle*; CD = *De Civitate Dei*.

Texts and Translations

LCC, vols. vi–viii.

C and CD in the Loeb Classical Library.

ET of C by F. J. Sheed. London, Sheed & Ward, 1934; New York, Sheed & Ward, 1942, often reprinted.

An Augustinian Synthesis, ed. E. Przywara. London and New York, Sheed & Ward, 1936, often reprinted.

Augustine of Hippo, *Selected Writings*, tr. Mary T. Clark. CWS 1985 (contains: parts of C, P, EpJ, T, CD, and other writings).

Studies

Brown, P., *Augustine of Hippo*. London, Faber, 1967; Berkeley, University of California Press, 1969.

Burnaby, J., *Amor Dei*. London, Hodder & Stoughton, 1938, 1947, 1960.

Butler, E. C., *Western Mysticism*. London, Constable, 2nd edn 1927; 3rd edn 1967; New York, Barnes & Noble, 1968.

Holte, R., *Béatitude et sagesse*. Paris, 1962.

Ladner, G. B., *The Idea of Reform*. Cambridge, Mass., Harvard University Press, 1959.

O'Donovan, O., *The Problem of Self-Love in St Augustine*. New Haven and London, Yale University Press, 1981.

Przywara, E., *Augustinisch*. Einsiedeln 1970 (discusses Augustine's influence).

teSelle, E., *Augustine, the Theologian*. London, Burns & Oates; New York, Herder & Herder, 1970.

Very full bibliography in C. Andresen, *Bibliographia Augustiniana* (Darmstadt 1962); see also Altaner.

We probably know more about Saint Augustine than anyone else in late antiquity: his *Confessions* give us a detailed account of his youth and early manhood, and tell us much of his thoughts and feelings; his letters and sermons are revealing of the man, and indeed there is little in what Augustine has left to us that does not reveal, beyond his teaching and ideas, the man himself. Even the *Soliloquies*, clearly intended as an academic exercise and not any kind of confession at all, give us, at one point, a glimpse of his still new struggle to live a life of chastity, and thus were not unjustly published in French in a series called *Ecrits intimes*. But this Augustine, who has revealed so much of himself, was one whose deepest conviction regarding man was that 'the human heart is an abyss' (P XLI.13), that 'man is a vast deep . . . the hairs on his head are easier by far to number than are his feelings, and the movements of his heart' (C IV.xiv.22). Man is unknown to himself, and still more unknown to anyone else: 'in the sojourning of this carnal life each one carries his own heart, and every heart is closed to every other heart' (P LV.9).

Nevertheless the facts of his life are these: Augustine was born at Thagaste in North Africa of a pagan father and a Christian mother, Monica, and received a Christian education. He then went to Carthage where he studied rhetoric. There he abandoned Christianity, probably repelled by the Christians' 'superstitious' demand for faith, and after reading Cicero's *Hortensius*, which inspired in him a lasting passion for philosophy, he joined the Manichees, attracted to them because they dispensed with faith and claimed to settle everything on the basis of reason. While he was in Carthage he took a mistress to whom he remained faithful for fifteen years and by whom he had a son, Adeodatus. In 383 he left Carthage for Rome, and about the same time became disillusioned with Manicheism. Very soon he went to Milan as professor of rhetoric where he fell under the spell of the bishop, St Ambrose. His reading of the Neoplatonists finally freed him from the spell of Manicheism and in 386 he was converted to Christianity, at the same time embracing a life of continence. After some months spent in seclusion at Cassiciacum with his mother and some friends, Augustine was baptized on Easter Eve, 387. In 388 he returned to Africa and again with some friends lived a kind of monastic life at Thagaste. While visiting the town of Hippo Regius in 391 he was seized by the people and ordained priest by Valerius, the aged bishop. In 395 he was consecrated bishop to succeed Valerius, which he did a year later on Valerius' death. The rest of his life was spent in Hippo, involved in the ecclesiastical affairs of North Africa and the Empire. Two issues especially beset him: from the beginning, Donatism, the schismatic church in North Africa which claimed that it was the true successor of the Church of St Cyprian, and that the Catholic Church had fatally compromised itself in the final great persecution under Diocletian

(303–12); and in the last twenty years of his life, the heresy of Pelagianism, which in Augustine's eyes and those of the Catholic Church preached a defective doctrine of grace. Augustine died on 28th August, 430, as the Vandals were besieging the city of Hippo.

A major influence on Augustine's understanding of Christianity and of the spiritual life was Neoplatonism (see pp. 97–9), though much of its influence came to him through Christian channels such as Ambrose and Marius Victorinus, an African rhetor who was converted to Christianity in Rome in the middle of the fourth century, as well as directly from Plotinus (in Latin translation, perhaps by Victorinus) and his biographer, Porphyry. The precise nature of this influence cannot be discussed here, but it can be safely said that what Augustine found in Neoplatonism was on the one hand a doctrine of the soul and of the way in which through purification and contemplation it can rise to God, and on the other (for this was characteristic of later Neoplatonism, if not of Plotinus) a sense of man's frailty and his need for some kind of assistance in his search for God. In other words, Neoplatonism freed Augustine from the spell of Manicheism by undermining both its doctrine of the materiality of the soul, and its rejection of authority and professed reliance on reason alone. Throughout Augustine's writings we find the path of the soul's ascent to God mapped out in Neoplatonic terms: it is a movement of withdrawal from the world and into oneself, a movement that involves purification and the acquiring of the virtues, leading to contemplation of God. In two early writings, *De Quantitate Animae* and *De Vera Religione*, he gives accounts of the soul's ascent through seven stages: the first account corresponds to the 'acts' or functions of the soul, from giving life to the body at the lower end to its highest function 'in the very vision and contemplation of truth', of which state 'great and peerless souls' – among whom is probably to be included Plotinus – have told us; the second is more an account of the soul's spiritual progress, first 'being taught by the rich stores of history which nourish by examples' (contained in the Scriptures), then turning from human affairs and attaining tranquillity, and beyond that reaching 'eternal rest and perpetual beatitude'. But very soon this Neoplatonic pattern yields rather surprising conclusions: in the *Confessions*, written only a little later, the accounts of Plotinian ecstasy (in VII.xvii.23, IX.x.23–5 [the vision at Ostia with his mother, Monica], X.xl.65) are less accounts of attainment, for they are shot through with the sense that what is revealed is beyond our grasp and Augustine is left with a consciousness of his own frailty: 'by weight of my imperfections I fall back again, and I am swallowed up by things customary: I am bound, and I weep bitterly, but I am bitterly bound' (C X.xl.65).

For Plotinus the soul's ascent to God was the 'flight of the alone to the

Alone', but for Augustine there is always the conviction that it is with others, in some kind of *societas*, that we are to seek God. His vision at Ostia grew out of a conversation with his mother, and throughout his life – at Cassiciacum, Thagaste and Hippo – he pursued his Christian life in a community. But there is an ambivalence here in Augustine which comes out clearly in a passage in the *Soliloquies*: 'But why, I ask, do you wish your friends to live and to live with you? That with one mind we may together seek knowledge of our souls and God. For in this way, if one makes a discovery he can without trouble bring the others to see it' (S I.xii.20). But reason goes on to ask, 'But if their presence hinders you from inquiry, will you not wish and strive if their attitude cannot be changed, not to have them with you?' To which Augustine replies, 'I confess that is so.' Augustine is convinced of the need for companionship, but his sense of the way in which 'every heart is closed to every other heart' makes it difficult for him to see how such companionship can yield anything in this life. We are all shut off from one another and communicate in an uncertain way by language and gesture: at the end of *De Magistro* Adeodatus sums up what he has learnt by saying, 'words do no more than prompt people to learn, and what appears to be the thought of the speaker expressing himself, really amounts to extremely little' (M XIV.46).

Both these characteristics of Augustinian spirituality – its use of the Neoplatonic doctrine of the soul's ascent, and the ambivalent attitude to companionship – lead us back to Augustine's conviction that our life here below is marked by darkness, a darkness that separates one person from another, a darkness that weighs people down and makes it impossible for them to ascend to God. It is a darkness that penetrates people's very being and hides them from themselves. In the *Confessions* Augustine explores with great sensitivity his conviction that man is unknown to himself, that, when he enters into himself, he enters 'a limitless forest full of unexpected dangers' (C X.xxxv.56), that he cannot be sure who he is or of what he is capable. Augustine speaks of a 'lamentable darkness' within himself 'of which the possibilities in me are hidden from myself' (C X.xxxii.48), and in moral struggle finds himself exclaiming 'which side will win I do not know . . . I just do not know' (C X.xxviii.39). It is this sense of darkness that lies behind Augustine's conviction of the necessity of grace, in opposition to the Pelagians. It was a Pelagian taunt that Augustine was still partly Manichee in his denial of human freedom, and we must pause and ask what truth there is in this accusation which has been repeated by many since. Manicheism was a form of Gnosticism (see pp. 93–4), believing that there are two ultimate principles of good and evil, of light and darkness, and that in the world there is eternal conflict between these two principles. Matter is evil, and in human beings there are trapped sparks of light which it is the purpose of religion to release. What Augustine says attracted him to Manicheism was its claim to provide an explanation based on reason, without any appeal to faith; but he must also have been concerned about the problems the Manichees were seeking to solve, especially the problem of evil. It is probably true to say then that a profound sense of the tragic dimension of evil attracted Augustine to Manicheism, and that this sense remained with him all his life: but that is not to say that he remained a Manichee in any sense.

It is this sense of darkness rendering humanity helpless that marks Augustine off from Greek spirituality – or from most Greek spirituality, as there are striking parallels here with the Messalianism of the Macarian Homilies (see pp. 160, 173). For the Macarian Homilies have a profound sense of the difficulty of self-knowledge, of the darkness that has descended on humanity as a result of the fall. We read there that

> when man transgressed the commandment and was exiled from Paradise, he was bound down in two ways and with two different chains. One was in this life . . . but besides that, in the hidden region, the soul was hedged and hemmed in and walled round, and bound with chains of darkness by the spirits of wickedness (XXI.2).

We might compare this with Augustine when he says,

> The enemy held my will; and of it he made a chain and bound me. Because my will was perverse it changed to lust, and lust yielded to become habit, and habit not resisted became necessity. They were like links hanging one on another – which is why I have called it a chain – and their hard bondage held me bound hand and foot (C VIII.v.10).

But on the whole Greek spirituality makes a more positive use of the Platonic and Neoplatonic understanding of the soul. The tripartite analysis of the soul – into the desiring, passionate and rational parts – becomes a diagnostic device helping one to understand the vices and so overcome them. That done, one attains *apatheia*, which corresponds closely to the tranquillity Augustine in his early writings saw as a state that opened out on to contemplation. This tripartite analysis of the soul, used to diagnose the soul's sickness, is found in Augustine too. In *De Moribus Ecclesiae* Augustine analyses the vices into carnal desire, pride (meaning here not the spiritual sin, but delight in the pomp and vainglory of the world), and curiosity, and cites 1 John 2.16 ('the lust of the flesh, the lust of the eyes, and the pride of life'), altering the order to bring it into line with the Platonic tripartition of the soul. The use of this verse as a guide to self-analysis remains with Augustine, but as early as *Confessions* X the biblical order has asserted itself, the Platonic tripartition is lost from view, and

Augustine is examining, without sparing himself, how far he is from the continence by which 'we are collected and bound up into unity within ourselves', the indispensable condition of being able to apprehend God. It is an analysis that spells out in detail how deeply Augustine is in need of grace, of the Mediator, and how impossible it would be for any ascetic discipline to bring him to a fit state to behold God.

It is this sense of darkness, this sense of human frailty, that forced Augustine to see the need for faith, which had kept him from Christianity. In the early dialogues we see this in his understanding of the relationship between authority and reason (*auctoritas, ratio*). To begin with, authority is seen as no more than a short cut: authority shows us what reason will later discover for itself. So he says, 'It is one thing to believe on authority, another to have reason to back you. Reliance on authority offers you an excellent short cut and eliminates toil' (Q VII.12). But there is a suggestion of a more abiding authority when Augustine says at the end of *De Magistro* that 'he alone teaches who when he spoke externally reminded us that he dwells within us' (M XIV.46), and this notion that with Christ, because he dwells in us and knows the secrets of our hearts, we have one who is not limited by the chancy nature of human communication, provides the key both to the place the incarnation occupies within Augustine's understanding, and to the place of the Scriptures in the Christian life. In the *Soliloquies* Augustine still spoke of 'yonder light, which does not deign to manifest itself to men shut up in a cave unless they can escape, leaving sensible things broken and dissolved' (S I.xiv.24); by the time of *De Libero Arbitrio* he will say that 'the Food of the rational creature became visible, not by changing his own nature but by adapting it to ours, in order that he might recall those who follow visible things to embrace the invisible', and speak of the soul 'which in its inward pride had forsaken him . . . imitating his visible humility' (L III.x.30). The humility of the incarnate Word shows us our way back to God: the way of humility. And the willingness to learn from the Scriptures, to submit ourselves to their authority, comes through humility. This process of learning *within* faith, coming to hold by reason what has already been professed by faith – the Augustinian *fides quaerens intellectum* (to use the phrase familiar from St Anselm) – from being a weapon against the Manichees, becomes a summary statement both of the soul's journey to God, and of the programme of Christian theology. As Henri de Lubac has remarked (in his important *Exégèse médiévale* 1/2, 533–5) the movement from *fides* to *intelligentia* characterizes most aptly the process of interpreting the Scriptures, and the plenitude and end 'of all the sacred Scriptures is the love of a Being which is to be enjoyed and of a being that can share that enjoyment with us' (DC I.xxxv.39). The twofold commandment to love God and our neighbour is the heart of what we are to learn from the Scriptures, and this emphasis on the centrality of the twofold commandment of love is both characteristic of Augustine and probably original to him (see O'Donovan, p. 4). Love then characterizes our duty, but it has another significance for Augustine: when we love we look beyond this changing world to the unchanging God, and we see men and women as essentially created in his image. In drawing our attention beyond this world, love makes us dissatisfied with this world: as early as the *Soliloquies* Augustine sees the importance of love as preventing us from being 'content with the world's darkness which through habit has become pleasant' (S I.vi.12). As he says later, 'The whole life of the good Christian is a holy longing' (EpJ IV.6).

This sense of darkness was an abiding conviction of Augustine's, but a critical realization of its seriousness came to Augustine in 396, when he wrote to Simplicianus, who succeeded Ambrose as bishop of Milan, in reply to some questions about the interpretation of some passages in St Paul's epistles. There he speaks of all humanity as a mass of sin, *massa peccati*, 'since, as the apostle says, "In Adam all die", and to Adam the entire human race traces the origin of its sin against God' (AdS II.16), and goes on to speak of God's electing some from this *massa peccati* for salvation, and not electing others. This sense of people finding their only natural solidarity in the *massa peccati*, so that redemption is purely a matter of God's initiative, of God's grace, is something that remains with Augustine and was indeed deepened in the course of the Pelagian controversy. He probably owes it to Tyconius, the greatest of the Donatist theologians, and also betrays the influence here of the Roman presbyter, known since the time of Erasmus as Ambrosiaster. It leads Augustine to an ever deeper sense of human dependence on God, a sense that in the darkness of this life one must live a life of faith and prayer, of continence which does not 'trust in the felicity of the world', and endurance which does not 'give way under the misfortunes of this world' (Serm. XXXVIII.i.1). In his late anti-Pelagian treatises Augustine stresses again and again how prayer, which is the heart of the Christian life, points to the Christian's dependence on the grace of God, a grace one cannot earn but can only beg. This was indeed the original meaning of the tag, *lex orandi lex credendi* (see DS 246). And it is a *blind* dependence: in the night of this life, it is not known who is elect and who is not, all are to be loved. It is not possible, as the Donatists thought, to have a church of the holy: the Church is a *corpus permixtum*. For this life there is a 'short and simple precept': 'Love and do what you will . . . Let love's root be within you, and from that root nothing but good can spring' (EpJ VII.8). On the basis of such a rule Augustine justified 'harsh and savage actions . . . performed for our discipline at the dictate of charity': actions which included the persecution of the Donatists. But the heart of the attitude he inculcates here is rather that we should act in love, and leave the fruit of such action to God, for it is only God who sees the human heart. So of St Paul's preaching Augustine says, 'But he knew that all these things which he was doing in the way of planting and watering openly were of no avail unless he who gives the increase in secret should give heed to his prayer on their behalf' (CG II.3). If in his anti-Pelagian polemic there often seems to be a crude recourse to authority in his appeal to the Pauline text, 'O the depth of the riches both of the wisdom and knowledge of God! How unsearchable are his judgements, and his ways past finding out!' (Rom. 9.33), to get him out of the moral difficulties his doctrine of predestination seems to land him in, the attitude behind it – of wonder and humility before the mystery of God – is at the heart of Augustinian spirituality:

> There is no sea so deep as these thoughts of God, who makes the wicked to flourish and the good to be afflicted – nothing so profound, nothing so deep; and in that deep, in that profundity, every unbelieving soul is wrecked. Dost thou wish to cross this deep? Move not away from the wood of Christ's cross. Thou shalt not sink; hold thyself fast to Christ (P XCI.8).

All this is summed up in his mysticism of the trinitarian soul's search for the trinitarian God, which was to be immensely influential in the West. It finds its fullest expression in the second half of that great work of his maturity, *De Trinitate*. The first half of *De Trinitate* is an exposition of the doctrine of the Trinity based on Scripture and tradition: it is a statement of faith, *fides*, a setting out of the deliverances of *auctoritas*. The second part is an attempt at understanding, an exercise in *fides quaerens intellectum*, meaning by that not simply an effort of elucidation, but primarily an attempt to see how the soul can come to contemplate God the Trinity, and in that way understand: not so much by knowing more and more about the Trinity, as knowing the triune God face to face. The key to his understanding of the soul's ascent to God lies in the doctrine, revealed in Scripture, that the soul is created in the image and likeness of God. But in his understanding of this Augustine marks a break with earlier tradition. In the theology of the Greek Fathers – and indeed in Ambrose and the early Augustine – it is the Word who is the image of God; human beings are created after the pattern of the Word, they are a derived image, created in accordance with the image of God. But Augustine rejects such an understanding of the image of God as subordinationist: the Son is God, not the image of God. The image of God must then be something other than God, and is indeed the highest spiritual substance which is constituted by the angels and by human souls. Such an image is a direct image of the trinitarian God, and must therefore itself be trinitarian. As an image it is related to its archetype, God, by being derived directly from him (by creation) and by seeking its fulfilment in him through a longing to return to contemplation of him (in this Augustine is drawing heavily on Plotinus' understanding of what an image is). The soul's 'restlessness till it rests in' God is part of what is meant by its being an image of God.

The soul's quest for God in *De Trinitate* begins in earnest in book VIII, and falls into two parts. In the first part (VIII–X) Augustine seeks to discover the true nature of a human being, and does this by using the doctrine of the Trinity already developed in books I–VII as a guide. If human nature is an image of the trinitarian God, then that image will be found in that part of it (and that part will be the true nature) in which there can be discerned a trinity reflecting the trinitarian nature of God. Since human nature as an image comes into play most clearly when humanity seeks to return to God, Augustine begins by looking at the human longing for truth, that truth which is God, for God is the light in which we know everything else (a conviction of Augustine's often referred to as his doctrine of illumination). He first develops a triad of the lover, the object of his love, and the love itself: but it is a triad, not a trinity, for there is no unity between the lover and his beloved. In book IX he seeks to discern a trinity in the mind's love of itself, and a trinity emerges when he draws on the mutual involvement of love and knowledge (for we cannot love what we do not know, nor properly know what we do not love) – the trinity of the mind, its self-knowledge and its self-love (*mens, notitia, amor*). Augustine shows that there is a real three-in-oneness here, a real image of the Trinity:

> and in these three, when the mind knows itself and loves itself, there remains a trinity, mind, love and knowledge; and it is confused by no mingling; although each is singly in itself, and all are wholly in one another, whether one in both or both in one, and so all in all (T IX.v.8).

The mind, self-knowledge and self-love: but self-knowledge, as no one knew better than Augustine, is hard to come by – how useful then is such a trinity? Augustine seems to have in mind here two errors: that of the Manichees, who thought the soul material, and that of the Neoplatonists who thought the soul divine. For both of them the trinity of mind, self-knowledge and self-love is an *unequal* trinity, a heretical trinity: only when a human being sees itself to be a created spiritual being does an orthodox, co-equal trinity emerge. And it is this that Augustine seeks to achieve, at a formal level, in book X of *De Trinitate*. Right from the beginning, in his first Christian work, *Contra Academicos*, Augustine had appealed to the mind's certainty of its existence, and life, and intellectual activity: even if one doubts, one is certain that one remembers, understands, wills and thinks (see T X.x.14). And it is among these indubitable intellectual activities that Augustine seeks his final trinity of memory, understanding and will (or love). Here he finds a triad of mutually co-inhering intellectual functions, which 'three constitute one thing, one life, one mind, one essence' (T X.xi.18). This is the trinity in which is revealed that a human being is the image of God, and it is this image that finds its fulfilment in the contemplation of God.

Books XI–XIV explore how this trinitarian image is to be restored to its archetype, the triune God. The method is familiar: it is the method of withdrawal and introversion. In book XI Augustine seeks to show what is involved in the soul's realizing its state as a purely spiritual trinity, by tracing a movement from an external trinity, involved in one's perception of the external world, inwards by progressive detachment from the external world. But this is less easy than it might seem: the mind can drain knowledge of the external world of its reality, but not so easily grasp invisible reality. In book XII Augustine introduces a distinction between knowledge and wisdom, *scientia* and *sapientia*: *scientia* is concerned with the world we perceive through the senses, *sapientia* with contemplation of eternal reality. What is needed then is that the soul relinquish *scientia* and embrace *sapientia*, but Augustine goes on to show that as a result of the fall humanity cannot, by its own powers, move the centre of its concern from the temporal to the eternal, from *scientia* to *sapientia*: humanity is too ensnared in its private and selfish enjoyment of the physical world to accomplish that. So in book XIII we come to consider faith, and the trinity discerned in the exercise of faith, the trinity of recalling, beholding and delighting in (*retentio, contemplatio, dilectio*): faith in the Son of God, who makes himself available to *scientia* in the incarnation, while remaining in himself the eternal object of *sapientia*.

> Our *scientia* is Christ, our *sapientia* is the same Christ. He introduces among us faith concerning temporal things, he shows truth concerning eternal things. Through him we rise to him, we pass through *scientia* to *sapientia*: we do not however move away from the one and the same Christ, 'in whom are hid all the treasures of wisdom and knowledge' (Col. 2.3) (T XIII.xix.24).

It is by humbly following Christ, the incarnate Word, that we come to contemplate eternal reality, not by ascetic exercises intended to withdraw us from temporal things and fit us for eternal things. It is not our own efforts at detachment, but our response to One who has come among us and loved us, that will draw us away from ourselves and centre our lives on God. Grace is for Augustine an attractive power which draws us to

God by implanting in us a 'delight in righteousness'. The Father draws us to himself by a kind of 'violence done to the heart', not however 'a rough or painful violence . . . It is sweet, its very sweetness draws' (Serm. 131.2).

In book XIV Augustine considers what is involved in the perfection of the image of God in humanity when through exercise of the trinity of faith the mind is purified and comes to contemplate God the Trinity. The image of God in the soul is memory, understanding and love, which is manifested (and can never be ultimately lost) when the mind remembers itself, loves itself and knows itself, but which is truly the image because it is the capacity the soul has to remember, know and love God – and it is in such cleaving to God that the image is perfected:

> When its cleaving to him has become absolute, it will be one spirit with him . . . The mind will be raised to the participation of his being, truth and bliss, though nothing thereby be added to the being, truth and bliss which is its own. In that being, joined to it in perfect happiness, it will live a changeless life and enjoy the changeless vision of all that it will behold (T XIV.xiv.20).

What is happening here is less the soul's ascent to God than the soul's submitting to be refashioned by God: 'the beginning of the image's re-forming must come from him who first formed it. The self which it was able to deform, it cannot of itself reform' (T XIV.xvi.22). It is a process which begins in the moment of baptism, and is perfected in a long gradual process of penitence and endurance: 'the cure's beginning is to remove the cause of the sickness: and that is done through the forgiveness of sins. Its furtherance is the healing of the sickness itself, which takes effect by gradual progress in the renewal of the image' (T XIV.xvii.23). The soul's return to God is the perfecting within it of the image of God in which it was created. It is a movement away from the 'land of unlikeness' (C VII.x.16) in which it finds itself as a result of the fall. But Augustine emphasizes in the last book (XV) of *De Trinitate* that the likeness to God we have discovered in humanity is no equality: it is a likeness between two utterly different beings, God and the creature, and so he says, fore-shadowing the language of the fourth Lateran Council (DS 806), that we must 'rather discern in its measure of likeness a greater unlikeness too' (T XV.xx.39). It is still a mysticism of the night, as Przywara has put it.

And yet if we look beyond this life to the day that will dawn in the Kingdom of heaven, we see that this night is at its deepest a night of the excess of light. There the walls that isolate people from one another will be pierced by the manifest glory of the Lord. In a letter to a young widow, consoling her in her loss, Augustine says:

> Even though your husband was well known to you, he was still better known

to himself, and that because, though you saw his bodily face . . . true knowledge of ourselves is inward, where no one knows what is of man save the spirit of man who is in him: but when the Lord comes, and illumines the hidden places of shadows and manifests the thoughts of the heart, then nothing of our neighbour will be hidden from us, nor will anything that is open to him be kept hidden from strangers, where there will be no strangers (Ep 92.2).

God will be apparent to us, and apparent in all: 'God will be so known by us and so present to our eyes that by means of the spirit he will be seen by each of us in each of us, seen by each in his neighbour and by each in himself' (CD XXII.29). There the true *vita socialis sanctorum* will become a reality; there the *sancta societas*, which Augustine prescribes in his monastic rule, and in which he hoped the *civitas Dei* would be manifest, will be realized. For Augustine the beatific vision is the consummation of the communion of saints in the city of God, where 'we shall rest and we shall see, we shall see and we shall love, we shall love and we shall praise. Behold what shall be in the end without end. For what else is our end except to reach the kingdom which has no end?' (CD XXII.30).

4 John Cassian

OWEN CHADWICK

Texts

Ed. M. Petschenig, CSEL 13 and 17.

Studies

Chadwick, O., *John Cassian*. London and New York, CUP, 1950; 2nd edn, 1968.
Rousseau, P., *Ascetics, Authority and the Church.*

John Cassian (*c.* 360–*c.* 432), probably from the Dobrudja, joined a monastery by the Church of the Nativity at Bethlehem. With his friend Germanus he got leave to visit the hermits and saints of Egypt. There he learnt much of spirituality from Evagrius of Pontus (see pp. 169–73). In 399 he left Egypt in the Origenist controversy, was ordained deacon at Constantinople by St John Chrysostom, and made treasurer at the cathedral. After Chrysostom's fall he carried official letters to Pope Innocent I. Perhaps driven again by the sack of Rome in 410, he settled in Marseilles and founded a monastery (St Victor) and a nunnery. In Southern Gaul he wrote books to explain the monastic ideal to the Gauls and so became a fundamental source for our knowledge of Egyptian spirituality.

The works were: (1) Three books on monks' dress and psalmody; (2) a book on the rules appropriate to a monastery; (3) eight books on the eight principal faults. Those twelve books were finally put together as *De Institutis coenobiorum et de octo principalium vitiorum remediis*. (4) Three books of *Conferences*, totalling in all twenty-four *Collationes*, in the form of reports of the addresses given in Egypt to him and Germanus by Egyptian hermits or coenobites. These *Conferences*, especially the first two parts (I–XVII), contain the essence of his spiritual teaching. The work makes as a whole the greatest corpus of teaching on spirituality to come out of the age of the Fathers.

The hermit's life is the highest life because the solitary is capable of continuous prayer. But one may not become a hermit unless one has served for years in a community and so learnt charity, obedience, tranquillity of mind and self-discipline. And the life of prayer is possible, in high measure even, for the soul in a community. For the analysis of the life of progress in virtue, and the life of contemplative prayer, Cassian possessed a very penetrating and rare ability for psychological analysis, especially of the nature and force of temptation; and with this he combined a profound knowledge of the Bible, derived from the sense of Egyptian monks that the scriptural texts, rightly prayed over, make up all that the experienced soul needs – not the inexperienced, for he will also need the guidance, in his understanding both of Scripture and of his own moral predicament, of some wise elder.

The junior must confess all his thoughts to his senior. Outside the penitential system of the Church, without priest and without absolution, the monks developed a system of confession and direction. It is easy but erroneous to read later development into Cassian's words. Neither in Basil nor in Cassian was the confession primarily penitential, though it was natural that the confession of gross sin should mean a more severe mortification. The confessor need not be a priest; and the manner in which our authors describe the practice suggests more an exercise for the younger than a universal medicine. There is no evidence that the seniors made regular confession though it was permissible. And the juniors must reveal their thoughts of every kind, good or bad, to receive comment and direction from their guide. The system was a version of the consultation found in the desert between 'a spirit-bearing' elder and a novice.

In the exposition of moral progress with the aid of Scripture, and of the wise and inspired, Cassian was a reasonable man. When he published his books for monks, a quarter of a century had elapsed since he had known Evagrius. He was working in a new milieu and with a different language. We see how the Evagrian pilgrimage of the soul looked when it was described in Latin prose. The key ideas reappear, in other words: the division into active life and contemplative life; the fight against the passions; the state of *apatheia*; the charity of the passionless man; the gateway to *gnosis*; the stripping of the mind in prayer. Most of the terminology occurs at the same points, with the same general significance (see pp. 170–2).

Yet the atmosphere feels different. Not only has he changed the emphasis at certain important points. In the process of translation a benefit accrued. Many of the technical terms came down after a history in Greek thinking. Words like *apatheia* and *gnosis* and *theoria* had a non-Christian as well as a Christian history. Their Latin equivalents were free from the faint reminiscence of Stoic or Gnostic or Platonist thought. He was very far removed from the fanaticisms or bizarre ascetic phenomena present in some of his sources. He relates few miracles but wants his men not to give them an excess of importance, for the moral law is growth and not sudden leaps. Loving the grace of God and his work of forgiveness as that without which progress of any kind is impossible, he laid much stress on our need to decide morally, and our need to discipline our own wills so that they decide rightly. Hence he was strong against St Augustine's doctrines of predestination and irresistible grace, and devoted one of the *Conferences* (XIII) to confute Augustine and explain what he took to be the proper doctrine of grace and free will (see pp. 140–1); and so gained the unfair title semi-Pelagian. It is clear that he thought of this as no digression from moral theology into dogmatic theology, for the true understanding of grace and free will he considered to be an integral part of the understanding of moral progress.

The movement of the soul he described as from multiplicity to singleness; or from complexity to simplicity; or from rushing anarchic motion to stillness. At the beginning the mind is assailed by storms of thoughts, and by demons, and is buffeted this way and that. At the summit the mind is still; concentrated on God, unceasing in the direction of its prayer. Therefore much of the moral discipline consists in the control and selection of thoughts in order to bring them nearer and nearer to simplicity; and at moments when this simplicity of apprehension is attained, the mind may experience a heavenly enlightenment or sense of fire, or even a loss of consciousness of self. The effects of contemplation are mentioned only occasionally. As in Greek and Augustinian thought, it brings union with God, by union of wills, though not in essence. The soul comes to the image and likeness of God, it feeds on the beauty and knowledge of God, it receives the indwelling Christ, it is filled by the Holy Spirit, it is illumined, it attains to the adopted sonship and possesses all that belongs to the Father. The soul is so filled that it begins to share in the love of the Blessed Trinity, to reach a state 'where God shall be all our love, and every desire and wish and effort, every thought of ours, and all our life and words and breath, and that unity which already exists between the Father and the Son, and the Son and the Father, has been shed abroad in our hearts and minds' (*Conferences*, X.7).

All this is conditioned by the ceaseless meditation upon Scripture in the background, and anchored in ejaculatory prayers consisting of scriptural texts. But when he speaks of the nature of contemplation, he urges the soul to pass from the earthly life of Jesus to a higher vision. There are souls who best contemplate 'Jesus still humble and in the flesh', but he thinks that these souls are not advanced. In this sense he interprets 2 Cor. 5.16: 'Though we have known Christ after the flesh, yet now henceforth know we him no more.' Christ's humanity has been 'absorbed' into divinity. The Origenist desire for prayer without images, together with the traditional doctrine that the contemplation of God does not mean 'Jesus-worship', would account satisfactorily for Cassian's interpretation of this verse. By the exhortation to pass from the life of Jesus to the glorified Lord, Cassian meant no more than Paul had meant. The monk never rises above his need of Christ. Cassian, and therefore desert tradition, believed that the soul shall behold God by meditating upon the revelation of the incarnate Lord.

Monasteries in southern Gaul, especially Lérins, drew from Cassian's influence. We find him much used by monastic legislators. Some monasteries made a rule out of *Institutes*, Books I–IV. The Rule of the Master used him largely; and then St Benedict canonized him as reading for Benedictines. Benedict ordered the reading of the *Conferences* after supper, and said that as his own rule was only a rule for beginners, those who wished to go on to the heights of the spiritual life should read the *Institutes* and the *Conferences*. Henceforth the influence of Cassian on Western spirituality was assured through the Benedictine Rule. Very early he was translated into Greek in summary or diluted forms, and in this way came into anthologies of Orthodox spirituality.

5 Benedict

PLACID SPEARRITT

Texts with commentary

RB 1980. The Rule of St Benedict, ed. T. Fry. Collegeville, 1981.
La Règle de Saint Benoît, ed. A. de Vogüé and J. Neufville. 7 vols., Paris, 1971–7.
Delatte, P., *The Rule of St Benedict. A Commentary*. London, Burns, Oates & Washbourne; New York, Benziger, 1921.

La Règle du Maître, ed. A. de Vogüé and others. 3 vols., Paris, 1964–5.
The Rule of the Master, tr. Luke Eberle. Kalamazoo, Cistercian Publications, 1977.

Studies

Bouyer, L., (ET) *The Meaning of the Monastic Life*. London, Burns & Oates; New York, Kennedy, 1955.

Butler, E. C., *Benedictine Monachism* (or *Monasticism*). London and New York, Longmans, Green, 1919; New York, Barnes & Noble, 1961.

de Vogüé, A., (ET) *The Rule of Saint Benedict: A Doctrinal and Spiritual Commentary*. Kalamazoo, Cistercian Publications, 1983.

Hume, G. B., *Searching for God*. London, Hodder & Stoughton, 1977; New York, Paulist Press, 1978.

Knowles, D., *Christian Monasticism*. London, Weidenfeld & Nicolson; New York, McGraw-Hill, 1969.

Leclercq, J., (ET) *The Love of Learning and the Desire for God*. 2nd edn rev., London, SPCK; New York, Fordham University Press, 1974.

Leclercq, J., Vandenbroucke, F., and Bouyer, L., (ET) *HCS*, vol. 2, *The Spirituality of the Middle Ages*. London, Burns Oates; New York, Seabury, 1968.

Louf, A., (ET) *The Message of Monastic Spirituality*. New York, Desclée, 1964.

McCann, J., *Saint Benedict*. Rev. edn, New York, Sheed & Ward, 1966.

Peifer, C., *Monastic Spirituality*. New York, Sheed & Ward, 1966.

Rees, D., ed., *Consider Your Call*. London, SPCK, 1978; Kalamazoo, Cistercian Publications, 1980.

Salmon, P., *The Abbot in Monastic Tradition*. Washington D.C., Consortium Press, 1972.

Wathen, A., *Silence: The Meaning of Silence in the Rule of St Benedict*. Washington D.C., Cistercian Publications, 1973.

Benedict was born about the year 480 in the neighbourhood of Nursia, some seventy miles north-east of Rome, and died as abbot of Monte Cassino around 547. Sent to Rome to study in his youth, he reacted against the moral corruption of his companions and, *scienter nescius et sapienter indoctus*, withdrew to live as a hermit for three years in a cave at Subiaco, not far from a cenobitic monastery. Sought out by disciples, he formed them into a colony of twelve monasteries, each with twelve monks and an abbot – an arrangement familiar from Egyptian monastic precedents, and perhaps modelled on the life of the twelve apostles with Jesus. He directed these monasteries for about twenty-five years until, driven out by persecution from an unholy priest in the area, he migrated with a few of his monks to Monte Cassino. There he spent his last seventeen years or so establishing his monastery, civilizing and converting a formerly pagan area, and composing his *Rule* for monks.

This account of his life is gathered or deduced wholly from the second book of the *Dialogues* of Gregory the Great. Gregory's stated purpose in this work is to recall the virtues and miracles exhibited by holy men and women in Italy within living memory. He attributes to Benedict a series of miraculous incidents, many of them with scriptural parallels, from which the conclusion is drawn that he was a man of God, filled with the spirit of all the saints.

During most of Benedict's life, Italy was ruled peaceably and justly by the Vandal Odoacer (476–89) and the Ostrogoth Theodoric (493–526). The ancient forms of government had survived the barbarian invasions, but social and religious order were still extremely weak. It is possible that a flight from decadence to security contributed to the strength of the monastic movement, for monasteries and hermitages were numerous. A flavour of monastic semi-Pelagianism might be attributed partly to this factor; and Benedict's theology is certainly free of the Arian sentiments often espoused by the barbarian invaders. The Gothic war (535–55) seems not to have disturbed the peace of Monte Cassino, and the first destruction of that monastery did not occur until *c.* 588, during the Lombard invasion.

Benedict lived his monastic life and wrote his *Rule* within a strong, though by his time a highly pluralist, tradition. It is probable that Antony of Egypt had followed already existing examples of eremitical life, but it was Athanasius' *Life of Antony* that had caused the monastic movement to spread widely and rapidly in both East and West. The developments initiated or conveyed by Pachomius, Basil, Jerome, Ambrose, Martin of Tours, the bishops from Lerins, Augustine and above all John Cassian were explicitly or implicitly present in the culture of the numerous monasteries of sixth-century Italy and Gaul. The large quantity of monastic literature from the fourth century onwards is characterized by extensive and highly complex borrowing, so that there are relatively few topics on which Benedict's treatment is not paralleled elsewhere.

Since the late 1930s the conviction has grown into virtual unanimity among scholars that the *Rule of Benedict* (RB) is dependent on the slightly earlier, anonymous *Rule of the Master* (RM). For the Prologue and chapters 1–7 of RB, on spiritual doctrine, the dependence amounts to transcription with some emendations, omissions and additions; the practical regulations of chapters 8–66 are often related to RM but show more independence; and there is an appendix mostly on fraternal relationships (chapters 67–73) which is not derived from RM. Some of the characteristics of Benedict are revealed by a study of how he has handled this major source. The length of RB is less than a third that of RM. The latter is given to much detailed prescription, which RB displaces by general principles and a wide recommendation to the abbot always to exercise discretion in applying those principles to the circumstances and the personalities of his monks. This recognition of the need for adjustment is no doubt one of the reasons for the pre-eminence gained by RB over all other Rules in the West in later centuries; unfortunately it has not always characterized later interpretations of the RB in theory and in practice.

It should perhaps be emphasized that Benedict, like all other early monastic writers, regarded his *Rule* as a document subordinate to, a means of insertion into, the wider monastic tradition. But that tradition further saw itself as wholly subordinate to a higher rule:

> All the ancient monks considered their real rule, in the sense of the ultimate determinant of their lives, to be not some product of human effort but the Word of God himself as contained in the Scriptures. Monasticism was simply a form of the Christian life itself, and hence it drew its inspiration from divine revelation (C. Peifer, in *RB 1980*, p. 85).

The RB is replete with scriptural citations and allusions, some of them interpreted with a freedom disconcerting to modern exegetes. They are there not as illustrations, but as norms governing the whole of monastic life, and governing the choice and treatment of the topics dealt with in the *Rule*.

'Listen, my son, to the precepts of the master, and incline the ear of your heart; welcome the admonition of a loving father and put it into practice . . .' These opening words of the Prologue set the tone of the *Rule*. As with the wisdom literature of the Old Testament, it is not a case of mere legislation but of firm guidance offered in generosity by a living person of long experience to a disciple whose heart is open and who is willing to change his ways of behaving. The Prologue stresses that both faith and good works will be required if the disciple is to profit in the monastery, 'the school of the Lord's service', and ends by placing perseverance until death into the context of Christ's paschal mystery: 'We shall by patience participate in the sufferings of Christ, so that we may also deserve to share in his kingdom.'

The *Rule* addresses itself (ch. 1) to cenobites, monks living together in community, doing their service under a rule and an abbot, though it acknowledges the excellence of the eremitical life provided that the hermit has first been long trained and tested in community life. Chapter 2 proceeds straight to the centre of Benedict's idea of monastic life: the abbot. If the spirituality of the monk is to be that of an obedient listener and follower in practice of the Word of God, the life of the monk needs an incarnational expression of that attitude, which is made available in concrete obedience to the person of the abbot. '*Christi enim agere vices in monasterio creditur*': he is believed (faith is necessary) to act as Christ's representative in the monastery. Not surprisingly then, the requirements are set high. The abbot must be conspicuous for wisdom and merit, learned in the Scriptures, a good teacher by his actions as well as by his words. He must as a good father love all alike, and therefore treat all differently, according to their need, their capacity and their response. He must both rule and serve, be severe but strive to be loved rather than feared. He must not be suspicious, restless, or over-demanding. Exercising discretion, the mother of virtues, let him so arrange all things that there be a standard to attract the strong without frightening off the weak. He should always put mercy above judgement; his function is to be *for* the brethren rather than *over* them (*prodesse magis quam praeesse*) (ch. 64).

Father, teacher, shepherd, physician, judge, steward of his community, the abbot is nonetheless himself subject to the rule: to the rule of God, the rule of Scripture, but also in all things to this present written *Rule*; yet he is encouraged in many matters to modify the provisions of the *Rule* as discretion requires. This attitude of a rather conservative respect for the letter combined with the freedom of discernment under God is, or should be, characteristic of all Benedictine spirituality. The fact that Benedict requires the combination in the abbot means that his abbot is not an absolute monarch, not a Roman *paterfamilias* with power of life and death. The basic model is that of the spiritual father in the Egyptian desert tradition, the spiritual director of individual disciples, but in RB of individuals seen very much as members of the community.

An integral part of the abbot's service of discernment is his listening to the expression of God's revelation through his own monks, especially through junior monks who are humble and obedient. In less important matters he should still not act without first taking the counsel of seniors. But in all matters he is ultimately to decide in the light of his own judgement, in the fear of God and in observance of the rule (ch. 3).

Before proceeding in chaps. 5–7 to the great trilogy of monastic virtues, obedience, silence and humility, Benedict inserts a chapter on the tools of good works. At first reading, and let it be said for some monks after many hundreds of readings, this list seems to be an inconsequent jumble of scriptural and other spiritual maxims of very varying degrees of profundity, not all of them conspicuously relevant to the monastic condition. The study of Adalbert de Vogüé, 'The Maxims of the Spiritual Art' (*The Rule of Saint Benedict: A Doctrinal and Spiritual Commentary*, pp. 77–90) has made it clear that they constitute a careful and deliberate statement of the whole Christian ascesis, structured around the two great commandments of Jesus with which they begin. They serve to recall to the abbot and to his monks the general Christian principles of discernment that must underlie the particularly monastic applications of obedience, silence and humility that are to follow. De Vogüé very credibly sees in this chapter a conscious and deliberate corrective on the part of RM and RB to the Evagrian, purist, monastic theory of John Cassian. This reading helps also to account for the frequent recourse in RM and RB to threats of hell and promises of heaven as motivations for our behaviour on earth: these writers remain close in mentality to the cruder imagery of the synoptic Gospels, even though Benedict will claim that the monk who begins and perseveres with these motives will soon arrive at the perfect love that casts out fear.

Obedience is the theme of chapter 5, but it is a theme that permeates the whole of the *Rule*. Right at the beginning of the Prologue it appears as fundamental:

> Welcome the admonition of a loving father and put it into practice, so that by the labour of obedience you may return to him from whom by the laziness of disobedience you had strayed.

The loving father addresses as son 'anyone renouncing the promptings of self-will'. Self-will as opposed to the will of God is a frequent preoccupation of the *Rule* (cf. *RB 1980*, p. 584), and renunciation of self-will would certainly be a candidate for the position of the strongest psychological motivation in Benedict's monasticism. The reference to Matt. 16.24–5 puts it in the context of the renunciation required by Jesus of all Christians:

> If any man would come after me, let him deny himself and take up his cross and follow me. For whoever would save his life will lose it, and whoever loses his life for my sake will find it.

RB asks for prompt obedience to monastic superiors 'as if the command were from God', and by quoting Luke 10.16, 'He who hears you, hears me', seems to justify what in later centuries became a widespread doctrine, that the command of the superior is the will of God for the subject. The *Rule* says that it is the desire of gaining eternal life that impels cenobites to *want* to have an abbot over them, to live not by their own judgement but by the decisions and commands of another. External obedience is acceptable to God only if it reflects interior willingness and indeed cheerfulness. Murmuring against orders given, even murmuring in the heart, is incompatible with obedience. If the command is extremely heavy or impossible to fulfil, the monk should explain his difficulty; but if the superior persists, he must obey (ch. 68). It is a hard saying to many modern ears, but there can be no doubt that total obedience is of the essence of Benedictine spirituality. 'It is not permissible for monks to have even their bodies or their wills at their own disposal' (ch. 33).

Two considerations may serve to distance this teaching from the quite devastating abuses of it that have certainly occurred in the course of monastic history. The first is that the *Rule* constantly threatens the abbot that he is in danger of hell if he allows his own will to supplant the will of God which he should be discerning in Scripture, in the whole monastic tradition, in his own obedience to the rule. The second can best be expressed in the words of an outstanding abbot of the twentieth century:

> Secure under the protection and guidance of their vow of obedience, St Benedict's monks could throw themselves into every detail of their life without doubt of its value in God's eyes and without anxious self-questioning about the wisdom or worthwhileness of their occupations. But they were not meant to be unreflective . . . He did not wish for a community of robots, but of men with active and interested minds and with wills at once strong and obedient (Herbert Byrne, 'St Benedict and his Spirit', in *Ampleforth and its Origins*, ed. J. McCann and C. Cary-Elwes [London, Burns Oates & Washbourne, 1952], p. 12).

Finally, chaps. 71 and 72 at the end of the *Rule* remind the reader that the good of obedience is not limited to obeying superiors: the reasons that justify the brethren in obeying their abbot should move them to compete also in obedience to one another. The motive for all true obedience is love, ultimately the love of God.

Silence is the second of the monastic virtues (ch. 6). Obviously it pre-empts the danger of sinful talk, but it is good to restrain speech even about good, holy and edifying topics, for a monk is by definition a disciple, and should want more to listen than to speak. His silence is an expression of his humility. Silence should characterize the monastery at all times, but especially at night; and in all places, but especially in the oratory and the refectory.

Monastic humility (ch. 7) is grounded in the general proclamation of Jesus: 'Everyone who exalts himself will be humbled, and he who humbles himself will be exalted' (Luke 14.11; 18.14). Benedict follows RM in presenting the theme in a somewhat obscure metaphor of a Jacob's ladder of twelve steps leading to heaven. The first step is to live constantly in the fear of God, unto whom all hearts are open and all desires known: hence not only bodily lusts, but also self-will are to be kept in check by the monks' awareness that their lives are lived out in the sight of God. Wilfulness is overcome by obedience, perseverance even under injustice, and humble confession of sin. The seventh step of humility is that a man believe in his heart that he is lower and of less worth than all others – perhaps one of the clearest of the many indications of the deep level at which Benedict is eliciting what he thinks necessary for one who desires to live by his *Rule*. The remaining steps call for the expression of this interior humility in deportment and in silence. Then when a monk has mounted all these steps, what began in the fear of God will soon be achieved in perfect love.

The novice-master must discover 'whether the novice is truly seeking God, whether he is zealous for the *opus Dei*, for obedience, for *opprobria*' (ch. 58). *Opprobria* can fairly be understood as occasions that will test and deepen his humility. And it can fairly be claimed that the two 'whether' clauses in this formula are intended to be equivalent. For a monk to seek God is to be humble, to be obedient, and to do the *opus Dei*, the work of God. Once the spiritual principles have been established in the Prologue and first seven chapters, the *Rule* devotes its attention to the ordering of the divine office, the *opus Dei*, which is the monk's chief work (chaps. 8–19).[1] The modern reader will be struck by the almost total absence of eucharistic liturgy from the *Rule*. It is unlikely that the Eucharist was celebrated except on Sundays and feast days. The divine office is clearly the liturgical staple of Benedict's monastic spirituality.

Chapter 58 contains the procedure for receiving new entrants to the community. There is no mention of 'vows', or of the three evangelical counsels, poverty, chastity and obedience. The practice of taking these vows in religious life was a much later development. Most Benedictine profession formulas still follow the pattern given in RB: the novice promises stability (in the community), *conversatio morum* (conversion to the monastic way of life), and obedience.

'Idleness is the enemy of the soul, and therefore the brethren ought to be occupied at fixed times in manual labour, and again at fixed times in *lectio divina*' (ch. 48). About six hours were to be spent in the former, about four in the latter each day. The monks should live by the labour of their hands: the monastery should be self-supporting. *Lectio divina*, sacred reading, limited almost exclusively to Scripture and to patristic works on Scripture, was intended to lead to *meditatio*, the turning over in the mind if not also on the lips of the texts read and often memorized during the *lectio*: the time of work was normally also time for *meditatio*.

Private prayer is hardly envisaged at all in the *Rule*, at least not in a sense clearly distinguishable from *meditatio* on the one hand and the silent pauses after the psalms for listening to the word of God on the other. In chapter 20, Benedict seems to equate prayer with petition. Since God is more interested in our purity of heart and our compunction than in our words, prayer should be short and pure, unless it is prolonged by

---

[1] An account of its structure and its wide influence can be found in *SL*, pp. 372–5; for a more detailed study, cf. Nathan Mitchell, 'The Liturgical Code in the Rule of Benedict', *RB 1980*, pp. 379–414.

the inspiration of divine grace. Benedict knew his Cassian well, and recommended his monks to read the *Conferences* of that author: so he was not averse to the exalted appreciation of prayer manifested in Abbot Isaac's two conferences on the subject. But the RB is only a little rule for beginners (ch. 73), and the humility Benedict finds at the centre of Christianity and places at the centre of monasticism is surely central also to the prayer of passive union so attractively expounded in Cassian's *Conference*, 10.6, 7, 11.

In RB there is no spirituality separable from the 'rest of life'. The whole life is wholly spiritual, because of the nature of the God who calls for it and because of the interior disposition of the monk who listens to the call. Likewise there is little or no spirituality in RB other than monastic spirituality. But because what is there is founded wholly in Scripture, it is not surprising that lay folk have profited through the centuries from the spirituality of the *Rule* and of the life that continues to be lived in monasteries according to the *Rule*. Again, it can be said that there has never been a specifically Benedictine 'school' of spirituality. Monks were not called Benedictines until there were other religious orders to distinguish them from. Benedict himself put no objection to reading any of the Fathers, provided they were orthodox. The majority of the monks and nuns who have lived under his *Rule* have continued to be fairly eclectic in the devotional spiritualities they have absorbed from their various cultural milieux.

The rise of the RB to predominance over all other monastic Rules in the West is no doubt partly accounted for by its intrinsic merits; but it was significantly helped on its way, notably by St Wilfrid (there is no evidence that Augustine brought it with him to Canterbury), St Boniface, and above all by St Benedict of Aniane, who under the auspices of the Emperor Louis the Pious imposed it on the monasteries of France and Germany in the early ninth century.

Later centuries were to fall into the trap of identifying the Benedictine 'thing' with the civilization of Europe, missionary monasticism, Cluniac liturgy, total enclosure for 'the contemplative life', the pursuit of excellence, Maurist scholarship, marginal eschatological witness, and half-a-dozen other ideals. All of these are compatible with, but none of them is necessary for, the spirit of humility that leads a man to want to live out his life under a rule and an abbot.

6 John Scotus Eriugena

EDWARD YARNOLD

Texts

Latin text in *PL* 122.
Sheldon-Williams, I. P., and Bieler, L., critical edn and ET of *Periphyseon*,
  Scriptores Latini Hiberniae, 7. Dublin, Institute for Advanced Studies,
  1968– . (ET) *On the Division of Nature*. Indianapolis, the Library of Liberal
  Arts, 1976.

Studies

Roques, R., 'Jean Scot Erigène', in *Dict. Sp.* 8.735–62.
Sheldon-Williams, I. P., 'Johannes Scottus Eriugena', in Armstrong, ch. 34.
Bibliography in *ODCC*, s.v. 'Erigena'.

John Scotus Eriugena (or Erigena) was born early in the ninth century in
Ireland, as his last two names imply. Whether it was his native country or
his adopted France that can claim credit for the breadth of his learning
and his knowledge of Greek, Charles the Bald made him Master of the
Frankish Palace School *c.* 846. Though his early work *De Praedestinat-
ione* (851) was condemned by two local councils, the King set him to make
a new Latin translation of the writings of Dionysius the Areopagite (see
pp. 184–9). Eriugena's version contributed greatly to the spread of the
Dionysian ideas in the West. He went on to translate other works of
Christian Neoplatonism by Maximus the Confessor and Gregory of
Nyssa. Many of these ideas he incorporated into his own 'Summa', a
work in dialogue form called the *Periphyseon*, to which later tradition
gave the name *De Divisione Naturae*. His death is generally assumed to
have occurred in the 870s.

   In the *Periphyseon*, which shows the influence of Augustine as well as
the Greek Christian Neoplatonists, two apparently contradictory insights
are held in tension. The first is the ineffability of God. Giving a justification, based on logic, for Dionysius' apophatic theology (see p. 188;
Eriugena coins the Latin words *apofaticus* and *catafaticus*), he asserts
that:

> Nothing can be said properly (*proprie*) of God, because he transcends all
> understanding . . . he is known better by not knowing; ignorance concerning
> him is true wisdom. It is more in accordance with truth and faith to deny
> anything of him than to affirm it (*Periphyseon*, i.66; *PL* 510B).

Affirmations can be made concerning God, but they can be true only metaphorically (*per metaphoram*) or analogically (*translate*); this is true even of statements concerning God's love (i.62; 504AB).

The second insight is that God is so closely related to his creatures that he is said more properly to be created in them than to create them (op. cit. iii.23; 689AB).[1] This is true not only of the Forms in the mind of God the Word, but even of individual created things. God 'descends' in created things so that a 'theophany' takes place (loc. cit.). But Eriugena also describes the Neoplatonic process by which God 'returns' to himself, gathering together the multiplicity of creation in a process of *'theōsis* or deification' (Introd. to translation of Maximus' *Ambigua*, PL 1195C–1196A). This return for human beings includes ascetic progress, but fundamentally consists of a Neoplatonist intellectual ascent (Roques, 749–50).

Eriugena develops this idea in a later work, the *Expositiones*, a commentary on Dionysius' *Celestial Hierarchy*:

> For the human mind (*animus* = *nous*) was not made for divine Scripture, for it would not have any need of Scripture if it did not sin; but for the sake of the human mind holy Scripture has been woven into various creeds and doctrines so that it may guide our rational nature, which has fallen by sin from the contemplation of the truth, on its return to its original height of pure contemplation (ii.1; 146C).

---

[1] Subsequent generations interpreted such sayings in a literal sense, and saw them as pantheistic. For this reason the *Periphyseon* was twice condemned by the Church in the thirteenth century and placed on the Index of prohibited books in the seventeenth.

IV

THE EASTERN FATHERS

A GREEK WRITERS FROM THE CAPPADOCIANS TO JOHN OF DAMASCUS

1 Introduction

KALLISTOS WARE

Bouyer, L., *The Spirituality of the New Testament and the Fathers* (*HCS* i: London, 1963).

Hausherr, I. (J. Lemaître), 'Contemplation chez les Grecs et autres orientaux chrétiens', in *Dict. Sp.* 2.1762–1872.

Hausherr, I., *Hésychasme et prière* (*OCA* 176: 1966).

Hausherr, I., *Etudes de spiritualité orientale* (*OCA* 183: 1969).

Louth, A., *The Origins of the Christian Mystical Tradition: From Plato to Denys*. Oxford, OUP, 1981.

Špidlík, T., (ET) *The Spirituality of the Christian East: A Systematic Handbook*. Kalamazoo, Cistercian Studies, 1985.

Williams, R., *The Wound of Knowledge*. London, DLT, 1979.

At the start of the fourth century Christianity entered upon a new era. With the conversion of the Emperor Constantine in 312 persecution ceased, apart from a brief interlude of renewed repression under the Emperor Julian 'the Apostate' (361–3). This dramatic change in Church–State relations, with Christianity now no longer proscribed but privileged and 'established', had a double effect upon prayer and spirituality. On the one side it led to an impressive elaboration of liturgical worship. Spacious churches were built, richly decorated, where the Eucharist could be celebrated with an outer magnificence impossible in the pre-Constantinian period. During the later fourth and the fifth centuries there was also a rapid development of pilgrimages, the cult of the saints, and devotion to the Blessed Virgin Mary. On the other side the ascetic spirit, present in Christianity from the start, now assumed a far more articulate form with the emergence of monasticism as an organized movement, distinct from the life of the local parish. Both the 'way of affirmation' and the 'way of negation', as they may be termed, became in this manner more sharply differentiated.

Yet the polarity between the city and the desert should never be exaggerated. Their interdependence is symbolized by the personal friendship existing, at the very start of monastic history, between St Athanasius, Archbishop of Alexandria, and the hermit St Antony. While monasticism could easily have developed along schismatic lines as an 'alternative Church', on the whole this did not in fact happen. Bishops in the fourth and fifth centuries, as well as being high-ranking functionaries within the civil structure of the Christian Empire, were also in many cases monks; the monks on their side contributed notably to the elaboration of liturgical worship, and in the eighth century played a leading part in the defence of the holy icons. The two 'ways' of affirmation and negation existed within a single, all-embracing framework of church life, and each presupposed the other.

In the later fourth century two specific 'currents' emerged in Eastern Christian spirituality, represented respectively by Evagrius of Pontus and the Macarian Homilies. Evagrius, a disciple of the Cappadocians – but at the same time deeply indebted to the Desert Fathers of Egypt, among whom his later years were spent – developed a systematic, 'intellectualist' spirituality, platonizing and Origenist in outlook. He defined prayer as 'the communion of the intellect (*nous*) with God', and regarded it in its higher stages as a state of 'pure' intellectuality, free from images, words and rational concepts. The Homilies, on the other hand, are unsystematic and 'affective' in approach; they do not advocate image-free prayer but allow full scope to the visual imagination, speaking in terms of the heart (*kardia*) rather than the intellect. The Homilies display marked affinities with the extreme ascetic movement known as Messalianism, which emerged in Mesopotamia and Syria in the last quarter of the fourth century, spreading rapidly throughout the Christian East. The Messalians (in Greek, 'Euchites': literally 'those who pray', from their insistence upon continual prayer) were accused by their critics of depreciating the value of the sacraments, and overemphasizing the role of visions, feelings and conscious experience in the life of prayer. While Messalian traits are undoubtedly present in the Homilies, there is much disagreement among specialists about the precise extent of Messalian influence upon Macarius.

Yet in reality the two 'currents' are less far apart than appears at first. When Evagrius, for example, spoke of the *nous*, he meant not only the reasoning brain but also, and more fundamentally, the apprehension of spiritual truth through direct, non-discursive insight; and Macarius understood by the heart not merely the emotions and affections but the deep centre of the human person. From the fifth century onwards there was a growing convergence between the two 'currents'. This tendency is to be seen already in St Diadochus of Photice, and is continued by St John Climacus and above all by St Maximus the Confessor.

2 The Cappadocians

ANDREW LOUTH

Texts and translations

Ascetic Works of St Basil, ed. W. K. L. Clarke. London, SPCK; New York and Toronto, Macmillan, 1925.
Basil, (ET) *On the Holy Spirit*, Crestwood, N.Y., St. Vladimir's 1980.
Basil, *On The Holy Spirit*, French tr. SC 17 bis.
From Glory to Glory, ed. H. Musurillo. New York, Scribner, 1961; London, J. Murray, 1962; selections from Gregory of Nyssa in ET with useful introduction by J. Daniélou.
Gregory of Nyssa, *Life of Moses*, tr. A. J. Malherbe and E. Ferguson. CWS 1979.
Gregory of Nyssa, *Life of Moses*, French tr. SC 1 ter.
Gregory of Nyssa, *On the Lord's Prayer and the Beatitudes*, ed. H. Graef, ACW XVIII.
Works of Gregory of Nyssa, critical edn by W. Jaeger et al. Leiden, 1921–   .

Studies

Amand, D., *L'Ascèse monastique de S. Basile*. Maredsous, 1948.
Clarke, W. K. L., *St Basil the Great*. CUP, 1913.
Daniélou, J., *Platonisme et théologie mystique*. 2nd edn Paris, 1953.
Morison, E. F., *St Basil and his Rule*. London, OUP; New York, H. Frowde, 1912.
Špidlík, T., *Grégoire de Nazianze: Introduction à l'étude de sa doctrine spirituelle*. Rome, 1971.
Völker, W., *Gregor von Nyssa als Mystiker*. Wiesbaden, 1953.
For further bibliography see s.v. in Quasten and Altaner.

The achievement of the Cappadocian Fathers in the realm of dogmatic theology is usually seen as that of consolidating the work of Athanasius and securing the acceptance throughout the Church of the dogmatic settlement of the Council of Nicaea: as Athanasius' life was spent in defending Nicene Orthodoxy, so the Cappadocian Fathers secured its final triumph at the Second Ecumenical Council, held at Constantinople in 381. What the Council of Nicaea meant for Athanasius can be summed up as on the one hand a clear recognition of the absolute ontological gulf separating the divine, which consisted simply of the three consubstantial persons of the Blessed Trinity, from the creaturely order, which has been created out of nothing by God, and on the other hand an understanding of redemption as wrought by God himself in the incarnation in which the Son shared the fragility of the human, created condition and offered humankind participation in his own blessed life: 'He was made man that

161

we might be made God', as Athanasius puts it in his *De Incarnatione*. Such an emphasis on the gulf between God and humankind called in question hellenistic ideas of human kinship with God, in virtue of which human beings could attempt to ascend to God – ideas found in Origen, for example. For Athanasius deification no longer meant restoration of our natural state but the realization of a new possibility offered to us by God through the incarnation. In Athanasius' own writings such traditional Greek concepts as contemplation (*theōria*), in which humans realize their kinship with God, fall into the background: the emphasis is on God's condescension to us rather than on our ascent to God. An important part of Athanasius' achievement was in his championing of the ascetic movement which saw such a remarkable growth in the fourth century. In his widely influential *Life of St Antony* (see p. 120) he presented an understanding of the ascetic life less in terms of a human search for God than as the way in which the war against the forces of evil, in which God had achieved the decisive victory through the cross and resurrection, was continued in the Church of his day.

Such a position as that of Athanasius in which orthodox theology and a demanding spirituality mutually inform one another lies behind the efforts of the Cappadocian Fathers. Basil the Great (*c*. 330–79) and his brother, Gregory of Nyssa (*c*. 335–*c*. 395), were the sons of devout parents. Basil received a good hellenistic education, studying finally in Athens where his friendship with the third of the 'Cappadocian Fathers', Gregory of Nazianzus (329–89), blossomed. He then forsook the world for the ascetic life and after a year spent visiting monasteries in Syria and Egypt, in 358 he settled as an ascetic at Annesis by the river Iris in Pontus, where Gregory of Nazianzus joined him from time to time. During his time there he founded a number of monasteries. In 370 Basil became bishop of Caesarea and for the rest of his life was at the centre of ecclesiastical administration and controversy. Gregory of Nazianzus shared Basil's education and his calling to the ascetic life, but was a very different kind of person, by temperament suited to a life of withdrawal and only with reluctance involved in matters of ecclesiastical politics. Gregory of Nyssa had a rather different background from the others: he did not have their brilliant educational career, but seems to have been taught by his brother. Originally destined for the priesthood, he became a teacher of rhetoric and married. Basil tried to persuade him to join him at Annesis, but there is no proof that he succeeded or that Gregory ever lived a monastic life: it would seem on the contrary that he continued to live with his wife even after he became a bishop in 372. It is Gregory of Nyssa who was the most brilliant intellectually of the Cappadocian Fathers: we find in him a depth and breadth of thought that surpasses the others. He seems to have played a decisive role at the Second Ecumenical Council, and in the years after that council enjoyed a brief period of influence and imperial favour.

All the Cappadocian Fathers manifest the influence of Origen (see pp. 115–19) and Neoplatonism, especially the thought of Plotinus (see pp. 96–9), as well as the influence, already mentioned, of Athanasius and the contemporary ascetic movement. Indeed towards the beginning of Basil's period of monastic retreat he and Gregory of Nazianzus prepared a collection of extracts from Origen's writings, called the *Philokalia*. Origen and Neoplatonism provide them with a conceptual framework within which their ascetic doctrine seems at times to fit very neatly, but the impact of Nicene orthodoxy is ever present, though it is perhaps only Gregory of Nyssa who sees clearly its bearing on spirituality and works out its implications thoroughly. It must not be forgotten either that the pressure of the Scriptures, which is the professed source of their ascetic theory and practice, is always felt and often gives a very different twist to what otherwise sounds very hellenistic.

Basil's principal ascetic work is the two sets of monastic rules: the *Longer Rules* (or *Detailed Rules: Regulae fusius tractatae* – abbreviated as F) and the *Shorter Rules* (*Regulae brevius tractatae* – B). Despite (or perhaps because of) his knowledge of Syrian and Egyptian monasticism, the kind of monasticism adumbrated in these rules is somewhat different, as we shall see. Others of Basil's writings important for his spirituality are: his letters, the treatise *On the Holy Spirit* (S), and not least his *Liturgy*, for the *Liturgy of St Basil*, still celebrated in the Eastern Orthodox Church, goes back to Basil himself, and indeed even further, for Basil's work was essentially that of revision. Gregory Nazianzen's writings comprise letters, sermons and a great deal of verse; but although the writings of the 'Theologian' have perhaps been more influential than those of the other two, it is difficult to avoid the impression that the Nazianzen only says more elegantly what is found expressed more deeply in the others. Gregory of Nyssa's intention in his spiritual writings was, as Werner Jaeger has shown, to give a mystical orientation to the monastic movement organized by his brother. His *De Instituto Christiano* sets out the fundamental spiritual doctrine of Basil, but his late writings, especially his *Commentary on the Song of Songs* (C) and the *Life of Moses* (M), develop what might be called the mystical vision informing such spiritual teaching.

Perhaps the simplest and most direct way to characterize the spiritual teaching of Basil, and a way that recalls that he was the author (or reviser) of the Liturgy that bears his name, is to say that it is essentially *eucharistic*: that is, humanity's relationship to God is to be one of thanksgiving. This comes out clearly at the very beginning of the *Longer Rules* when he discusses the nature of love towards God. This is something natural, implanted in us by God at our creation, which cannot be taught, but is rather a spontaneous response to the divine beauty and the divine goodness. In a passage which, as Lowther Clarke remarks, recalls in its language the *anaphora* of the Liturgy of St Basil, Basil runs through all that God has done for humankind, from creation to redemption, and concludes:

> When I think of all this . . . I fall into a fearful shuddering and terror, lest haply through carelessness of mind or absorption in vain things I should fall from the love of God and become a reproach to Christ (F 2:339B).

Corresponding to the eucharistic *anamnēsis*, the heart of man's spiritual life is the remembrance (*mnēmē*) of God and thanksgiving for his gifts to us. So in the *Shorter Rules* we read: 'For what cause does a man lose the continuous remembrance of God? By becoming forgetful of God's benefits and insensitive towards his Benefactor' (B 244). There is, however, another way in which the Liturgy seems to be significant for Basil's understanding of the spiritual life. Like Origen, he sees the Spirit peculiarly at work in the sanctification of the Christian, in the renewal of the image in which humankind was created. So in a letter to his monks he sums up the progress of the soul thus: 'The mind being enlightened by the Spirit looks up to the Son, and in him as in an image beholds the Father' (*Ep.* 226). This working of the Spirit is hidden: it is not explained in written formulations but witnessed to in the unwritten tradition of the Church – an unwritten tradition which, as Basil explains in his work *On the Holy Spirit*, consists almost entirely of liturgical practices, so that it is in taking part in the liturgy that the Spirit brings to people 'understanding of spiritual gifts . . . and the summit of their desires: to become God' (S ix.23).

The way by which, according to Basil, this is to be pursued is expressed concisely in a letter (*Ep.* 2) he wrote at the beginning of his time of retreat at Annesis, encouraging Gregory of Nazianzus to join him there. The aim of the ascetic life is to 'keep the mind in tranquillity (*hēsuchia*)' and the way to attain this is to avoid distraction. To achieve this it is necessary to separate onself from the world altogether, which means a severance of the soul from sympathy with the body and a readiness to receive in one's heart the impressions engendered there by divine instructions. To this end solitude (*erēmia*) is the greatest help 'since it calms our passions and gives reason leisure (*scholē*) to sever them completely from the soul'. On the positive side, the 'discipline of piety', that is the daily round of prayer and praise by which the ascetic 'imitates on earth the anthems of the angels' choirs', nourishes the soul with divine thoughts and brings it to a condition of joy, free from grief. Through this practice of tranquillity the soul is purified and, withdrawing into itself, ascends to the contemplation of God. Ravished by the divine beauty, the soul applies itself through reading and meditating on the Scriptures to the acquisition of the virtues. So God comes to dwell in the soul by our holding God continually in the memory, and we become temples of God. There is much in this that reminds one of hellenistic philosophical ideals, especially when one contrasts this life of withdrawal and leisure given over to contemplation with the picture of the life of the desert fathers with their dramatic struggle against the onslaughts of the demons (about whom Basil is noticeably silent). But one point of contrast with the desert fathers brings out the special contribution of Basil to the history of monasticism, and that is his rejection of the eremitical life in favour of the coenobitical life.

The seventh of the *Longer Rules* is a long attack on the solitary life and a defence of the ideal of the coenobitical life, life in community. With the desert fathers the solitary hermit appears to have been the supreme vocation, and even the *coenobia* of Pachomius (see pp. 128–30) seem more like encampments of hermits than an attempt at community life as a good in itself. Evagrius (see pp. 168–73), a friend of the Cappadocians who was ordained to the diaconate by Basil, reflects this estimate of the eremitical life in the prologue to his *Praktikos*, where he depicts the solitary as one who fights hand to hand with the demons. For Basil the solitary life is a dangerous temptation, for the aim of the Christian life is love, whereas 'the solitary life has one aim, the service of the needs of the individual', which is 'plainly in conflict with the law of love'. 'Whose feet wilt thou then wash?' exclaims Basil, 'Whom wilt thou care for? In comparison with whom wilt thou be last if thou livest by thyself?' But, further, the solitary will have no one to correct him for his defects, and (what is perhaps for Basil the most serious point) the solitary will neither be able to share his spiritual gifts with others, nor benefit from theirs. (Basil's concern for spiritual gifts is one of several points in which he invites comparison with the contemporary Messalian movement (see p. 160).) Basil compares the solitary to the man in the parable who buried his one talent. For Basil the mutual support and correction provided only by a community are essential to the life of the monk: something developed further in his stress on the place of spiritual direction. In the communities there are to be monks 'entrusted with the task of caring for weak souls tenderly and sympathetically', and to them all things, 'even the secrets of the heart', are to be made known. This is not exactly sacramental confession – for it is not just *sins* that are confessed, nor is there any evidence that such confessors were to be priests – but it is a means, pastoral and practical, of healing the wounds inflicted by sin. Life in such communities was to be severe, but there was no place for the exceptional severities of the desert. The principal means of asceticism was obedience to the superior (or the senior monks), for the aim of asceticism is to strike at the root of self-will. Basil lays great stress too on the importance of continence (*enkrateia*) which he praises as 'the beginning of the spiritual life, the introducer of eternal blessings' (F 17), the one commandment round which 'all the commandments are grouped as in a chorus' (F 16). The mutual love that such communities existed to foster was not confined to their members: the monasteries ran hospitals and were places of hospitality and relief for the poor and needy.

In the *Rules* Basil quotes frequently from the books of Proverbs and Ecclesiastes, but once only from the Song of Songs when he speaks of the yearning the divine beauty arouses in the soul, a yearning so keen and intolerable that the soul cries out with true affection, 'I am wounded with love!' (F 2:337B). Origen regarded the three books of wisdom – Proverbs, Ecclesiastes and the Song of Songs – as belonging to the three successive stages of the soul's spiritual ascent, and in this he is followed by Gregory of Nyssa: the early stages, which Basil is principally concerned with in his *Rules*, correspond to Proverbs and Ecclesiastes; beyond lies the fruition of the soul's life with God of which the Song of Songs sings, and with which Gregory of Nyssa is principally concerned, especially in his commentary on that book. For Origen the three stages of the soul's ascent were the movement away from sin in which the soul learns the virtues, the stage of natural contemplation in which the soul sees the created order in God, and beyond that contemplation of God himself (which Evagrius, who follows Origen closely, called *theologia*, a usage sometimes found in Gregory of Nyssa). For Origen this was a movement of increasing illumination: the soul moves from darkness to light to still greater light. Gregory of Nyssa takes over Origen's three stages, but for him they are a movement from light to darkness. In speaking of the three stages he often compares them with three stages in the life of Moses (his whole treatise, the *Life of Moses*, is built round this idea): the revelation at the Burning Bush, and then Moses' two ascents of Mt Sinai, the first into the cloud, the second into the darkness where he asked to see God face to face (see C xi:1000–1). Moses moves from the revelation of light (*phōs*), to the darkness of the cloud (*nephelē*), and beyond that to the thick darkness (*gnophos*) 'where God dwells'. The reason for this reversal of Origen is quite simple. For Origen the soul's ascent to God was its restoration to its original state, a movement from the darkness and confusion of its fallen state; for Gregory the soul's ascent to God is its drawing closer and closer to One who is utterly different from it, One who is absolutely unknowable because there is no natural kinship between the Creator God and his creatures. In this Gregory is exploring the consequences of the orthodoxy of Nicaea with greater consistency than the other Cappadocian Fathers, neither of whom develops the radical implications of the doctrine of *creatio ex nihilo* (creation from nothing): they remain, with Evagrius, closer to the doctrine of Origen. For Gregory of Nyssa the doctrine of God's unknowability means that the soul's ascent to God is an ascent into the divine darkness.

Although in speaking thus of the divine darkness Gregory is drawing on Philo (see pp. 94–6), he goes beyond him in the way he explores the implications of this theme for the spiritual life. We cannot *see* in the dark, but for the Platonic tradition contemplation was an attempt to understand the way the intellect (*nous*) grasps true reality by analogy with sight, the 'keenest of the senses' (*Phaedr.* 250D; cf. *Rep.* vi.508B). To say that the closer we come to the truest of all reality, God, the darker it gets, is to overthrow all this. And this is what Gregory does, and he explores its implications. Plunged into the dark, we feel terror and giddiness: the soul which comes close to God finds itself as it were on the edge of 'the slippery, steep rock that affords no basis for our thoughts' (*Hom.* vi on the Beatitudes). Gregory depicts vividly the bewilderment, despair and longing that possesses the soul that seeks God. In the dark we can form no finished conception of what is there: this experience is interpreted by Gregory in terms of an endless longing for God, continually satisfied yet always yearning for more, which the soul knows that embarks on the search for the unknowable God. Daniélou has called this experience *epectasis* – a continual reaching out after God. So Moses learns that 'the true vision of God consists in this, that the soul that looks up to God never ceases to desire him' (M ii.233). And since in the dark we cannot see, Gregory is led, encouraged by the sensuous imagery of the Song of Songs, to try and express the experience of the divine darkness by drawing on the analogy of the other senses: of smell, taste and touch (not, significantly, hearing). For Gregory the experience yielded by these spiritual senses is basically one of obscure, but certain, presence – and a presence that is disclosed to us, rather than something we seek out. The soul is

> encompassed by a divine night, during which the Spouse approaches, but does not reveal himself . . . He gives the soul some sense of his presence, even while he eludes her clear apprehension, concealed as he is by the invisibility of his nature (C x: 1001BC)

This obscure sense of presence, of possession, or rather of being possessed, is most adequately understood as the soul's awareness of her being the object of God's love, a love which awakens within herself a passionate response of love as she senses the beauty of God which transcends any apprehension:

> the bride then puts the veil from her eyes and with pure vision sees the ineffable beauty of her Spouse. And thus she is wounded by a spiritual and fiery dart of love (*erōs*). For *agapē* that is strained to intensity is called *erōs* . . . The bride glories in her wound, for the point of this spiritual yearning has pierced to the depths of her heart. And this she makes clear when she says to the other maidens: I am wounded with love (C xiii: 1048CD).

The mysticism of the divine darkness in which the soul is united in love with the unknowable God is the summit of the spirituality of the Cappadocians, a spirituality the lineaments of which are derived from their reflections on the nature of the Christian God which helped shape the Church's dogmatic tradition.

3 Evagrius and Macarius

SIMON TUGWELL

EVAGRIUS (*with abbreviations*)

A = *Antirrhētikos*; B = the eighth letter in the collection of Basil's letters; G = *Gnōstikos*; K = *Kephalaia Gnōstika*; L = Letters; M = works edited by J. Muyldermans in *Muséon* 44 (1931) (M[1]) and 51 (1938) (M[2]); N = *Nonnenspiegel*; O = *De Oratione* (text taken essentially from MS Paris, Coislin 109); P = *Praktikos*; S = J. Muyldermans, *Evagriana Syriaca*. Louvain, 1952.

Evagrius Ponticus, *Praktikos*; *Chapters on Prayer*, ET J. E. Bamberger. Spenser, Mass., Cistercian Publications, 1970.

Guillaumont, A. and C., ed., *Evagre le Pontique: Traité Pratique*, SC 170–1; contains a critical edition of the *Praktikos* and a substantial bibliography of Evagrius' works.

Hausherr, I., *Les leçons d'un contemplatif*. Paris, 1960.

Palmer, G. E. H.; Sherrard, P.; Ware, K. T., ed. (ET) *The Philokalia*, vol. 1 (London and Boston, Faber, 1979), pp. 29–71.

Tugwell, S., *Ways of Imperfection* (London, DLT, 1984), pp. 25–36.

MACARIUS (*with abbreviations*)

B = Makarios/Symeon, *Reden und Briefe*, ed. H. Berthold. Berlin, 1973.

C = E. Klostermann and H. Berthold, ed., *Neue Homilien des Makarius/Symeon*. Berlin, 1961.

H = H. Dörries, E. Klostermann and M. Kroeger, ed., *Die 50 geistlichen Homilien des Makarios*. Berlin, 1964.

H 51 = G. L. Marriott, *Macarii Anecdota* (Cambridge, Mass., Harvard University Press, 1918), pp. 19–23.

GL = W. Jaeger, *Two Rediscovered Works of Ancient Christian Literature*. Leiden, 1965.

(ET) *Fifty Spiritual Homilies* tr. A. J. Mason. London, SPCK; New York, Macmillan, 1921.

(French tr.) *Neue Homilien des Makarius/Symeon* tr. V. Desprez. Sources chrétiennes 275. Paris, 1980.

Desprez, V. and Canévet, M., 'Macaire', *Dict. Sp.* 10 (1977), cols. 20–43.

Dörries, H., *Die Theologie des Makarios/Symeon*. Göttingen, 1978.

Tugwell, S., *Ways of Imperfection* (London, DLT, 1984), pp. 47–58.

Fourth-century monasticism produced two influential writers, Evagrius Ponticus (*c.* 345–99) in Egypt, and 'Macarius'. Though they are often contrasted, their interests overlap significantly. Both are concerned to internalize monasticism and to resist spiritual one-upmanship and complacency (Evagrius S ii; Macarius H 3.3; 17.13; GL p. 289); both stress humility and fraternal charity and service, particularly the service of teaching (Evagrius G 110, 136 etc.; O 40, 123f; Macarius B 4.11; 16.2),[1] though they are aware of the dangers involved in teaching (Evagrius O 25, A 'Vainglory' 9; Macarius C 10.2). Both agree that prayer is the paramount virtue (Evagrius O 150; Macarius H 3.3; GL pp. 268f, 287–9).

EVAGRIUS

Evagrius was born in Pontus, where he knew Basil and Gregory Nazianzen, whose disciple he claimed to be. He was ordained lector by Basil and deacon by Gregory, and accompanied Gregory to Constantinople in 380. A promising church career was cut short by an ill-advised love-affair, and he fled to Melania the Elder in Jerusalem. She eventually persuaded him to become a monk in Egypt. After two years in Nitria, he settled, *c.* 385, in Kellia, where he stayed until his death.

A letter written from Constantinople (B) already contains hints of his later doctrine, and shows him to be a man of daring intellect, more unreservedly Origenistic than any of the Cappadocians. Like Origen, he sees the Christian life as involving three essential ingredients, which he names *praktikē* (the cultivation of the virtues), *phusikē* (the contemplation of created beings) and *theologikē* (the knowledge of God) (B 4; P 1). His speculative interests can only have been encouraged by Melania, and in

---

[1] Contrast the Syriac Isaias XXV 64a ('Instructing your neighbour is the downfall of your soul'), and Theodore of Pherme, *Apophthegmata* 15, 20, 21, whose sentiments are echoed in less extreme form in other monastic texts.

Egypt he attached himself to the intellectualist monks, among whom he became a leader. But he also immersed himself in the ascetic traditions of the desert, and his most influential achievement was to provide a more theoretical account of these traditions. He was one of the shrewdest psychologists of antiquity. But his intellectual audacity led him beyond the bounds of orthodoxy, and he was condemned in 553. As a result, much of his writing was lost in the original Greek and is known only in Syriac translation. Many of his ascetic works survive in Greek under the name of Nilus, and in some cases the attribution to one author or the other is still uncertain.

His works consist chiefly of disconnected propositions (*kephalaia*) rather than systematic exposition. Combined with his avowed intention to veil his more advanced teaching (P Prol., *PG* 40.1285B), this procedure makes it hazardous to systematize his views, and his meaning is often obscure. He is clearest when dealing with *praktikē*, and it is this part of his doctrine which the monastic tradition accepted with least reserve (cf. Barsanuphius, *Letter* 602).

In the beginning, according to Evagrius, God created pure intellects, united with himself and with one another. They were endowed with free will and, through inattentiveness, they all turned away from God, except for the mind of Christ, which never fell from union with the Word. This initial movement broke their unity with God and with each other. To catch them as they fell, God created the bodily universe; those who fell furthest became demons, those who fell least became angels, those in between became human souls. All were given appropriate bodies, which were not a punishment but a means of healing ('Body is the friend of the soul', S xii.13). At the end, bodies and plurality will be abolished.[1]

Evagrius' whole spirituality is orientated towards the restoration of knowledge of God and unity. The seeds of good remain in fallen creatures; though they are capable of evil, there is nothing evil in their nature (K i.39; L 30, 45). Recovery begins with faith, which is present even in those who do not believe; faith, when activated, leads to fear of God, which leads to self-discipline and the attempt to practise the virtues. Full practice of the virtues leads to the overcoming of the passions (*apatheia*), resulting in charity, which is 'the door of knowledge' (P Prol., 81, 84), enabling the mind to proceed, through the understanding of bodily reality to the understanding of unbodily reality (including the mind itself), and from there to union with God (O 52, 132; K iii. 61).

Apatheia, for Evagrius, is neither the highest goal nor is it indefectible. It is present in part whenever we are not bothered by some particular

[1] See A. Guillaumont, *Les 'Kephalaia Gnostica' d'Evagre le Pontique* (Paris 1962), pp. 37–9, 103–17.

passion, and in full when we are bothered by no passions (P 60). But much the same temptations recur throughout our lives.

There are four sources of trouble: things, thoughts (*logismoi*), passions and demons. Demons orchestrate a whole campaign against us, using many wiles, which Evagrius exposes. They cannot see into our minds, but they are quick to observe our reactions (*PG* 79.1232B). They cannot constrain us to sin (P 80), and their power over our minds depends on ourselves. Similarly things only harm us because of our wrong attitudes to them (*PG* 79.1221C). The essential enemy is the passions, the sicknesses of the soul (P 55f; L 52). These are by definition disordered affections, and *apatheia* does not mean the suppression of any of the soul's powers, but their healthy functioning, so that we *desire* virtue, use the energy of *anger* to fight for it against all opposition, and apply our *reasoning power* to the contemplation of reality (P 86).

The passions are obviously stirred by things and people, so withdrawal from external situations which might tempt us is a useful preliminary (N 6; *PG* 79.1150). But the hermit who has so withdrawn is faced with what always was the essential struggle, the struggle with *thoughts*, because, strictly speaking, it is they that stir passions (P 48). All harmful thoughts spring from self-love (M¹, p. 379, no. 53), and they all involve a false notion of God (M¹, p. 379, no. 49). Evagrius isolates eight generic types of *logismos*, of which he gives colourful and perceptive descriptions: thoughts of gluttony, fornication, love of money, depression (*lupē*), anger, listlessness (*akēdia*), vainglory and pride (P 6ff; *PG* 79.1145ff). This analysis was taken over by Cassian and later adapted to produce the familiar seven deadly sins.

At first we fight these thoughts 'in the dark', resisting them as best we can (P 83). Evagrius indicates the standard ascetic precautions. He also provides an armoury of scriptural texts in his *Antirrhētikos* to be used against various thoughts. He recommends that, before praying against thoughts, we should address them angrily, because anger dispels all thoughts (P 24, 42; *PG* 79.1217D; M¹, p. 54, no. 24). But these practical remedies cannot produce a complete cure. We need also to understand the powers and workings of our soul (P 79; K ii.9; L 11, 25). Once we have a certain self-control, we should sometimes allow thoughts to linger for a while, without challenging them, so that we can learn more about them (P 36, 43, 50; *PG* 79.1209–12), and thereafter we fight with greater understanding (P 83).

Apatheia is shown in an ability to face things, memories and dreams, without being ruffled. And at this point the mind 'begins to see its own light' (P 64, 67; K v.15). The pure mind is 'the place of God' and it can be seen as 'rather like sapphire and the colour of the sky' (cf. Exod. 24.10;

PG 79.1221B). This vision of the mind's own luminosity probably does not mean any psychic experience of light; Evagrius is thinking more of the translucency of a mind which is undisturbed by passions (K v.39), enabling it to see things for what they are ('human' thinking) and then to probe the rationale (*logoi*) of things ('angelic' thinking) (G 107; *PG* 79.1209AB). From there it moves on to consider spiritual beings, which is the higher *phusikē*.

Three temptations are important at this level. First, vainglory, which preys on all our achievements and virtues (P 30f; *PG* 79.1160CD; 1217B). Then anger, which is the besetting temptation of contemplatives and which completely obscures the mind's light (P 24, 63; O 24; K iv.47; v.27; M¹, p. 56, no. 56; M², p. 201, no. 10). Thirdly, because the contemplation of things is, once we have tasted it, far more enjoyable than things themselves (K ii 10; L 53), there is the temptation to settle down there, instead of moving on towards God. Just because we have reached *apatheia*, we have not yet reached 'the place of prayer'; we may be investigating things or contemplating the rationale of things or enjoying the knowledge of spiritual beings, but all of these involve a diversification of the mind, if not also a shaping of the mind, and either way we shall be far from the simplicity and formlessness of God (O 56–8; *PG* 79.1228–9).

Prayer is the highest and most proper activity of the mind (O 35, 83f), but, paradoxically, it means, at its purest, 'the putting away of thoughts' (O 71). God has no shape or form or complexity, and the mind, to be united with him, must also shed shapes and forms (G 143; L 39; O 67ff, 114f). Demons will try to make us accept some visionary form as being God, but this is sheer vainglory (O 73f, 116). In pure prayer, the mind is illumined only by the light of the Holy Trinity (M¹, pp. 374, no. 4; 377, no. 27). This means that it has passed beyond the light of contemplation of bodily beings and their *logoi* and beyond the knowledge of spiritual beings, including itself. God is not in any ordinary sense an *object* of knowledge, he *is* 'substantive knowledge' (L 29; K iv.77, 87; v.55f). In the highest prayer there is no more consciousness of ourselves than there is when we are asleep (*PG* 12.1644).[1] God is not bounded by any definition or localization or particularization, so our knowledge of him too is unbounded in such a way that it can also be described as 'unbounded ignorance' (G 131; Ki.71; iii.63). This is perhaps why Evagrius uses the word 'prayer': all that is left to the formless mind is an intense yearning for God (O 53, 62, 119; K iv.50), which is, in a rarefied sense, a kind of petition. The whole spiritual life is directed towards this goal, and the

---

[1] For the ascription to Evagrius, see M. J. Rondeau, *Orientalia Christiana Periodica* 26 (1960), pp. 307–48.

whole strategy of the demons is designed to prevent us from getting there (O 50f; L 1, 17).

In spite of the condemnation of Evagrius' speculative adventures, he had a profound influence on Eastern and Western spirituality. His ascetic doctrine, through Cassian, Palladius and the *Historia Monachorum*, was diffused anonymously; his *Praktikos*, under his own name, and his *De Oratione*, under the name of Nilus, continued to be widely used. He was a major influence on Eastern writers like Diadochus and Maximus the Confessor, who transmitted much of his teaching to the Byzantine church.

MACARIUS

The writings ascribed to 'Macarius' have had a wide and lasting influence among Greeks, Syrians, Russians, Franciscans, Jesuits, Pietists, Methodists and even neo-Pentecostals. But there are considerable scholarly problems. Four collections of Macarian material survive in Greek, but the work of critical editing is far from complete and the study of the relationships between the different collections has hardly begun. The identity of the author is unknown, but it is safe to situate him between the mid-fourth and the mid-fifth centuries, within the monasticism of Mesopotamia or Asia Minor, probably within Basil's sphere of influence. Since the discovery that the condemned Messalian *Askētikon* is at least closely related to Macarius, there has been a tendency to regard Macarius as Messalian, and to identify him with a minor Messalian leader, Symeon (a few MSS identify the author as 'Symeon'), but this identification is doubtful, and H. Dörries has now argued that Macarius is, if anything, *anti*-Messalian, even if the Messalians did make use of him.[1]

Macarius' doctrine is based on a profound awareness of the effects of sin.

> The whole phenomenal world, from kings to paupers, is in a state of disturbance and confusion and strife, and none of them knows why, none of them realises that it is the evil which entered in through Adam's disobedience, the 'sting of death', showing itself in all these things. Sin, which thus sneaked in, is a rational power of Satan, a rational substance, and it sowed all these evils, working secretly in the inner man, in the mind, fighting by means of thoughts (H 15.49).

Macarius rejects the notion that baptism in principle rids us of sin (H 15.14); sin is far more radical and persistent than many people believe (H

---

[1] H. Dörries, *Die Theologie des Makarios/Symeon* (Göttingen 1978), pp. 12f. Other references in the text are to this extremely useful and well-documented study. For a different assessment of Messalianism, see above, pp. 138, 160.

45.1; 51.2). There can be no brisk 'On with the new man, off with the old!' (H 15.41). A long process of growth is required to bring us to perfection. Baptism gives us an 'image of perfection', but this has to mature slowly, just as a baby is, in one sense, fully formed, but still has to grow (B 43; GL, p. 236). The immediate result of baptism is that there are now two 'personae' at work in us (B 4.5; GL, p. 246). Sin and grace coexist in us (B 16). The important thing is that we should side with grace (H 4.1; GL, p. 245f). Even if sin still controls our actions and many of our thoughts, we can and must refuse to align ourselves with it (C 26.3). This means resisting as alien to us even the slightest stirring of disorder in our minds and wills; it is a mistake to disregard such things as 'only natural' (H 15.49; GL, p. 241; C 25.1). But the result of this endeavour is to learn that we cannot root out sin for ourselves; only God can do that (H 3.4). Therefore we must pray, persisting shamelessly like the woman pestering the unjust judge in the parable (H 1.12; 4.26f; C 16.7). And God will deliver us speedily, as he promised; if he seems to delay, we must realize that it is already a great grace to go on praying and struggling (B 2.4).

Fallen humanity is not only sinful, it is benighted (C 1.3; 18.1). The first grace is that of revelation: Christ enables us to see clearly what we are by embodying human perfection in himself, by teaching us in the Scriptures and by ordering our circumstances to reveal our own condition to ourselves (a process in which even our enemies help) (B 37.4f; 39.1–3; 54.2; H 51.2).

What we learn from this is an extremely high ideal of perfection. At times Macarius seems to imply that, by grace, we can attain to this ideal in this life, but what matters is that we should believe that God's commandments and promises are realistic, even if perfection comes only after this life (GL, p. 291; C 10.3). The reason for stressing how high the ideal is is to prevent complacency: however far we have got, there is still further to go (GL, p. 254; C 1.3; 7.6). Nothing less than complete integrity will suffice (C 1.2). Macarius says he has never met anyone who has achieved this (B 4.9).

Macarius lays stress on experience. But the primary experience is that of evil (Dörries, pp. 199ff). The desired experience of grace is the gradual cessation of evil, so that the practice of virtue, especially charity and prayer, becomes easy and natural. Virtue and the fruits of the Spirit should come to be as perceptible to us as sin is. Visions and such phenomena are valuable, but only if they help our quest for perfect charity (cf. Dörries, pp. 289–302).

Constant prayer is essential for all believers, and some people may devote themselves to it full-time. But Macarius seems to be thinking more of a battle in prayer than of contemplative peace (GL, p. 272;

Dörries, p. 267). And he warns that absorption in mystical joys may be a temptation against fraternal charity (Dörries, p. 297). And if praying people disdain or neglect the humble brethren who provide for their bodily needs, their prayer becomes devilish (GL, pp. 273ff).

In all eventualities, we should run to grace as a chick runs to its mother (B 3.6). It is the Holy Spirit, or grace, that is the essential maker of our progress. 'As a bee makes a honeycomb secretly in a sieve, so grace secretly makes love of itself in men's hearts, changing them from bitterness to sweetness, from roughness to smoothness' (H 16.7). But we also need to struggle, because this is the sign that we are serious in praying for grace; if we do not want virtues enough to fight for them, we shall be incapable of retaining them, even if we are given them (H 19.6). Neither good nor evil constrains us: they appeal to our free will (H 27.22). So the effort of our own will is necessary as well as our prayer.

4 The Origins of the Jesus Prayer: Diadochus, Gaza, Sinai

KALLISTOS WARE

Texts and Translations

Diadochus, *Hundred Gnostic Chapters*, Greek text and French tr. E. des Places, SC 5, 3rd edn, 1966; ET G. E. H. Palmer, P. Sherrard, K. Ware, *The Philokalia*, vol. i (London and Boston, Faber, 1979), pp. 252–96.

Barsanuphius and John, *Questions and Answers*, Greek text ed. Nicodemus of the Holy Mountain/S. Schoinas (Volos, 1960); critical edn and ET (incomplete) D. J. Chitty (PO xxxi, 3, 1966); French tr. L. Regnault and P. Lemaire (Solesmes, 1972).

Dorotheus, *Life of Dositheus*, Greek text and French tr. L. Regnault, SC 92 (1963), pp. 122–45.

The Life of Abba Philemon, Greek text in *Philokalia tōn ierōn nēptikōn*, vol. ii (Athens, 1958), pp. 241–52; ET *The Philokalia*, vol. ii (1981), pp. 344–57.

John Climacus, *The Ladder of Divine Ascent*, Greek text PG 88. 632–1208; ET C. Luibheid and N. Russell, with introduction by K. Ware. CWS 1983.

Hesychius of Sinai, *On Watchfulness and Holiness*, Greek text PG 93. 1480–1544; ET *The Philokalia*, vol. i, pp. 162–98.

Philotheus of Sinai, *Forty Texts on Watchfulness*, Greek text in *Philokalia tōn ierōn nēptikōn*, vol. ii, pp. 274–86; ET *The Philokalia*, vol. iii (1984), pp. 16–31.

Studies

The Jesus Prayer: I. Hausherr, (ET) *The Name of Jesus*, Cistercian Studies Series 44 (Kalamazoo, 1978); A Monk of the Eastern Church [L. Gillet], (ET)

The Prayer of Jesus (New York, 1967); P. Adnès, in *Dict. Sp.* 8. 1126–50; on monologic prayer, see L. Regnault, in *Irénikon*, 47 (1974), pp. 467–93; on the Coptic evidence, see A. Guillaumont, in *ECR*, 6 (1974), pp. 66–71.

Barsanuphius: D. J. Chitty, *The Desert a City* (Oxford, Blackwell, 1966), pp. 132–40.

Hesychius: J. Kirchmeyer, in *Le Millénaire du Mont Athos*, vol. i (Chevetogne, 1963), pp. 319–29.

Between the fifth and the eighth centuries a method of prayer emerged which has proved deeply influential in the Christian East: the remembrance or invocation of the name of Jesus, commonly termed the 'Jesus Prayer' or 'Prayer of Jesus'. This takes the basic form of a short sentence addressed to Jesus Christ and designed for frequent repetition. The standard phrasing of it runs, 'Lord Jesus Christ, Son of God, have mercy on me'; but there are many variations. It is, however, unusual in the Christian East to repeat the name 'Jesus' entirely on its own. Round the use of this brief 'arrow prayer' a Jesus-centred spirituality has gradually developed, in which four main elements can be distinguished:

1. Devotion to the Holy Name 'Jesus', which is felt to act in a semi-sacramental way as a source of power and grace.

2. The appeal for divine mercy, accompanied by a keen sense of compunction and inward grief (*penthos*).

3. The discipline of frequent repetition.

4. The quest for inner silence or stillness (*hēsuchia*), that is to say, for imageless, non-discursive prayer.

The last three of these elements can all be found in monastic sources from fourth-century Egypt (see 'The Desert Fathers', pp. 119–30; 'Evagrius', pp. 168–73). The *Apophthegmata* or *Sayings of the Desert Fathers* assign a central importance to the second element, *penthos*. 'This is a man's chief work,' says St Antony, 'always to blame himself for his sins in God's sight' (Alphabetical collection, Antony 4). When asked what he is doing in his cell, the monk can briefly reply, 'I am weeping for my sins' (Dioscorus 2); for 'the monk should always have *penthos* in his heart' (Poemen 26).

The third element, the use of short phrases frequently repeated, is also emphasized in the *Apophthegmata*. Mindful of Paul's injunction to 'pray without ceasing' (1 Thess. 5.17), the early monks strove at all times to preserve *mnēmē Theou*, the 'remembrance of God' or sense of the divine presence – while performing manual labour, when eating, even when talking with others or resting. Like St Basil (see p. 164), they looked on this *mnēmē* as the heart of the spiritual life. To assist them in maintaining the constant awareness of God, it was their practice to repeat aloud or inwardly a verse from Scripture, especially from the Psalms. Abba Lucius used the first verse of Psalm 51, 'Have mercy upon me, O God . . .' (*Apophthegmata*, Lucius 1); Abba Isaac, as reported by St John Cassian, recommended the continual recitation of Psalm 70.1, 'O God, come to my aid; O Lord, make haste to help me' (*Conferences*, x.10). In other cases the phrase could be of a monk's own devising. Abba Apollo, for example, repeated the words, 'As man, I have sinned; as God, forgive' (*Apophthegmata*, Apollo 2): here the second element, sorrow for sin, is very marked. From the time of John Climacus (seventh century), the repetition of short phrases in this manner has been known as 'monologic prayer', that is, prayer of a single *logos*, a single word or phrase. While the name of Jesus figures occasionally in the 'monologic prayers' employed by the fourth-century desert fathers, it enjoys no special prominence. A wide variety of formulae prevails, and there is as yet no trace of a spirituality centred particularly upon the Holy Name. The early Egyptian desert, then, provides evidence for the second and third of our four elements, but not for the first.

There is evidence in early monastic Egypt also for the fourth element, non-discursive prayer, if not among the Coptic monks, then at any rate in the writings of Evagrius. Prayer, so he teaches, is 'the putting away of thoughts' (*On Prayer*, 71) – not of sinful and impassioned thoughts only but, so far as possible, of *all* thoughts: the intellect (*nous*) is to become simple and 'naked', free from shape or form, wholly unified, transcending the division between subject and object. But, although commending the use of 'brief but intense prayer' (*On Prayer*, 98), and also in the *Antirrhē-tikos* the repetition of verses from the Psalms as a weapon against the demons, Evagrius does not link this specifically with the 'putting away of thoughts'. Thus the fourth element, non-discursive or 'apophatic' prayer, is not as yet explicitly connected with the third, the discipline of repetition. Evagrius does not attach any special significance to the name of Jesus.

The real beginnings of a distinctive spirituality of the Jesus Prayer must therefore be sought in the fifth rather than the fourth century. St Nilus of Ancyra (d. *c.* 430), in the course of his voluminous correspondence,[1] advocates the 'invocation' or 'remembrance' of the name of Jesus, urging that this should be so far as possible continuous (*Letters*, ii.140, 214; iii.273, 278); but these are only brief allusions made in passing. Far more important in the history of the Jesus Prayer is St

[1] There are problems of authenticity: see A. Cameron, in *Greek, Roman and Byzantine Studies* xvii (1976), pp. 181–96.

Diadochus, Bishop of Photice in northern Greece (second half of the fifth century). He acts as a decisive 'catalyst': although the second element, *penthos*, is not particularly prominent in his teaching, he establishes an explicit connection between the other three elements, treating the constant repetition of the name of Jesus precisely as a means of entry into non-discursive, imageless prayer. Diadochus is influenced both by Evagrius and by the Macarian Homilies – the first in a long series of Eastern Christian writers to effect a synthesis between these two complementary 'currents'. From Evagrius he inherits, among other things, an understanding of prayer as the 'putting away of thoughts'; from the *Homilies* he derives an 'affective' emphasis upon the spiritual senses, upon feelings and conscious experience, while at the same time he is firmly opposed to the more extreme Messalian views.

In consequence of the fall, so Diadochus teaches, the 'perception' of the human soul has become divided into two contrary tendencies (*Chapters* 24–5), and this division has affected both the will (78) and the memory (88). At the same time the intellect (*nous*) suffers from restlessness, 'requiring of us imperatively some task that will satisfy its need for activity' (59). How are we to unify our inner faculties and bring them to stillness, while at the same time providing the ever-active intellect with an appropriate occupation? The will, he answers, is to be unified through the practice of the 'active life' (in the Evagrian sense); the memory, through the 'remembrance' (97) or 'invocation' (85) of Jesus, which will satisfy the intellect's 'need for activity' while overcoming its fragmentation. 'We should give it nothing but the prayer *Lord Jesus* . . . Let the intellect continually concentrate on this phrase within its inner shrine with such intensity that it is not turned away to any mental images' (59). Here Diadochus clearly connects the invocation of Jesus with the attainment of imageless prayer. He seems to envisage, not merely the 'remembrance' or 'recollection' of Jesus in a diffused sense, as some have held, but an actual invocation through a specific formula of prayer. Perhaps other words also followed the phrase *Lord Jesus*, but if so he has not told us what they were.

Significantly Diadochus says '*nothing* but the prayer *Lord Jesus*'. The diversity of monologic formulae, as found in fourth-century Egypt, is now giving place to a greater uniformity. The repetition needs to be unvarying, so as to bring the intellect from fragmentation to unity, from a diversity of thoughts and images to a state of single-pointed concentration. While itself an invocation in words, by virtue of its brevity and simplicity the prayer *Lord Jesus* enables us to reach out beyond language into silence, beyond discursive thinking into intuitive awareness. Through habitual use, Diadochus states, the prayer becomes ever more spontaneous and self-acting, an organic part of us, as with a child instinctively 'calling for his father even when asleep' (61). For Diadochus, indeed, this is more than a mere analogy, for he sees the Jesus Prayer as an eminently effective weapon against the demons when we are on the threshold between waking and sleeping (31). The invocation of Jesus leads, so he teaches, to a vision of the 'light of the intellect' and at the same time to a feeling of 'warmth in the heart' (59). Here his double debt to Evagrius and the Macarian *Homilies* is evident: the intellect's vision of its own light is a characteristically Evagrian theme (see *Praktikos* 64), while his words about the feeling of warmth recall the 'affective' spirit of the *Homilies* with their imagery of fire.

Diadochus, then, combines the Evagrian insistence upon 'pure' or non-discursive prayer with the practice of *monologia* or frequent repetition, as used by the desert fathers; and at the same time he treats the name of Jesus as the focal point of this repetition. In this way he takes a decisive step forward by proposing a practical method for attaining imageless prayer, which is something that Evagrius himself had failed to do; and he endows this method with a powerful force of attraction by centering it upon the Holy Name.

In the early part of the following century the tradition of the Jesus Prayer is continued by St Barsanuphius and St John, two hermits living close to a monastery outside Gaza, who gave spiritual guidance both to the monks of the monastery and to a wide circle of outside visitors, clerical and lay. In the sources they are described respectively as 'the Great Old Man' and 'the Other Old Man'. Since they refused to meet anyone except the abbot of the monastery, their disciple Seridus, all questions had to be submitted in writing, and their answers were likewise given in writing. Nearly 850 of these questions and answers survive, and there is no other patristic source providing such vivid, first-hand insight into the ministry of spiritual direction in the early Church.

The two Old Men of Gaza are openly hostile to Origen and Evagrius (*Questions and Answers* 600–7).[1] They stand, not in the speculative, platonizing line of Alexandria but in the pragmatic tradition of the *Apophthegmata*. They have many practical suggestions to make concerning humility, obedience and the excision of self-will. While urging the need to watch over the thoughts (*logismoi*), they do not envisage prayer as imageless and non-discursive. For them, as for the desert fathers, prayer and the remembrance of God should be so far as possible unceasing, and in this connection they recommend the constant repetition of short phrases. But, unlike Diadochus with his insistence upon uniformity,

---

[1] References are given according to the Chitty/Regnault numbering (somewhat different from the Nicodemus/Schoinas enumeration).

Barsanuphius and John suggest a variety of formulae: among others, 'Lord Jesus Christ, have mercy on me' (175, 446) – this is close to what was termed above the 'standard phrasing'; 'Jesus, help me' (39, 268); 'Master Jesus, protect me and help my weakness' (659); 'Lord Jesus Christ, save me from shameful passions' (255). Although also commending short prayers without the word 'Jesus', in general they attach paramount value to the Holy Name. Even when not referring specifically to monologic prayer, their letters are full of remarks such as 'Cry out to Jesus' (148), 'Run to Jesus' (256), 'Let us awaken Jesus' (182).

The chief disciple of Barsanuphius and John is Dorotheus, who around 540 founded his own monastery not far from Gaza. In his main work, the *Instructions* – widely read in the West, and used in particular by the early Jesuits – he adopts a practical approach similar to that of his two teachers, attaching central importance to humility, but he is more open to Evagrian influence than they are. The invocation of Jesus is not mentioned in the *Instructions*, but it plays a notable role in one of Dorotheus' other works, the *Life of Dositheus*. Coming as a boy to the monastery of Abba Seridus, Dositheus is entrusted to Dorotheus' care, and he is taught to preserve the 'remembrance of God' by saying continually 'Lord Jesus Christ, have mercy on me', and then at intervals 'Son of God, help me' (10). Here, as in Barsanuphius and John, more than one formula is proposed; indeed, the second phrase does not in fact include the name of Jesus. When Dositheus falls gravely ill, Dorotheus tells him to keep saying the Prayer as long as he can. But when he finally grows too weak, Dorotheus says: 'Then let the Prayer go; just remember God and think that he is in front of you' (10). Thus the actual saying of the Prayer, however important, is only a means to an end: what really matters is the unceasing remembrance of God. Continual prayer does not mean merely the continual saying of prayers; it may also take the form of an implicit state rather than a series of outward acts.

The standard form of the Jesus Prayer, 'Lord Jesus Christ, Son of God, have mercy on me' – combining the two formulae in the *Life of Dositheus* – is first found in the *Life of Abba Philemon*. He was an Egyptian monk, living perhaps in the sixth century, but possibly one or two centuries later than this. In his spiritual teaching Philemon is indebted to both Evagrius and the *Apophthegmata*, but his chief master is Diadochus. Yet he is far less definite than either Evagrius or Diadochus about the need for 'pure', non-discursive prayer. He places strong emphasis on inward grief (*penthos*) and on stillness (*hēsuchia*). 'Inner work' or 'secret meditation' are to be continual, a point to which he attaches the utmost importance: here, as so often, the influence of 1 Thess. 5.17 is evident. The Jesus Prayer is seen as a way of maintaining this continual remembrance: 'Without interruption, whether asleep or awake, eating, drinking, or in company, let your heart inwardly and mentally at times be meditating on the Psalms, at other times be repeating the prayer, "Lord Jesus Christ, Son of God, have mercy on me"' (ET, p. 348). As this passage makes clear, Philemon is less strict than Diadochus in requiring uniformity, for the use of the Jesus Prayer is to be combined with meditation on the Psalms. Alongside the standard formula, as given above, Philemon also commends the shorter version found in Barsanuphius and Dorotheus, 'Lord Jesus Christ, have mercy on me', and sometimes he simply repeats 'Lord, have mercy'.

The Jesus Prayer is also recommended by three writers associated with Sinai: St John Climacus (seventh century) and his two followers St Hesychius (?eighth–ninth century) and St Philotheus (?ninth–tenth century). Some modern specialists regard the Jesus Prayer as distinctively an expression of what they term 'Sinaite spirituality', but this is misleading. As we have seen, the earliest evidence of the Prayer's use comes from elsewhere; Sinai plays the role of transmitting rather than originating. None of the three Sinaite authors specifies a precise formula or formulae for use when saying the Prayer.

Climacus occupies in ascetic theology a position similar to that occupied in Christology by his contemporary Maximus the Confessor (see pp. 190–5). Both are synthesizers, drawing together and creatively integrating the disparate strands in previous tradition. Climacus' work, *The Ladder of Divine Ascent*, forms in this way a first, and remarkably successful, attempt to produce a 'directory' of monastic spirituality, and as such it still remains widely popular. While written initially for monks – it is normally read in monasteries every year during Lent – it is also valued by many Orthodox lay people. Climacus draws heavily upon the *Apophthegmata* and at the same time, like Diadochus, he combines the Evagrian and Macarian 'currents'. From Evagrius he derives much of his technical vocabulary and his practical teaching, while discarding the speculative, Origenist aspect of Evagrianism. He does not quote the Macarian *Homilies* explicitly, but he is close to them in his repeated emphasis upon direct personal experience. Most of all he is indebted to the Gaza 'school' – to Barsanuphius, John and Dorotheus – although never mentioning them by name. There are no clear traces of any influence from Dionysius.

Most of the *Ladder* is concerned with the 'active' life – with the struggle against the passions and with the acquisition of such primary virtues as obedience, humility and discernment (*diakrisis*). There is an important section, Step 7, on 'joy-creating sorrow' and the gift of tears, which is seen as renewing the grace of baptism. Tears are not only an expression of penitence, but a loving response to divine forgiveness: they are 'sweet' as well as 'bitter'. 'Dispassion' (*apatheia*) is closely linked with love. To this last Climacus devotes the final section, Step 30, and in language that recalls Maximus he extols it as the ultimate end of all spiritual striving. The last words of the *Ladder* are from 1 Cor. 13.13: 'Love is the greatest of them all'.

In his teaching on prayer, Climacus underlines the value of using few words: 'Pray in all simplicity. The publican and the prodigal son were reconciled to God by a single utterance.' Our aim should be *monologia*, brevity, not *polulogia*, garrulousness (Step 28 [1129D, 1132AB]; ET, pp. 275–6). He makes only three allusions to the Jesus Prayer in the *Ladder*, and so this cannot be considered a central theme of the work as a whole; but these three references have proved remarkably influential. He is the first Greek writer to use the actual phrase 'Jesus Prayer' (*Iēsou euchē*); he terms it 'monologic' (*monologistos*), and like Diadochus he advises its use as we drop off to sleep (Step 15 [889D], p. 178). He sees it as an effectual weapon against the demons: 'Flog your enemies with the name of Jesus' (Step 21 [945C], p. 200). Most significantly of all, he connects the Prayer with stillness (*hēsuchia*): 'Stillness is the putting away of thoughts . . . Stillness is unceasingly to worship God and wait on him. Let the remembrance of Jesus be united with your breathing. Then you will appreciate the value of stillness' (Step 27 [1112A–C], pp. 269–70). Note the clear insistence here upon continuity: prayer is to be as constant as breathing. Note also the way in which Climacus adapts Evagrius' phrase, 'Prayer is the putting away of thoughts' (*On Prayer*, 71): for the author of the *Ladder*, as for Diadochus, the invocation of the Holy Name is a means of entry into the inner silence of the heart, a way of attaining non-discursive prayer.

Whereas Climacus refers only occasionally to the Jesus Prayer, Hesychius makes it the central and recurrent theme throughout his work *On Watchfulness and Holiness*. The term 'watchfulness' (in Greek, *nēpsis*: sometimes rendered 'sobriety') he understands in a wide-ranging sense: it means vigilance, attentiveness, keeping guard over the thoughts and the heart, but also embraces the whole practice of the virtues (1–6).[1] The chief way of maintaining watchfulness is to call upon Jesus: 'Attentiveness is the heart's stillness (*hēsuchia*), unbroken by any thought. In this stillness the heart breathes and invokes, endlessly and without ceasing, only Jesus Christ the Son of God' (5). In his teaching on the Jesus Prayer – a phrase that he frequently employs – Hesychius stresses two things in particular. So far as possible, the invocation is to be continual, and it is to be without thoughts or images: for him, as for Diadochus and Climacus,

[1] References follow the *Philokalia* numbering; *PG* follows a different system.

it is a path of ascent to 'pure' prayer in the Evagrian sense. Hesychius writes of the Jesus Prayer in an outstandingly attractive manner, stressing the sense of joy, sweetness and light that it brings to the heart: 'The more the rain falls on the earth, the softer it makes it; similarly, the more we call upon Christ's Holy Name, the greater the rejoicing and exultation that it brings to the earth of our heart' (41). There is much in Hesychius that recalls the fervent devotion to the name of Jesus expressed by Western medieval writers such as St Bernard of Clairvaux (see pp. 287–8) or Richard Rolle of Hampole (see pp. 330–2).

Philotheus follows closely in the steps of his Sinaite predecessors, seeing the Jesus Prayer as a means of 'gathering together' the fragmented self: 'Through remembrance of Jesus Christ concentrate your scattered intellect' (*Texts on Watchfulness*, 27). This 'remembrance' leads to a vision of light in the heart: 'Invoked in prayer, Jesus draws near and fills the heart with light' (29); 'at every hour and moment let us guard the heart with all diligence from thoughts that obscure the soul's mirror; for in that mirror Jesus Christ, the wisdom and power of God the Father, is delineated and luminously reflected' (23). The Greek word for 'luminously reflected' is *phōteinographeisthai*, literally 'photographed': the pure soul is a photographic plate, on which is marked the divine light of Christ. Here Philotheus points forward to the 'light mysticism' of St Symeon the New Theologian and St Gregory Palamas.

All three Sinaite authors link the invocation of Jesus with the breathing: 'Let the remembrance of Jesus be united with your breathing' (Climacus, Step 27); 'Let the Jesus Prayer cleave to your breathing' (Hesychius, 182; cf. 5, 170, 187, 189); 'We must always breathe God' (Philotheus, 30). Is such language merely metaphorical, or does it point to a specific technique whereby the recitation of the Jesus Prayer was co-ordinated with the rhythm of the breathing? It is hard to say. There are passages in the Coptic Macarian cycle (?seventh–eighth century) which indicate more than a mere analogy, clearly implying some kind of breathing technique. But in the Greek tradition the first unambiguous references to such a technique are to be found only in the thirteenth century, in pseudo-Symeon and Nicephorus the Hesychast (see pp. 244–5).

Between the fifth and the eighth centuries, then, the Jesus Prayer emerged in the Christian East as a recognized spiritual 'way'. By modern Western writers it is sometimes termed a 'Christian mantra', but this could give rise to confusion. The Jesus Prayer is not simply a rhythmic incantation, but an invocation addressed directly to the person of Jesus Christ, and it presupposes conscious, active faith in him as only-begotten Son of God and unique Saviour. It is not, however, a form of discursive meditation upon particular incidents in Christ's life, but has as its aim to bring us to the level of *hēsuchia* or stillness – to a state of intuitive, non-discursive awareness in which we no longer form pictures in our mind's eye or analyse concepts with our reasoning brain, but feel and know the Lord's immediate presence in a direct personal encounter. 'Prayer is the communion of the intellect with God', states Evagrius. 'What state, then, does the intellect need so that it can reach out to its Lord without deflection and commune with him without intermediary?' (*On Prayer*, 3). The Jesus Prayer seeks to achieve precisely that: to commune with the Lord Jesus face to face *without intermediary*.

The references to the Jesus Prayer in the early period, while influential upon later Byzantine spirituality, are scattered and relatively infrequent. There is no reason to believe that its use at this time was universal or even widespread. It is nowhere mentioned by Dionysius the Areopagite, Maximus the Confessor or Isaac of Nineveh, nor during the eleventh century in the authentic writings of Symeon the New Theologian or in the vast anthology known as Evergetinos. It is not until the fourteenth century that its employment in the Byzantine and Slav world becomes frequent, and even then it is largely restricted to certain monastic centres. Only in our present twentieth century has it come to be adopted on a large scale by Orthodox lay people (see p. 272). Indeed, allowing for its contemporary popularity among Western Christians as well as Orthodox, it can be claimed with confidence that never before has the Jesus Prayer been practised and loved as much as it is today.

5 Denys the Areopagite

ANDREW LOUTH

Texts and Translations

PG, vols 3–4.
Celestial Hierarchy, in SC 58 bis (also good bibliography).
French trans., M. de Gandillac, *Oeuvres complètes du Pseudo-Denys l'Aréopagite*. Paris, 1943, reprinted 1980.

Studies

von Balthasar, H. U., *Herrlichkeit* II/1 (Einsiedeln, 1962), pp. 147–214 [ET pp. 144–210].
von Ivánka, E., *Plato Christianus* (Einsiedeln, 1964), pp. 225–89.
Roques, R., 'Contemplation' and 'Denys', in *Dict. Sp.*, 2. 1777–87, 1885–1911; 3. 244–86.

Roques, R., *L'Univers dionysien*. Paris, 1954.
Rorem, P., *Biblical and Liturgical Symbols within the Pseudo-Dionysian Synthesis*. Toronto, 1984.
Sheldon-Williams, I. P., in Armstrong, pp. 457–72.
Völker, W., *Kontemplation und Ekstase bei ps.-Dionysius Areopagita*. Wiesbaden, 1958.

Denys (or Dionysius) the Areopagite is a unique case in the history of theology: one who exercised a vast influence over succeeding generations, despite (or because of) his pseudonymity. The works attributed to him – the *Divine Names* (abbreviated as DN), the *Mystical Theology* (MT), the *Celestial Hierarchy* (CH) and the *Ecclesiastical Hierarchy* (EH), and ten letters – were first brought on to the theological scene in the sixth century by Monopyhysite theologians to support their case against the Orthodox. Claiming to come from the first century, from the Denys converted by St Paul's speech on the Areopagus, they were quickly rejected by the Orthodox on the grounds that the writings of such a supposed companion of the apostles were unknown to Athanasius, Cyril, or indeed any of the Fathers. But almost as quickly their spiritual power was felt by the Orthodox, and by the next century his authority was accepted both in the West and in the East, Maximus the Confessor (see pp. 190–5) playing an important part in their acceptance. The Areopagitical writings have strong affinities with the Neoplatonism of Proclus (410–85, see pp. 99–101) – though such is the nature of late Neoplatonism and our knowledge of it that it cannot be ruled out that Denys and Proclus depend on some common source – and would not be out of place in the Monophysite circles where they were first cited (though there is nothing unequivocally Monophysite about their content), so that it seems reasonable to suppose that they belong to the late fifth century and come from a Syrian and Monophysite background.

The affinities with Proclus are manifest in the very cumbersome and overloaded language, the metaphysics with the notion of a God 'beyond being', all of whose attributes are 'transcendent' (so that the prefix *hyper* is much used) and the threefold analysis of existence into Being, Life and Intelligence, and the idea of a threefold movement from rest (*monē*) in God, out in procession (*proodos*) and back in return (*epistrophē*). In fact in Denys, as in Proclus, the tendency to see triads everywhere is somewhat overwhelming. Another affinity is seen in the interest in, and use of the language of, *theourgia*: for Proclus a kind of magic that helps the soul on its way to God – indispensable as he regards theurgical power as 'better than any human wisdom or knowledge'; in Denys the language of theurgy is applied to the Christian sacraments.

Denys' picture of reality recalls much that we find in Proclus. He has three levels of reality: God, the angelic (or celestial) hierarchy, and the ecclesiastical hierarchy, in descending order. Each level is triadic. God (or the Thearchy, as he habitually calls him) is the Blessed Trinity of Father, Son and Holy Spirit. The angelic hierarchy consists of three ranks, each containing three orders of beings: the first rank consists of seraphim, cherubim and thrones; the middle rank of dominations, powers and authorities; the lowest of principalities, archangels and angels. The ecclesiastical hierarchy (itself seen as being midway between the 'legal' hierarchy of the Old Testament and the celestial hierarchy) consists again of three ranks of three: first the rank of the mysteries into which we are initiated – baptism, the Eucharist or synaxis, and the mystery of oil; secondly the rank of those who perform the mysteries – the bishops (or hierarchs), the priests, and the deacons or ministers; and thirdly the rank of those who are being initiated – the monks, the laity (called the contemplative order), and the lowest rank of those not yet initiated, or who have spoilt their initiation – the catechumens, the penitents and the possessed.

Hierarchy is defined by Denys as a 'sacred order and knowledge and activity which is being assimilated as much as possible to likeness with God and, in response to the illuminations that are given it from God, raises itself to the imitation of him in its own measure' (CH III.1: 164D). The qualifications, 'as much as possible' and 'in its own measure' (reminiscent of Plato's *kata to dunaton*) have a precise significance here, for they refer to the way in which each being is to fulfil its own role in the hierarchy as perfectly as possible. The hierarchies are static: one 'ascends' to God by perfecting one's role in them, not by climbing up them. The movement within the hierarchies – from priest to bishop, for example – is not a movement towards God except in so far as it is the fulfilment of one's vocation. It is, for Denys, the monks, on the lowest rank of the ecclesiastical hierarchy, who symbolize the 'transcendence of all division in a Godlike unity and the perfection of the love of God' – presumably the aim of all.

How this process of 'assimilation to likeness with God' or deification (*theōsis*) or union (*henōsis*) is effected is explained by what Denys calls 'theology'. Here too there is a triad – symbolic, cataphatic, apophatic – and to explain it we must introduce another triad, that of purification, illumination and perfection or union (*katharsis, phōtismos, teleiōsis* or *henōsis*). The latter triad was destined to become almost canonical in the language of mysticism, and though it has antecedents, this precise form is due to Denys. *All* engagement with God has this threefold character: purification of all that hinders our approach to God, the gift of illumination coming from God, and then as we are assimilated to this, union with

God. The three theologies are the three ways in which our union with God is furthered, for *theologia* has for Denys its full patristic sense, not so much knowledge about God, as knowledge of God through communion with him and union with him, knowing by 'being known'. The three theologies may be regarded as corresponding to the fundamental metaphysical triad we have already mentioned – that of rest, procession and return – apophatic theology to rest, God in himself; symbolic theology to procession, God's movement outwards in creation and care for his creation; cataphatic theology to our return to God in loving response to his love.

Symbolic theology corresponds to procession, emanation: that means that symbolic theology is concerned with the 'conversion of what is taken from the realm of the senses to the service of the divine' (MT III), that is with seeing God in material things, and with seeing how material things bear God, either by a natural likeness, or by their inspired use as metaphor of God in the sacred Scriptures, or (most importantly) by their use in the sacraments of the Church. Symbolic theology then yields a vision of the world as bearing God to us: by sensitive attunement to symbolic reality we can see the world as full of God. By the 'world' Denys means, on the one hand, the natural world, and, on the other, the use of the material order in the sacraments of the Church: he has nothing to say about society and the political order; strangely, for one who seems to belong so much to the Byzantine world, he is oblivious of the Emperor. In his exposition of the various sacramental rites in his *Ecclesiastical Hierarchy* Denys moves from an account of those involved, through an account of the rite itself, to a 'contemplation' (*theōria*) of its significance. For this Denys has been accused of reducing the whole sacramental life of the Church to a system for individual enlightenment. But this seems to overlook two things: first, that the sacraments are *theourgia* as well as *theōria*, to use Denys' terms – they convey grace as well as disclosing to us deeper reality; and secondly, that *theōria* need not have individualistic overtones read into it. Denys sees the hierarchies as a *society*, mutually supporting and supported, albeit a sacral society, and the sacraments are symbolic dramas, re-enacting the events of our redemption, in which all participate. (To participate by *beholding* only seems a shortcoming to the busy Western mind.) How seriously symbolic theology takes the material order is seen in the 'contemplation' concerning the order of the laity, which discusses the burial rites: 'thearchic purification' is given both to the soul and to the body, to the soul in pure contemplation, and to the body by holy anointing, whereby the whole man is sanctified and the most complete resurrection announced (EH VII.iii.9: 565BC). But Denys emphasizes too that symbolic theology leads us beyond itself:

distinguishing between 'like' and 'unlike symbols' (symbols that resemble what they symbolize and those that do not), Denys expresses his preference for 'unlike symbols' which force the soul to rise above the symbols to what is symbolized by them.

If symbolic theology is the theology of procession, cataphatic theology is the theology of return: in cataphatic theology we seek to return our concepts to God by ascribing to God what he has revealed of himself. Denys puts this more precisely by saying that in cataphatic theology we celebrate (*humnein*) the nature of God that is revealed in his movement towards us in creation and redemption: it is concerned with the perfecting of our praise of God. The treatise on the *Divine Names* is devoted to this subject: after discussing the terms we use to praise the Triune Majesty of God, Denys moves on to consider the attributes of God, beginning with his goodness and ending with his unity. The order of the attributes thus discussed and the nature of the discussion owes a good deal to Denys' Neoplatonic background; indeed the first example of such a discussion of the divine attributes as the *Divine Names* is found in Proclus, in the first book of his *Platonic Theology*. Cataphatic theology then concerns the terms we use, the affirmations we make, in our praise of God: but throughout the *Divine Names* we are constantly reminded that our affirmations fall short of God, that none of our concepts can reach him who is unknowable, and this leads to the realization that 'the most divine knowledge of God' is 'that he is known through unknowing . . . when the understanding withdraws from all, and abandons itself, and is united with the dazzling rays' (DN VII.3: 872AB).

Both symbolic and cataphatic theology then point beyond themselves to a state where symbols and concepts are transcended and God is known by unknowing. This is apophatic theology, the theology of rest, the subject of the *Mystical Theology*. Here Denys draws on the apophatic tradition already developed in Philo (see pp. 94–6) and Gregory of Nyssa (see pp. 166–8); indeed he seems to be directly indebted to Gregory, for in his account of Moses' ascent into the darkness where God is (in MT 1.3) he uses language which presumes knowledge of Gregory's interpretation of this episode. In the darkness the intellect passes beyond any active knowledge, whether from the senses or by concepts, and is reduced to 'complete speechlessness'; 'united in his highest part in passivity (*anenergēsia*) with him who is completely unknowable, he knows by not knowing in a manner that transcends understanding' (MT I.3: 1001A). This activity of negating is partly something we do – Denys uses Plotinus' analogy of the way a sculptor cuts away in order to reveal a hidden beauty (MT II: 1025B; cf. *Enn.* I.6.9.6ff) – but more deeply, in the darkness of unknowing, the soul submits to God and, as Denys says of his master Hierotheus, 'suffers' divine things and 'through sympathy with them is perfected to an untaught and hidden faith concerning them and union with them' (DN II.9: 648B). This state of utter passivity is sometimes expressed by speaking of a 'pure and absolute ecstasy' in which the intellect goes out of itself and is united to 'the ray of Divine Darkness that is beyond being'. It is not however the negative side of ecstasy that Denys stresses, but its positive aspect as an ecstasy of love, as union and deification. Love (*erōs* or *agapē*) is 'a power that unites and binds together and effects an indissoluble fusion in the beautiful and the good' (DN IV.12: 709C) and is ecstatic in that 'those who are possessed by this love belong not to themselves, but to the objects of their longing' (ibid.: 712A). In its ecstasy the soul meets God's own ecstatic love for his creation, for Denys asserts as something amazing but true that 'the Source of all things himself, in his wonderful and good love for all things, through the excess of his loving goodness, is carried outside himself, in his providential care for all that is, so enchanted is he in goodness and love and longing' (DN IV.13: 712AB). Even here where Denys reveals his deepest inspiration to be the Christian doctrine that God is love, there is manifest the influence of Proclus, for the language of 'providential care' recalls Proclus' idea of God's 'providential love' (*erōs pronoētikos*). Denys' fusion of Christianity and Neoplatonism is no cobbling together betraying both, but a union of their deepest concerns. Nor are the three 'theologies', the three ways to communion with God and union with him, potentially at odds with one another, for they are *all* rooted in Denys' conviction that the Christian God who creates *ex nihilo* is of a totally different order of reality from his creatures and thus unknowable. And since he is unknowable, he 'is known in all things, and apart from all things . . . Therefore everything may be ascribed to him at one and the same time, and yet he is none of these things' (DN VII.3: 872A; V.8: 824B).

Such is Dionysian spirituality: a spirituality deeply sensitive to the manifold variety of God's manifestation of his inexhaustible being in creation and redemption, and at the same time a spirituality that longs to encounter God in himself in the mysterious darkness of unknowing. It was destined to have a profound influence in both East and West, and if in the East the balance is better preserved, in the West it was a constant source of fresh inspiration.

6 Maximus the Confessor

ANDREW LOUTH

Texts and translations

Text of C by A. Ceresa-Gastaldo (Rome 1963); trans. (together with LA and good intro. and notes) by P. Sherwood (ACW XXI) and (together with TE and PN) in *The Philokalia*, tr. and ed. G. E. H. Palmer, P. Sherrard and K. T. Ware, vol. II (London and Boston, Faber, 1981).
Maximus the Confessor, *Selected Writings*, tr. G. C. Barthold. CWS 1985 (contains C, PN, TE and M).

The abbreviations are explained in the course of this chapter.

Studies

von Balthasar, H. U., *Kosmische Liturgie*. Einsiedeln, 2nd edn, 1961 with trans. of M and C.
von Balthasar, H. U., (French trans.) *Liturgie cosmique*. Paris, 1947.
Garrigues, J. M., *Maxime le Confesseur*. Paris, 1976.
Hausherr, I., *Philautie*. Rome, 1952.
Léthel, F.-M., *Théologie de l'agonie du Christ*. Paris, 1979.
Riou, A., *Le monde et l'église*. Paris, 1973, with trans. of PN and the first century of TE.
Thunberg, L., *Microcosm and Mediator*. Lund, 1965.

For further bibliographies, see Garrigues, Riou, Thunberg.

Maximus the Confessor is one of the most important and influential theologians of the late patristic period. He represents the period of consolidation in the seventh century, when in the East the wisdom of the earlier patristic period, both in dogmatic theology and in spirituality, was being drawn into an impressive synthesis. Maximus' contribution to both dogmatic development and spirituality was profound: as a theologian he stood out, almost alone, against the threat of Monothelitism, and a measure of his importance as a spiritual writer can be seen in his being assigned more space than anyone else in the *Philokalia* of St Nicodemus of the Holy Mountain and St Macarius of Corinth (163 pages out of 1,206 in the *editio princeps*: most of the second volume of the English translation).

Born in 580, Maximus received his education during the years when Gregory the Great was Pope. After a good education, including instruction in philosophy – Plato and Aristotle and their (largely Neoplatonic) commentators – he entered the imperial service, becoming first secretary to the Emperor Heraclius. Probably about 613–14 Maximus withdrew from the world and became a monk at the monastery of Chrysopolis on the Asiatic shore across from Constantinople. About ten years later he left his first monastery for that of St George at Cyzicus. In 626 with the Persian advance he fled first to Crete and then to Africa, where he stayed for many years. Maximus played a leading role in opposing the heresies of Monoenergism and Monothelitism. In 645 he went to Rome and had an important part in the Lateran Council of 649 which condemned Monothelitism. In 653 he was arrested by the imperial authorities for his continued opposition to the heresy, was finally condemned in 662 at Constantinople, after which he was flogged, his tongue plucked out and his right hand cut off. He died on 13th August 662, an exile in the Caucasus. Within twenty years he was vindicated: at the Sixth Ecumenical Council held at Constantinople in 681.

Maximus' writings are somewhat unsystematic, consisting of a large number of responses to particular questions raised about difficulties in Scripture or (more usually) in the Fathers, especially Gregory of Nazianzus and Denys the Areopagite, or problems on particular dogmatic questions. Writings of a more directly spiritual nature are his book on the *Ascetic Life* (abbreviated as LA), his *Centuries on Charity* (C), his *Centuries on Theology and the Incarnation* (TE), a short *Exposition of the Lord's Prayer* (PN) and an important commentary on the Liturgy, the *Mystagōgia* (M). Despite the unsystematic nature of his writings, Maximus' vision is a highly successful attempt at a synthesis drawing together the most important strands in late patristic thought – the Origenist tradition, which continued to exercise a powerful attraction especially through Evagrius (see pp. 168–73) and his followers, and the relatively new tradition stemming from Denys the Areopagite (see pp. 184–9); recent research (Riou, Garrigues) has drawn attention to the importance for Maximus of the tradition of Macarian spirituality (see pp. 173–5). The Maximian synthesis is no uncritical amalgam: in his hands the Dionysian tradition is rid of the suspicion of emanationism that sometimes (though falsely) attaches to it, and Origenism is thoroughly 'demythologized' – the myths of the pre-existence and cosmic fall of souls are rejected. Maximus' receptivity to Macarian influence is very selective: he takes over some of the language and ideas characteristic of the Homilies, but there is little trace of the Messalianism that informs the Homilies;[1] indeed Maximus' affinities in this direction look as if they may have been mediated by Diadochus of Photice (see pp. 178–9), who bears the mark not only of Macarianism, but of a sharp reaction against Messalianism too. There is perhaps evidence for such a link between Diadochus and Maximus in the way they combine Evagrianism with a spirituality rooted

[1] However, a different assessment of the Macarian Homilies is given above, p. 173.

in baptism by the use of categories drawn from the Macarian Homilies: indeed Riou speaks of this Macarian or Diadochan strain as providing Maximus with

> the axis of integration and synthesis for the Origenist and Dionysian systems: baptismal grace of filial adoption embraced in a synergy with the human will, the primacy of love in deification, the prayer of the heart and the pneumatological dimension – all themes typically Macarian (Riou, pp. 39f).

In his understanding of the first stage of the spiritual life – the struggle to overcome vices and temptations and to acquire virtue (*praktikē*) – Maximus follows Evagrius very closely; none the less Maximus' teaching here breathes a different spirit. Evagrius, for instance, makes hardly any reference to our Lord; Maximus on the contrary sees the Christian life as an imitation of Christ (LA 1–3) – so when he speaks of the Christian's struggle with the demons he recalls our Lord's temptation in the wilderness (C ii.13), and in one remarkable passage he passes directly from the idea that the Christian is to imitate God's love to reference to God's passion as inviting us to follow him:

> God alone is good by nature, and only the imitator of God is good through conformity of will. His purpose indeed is to join the wicked to the good by nature that they may become good. Therefore, reviled, he blesses them; persecuted, he endures; slandered, he entreats; put to death, he intercedes. He does everything in order not to fall from love's purposes (C iv.9).

Maximus draws on the Evagrian understanding of the eight principal vices or temptations (*logismoi*), but here too there is a difference of feel. Evagrius is almost exclusively concerned with the way in which temptation disturbs the soul and prevents it from praying; Maximus is more aware of the effect of our behaviour on others. 'If you wish not to fall off from God-like love, neither allow your brother to go to sleep with grief against you, nor do you go to sleep grieved against him' (C I.53). It is perhaps significant that Maximus has a good deal to say about *envy* – not one of Evagrius' eight *logismoi*, though it was included in the Western list of seven deadly sins – for envy is about our relations with others. Maximus is however in basic accord with Evagrius in his use of the tripartite analysis of the soul – into the intellect (*nous*), the passionate part (*thumos*) and the desiring part (*epithumia*) – as a diagnostic device: for him the desiring part of the soul is quelled by continence (*enkrateia*), the passionate part by love (rather than meekness, as in Evagrius), and the intellect by prayer (LA 19; C iv.80, etc.). He agrees with Evagrius in finding the battle against the passionate part the hardest (C i.66): thus its remedy is love, the most basic virtue. They agree too in seeing the goal of this struggle against the passions as *apatheia*, passionlessness or dispassion or serenity. But whereas for Evagrius *apatheia* means the destruction of the passions (though not of the soul's powers; see p. 170), Maximus seems rather to envisage their transformation. In C iii.68 Maximus discusses the danger of a merely negative attitude to the passions: in itself it leads to a state of indifference, in which one is 'drawn neither to human things, nor to the divine'. There is need, he says, for 'the blessed passion of holy love' (C iii.67). Early on in the *Centuries on Charity* Maximus says, 'As memory of fire does not warm the body, so faith without charity does not effect illumination of knowledge in the mind' (C i.31). Maximus here seems to be drawing on characteristically Macarian themes and to foreshadow Symeon the New Theologian. Maximus is quite explicit about how in contemplation of God the intellect is not detached from the irrational parts of the soul, which, on the contrary, still have a role to play, when he says:

> For him whose mind is continually with God, even his desiring part is increased above measure into divine *erōs*, and the entire passionate part changed into divine *agapē* (C ii.48).

Such an understanding of *apatheia* represents no inconsistency or contradiction on Maximus' part, for he defines passion (*pathos*) not as *any* movement of the irrational part of the soul but as 'a movement of the soul *contrary to nature*' (C ii.16). *Apatheia* is then the restoration of the soul to its true nature. In this state the intellect is able to contemplate, thoughts that occur to it do not engage the passions (in the bad sense) but remain 'mere thoughts' (*psila noēmata*). In this and in his understanding of the way the intellect now is to progress through a series of 'contemplations', by way of natural contemplation, to contemplation of God, he follows Evagrius. But in his account of such contemplation of God he combines Evagrian language about how the intellect becomes aware of its own splendour (C iii.97; iv.56, 79) with the Dionysian language of ecstasy. In this, the 'sabbaths of sabbaths', the intellect 'is through ecstasy of love clothed entirely in God alone, and through mystical theology is brought altogether to rest in God' (TE i.39); it 'attains through unknowing the very principle of the divine unity' (TE ii.8). Maximus can speak of this state using the Macarian language of the heart (*kardia*):

> A pure heart is one which offers the mind to God free of all image and form, and ready to be imprinted only with his own archetypes, by which God himself is made manifest (TE ii.82).

It is not only in his understanding of the ecstatic union of the mind with God in unknowing that Maximus displays the influence of Denys. The triad of purification, illumination and perfection is found in him, and applied to the threefold order of the apostolic ministry in a Dionysian way

(C ii.21). But the influence of Denys is most profoundly felt (and acknowledged) in his work on the Divine Liturgy, the *Mystagōgia*. It is misleading to say, as Riou does (p. 160), that Maximus' interpretation of the liturgy recalls less Cyril of Jerusalem and Theodore of Mopsuestia than the elaborately allegorical interpretations of the liturgy found in the Western Middle Ages; for those latter are individualistic and highly arbitrary, whereas Maximus stands in a tradition and, in common with that entire Byzantine tradition, interprets the Eucharist as the action of the whole Church, with a sense of the dramatic structure of the rite as a unity, and in particular a profound appreciation of its eschatological orientation. The first part of the *Mystagōgia* speaks of the symbolism of the Church, which in its unity in diversity is an image of God, and, in the division of the Church building into the sanctuary (*hierateion*) and the nave (*naos*), reflects similar divisions in the cosmos (between the invisible and visible orders), the physical world (heaven and earth), man (body and soul), soul (contemplative intellect and practical reason), Scripture (mystical and literal meaning). This system of mutual reference gives the celebration of the Eucharist, to which the division of the Church lends structure and movement, a range of meaning from the cosmic, to the community, to the movement of the individual soul towards God. This mutual lending of meaning is perhaps the most important part of Maximus' teaching. In his interpretation of the detail of the action of the liturgy, there is a vivid sense of the Church standing on the brink of the age to come, looking for the 'future harmony of all with one another in the time of the revelation of the ineffable good things which are to be' (M xviii), in which the whole cosmos is to take part.

The goal of the spiritual life is, for Maximus, deification (*theōsis*), and the foundation of this is laid for all Christians in their baptism:

> Baptized in Christ through the Spirit, we receive the first incorruption according to the flesh. Keeping this original incorruption spotless by giving ourselves to good works and by dying to our own will, we await the final incorruption bestowed by Christ in the Spirit (TE i.87).

As with Diadochus, the Christian life is seen by Maximus as the bringing to perfection of baptismal grace, and in that process we are called to play our part by working together with the grace of the Holy Spirit. Deification is becoming God, and if God is love, it means then being perfected in love:

> the mind, joined with God and abiding with him through prayer and love, becomes wise, good, powerful, benevolent, merciful, long-suffering; in a word, it contains in itself practically all the divine attributes (C ii.52).

1 Transfiguration icon (*see p. 248*)

2   The Ladder to Heaven icon

3　A hesychast at prayer (*see pp. 244, 247*)

4　St Hildegard of Bingen (*see p. 290*)

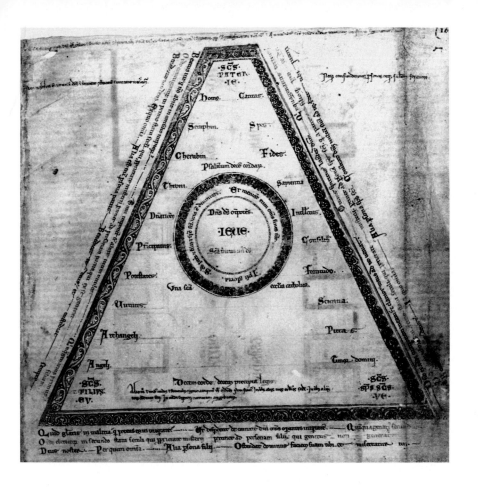

5   The ten-stringed psaltery of Joachim of Fiore (*see p. 293*)

6 St Francis of Assisi (*see p. 301*)

7 Dante (*see p. 309*)

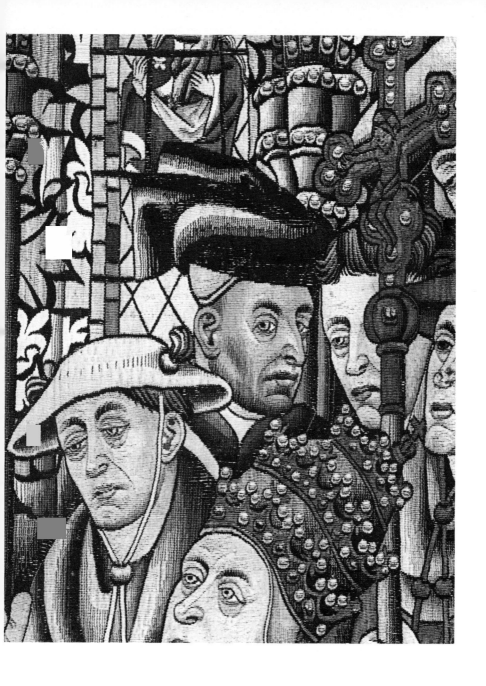

8   The 'omnivoyant' eye. See Nicholas of Cusa (*p. 327*)

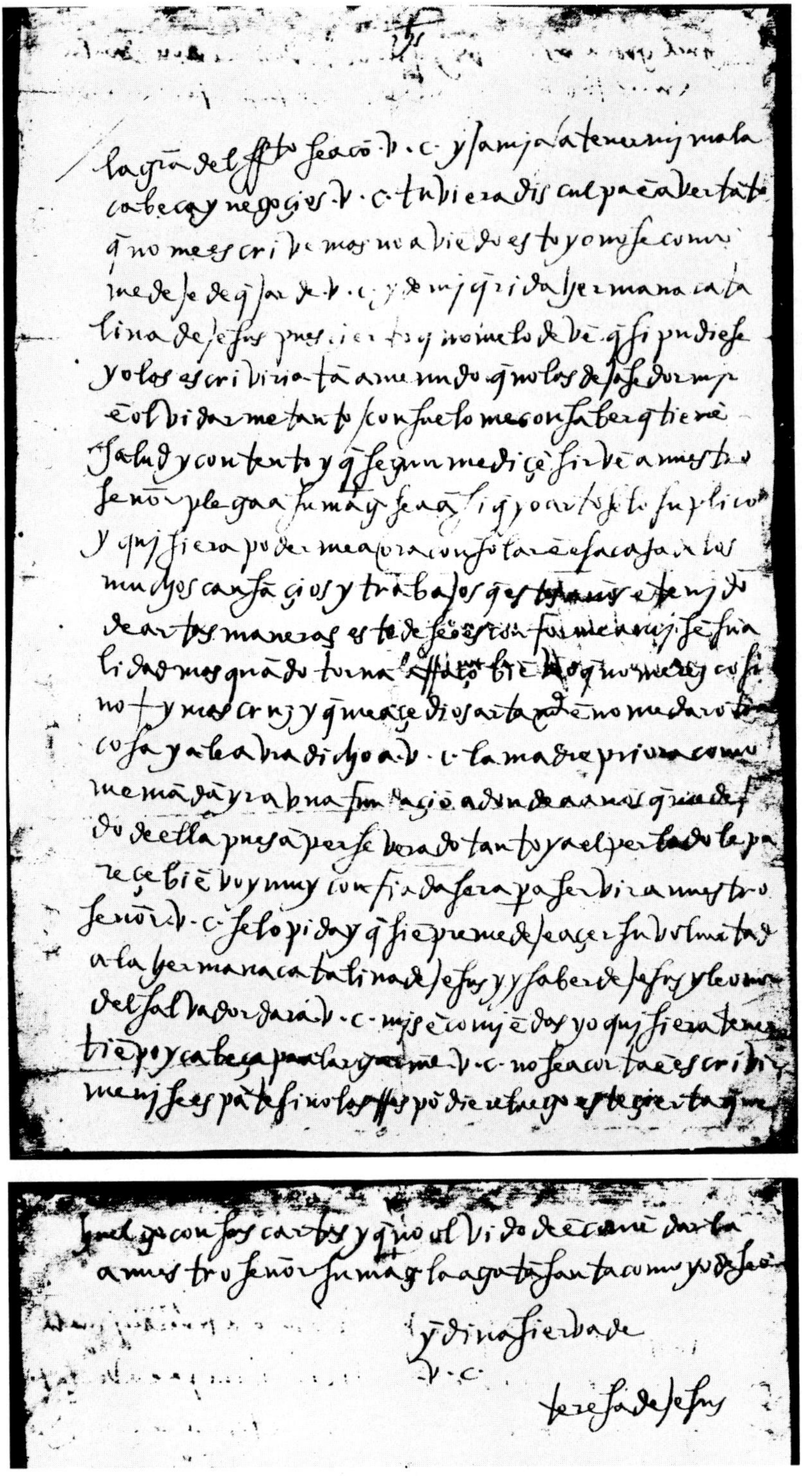

9 A letter by St Teresa of Avila (*see p. 363*)

But the real meaning of deification is seen only when we reflect that our becoming God is the counterpart of God's becoming man. It is not a natural possibility, but the response to God's gift of love in the incarnation. More precisely, as the incarnation is the becoming man of the Son of God, so our deification is becoming God as sons and daughters through the Spirit and thus sharing in the life of the Trinity: so in the *Mystagōgia* Maximus lays particular stress on the saying of the Lord's Prayer, a symbol of our adoption as sons and daughters by the grace of the Spirit. In his exposition of the Lord's Prayer he says,

> The Word bestows adoption on us when he grants us that birth and deification which, transcending nature, comes by grace from above through the Spirit. The guarding and preserving of this in God depends upon the resolve of those thus born.

We are called on to co-operate with God's grace. This co-operation is the pursuit of *apatheia*, which Maximus sees as our answering response to the *kenōsis* of the Word of God in the incarnation:

> Moreover, by emptying themselves of the passions they lay hold of the divine to the same degree as that to which, deliberately emptying himself of his own sublime glory, the Word of God truly became man (PN 877A).

The spirituality of Maximus is then a rich synthesis within which many apparently conflicting traditions find a place, but a synthesis which is based on a profound understanding of the mystery of God's love for us in the incarnation of his Son.

7 The Spirituality of the Icon

KALLISTOS WARE

Texts and Translations

John of Damascus, *In Defence of the Holy Icons*, Greek text ed. B. Kotter (Berlin, 1975); ET D. Anderson (Crestwood N.Y., St Vladimir's Seminary Press, 1980).
Theodore the Studite, *On the Holy Icons*, Greek text *PG* 99. 328–436; ET C. P. Roth (Crestwood N.Y., St Vladimir's Seminary Press, 1981).

Studies

Alexander, P. J., *The Patriarch Nicephorus of Constantinople*. Oxford, Clarendon, 1958.
Evdokimov, P., *L'art de l'icône*. Paris, 1970

Mathew, G., *Byzantine Aesthetics*. London, J. Murray, 1963.
Ouspensky, L., (ET) *Theology of the Icon*. Crestwood N.Y., St Vladimir's
Seminary Press, 1978.
Ouspensky, L. and Lossky, V., (ET) *The Meaning of Icons*. Boston, Mass.,
Boston Book and Art Shop, 1969.
von Schönborn, C., *L'icône du Christ*. Fribourg, 1976.

From 726 until the middle of the ninth century the Byzantine world was
convulsed by the Iconoclast controversy. The use of icons in the
Church's worship was formally endorsed at the seventh Ecumenical
Council (787), although the conflict only came to an end with the definitive restoration of the icons to the churches in 843 – the 'Triumph of
Orthodoxy', as it came later to be known. The dispute concerned both the
legitimacy and the *veneration* of icons. Is it permitted to make icons –
pictorial representations of Christ, the Mother of God, the saints and the
angels – and to place these icons in the church and the home? And, if such
icons are permitted, should they also be venerated? Should incense be
offered before them and candles lit, should they be carried in procession,
should the faithful make prostrations in front of them and kiss them? To
these questions the Eastern Church ended by returning a strongly affirmative answer. The chief defenders of the icons during the controversy
were St John of Damascus (d. *c.* 749), who lived outside the Byzantine
Empire under Arab rule, and St Theodore the Studite (759–826), abbot
of the monastery of Studios in Constantinople.

The Iconoclast controversy raised a number of related issues. First,
there was the charge of *idolatry*, made against the iconodules ('icon-
venerators'). To this they responded by drawing a clear and emphatic
distinction between *latreia*, the worship that may rightly be ascribed to
the three persons of the Trinity alone, and *schetikē timē*, the 'relative
honour' that may be given to created persons or objects associated with
God. Icons are not to be worshipped, but merely honoured.

Secondly, complex questions of *Christology* were involved, and it was
to these that most of the polemics on both sides were devoted. The
iconodules argued that it is not only legitimate but essential to make an
icon of Christ; to refuse to do so is to imply that his body, and so his
humanity, is somehow unreal. Icons, as the Council of 787 put it, are a
'guarantee that the incarnation of God the Word is true and not illusory'.

Linked with this was the Christian doctrine of *creation*. Icons
safeguard not only the authenticity of Christ's material body but also the
Spirit-bearing potentialities of all material things. The iconoclasts ('icon-
smashers'), so the opposite side claimed, wanted to restrict the worship of
God to the mind alone, failing to allow sufficiently for the 'materialism' of
Christianity. 'I shall not cease to honour matter,' John of Damascus

protests, 'for it was through matter that my salvation came to pass . . . Do not despise matter, for it is not despicable; nothing is despicable that God has made' (*In Defence of the Holy Icons*, I. 16; ET, pp. 23–4). Human beings are not saved *from* but *with* the material world; through human-kind the material world is itself to be redeemed and transfigured.

This in turn has implications, fourthly, for the doctrine of the *human person*. In the words of Theodore the Studite, 'The fact that the human person is made in the image and likeness of God means that the making of icons is in some way a divine work' (*On the Holy Icons*, III. ii, 5; ET, p. 101). Each man or woman is a creator after the image of God the Creator, a 'sub-creator' in J. R. R. Tolkien's phrase. Each is priest of the created order, refashioning material things, revealing God's glory in them, and so giving them a voice and making them articulate in the divine praise. Iconography bears witness to the royal priesthood that is the prerogative of every human being. To make an icon from plaster or cubes of stone, from wood or paint, to sanctify that icon and to incorporate it in the worship of God, is to call down his blessing also upon all other forms of human art and craftsmanship.

But what, more particularly, is the function of icons in prayer and worship? The art of the icon is, first and foremost, a liturgical art. The icon is not merely a piece of decoration but a part of the liturgy. Outside the context of prayer it ceases to be an icon and becomes – what is by no means the same thing – a picture on a religious subject. Within the context of prayer it is not just a 'visual aid' but fulfils a sacramental function, constituting a channel of divine grace: as the seventh Ecumeni-cal Council affirms, 'When we honour and venerate an icon, we receive sanctification.' Viewed in these terms, the icon acts as a point of meeting, a place of encounter: 'The icon is termed a door' (*The Life of St Stephen the Younger*, PG 100.1113A). By virtue of the icon the worshipper enters the dimensions of sacred time and space, and so is brought into a living, effectual contact with the person or mystery depicted. The icon serves not as a mere reminder only but as a means of communion. Surrounding the congregation on every side, the icons ensure that the communion of saints is not simply an article of faith but a fact of immediate experience. The church walls become windows into eternity. Present through their icons, the Mother of God, the angels and the saints become fellow-worshippers with the living, concelebrants in the same liturgical act.

In this connection it should be remembered that an icon is not neces-sarily a separate panel of wood, but may be a mosaic or fresco on the wall,[1] organically part of a single pattern embracing the place of worship

---

[1] In Orthodox practice icons are normally two-dimensional, but the use of free-standing, three-dimensional statues is not altogether unknown. Although modern Orthodox

in its entirety. In this way the church building as a whole is felt to be one great icon. To use a phrase much loved by the Christian East, it is 'heaven on earth': in the words of Patriarch Germanus of Constantinople (d. *c.* 733), 'The church is an earthly heaven, in which the heavenly God lives and moves' (*Commentary on the Divine Liturgy*, 1). 'It is as if one had entered heaven itself', remarked Patriarch Photius (d. *c.* 895) of a newly-consecrated church (*Homily* x, 5). The spirituality of the icon also extends beyond the church into the home: in each Orthodox household there is traditionally an icon corner or shelf, before which lamps are lit, incense is offered, and the family prayers are said; and this too is felt as 'heaven on earth'.

Through the liturgical art of the icon, God is experienced not only as truth and love but also as *beauty*. 'Beauty will save the world', affirms Feodor Dostoevsky (1821–81); and Fr Sergei Bulgakov (1871–1944) states, 'Beauty is an objective principle in the world, revealing to us the divine glory . . . Art brings about the transfiguration of the world and renders it conformable to its true image . . . Things are transfigured and made luminous by beauty; they become the revelation of their own abstract meaning' ('Religion and Art', in *The Church of God*, ed. E. L. Mascall [SPCK, 1934], pp. 176–7). In this way the icon constitutes the firstfruits of the cosmic transfiguration that will come to pass on the Last Day.

Within the tradition of Eastern Christendom, then, there exist two ways of praying, the one iconic and the other non-iconic. There is, first, on both the corporate and the private level, the way of 'cataphatic' prayer, making full use of the imagination, of poetry and music, of symbols and ritual gestures; and in this way of praying the holy icons have an essential place. Secondly, there is the way of 'apophatic' or hesychastic prayer, transcending images and discursive thought – a way commended by Gregory of Nyssa, Evagrius, Dionysius and Maximus, and expressed also in the practice of the Jesus Prayer (see pp. 175–84). These two ways are not alternatives, still less are they mutually exclusive, but each deepens and completes the other.

---

writers sometimes condemn the use of statues, in the eighth/ninth-century iconodule sources no doctrinal significance is attached to the distinction between two- and three-dimensional religious art.

B THE SYRIAC TRADITION

SEBASTIAN BROCK

INTRODUCTION

Colless, B., 'The place of Syrian mysticism in religious history', *Journal of Religious History*, 5 (1968), pp. 1–15.

Smith, M., *Studies in Early Mysticism in the Near and Middle East*. London, Sheldon, 1931.

Vööbus, A., *History of Asceticism in the Syrian Orient*. CSCO 184, 197 (1958, 1960).

EARLY WRITERS TO *c.* 400

GENERAL

Brock, S. P., 'World and Sacrament in the writings of the Syrian Fathers', in *Sobornost*, 6:10 (1974), pp. 685–96.

Brock, S. P., *The Holy Spirit in the Syrian Baptismal Tradition*. Syrian Churches Series 9. Paderborn, Ostkirchendienst, 1979.

Brock, S. P., 'The prayer of the heart in Syriac tradition', in *Sobornost/ECR*, 4 (1982), pp. 131–42.

*Murray, R.,[1] *Symbols of Church and Kingdom*. CUP, 1975.

ODES OF SOLOMON AND ACTS OF THOMAS

Charlesworth, J. H., (ET) *The Odes of Solomon*. Oxford, Clarendon, 1973; Missoula, Scholar's Press, 1977.

Klijn, A. F. J., *The Acts of Thomas*. Leiden, Brill, 1962.

APHRAHAT

Brock, S. P., 'Aphrahat on Prayer', *Annual of the Leeds University Oriental Society*. Leiden, Brill, forthcoming.

Gwynn, J., in *A Select Library of Nicene and Post-Nicene Fathers*, II.13. Oxford, 1898; repr. Grand Rapids, Eerdmans (ET of Dem. 1, 5, 6, 8, 17, 21, 22).

Hausherr, I., *Dict. Sp.* 1. 746–52.

EPHREM

(a) *ET*

*Brock, S. P., *The Harp of the Spirit*. Studies Supplementary to *Sobornost*, 4 (1975).

Gwynn, J. (see above).

---

[1] Asterisked works contain a helpful bibliography; for further details see I. Ortiz de Urbina, *Patrologia Syriaca* (Rome, 1965), supplemented by the bibliography for 1960–70 in *Parole de l'Orient*, 4 (1973), and for 1971–1980 in *Parole de l'Orient*, 10 (1981–2).

Morris, J. B., *Selected Works of St Ephrem the Syrian*. Oxford, Parker, 1847 (LF).
McVey, K., ed., (ET) *St Ephrem: the Hymns*. CWS XLIII.
(Translations of individual hymns, by R. Murray and S. P. Brock, will be found in recent numbers of *ECR* and *Sobornost*.)

(b) *Studies*

*Beck, E., *Dict. Sp.* 4. 788–800.
Brock, S. P., 'The poet as theologian', in *Sobornost*, 7:4 (1977), pp. 243–50.
*Brock, S. P., *The Luminous Eye: the Spiritual World Vision of St Ephrem*. Rome, C.L.I.S., 1985.
Murray, R., 'The theory of symbolism in St Ephrem's theology', in *Parole de l'Orient*, 6/7 (1975/6), pp. 1–20.

LIBER GRADUUM

Latin translation in M. Kmosko, *Patrologia Syriaca* 3 (1926).
Guillaumont, A., *Dict. Sp.* 9. 749–54.
Guillaumont, A., 'Situation et signification du "Liber Graduum" dans la spiritualité syriaque', in *OCA* 197 (1974), pp. 311–22.

FIFTH TO SIXTH CENTURIES

(a) TRANSLATIONS FROM GREEK

MONASTIC WRITINGS FROM EGYPT

Budge, E. A. W., *Stories from the Holy Fathers*. OUP, 1934.
Budge, E. A. W., *The Wit and Wisdom of the Christian Fathers of Egypt*. OUP, 1934.
Chitty, D. J., *The Letters of Ammonas*. Oxford, Fairacres Publication 72, 1979.
Draguet, R., *Les formes syriaques de la matière de l'histoire lausiaque*. CSCO 389–90, 398–9 (1978).
Draguet, R., *La vie primitive de S.Antoine conservée en syriaque*. CSCO 417–8 (1980).

MACARIAN HOMILIES

Strothmann, W., *Die syrische Überlieferung der Schriften des Makarios*. Wiesbaden, 1981.

EVAGRIUS

Guillaumont, A., *Les six centuries des 'Kephalaia gnostica' d'Evagre le Pontique*. PO 28, 1958.
*Guillaumont, A., *Les 'Kephalaia gnostica' d'Evagre le Pontique et l'histoire de l'Origénisme chez les grecs et les syriens*. Paris, 1962.
Muyldemans, J., *Evagriana Syriaca*. Louvain, 1952.

DIONYSIAN CORPUS

Strothmann, W., *Das Sakrament der Myron-Weihe in der Schrift de Eccl. Hier. des Ps. Dionysios Areopagita.* Wiesbaden, 1977.

ABBA ISAIAH

Draguet, R., *Les cinq recensions de l'Ascéticon syriaque d'Abba Isaie.* CSCO 289–90, 293–4 (1968).
Chitty, D. J., 'Abba Isaiah', in *JTS* 22 (1971), pp. 47–72.

(b) SYRIAC WRITERS

JOHN THE SOLITARY

*Bradley, B., in *Dict. Sp.* 8. 764–74.
*Brock, S. P., 'John the Solitary, on Prayer', in *JTS* 30 (1979), pp. 84–101.
Hausherr, I., *Jean le Solitaire, Dialogue sur l'âme et les passions de l'homme*, in *OCA* 120 (1939).
Lavenant, R., *Jean d'Apamée, Dialogues et traités.* SC311 (1984).

PHILOXENUS

Budge, E. A. W., *The Discourses of Philoxenus.* London, Royal Society of Literature, Asher, 1894.
Lavenant, R., *La lettre à Patricius de Philoxène.* PO 30 (1963).
Tanghe, A., 'Memra de Philoxène sur l'inhabitation du Saint Esprit', *Le Muséon*, 73 (1960), pp. 39–71.

JACOB OF SERUGH

Brock, S. P., 'Jacob of Serugh on the Veil of Moses', in *Sobornost/ECR*, 3:1 (1981), pp. 70–85.
Connolly, R. H., 'Two Homilies on the Eucharist', in *Downside Review*, 27 (1908), pp. 278–87; and 29 (1910), pp. 260–70.
*Graffin, F., in *Dict. Sp.* 8. 56–60.

STEPHEN AND 'HIEROTHEOS'

*Guillaumont, A., in *Dict. Sp.* 4. 1481–88.
Marsh, F. S., ed and trans., *The Book of the Holy Hierotheos.* London, Text and Translation Society, Williams & Norgate, 1927.

EAST SYRIAN WRITERS, LATE SIXTH TO EIGHTH CENTURIES

GREGORY OF CYPRUS

Hausherr, I., 'Gregorii Monachi Cyprii De Theoria Sancta', in *OCA* 110 (1937).
Kirchmeyer, J., in *Dict. Sp.* 6. 920–22.

MARTYRIUS

De Halleux, A., *Martyrius (Sahdona): Oeuvres spirituelles*. CSCO 200–1, 214–15, 525–5.
*Leloir, L., in *Dict. Sp.* 10. 737–42.

ISAAC OF NINEVEH

Wensinck, A. J., *Mystic Treatises by Isaac of Nineveh*. Amsterdam, 1923; Wiesbaden, 1969. (A new translation is to appear shortly.)
Brock, S. P., 'St Isaac of Nineveh and Syriac spirituality', in *Sobornost*, 7:2 (1975), pp. 79–89.
Brock S. P., 'St Isaac of Nineveh', in *The Way* (Jan. 1981), pp. 68–74.
*Khalifé-Hachem, E., in *Dict. Sp.* 7. 2041–54.

DADISHO, SIMEON

Draguet, R., *Commentaire du livre d'Abba Isaie par Dadisho Qatraya*. CSCO 326–7 (1972).
Mingana, A., *Early Christian Mystics*. Manchester, John Rylands Library Bulletin, 1927–32; Woodbrooke Studies, 7 (1934).

JOSEPH HAZZAYA

Mingana, A., (see above).
Olinder, G., *A Letter of Philoxenus of Mabbug* [in fact Joseph] *sent to a Friend*. Göteborg, 1950. French transl. by F. Graffin in *L'Orient Syrien*, 6 (1961), pp. 317–52, 455–86; 7 (1962), pp. 77–102.
*Beulay, R., in *Dict. Sp.* 8. 1341–9.
Guillaumont, A., 'Sources de la doctrine de Joseph Hazzaya', in *L'Orient Syrien* 3, (1958), pp. 3–24.
Sherry, E. J., 'The life and works of Joseph Hazzaya', in *The Seed of Wisdom: Essays in honour of T. J. Meek*, ed. W. S. McCullough (Toronto, University of Toronto Press, 1964), pp. 78–91.

JOHN OF DALYATHA

Beulay, R., *La collection des lettres de Jean de Dalyatha*. PO, 39 (1978).
*Beulay, R., in *Dict. Sp.* 8. 449–52.
Colless, B., 'The mysticism of John Saba', in *OCP 39* (1973), pp. 83–102.

LATER WRITERS

JOSEPH BUSNAYA

Chabot, J. B., in *Revue de l'Orient Chrétien*, 4 (1899), pp. 380–415; 5 (1900), pp. 118–33.

BARHEBRAEUS

Wensinck, A. J., *Bar Hebraeus' Book of the Dove, together with some chapters from his Ethicon*. Leiden, 1919.

MAS'UD

Van Helmond, B. L., *Mas'oud du Tour 'Abdin, un mystique syrien du XVe siècle.*
Louvain, 1942.

INTRODUCTION

From an early date Syriac (a dialect of Aramaic) came to serve as the
literary language of the majority of Christians living in the eastern prov-
inces of the Roman Empire (modern south-east Turkey and Syria) and in
the Persian Empire (modern Iraq and western Iran); it continues in use
up to the present day as the liturgical language of three Oriental
Orthodox Churches (Maronite, Syrian Orthodox, Church of the East).

The beginnings of Christianity in these areas are very obscure, and
Syriac writings which can safely be dated earlier than the fourth century
are rare. The golden age of Syriac literature spans the fourth to the
seventh centuries. As far as writers on spirituality are concerned, four
fairly well-defined periods can be discerned:

1. Early writers to *c.* 400. During this (pre-monastic) period Syriac
Christianity is still only barely hellenized, and its great significance lies in
the fact that it thus serves as the only extant witness to a genuinely semitic
form of Christianity, as yet virtually untouched by Greek thought patterns. The period culminates with the writings of St Ephrem, a religious
poet of outstanding importance.

2. Fifth and sixth centuries. These two centuries witnessed the ever-
increasing hellenization of Syriac Christianity, and it is ironic that, at the
moment when the Arab invasions cut off Syriac Christianity from the
Byzantine world (early seventh century), Greek influence on Syriac
writers was at its strongest. The christological controversies of these
centuries effectively divided up the Syriac world into three separate
ecclesiastical traditions, the Chalcedonian, the Syrian Orthodox, and the
Church of the East; the former two were chiefly represented in the eastern Roman Empire, while the last was almost entirely confined to the
Persian Empire. As far as spiritual literature was concerned, however,
ecclesiastical boundaries had little effect on its dissemination. A number
of translations of Greek spiritual writings, made during this period (notably those of the *Apophthegmata*, the Macarian Homilies, Evagrius and
the Dionysian corpus), were to exercise a profound influence on subsequent Syriac writers of every tradition.

3. The end of Sassanid rule and the first two centuries of Islam witnessed
an astonishing flowering of mystical writers in the Church of the East,

and the works of one of these, Isaac of Nineveh, were subsequently translated into Greek as well as into Arabic. Isaac has proved very influential up to the present day (especially on Mount Athos and in the contemporary monastic revival in the Coptic Orthodox Church). How far these East Syrian mystics also influenced the early Sufi tradition in Islam (see pp. 498–503) remains unclear. There also exist fragmentary Sogdian translations of some of these writers.

4. Although a number of later works on the spiritual life in Syriac survive, very few of these have been published; one of them, the *Book of the Dove*, by the famous polymath Barhebraeus, exhibits the influence of Islamic mystics. During the seventeenth to nineteenth centuries European missionaries translated several classics of Western spirituality into Syriac.

Several important writers within these four periods have only recently come to be better known, and in some cases major works still remain unpublished; this applies above all to John the Solitary and John of Dalyatha.

Certain prominent themes recur throughout much of this literature.

1. Early writers regularly see baptism as the return to Paradise and the potential recovery of the 'robe of glory'[1] lost by Adam (humanity) at the fall; the recovery is only finally realized at the resurrection, though the holy can anticipate this in the present life. Eschatological Paradise is far more glorious than the primordial, since the holy will there be granted the divinity which Adam and Eve would have been given had they kept the commandment.

2. The betrothal of the Church to Christ takes place at his baptism; so too Christian baptism is understood as the betrothal of the soul to Christ the Bridegroom. This helps explain the encratite slant of early Syriac Christianity, with its emphasis on virginity and the ideal of the *ihidaya* (which may underlie the earliest usage of *monachos*), meaning single, celibate, single-minded, and especially follower of Christ the *ihida*, 'Only-Begotten'.

3. The following are very common:
—the ideal of *shaphyutha*, 'limpidity, lucidity, clarity, serenity, smoothness', etc., applied to the heart or mind.
—fire as a symbol of the divinity, and the terminology of 'mingling, mixing' used of the interaction between God and creation.

---

[1] The whole of salvation history is regularly expressed in terms of clothing imagery.

—the perception of an analogy between the activity of the Holy Spirit at the Annunciation, the eucharistic epiclesis and mystical experience of the soul (especially from the sixth century onwards).[1]

EARLY WRITERS TO *c.* 400

Two early texts are important. The Odes of Solomon (late second century?) are short lyrics in which the baptismal experience of the Odist is often identified with that of Christ. The Acts of Thomas (third century?) well illustrate the ideal of virginity; they incorporate two earlier poems, the hymn of the Bride of Light (Church), and the famous hymn of the Soul or Pearl.

APHRAHAT

Aphrahat 'the Persian sage' (mid fourth century) wrote twenty-three *Demonstrations* on a variety of topics including Faith (no. 1), Love (2), Fasting (3), Prayer (4), 'Members of the Covenant' (6), Penitents (7) and Humility (9). These have a strong biblical orientation (Aphrahat calls himself 'a disciple of the Scriptures'). No. 4 (the earliest Christian treatise on prayer, as opposed to treatises which deal with the Lord's Prayer) seeks to show how prayer is acceptable only if it stems from 'purity of heart'. No. 6 deals with a distinctive feature of early Syriac Christianity: it appears that originally the term 'covenant' designated the entire baptized community, who had also undertaken certain ascetic vows (notably chastity) at baptism; by Aphrahat's time, however, the 'sons and daughters of the covenant' (the translation 'monks' in Gwynn is anachronistic) represented an ascetic group within the baptized community, consisting of people who were either celibate ('virgins', used of both men and women) or married couples who had renounced intercourse (designated *qaddishe*, lit. 'holy', based on Exod. 19.10, 15). *Dem.* 6 also discusses the indwelling of the Holy Spirit and the problem of post-baptismal sin.

Aphrahat's writings were known to several later Syriac writers. A complete Armenian translation (attributed to Jacob of Nisibis) exists, and individual Demonstrations were translated into Arabic, Georgian and Ethiopic.

EPHREM

The poet Ephrem (*c.* 306–73) is the finest representative of Syriac symbolic theology and its pre-monastic spirituality. Until 363, when he had to move to Edessa, he lived in Nisibis. Later tradition anachronistically portrayed him as a monk living in a cave outside Edessa, but in fact his life

[1] cf. my 'Passover, Annunciation and Epiclesis', *Novum Testamentum*, 24 (1982).

was spent within the urban community he served as a deacon and teacher.

His writings comprise: (1) prose works (including several biblical commentaries);[1] (2) artistic prose (including a meditation on judgement, the *Letter to Publius*);[2] and (3) poetry, for which he is chiefly famous. The main poems are preserved in a series of hymn cycles; several were written specifically for women to sing.

The hymns offer an essentially sacramental view of the Christian life, with great emphasis on baptism as the point of entry. Everything in Scripture and creation is capable of directing the eye of faith to Christ, himself the manifestation of God's hiddenness. This is made possible by the inherent presence in everything of types and symbols (lit. 'mysteries'),[3] which act as pointers towards God. This anagogic process, leading the mind to a state of wonder and praise, is itself possible only because God initially descended to meet the human condition, first by allowing himself to be 'clothed in human language' and in symbols, and then by actually 'clothing himself in a human body'. There is thus a state of creative tension between the utter transcendence and the total immanence of God, a state which Ephrem describes by a whole series of paradoxes. The continuing sanctifying immanence of God in the sacraments of baptism and the Eucharist serves as a pattern for his immanence, equally sanctifying, in the 'symbols' contained in creation and Scripture.[4]

As an exponent of symbolic theology Ephrem abhors all literalism and definitions: these he regards as static and deadening in their effect. His is, rather, an essentially positive and dynamic vision; it is a world-view which involved him actively in the world around him (the one well-attested episode in his life concerns his efforts in his old age to distribute food to the poor during a famine).

Ephrem exercised a strong influence on later Syriac writers. Several of his works were translated into Arabic and Greek (though many of the extant Greek, Latin and Slavonic writings attributed to him are not by him).

LIBER GRADUUM

Thirty anonymous homilies entitled the *Book of Steps* (or *Ascents*) constitute the earliest corpus of Syriac writings specifically on the spiritual life; the author probably wrote in the Persian Empire during the fourth

[1] French trans. of the Commentary on the Diatessaron in *SC* 121.
[2] ET in *Le Muséon*, 89 (1976), pp. 261–305.
[3] In common with most Church Fathers Ephrem has a very 'strong' view of symbolism: what is symbolized is actually present in some sense in the symbol.
[4] Although expressed in a totally different way, Ephrem's theology of names in some respects anticipates that of the Dionysian corpus.

century. Their editor held them to be Messalian, but the distinctive Messalian aberrations are absent, and it is preferable to see the work as belonging to the sort of milieu out of which Messalian tendencies grew. It has some features in common with the Macarian Homilies, but there are no direct literary connections.

Two basic stages are distinguished: of the 'upright', and of the 'perfect'. The upright follow the 'small commandments' of active charity, while the perfect keep the 'great commandments' of total renunciation: they 'fast from the world', being 'strangers' to it; theirs is a life of continual prayer, self-emptying, profound humility and compassion for others. The upright have received the 'pledge' of the Spirit, whereas the perfect have received the fulness. Progress in the spiritual life is represented by the increase of the 'pledge of the Spirit' until the point of plenitude is reached: this is the 'baptism in fire and the Spirit'.

Homily 12 (ET in Murray, *Symbols*, pp. 264–8) offers a threefold view of the Church: worship takes place visibly at the public level, and invisibly at the altar of the heart and at the heavenly altar of the Church above; there is a progression through (but not beyond) the visible Church to the invisible Church of the heart and thence to the heavenly Church.

Among later writers Philoxenus clearly knew the *Liber Graduum*.

FIFTH TO SIXTH CENTURIES
TRANSLATIONS FROM GREEK

Many Greek patristic writings were translated into Syriac, and among these were four groups of texts which influenced, in varying degrees, almost all subsequent Syriac writers.

MONASTIC WRITINGS FROM EGYPT

Although Syriac Christianity had developed its own particular type of ascetic life as a form of proto-monasticism, from the late fourth century onwards this rapidly came to be overshadowed by the prestige of Egyptian monasticism. Syriac translations of the *Lausiac History*, the *Historia Monachorum* and collections of *Apophthegmata* were probably available by *c.* 500 and proved very popular. In the seventh century much of this material was incorporated into the *Paradise of the Fathers*, compiled by the East Syrian monk Ananisho (ET by Budge, *Stories from the Holy Fathers*). Other Egyptian texts translated into Syriac include the Letters of Ammonas, Lives of Antony, Pachomius, Macarius and others.

MACARIAN HOMILIES (see pp. 173–5).

Two independent translations are known. The first consists of an ill-defined group of twenty-three texts, attributed to Macarius the Egyptian and Macarius the Alexandrian, found in numerous manuscripts; the majority of these correspond to homilies or parts of homilies in one or other of the Greek collections, though some texts have no Greek parallel, or are known only from other sources.[1] The second translation, in a single Sinai manuscript, contains twenty-three texts, only six of which overlap with texts in the other translation; although almost all correspond to Greek texts, there is again no clear pattern of relationship with extant Greek collections.

EVAGRIUS

Syriac and Armenian preserve several writings of Evagrius whose Greek original has been lost as a result of the condemnation of his teaching in 553 (see pp. 169–70). Of particular interest are the two Syriac versions (both late fifth century?) of the *Kephalaia Gnostica*: in one version (in a single manuscript) we have an unexpurgated form of Evagrius' text, while in the other (much more influential)[2] version the more outspoken Origenist elements have been expunged.[3] The widespread influence of Evagrius' works (in an expurgated form) on later Syriac writers has been traced by Guillaumont.

THE DIONYSIAN CORPUS

(See pp. 184–9), where the abbreviations used below are explained).
Two Syriac translations survive. The first was probably made by Sergius of Reshaina (d. 536), who added his own preface;[4] the second was a revision of the first by Phocas of Edessa (late seventh century). The ordering of the texts in the two translations differs: the sixth century one has DN CH MT EH Epp., while the revision has three introductions (by the translator, John of Scythopolis, and George of Constantinople), CH EH DN MT Epp. A second edition of the revision, made by Cyriacus of Edessa in 766/7, reverts to the older order and adds Sergius' preface. There are several Syrian Orthodox commentaries and scholia. An edition of both translations (with scholia) is being prepared at Göttingen.

OTHER WRITINGS

Other Greek writers whose works proved influential in Syriac translation include Abba Isaiah, Mark the Monk, and Nilus. Isaiah's *Ascēticon* sur-

---

[1] See the table in Strothmann II, pp. xlii–xliii.
[2] There exist commentaries by Babai (East Syrian, d. 628) and Dionysios bar Salibi (Syrian Orthodox, d. 1171).
[3] Joseph Hazzaya, the only writer who refers to the unexpurgated text, held that it had been 'interpolated and filled with all sorts of blasphemies'.
[4] French trans. in *L'Orient syrien*, 5 (1960) and 6 (1961).

vives in five Syriac recensions, and was commented on by Dadisho and an anonymous writer. A lost work by Theodore of Mopsuestia on the spiritual life influenced several East Syrian writers (Dadisho preserves some quotations).

SYRIAC WRITERS

JOHN THE SOLITARY

A considerable number of writings survive attributed to 'John the Solitary' (*iḥidaya*), who may have come from Apamea. This John is certainly to be distinguished from John of Lycopolis, and probably from two Johns of Apamea accused by later writers of heresy. Nothing is known of his life; he probably belongs to the first half of the fifth century.

Only part of his writings has been published, but it is clear that he is an author of major importance who was much read by later writers. The main works published so far include (1) *Letters to Theodoulos* (ed. Rignell), (2) *Letters on True Perfection* and *On the Mystery of Baptism* (ed. Rignell), (3) *Dialogues on the Soul* (ed. Dedering), (4) *Dialogues with Thaumasios* (ed. Strothmann), and (5) *On Prayer and Inner Silence* (ed. Brock). Of his unpublished works the most widely read was a letter to Hesychios on the spiritual life (ET S. Brock, Kalamazoo, Cistercian Publications, forthcoming).

The *Dialogues on the Soul* lay down a tripartite pattern of the spiritual life (based on 1 Cor. 3.3) that was to prove very influential: the stage of the body (*pagranutha*), of the soul (*napshanutha*), and of the spirit (*ruḥanutha*). The letters are primarily concerned with advanced teaching on 'the new life' of the resurrection which the Christian should strive to anticipate in this life following the 'resurrection' that takes place at baptism.

PHILOXENUS

Philoxenus, the ardent anti-Chalcedonian bishop of Mabbug (d. 523), stands at the point of intersection between Greek and native Syriac traditions both in matters of theology and of spirituality; in each field he produced a remarkably original synthesis. His most important writings on spirituality are (1) thirteen *Discourses* (concentrating on the beginnings of the ascetic life), (2) a work on the *Indwelling of the Holy Spirit*, and (3) the *Letter to Patricius*.[1] This last is a reply to Patricius who evidently sought to achieve 'contemplation' and impassibility without building on the 'lesser commandments'; there is a Greek translation,

[1] The letter on the three stages of the spiritual life, attributed to Philoxenus, is probably by Joseph Hazzaya (see below).

attributed to Isaac. Although the influence of Evagrian terminology is often present, Philoxenus has everywhere preserved a conceptual framework that is essentially biblical.

For Philoxenus (as for earlier Syriac writers) baptism is the focal point,[1] being the entry into a new mode of existence, the spiritual (*ruhanutha*); this takes place 'through grace', but only comes to be realized at a subsequent point in time, when God's grace is met by the human 'will'. Thus Philoxenus sees the Christian as undergoing three 'births', natural birth, baptism 'when someone becomes a child of God by grace', and the third (which he sometimes calls 'a second baptism') 'when someone is born of their own will out of the bodily way of life (*pagranutha*) into the spiritual, where self-emptying of everything is the womb that gives birth' (*Discourse*, 9; cf. *Letter to Patricius*, 97).

JACOB OF SERUGH

The Syrian Orthodox poet Jacob, bishop of Batnan da-Serugh (d. 521), is chiefly famous for his verse homilies where he intermingles biblical and sacramental typology in a highly creative manner. His poetry, though more diffuse than Ephrem's, belongs to the same essentially semitic world of symbolic theology. His prose letters include several on the inner life (e.g. 7, 11, 38, 39, 42).[2]

STEPHEN BAR SUDHAILI AND 'HIEROTHEOS'

The Origenist monk Stephen of Edessa (active early sixth century) evidently taught a kind of eschatological pantheism, strongly influenced by Evagrius' more speculative writings.

The view of some later Syriac writers that Stephen was the author of *The Book of the Holy Hierotheos* is probably correct. This Hierotheos purports to be the revered teacher of that name, mentioned in the Dionysian corpus. Earlier scholars who accepted this claim consequently held the work to be a forerunner of the corpus; it has subsequently been shown, however, that the work is later than, and dependent on, the Dionysian writings (though the influence of Evagrius is in fact far stronger). It is almost certainly not a translation from Greek, as its preface claims.

The book describes the ascent of the mind (following the pattern of Christ's life), ultimately going beyond 'union' to 'commingling' with the divinity.

---

[1] cf. A. Grillmeier, 'Zur Tauftheologie des Philoxenus von Mabbug und ihre Bedeutung für die christliche Spiritualität', in *Studies in honour of P. Smulders* (Assen, 1981), pp. 137–75.

[2] French trans. of no. 11 in *Parole de l'Orient* 3 (1972).

BABAI

From within the Persian Empire comes one work which may date from the late fifth century, by 'Babai whom Barsauma killed', addressed to Cyriacus; possibly the Catholicos Baboway (d. 484) is meant. The author was evidently a convert from Zoroastrianism and the work[1] consists of guidelines for the monastic life interspersed with homely examples taken from fables and proverbs, perhaps imitating the older Wisdom instruction literature.

EAST SYRIAN WRITERS
LATE SIXTH TO EIGHTH CENTURIES

The mid sixth century witnessed a monastic revival in north Mesopotamia which was to produce an extensive literature on spirituality in the Church of the East over the next couple of centuries. The earliest representatives are: (1) Abraham of Nethpar, whose works are largely unpublished; (2) Shubhalmaran ('Praise to our Lord'), Bishop of Karka d-Beit Slokh (Kerkuk) and author of 'The Book of Parts' (ET by D. Lane in preparation); (3) Babai the Great (d. 628), the East Syrian theologian *par excellence*, and author of a *Book of Perfection* (lost) and a commentary on Evagrius' *Kephalaia Gnostica* (ed. Frankenberg, 1912); and (4) Gregory of Cyprus, a monk from northern Mesopotamia who spent some time in Cyprus (later tradition wrongly placed him in the fourth century). Gregory is the author of seven monastic treatises and a collection of letters; the only treatise so far published is his *De Theoria Sancta*, which seeks to correct certain misconceptions about 'contemplation' and to put forward the true teaching of the 'sages' on the subject.

MARTYRIUS

Martyrius, the author of a long work entitled *The Book of Perfection*, can be identified with Sahdona (which 'Martyrius' translates), a bishop who was violently attacked by East Syrian writers for his 'Chalcedonian' theological views (he was expelled from the Persian church and took refuge near Edessa).

Throughout his book Martyrius lays emphasis on the centrality of love, on the need for purity of heart and the interiorization of the ascetic effort. It is a work of evident religious fervour, and is remarkable both for its freshness of approach and for its strongly biblical orientation; the latter is brought out by the very large number of biblical quotations and allusions (far more than in the works of his contemporaries), and by the emphasis on the heart as the focal point of the inner person, rather than

[1] ET S. Brock, Kalamazoo, Cistercian Publications, in preparation.

the mind, as was becoming the norm under the influence of the Evagrian and Dionysian traditions.

There also survive five letters to monks, and some maxims. The fifth letter is to someone who complained that *The Book of Perfection* did not contain directives on the more advanced stages of contemplation; in reply Martyrius offers some advice, but it is clear that he is unwilling to tread on such delicate ground.

ISAAC OF NINEVEH

Isaac of Nineveh, or 'the Syrian', is the best known of Syriac writers on spirituality, and thanks to early translations into Greek and Arabic he has proved influential outside as well as within the Syrian churches. Extremely little is known of his life: he originated from Qatar (Persian Gulf) and was consecrated Bishop of Nineveh some time between 660 and 680, only to retire after five months to live a life of solitude.

Isaac's main surviving work is entitled *The First Part of the Teaching of Mar Isaac on the Monastic Life*, in 82 chapters; this is the work translated by Wensinck. The ninth-century Greek translation, made at the monastery of St Saba (Palestine) and printed first in 1770, has a different ordering of chapters.[1]

Isaac is not a systematic writer, and he draws on both the intellectualist traditions of Evagrius and Dionysius and the more experiential ones of the Macarian Homilies and the native Syriac writers. The absolute prerequisite for the spiritual life lies in renunciation of the 'world', by which Isaac understands the 'self' as much as the external world. The Christian life is essentially seen as the imitation of Christ, and, since Christ 'clothed himself in humility', so the Christian must 'compel himself' to put on profound humility, for only then will the heart become truly compassionate. Isaac probably owes much to John the Solitary, whose threefold pattern of the spiritual life he adopts and adapts: for Isaac the second stage ('of the soul') aims at restoring the soul to its original state of impassibility, while the third stage ('of the spirit') goes beyond all that human nature is capable of, and lies entirely as a gift from God; it represents a state encountered only extremely rarely, and is characterized by a movement beyond 'pure prayer' to one of total rest, where the will is taken over by the Spirit; it is a state which coincides with the life of the resurrection.

Isaac's writings were widely read by members of all ecclesiastical traditions (objectionable names, such as that of Theodore of Mopsuestia,

---

[1] See Wensinck, p. xiv, and (in more detail) K. Deppe in *P. de Lagarde und die syrische Kirchengeschichte* (Göttingen, 1968), pp. 48–57. The lost *Second Part* of Isaac's writings has recently been found.

were altered by Syrian Orthodox and Melkite scribes). From Greek derives (1) the Latin *De contemptu mundi*, first printed 1506, and (2) the Slavonic, from which excerpts were incorporated into the Russian edition of the *Philokalia*.[1]

DADISHO AND SIMEON

In his *Early Christian Mystics* Mingana includes works by two contemporaries of Isaac, Simeon 'the graceful' (d-Taybutheh) and Dadisho of Qatar; both belong to the monastic world of northern Iraq. Simeon's work represents the fusion of various traditions of spirituality characteristic of all East Syrian writers of the period; a notable feature is his interest in physiology and his emphasis on the interrelationship between the individual and the rest of creation. Of Dadisho's writings his lengthy commentary on Abba Isaiah's *Askēticon* and a treatise on solitude and prayer have been published; the latter is addressed to monks who adopt the eremitical life for certain periods, offering practical advice on how to achieve the goal of 'pure prayer'.

JOSEPH HAZZAYA

Joseph Hazzaya ('the seer') was born *c*. 710–13 of Zoroastrian parents. Taken captive as a child, he was eventually converted by the example of some local monks, and on being freed he became a monk himself. Only a few of his surviving writings have been published, notably some texts included in *Early Christian Mystics* (some are under the name of his brother Abdisho), and a long letter on the three stages of the spiritual life, wrongly attributed to Philoxenus.

Although he has been called 'le théoricien par excellence de la mystique nestorienne' (Beulay), it is clear that his writings are based on personal experience. His synthesis of the various traditions provides the following correspondences: (1) 'stage of the body' (the terminology derives from John the Solitary), concerned with external practices, fasts, vigils, psalmody, etc.; this belongs to the cenobitic life and its aim is 'purity'; it corresponds to the Evagrian *praktikē* and the Dionysian 'purification'. (2) 'Stage of the soul', concerned with the interior virtues such as humility, patience; this stage belongs to the solitary life, and its aim is *shaphyutha*, 'lucidity', etc.; it corresponds to the Evagrian 'natural contemplation' and the Dionysian 'illumination'. (3) 'Stage of the spirit', concerned no longer with the activities of the senses or the soul, but with those of the mind; characteristic of this stage, which represents 'perfection', is the vision of the formless light of the Trinity and of the risen

[1] ET in E. Kadloubovsky (or Kadleigh) and G. E. H. Palmer, *Early Fathers from the Philokalia* (London, Faber, 1954), pp. 181–280.

Christ; the stage corresponds to the Evagrian *theologia* and the Dionysian 'unification'.

JOHN OF DALYATHA

John of Dalyatha, or 'the Elder' (Saba), belonged to the monastic circles in early eighth-century northern Iraq which were misguidedly accused of Messalianism (see pp. 160, 173) by the authorities of the Church of the East, and his writings were condemned (along with those of Joseph) at a synod in 786/7. Of his surviving works the most important are the homilies and the letters (only the latter have been published).[1]

John is an unsystematic writer with an intuitive approach. Although there is the usual veneer of Evagrian language, he is closest to the experiential tradition of spirituality. The mystical life is for him the fruit of baptism and the Eucharist, representing an anticipation of the resurrection (a constant theme of the native Syriac tradition). His letters for the most part deal with an advanced stage in the spiritual life, and are notable for the fervour of their expression and the vivid imagery of the spiritual senses; he frequently breaks out into prayer.

Despite their condemnation his works were widely read, and were also well known in Syrian Orthodox and Melkite circles as well. There are Arabic and (partial) Greek[2] translations.

LATER WRITERS

The later period of Syriac spirituality has been little studied and only three works are available in translation.

Chapter 8 of the *Life* of the East Syrian monk Joseph Busnaya (d. 979) by his pupil John bar Kaldun contains an outline of Joseph's instructions to monks, starting from the noviciate and ending with a description of the 'three stages' (following Joseph Hazzaya's pattern).

Barhebraeus (1225/6–1286), 'Maphrian of the East' (an office second only to that of the Syrian Orthodox Patriarch), was a man of ecumenical vision, besides being one of the most learned writers of his time. Towards the end of his life he experienced a religious crisis, becoming aware of the contrast between his high office and the inadequacy of his spiritual life; in response he turned to 'the writings of the initiated, Abba Evagrius and others', and in due course wrote the *Ethicon*, containing directives for Christian living (lay as well as monastic), and the *Book of the Dove*, intended as a guide for monks who have no spiritual director. The first

---

[1] ET of the homilies by B. Colless is promised.
[2] Homilies 1,18,20 and Letter 18 (rules for novices; this also appears as no. 24 of the Teachings of Dorotheus: see I. Hausherr *OCP* 6 [1940], pp. 220–1).

and second sections of the *Book of the Dove* deal with conduct in the monastery and in the cell, while the third concerns the higher stages of spiritual life, and the fourth (with an autobiographical preface) consists of a century of sayings to illustrate 'a part of what the flash of lightning revealed to me in the darkness of night'. In these works Barhebraeus shows the influence of Al-Ghazali (see pp. 502–3).

From the late fifteenth century comes Mas'ud's *Book of the Spiritual Ship*, written in verse.

Almost no Syriac writings of the Ottoman period have been published. The seventeenth to nineteenth centuries saw several translations into Syriac of Western spiritual classics, such as Thomas à Kempis' *Imitation of Christ* (1715, printed 1857; modern Syriac translation by P. Bedjan,[1] 1885), and John Bunyan's *Pilgrim's Progress* (modern Syriac, published by the American Presbyterian Mission, Urmi, 1848).

---

[1] Among Bedjan's large output was a modern Syriac *Manuel de piété* (1886, 1893).

V

INSULAR TRADITIONS

1 Celtic Spirituality

DIARMUID O'LAOGHAIRE

GENERAL HISTORICAL BACKGROUND

Dillon, M., and Chadwick, N. K., *The Celtic Realms*. 2nd edn, London, Weidenfeld & Nicolson, 1973.

Jackson, K. H., *Studies in Early Celtic Nature Poetry*. CUP, 1935.

Jackson, K. H., *A Celtic Miscellany* (ed. and trans.). London, Routledge & Kegan Paul, 1979; Cambridge, Mass., Harvard University Press, 1951.

Powell, T. G. E. *The Celts*. 2nd edn, London and New York, Thames & Hudson, 1980.

Raftery, J., *The Celts*. Cork, 1964.

Rees, A. and B., *Celtic Heritage*. London, Thames & Hudson; New York, Grove Press, 1961.

GENERAL HISTORY OF CELTIC SPIRITUALITY

Bulloch, J. B., *The Life of the Celtic Church*. Edinburgh, St Andrew Press, 1963.

Chadwick, N. K., *The Age of the Saints in the Early Celtic Church*. OUP, 1961; with corrections, 1963.

Duckett, E., *The Wandering Saints*. London, Collins, 1959 = *The Wandering Saints of the Early Middle Ages*, New York, Norton, 1959.

Gougaud, L., *Christianity in Celtic Lands*. London, 1832.

MacNeill, J. T., *The Celtic Churches. A History, A.D. 200 to 1200*. Chicago, University of Chicago, 1974.

SPECIFIC CHURCHES AND SPIRITUALITIES

Ashley, A., *The Church in the Isle of Man*. London, St Anthony's Press, 1958.

Bieler, L., *Ireland: Harbinger of the Middle Ages*. OUP, 1963.

Chadwick, N. K., *Early Brittany*. Cardiff, University of Wales Press, 1969.

Curran, M., *The Antiphonary of Bangor*. Dublin, Irish Academic Press, 1983.

Daniel-Rops, H., ed., (ET) *The Miracle of Ireland*. London, Burns, Oates & Washbourne; Dublin, Clonmore & Reynolds; Baltimore, Helicon Press, 1959.

Dodd, B. E., and Heritage, T. C., *The Early Christians in Britain*. London, Longmans, 1966.

Essays on aspects of Celtic monasticism, in *Monastic Studies* 14. Montreal, 1983.

Godel, W., (ET) 'Irish Prayer in the Early Middle Ages'. *Milltown Studies*, Dublin, 1979–1982.

Gwynn, E. J., 'The Teaching of Mael-ruain'. *Hermathena*, vol. 44, 2nd supplemental vol. (Dublin, Hodges, 1927), 1–63.

Gwynn, E. J., and Purton, W. J., 'The Monastery of Tallaght'. *Proceedings of the Royal Irish Academy*, 29, C, 115–79 (1911).

Hughes, K., *The Church in Early Irish Society*. London, Methuen, 1966.

Kenney, J. F., *The Sources for the Early Irish History of Ireland*. I. *Ecclesiastical*. 2nd edn, Dublin and New York, Columbia University Press, 1977.

Largillière, R., *Les Saints et l'organisation chrétienne primitive dans l'Armorique Bretonne*. Rennes, 1925.

Maher, M., ed., *Irish Spirituality*. Dublin, Veritas, 1981.

McNally, R. E., ed., *Old Ireland*. Dublin, Gill; New York, Fordham University Press, 1965.

O'Dwyer, P., *Céli Dé Spiritual Reform in Ireland, 750–900*. Dublin, Taillura, 1981.

O'Dwyer, P., *Devotion to Mary in Ireland, 700–1100*. Dublin, Carmelite Publications, 1976.

Plummer, C., *Irish Litanies*. Henry Bradshaw Society, vol. 62, London, 1925.

Ryan, J., *Irish Monasticism*. London, Longmans, 1931; Shannon, Irish University Press; Ithaca, N.Y., Cornell University Press, 1972.

Victory, S., *The Celtic Church in Wales*. London, SPCK, 1977.

INDIVIDUAL SAINTS

Anderson, A. O. and M. O., ed. and (ET), *Adamnan's Life of Columba*. London, and New York, Nelson, 1961.

Baring-Gould, S., *The Lives of the British Saints*, vols. i–iv. London, C. J. Clark, 1907–13.

Bede, *Historia Ecclesiastica Gentis Anglorum*, ed. and (ET) B. Colgrave and R. A. B. Mynors. OUP, 1969 (much reference to Irish saints).

Bieler, L., *The Life and Legend of St Patrick*. Dublin, Clonmore & Reynolds, 1949.

Bieler, L., *Libri Epistolarum Sancti Patricii Episcopi* I, II. Dublin, Irish Manuscripts Commission, 1952.

Doble, G. H., 'Cornish Saints' Series, Long Compton, King's Store Press, 1927–41. Reprinted as *The Saints of Cornwall*, Truro, Dean and Chapter, 1960.

Mélanges Colombaniens, *Actes du Congrès International de Luxeuil, 20–23 juillet, 1950*. Paris, 1951.

Mould, D. D. C. Pochin, *The Irish Saints*. Dublin, Clonmore & Reynolds; London, Burns & Oates, 1964.

O'Kelleher, A., and Schoepperle, G., *Betha Colaim Chille: Life of Columcille compiled by Manus O'Donnell in 1582*. Chicago, J. A. O'Donnell, 1918.

Plummer, C., *Vitae Sanctorum Hiberniae* I, II (text and ET). Oxford, Clarendon, 1910.

Plummer, C., *Bethada Naém nÉrenn* I, II (text and ET). Oxford, Clarendon, 1922.

XIIIᵉ Centenaire de Saint Fiacre. *Actes du Congrès*, Meaux, 1970.

Walker, G. S. M., *Sancti Columbani Opera* (with trans.). Dublin, Institute for Advanced Studies, 1957.

OTHER RELEVANT TEXTS

Bieler, L., ed., *The Irish Penitentials*. Dublin, Institute for Advanced Studies, 1963.

Bischoff, B., (ET) 'Turning Points in the History of Latin Exegesis in the Early Middle Ages'. *Proceedings of The Irish Biblical Association*, 1976, 74–160.

Carney, J., *The Poems of Blathmac*. Dublin, Educational Co. of Ireland, 1964.

Flower, R., *The Irish Tradition*. Oxford, Clarendon Press, 1947.

Henry, F., *Irish Art in the Early Christian Period to 800 A.D.* London, Methuen; Ithaca, Cornell University Press, 1965.

Henry, F., *Irish Art during the Viking Invasions, 800–1020 A.D.* London, Methuen; Ithaca, Cornell University Press, 1967.

Henry, F., *Irish Art in the Romanesque Period, 1020–1170 A.D.* London, Methuen; Ithaca, Cornell University Press, 1970.

Kuypers, A. B., *The Book of Cerne*. CUP, 1902.

Murphy, G., *Early Irish Lyrics*. Oxford, Clarendon, 1956.

The works of Kenney and Ryan cited above contain extensive bibliographies.

We speak of the spirituality of the six Celtic lands before the coming of the Normans (or Anglo-Normans, as in the case of Ireland, who arrived there in 1169), namely, Ireland, Scotland, Wales, Cornwall, Brittany and the Isle of Man. Ireland, Scotland and the Isle of Man could be regarded as a unit, but we have very little knowledge of the Isle of Man. The other three Brythonic lands can likewise be regarded as a unit within the whole Celtic complex. Of all the countries Ireland is by far the best documented in itself and in its relations with Irish foundations in Scotland and Northumbria. However, in terms of spirituality, most of what we say of Ireland can be applied to all the other Celts. A symbol of that unity could be the *Penitentials*,[1] where we have gathered matter from Ireland, Wales and Brittany. Sometimes, of course, that might mean just copying in Brittany of Irish matter, but that fact alone shows the unity, and in what deeply concerns the progress of the soul.

Ireland, unlike Britain, was never subject to Rome or Roman law. Her first full contact with Rome, then, was through the Christian faith. Saint Patrick, a Roman Briton, is the only known apostle of Ireland,[2] although it seems he laboured mostly in the northern half of the country. There were Christians in Ireland before he came, but what evangelizers there were left us nothing in writing, whereas we have two authentic and most precious documents from the fifth-century Patrick. It is doubtful if any evangelizer left such a lasting imprint on his spiritual children as did

---

[1] ef. Bieler, *The Irish Penitentials*.

[2] There was Palladius, of course, but all we know of him is that he was sent 'to the Irish who believed in Christ' (Prosper of Aquitaine).

Patrick. As we will see, some of his outstanding traits were reproduced in the Irish. So, he speaks many times of being an exile till death for Christian Ireland; his writings abound with quotations and echoes from Scripture, notably from St Paul; in his *Confession* he speaks of his constantly repeated prayer out in the open, day and night, no matter how harsh the weather, when a slave in Ireland (*Conf.* 16).

It is a remarkable fact that in less than a hundred years after Patrick the Church in Ireland was not diocesan but monastic, and although obviously not lacking bishops, was governed by abbots of important monasteries – who might also be bishops. So it was also in the other Celtic lands, with some variations where Roman influence was greater. Saint Patrick himself tells us how astonished he was at the numbers of his newly-baptized who chose to be monks and virgins of Christ. Presumably unorganized, they were the predecessors of thousands such in monasteries and convents throughout the land.

In these monasteries prayer, study and manual labour were cultivated with great diligence; and study, above all, meant study of the Scriptures. The psalms were held in the greatest veneration and it is a commonplace in the lives of the saints to read that young children were sent to read their psalms with some holy man. The whole spirituality was deeply scriptural. To this day, we have visible proof of the honour and love lavished on the word of God. In Ireland we have the Book of Kells from the eighth or ninth century, an incomparable shrine of the four Gospels, and the high crosses on which are depicted the history of salvation, all summed up in the cross itself, from Adam and Eve to the death and resurrection of Christ and his second coming. Saint Illtud, the British saint, born perhaps in Brittany, in the fifth century, can be considered typical in his devotion to the Scriptures. We are told of him in the early seventh-century life of that other great saint Samson, who from his native Britain (or Wales) went a pilgrim to Brittany, there to labour with great success. Illtud, we are told, was the most learned of all the Britons in the knowledge of Scripture, both the Old and the New Testaments. Another such was Saint Adamnan from the seventh century, successor of Saint Colm Cille (Columba) as abbot in Iona and his biographer. Of him Bede wrote in his *Ecclesiastical History of the English People*: 'He was a good and wise man with an excellent knowledge of the Scriptures' (V.15). Bede, who so loved the Irish, is an important witness to the place Scripture held in Ireland. He tells us of the holy English priest, Egbert, who 'had lived long in exile in Ireland for the sake of Christ and was most learned in the Scriptures . . .' (III.4), and of Agilbert, a Gaulish bishop, 'who had spent a long time in Ireland for the purpose of studying the Scriptures' (III.7). Professor Bernhard Bischoff in our own time is showing us the remarkable extent of Irish scriptural studies on the Continent in the early Middle Ages.[1]

The height of asceticism among the Celts was considered to be exile and perpetual pilgrimage for the sake of Christ. We have just seen how Bede makes use of the phrase. We have no evidence that the Irish monks knowingly imitated Patrick in this. Their exemplar, as in so many things, came from the Scriptures – Abraham, commanded by God to leave his own land and people for the Promised Land. Exile could be imposed as a penalty under the law for crime, and perhaps the thought of penance for sin entered into this Christian exile, but the motive usually given is positive and personal – for the sake of Christ, for the eternal fatherland, etc. It has often been noted that the motive did not seem to be missionary, but ascetic. However, we note that Saint Aidan, as Bede tells us, came from Iona at King Oswald's request to evangelize Northumbria in the early seventh century. Bede, once again, tells us of Saint Fursa that he came from Ireland to East Anglia

> to live the life of a pilgrim for the Lord's sake, whenever opportunity offered. When he came . . . he . . . followed his usual task of preaching the gospel. Thus he converted many both by the example of his virtues and the persuasiveness of his teaching, turning unbelievers to Christ and confirming believers in his faith and love (III.18).

Saint Columbanus himself, but in a letter written to his disciples in Luxeuil, when he had been expelled from there, says, 'It was in my wish to visit the heathen and have the gospel preached to them' (Walker, *Sancti Columbani Opera*, pp. 30–1). Since the Irish monks at home were used to ministering to the people it would have come naturally to them to do so abroad, nor could they pretend to be pilgrims for Christ if they were to neglect those in need of Christ. Indeed we have a verse from the *Rule* attributed to Saint Ailbhe:

> Their Father is noble God,
> their mother is holy Church;
> let it not be mouth-humility,
> let everyone have pity on his fellow.

Saint Colm Cille was the first great exile for Christ (his biographer, Adamnan, gives us the motive) and is regarded as the exile *par excellence*. In the many poems attributed to him there is much nostalgia for his homeland. In the early sixteenth-century *Life* which contains much from Adamnan and much that is legend we have a passage that we may confidently take as representing the mind and heart of those exiles:

[1] cf. 'Turning Points in the history of Latin exegesis in the Early Middle Ages'.

When Colm Cille was going into exile to Scotland, Mochonna, this holy child of whom we have spoken, said that he would go with him. 'Don't go,' said Colm Cille, 'but remain with your father and mother in your own country.' 'You are my father,' said Mochonna, 'and the Church is my mother, and the place in which I can give most service to God is my country,' said he, 'and since it is you, Colm Cille, who have bound me to Christ, I will follow you till you bring me to where he is.' And then he took the vow of pilgrimage.[1]

This ascetic desire, and love of God, took the Celts to all kinds of remote isles, even to the Faroes and Iceland, as well as to the nearer offshore islands of Britain, Ireland and Brittany. The *Anglo-Saxon Chronicle* for the year 891 or 892 gives a completely typical example of three Irishmen whom it names, who in utter trust in God put to sea without oars and landed in Cornwall. Within their own lands also remote places were sought out. Hence the place-name 'Díseart' in Ireland (where there are more than eighty such) and Scotland, and 'Dyserth' in Wales for those desert-places. Of course, there were definite places of pilgrimage, notably Jerusalem and Rome. In fact, the Irish word 'rómh' or 'ruamh' (from 'Roma') became a common noun, meaning a holy burying-ground, and therefore a place of pilgrimage, and we are told of soil being brought from the graves of Peter and Paul and other saints to spread in Irish graveyards.

The faith had been planted in Ireland without martyrdom, although Patrick was ready for it and went daily in danger of his life (*Conf.* 35, 37, 55). However, we find the ideal of martyrdom expressed, in both Latin and Irish texts, in terms of white, blue and red martyrdom. White martyrdom was the daily living of the ascetic life for Christ's sake; red, of course, meant the shedding of blood and death itself for Christ's sake. Blue martyrdom, which seems to have been a particularly Irish development, stood for the way of the penitent in penance, in bewailing of sins and in labour. Clare Stancliffe recently has argued very well that lay penitents could qualify to rank with the martyrs and monks, leaving as an open question whether their penitence was lifelong or for a fixed number of years.[2]

The principle *contraria contrariis sanantur*, contraries are cured by their contraries, popularized by John Cassian, was adopted wholeheartedly, first perhaps by the Welsh, and through them by the Irish. In the *Penitential* of Finnian we have the oft-repeated counsel:

---

[1] O'Kelleher-Schoepperle, *Betha Colaim Chille*, p. 136.
[2] Stancliffe, C., 'Red, white and blue martyrdom', in *Ireland in Early Mediaeval Europe. Studies in memory of Kathleen Hughes*, ed. David Dumville (CUP, 1982), pp. 21–46. Also relevant is Pádraig P. Ó Néill, 'Background to the Cambrai Homily', in *Ériu* (Dublin, 1981), pp. 137–48.

But, by contraries . . . let us make haste to cure contraries and to cleanse away these faults from our hearts and introduce heavenly virtues in their place; patience must arise for wrathfulness; kindliness, or the love of God and of one's neighbour, for envy; for detraction, restraint of heart and tongue; for dejection, spiritual joy; for greed, liberality.[1]

These *Penitentials* were for the laity as well, and could be severe enough, and restrictive, for instance in such a thing as marital intercourse. We know that they had a great influence abroad, and if the Irish did not introduce private penance there, at least they greatly extended its use, and after Saint Columbanus it seems to have become the norm. No doubt the practice of *anamchairdeas*, spiritual direction, literally 'soul-friendship', exercised by the *anamchara* or 'soul-friend' – also for lay people – was a great help towards fervour of life and the promotion of private penance and confession. 'Colainn gan cheann duine gan anam-chara' (a person without a soul-friend is a body without a head) was a very telling and common maxim. Here it is right to note the constant stress on purity of heart. A tonsured head, went an ancient verse, is not pleasing to God unless the heart, too, be tonsured. The *Penitentials* and the monastic Rules consistently deal with that issue, as we have just seen, for example, in Finnian's words. So Gildas in the *Preface on Penance* attributed to him tells the repentant cleric to 'at all times deplore his guilt from his inmost heart'.[2]

The practice of soul-friendship is of a piece with the general attitude towards the spiritual and monastic life. Allowance was always made for the individual. Even in the same monastery and under the same Rule the Holy Spirit must be allowed to lead as he wills. In the *Rule of Mochuda* we read: 'Different is the condition of everyone, different the nature of the place, different the law by which food is diminished or increased.'[3] The austere Columbanus himself stresses that principle. He speaks of the choir office: 'Although the length of time standing or singing may be various, yet the identity of prayer in the heart and mental concentration that is unceasing with God's help will be of a single excellence.'[4] We are reminded of the famous ninth century quatrain, composed perhaps by a disillusioned pilgrim: 'Techt do Róim . . .'

> To come to Rome:
> much labour, little profit –
> the King you seek here
> you will not find him unless you bring him with you.

[1] Bieler, op. cit., p. 85.
[2] ib. p. 61.
[3] Quoted in Hughes, *The Church in Early Irish Society*, p. 183.
[4] Walker, op. cit., pp. 132–3.

One rightly associates corporal austerity with Celtic spirituality. It is summed up in the rather muddled life of Saint (or Saints) Padarn, where we read that his father came to Ireland there to spend his life in watching and fasting, praying day and night with genuflexions. Bede, in a number of places in his *History*, speaks with admiration of the ascetic life led by the Irish monks, especially Aidan, in his own Northumbria. In addition to the ordinary season of Lent, the Lent of Jesus, as they called it, the Irish also observed the Lent of Elias in winter and that of Moses after Pentecost. We note again the love of Scripture and of the holy ones of the Old Testament, who were also celebrated liturgically. The body was made to offer its meed of praise to God. The *crosfhigheall* or cross-vigil, praying with outstretched arms for long periods, was very popular. When we read that a bird came and nested in the outstretched hands of a saint, we may perhaps conclude that such a mystical state was not unknown. As regards genuflexions, to which we may add frequent signs of the cross, it was not uncommon to see such in our own time in churches and pilgrimages. Praying the psalms in ice-cold water is mentioned so often that, as Dr Bieler said, it may well have been an ascetic practice. In all such austerities we find the motive to be love of God, and we cannot exclude what is called the folly of the cross. The ancient penitential pilgrimage to Loch Dearg with its three-day fast is still very much alive, as well as the pilgrimage to Cruach Phádraig, the mountain of penance traditionally associated, as is Loch Dearg, with St Patrick. In the ancient tradition also were the penitential practices in our day of Father Willie Doyle and the holy layman, Matt Talbot.

We have a large body of prayer, both in Irish and Latin, and mostly in verse. There are quite a number of very heartfelt and prolix prayers of repentance in Latin, as well as prayers in Irish in disciplined verse. There are also litanies to which the Irish were very given. There was no objection to repetitious prayer. A feature of prayer in general is that so much of it is loosely litanic in form. The *lorica* or breastplate prayer, such as the well-known ninth-century Breastplate of Saint Patrick, was very popular. The *lorica* may well have been pagan in origin, as a charm against natural phenomena and evil spirits, but as a Christian prayer it has also the interior and Christian dimension. These prayers convey a sense of completeness, for example, in enumerating the members of the body, external circumstances, all the various groups of the heavenly and earthly Church, represented by the outstanding saints. Everything, external and internal, was to be under the sway of God. Here is one of the *loricae*, that of St Fursa, the language of which dates from about the ninth century:

> May the yoke of the Law of God be upon this shoulder,
> the coming of the Holy Spirit on this head,

the sign of Christ on this forehead,
the hearing of the Holy Spirit in these ears,
the smelling of the Holy Spirit in this nose,
the vision that the people of heaven have in these eyes,
the speech of the people of heaven in this mouth,
the work of the Church of God in these hands,
the good of God and of the neighbour in these feet.
May God dwell in this heart
and this person belong entirely to God the Father!

The Last Judgement is prominent in Celtic, and especially (there are more documents) in Irish spirituality, but I think some authors err when they speak of it, and of an avenging God, as being dominant features.[1] The intimate and human side of that spirituality (which are still characteristic of it) must be stressed. About the mid-seventh century arose the reforming movement of the *Céili Dé* (Servants of God) which sought to revitalize the ancient asceticism. That movement, which fostered the eremitical life, and which might to some extent be called today 'puritanical', produced the most beautiful of lyrical and nature poetry and other works of religious art. Many of the lyrics are actually prayers. The purity of vision and language in that poetry is as if their great detachment from created things had helped the poets to share in the Creator's own vision of his creation.

The poems of Blathmhac (*c.* 750)[2] in honour of our Lady and her Son show a great tenderness and humanity. The poet asks Mary to come to him that he might lament with her the death of her beautiful Son. He speaks of consoling her heart. The poet tells that when our Lord after his death returned to heaven and 'when the household of heaven welcomed their true heart, Mary, your beautiful Son broke into tears in their presence'. Not till almost half a millennium later, when the humanity of the suffering Christ came to be stressed, do we come across such tender language in this part of Christendom. In another well-known poem (*c.* 800) God himself is addressed as 'mu chridecán', my little heart.[3] Again, there is the poem in which St Íde welcomes to her little hermitage 'Ísucán', the Infant Jesus (*c.* 900).[4] The poem is full of diminutives such as a mother would use with her child, one of the verbs even being in a completely untranslatable diminutive form! (It would be pleasant, if we had space to recount some of the whimsical stories that show so long before St Francis himself what intimate relations the saints had with the animals.)

[1] e.g. Godel, op. cit.
[2] Ed. Carney.
[3] Murphy, *Early Irish Lyrics*, pp. 112–13.
[4] id., pp. 26–7.

So then, although we find many prayers to the Trinity and much stress on the majesty of God (cf. Columbanus, but also note how he speaks of Christ and also what we might term his warm, mystical passages), all that is well balanced by constant reference to the humanity of Christ. He is 'Ri' (King), certainly, as is his Father, but in the Irish sense of the term, where the king in each of the hundred or so statelets (*tuatha*) was one of his people and in their midst, and closely related to not a few of them. In modern traditional prayers 'Ri' is still the commonest of terms in addressing Christ or his Father. This aspect of Christ is completed, as it were, in the very corporate (which does not exclude the individual) Christianity of the old Irish. In particular, I suppose the institution of the *tuath*, with the great stress on kindred, was a help towards realizing the Church as the Body of Christ (Christ himself has always been referred to as 'Mac Mhuire', the Son of Mary, or anciently in Welsh also, 'Mab Mair'). Very significant is the word *muintir*, meaning 'family' and derived from the Latin *monasterium*. The monastery fitted splendidly into the close-knit native society. The derived adjective, *muinteartha*, means 'friendly, intimate, affectionate' – 'familiar' (in the radical and best sense). Hence, when it came to hospitality and almsgiving, not to mention other ways of doing 'the good of God and the neighbour', it is not surprising to see the famous passage in Matthew 25 so often repeated.

2 The Anglo-Saxon Tradition

MILTON MCC. GATCH

Aldhelm: The Prose Works, trans. M. Lapidge and M. Herren. Ipswich and Cambridge, D. S. Brewer; Totowa, N. J., Rowman & Littlefield, 1979.

Bede's Ecclesiastical History of the English People, ed. B. Colgrave and R. A. B. Mynors. Oxford Medieval Texts. Oxford, Clarendon, 1969 (= *HE*).

Blair, P. H., *An Introduction to Anglo-Saxon England*. 2nd edn, CUP, 1977.

Butler, E. C., *Western Mysticism*. London, Constable, 1922.

Duckett, E. S., *Anglo-Saxon Saints and Scholars*. New York, Macmillan, 1947.

Emmerson, R. K., *Antichrist in the Middle Ages*. Manchester University Press, 1981.

English Historical Documents, ed. D. C. Douglas. Vol. 1 (*c*. 500–1042) ed. D. Whitelock. 2nd edn, London, Methuen, 1979 (= *EHD* I).

Gatch, M. McC., *Loyalties and Traditions*. New York, Pegasus, 1971.

Gatch, M. McC., *Preaching and Theology in Anglo-Saxon England: Aelfric and Wulfstan*. University of Toronto Press, 1977.

Godfrey, C. J., *The Church in Anglo-Saxon England*. CUP, 1962.

Ritzke-Rutherford, J., 'Anglo-Saxon Antecedents of the Middle English Mystics', in *The Medieval Mystical Tradition in England*, ed. M. Glasscoe (University of Exeter, 1980), pp. 216–33.

Swanton, M. ed., and comp., *Anglo-Saxon Prose*. London, Dent, 1975.

The history of spirituality among the Christians of Anglo-Saxon England has not been the subject of separate studies; the ground has not been carefully or systematically charted, and there are no comprehensive anthologies of the materials that should be reviewed by students of the period. Here primary attention will be given to two major figures who lived at the turn of the seventh and eighth centuries, and reference will be made as well to major developments from the end of the ninth to the beginning of the eleventh centuries.

Pope Gregory the Great sent missionaries to England in 597. There had been Christians in Roman Britain, whose descendants had been unable or unwilling to convert the pagan Anglo-Saxon settlers; but Gregory's mission and later missions in the seventh century brought about the conversion of the Saxon kings and their subjects. As a result, although missionaries from Ireland played a very important role in the conversion and in the establishment of a distinctive Anglo-Saxon Christian culture, Anglo-Saxon Christians looked with special fondness to Rome and to the Latin Fathers, of whom Gregory I was himself the last. King Alfred (d. 899) was later to refer to Gregory as 'the best of the Romans, wisest man, most famous for deeds of glory' (*EHD* I. no. 226(b)). In the following study, the Anglo-Saxon spiritual teachers will be seen turning again and again for guidance to the Latin Fathers, to the traditions of biblical exegesis, and to monasticism – all of which they knew first and most definitely through Gregory and others from Rome.

ALDHELM

According to the twelfth-century historian, William of Malmesbury, Aldhelm first studied with one Máeldub, a scholar of Irish birth. This assertion cannot be verified, although it is certain that Aldhelm was already a learned man when he went to Canterbury as a pupil of Abbot Hadrian, the associate of the Greek-born Archbishop of Canterbury, Theodore of Tarsus. Aldhelm's affectedly learned literary style, which used to be regarded as 'Hisperic' or Irish, is now recognized as having continental sources.[1] Aldhelm became Abbot of Malmesbury by 673 or

---

[1] Unless otherwise noted, biographical and interpretative material on Aldhelm is based on the introduction to *Aldhelm: the Prose Works*. The authoritative edn is R. Ehwald, *Aldhelmi Opera Omnia*, Monumenta Germaniae Historica, Auctores Antiquissimi, XV (Berlin, 1919).

674 and died in 709 or 710 after having served for about three years as the first bishop of the new see of Sherborne. William of Malmesbury had access to one important source for the life of Aldhelm which no longer survives, the *Handbook* of King Alfred the Great.[1] Alfred recorded that Aldhelm was gifted as a poet in the native tongue of the West Saxons. Because the layfolk who attended Mass at the monastic church of Malmesbury did not wait for the instruction that followed the Mass, Aldhelm is said to have waylaid them at the bridge over the river Avon, singing at first 'merry songs' and later psalms. Nothing of Aldhelm's verse in Old English survives, although it is arguable that there are traces of Anglo-Saxon poetic practice to be discerned in his Latin verse,[2] and a strong sense of his spiritual teachings can be gained from his Latin writing.

Three Latin prose works of Aldhelm may be mentioned here as evidence of his teaching on Christian spirituality. The first is a letter of uncertain date (perhaps 677) to abbots who were subject to Wilfrid, the ill-starred and controversial bishop who had been the champion of Roman ecclesiastical custom at the Synod of Whitby in 664.[3] Aldhelm's letter, written during one of Wilfrid's several periods of involuntary exile from his ecclesiastical posts, is supportive of Wilfrid. It states firmly the standard of loyalty Aldhelm thinks appropriate on the part of clergy towards their superiors. As though there had been an earthquake, the church has been shaken by turbulence leading to Wilfrid's expulsion from his see. The clergy are members of the same tribe as Wilfrid, who is their superior and lord. Aldhelm believes that 'the necessity of event requires that you along with your own bishop . . . be [voluntarily] expelled from your native land and go to any transmarine country in the wide world that is suitable'. The bishop has reared and cared for his clergy 'like a wet-nurse' from infancy to maturity. When the leader of bees leaves the hive, his cohorts follow. It is a law of nature, then, that the subject 'obeys the precept of its leader in the recurring course of time'. Aldhelm continues with a second example from secular life in his own times:

> If worldly men, exiles from divine teaching, were to desert a devoted master, whom they embraced in prosperity, but once the opulence of good times began to diminish and the adversity of bad fortune began its onslaught, they preferred the secure peace of their dear country to the burdens of a banished

[1] Duckett, pp. 41–2.
[2] M. Lapidge, 'Aldhelm's Latin Poetry and Old English Verse', in *Comparative Literature*, 31 (1979), pp. 209–31.
[3] Trans. in *Prose Works*, pp. 168–70, with introduction at pp. 150–1. Incomplete trans. in *EHD* I. no. 165.

master, are they not deemed worthy of the scorn of scathing laughter and the noise of mockery from all?

Aldhelm is striking the theme of loyalty: much as Tacitus described the loyalty of the *comitatus* system in the *Germania*, Aldhelm describes the expectations of loyalty between lord and dependant in secular life; and he applies the same standard to the relationship of lower clergy to their ecclesiastical superiors that secular society applied to kinship and lord-ship. If one remembers Alfred's tale about Aldhelm singing in the secular manner to the layfolk of Malmesbury and at the same time has in mind the imagery of the letter to the followers of Wilfrid, it is difficult to refrain from associating Aldhelm's spirituality with that of the greatest poem of the Anglo-Saxon era, *Beowulf*, or with *The Dream of the Rood* or the elegies of the Exeter Book, notably *The Wanderer* and *The Seafarer*. In all of these poems the motif of loyalty looms large, as also does the notion that the Christian's life in the world is an exile from the true homeland, lived by the follower of Christ in obedience and loyalty to the Lord, who was himself a voluntary exile for the sake of those he loved. The monastic or ascetic life was regarded as another and more rigorous form of voluntary exile.

Another letter shows Aldhelm as spiritual instructor in a far more learned mien, although the recipient was a layman. Even the title of the letter, 'Epistola ad Acircium', is abstruse: Acircium ('from the north') is a nickname for Aldfrith, king of Northumbria (685–705), who was probably Aldhelm's godson.[1] The document is a compendium. After an elaborate greeting in praise of the king, one finds a discourse on the symbolic meanings of the number seven, followed by a treatise on Latin prosody or metrics and a collection of one hundred riddles, the *Enig-mata*.[2] In a sense, each section of the 'Epistola and Acircium' is intended to inculcate true piety; but the treatise on the mysteries of the number seven does so most clearly and in a way quite recognizable to readers of patristic commentary.

This sevenfold measure of intervals, I say, came to be sacred from the very first beginning of the new-born world. For not only the entirety of all creation, which the revolving and moving pinnacle of the heavens and the double hemispheres gird, is said to have been brought into being in a multitude of forms in the sevenfold course of a single week, when he who lives in eternity made all things simultaneously in a single stroke; but also the hoped-for rest of future promise and the perennial felicity of the blessed life, which shall be paid to each and every one according to the amount of his merits, is granted to the

[1] Trans. and introd., ibid., pp. 31–47.
[2] For repr. of Pitman's trans. of *Enigmata*, see CCSL 133, pp. 359–540.

innocent and those free of the offence of sin only through a sevenfold increment of times, one thousand in number, after the throng of the impious has been separated.

Stylistically less accessible than much similar teaching on the spiritual significance of numbers, Aldhelm's treatise is typical in its contemplation of the hints concerning salvation contained in sevens from the days of creation, throughout Scripture and in the life of the Church (in the sacraments and the gifts of the Spirit), to the signs of the Apocalypse, 'sevenfold and sevenfold – in inscrutable recurrence'.

The final work of Aldhelm to be mentioned here is the prose treatise on virginity.[1] *De Virginitate* is addressed to the abbess Hildelith and other nuns of the monastery at Barking, one of a number of double-houses or communities of both monks and nuns under the leadership of a woman, usually of noble lineage. St Paul, it will be recalled, held that virginity was a high state and to be preferred to marriage if one was not already married and could keep the flesh under control; but it was not permitted by the apostle to put aside a marriage partner in order to embrace religious chastity. Nevertheless, it became a custom in Anglo-Saxon England for noble persons, usually women, to forsake their spouses for the monastic life, a practice that Archbishop Theodore apparently sanctioned, citing canons of the Eastern Church. In Aldhelm's treatise, local custom is upheld; and the more usual schema of the three states of chastity for women (virginity, widowhood and marriage) is altered so that others may be added to widows, under 'chastity'. Virgins are those who have never been harmed 'by any carnal defilement'; chastity includes those who, 'having been assigned to marital contracts, . . . scorned the commerce of matrimony for the sake of the heavenly kingdom'; and marriage exists 'for propagating the progeny of posterity' (cap. 19). A loosely-structured treatise, *De Virginitate* is an effort to teach nuns about a central tenet of the ascetic life which they have embraced.

Aldhelm, then, adopted as metaphors for his spiritual instruction images that were widely used in the secular discourse of his people; yet he also delighted in the traditions based in patristic writing of abstruse and symbolic approaches to spiritual teaching; and he reflected upon the tenets of monastic spirituality, adapting his teaching to the practices of Anglo-Saxon monasticism.

BEDE

The Venerable Bede, who died in his sixties in 735, is rivalled only by Aldhelm as the greatest scholar of his time. Known in our time primarily

[1] Trans. and introd. in *Prose Works*, pp. 59–132. Aldhelm also wrote a verse *De Virg*.

for his *Ecclesiastical History of the English People*, he was above all a monastic teacher and biblical exegete; and his literary or scholarly calling is inseparable from his primary vocation to the monastic life, to which he was dedicated by his parents at the age of seven. Bede's educational works, notably in grammar and computistics, are 'purely vocational in purpose . . . At each level of instruction, the novice was taught whatever might be of use . . . as an aspirant to wisdom' within the context of monastic discipline and spirituality.[1] So, too, the sermons on Scripture for use in the monastic community and the great volumes of biblical exegesis are firmly rooted in the highest traditions of patristic scholarship, most notably in the work of Augustine and Gregory the Great. For Bede, the monk and exegete, contemplation of Scripture is the basis of the spiritual life.[2]

The *History* is also a work of Christian spirituality, for in its pages one learns of both the external and the spiritual lives of the English, deriving either cautionary or exemplary guidance for one's own life (*HE*, pref.). All of one's life is to be spent in contemplation of death and the eternal life. Bede's pupil Cuthbert, in a letter reporting the manner of Bede's death, quotes in Old English a short poem that Bede recited frequently on his deathbed:

> Before the journey that awaits us all,
> No man becomes so wise that he has not
> Need to think out, before his going hence
> What judgement will be given to his soul
> After his death, of evil or of good.[3]

Bede's spirituality is, like the *Death-Song*, deeply eschatological.

Although much could be said about the spiritual teachings of Bede, it may be best in the present, limited context to discuss a profound example of lay spirituality related by Bede: the miracle story of an illiterate lay servant of the double-house of Whitby under the abbess Hilda, who learned the art of contemplation and the art of communicating the fruits of his contemplation to others. The story of Caedmon (*HE*, iv.24) involves the composition of the first Christian verse in English. It was the custom after festive meals to pass the harp about the table to all participants so that each could sing a song to entertain the company. Such songs

---

[1] M. H. King, '*Grammatica Mystica*: A Study of Bede's Grammatical Curriculum', in *Saints, Scholars and Heroes: Studies . . . in honour of Charles W. Jones*, ed. M. H. King and W. M. Stevens (Collegeville, St. John's Abbey; Ann Arbor, University Microfilms, 1979–   ), vol. 1, pp. 145–59, on p. 153.

[2] See Gatch, *Loyalties*, pp. 83ff., for discussion of Bede's exegesis.

[3] Trans. R. Hamer, *A Choice of Anglo-Saxon Verse* (London, Faber, 1970), p. 127. Full text of Cuthbert's letter printed in *HE*, pp. 580ff.

may have been either traditional poems memorized by the singer or verses composed on the occasion and performed on the spot. In either case, all were apparently expected to be able to recite or to compose poems on traditional subjects no matter what their social rank or education. But Caedmon always left feasts as the harp approached his place at table because he could not perform. Once when he absented himself in this way, Caedmon went to the cattle barn, where he was assigned the watch for the night. In his sleep, he dreamt that someone called upon him to sing:

> 'Caedmon,' he said, 'sing me something.' Caedmon answered, 'I cannot sing; that is why I left the feast and came here because I could not sing.' Once again the speaker said, 'Nevertheless you must sing to me.' 'What must I sing?' said Caedmon. 'Sing', he said, 'about the beginning of created things.' Thereupon Caedmon began to sing verses which he had never heard before in praise of God the Creator, of which this is the general sense: 'Now we must praise the Maker of the heavenly kingdom, the power of the Creator and his counsel, the deeds of the Father of glory and how he, since he is the eternal God, was the Author of all marvels and first created the heavens as a roof for the children of men and then, the almighty Guardian of the human race, created the earth' . . . When [Caedmon] awoke, he remembered all that he had sung while asleep and soon added more verses in the same manner, praising God in fitting style.

By divine intervention, it was believed, the herdsman who had not been able to master the art of composing or reciting secular verse had not only mastered the art of poetry but also – and this seems the locus of the miraculous aspect of the event in Bede's mind – had applied the traditional methods of composing poetry to a new subject-matter for which there were no traditional forms of expression; the praise of the Christian God.

The abbess Hilda and her advisers heard of this and, upon investigation, agreed that Caedmon had learned to sing through divine grace. They tested him further by having read to him a passage, probably from Scripture, and asking him to make a song of it. He went off for the night and returned in the morning with a song that passed the test. Caedmon was then tonsured and made a member of the monastic community. There he lived, composing songs on the whole range of biblical history and Christian hope, to the time of his death. Describing the manner in which Caedmon contemplated and appropriated the materials that he reworked into English verse, Bede uses language appropriate to his former occupation as a cowherd: 'He learned all he could by listening . . . and then, memorizing it and ruminating over it, like some clean animal chewing the cud, he turned it into the most melodious verse.' The root meaning of *ruminatio* is the act of chewing over again, as cattle chew cud, although the figurative sense of the word is at least as old as Cicero. The contemplation and appropriation of the spiritual sense of Scripture was at the centre of the monastic piety transmitted to the Anglo-Saxons by Gregory the Great in the mission of 597 and by travellers to and from Rome in the seventh century. In Bede's account of Caedmon we see this spiritual tradition not only made available to an unlearned layman but also, as though by miracle, expressed in English verse, which had never known the like songs before.

THE VIKING AND POST-VIKING PERIODS

The level of sophistication achieved by English Christians in the generation of Aldhelm and Bede, born respectively within one half and three-quarters of a century after the arrival of the Gregorian mission in 597, was truly remarkable. Few if any scholars in all of Europe could match their standard. And Anglo-Saxon Christian scholars who went to the Continent in the eighth century, of whom Alcuin of York was the most famous, were seminal in the so-called Carolingian Renaissance. Yet the Viking attacks, which began at Lindisfarne, the holy island of St Cuthbert, in 793 and continued throughout the ninth century, came perilously close to obliterating Christian learning in England and, with it, both monasticism and the contemplative way of life. In his preface to a translation of the *Book of Pastoral Care* of Gregory the Great (*EHD* I. no. 226[a]), King Alfred the Great expressed the belief that a lapse in the earlier standard of learning was a direct cause of the divine retribution brought by the Viking scourge: 'Remember what temporal punishments came upon us, when we neither loved wisdom ourselves nor allowed it to other men; we possessed only the name of Christians, and very few possessed the virtues.' Loss of sound knowledge of Latin was one factor in the decline of cultured spirituality that brought on the disaster, and Alfred tried to remedy the situation in part by encouraging a series of translations of basic works into Old English. The translations most securely associated with the king himself are all works connected with spirituality: the *Pastoral Care*, a guide to spiritual directors; the *Consolation of Philosophy* of Boethius, the great reflection upon the problem of evil; and the *Soliloquies* of Augustine, which Alfred apparently had hoped would contain an elucidation of the soul's post-mortem knowledge of God.

In the incomplete preface to the *Soliloquies* (*EHD* I, no 237[a]), Alfred used the metaphor of gathering building materials for a wooden structure to illustrate his understanding of the nature of spiritual wisdom:

> For I advise each of those who is strong and has many wagons, to plan to go to the same wood where I cut these props, and fetch for himself more there, and

load his wagons with fair rods, so that he can plait many a fine wall, and put up many a peerless building, and build a fair enclosure with them; and may dwell therein pleasantly and at his ease winter and summer, as I have not yet done.

If one builds well on land leased by the lord in earthly life, full title to the land and house may ultimately be the reward. So, too, in the spiritual life one may gain title to the eternal home. To judge both from the materials that were translated and from the references in the preface to the *Soliloquies*, Alfred believed firmly that the wisdom of the past was the surest guide to spiritual wisdom, and the central figures for his researches were the great Western doctors, Augustine and Gregory. In this respect, as in others, he was the continuator of the tradition of spirituality of his forebears.

No great literature worthy of the spiritual traditions of the early Christian period of Anglo-Saxon England or of his own efforts survives from the death of Alfred to the introduction of monastic reform in the reign of Edgar (959–75). The reform, in which Edgar was supported by Dunstan, Archbishop of Canterbury, and Aethelwold, Bishop of Winchester, among others, is important in the history of spirituality because it introduced into England the principles for monastic practice developed on the Continent some years before, notably at Cluny (see p. 285). The reform, which urged obedience to the *Rule of St Benedict*, also encouraged elaboration of the monastic liturgy. As a side effect of this, there was a tendency for spirituality to shift from contemplation of Scripture to meditation upon the liturgy itself.[1]

Towards the end of the tenth century, initially perhaps at the instigation of the king and the bishop and monasteries of Winchester, there appeared a significant body of writing in English prose, which increasingly took the form of sermons and other devotional writings designed to edify the faithful. In the sermon literature Anglo-Saxon spirituality, which had always been strongly eschatological, assumed an apocalyptic tone. One of the *Blickling Homilies* observes that 971 years of the sixth age of history have passed and the end of the age is approaching.[2] Abbot Aelfrid in the Preface to the First Series of his *Catholic Homilies* (990) speaks of the importance of teaching the people so that they may be prepared for the Last Judgement. He continues with a description of the travails of the last times and describes the age of Antichrist (*EHD* I. no.

---

[1] Gatch, *Loyalties*, pp. 61–74. Although it is conceivable (as Ritzke-Rutherford argues) that the work of John Scotus Eriugena (and, hence, pseudo-Dionysius) was known in Alfred's circle or in Aelfric's time, I believe the elaborated monastic liturgy was the most important development in Anglo-Saxon spirituality of the tenth century.

[2] Ed. R. Morris, *Blicking Homilies*, Early English Text Society, Original Series 58, 63, 73 (London, 1874–80; repr. OUP, 1967), p. 115.

239[a]). The most famous of the sermons is the *Sermo Lupi ad Anglos* of Wulfstan, Archbishop of York (d. 1023):

> Beloved men, realize what is true: this world is in haste and the end approaches; and therefore in the world things go from bad to worse, and so it must of necessity deteriorate greatly on account of the people's sins before the coming of Antichrist, and indeed it will then be dreadful and terrible far and wide throughout the world (*EHD* I. no. 240).

Both Aelfric and Wulfstan probably had access to the great treatise of apocalyptic spirituality of their time, the *Letter on the Origin and Time of the Antichrist* of Adso of Montier-en-Der.[1] Both avoided the excesses of specificity in Adso, however, and neither of them pursued Adso's prime innovation, which was to model his account of the life of Antichrist on a saint's life. Like the other writers of sermons in Old English during the tenth and eleventh centuries, they laid great stress on the imminence of judgement and the urgency of life in history. In spirituality lay the hope for protection against the possibility of disaster at the great Doom.

[1] Trans., and ed., B. McGinn, *Apocalyptic Spirituality* (CWS 1980), pp. 89–96.

VI

THE EASTERN TRADITION
FROM THE TENTH TO THE
TWENTIETH CENTURY

A   GREEK

1   Symeon the New Theologian

KALLISTOS WARE

Texts and Translations

There is a critical Greek text, with French tr., in SC (9 vols. so far; one to follow); the main writings exist also in ET.

(i) *Chapters* [*Theological, Gnostic and Practical Chapters*], ed. J. Darrouzès and L. Neyrand, SC 51 (2nd edn, 1980); ET P. McGuckin, Cistercian Studies Series 41 (Kalamazoo, 1982).

(ii) *Catecheses* or *Discourses*, ed. B. Krivochéine and J. Paramelle, SC 96, 104, 113 (1963-5); ET C. J. de Catanzaro, CWS XXI.

(iii) *Theological Treatises*, ed. J. Darrouzès, SC 122 (1966); ET McGuckin (see i above).

(iv) *Ethical Treatises*, ed. J. Darrouzès, SC 122, 129 (1966-7).

(v) *Hymns*, ed. J. Koder and J. Paramelle, SC 156, 174, 196 (1969-73); also ed. A. Kambylis (Berlin, 1976); ET G. A. Maloney (Denville, N.J., Dimension Books, no date).

(vi) *Letters*: to appear in SC. For *Letter* i (*On Confession*), see K. Holl, *Enthusiasmus und Bussgewalt beim griechischen Mönchtum: Eine Studie zu Symeon dem neuen Theologen* (Leipzig, Hinrichs, 1898), pp. 110-27 (Greek text only).

(vii) *Life* of St Symeon by Nicetas Stethatos: Greek text and French tr. I. Hausherr and G. Horn, Orientalia Christiana 12 (45) (Rome, 1928).

Studies

Krivochéine, B., *Dans la lumière du Christ. Saint Syméon le Nouveau Théologien 949-1022, Vie – Spiritualité – Doctrine.* Chevtogne, 1980.

Maloney, G. A., *The Mystic of Fire and Light: St. Symeon the New Theologian.* Denville, N.J., Dimension Books, 1975.

Völker, W., *Praxis und Theoria bei Symeon dem neuen Theologen.* Wiesbaden, Steiner, 1974.

'He became man that we might be made god'; he became 'incarnate' that we might be 'ingodded'. So St Athanasius of Alexandria sums up the message of salvation in Christ (*De Incarnatione*, 54). The Eastern

235

Orthodox tradition has sought to give full emphasis to both parts of his statement. 'He became man': the implications of this were explored more especially by the Greek Fathers from the fourth to the seventh centuries. What does it mean to affirm that Jesus Christ is fully God, truly human, and yet a single undivided person? It was in response to this three-sided question that the first six Ecumenical Councils, from Nicaea I (325) to Constantinople III (680), developed the classic expression of Trinitarian theology and Christology. In the centuries that followed, the main focus of attention shifted from the first to the second part of Athanasius' *dictum*: '. . . that we might be made god'. What are the effects of the divine incarnation in the life of the Christian? What is signified by the fulness of 'ingodding' or 'deification' (*theōsis*)? How is it possible for the human person, without ceasing to be authentically human, to enjoy direct and transforming union with God in his glory? These are the master themes of later Byzantine theology and spirituality.

Two writers in this period stand out with particular prominence: in the eleventh century, St Symeon the New Theologian, and in the fourteenth, St Gregory Palamas. Each is rooted in the past, but both are at the same time explorers, developing the earlier tradition in fresh ways. From the ninth century onwards Greek Christianity tended to be strongly conservative, and all too often its spokesmen remained content with a barren 'theology of repetition'. Typical of this outlook is the somewhat discouraging comment of the Byzantine scholar Theodore Metochites (d. 1332), 'The great men of the past have expressed everything so perfectly that they have left nothing more for us to say' (*Miscellanea*, preface: cited in S. Runciman, *The Last Byzantine Renaissance*. CUP, 1970, p. 94). There was in the Greek East nothing equivalent to the startling rediscovery of Aristotle and the dynamic evolution of scholasticism in the West during the twelfth and thirteenth centuries; in the East the patristic period of theology continued uninterrupted until 1453, and indeed beyond. But, throughout the twelve hundred years of Byzantium, alongside continuity there is also change; and the finest representatives of later Byzantine thought, such as Symeon and Palamas, succeed in combining loyalty to the past with creative originality.

Later Byzantine spirituality is marked above all by three features:

1. A strong insistence upon the *divine mystery* and so upon the apophatic approach to God; he is utterly transcendent, beyond all concepts and images, beyond all human understanding.
2. A balancing sense of the nearness as well as the otherness of the Eternal; not only transcendent but immanent, God can be known here and now, in this present life, through *direct personal experience*.

3. A preference for the symbolism of *light* rather than darkness; mystical union with God takes above all the form of a vision of divine radiance, the dominant 'model' being Christ transfigured upon Mount Tabor.

St Symeon the New Theologian (949–1022) exemplifies all three of these features, but more particularly the second. In a manner altogether exceptional in the Christian East – for there is in Greek patristic literature no autobiographical work equivalent to the *Confessions* of St Augustine – Symeon refers explicitly to his own personal experiences. Enthusiastic, unsystematic, he is a 'theologian', not in the modern academic sense, but rather according to the older understanding of the term: a man of prayer, of personal vision, who speaks about the divine realm, not in a theoretical fashion, but on the basis of what he has himself seen and tasted. The designation 'new' in his title, according to the most persuasive interpretation, implies a comparison first of all with St John the Evangelist or the Divine (in Greek, *theologos*, 'the Theologian'), and then with St Gregory of Nazianzus, 'Gregory the Theologian' as he is known in the Christian East. The name 'New Theologian' means, then, that St Symeon in the eleventh century renewed the tradition of mystical prayer to which St John bore witness in the first century and St Gregory of Nazianzus in the fourth.

Destined originally for a political career, at the age of fourteen Symeon the New Theologian passed under the influence of a monk at the monastery of Studios in Constantinople, also named Symeon, known as *Eulabes*, 'the devout'. Profoundly marked by the example of his own spiritual father, in his teaching the younger Symeon stresses the vital need for living, personal direction in the spiritual life. He would have agreed with the Hasidic master Rabbi Jacob Yitzhak that 'the *way* cannot be learned out of a book, or from hearsay, but can only be communicated from person to person' (M. Buber, [ET] *The Tales of the Hasidim* [New York, Shocken Books, 1947], vol. i, p. 286). The importance of the spiritual father is, indeed, a recurrent theme throughout later Byzantine spirituality: 'Above all else', say Kallistos and Ignatios Xanthopoulos (fourteenth century), 'search diligently for an unerring guide and teacher' (*On the Life of Stillness*, § 14).

When Symeon was aged about twenty and still a layman, he received the first in a series of visions of divine light. Seven years later he became a monk. For a quarter of a century he was abbot of the monastery of St Mamas in Constantinople; his last thirteen years were passed outside the city, in a small hermitage on the opposite shore of the Bosphorus. Thus the central and most creative period of his life was spent, not in seclusion, but as superior of a busy community in the heart of the imperial capital;

he is an 'urban Hesychast', a mystical theologian who combines inner prayer with pastoral and administrative work. In his understanding of monastic life he blends the cenobitic approach of St Basil the Great and St Theodore the Studite with the more solitary, eremitic spirit of St John Climacus. During his life and after his death he aroused sharp controversy – in particular, because of the cult that he rendered to his spiritual father as a saint, without waiting for official approval, and because of his views on priesthood and confession – but the Byzantine Church ended by canonizing him.

Symeon displays an especially close affinity with the *Spiritual Homilies* attributed to Macarius. Whatever the truth about the supposed Messalian character of the *Homilies* (cf. p. 160), there is no good reason to attribute to the New Theologian the kind of Messalianism that might be suspected of heresy. What Symeon shares with the *Homilies* is above all an emphasis upon conscious, personal awareness of Christ and the Spirit. Christianity, so he is passionately convinced, involves much more than a formal, dogmatic orthodoxy, than an outward observance of moral rules. No one can be a Christian at second hand; the tradition has to be *relived* by each one of us without exception, and each should *feel* the indwelling presence of the Holy Spirit in a conscious, palpable manner:

> Do not say, It is impossible to receive the Holy Spirit;
> Do not say, It is possible to be saved without him.
> Do not say, then, that one can possess him without knowing it.
> Do not say, God does not appear to men,
> Do not say, Men do not see the divine light,
> Or else, It is impossible in these present times.
> This is a thing never impossible, my friends,
> But on the contrary altogether possible for those who so wish
> *(Hymn XXVII, 125–32).*

If in this passage and elsewhere Symeon comes close to identifying the reality of grace with the conscious feeling of grace, as the Messalians were accused of doing, he does sometimes allow for a real yet hidden activity of the Spirit on an unconscious level (see, for example, *Chapters*, III, 76). The aim, however, is always to advance beyond this unconscious grace to the point of explicit awareness, at which we experience the Spirit 'in a conscious and perceptible way', with what he calls the 'sensation of the heart'. In the passage quoted above, it is significant that Symeon vehemently repudiates any suggestion that the *charismata* granted to holy men and women in the past are no longer accessible to Christians in the present time. For him this was the worst of all heresies, implying as it does that the Spirit has somehow been withdrawn from the Church. We are in exactly the same situation as the first Christians, he protests; if grace is not as apparent among us today as it was once among them, the sole reason is the weakness of our faith.

Symeon applies this teaching about direct experience more especially to confession and absolution. Who, he asks in his letter *On Confession*, is entitled to 'bind and loose'? The answer is surprising. There is one essential qualification, and one only, which enables a person to act as confessor and spiritual father, and that is a conscious awareness of the Holy Spirit:

> Do not try to be a mediator on behalf of others until you have yourself been filled with the Holy Spirit, until you have come to know and to win the friendship of the King of all with conscious awareness in your soul (*Letter* i, 10: Holl, p. 119).

From this Symeon draws a double conclusion: negatively, that anyone who lacks this conscious awareness – even though he may be bishop or patriarch – should not, and indeed cannot, exercise the ministry of confession; positively, that lay monks who possess such awareness, even though not in holy orders, may be called to exercise this ministry.

Most Orthodox would hesitate to go the whole way here with Symeon. It is true that in the Christian East, from the fourth century up to the present, there have been many instances of lay monks acting as spiritual fathers. Symeon's own 'elder', Symeon the Studite, was not a priest – although the New Theologian himself was – and many of the leading spiritual fathers on the Holy Mountain of Athos today are likewise lay monks; within Orthodoxy the ministry of eldership is at times exercised equally by nuns who act as spiritual mothers. But is this ministry of eldership or spiritual direction identical with the sacrament of confession, strictly defined? Although Symeon makes no distinction between the two, many other Orthodox would wish to do so. One point, however, emerges unambiguously from Symeon's answer about confession: the high significance that he attaches to direct personal experience of God.

This direct experience takes the form, in Symeon's teaching, more especially of the vision of divine light. Here Symeon, speaking of himself in the third person, describes the first such vision that he received:

> While he was standing one day and saying the prayer *God be merciful to me a sinner* (Luke 18:13), more with his intellect than with his mouth, a divine radiance suddenly appeared in abundance from above and filled the whole room. When this happened, the young man lost all awareness of his surroundings and forgot whether he was in a house or under a roof. He saw nothing but light on every side, and did not even know if he was standing on the ground . . . He was wholly united to non-material light and, so it seemed, he had himself been turned into light. Oblivious of all the world, he was

overwhelmed with tears and with inexpressible joy and exultation (*Catechesis* XXII, lines 88–100).

Note how Symeon's experience combines sorrow with joy. Before the vision he prays for mercy, and when the vision comes he sheds tears; yet they are tears not of penitence only but of rejoicing. The light that enfolds him is evidently far more than a metaphorical 'light of the understanding'. It is an existent reality, and yet at the same time it is not a physical and created light, but spiritual and divine; as he affirms throughout his writings, the light is God himself. This divine light has upon Symeon a transforming effect; he is taken up into that which he contemplates, and is himself 'turned into light'. Yet, though transfigured, he does not lose his personal identity, but is never so truly himself as when within the light. If the account of Symeon's first vision might seem to suggest that the light is impersonal, elsewhere he insists upon the personal presence of Jesus within the divine radiance: the Lord speaks to him from the light, and the vision involves a dialogue of love between them. Symeon's light-mysticism is not just 'photocentric' but Christocentric.

Although Symeon almost always describes the mystical union in terms of light, not of darkness, he is at the same time an apophatic theologian, frequently applying negative language to God; the first of the three features mentioned above is present as well as the second and the third. 'You are higher than all essence,' he says to the Creator, 'than the very nature of nature, higher than all ages, than all light . . . You are none of the things that are, but above them all' (*Hymn* XV, 67–71). Yet, while 'invisible, unapproachable, beyond our understanding and our grasp' (XV, 75), God has at the same time become truly human and is known by the saints in a vision face to face. To express this double truth that God is at once transcendent and immanent, unknown yet well known, the fourteenth-century Hesychasts make use of the distinction between the divine essence and the divine energies: although beyond all understanding in his essence, God reveals himself and enters into personal communion with us through his energies. Sometimes Symeon likewise employs this distinction (e.g. *Hymn* XXIV, 11; XXXI, 6–7), but elsewhere he ignores it, stating that humans can partake even in the very essence of God (e.g. *Hymn* VII, 25–29). His usage is not consistent, and it would be misleading here to read back into his thought the more developed position of the later period. In general, however, he exercised an important influence on the fourteenth-century Hesychasts.

Three other points call for mention:

First, an absence: there is no reference in Symeon's authentic writings to the Jesus Prayer. Here again a difference should be noted between Symeon and the later Hesychasts.

Secondly, Symeon's vision of the spiritual way, as well as being Christocentric, is also deeply sacramental. In particular, he refers to the Eucharist in strongly realistic terms:[1]

> My blood has been mingled with your Blood,
> And I know that I have been united also to your Godhead.
> I have become your most pure Body,
> A member dazzling, a member truly sanctified,
> A member glorious, transparent, luminous . . .
> What was I once, what have I now become! . . .
> Where shall I sit, what shall I touch,
> Where shall I rest these limbs that have become your own,
> In what works or actions shall I employ
> These members that are terrible and divine?
> (*Hymn* II, 13–29).

Thirdly, Symeon displays a profound reverence for the body, which he sees in Hebraic, biblical terms as an integral part of the human person – to be sanctified, not hated and repressed. This was something that he had learnt from his spiritual father Symeon the Studite, of whom he says:

> He was not ashamed of the limbs of anyone,
> Or to see others naked and to be seen naked himself.
> For he possessed the whole Christ and was himself wholly Christ;
> And always he regarded all his own limbs and the limbs of everyone else,
> Individually and together, as being Christ himself
> (*Hymn* XV, 207–11).

Here, as in the account of his first vision of the divine light and in his words of thanksgiving after Holy Communion, we see how for Symeon the *total* person, body and soul together, is hallowed and permeated by grace and glory. A monk and an ascetic, he yet has no sympathy for the platonizing or Gnostic outlook that depreciates the body, excluding it from the process of salvation. In Symeon's eyes ascetic self-denial is a battle not against but for the body.

Vivid, full of personal warmth, St Symeon the New Theologian is an unusually attractive writer. His spirituality is perhaps expressed most eloquently in the fifty-six *Hymns of Divine Love* written towards the end of his life, from which we have quoted more than once. A theologian-poet, in the long line extending from St Ephrem the Syrian, through Dante, St John of the Cross, Milton and Blake, up to T. S. Eliot and

---

[1] But the metrical prayer commencing *From polluted lips* . . ., used by Orthodox before communion and commonly attributed to Symeon the New Theologian, is almost certainly not his work but that of his contemporary St Symeon Metaphrastes ('the Translator').

Edwin Muir in our own century, he exemplifies the close link existing between theology and poetry. Often it is the poets who are the best theologians of all. It would be good for the Church if we paid them greater heed.

2 The Hesychasts:
Gregory of Sinai, Gregory Palamas
Nicolas Cabasilas

KALLISTOS WARE

Texts and Translations

Nicephorus of Mount Athos, *On Vigilance and the Guarding of the Heart*, Greek text *PG* 147. 945–66; ET E. Kadloubovsky and G. E. H. Palmer, *Writings from the Philokalia on Prayer of the Heart* (London, Faber, 1951), pp. 22–34.

Pseudo-Symeon, *Method of Holy Prayer and Attentiveness*, Greek text and French tr. I. Hausherr, *La méthode d'oraison hésychaste*, Orientalia Christiana 9, 2 (36) (Rome, 1927), pp. 150–72; ET Kadloubovsky and Palmer, *Writings*, pp. 152–61.[1]

Gregory of Sinai, Greek text *PG* 150. 1240–1345; ET Kadloubovsky and Palmer, *Writings*, pp. 37–94; *Discourse on the Transfiguration*, Greek text and ET D. Balfour: reprint (Athens, 1983) from the journal *Theologia*.

Gregory Palamas, Greek text P. K. Christou, 3 vols. (in progress) (Thessalonica 1962–70): for works not yet included in this, see *PG* 150–1 and the edition of the *Homilies* by S. Oikonomos (Athens, 1861). For *Triads in Defence of the Holy Hesychasts*, cf. Greek text and French tr. J. Meyendorff (*Spicilegium Sacrum Lovaniense* 30–31: Louvain, 2nd edn, 1973). ET of *Triads* (selections only) N. Gendle, CWS 1983.

Kallistos and Ignatios Xanthopoulos, *On the Life of Stillness and Solitude*, Greek text *PG* 147. 636–812; ET Kadloubovsky and Palmer, *Writings*, pp. 164–270.

Nicolas Cabasilas, *The Life in Christ*, Greek text *PG* 150. 493–725; ET C. J. de Catanzaro (Crestwood, N.Y., St Vladimir's Seminary Press, 1974); *A Commentary on the Divine Liturgy*, Greek text and French tr. S. Salaville and others, SC 4 (2nd edn, 1967); ET J. M. Hussey and P. A. McNulty (London, SPCK, 4th edn, 1978).

---

[1] The Kadloubovsky-Palmer rendering of Nicephorus and Ps.-Symeon (as also of Gregory of Sinai and Kallistos and Ignatios Xanthopoulos) is based on the nineteenth-century Russian version by Theophan the Recluse, not on the original Greek; this results in some inaccuracies. For more exact translations, made directly from the Greek, see J. Gouillard, *Petite Philocalie de la Prière du Coeur* (Paris, 1953).

Studies

GENERAL

V. Lossky, (ET) *The Mystical Theology of the Eastern Church.* London, J. Clarke, 1957.

Lossky, V., (ET) *The Vision of God.* London, Faith Press, 1963.

Lossky, V., (ET) *In the Image and Likeness of God.* Crestwood, N.Y., St Vladimir's Seminary Press, 1974.

Meyendorff, J., *Byzantine Theology: Historical Trends and Doctrinal Themes.* New York, Fordham University Press, 1974; London, Mowbray, 1975.

GREGORY OF SINAI

Ware, K., 'The Jesus Prayer in St Gregory of Sinai', *ECR* 4 (1972), pp. 3–22.

GREGORY PALAMAS

Krivochéine, B., *The Ascetic and Theological Teaching of Gregory Palamas.* Reprint from *The Eastern Churches Quarterly,* London, 1954.

Mantzaridis, G. I., *The Deification of Man: St Gregory Palamas and the Orthodox Tradition.* Crestwood, N.Y., St Vladimir's Seminary Press, 1984.

Meyendorff, J., (ET) *A Study of Gregory Palamas.* London, Faith Press, 1964.

Meyendorff, J., (ET) *St Gregory Palamas and Orthodox Spirituality.* Crestwood, N.Y., St Vladimir's Seminary Press, 1974.

NICOLAS CABASILAS

Lot-Borodine, M., *Un maître de la spiritualité byzantine au XIVe siècle: Nicolas Cabasilas.* Paris, 1958.

Nellas, P., *The Vocation of the Human Person,* part 2. Crestwood, N.Y., St Vladimir's Seminary Press, 1985.

Völker, W., *Die Sacramentsmystik des Nikolaus Kabasilas.* Wiesbaden, 1977.

The fourteenth century is an era of exceptional significance in the history of Greek Orthodox spirituality, a time of both crisis and creative development, when the tradition of prayer known as 'Hesychasm' was called in question, reaffirmed and deepened.

The term 'Hesychasm' can be used in a variety of ways. It is derived from the Greek word *hēsuchia,* meaning 'quiet' or 'stillness'. In principle, therefore, Hesychasm might be termed 'Byzantine Quietism'; but this is confusing, since many of the distinctive opinions of the seventeenth-century Western Quietists are not characteristic of the Greek Hesychasts. The word 'Hesychast' may be used in an exterior and spatial sense, to denote a hermit or solitary as contrasted with a monk in a cenobitic community. But more commonly it is employed in an interior sense, to indicate one who practises inner prayer and seeks silence of the heart. If understood in this way, the title 'Hesychast' can be applied to many writers earlier than the fourteenth century, such as St Maximus the Confessor or St Symeon the New Theologian. On the whole, however, the word is used more narrowly, to mean one who practises the Jesus Prayer, and who in particular adopts the so-called 'physical technique' connected with the Prayer. Yet more specifically, 'Hesychasm' may signify those who, during the middle of the fourteenth century, supported St Gregory Palamas and accepted the distinction that he drew between the essence and the energies of God. Thus the 'Hesychast controversy' means the dispute in which Palamas was involved during 1337–47.

The physical technique, which constituted one of the points at issue in this controversy, is in fact somewhat older than Palamas himself. Allusions to some kind of method linking the Jesus Prayer to the rhythm of the breathing are perhaps to be detected in Greek authors of the seventh to ninth centuries such as Climacus and Hesychius, and can certainly be found in Coptic sources dating from the same period (see p. 183). The first developed description of such a method in the Greek sources, however, dates only from the late thirteenth century, in the work *On Vigilance and the Guarding of the Heart* by Nicephorus the Hesychast, a monk of Mount Athos. There is a closely similar description in a text attributed to Symeon the New Theologian, entitled *Method of Holy Prayer and Attentiveness*; it is now generally agreed that Symeon cannot be the author of this, and very possibly it is also by Nicephorus.

Nicephorus recommends that the Jesus Prayer be recited with the words 'Lord Jesus Christ, Son of God, have mercy on me', that is to say, using the standard formula first found in the *Life of Abba Philemon* (see p. 180). There are three main features in the physical technique that he and Ps.-Symeon describe:

1. A particular *bodily posture* is enjoined. The aspirant is to sit with his head bowed, 'resting your beard on your chest and directing your bodily eye together with your entire intellect (*nous*) towards the middle of your belly, that is, towards your navel' (Ps.-Symeon, in Hausherr, p. 164). Other texts suggest that the gaze is to be fixed on the place of the heart. Gregory of Sinai specifies that the monk should sit on a low stool about nine inches high. In any case the shoulders are bowed and the back is bent; contrast the 'lotus' position in Yoga, where the back is straight. The adoption of a seated position would have appeared more surprising to a Byzantine than it does to a contemporary Westerner, for in the Christian East the normal position for prayer has always been to stand (see Plate 3).

2. The *rhythm of the breathing* is to be slowed down: 'Restrain the inhalation of your breath through the nose, so as not to breathe in and out

at your ease' (Ps.-Symeon, p. 164). Nicephorus and Ps.-Symeon imply that this slowing-down of the respiration *precedes* rather than accompanies the recitation of the Jesus Prayer; the control of the breathing is a preliminary exercise, designed to secure calmness and concentration before the actual invocation of the Holy Name has commenced. Not until the end of the fourteenth century, in the teaching of Kallistos and Ignatios Xanthopoulos, is it clearly implied that the tempo of the breathing should be co-ordinated with the actual words of the Prayer (*On the Life of Stillness*, §25). In modern Orthodox practice it is usual to say the first part of the Prayer, 'Lord Jesus Christ, Son of God', while breathing in, and the remainder while breathing out; but there are several variations. According to the anonymous nineteenth-century Russian work *The Way of a Pilgrim* (tr. R. M. French [SPCK 1954], pp. 19–20, 102), the recitation of the Prayer may be connected with the beating of the heart; but nothing is said of this in the Byzantine sources.

3. As he controls his breathing, the one who prays is at the same time to *search inwardly for the place of the heart*. He is, says Nicephorus, to imagine his breath entering through the nostrils and then passing down within the lungs until it reaches the heart. In this way he is to make his intellect (*nous*) descend with his breath, so that intellect and heart are united. The effect of this will be a sense of joyful homecoming, like that of a man, 'long absent abroad, who cannot restrain his gladness on once more meeting his wife and children'. When the intellect has found the place of the heart, 'accustom it not to come out quickly. At first it grows very weary of being narrowly enclosed within; but, having once become used to this, it no longer yearns to wander abroad. For the kingdom of heaven is within us' (*PG* 147. 964A). Having found the place of the heart, one then commences the recitation of the Jesus Prayer. Thus, as with the control of the breathing, the inward exploration precedes the actual saying of the Prayer. Established within the heart, the *nous* beholds itself 'entirely luminous' (Ps.-Symeon, p. 165). This is a vision, not of the uncreated light of the Godhead, but of the intrinsic luminosity of the human intellect; a similar vision of the light of the *nous* is mentioned by Evagrius (*Praktikos*, 64) and by Diadochus (*Chapters*, 59). 'From this moment onwards', Ps.-Symeon continues, 'as soon as a thought arises, before it comes to completion and assumes a form, the intellect expels and destroys it by the invocation of Jesus Christ' (p. 165). In this way the physical technique, combined with the Jesus Prayer, is a help in keeping guard over the heart and expelling thoughts from it. The aim, as in Evagrius and Diadochus, is to acquire a state of inner simplicity, free from images and discursive thinking.

The accounts of the 'method' in Nicephorus and Ps.-Symeon lack subtlety and sophistication, and are surely too crude in the correlation that they posit between physical processes and mental acts of prayer. Nevertheless the bodily technique rests ultimately upon a sound theological principle: the human person is a single unity, and therefore the body as well as the soul has a positive, dynamic part to play in the task of praying. The references to the heart should not be understood too literally. In Nicephorus and Ps.-Symeon, as in Scripture and the Macarian *Homilies*, the heart signifies not merely the physical organ in the chest, and not merely the emotions and affections, but the deep centre of the human person as a whole, the point where created humanity is most directly open to uncreated love. 'Prayer of the heart', therefore, means not just 'affective prayer' but prayer of the entire person. Phrases such as 'finding the place of the heart' or 'descending with the intellect into the heart' signify a state of reintegration, in which the one who prays is totally united with the prayer itself and with the Divine Companion to whom the prayer is addressed. The aim is to become like St Francis of Assisi, as described by Thomas of Celano: *totus non tam orans quam oratio factus*, 'with his whole being, not so much saying prayers as himself turned into prayer'.

While commending the physical technique, Nicephorus did not regard it as indispensable, but saw it as no more than an accessory, useful to some but not obligatory upon all; indeed, none of the Hesychasts imagined that the bodily 'method' constitutes the essence of prayer. There are striking parallels between the 'method', as found in Nicephorus, and the techniques used in Yoga and Sufism (cf. pp. 507, 500), which also involve control of the breathing and concentration of the attention upon specific psychosomatic centres. It is possible that the Byzantine Hesychasts were influenced by the Sufis, but conclusive evidence of this is so far lacking.

The immediate influence of Nicephorus seems to have been limited. At any rate, when St Gregory of Sinai (d. 1346) came to Mount Athos in the early years of the fourteenth century, less than a generation after Nicephorus' death, it was only after long searching that he found anyone experienced in *hēsuchia* and inner prayer; according to Gregory's biographer Patriarch Kallistos – who is perhaps exaggerating a little – virtually all the monks of the Holy Mountain at that time devoted their efforts exclusively to fasting and other forms of ascetic effort. Gregory himself had learnt about inner prayer while in Crete, prior to reaching Athos. He left the Holy Mountain around 1335, taking no direct part in the subsequent Hesychast controversy at Constantinople, but spending his last years at Paroria, on the borders between the Byzantine Empire and Bulgaria. His disciples were instrumental in propagating Hesychast teaching throughout Bulgaria, Serbia and Russia, and Gregory forms in this way an important connecting link between the Greek and Slav worlds.

In his spiritual teaching Gregory of Sinai assigns a central place to the Jesus Prayer. He recited it in the standard form, 'Lord Jesus Christ, Son of God, have mercy on me'; his biographer Kallistos tells us that he used also to add at the end the words 'a sinner', a practice widespread in modern Orthodoxy. Gregory also suggests the use of shorter forms: one may alternate between 'Lord Jesus Christ, have mercy on me' and 'Son of God, have mercy on me'. But he issues a warning against changing the form of words too often: 'Trees that are constantly transplanted do not bear fruit' (*PG* 150. 1316B).

Gregory recommends the physical technique, as found in Nicephorus: 'Sit down on a low stool . . . compress your intellect, forcing it down from your brain into your heart, and retain it there within the heart. Laboriously bow yourself down, feeling sharp pain in your chest, shoulders and neck . . . Control the drawing-in of your breath . . . So far as possible, hold back its expulsion, enclosing your intellect in the heart' (1316AB). It is interesting that Gregory says 'feeling sharp pain': he acknowledges that the posture recommended will prove highly uncomfortable. Control of the breathing helps to control the thoughts: 'The retention of the breath, with the mouth kept tightly closed, controls the intellect, but only partially, for it becomes dispersed once more' (1332B). Here, as in Nicephorus and Ps.-Symeon, the physical technique is a way of keeping guard over the heart. But the purely physical aspect, so Gregory insists, is not to be unduly emphasized. The aim is always the concentration of the mind: 'Closing the mouth a little, control the respiration of the intellect and not that of the nostrils, as the uninstructed do' (1344B).

Following earlier tradition, Gregory urges that the use of the Jesus Prayer should be so far as possible continuous. Like Diadochus and Hesychius, he sees it as a way of attaining image-free, non-discursive prayer: 'Always keep your intellect free from images, naked of concepts and thoughts', he says (1341D). The imagination or *phantasia* is to be restrained; otherwise one may find that one has become 'not a Hesychast but a phantast' (1284A). But, while images and thoughts are to be excluded, not all feelings should be rejected. Rightly practised, the Jesus Prayer leads to a sense of joyful sorrow (*charmolupē*) – here Gregory draws upon Climacus – and to a feeling of warmth (*thermē*) that is not physical but spiritual: 'The true beginning of prayer is a feeling of warmth in the heart' (1324AB). From these feelings of compunction and warmth the aspirant ascends to the 'contemplation of the divine light' that was manifested to the three disciples at the transfiguration on Tabor (1300C) (see Plate 1). Although Gregory does not discuss in detail the theological meaning of this light, it is clear that he has in view, not just a vision of the created light or intrinsic luminosity of the intellect, as in Ps.-Symeon, but a vision of the uncreated light of the Godhead, as in Palamas.

Gregory of Sinai sets the Jesus Prayer firmly in a sacramental context. Prayer, he says, is 'the revelation of baptism' (1277D), and this is true in particular of the Jesus Prayer. It is in no sense an alternative to the normal sacramental life of the Church, but precisely the means whereby sacramental grace takes fire within us. As Christians we have all received the Holy Spirit 'secretly' at our baptism, but most of us are unconscious of his presence; the Jesus Prayer enables us to become aware of this 'secret' baptismal indwelling in an active and conscious manner. With his appeal to the feeling of warmth, to the conscious experience of baptismal grace, Gregory of Sinai takes his place in the 'affective' tradition of Eastern spirituality, extending back through Symeon the New Theologian to Diadochus and the Macarian *Homilies*.

In Gregory of Sinai's contemporary and friend on Mount Athos, St Maximus of Kapsokalyvia – the name means 'burnt huts': it was Maximus' practice to move from place to place, each time burning down the simple cell in which he was living – the Jesus Prayer is linked especially with the person of the Mother of God (the *Theotokos*). Maximus' disciple, Theophanes of Vatopedi, reports him as saying:

> One day, as with tears and intense love I kissed her most pure icon, suddenly there came a great warmth in my breast and my heart, not burning me up but refreshing me like dew, and filling me with sweetness and deep compunction. From that moment my heart began to say the Prayer inwardly, and at the same time my reason with my intellect holds fast the remembrance of Jesus and of my *Theotokos*; and this remembrance has never left me (*Life* 15: in *Analecta Bollandiana* 54 [1936], p. 85).

The way in which the Jesus Prayer is here associated with the Virgin Mary is unusual, but not in itself surprising in view of the prominent place assigned to our Lady in all Orthodox worship. Maximus' references to the feeling of warmth reflect the same 'affective' approach as is found in Gregory of Sinai. Maximus agrees with Gregory also in what he says about the vision of divine light: the Holy Spirit transports the aspirant in ecstasy 'to the non-material realm of inconceivable divine light'; his intellect is 'kindled into flame by the fire of the Godhead, and it is dissolved in its thoughts and swallowed up by the divine light, becoming itself entirely divine light of surpassing radiance' (*Life* 15: pp. 86–7). It is clear that Maximus envisages here, not merely a physical light of the senses or the natural luminosity of the intellect, but the uncreated light of God himself. In Maximus' view, as in that of Symeon, the light has a transforming effect, and the visionary is taken up into the glory that he contemplates. According to the testimony of those who knew him personally, this happened to Maximus himself, who used to be seen surrounded by dazzling radiance.

The spiritual tradition represented by Symeon the New Theologian, Nicephorus, Gregory of Sinai and Maximus of Kapsokalyvia, was called in question and challenged during the decade 1337–47, in what is known as the Hesychast controversy. The attack on Hesychasm was launched by a learned Greek from South Italy, Barlaam the Calabrian (*c.* 1290–1348), who was answered by a monk from the Holy Mountain, St Gregory Palamas (1296–1359). Unlike Symeon the New Theologian, with his urban cenobitic background, Palamas had spent most of his monastic life prior to 1337 at remote hermitages in the 'desert'. Although it is sometimes suggested that Barlaam was influenced by Western Nominalism, he seems in fact to have been fundamentally a Greek in culture and education, and at any rate until his defeat in 1341 he regarded himself as a loyal member of the Orthodox Church, in his writings frequently attacking Latin theology. The controversy between him and Palamas was not a dispute between the Latin West and the Greek East, but essentially a conflict *within* the Greek tradition, involving two different ways of interpreting Dionysius the Areopagite (cf. pp. 184–9). For Barlaam, the Areopagite was a philosophical theologian, using negative, apophatic language to affirm, on the level of reasoned argument, the radical transcendence of God. For Palamas, the Areopagite was above all a mystical theologian; the 'unknowing' of which the Dionysian writings speak is not merely a philosophical theory, for within and beyond the 'unknowing' they affirm a direct and personal experience of union with the divine. It is here, over the question whether or not direct experience of God is possible here and now, in this life, that the basic difference between Palamas and Barlaam should be situated.

Palamas' standpoint was upheld by a synod at Constantinople in 1341. Barlaam now withdrew from the controversy and returned to Italy, but the anti-Hesychast position continued to be urged, although on somewhat different grounds, by Akindynos and Nicephorus Gregoras. Political factors prolonged and complicated the debate, but the Palamite teaching was eventually vindicated at two further councils in Constantinople (1347, 1351). Palamas himself was appointed Archbishop of Thessalonica in 1347, taking up residence in 1350; thus, after an early life of semi-eremitic solitude, he spent his last years not in the desert but in the city, charged with heavy pastoral duties. He illustrates the connection often existing between mysticism and society. He was canonized in 1368, only nine years after his death.

Barlaam's indictment of Hesychasm involves three main points:

1. *The knowledge of God.* Underlining the divine incomprehensibility, Barlaam argues that our knowledge of God during the present life is indirect, through Scripture and church tradition, through signs and symbols. He therefore denies the Hesychast claim to attain in this life a direct experience of the divinity and unmediated union with him.

2. *The vision of God.* Since direct experience of God is not possible in this life, it follows that the light which the Hesychasts claim to see with their bodily eyes cannot be the uncreated light of the Godhead; it must be a physical and created light.

3. *The physical technique of the Hesychasts.* Denouncing this as materialistic and grossly superstitious, Barlaam labels the Hesychasts *omphalopsychoi*, 'those who locate the soul in the navel'.

The first and second points pose the basic question of our relationship as human persons to the divine realm: in what way is the hidden God revealed? They involve also our understanding of eschatology: here Barlaam is 'futurist', reserving the vision of God to the age to come, whereas Palamas' eschatology is 'realized' or, more exactly, 'inaugurated' – the pledge and firstfruits of the future age can be experienced already in this present life. The second and third points both raise the further issue of the role of the body within the spiritual life: Barlaam attacks the Hesychasts' claim to see the divine light with or through the bodily eyes, as also their attempt to harness the bodily organism to the task of praying. Platonist in his approach, in both cases he repudiates what he sees as the materialism of the Hesychasts.

What is Palamas' answer? On the first point, he agrees with Barlaam that God is indeed unknowable. Using the apophatic language characteristic of Dionysius, he speaks of God as 'the beyond-essence, anonymous, surpassing all names' (*Against Akindynos*, II, xiv, 63), who 'in a manner beyond all being transcends every being' (*Triads*, I, iii, 8). But, where Barlaam stops short at the divine unknowability, Palamas goes a step further. He draws a distinction between the *essence* or inner being of God, and his *energies* or acts of power. The essence indicates the divine transcendence and otherness; and as such it remains unknowable not only in the present life but in the age to come, not only to humankind but to the angels – it is *radically* unknowable. Never in all eternity shall we come to know God's essence – that is to say, never shall we come to know God in the manner that he knows himself – simply because he is Creator and we are creatures. Even in heaven the distinction between the uncreated and the created still prevails. But, unknowable in his essence, God is dynamically disclosed to us in his energies, which permeate the universe and in which we humans can directly participate, even in this present life. These energies are not an intermediary between God and man, but the living God himself in action; and so, sharing in the divine energies, the saints are indeed enjoying the true vision of God 'face to face'.

Barlaam considered that Palamas, in thus differentiating between the essence and the energies of God, was introducing a division into the Godhead, thereby impairing the divine simplicity; and so the Calabrian accused him of 'ditheism'. Akindynos charged Palamas more particularly with innovation: in his view the essence–energies distinction, as drawn by Palamas, is not to be found in earlier tradition. Both these charges have been repeated by Western critics of Palamism from the fourteenth century up to our own time, although there are also many contemporary Roman Catholics who see nothing heretical in his teaching. For his part Palamas considers that the essence–energies distinction no more destroys the divine indivisibility than does the distinction between the three persons of the Trinity; and he also argues that the distinction can claim a sound pedigree, employed as it is (in his opinion) by the Cappadocians, Dionysius and Maximus the Confessor. How far Palamas has correctly interpreted the earlier patristic tradition remains a matter for continuing dispute among modern specialists.

The essence–energies distinction-in-unity is for Palamas a way of holding in balance both transcendence and immanence, both the otherness and the nearness of God. He wishes to exclude pantheism, and yet to uphold the reality of direct personal communion with God. Because we participate in God's energies, not in his essence, the mystical union is a union without confusion. *Theōsis* signifies the glorification but not the absorption of our created personal identity.[1]

The term 'energy' has a somewhat abstract and elusive flavour: what does it really signify? Fortunately Palamas also uses words with a more specific connotation. First, the uncreated energies, in relation to us humans, can be termed divine *grace*; the Palamite doctrine of energies is in fact an Eastern theology of grace. Secondly, the *light* which the Hesychasts behold in prayer – and here we come to the second point in Barlaam's attack – is to be interpreted as a manifestation of the divine

[1] The criticisms of the *theōsis* doctrine by, for example, B. Drewery in P. Brooks, ed., *Christian Spirituality: Essays in Honour of Gordon Rupp* (London, SCM, 1975), pp. 35–62, are not applicable to the Palamite position, correctly understood.

energies. The vision of light is the vision of God himself; of God, however, in his energies and not in his essence. What the saints see is the same uncreated light that shone from Christ at the transfiguration on Mount Tabor, and that will shine from him equally at his second coming.

Of this light, Gregory affirms seven things:

1. It is a 'non-material' light (*Triads*, III, i, 22) – this recalls Symeon's description (see p. 240) – 'a light that is noetic and intelligible, or rather spiritual' (*Triads*, I, iii, 10), not a physical light of the senses.

2. Although non-material, the light is not merely imaginary or symbolic; it is not just a metaphorical 'light of knowledge' but is 'hypostatic', an existent reality (*Triads*, I, iii, 7).

3. Although the light is not a physical light of the senses, it can be perceived through the senses, provided that they are transformed by the grace of the Holy Spirit; for the human person is an integral unity, and the body shares with the soul in the vision of God. Thus the three disciples on Mount Tabor beheld the glory of the transfiguration through their bodily eyes; and the righteous at the resurrection of the body on the last day will likewise see the glorified Christ through their physical senses. Yet what enables us to see the divine light is not the organs of sense-perception by virtue of their own intrinsic power, but rather the grace of God that is active within them. None can behold the light except those who are spiritually prepared so to do; that is why Christ was transfigured before three disciples only, not before the crowds. In this way the light is to be termed both 'invisible' and yet 'visible' (*Triads*, I, iii, 16).

4. The light is not created but uncreated and divine; it is the light of the Holy Trinity, Father, Son and Spirit. But, while the light is God, it is God in his energies, not in his essence; it is God's glory, not his inner nature. Because it is divine and is God himself, the light divinizes the beholder, conferring upon him the gift of *theōsis*.

5. The light is infinite, 'like an ocean without limits' (*Triads*, III, i, 33), and so human beings will never see the whole of it, either in this life or in the age to come. God is indeed truly revealed in his divine energies, but he is never exhaustively revealed. In this way Palamas allows for St Gregory of Nyssa's notion of *epektasis* or unending progress. Perfection is to be seen not in static but in dynamic terms: the blessed never reach a point where their pilgrimage comes to an end, but through all eternity they continue to advance further and further into the love of God.

6. The light may rightly be termed both radiance and darkness. Taking

up the statement of Dionysius the Areopagite, 'The divine darkness is the unapproachable light in which God is said to dwell' (*Letter* 5: *PG* 3. 1073A), Palamas says that 'in the strict sense it is light', for it is a supremely positive reality; but, 'by virtue of its transcendence', it is experienced by us as 'darkness' (*Triads*, II, iii, 51). So, like the Areopagite, he combines 'solar' and 'nocturnal' symbolism: 'Even though it is darkness, yet it is surpassingly bright; and in that dazzling darkness, as the great Dionysius says, things divine are granted to the saints' (*Triads*, I, iii, 18).

7. Palamas, like Symeon, believes that the light has a transforming effect upon the beholder. Just as Western saints who receive the *stigmata*, such as Francis of Assisi, enter physically into the mystery of the cross, so in the Byzantine East – where the phenomenon of stigmatization is unknown – the saints in their bodily experience enter rather into the mystery of the transfiguration. Taken up into the uncreated splendour, they themselves shine outwardly with the divine radiance that they contemplate, 'transfigured from glory into glory' (2 Cor. 3.18): 'Participating in that which surpasses them they are themselves transformed into it . . . the light alone shines through them and it alone is what they see . . . and in this way God is all in all' (*Triads*, II, iii, 31). This glorification of the body, while reserved in its plenitude to the last day, is partially anticipated even in this present life.

Palamas' understanding of the divine light, as will by now be apparent, is strongly eschatological. He sees it as the light not only of Tabor but of the *parousia*, and so he regards the vision of the uncreated light as a foretaste of the age to come, as the firstfruits of eternal life. It will also have become clear that, in his understanding of the vision of God, Palamas is upholding a doctrine of the human person that is not dichotomist but holistic, not Platonist but biblical: the human being is not in his view a soul dwelling temporarily in a body but an integrated whole of mind and matter together, and therefore the body shares with the soul in the experience of the divine light. Citing Maximus the Confessor, Palamas affirms a doctrine of total redemption: 'The body is deified along with the soul' (*Triads*, I, iii, 37). Appealing to the incarnation, he insists that Christ took not only a human soul but a human body, and so 'he has made the flesh an inexhaustible source of sanctification' (*Homily* 16: *PG* 151. 193B). Even the passionate aspect of our personhood is to be consecrated to God: Palamas speaks of 'blessed passions' (*Triads*, II, ii, 12), and argues that *apatheia* or 'dispassion' involves not the 'mortification' (*nekrōsis*) but the 'redirection' (*metathesis*) of the passions (*Triads*, III, iii, 15).

This brings us to the third point in Barlaam's polemic, his attack on the physical technique used in combination with the Jesus Prayer. Palamas does not in fact attach particular importance to this technique, considering it suitable primarily for 'beginners' (*Triads*, I, ii, 7; II, ii, 2). But he regards it as theologically defensible, based as it is upon a biblical anthropology which treats human nature as a single whole. Body and soul interact upon each other, and the outer affects the inner: 'Through our bodily posture we train ourselves to be inwardly attentive' (*Triads*, I, ii, 10). If body and soul are in this way essentially united – if, moreover, the body will rise again from the dead at the last day, and is capable of sharing even now in the vision of God – then the body should also be employed to the full at every stage upon the journey of prayer.

Such are the *leitmotifs* of St Gregory Palamas' spiritual teaching. 'Unknown, yet well known', God is utterly transcendent in his essence, yet directly revealed in his uncreated energies. Humans are united with these energies, even during this present life, through the vision of divine light. In this vision the body shares together with the soul – once more, in this present life as well as in the age to come. Body and soul co-operate likewise in the practice of the Jesus Prayer with the accompanying physical technique. In all this Palamas, like Symeon, emerges plainly as a theologian of personal experience. Christianity is not merely a philosophical theory or a moral code, but involves a direct sharing in divine life and glory, a transforming union with God 'face to face'.

Towards the end of the fourteenth century, after the heat of the Palamite controversy had died down, the Hesychast teaching on the Jesus Prayer was summarized in a balanced and tranquil way by St Kallistos and St Ignatios Xanthopoulos in their work *On the Life of Stillness and Solitude*. Their approach is close to that of Gregory of Sinai. Like him, they see the aim of the spiritual life as the ever-increasing 'manifestation' of the grace of baptism: 'Our final end . . . is to return to that perfect spiritual re-creation by grace which was conferred upon us at the outset as a free gift from above by the holy font' (§4). They attach cardinal importance also to the Eucharist: communion should be 'continual' (§91), even daily (§92), for 'these are the things that the enemies fear most of all: the cross, baptism, communion' (§92). In the spiritual life they assign a privileged place to the Jesus Prayer: 'The beginning of all work pleasing to God is the invocation with faith of the saving name of our Lord Jesus Christ' (§8). The Prayer may be accompanied by the physical technique, with control of the breathing, but this is no more than an accessory or 'aid' (§24). The invocation should be without 'thoughts' or the use of the imagination (§25), and should be so far as possible continual:

This all-holy and most sweet name should be our uninterrupted task and study, and we should always carry it with us in our heart, in our intellect, and on our lips. In it and with it we should breathe and live, sleep and wake, move and eat and drink, and in short do everything (§13).

Kallistos and Ignatios, like Gregory of Sinai, are writing with monks in mind. But the Hesychast teaching was never restricted to an exclusively monastic *milieu*. Gregory of Sinai sent his disciples back to the city from the desert, to act as guides to lay people, and Gregory Palamas, in a sharp dispute with a certain monk Job, insisted that Paul's injunction 'Pray without ceasing' (1 Thess. 5.17) is addressed to every Christian without exception. The links of Hesychasm with the wider culture of the day are exemplified in particular by Palamas' contemporary and friend St Nicolas Cabasilas (*c.* 1320–*c.* 1391). Highly educated, pursuing in his earlier years a political career, Cabasilas to the best of our knowledge was never ordained or professed a monk. Although he wrote a short tract in support of Palamas against Gregoras, in his two main works, *The Life in Christ* and *A Commentary on the Divine Liturgy*, Cabasilas avoids all explicit reference to specifically Hesychast themes, such as the Jesus Prayer, the light of Tabor, or the uncreated energies. He expounds the spiritual way simply in terms of the sacraments: 'life in Christ' is nothing else than 'life in the sacraments', and this is accessible to each one alike, whether monastic or married, whether priest, soldier, farmer or the mother of a family. Like Palamas, he sees continual prayer as the vocation of all: 'It is quite possible to practise continual meditation in one's own home without giving up any of one's possessions' (*The Life in Christ*, 6; ET, p. 174). Hesychasm is in principle a universal path.

3 The Hesychast Renaissance

KALLISTOS WARE

Texts and Translations

St Nicodemus of the Holy Mountain and St Macarius of Corinth, *The Philokalia*: Greek text, 3rd edn, 5 vols. (Athens, 1957–63); ET (from the original Greek) G. E. H. Palmer, P. Sherrard and K. Ware, in progress, 3 vols. so far (London and Boston, Faber, 1979–84); partial ET (from Russian) E. Kadloubovsky and G. E. H. Palmer, *Writings from the Philokalia on Prayer of the Heart* (London, Faber, 1951); *Early Fathers from the Philokalia* (London, Faber, 1954).

St Nicodemus of the Holy Mountain and Theophan the Recluse, *Unseen*

Warfare, ET (from Russian) E. Kadloubovsky and G. E. H. Palmer, with introd. by H. A. Hodges (London, Faber, 1952).

Study

K. Ware, 'Philocalie', in *Dict. Sp.* 12.1336–52.

From the fall of Constantinople (1453) until the early nineteenth century, the entire Greek Orthodox world lay under the domination of the Ottoman Turks. In theology and spirituality, as in all aspects of church life, this was for the most part a time of rigid traditionalism. Oppressed beneath a non-Christian regime, the Greeks adopted a defensive stance, holding fast as best they could to their patristic heritage, but making little effort dynamically to develop it. Some of the higher clergy and lay theologians in the Turkish period, especially those who received a Roman Catholic or (less commonly) a Protestant education in the West, introduced Western categories into their thinking. But this had little effect upon the outlook of most monks, of the parish clergy and of the less educated laity. Their spirituality was based, as it always has been in the Christian East, upon the Sunday celebration of the Divine Liturgy or Eucharist. Despite the infrequent reception of Holy Communion – perhaps no more than three times a year, careful preparation being required through fasting and abstinence – the spiritual life of the laity remained none the less strongly eucharistic. Through the annual cycle of feasts and fasts, closely integrated with the agricultural year, and particularly through special blessings of wheat, wine and oil, of homes and crops, the liturgical life of the Church permeated the daily experience of the people. In Orthodox spirituality of the Turkish era, as in the periods before and since, an important role was played by devotion to the Mother of God and the saints, and by the holy icons.

The most significant development in Greek spirituality during the *Turcocratia* is the 'Hesychast renaissance', as it may be termed, during the second half of the eighteenth century. This was set in motion by a group of monks, linked primarily with the Holy Mountain of Athos, known as the 'Kollyvades', from the Greek word *kollyva*, meaning the plate of boiled wheat eaten at memorial services for the dead. They acquired this *sobriquet* because of their insistence upon the strict observance of the rules governing such services. This reflected their more general attitude, which was one of faithful loyalty to church tradition. Reacting against the ideas of the Western 'Enlightenment' that were beginning to spread among educated Greeks, they believed that a regeneration of the Greek nation could come only through a return to the Fathers: it was here alone, they were convinced, that the true roots of

Orthodoxy were to be found. Yet their traditionalism was never blind or inflexible. Thus, for example, at a time when infrequent communion was the all but universal norm, they were fervent supporters of frequent or, as they termed it, 'continual' communion.

Chief among the Kollyvades were St Nicodemus of the Holy Mountain (1749–1809) and St Macarius of Corinth (1731–1805). Despite his Orthodox traditionalism, Nicodemus was also willing to make use of Roman Catholic works of spirituality, and he produced adaptations in Greek of Lorenzo Scupoli's *Spiritual Combat* and Ignatius Loyola's *Spiritual Exercises* (as edited by G. P. Pinamonti). What Nicodemus seems to have found valuable in such volumes was their use of discursive meditation, allowing full scope to the imagination; this, he felt, helpfully supplemented the type of image-free, non-discursive prayer commended by Hesychasm. But the main work edited jointly by Nicodemus and Macarius, the *Philokalia* (Venice, 1782), draws exclusively upon Eastern sources. Literally the title means 'love of beauty' – love, more particularly, of God as the source of all things beautiful. This vast collection of spiritual texts dating from the fourth to the fifteenth century has proved deeply influential in modern Orthodoxy. A Slavonic edition by Blessed Paissii Velichkovsky appeared at Moscow in 1793; Russian versions by Bishop Ignatii Brianchaninov and Bishop Theophan the Recluse followed in the nineteenth century. Through numerous translations into Western languages during the last thirty years, the work's influence has extended widely into the non-Orthodox world.

The selection of texts in the *Philokalia* was no doubt made in part for pragmatic reasons. Nevertheless the book as a whole, without being systematic, presents a specific and coherent view of the Christian life. The main features of the 'Philokalic' spirituality are these:

1. Although the texts included are almost entirely by monks, writing for a monastic audience, the editors intended the book for all Christians, monks and laity alike.

2. The need for personal direction by an experienced spiritual father is frequently emphasized.

3. There is throughout the work a close link between spirituality and dogma. The life of prayer is set firmly in the context of Trinitarian theology and Christology.

4. The main centre of interest is the inner purpose of the spiritual way, not the outward observance of ascetic rules. Key concepts throughout the work are vigilance or sobriety (*nēpsis*), attentiveness (*prosochē*), stillness (*hēsuchia*), and the continual remembrance of God. As a means to the

attainment of stillness and unceasing prayer, the invocation of the name of Jesus is especially recommended. The Jesus Prayer helps the aspirant to keep guard over intellect and heart, to unite the two together, and so to achieve a state of communion with God on a level free from concepts and images.

5. Although containing a paraphrase of certain Macarian writings, the *Philokalia* draws mainly upon writers in the tradition of Evagrius and Maximus the Confessor. Nothing is included by the Cappadocians or by Dionysius the Areopagite. Among the authors from the later Byzantine period are Symeon the New Theologian, Nicephorus the Hesychast, Gregory of Sinai, Gregory Palamas, and Kallistos and Ignatios Xanthopoulos (but not Nicolas Cabasilas).

Through the persisting influence of the *Philokalia* and similar books in the Greek and Slav world, the Hesychast renaissance has continued up to the present day. The Philokalic 'thread' represents, in the eyes of many, the most creative element in contemporary Orthodox spirituality.

B RUSSIAN

SERGEI HACKEL

GENERAL

The Art of Prayer. An Orthodox Anthology, comp. Igumen Chariton of Valamo, ET E. Kadloubovsky and E. M. Palmer, ed. T. Ware. London, Faber, 1966.

Behr-Sigel, E., *Prière et sainteté dans l'Eglise russe*. Paris, 1950.

Evdokimov, P., *Le Christ dans la pensée russe*. Paris, 1970.

Fedotov, G. P., *The Russian Religious Mind* (vol. i: *Kievan Christianity, the tenth to the thirteenth centuries*; vol. ii: *The Middle Ages, the thirteenth to the fifteenth centuries*). Cambridge, Mass., Harvard University Press, 1946–66 (= *RRM*).

Fedotov, G. P. ed., *A Treasury of Russian Spirituality*. Sheed & Ward, New York, 1948; London, 1950 (= *TRS*).

Gorodetzky, N., *The Humiliated Christ in Modern Russian Thought*. London, SPCK, 1938.

Grunwald, C. de, (ET) *Saints of Russia*. London, Hutchinson; New York, Macmillan, 1960.

Kologrivof, I., *Essai sur la sainteté en Russie*. Bruges, 1953.

Kovalevsky, P., (ET) *Saint Sergius and Russian Spirituality*. Crestwood, N.Y., St Vladimir's Seminary Press, 1976.

Rouët de Journel, M., *Monachisme et monastères russes*. Paris, 1952.

Smolitsch, I., *Russisches Mönchtum. Entstehung, Entwicklung und Wesen, 988–1917*. Wurzburg, 1953.

Tysckiewicz, S., *Moralistes de Russie*. Rome, 1951.

Tysckiewicz, S., and Belpaire, T., ed., *Ecrits d'ascètes russes*. Namur, 1957.

PARTICULAR WORKS: MEDIEVAL

Anon., 'The Tale of Boris and Gleb', tr. S. Hackel, *Eastern Churches Review*, 6/1 (1972), pp. 23–35.

Avvakum [Petrov], Archpriest, (ET) *The Life written by himself*. Ann Arbor, 1979; also: *La vie de l'archiprêtre Avvakum*, tr. P. Pascal. Paris, 1938.

Kliuchevsky, V. O., (ET) 'St Sergius: the Importance of his Life and Work', *Readings in Russian History*, ed. S. Harcave (New York, Crowell, 1962), i. 153–64.

Lilienfeld, F. von, *Nil Sorskij und seine Schriften*. Berlin, 1963.

Maloney, G., *Russian Hesychasm. The Spirituality of Nil Sorskij*. The Hague and Paris, Mouton, 1973.

Nestor, (ET) 'The Life of St Theodosius', *TRS*, pp. 15–48.

Nilus [= Nil Sorskii], St, (ET) 'The Tradition to the Disciples', 'The Monastic Rule', 'Last Will', *TRS*, pp. 90–133. See also Maloney, *Russian Hesychasm*, pp. 245–68 (Nil Sorskii, Nine Letters).

(ET) *The Rule of Joseph of Volokolamsk*. Kalamazoo, Cistercian Publications, 1982.

Špidlík, T., *Joseph de Volokolamsk. Un chapitre de la spiritualité russe.* Rome, 1956.
(ET) *The 'Vita' of St Sergii of Radonezh.* Belmont, Mass., Nordland Pub. International, 1980.

PARTICULAR WORKS: POST-PETRINE

Alexander [Semenov-Tian-Chansky], Bishop, (ET) *Father John of Kronstadt.* Crestwood, N.Y., St Vladimir's Seminary Press, 1979.
Anon., (ET) *The Way of a Pilgrim,* tr. R. M. French. London, SPCK, 1960.
Beausobre, I. de, *Flame in the Snow: A Russian Legend.* London, Constable, 1946.
Behr-Sigel, E., 'Le moine dans la ville. Alexandre Boukharev (1822–1871)', in *Revue d'Histoire de la Spiritualité,* 52 (1976), pp. 49–88.
Behr-Sigel, E., *Alexandre Boukharev. Un théologien de l'Église Orthodoxe russe en dialogue avec le monde moderne.* Paris, 1977.
Brianchaninov, I., (ET) *On the Prayer of Jesus.* London, Watkins, 1952.
Brianchaninov, I., (ET) *The Arena: An Offering to Contemporary Monasticism.* Madras, 1970.
Chetverikov, S., (ET) *Starets Paisii Velichkovskii. His Life, Teachings, and Influence on Orthodox Monasticism.* Belmont, Nordland, 1980.
Dunlop, J. B., *Staretz Amvrosy: Model for Dostoevsky's Staretz Zossima.* Belmont, Nordland, 1972; London, Mowbray, 1975.
Elchaninov, A., (ET) *The Diary of a Russian Priest.* London, Faber, 1967.
Gorodetzky, N., *Saint Tikhon Zadonsky: Inspirer of Dostoevsky.* London, SPCK, 1951; see also *TRS,* pp. 186–241.
Graham, S., *With the Russian Pilgrims to Jerusalem.* London, Macmillan, 1913.
Grisbrooke, W. J., ed. and ET, *Spiritual Counsels of Father John of Kronstadt.* London, J. Clarke, 1967.
Hackel, S., *Pearl of Great Price. The Life of Mother Maria Skobtsova, 1891–1945.* London, DLT; Crestwood, N.Y., St Vladimir's Seminary Press, 1981.
Lossky, V., [A series of articles on *startsy*] *Contacts,* 33 (1960), pp. 163–76; 34 (1961), pp. 99–107; 37 (1962), pp. 9–19; 40 (1962), pp. 219–36.
Macarius, or Makariï, Starets of Optino, (ET) *Russian Letters of Direction, 1834–1860,* ed. I. de Beausobre. London and Westminster, Md., Dacre, 1944.
Pascal, P., *Avvakum et les débuts du raskol.* Leningrad, 1938.
Saward, J., *Perfect Fools.* OUP, 1980.
Seraphim of Sarov, (ET) *Concerning the Aims of the Christian Life.* London, SPCK, 1936. See also *TRS,* pp. 246–79.
Sofrony, Archimandrite, (ET) *The Undistorted Image: Staretz Silouan (1866–1938).* London, Faith Press, 1958.
Špidlík, T., *La Doctrine spirituelle de Théophane le Reclus.* Rome, 1965.
Smolitsch, I., *Leben und Lehre der Startzen.* Vienna, 1936; (French trans.) *Moines de la Sainte Russie.* Paris, 1967.

The Russian state of the late tenth century received its Christianity at the hands of the Byzantine Church. Subsequent accounts of the decision-making which led to the conversion of the Kievan ruler Vladimir, his entourage and (eventually) his people stress the importance of liturgical experience in the process. According to the Russian Primary Chronicle, Prince Vladimir sent envoys throughout the known world to assess the worth and appropriateness of various religions. Judaism and Islam were both found wanting, as was Western Christianity. But in the capital of the Byzantine Empire, Vladimir's envoys were overwhelmed by a Eucharist which was celebrated for them at the great cathedral of Hagia Sophia. 'We knew not whether we were in heaven or earth', they are reported to have said, 'for on earth there is no such beauty, and we do not know how to describe it. We know only that God abides there among people . . .'[1]

Throughout the succeeding centuries, the eucharistic Liturgy was to be the Russian Orthodox Christians' main gateway to religious experience. It was to provide them with the model, the framework and the focus of their spiritual life. That liturgical reforms were to be few and largely of peripheral importance ensured the stability of that framework down to the present day; that the liturgical language (Church Slavonic) was related to the vernacular ensured that the focus was all the sharper. The Slavs of eastern Europe, the beneficiaries of the translation work initiated by St Cyril and St Methodius in the ninth century, did not have to master one of the three international (and to them alien) tongues of Christendom – Hebrew, Greek or Latin – in order to engage in prayer.

Not that worship was simply a question of language. In a way difficult to measure, the worshipper (then as now) was inevitably and deeply affected by the dramatic or visual expression of the Christian faith. Thus the icons which furnished every church (and in due course every home) provided each person with specific focal points where the divine presence could be encountered. The painting of icons itself came to be regarded as a spiritual exercise, even as a path to sanctity (see pp. 195–8). The greatest of Russian icon-painters, Andrei Rublev (?1360–1430) is venerated as a saint in the region where he worked, though the only evidence that survives of his sanctity is the product of his brush.

But it would be misleading to represent the Russian path to holiness as principally aesthetic, euphoric or ecstatic. Participation in eucharistic worship and icon-painting alike demand discipline, not to say ascesis. These in their turn are based on explicit doctrine and systematic prescriptions. And while there is a whole category of saints – the Fools for Christ's sake (see pp. 267, 269) – who in their time firmly (indeed brazenly) rejected the rules and regulations of the Church in the furtherance of their particular form of spirituality, there were others – like St

[1] *Povest' vremennykh let*, ed. V. P. Adrianova-Peretts (Moscow-Leningrad, 1950), i. 75.

Iosif (Joseph) of Volokolamsk (1439–1515) – who were to argue that it was firm adherence to canon law and the liturgical *typikon* which was most conducive to salvation. Both canon law and *typikon* were adopted in translation from Byzantium, together with liturgical and iconographic models.

Through their Byzantine teachers, the Russians also gained access to the monastic tradition. In part, they depended on such centres as Mount Athos and the Studios Monastery in Constantinople. Indeed, the Studite Rule, which early came to Russia (it was adopted by the influential Kievan Caves monastery in the mid eleventh century), remained the norm for centuries to come. At the same time, the Russians were almost equally aware of more ancient monastic traditions. At first it was not clear whether the more extreme asceticism of the Syrian world or the more moderate model of the Palestinians was to be preferred.

The founder of the Kievan Caves monastery, St Antonii (d. 1073), gained his early training on Mount Athos itself. On his return to Kiev he settled as a hermit in a cave, and it was there that a community grew up around him. The same asceticism that had earlier brought him to this cave caused him eventually to leave it for greater isolation in another. Little is known about Antonii since no Life survives. But it could be argued that many of his attitudes were to be perpetuated in those Lives of his successors which were to be included in the Kievan Caves *Paterikon* (11th–13th centuries). Here there is talk of rigorous fasting, stern asceticism in seclusion, the use of penitential iron chains.[1] It is possible that Theodoret of Cyr's (translated) *Philotheus* may have brought Syrian models for such commitment to the attention of the Kievan monks. In any case, a 'Syrian' cast of mind may be detected in them.

Their way of life was not to prevail in Russian monasticism as a whole. Even within the confines of the one community there was already a compensatory or rather countervailing force at work. Its finest representative was St Feodosii (Theodosius) (d. 1074). He it was who in 1062 brought the community as a whole out from the caves; he it was who introduced the cenobitic Studite rule at Kiev (and, unwittingly, elsewhere).

Feodosii was the model of moderation. 'Real humility and great gentleness' were among his principal characteristics.[2] He practised asceticism, but surreptitiously. He admonished the Kievan ruler for his hedonism, while yet attending his feasts. Altogether he addressed himself not only to his community, but also to the outside world. His monastery provided shelter for the most deprived members of Kievan society, and

---

[1] E. Benz, ed., *Russische Heiligenlegenden* (Zurich, 1953), pp. 174–243.
[2] 'A Life of St Theodosius' by the monk Nestor (11th century) in *TRS*, p. 33.

provided a weekly ration of bread for its prisons. Yet he was not merely an agent of the establishment. When circumstances dictated it, and at some risk, he was prepared to criticize the prince's political pretensions as well as his personal way of life. Thus he paved the way for such daring critics of the powers-that-be as St Filipp (Philip), Metropolitan of Moscow (1507–69),[1] and Tikhon, Patriarch of Moscow and All Russia (1865–1925).[2] The one was to challenge Ivan the Terrible and his *Oprichnina*, the other Lenin, his government and Party.

In his humility, Feodosii wore tattered clothes and willingly performed those menial tasks from which, as abbot, he would normally have been exempt. Even as a youth he had insisted that 'Our Lord Jesus Christ became poor and humbled himself, offering himself as an example, so that we should humble ourselves in his name' (*TRS* p. 20). The life of his maturity was to provide ample justification for the application of the term 'kenotic' to describe it (*RRM* i.127–31). It was no beatific vision which motivated or (with one possible exception in the very last moments of his life) rewarded him (*TRS* p. 48): rather was he guided by his perception of the divine image in his fellow human beings, waiting to be served and redeemed.

Feodosii made such an impact on his contemporaries that he was canonized almost immediately after his death (1108). Just before he died he had been able to participate in the very first canonization (St Boris and St Gleb, 1072) to dignify the infant Russian Church. Boris and Gleb were two children of that same Vladimir who had been instrumental in bringing about its establishment (988): they were to be among the first to suffer death in loyalty to its beliefs (1015). Not that the beliefs themselves were challenged. Boris and Gleb were killed in an attempt by their half-brother to secure the Kievan throne. According to the accounts of their death, their achievement was to accept death as it came to them, rather than fight for the throne or even offer resistance to the rival claimant. Thus they underwent their passion in all innocence and in a Christlike manner.[3] Their canonization initiated a specifically Russian cult of 'passion-bearers'; several other such sufferers were to be added to the calendar in due course.[4] But even in the immediately succeeding age the beauty of their non-resistance was clearly misunderstood. The two saints

[1] See G. P. Fedotov, *St Filipp: Metropolitan of Moscow – Encounter with Ivan the Terrible* (Belmont, Nordland, 1978).

[2] See Johannes Chrysostomus, *Patriarch Tichon, 1917–1925* (*Kirchengeschichte Russlands der neuesten Zeit* (i) (Munich, 1965).

[3] See (ET) 'The Tale of Boris and Gleb' (11th century), in *Eastern Churches Review*, 6/1 (1972), pp. 23–35.

[4] A brief survey of them is given in *RRM*, i. 105–10.

were most frequently to be commemorated as militant defenders of the Russian land.

It was a land which suffered persistent incursions on its eastern borders from a variety of foes. However, nothing was to match the violence, extent and duration of the Mongol conquest. Mongol suzerainty was established by the end of the 1230s, and it was to last for more than two centuries. The first Mongol rulers were to prove exceptionally tolerant in matters of religion; but their troops were often indiscriminate in the violence they wrought. The preachers and chroniclers of the thirteenth century spoke of the invasion as a divine retribution for the sins of the people. Yet the destruction of those centres of civilization where church life had been firmly established over the previous centuries may also be said to have had positive repercussions. Not least of these was the eventual diffusion of monastic life into the sparsely inhabited and uncultivated regions of central and northern Russia. This diffusion involved a renewal of monastic life which is closely (though not exclusively) associated with the name of St Sergii (Sergius) of Radonezh (?1314–92). An expression of this renewal was the foundation of about one hundred and fifty monasteries within his lifetime and that of his immediate disciples.

It is remarkable that so reticent a monk should have made so indelible an impression not only on the monastic world of his time, but on the shaping of his country's history as whole. Sergii's monastic house, which began as a hermitage in the wilds for his brother and himself, became in due course the best endowed and most renowned of Russian monasteries. His relics became the focus of a national pilgrimage down to the present day. Yet he wrote nothing, was not known as an orator, was weak in administration. Above all, it was his radiant integrity which contemporaries cherished.

In his outward humility he resembles Feodosii of Kiev. But in his inner life a new ingredient may be detected. It was during Sergii's time that Byzantine and east European Hesychasm was beginning to penetrate Muscovy (see pp. 242–55). Little is known about Sergii's method of prayer. But that a hesychast experience of divine light may have been one of its fruits is certainly suggested in his *Life*. The same *Life* also describes his vision of the Mother of God. However, though he began his monastic life as a hermit and ended it with visionary experiences like these, he neither preached nor practised indifference to secular affairs. Indeed, he acted as the adviser (at times the emissary) of his ambitious ruler. Yet although his capacity for this kind of work was recognized by an offer to become Metropolitan of Moscow in 1378, his commitment to a life of prayer led him firmly to refuse it. It was the monk, rather than the diplomat, who responded with the question, 'What am I, but a sinner and the least of men?'[1] Throughout his life he had sought to be 'the least of all and the servant of all' (cf. *RRM* ii.208).

The fifteenth century was to see the development of Hesychasm on Russian soil. Transmission of its teachings was as much by living example as by written prescription. To compensate for the silence of the silentiaries it is necessary to look to the icon-painting of the period. Even the Russian texts which do survive are at several removes from the reality to which they refer since they are not only deliberately impersonal, but largely borrowed or adapted from translated Greek sources (including the works of Saints Dorotheos, Symeon the New Theologian and Gregory of Sinai). Such were the writings of St Nil of Sora.

Like Antonii of Kiev before him, Nil served an apprenticeship on Athos. Later, at his retreat in the northern reaches beyond the Volga, Nil created a loosely-organized *skete*, a 'brotherhood of one spirit'.[2] There he taught his fellow monks ('brothers' rather than 'disciples': loc. cit.) how to combat the passions; there also he succinctly (and perhaps for the first time in Russia, in so far as his was an original compilation) expressed the hesychast teaching on prayer of the heart and on the experience of the divine light. Central to this, he argued, is the measured endeavour 'to maintain our mind in silence, remote even from such thoughts as may seem legitimate'.[3]

> Let us constantly look into the depths of our heart, saying, 'Lord Jesus Christ, Son of God, have mercy upon me' . . . Recite the prayer attentively in this manner, standing, sitting or reclining. Enclose your mind into your heart and, moderating your respiration so as to draw breath as seldom as possible . . . call upon God with fervent desire, in patient expectation, turning away all thoughts' (loc. cit.).

Such prayer can lead the practitioner (whether monk or lay person) beyond prayer: 'The soul is drawn to what is divine, and through [an] ineffable union becomes like God, being illumined in its movements by the light from on high'; then 'it forgets itself and all earthly things, and is affected by nothing' (*TRS* p. 104). Nil's own experience of such 'a foretaste of beatitude' (loc. cit.) may perhaps be assumed. But he himself prefers to veil it behind the words of St Symeon the New Theologian:

> I behold a light which the earth does not possess, glowing in my cell, I see it as I sit on my couch. Within my own being I gaze upon the Creator of the world, and I converse with him, love him and feed on him, am nourished only by this

[1] 'The life of St Sergius', by St Epiphanius, his disciple; abbreviated ET in *TRS*, pp. 78–9. Full text: (ET) *The 'Vita' of St Sergii of Radonezh*. Belmont, Nordland, 1980.

[2] Nil Sorskii, 'The Tradition to the Disciples', in *TRS*, p. 90.

[3] Nil Sorskii, 'The Monastic Rule', in *TRS*, p. 100.

vision of God. And uniting myself with him, I rise above the heavens . . .
Where the body is at such a time I do not know.[1]

It is only 'God in his mercy [who] diminishes his grace for a while in his saints, to let them care for the brethren through preaching and example' (Nil, 'Rule', *TRS* p. 105).

Nil himself was to preach to the outside world on one notable occasion, the Moscow Council of 1503. The Council had before it a political and economic question, though Nil's contribution to the debate was a characteristically spiritual one. Should monastics own land and exploit peasant labour? In Nil's view, the vow of poverty precluded any such thing. Had his view prevailed, the subsequent expropriations of monastic lands (whether under Catherine II or V.I. Lenin) would have been forestalled. As it was, the alternative view prevailed, and the Possessors' party, headed by St Iosif of Volokolamsk (1439–1515) gained the ear of the Muscovite establishment. Many of Nil's Non-possessors were to be hounded in the years to come. As they retreated further into obscurity, so was their teaching eclipsed.

Iosif himself, following in the footsteps of the stern St Pafnutii of Borovsk (d. 1477) (*RRM* ii. 285–301), reflected a different aspect of the Feodosii–Sergii legacy. It was Sergii who had urged his monks, 'Do not neglect to show hospitality to strangers' (Heb. 13.2). Iosif sought to emphasize this aspect of monastic life and it was by reference to it that he justified monastic land-holdings. A monastery should be in a position to provide shelter and food in emergencies. Charity and social work should be institutionalized in order to be most effective. To this end, the monastery itself should be rigorously organized. Though the Jesus Prayer was recommended, the corporate element in spiritual and liturgical life was emphasized above all. Strict observance of the monastic Rule (Joseph published his own)[2] was of paramount importance. Hierarchy should moderate or displace fraternity. In such a setting, the dangers of rigorism and ritualism were not easy to avoid. The correct fulfilment of charitable and liturgical obligations was held to be meritorious in its own right: 'Everything has to be done decorously and in order.'[3] The pattern established by St Iosif was to have a lasting and often stifling effect on Russian spirituality in the years, even the centuries, that followed.

It is hardly surprising that Iosif's sixteenth century was to see the heyday of that alternative form of spirituality which involved the criti-

---

[1] Quoted in A. S. Arkhangel'skii, *Nil Sorskii i Vassian Patrikeev, ikh literaturnye trudy v drevnei Rusi*, 1 (St Petersburg, 1882), p. 101; cf. *TRS*, pp. 104–5.
[2] *The Rule of Joseph of Volokolamsk*, tr. D. Goldfrank. Kalamazoo, Cistercian Publications, 1982.
[3] Iosif of Volokolamsk, 'Rule', quoted in *RRM*, ii.312

cism, ridicule and rejection of all proprieties. The life of a Fool for Christ's sake was necessarily anti-institutional, since anarchic. It involved the voluntary acceptance of a guise of folly, not to say madness, and therefore also of any consequent humiliation. As the Fool distanced himself from society, so was he the freer to perceive its failings and to point them out. At its purest and its most prophetic, here was kenoticism at its most extreme. Even Ivan the Terrible was reputed to have heeded the parabolic supplications of St Vasilii (Basil) the Blessed (d. 1552) and/or St Nikolai of Pskov (d. 1576). But the church establishment, as if to discourage the practice of such folly, was to permit no new canonizations of Fools after the early years of the eighteenth century. Authentic Folly for Christ's sake was not inhibited thereby, though its practitioners suffered more than before at the hands of the state; nor were the laity dissuaded from their (often undiscriminating) veneration of them.[1] Among comparatively recent Fools was a disciple of St Serafim of Sarov, the nun Pelagia Serebrenikova (d. 1884).[2]

Aleksei Bukharev (1822–71) is also often added to the list of modern Fools. His supreme act of folly was to abandon his monastic state (therefore also his priesthood) (1863), and willingly to incur all the ensuing restrictions on residence and employment which the state Church of the day imposed. The dictum of St Serafim of Sarov (1831) to the effect that 'the Lord listens equally to the monk and the layman' was far from being heeded in a case like this (*TRS* p. 278). Yet Bukharev's setting aside of his monastic vows, together with his subsequent marriage, were intended to give room for Christ's grace to inform all 'the needs and infirmities of earthly life', including its physical aspect.[3] He felt impelled to seek Christ 'about the city in the streets, and in the broad ways' (Song of Sol. 3.2). For his part, the average church member could be brought to new spiritual insights 'because those others, in their gracious love, offer themselves to the hard *death* of frank madness in the eyes of men' (ibid. pp. 120–1). Their folly, achieved at the cost of their own freely conceded dignity, could thus become a missionary tool.

The Fools necessarily practised their folly in isolation and *ad hoc*. Their influence was not sufficient to moderate the ritualism which tended to weigh down Russian spirituality from the days of Iosif of Volokolamsk. The elation with which Vladimir's envoys had once discovered the Liturgy at Hagia Sophia was now too often reduced to gratification at the

[1] Dostoevskii provides a description of such veneration in *The Devils*, ii.5.2.
[2] On Fools for Christ's sake see I. I. Kovalevskii, *Iurodstvo o Khriste i Khrista radi iurodivye Vostochnoi i Russkoi Tserkvi* (Moscow, 1895); *RRM*, ii pp. 316–43; and below, pp. 601–2. On Pelagia see Kovalevskii, *Iurodstvo*, pp. 144–9.
[3] A. M. Bukharev, quoted in N. Gorodetzky, *The Humiliated Christ in Modern Russian Thought*, p. 125.

proper adherence to rubrics. The outer and visible form was treasured at the expense of the inward and spiritual grace.

When, towards the middle of the seventeenth century, the time came lightly to revise certain liturgical texts and practices, an astonishingly fierce resistance was generated even to the most minor reforms. It was deemed unacceptable for the patriarch merely to decree that the name of Jesus should be spelled differently or that the sign of the cross should now be made with three fingers rather than two. In each case it was sensed that there was something sacred and iconic about the inherited form. To challenge the detail might in due course lead to rejection of the whole. The defenders of the old ways came to be known as Old Ritualists;[1] but it was tradition in its entirety which they sought to safeguard, not merely its surface manifestations. Tens of thousands contested the innovations, broke with the official Church (1666–7), and willingly accepted the suffering imposed on them by the state in what they took to be the last days. It was this suffering, above all, which often transformed and ennobled their rigoristic stance. The Old Ritualists were led by some remarkable figures, most memorable among them Archpriest Avvakum Petrov (?1620–82). Avvakum's superlative autobiography (see bibliography; abridged ET in *TRS* pp. 137–81) provides a vivid picture of that seventeenth-century spirituality which he believed to be eternally valid and immutable. His imprisonment and execution set a martyr's seal on his stance. The schism which he helped to precipitate remains unhealed.

Avvakum feared secularization; he rejected the incipient westernization of Russia which was its motive force. By the end of the century the reforms of Peter the Great were to favour both, and the Orthodox establishment itself was to be dominated by figures such as Archbishop Feofan (Theophanes) Prokopovich (1681–1736), who were Western-minded to an unprecedented degree.[2] Their eclectic spirituality (which was soon to permeate the newly-established seminaries) was to give rise to few monuments of lasting importance.

A rare exception was provided by the life and (to a lesser degree) the works of St Tikhon of Zadonsk (1724–83). The influences of German pietism (in the person of Joseph Arndt) and of evangelical Anglicanism (Joseph Hall) are to be traced in his writings: these are curiously evangelical (and somewhat emotional) in tone, while yet Orthodox in substance. But it is in his personal life that his true dignity was revealed. He was to be remembered less as a bishop (he resigned his seat prematurely in 1768) than as a solitary seeker after truth, the counseller and benefactor of the

[1] More commonly remembered as 'Old Believers'.
[2] On Feofan, see J. Cracraft, 'Feofan Prokopovich', in J. G. Garrard, ed., *The Eighteenth Century in Russia* (Oxford, Clarendon, 1973), pp. 75–105.

poor in spirit.[1] According to his tombstone 'he appeared as the image of virtue by his word, life, love, spirit, faith and purity' (op. cit., p. 70). But to himself he appeared as a sinner. He would lie prostrate for hours, uttering prayers like, 'Lord have mercy. Be patient with our sins. Hear us, Lord' (ibid., p. 53). Even so, a local Fool for Christ's sake found Bishop Tikhon seated in his yard, slapped him in the face, and shouted, 'Don't think highly of yourself'. It is typical of Tikhon that he rewarded him with a regular payment of several kopecks per day (ibid., p. 64). In fact, Tikhon's danger was that he frequently thought too little of himself. 'What we need in such a case is, as St Paul said in Romans 4.18, against hope to believe in hope', he wrote once (ibid., p. 83). Nevertheless, 'I do not despair of salvation in Christ', he reassured himself in a letter. 'He does not judge sinners, but unrepentant sinners. When the thought overpowers us: how can we be with the apostles, prophets, martyrs, and other great saints who shine with such virtues? Let us thus answer our doubt: we desire to be with the thief, who at the very end of his life uttered only one cry of repentance and was heard' (ibid., p. 82). In the tradition of the Non-possessors, he was able to conclude his will with the words, 'As I have no possessions I leave nothing behind' (ibid., p. 91). Whatever came to him as bishop's salary or pension he had long since given to the needy.

However, the most authentic and extraordinary representative of St Nil's tradition was St Serafim of Sarov (1759–1833). During the main part of his monastic career he was to retire progressively into ever greater solitude. Ten years of unceasing prayer in a hermitage which he established near his monastery (during which a vigil of about three years was spent in the manner of a stylite (pillar hermit), standing or kneeling on rock) culminated in the five years of seclusion which he spent immured in the monastery itself. But when he emerged from his cell on 25 November 1825, the abundant reserves which he had built up in silence and in prayer of the heart were made available to all. Thousands flocked to consult him. His ministry involved a harmonious blend of tradition with inspiration; he was the epitome of a *starets*, though no one had groomed him for the role.

Central to his teaching was the conviction that the aim of life should be the acquisition of the Holy Spirit, 'whereas prayer, vigil, fasting, and other Christian practices, however good they are in themselves . . . serve

[1] As if anticipating the decision of Bukharev, Tikhon regretted that Russian regulations required him to retain his bishop's rank and prerogatives: 'If it had been possible I should have resigned not only my rank but even the hood and cassock; I should have gone to some remote community, there to do menial jobs as a peasant' (V. Chebotarev [Tikhon's cell attendant], quoted in N. Gorodetzky, *Tikhon Zadonsky*, p. 53).

only as the necessary means for achieving it'.[1] To N. A. Motovilov, who visited him at his hermitage in 1831, Serafim was able to reveal what it meant to be 'in the fullness of the Holy Spirit' (a term of St Macarius of Egypt which he made his own) (ibid., p. 129; *TRS* p. 277). Motovilov recounts how he perceived a mysterious light which emanated from Serafim and enveloped him. 'Your face has become brighter than the sun', he said to Serafim, 'and my eyes ache'. He received the startling response, 'You too have become as radiant as I am myself. You yourself are now in the fullness of the Spirit of God, or else you in your turn would not be able to see me as I am' (ibid., p. 124; *TRS* p. 274). Nil Sorskii would have understood such an exchange, as would the Hesychasts on whom he drew.

St Serafim did not intend that his pastoral role should end with his death. Nil Sorskii had asked for his body to be cast into the wilderness to be devoured by beasts and birds 'for that body has greatly sinned before God and is unworthy of burial'.[2] By contrast, Serafim gave the following instructions:

> When I am no longer with you, come to my grave. Whenever you have the time, come, the more often the better. Whatever you have on your mind, whatever happened to you, come to me, and bring whatever sorrow you have with you to my grave. Fall down on the earth, as you would to someone living, and tell me all there is to tell, and I shall hear you, all your sorrows will fly away and pass. As you always spoke to the living person, so also here. For you I am alive and shall be for ever.[3]

Thus he gave vivid expression to the Orthodox teaching on the communion of saints.

The publication of the *Philokalia* (1782) and its partial translation into Slavonic by Paisii Velichkovskii (1793) made readily available a wide range of patristic and hesychast texts for Serafim and his contemporaries.[4] This great work, as well as the personal example of the saintly Paisii, laid the foundations for a revival of the monastic life (much threatened and restricted since the time of Peter) and, in particular, for a remarkable development in the field of spiritual counselling. The role of *startsy* was revived and with it the practice of that prayer of the heart which had been central to Serafim's endeavours. Paisii Velichkovskii

[1] N. A. Motovilov's conversation with St Serafim, quoted in V. N. Il'in, *Prepodobnyi Serafim Sarovskii* (Paris, 1930; New York, Knigoizdatel'stvo 'Put'' zhizni, 1973), p. 113; also *TRS*, p. 266.

[2] Nil Sorskii's Last Will, *TRS*, p. 133.

[3] Quoted in V. N. Il'in, *Serafim*, p. 61. However, the relics of St Serafim (formerly at Sarov) were to disappear in the chaos of the 1920s.

[4] See (ET) *The Philokalia: The Complete Text*, ed. G. E. H. Palmer, P. Sherrard, K. Ware. See above, p. 267.

(1722–94), though Russian by birth and upbringing, had worked for most of his life on Athos and in Moldavia.[1] It was his Russian disciples (such as *starets* Vasilii Kishkin [1745–1831]) who brought his influence to bear on his homeland. Nowhere was it to prove more fruitful than at the monastery of Optino (Optina pustyn') near Kozel'sk. Here a succession of *startsy* was to guide seekers after truth in the course of the century between the 1820s and the 1920s. Where possible, such *startsy* based their counsels on the daily revelation of their client's thoughts. Notable among them were Leonid Nagolkin (1768–1841),[2] Makarii Ivanov (1788–1860)[3] and Amvrosii Grenkov (1812–91).[4] Their advice, founded though it was on absolute principles, tended to be personal and specific. As *starets* Makarii wrote to one correspondent,

> What I write to you, I write for you alone, and I must ask you to refrain from passing any of it on to others as a general rule of conduct for all. It is nothing of the kind. My advice to you is fashioned according to your inner and outer circumstances. Hence it can be right only for you.[5]

Thus, despite the undoubted importance (for some, the centrality) of the Jesus Prayer, Makarii would still write to one of his correspondents:

> It was a mistake for you to practise mental prayer and prayer of the heart. All this is beyond your strength, outside the scope of your capacities, incompatible with your circumstances . . . Because of all this I strongly advise you to stop all practice of the Jesus Prayer. Instead, read or recite – under the direction of your confessor – psalms, penitential canons, litanies and so on. Go to church as frequently as possible; live humbly, according to the admonitions of your conscience; and carefully, according to the commandments of our Lord. In other words, lead the life of an ordinary, God-fearing member of the Christian laity (ibid., pp. 97–8).

Similarly, while monastics should abstain altogether from meat, there was no requirement for others to follow suit, however strictly they might keep the usual fasts:[6] 'You also wish that you could have long ago given

---

[1] See S. Chetverikov, *Starets Paisii Velichkovskii.*

[2] See V. Lossky, *Contacts* 34 (1961), pp. 99–107.

[3] See V. Lossky, *Contacts* 37 (1962), pp. 9–19. Also Macarius, *Russian Letters of Direction, 1834–1860.*

[4] See V. Lossky, *Contacts* 40 (1962), pp. 219–36. Also J. B. Dunlop, *Staretz Amvrosy.*

[5] Macarius, *Russian Letters of Direction*, p. 25.

[6] Abstinence from all products of animal origin during four extended Lenten periods, as well as on the Wednesday and Friday of virtually each week. For 'it is only by a slow and patient effort that man discovers that he "does not live by bread alone" – that he restores in himself the primacy of the spirit' (A. Schmemann, *Great Lent*, Tuckahoe, N.Y., St Vladimir's Seminary Press, 1969, p. 50). In the words of Nil Sorskii, 'When the stomach is under control by prudent, intelligent constraint, then there comes into the soul a whole array of virtues' (Nil's Rule, quoted in G. Maloney, *Russian Hesychasm*, p. 86).

up eating meat. Since, in your case, this is one more occasion for pride, it is not good . . . Avoid making idols either of things or of practices' (ibid., p. 98). Above all, he counselled humility: 'All human misfortunes and all un-Christian actions spring from pride; all good comes from humility' (ibid., p. 102); 'Humble yourself and find peace' (ibid., p. 64). The moderation and appropriateness of such advice could be said to provide a model for each confessor in his parish church.

There were other spiritual authorities who deserve to be remembered, among them two bishops, the morose Ignatii Brianchaninov (1807–67) and the exceptionally engaging Feofan Govorov, known as the Recluse (1815–94).[1] Prolific, erudite and authoritative as they were, neither was to gain as much of a popular following in due course as the anonymous Pilgrim, whose sophisticatedly unsophisticated work on his practice of the Jesus Prayer first appeared in 1884, and has since brought this aspect of Orthodox spirituality to the attention of readers throughout the world (ET: *The Way of a Pilgrim*). Bishops Ignatii (1857) and Feofan (1877) were both (separately) Russian translators of the *Philokalia*. The Pilgrim was its avid reader. Each in his own way sought to 'pray without ceasing' (1 Thess. 5.17). It was, indeed, this phrase of St Paul's which first sent the Pilgrim on his search for the prayer of the heart. Eventually, the practice of this prayer was to lead him to apprehend the world as if it were transfigured.

> The prayer of the heart provided me with such delight, that I doubted if there were anyone happier than I on earth, or if there could be greater and finer delight in the very kingdom of heaven. Not only did I feel this in my innermost soul, but also all that was around me appeared to me in a delightful form, and all prompted me to love God and to thank him; people, trees, plants, animals, everything was akin to me, on all I found the impress of the name of Jesus Christ.[2]

But this was a by-product of the prayer, not its purpose. 'Let us not seek pleasure or visions', counselled Ignatii Brianchaninov. Rather, 'let us practise the prayer of Jesus disinterestedly, with simplicity and purity of intention, with penitence as our objective, with faith in God, with complete surrender to the will of God . . .'[3] In the process, pride or self-esteem must be avoided. 'The Holy Fathers wrote, "Do not measure yourself"', wrote Feofan the Recluse.

---

[1] Excerpts from their writings are to be found in Igumen Chariton of Valamo, (ET) *The Art of Prayer. An Orthodox Anthology* (London, Faber, 1966). On Feofan see T. Špidlík, *La Doctrine spirituelle de Théophane le Reclus*; also S. Bolshakoff, *Russian Mystics* (Kalamazoo, Cistercian Publications; Oxford, Mowbray, 1977), pp. 196–221.

[2] *Otkrovennye rasskazy strannika dukhovnomu ottsu* (Paris, 1948), p. 107; cf. *TRS*, p. 342.

[3] Ignatius Brianchaninov, *On the Prayer of Jesus*, p. 113.

If you think you can decide any question about your progress, it means that you are beginning to measure yourself to see how much you have grown. Please avoid this as you would avoid the fire (quoted in Chariton, *Art of Prayer*, pp. 158–9).

The Way of a Pilgrim incidentally provides an introduction to the extended (sometimes lifelong) pilgrimages which were formerly undertaken by numerous Russians of the peasant milieu. The pilgrimage to Jerusalem was particularly favoured,[1] but there were also destinations nearer home, sanctified by sacred icons, wells or relics. At best, extended pilgrimage might be said to correspond to a perpetual inward quest for the Kingdom of God, and this more than anything could provide justification for what, in a different context, has been called 'a Beduinization of the ascetic life'.[2] But it could not replace this quest, and too frequently it might distract attention from it. 'For someone who has not yet found the way to enter within himself, pilgrimages to holy places are a help', wrote Feofan to one of his correspondents.

But for him who has found it they are a dissipation of energy, for they force him to come out from the innermost part of himself. It is time for you now to learn more perfectly how to remain within. You should abandon your external plans (Chariton, *Art of Prayer*, p. 106).

A different category of reader learned of Russian spirituality through the medium of Russian fiction. A number of nineteenth-century writers dwelt thoughtfully on aspects of popular piety, even when this was inimical to them. Their works had a wider circulation in nineteenth-century Russia than the Pilgrim's.

P. I. Mel'nikov-Pecherskii (1819–83) concentrated on the Old Ritualists.[3] N. S. Leskov (1831–95) explored the world of Old Ritualists and sectarians alike, as well as that of the Orthodox.[4] But the most renowned of the novelists who dwelt on religion was undoubtedly F. M. Dostoevskii (1821–81). In his own estimation and in that of many of his critics, he was a spokesman of Orthodoxy. Most transparently Orthodox of all, so it was suggested, were the teachings of *starets* Zosima in *The Brothers Karamazov*. Had not Dostoevskii modelled Zosima on Amvrosii of

[1] S. Graham, *With the Russian Pilgrims to Jerusalem*. London, Macmillan, 1913; Archimandrite Spiridon, *Mes Missions en Sibérie* (Paris, 1950), pp. 20–54.
[2] P. Brown, *Society and the Holy in Late Antiquity*. London, Faber; Berkeley, University of California, 1982.
[3] P. I. Melnikov-Petcherski, *Dans les forêts*, French trans. Paris, 1957.
[4] Much of his work is available in German: N. S. Leskov, *Gesammelte Werke* tr. J. von Guenther et al. (Munich, 1924–7); (ET) N. S. Leskov, *The Cathedral Folk* (London, John Lane; New York, Knopf, 1924). See also M. L. Rössler, *Nikolai Leskov und seine Darstellung des religiösen Menschen* (Weimar, 1939).

Optino, whom he had visited? It was too easily forgotten that the monks of Optino had been among the first to cast doubts on Zosima's authenticity. A careful examination of something like Zosima's curious veneration of the earth is likely to confirm such doubts.[1] Clearly Dostoevskii poses religious problems in his works. Whether his characters propound Orthodox answers to them – or even answers at all – remains less clear. Even so, his writings were to play a critical role in awakening a concern for religious questions in the largely secularized Russian intelligentsia at the turn of the century. In time, it was this same intelligentsia which was to bring a new vitality to Russian church circles in the Emigration after the Revolution of 1917.[2]

Dostoevskii's Zosima was a monk, as might have been expected: the monasteries and hermitages of the past had generally provided most of Russia's spiritual guides. An Avvakum might be a married parish priest, but he was certainly an exception among such guides. Bukharev was *sui generis* and can hardly be said to provide an alternative, non-monastic model. But it was one of Bukharev's and Dostoevskii's contemporaries who most dramatically demonstrated that the secular parish clergy were also capable of developing a specific form of spirituality and of deeply affecting their milieu thereby. This was Fr Ioann (John) Sergiev (1829–1908), usually known (by the name of the parish which he served throughout his working life) as John of Kronstadt.[3]

At the heart of Fr John's life was prayer. But he placed as much emphasis on the regular liturgical (and in particular the eucharistic) prayer of the Church as on the Jesus Prayer. In his estimation, 'Everything that the Church puts into our mouths and hearing is truth, the breathing or teaching of the Holy Ghost.'[4] Like those early Russian visitors to Hagia Sophia, he was convinced that

> the spiritual tranquillity of blessedness which we sometimes experience in God's temple . . . is a foretaste of that infinite bliss which those will experience who will eternally contemplate the unspeakable beauty of God's countenance (ibid., p. 367).

At the same time, prayer is far more than the passive reception of the Church's liturgical life. Prayer needs to be daring, sincere, attentive,

---

[1] See the contribution by S. Hackel to *New Essays on Dostoyevsky*, ed. M. V. Jones and G. Terry (CUP, 1982), pp. 139–68.

[2] A general study of some outstanding personalities of the Emigration is given in N. Zernov, *The Russian Religious Renaissance of the Twentieth Century* (London, DLT; New York, Harper & Row, 1963). See also S. Hackel, *Pearl of Great Price*.

[3] See also the writings of another remarkable pastor, Fr Alexander Elchaninov (1881–1934), *The Diary of a Russian Priest*. Extracts in *TRS*, pp. 421–85.

[4] John Sergieff, 'My Life in Christ', *TRS*, p. 376.

unrelenting, inward. It needs to be personal in its commitment; even, at times, in its language. Moments of deadly darkness or spiritual anguish should not lead to despair: 'Remember that if the Divine light has been cut off from you, it always shines in all its splendour and greatness in God himself, in God's Church, in heaven and in earth' (ibid., p. 359). Committed prayer cannot but be efficacious. Indeed, 'as often as I prayed with faith, the Lord always heard me and fulfilled my prayers' (ibid., p. 362). Thus it was that Fr John gained considerable renown as a thaumaturge. So much so, that even in his life-time the foundations were laid for an unofficial cult, which eventually found expression in a sect of 'Johnites' (*Ioannity*). The sect's equation of John of Kronstadt with the Christ of the Second Coming cast a shadow on Fr John's reputation. However it was principally his simplistic espousal of right-wing causes which, in Soviet times, led not only to the barricading of his tomb against would-be pilgrims but, eventually, also to the destruction of his remains.

It need hardly be said that the Revolution of 1917 brought more restrictions than this on religious observance. All that had been built up and, too often, taken for granted over the preceding centuries was to be challenged and disrupted. In terms of church-state relations, the country moved abruptly from the Constantinian age into an age of persecution. The path of the martyr and confessor became a normative one for many. Traditional spirituality was to be tested to the full in the prisons and camps of the succeeding decades, and it was not found wanting. Those who used the period of disarray to promote revised services or canons (and who went into schism with the formerly established Church in the process) failed to carry the mass of the church membership with them, and in due course forfeited even that support of the state authorities which they had earlier courted and obtained. By contrast, monastic spirituality was not eroded by the closure of virtually all monasteries by 1939, any more than was the liturgically oriented spirituality of the laity by the drastic reduction of open churches from over 54,000 in 1917 to a matter of hundreds in 1939.[1] Worship was driven underground. At the same time, as one monastic priest was able to comment in retrospect (and with a quiet smile) after decades of 'bonds and imprisonment' (Heb. 11.36), 'the word of God is not bound' (2 Tim. 2.9).[2] For those who bore witness (*martyria*) to this word were now diffused throughout society, more especially among its most deprived members. That they were now 'without form or comeliness' served only to emphasize the integrity of their message. As a leading bishop (Metropolitan Arsenii of Novgorod) was

---

[1] Official estimates of the year 1939 give the figure 4,225; but many commentators prefer to modify this figure and to refer to 'several hundreds'.

[2] Archimandrite Tavrion Bototskii (1898–1978), private conversation.

able to foresee at the very outset of this period, in February 1918, 'The host of martyrs illumines our path and demonstrates that strength which no persecution can undermine'.[1]

The institutional revival of the Church in the 1940s and 50s was in itself less important than that by which it was informed: that spiritual vigour, that inward renewal which was the fruit of persecution. Thus, although the Church which emerged was yet to experience renewed suppression under Nikita Khrushchev at the beginning of the 1960s, she was yet able to affirm then, through her patriarch, what she had believed throughout. 'For what significance can there be', asked Patriarch Aleksii in 1960,

> in all the efforts which human reason directs against Christianity when its two thousand year old history speaks for itself, when all enemy assaults were foreseen by Christ himself, who gave an assurance of the Church's perpetual stability and said that 'the gates of hell shall not prevail' against his Church?

And he concluded, 'We Christians know how we must live in order to serve people, and our love cannot be diminished by any circumstances whatsoever.'[1]

[1] Metropolitan Arsenii, speech at the Russian Church Council (1917–18), quoted in L. Regel'son, *Tragediia Russkoi Tserkvi* (Paris, 1977), p. 43.

[2] Patriarch Aleksii [of Moscow], 'The Gates of Hell shall not prevail', in *Sourozh*, 1 (1980), pp. 15–16.

VII

THE MEDIEVAL WEST

A MONASTIC SPIRITUALITY

1 Gregory the Great

BENEDICTA WARD

Texts

St Gregory, *Opera Omnia, PL* 75–79.
Gregorii Magni Dialogi, ed. U. Moricca. Rome, 1924.

Critical Editions

Homiliae in Hiezechielem Prophetam, ed. M. Adriaen. CCSL, 1971.
Moralia in Job, 2 vols., ed. M. Adriaen. CCSL, 1979.
Registrum Epistolarum, ed. P. Ewald and L. M. Hartmann. Monumenta Germaniae Historica, Ep. i–ii, 1891–99.

Translations

(French) *Morales sur Job*, R. Gillet and A. de Gaudemoris. SC, 1952.
(English) *Dialogues*, trans. O. J. Zimmerman. FC, 1959.
Morals on the Book of Job. LF, 4 vols., 1847.

General

Butler, E. C., *Western Mysticism*. 3rd edn, London, Constable, 1967; New York, Barnes & Noble, 1968.
Dudden, F. H., *Gregory the Great: His Place in History and Thought*, 2 vols. London, Bombay, New York, Longmans Green, 1905.
Evans, G. R., *St Gregory the Great*. OUP, 1985.
Leclercq, J. (ET) *Love of Learning and Desire for God.* 2nd edn, London, SPCK; New York, Fordham University, 1974.

One of the Latin doctors of the Church, Gregory (*c.* 540–604) was the son of a Roman senator and became prefect of the city in 573. He sold his property, gave the proceeds to the poor and commenced a life of austerity. He went to Constantinople for seven years as *apocrisiarius* from 578 to 585; after his return, he lived in the monastery of St Andrew in Rome until his election as Pope in 590. His decisive action as Pope led him to conclude an agreement with the Lombard invaders of Italy, 592–3, which further established the independence of Rome from the Emperor in Constantinople and his representative, the exarch of Ravenna. Gregory's able administration of the lands of the Church led to the establishment of the machinery of the medieval papacy and the articulation of its authority in the West. His missionary zeal caused him to send Augustine on a mission to England; and his monastic interests produced the *Life and Miracles of St Benedict*, the second book of the *Dialogues*, one of the most influential texts of the Middle Ages.

Gregory's writings are of a pastoral rather than a speculative nature. His *Liber Regulae Pastoralis* (*c.* 591) gives directions for the conduct of bishops especially in relation to their care of the clergy; it became the text-book of the medieval episcopate and was translated into English by King Alfred. The *Dialogues* (*c.* 593) relates accounts of sanctity in Gregory's contemporaries for the encouragement of his readers; it became a model for later hagiographical writing. His exegesis of the *Book of Job* (*Moralium Libri* XXV), his homilies on the Gospels, and in particular his commentary on the Book of Ezekiel, interpret the Scriptures in a mystical as well as a moral sense. He also wrote letters which provide information about pastoral and moral affairs in many spheres. He encouraged changes and development in the liturgy and in its music, providing several prayers for liturgical use, though the Gregorian Sacramentary is a later compilation; his homilies provided texts for use in the readings at Vigils for centuries.

Gregory's teaching on prayer reflects the influence of Augustine of Hippo but with a practical bent, suited to his own temperament and times. His comments on the nature of contemplation in the *Moralia* and in the *Homilies on Ezekiel* profoundly influenced the monastic world of the Middle Ages. He bridges the gap between the patristic world and the Middle Ages, with his structured reflections upon Christian life and doctrine in a dialectic of presence and absence, faith and knowledge, dark and light. Almost all the later vocabulary of the West concerning the spiritual life has its origin in Gregory's assimilation and rewriting of the vocabulary of Cassian and Augustine. He provided in Latin a sacred philosophy which was universally used in the West. His doctrine of prayer cannot be separated from his concept of the Christian life as exile and pilgrimage, a process of detachment from the world by desire for God. He describes first of all humanity's state as that of sinners, lacking peace, alienated from God, attached to earth as if by a weight, caught in a state of mutability which ends in death. Understanding of this leads to humility and compunction, fear of hell and the desire for salvation. The action of God pierces the heart, stirring people out of their lethargy, to the tears of repentance and of desire for God. This leads to the obscure realization of God, constantly found and lost, acting within human beings for their salvation. Through tribulation, suffering, temptation, our 'spiritual senses', i.e. the eyes of the heart, the ears of the heart, become open towards God, so that the soul is released to 'fly towards God on spiritual wings' (*Hom. in Ez.* II. 12). Human progress towards God is without limits, but it is also already realized from the beginning as unity with him: 'merely to love things above, already to mount on high' (*Mor.* XV. 53). This realization of unity with God in the soul produces fruit in the service of God and of humanity. It does not lead to the full vision of God in this life, but the whole of life in this world becomes a way of salvation leading to complete knowledge of God after death.

The idea of a whole life of prayer lived towards God includes the notion of union with God as transfiguring the whole of creation, giving people a new perspective towards this world. This theme is given expression in the *Moralia* but its most vivid demonstration is found in Gregory's account of the life of Benedict of Nursia. Benedict is presented as *vir dei*, the ideal of Christian as well as of monastic life. In the second book of the *Dialogues*, Gregory comes to the climax of his presentation with a description of Benedict at prayer:

> The man of God was standing at his window, where he watched and prayed while the rest were still asleep. In the dead of night he suddenly beheld a flood of light shining down from above more brilliant than the sun and with it every trace of darkness cleared away . . . the whole world was gathered up before his eyes in what appeared to be a single ray of light (*Dialogues*, 34).

Gregory comments:

> The light of holy contemplation enlarges and expands the mind in God until it stands above the world. In fact the soul that sees him rises even above itself, and as it is drawn upwards in his light all its inner powers unfold.

This theme of transfiguration in God by prayer reaches its proper climax, however, in Gregory's account of the vision seen by two monks at the death of St Benedict: 'They both saw . . . a magnificent road . . . From his monastery it stretched eastwards in a straight line until it reached up into heaven', and they were told, 'this is the road taken by blessed Benedict, the Lord's beloved, when he went to heaven'. The message contains the essence of Gregory's teaching about prayer: the whole life gradually freed from the bonds of earth and seeing all things in perspective in the light of God, and thus taking the 'straight road' to heaven, where the vision of God, full union with him, is fulfilled after death. In this image of the *vir dei*, Gregory presents one of the main themes of Western spirituality, the continual conversion of the soul throughout life, which enables a person to see things 'in the light of God', but makes no claim to the immediate vision of God in this life:

So long as we are beset by the corruptions of the flesh, we in no wise behold the brightness of the Divine power as it abides unchangeable in itself, in that the eye of our weakness cannot endure that which shines above us with intolerable lustre from the ray of his eternity (*Moralia*, v, 52).

The soul illuminated by the light of God, sees its own weakness and what is contrary to God in itself and continues more ardently the process of repentance, in a dialectic of self-knowledge and the knowledge of God by love. This teaching permeated the monastic Middle Ages in the West, giving both the theology and the vocabulary to the barbarian Christians for them to use and develop.

2 Anselm of Canterbury

BENEDICTA WARD

Texts

Opera Omnia, ed. F. S. Schmitt, 6 vols. Edinburgh and London, Nelson, 1946–61.
Eadmer, *Vita S. Anselmi*, ed. and trans. R. W. Southern. London and New York, Oxford Medieval Texts, T. Nelson, repr. 1972.
Memorials of St Anselm, ed. R. W. Southern and F. S. Schmitt. London, Auctores Britannici Medii Aevi, i, 1969.

Translations

Hopkins, J., and Richardson, H., *Anselm of Canterbury* (selected works in ET), 4 vols. Toronto and New York, Edwin Mellen, 1974–6; London, SCM, 1974– .
Ward, B., *Anselm's Prayers and Meditations, with the Proslogion* (in ET). Harmondsworth, Penguin Classics, repr. 1980, with introd.

Studies

Evans, G. R., *Anselm and Talking about God*. OUP, 1978.
Southern, R. W., *St Anselm and His Biographer*. CUP, 1963.
Wilmart, A., *Auteurs spirituels et textes dévots du moyen âge latin* (Paris, 1932), pp. 162–201.

Anselm was born in Aosta *c.* 1033; he left home after the death of his mother and spent three years in northern France before becoming a monk in the abbey of Bec in Normandy. He was in turn prior and abbot, until he became Archbishop of Canterbury in succession to Lanfranc under William Rufus and Henry I. He was twice in exile during that time and died at Canterbury on the Wednesday of Holy Week, 1109.

Anselm was a man of independent and original mind, which he applied to the task of analysing and expounding lucidly major issues in philosophy and theology. His most famous philosophical work is the *Proslogion*, which bases the so-called ontological argument on the proposition, 'God is that than which nothing greater can be thought'. The *Monologion* and the *Proslogion* were written at Bec, 1076–8; four theological treatises, *De Grammatico, De Veritate, De Libertate Arbitrii*, and *De Casu Diaboli* were composed between 1080 and 1090. *De Incarnatione Verbi*, written against Roscelin, occupied him 1092–4 and his major theological work on the Atonement, *Cur Deus Homo*, was completed in exile, 1094–8. *De Conceptu Virginali* followed, 1099–1100, and *De Processione Spiritus Sancti* was composed in 1102, based on Anselm's participation in the Council of Bari. The Letters on the Sacraments (1106–7) and *De Concordia* (1107–8) were his last works. Anselm was also a prolific letter-writer and his letters, together with records of his miracles and his conversational expositions of doctrine, published in *Memorials of St Anselm*, complete his known works. His biography was written by his friend Eadmer, both in the *Historia Novella in Anglia*, an account of his public life, and in the *Vita S. Anselmi*, a more private and personal presentation.

In addition to his theological expositions, Anselm wrote and circulated several *Prayers and Meditations*, mostly composed while he was at Bec. It is in these last that Anselm's principal contribution to spirituality is to be found; but his spiritual and theological writings are not mutually exclusive. His treatise on the atonement, for instance, was explicitly related to his devotional writings by a *Meditation on Human Redemption*, which summarized in the form of a prayer the doctrine expounded in *Cur Deus Homo*. The *Proslogion* itself was written in the form of a meditation. Moreover, it contains not only the specifically Anselmian approach to the relationship between prayer and thought ('faith seeking understanding') but also a demonstration of the method of withdrawal into solitude, for intense self-examination leading to compunction and adoration, which is also involved in the *Prayers and Meditations*. The major part of the *Proslogion* is a meditative prayer arising from Anselm's consideration of the being of God, rising to a climax of adoration in the last sections on the nature of heaven.

The *Prayers and Meditations* offered a new style in devotional literature. Most of them are addressed to a saint and take the form of a meditation upon the saint in relation to Christ and to the person praying; each begins with a section of self-abasement and repentance, followed by compunction, and adoration for the fact of salvation in Christ. They are expressed in a highly-wrought prose, the function of which is to stir the mind to attention and so to provoke emotion that the will can be moved to action. The *Prayers* were sent to various friends at their request, and with some of them went letters explaining how they were to be used, a method also set out in a Preface to the *Prayers and Meditations*, which is attributed to Anselm. The *Prayers* introduced into the tradition of Christian devotion a new attention to words as a means of personal involvement in prayer, and gave a central place to emotion in the act of praying. The basic pattern of prayer has its roots in the ancient tradition of *penthos*, compunction, but the presentation was new.

The *Prayers* were admired and used by Anselm's contemporaries; their unique combination of clarity of thought and intensity of feeling made them popular to such an extent that they at once received the flattery of widespread imitation. They were soon surrounded by a mass of imitative material, and it was not until the middle of the present century that the eighteen genuine prayers and three meditations of Anselm were distinguished and presented as part of his works in a critical edition. Anselm's lifetime covered one of the most momentous periods of change in the thought of Western Europe, and there was no side of this that he left untouched. Though he did not seek to make innovations, Anselm's influence upon devotion was perhaps the most fundamental and long-lasting of all the changes which he stimulated.

B THE NEW ORDERS

BENEDICTA WARD

GENERAL

Bouyer, L., (ET) *The Meaning of the Monastic Life*. London, Burns Oates; New York, Kennedy, 1955.
Heimbucher, M., *Die Orden und Kongregationen der Katholischen Kirche*. 4th edn, Paderborn, 1934 (bibliography).
Knowles, M. D., *Christian Monasticism*. New York, McGraw-Hill, 1969.

CAMALDOLESE

Texts

Catechesimo Camaldolesi. Edizioni Camaldoli, 1951.
Giabbani, A., *L'Eremo*. Brescia, Morcelliana, 1945.

Individuals

St John Gualbert, *Vita*, by Andrew of Strumi. *AS*, July iii, pp. 343–65.
St Peter Damian, *Opera Omnia*, *PL* 144, 145. *AS*, Feb. iii, pp. 416–27.

Translations

St Peter Damien, Selected Writings on the Spiritual Life, trans. Patricia McNulty. London, Faber, 1959.
Textes primitifs camaldules, tr. L. A. Lassus, introd. D. Giabbiana. Namur, 1961.
St Romuald, Vita, by Peter Damian. *AS*, Feb. ii, pp. 104–24.
Anal. Boll. 31 (1912), pp. 76ff.
La Vie du Bienheureux Romuald, ed. D. Giabbani, in *Textes primitifs*.

General

Mazis, A. des, 'Camaldoli', in *DHGE*, vol. xi (1949) with bibliography.

CARTHUSIANS

Texts

Laporte, M., *Aux sources de la vie cartusienne*. La Grande Chartreuse, 8 vols, 1960–70.

Individuals

St Bruno, Life. *AS*, Oct. iii, pp. 503ff.
Bruno, Guigo and Anthelmus, *Lettres des premiers Chartreux*. Paris, SC 88, 1962.
Guigo I, *Meditations*, *PL* 153. 601–31.
Meditationes Guigonis prioris Cartusiae, ed. and Fr. trans. A. Wilmart. Paris, 1936.

(ET) Jolin, J., *Meditations of Guigo*. Milwaukee, Marquette University, 1951.
Guigo II, *Scala Paradisi* and *Liber de quadripertito exercitio cellae, PL* 153. 185–884.
Guigo II, (ET) Colledge, E., and Walsh, J., *The Ladder of Monks*. Oxford, Mowbray; Garden City, N.Y., Doubleday (Image Books), 1978.
Adam of Dryburgh, *Life of St Hugh of Lincoln*, ed. and trans. D. Douie and H. Farmer. London and New York, Nelson, 1961–2.
Adam of Dryburgh, *Liber de quadripertito exercitio cellae. PL* 153, 799–884.

General

Leclercq, J., 'St Bruno, Guigo and the Chartreuse', in *The Spirituality of the Middle Ages, HCS*, vol. 2. pp. 150–61.
Thompson, E. M., *The Carthusian Order in England*. London, SPCK; New York and Toronto, Macmillan, 1930.

CISTERCIANS

Early documents

Les Plus Anciens Textes de Cîteaux, ed. with text and French trans. J. de la Croix Bouton and J. B. van Damme. Achel, 1974.

Individuals

St Bernard, *Opera Omnia*, ed. J. Leclercq, C. H. Talbot, H. M. Rochais. Rome, 1957–9.
For further works cf. L. Janauschek, *Bibliographia Bernardina*. Vienna, 1891.
Aelred of Rievaulx, *Opera Omnia*, ed. A. Hoste and C. H. Talbot. CCCM 1971.

Translations

Texts by Bernard, Aelred, William of St Thierry, and other notable Cistercian writers are available in the series Cistercian Fathers (Kalamazoo, Spencer, Mass., and Washington).

General

Donkin, R. A., *Cistercian Bibliography*. Rochefort, 1969.
Gilson, E., (ET) *The Mystical Theology of St Bernard*. London and New York, Sheed & Ward, 1940.
Lekai, L., *The White Monks*. Okauchee, Wis., Cistercian Fathers, 1953.
Merton, T., *The Silent Life*. London, Burns Oates; New York, Farrer, Strauss & Cudahy, 1957.

CANONS

Colvin, H. M., *The White Canons in England*. Oxford, Clarendon, 1951 (bibliography).
Dickinson, J. C., *The Origins of the Austin Canons*. London, SPCK, 1950.
Petit, R. P. F., *La Spiritualité des Prémontrés aux XIIᵉ et XIIIᵉ siècles. Études de théologie et d'histoire de spiritualité* X, 1947.

Robert of Bridlington, *The Bridlington Dialogue*. London, Mowbray, 1960.

Gilbertines

Foreville, R., *Un Procès pour la canonisation de S. Gilbert de Sempringham*. Paris, 1943.

Graham, R., *St Gilbert of Sempringham and the Gilbertines*. London, Stock, 1901.

KNIGHTS TEMPLAR

Seward, D., *The Monks of War*. London, Eyre Methuen; Hamden, Conn., Archon books, 1972.

HERMITS

Leyser, H., *Hermits and the New Monasticism*. London, Macmillan, 1984.

WOMEN VISIONARIES

Elizabeth of Schonau, *Vita. AS*, June iv, pp. 499–532.
Elizabeth of Schonau, *Works. PL* 195. 119–208.

Further bibliography in *Dict. Sp.*, under individual entries.

By the end of the eleventh century, monastic life in western Europe was becoming diversified in a number of ways, and with it went new emphases in devotion. While the traditional understanding of monasticism and its spiritual basis continued in such great abbeys as Cluny, Gorze, Bec, Canterbury, though with awareness there also of the currents of change, new forms of monasticism appeared, exercising a decisive influence on the Church. The great increase in numbers and influence of the new monks, and their close association with the Gregorian reform movement, led to a monasticizing of spirituality throughout the Church, in which the ascetic spirituality of the monks became the norm for the devout Christian and especially for the clergy. This monasticizing of spirituality makes the twelfth century a turning point in the history of western thought; it is therefore important to look at its basis, which resides in the change in spirituality among the monks themselves in some of their main concerns.

Underlying the various new orders was a movement which reaffirmed the ancient tradition of hermit life as a valid expression of monastic spirituality. This impulse was widespread and characterized by the desire for a simple, solitary life without many of the structures of established monastic houses and their involvement with society. Poverty, solitude, silence, fasting, manual work characterized these new ventures; their inspiration was the literature surviving from fourth-century monasticism, interpreted according to the outlook of the eleventh and twelfth centuries. This movement took two forms: there were many hermits, living alone in individual solitude; there were, secondly, groups of monks living together in corporate solitude. These groups overlapped and produced the new orders of the twelfth century.

The first leader of a significant group of solitaries was Romuald of Ravenna (950–1027), who left a traditional Cluniac monastery with the specific intention of living a kind of monastic life on the pattern of Egyptian solitude. He created the 'desert' of Camaldoli near Arezzo, with a community of monks living in small houses and meeting for prayer and meals. A younger contemporary, John Gualbert (990–1073), also formerly a Cluniac monk, lived first at Camaldoli, then formed a similar group at Vallombrosa near Florence. A third monk who was a dominant influence on these reformers was Peter Damian, who expressed in his writings the extreme of the ideal behind their efforts.

A similar pattern of life was established at the Grande Chartreuse by Bruno of Cologne, at first master and chancellor in Rheims, then one of a number of hermits living in the forest of Colan. The life lived in the remote mountain valley by the Carthusians followed the pattern of individual houses for the monks, with prayer and meals in solitude and corporate meetings only at the week-ends. At both Camaldoli and the Grande Chartreuse, monks or *conversi* living a community life were essential to support the solitaries. A description given by Guibert of Nogent of the first Carthusians expresses the life and its spirituality very well, and can be applied both to Camaldoli and to other similar movements, e.g. the Grandmontines:

> The church stands upon a ridge . . . Thirteen monks dwell there, who have a convenient cloister in accordance with cenobitic tradition, but do not live together as other monks. Each has his own cell round the cloister and in these they work, sleep and eat. On Sundays they receive the necessary bread and vegetables, which is their only kind of food and is cooked by each in his cell; water for drinking and other purposes is supplied by a conduit . . . There are no gold or silver ornaments in their church, except a silver chalice. They do not go to the church for the usual canonical hours as we do but only for certain of them. They hear mass, unless I am mistaken, only on Sundays and solemnities. They hardly ever speak and if they want anything they ask for it by a sign. If they ever drink wine it is so watered as to be scarcely better than plain water. They wear a hair-shirt next to the skin and their other garments are thin and scanty. They live under a prior, and the bishop of Grenoble acts as their abbot and provisor . . . Lower down the mountain there is a building containing twenty most faithful lay-brothers who work for them. Although they observe the utmost poverty, they are getting together a very rich library (Guibert of Nogent, *PL* 156. 853ff).

A third, but more influential, company of 'new monks' were the Cistercians. A group of twenty monks from the monastery of Molesmes, led by the abbot Robert, who like some of the others had already experienced hermit life elsewhere, left the abbey and began again in the 'desert' of Cîteaux in 1098. There, under the leadership of Alberic (d. 1109) and Stephen Harding (d. 1134), they followed the same ideals of corporate solitude and austerity, declaring that they wished to follow the *Rule of St Benedict* 'to the last dot'. The influence of ideals of early Egyptian asceticism is seen in a description by William of St Thierry (d. 1148) of the early monastery at Clairvaux:

> Even I, unworthy as I am, when I had been with them for a few days wondered, for wherever I turned my gaze it was as if I saw a new heaven and a new earth, and that which of old was sown by our fathers, the ancient monks of Egypt, showed new shoots in these men in our times (*Life of St Bernard, PL* 185.247).

This, however, was no archaic imitation of monastic Egypt but a new form of monastic life, which referred to those earlier ideals to justify new practices of asceticism. Several new trends took definite shape at Cîteaux; for instance, the *conversi*, the lay brothers, became a definite part of the community, as brothers not bound by the choir office, but occupied with manual labour. This in turn led to a certain non-intellectual slant in Cistercian spirituality and a concern with work out of doors rather than in the scriptorium. The constitution of the Cistercians as an Order, in which the houses were related to one another in an international structure, was also new, and gave to their spirituality the notion of a 'Cistercian spirit', as distinct from the spirit of monasticism. This could seem exclusive and perfectionist and was to earn the Cistercians criticism later.

The spirituality of Cîteaux received a new impetus through the membership of St Bernard of Clairvaux, the dominant spiritual influence in Europe at this time. In his works and by his leadership, Bernard gave to the Cistercians as a central theme their specific concern with the analysis of the soul in its relationship to God. Expressed with fervour and analysed with acute perception, the relationship of the soul with God received from Bernard one of the finest expressions in Western literature. Bernard (*c*. 1090–1153) came to Cîteaux in 1113 with thirty other young men from Burgundy, some of them his own brothers. Two years later, he was sent by Stephen Harding to establish a monastery at Clairvaux of which he became abbot. In his life and teaching and in his writings Bernard proposed, with fervour and clarity, a mystical theology of love and knowledge which established a school of spirituality of immense power and lasting influence. Following the teaching of Augustine and Gregory the

Great, Bernard set out a psychological exploration of the soul, an inner pilgrimage, through which the individual could experience the love of God. In his treatise *On the Love of God*, he analyses this progress in terms of four degrees of love, a carnal love of self, a mercenary love of God for what he gives to that self, a filial love of God out of duty, and a wedded love of God, in which the soul loves God for himself and itself because it is loved by him. In his commentary on the Song of Songs, Bernard urges the process of conversion, compunction, and the purification of the heart to desire God in terms of the imagery of the Song of Songs, making the pursuit of love the sole aim of the monk: 'Remain alone, in order to preserve yourself for him whom alone of all things you have chosen for yourself among all' (*Song of Songs*, XL.4). The characteristic emphasis of Bernard, however, is in a further stage, in which he sees action as the fruit and overflow of this intimacy of the soul with God:

> In the first place we ought to have compunction; secondly, devotion; thirdly, a hard-working penitence; fourthly, works of piety; fifthly, earnestness in prayer; sixthly, the repose of contemplation; and in the seventh place, the fullness of charity (*Song of Songs*, XVIII.6).

The effects of union with God in prayer make the soul entirely flexible and ready to act as God directs, though only from this direction of love:

> If then you are wise you will show yourself rather as a reservoir than as a canal. For a canal spreads abroad the water it receives, but a reservoir waits until it is filled before overflowing and thus communicates without loss to itself its superabundant water (*Song of Songs*, XVIII.3).

Inspired by the passionate eloquence of Bernard, other Cistercian writers continued these themes. William of St Thierry, a Benedictine who transferred to the Cistercian order late in life, was a theologian of acute insight and formidable power, who gave a more ordered exposition to the inspired ideas of Bernard; his *Enigma of Faith* and *Mirror of Charity*, as well as his *Golden Letter* to the Carthusians, are among the classics of this school of spirituality. In England, Aelred of Rievaulx (*c.* 1109–1167) earned the title 'Bernard of the North' by his exposition of the characteristic Bernardine themes. In his *Mirror of Charity* and above all in his treatise on *Friendship*, the theme of love is analysed further, in terms of a characteristically Cistercian awareness of friendship as an image of the relationship of the soul with God.

The impact of Bernard and the Cistercian spiritual school was so great and their polemic so persuasive that it is not always remembered that similar ideals were common to monks in the eleventh and twelfth centuries in general and that the new ideas had their effect also on established monastic houses. In this period, for instance, an increased simplicity of life characterized Benedictine houses such as Cluny, where action and prayer were related, in liturgical prayer offered on behalf of society. This reached its finest expression in the Cluny of St Hugh (d. 1109) and was given many of the overtones found among the Cistercians during the abbacy of Peter the Venerable (d. 1156). One aspect of this spirituality was increased prayer for the dead, which received expression at Cluny in the Office of the Feast of All Souls, and which continued to infiltrate monastic spirituality among the new orders, whether in the widespread use of the Office of the Dead as a daily accompaniment to the choir office, or in the increase in association of the laity with the monks in confraternities for prayer for the dead. At Cluny, as at Cîteaux, charity towards the living also claimed to be based on the concept of prayer as a 'reservoir', especially in the activity of preaching, teaching and mission.

One of the least easily understood of the new orders which were influenced by St Bernard was the order of Knights of the Temple, the Templars. During the First Crusade, a group of knights from Northern France, led by Hugh de Payen, bound themselves by a solemn vow to protect pilgrims on the road to the Holy Land. They lived as monks in part of the Temple of Solomon and secured the approbation of St Bernard in his treatise *In Praise of the New Knighthood*, where he presents the spirituality of the monks of war as the consecration of the warring profession to the service of God, through the protection of pilgrims and the destruction of pagans, by men living the ascetic life of monks. A similar group of monk-knights formed the Knights of the Order of the Hospital of St John in Jerusalem (later called the Knights of Rhodes and the Knights of Malta) for similar purposes and with a parallel, and at times conflicting, history. Both were bound by monastic vows and their work was the protection and service of pilgrims, especially of the sick; in both cases, these monks eventually formed a regular army in the crusading warfare in Palestine. The idealism of the Templars and Hospitallers was a part of the general ideal of the Crusades, in which the activity of warfare for a time assumed the status of a spiritual combat.

The idea of an ascetic life leading to service of others on the basis of a life of prayer produced the military orders; it also led to the institution as an order of the Canons Regular of St Augustine. The Premonstratensians (the White Canons) were founded by St Norbert in 1120; they were greatly influenced by the Cistercians, especially through the friendship between their founder and St Bernard. Instead of the Rule of St Benedict, the canons based their life on the so-called Rule of St Augustine (precepts contained in Augustine's *Letter* 211). Canons attached to cathedrals and churches, living some degree of common life, had existed for many centuries, but in the eleventh and twelfth centuries they were influenced by the prevailing trends in monasticism, and formed more definite congregations, with austerities in line with the Cistercians. They were eventually indistinguishable from monks, except for their primary concern with the care of souls, through the liturgy and through teaching. Originally clerks bound by religious vows and in touch with either the cathedral or a parish church, in the eleventh century they became a major element in the reform of the clergy, and developed a more strict and communal life. Many of them gave their allegiance to the abbey of St Victor in Paris, founded by William of Champeaux in 1108. Here a major school of spirituality developed, under the influence of Hugh, Richard and Adam of St Victor. Their analysis of contemplation, of immense influence in the next years, was based upon bible study, in the ancient tradition of monks, but with a knowledge of the techniques of the schools and a thorough experience of the exploration of the soul according to the tradition of St Bernard.

Other canons were also part of communities, notably the Gilbertines in England. Founded by St Gilbert of Sempringham (*c.* 1083–1189), the Gilbertines were the only indigenous English religious order; it was remarkable for combining several religious rules in one order. The nuns followed the Rule of St Benedict, and were assisted by lay sisters and brothers who used the customs of the Cistercian lay brothers, while the canons, who formed the fourth part of the group, were Augustinians. This 'double community' for both men and women has left no successors and has few literary memorials, but formed part of the general resurgence of religious life in this period, as a 'way of perfection, whose foundation is the depth of humility'.

Another aspect of the life of prayer emerges in this period in the lives of women visionaries, a genre which was to flourish later in the lives and writings of Catherine of Siena, Catherine of Genoa, and Julian of Norwich. In this period Hildegard, the abbess of the Benedictine community of nuns at Bingen, produced her accounts of visions in her *Scivias*, remarkable both for the beauty and mysteriousness of her imagery and for the mixture of practical scientific observation with which they are interlaced. Her rebukes and warnings to contemporaries are based on a thorough knowledge of the Scriptures, which sees the world as a sign of the Kingdom. She was defended from her critics by the Cistercian Pope Eugenius III and by St Bernard, who insisted to the Council of Trier (1147) that 'so remarkable a lamp should not be put out'. Her writings had little influence on the spirituality of the twelfth century, except in the case of Elizabeth of Schonau and her brother and director, Egbert. Elizabeth (d. 1184) entered the double Benedictine monastery of

Schonau as a nun in 1137 and after a long and exhausting illness had a series of ecstatic visions in which she conversed with Christ, St Mary and other saints and angels. Following the mysteries of the liturgical year, she, like Hildegard, delivered admonitions to the Church and especially to the clergy, in the form of three series of visions, and also in many letters. This charismatic and visionary spirituality was to flourish again later in England, Spain and the Low Countries, but begins in the late eleventh and early twelfth centuries with these remarkable women.

The changes in monastic spirituality in this period were of profound importance for the devotional life of Europe. Many of those concerned with reform in the Church in this period were also monks of the new orders or under their influence, and saw monastic life as the ideal Christian way. This led to the monasticization of Christian spirituality to an exaggerated extent, the effects of which are still apparent. The contact of monastic spirituality with a wider circle than the monks themselves, however, led to a greater vigour in the art of prayer, and produced some of the most beautiful devotional works of the Middle Ages, e.g. *Jesu dulcis memoria*, and the *Salve Regina*. The underlying motive of desire for God which characterized this new spirituality is perhaps best expressed in the hymn *O quanta qualia*, by one who was himself the epitome of the tensions and glories of the age:

> O what their joy and their glory must be,
> Those endless sabbaths the blessèd ones see!
> Crowns for the valiant; for weary ones rest;
> God shall be all and in all ever blessed.
> Truly Jerusalem name we that shore,
> Vision of peace that brings joy evermore!
> Wish and fulfilment can severed be ne'er,
> Nor the thing prayed for come short of the prayer.
> (Peter Abelard, d. 1142)

C JOACHIM OF FIORE

MARJORIE REEVES

Apocalyptic Spirituality, ed. and trans. B. McGinn. CWS 1980, pp. 97–148.

Bloomfield, M., 'Joachim of Flora', *Traditio*, 13 (1957), pp. 249–311.

Bloomfield, M., 'Recent Scholarship on Joachim of Fiore and His Influence', in *Prophecy and Millenarianism*, ed. A. Williams, Harlow, Essex, Longman, 1980.

(Both of Bloomfield's articles are bibliographical.)

Crocco, A., *Gioacchino da Fiore e il Gioachismo*. Naples, 1976.

Lubac, H. de, *La Postérité spirituelle de Joachim de Flore*. Vol. i, Paris, 1979; vol. ii, Paris, 1981.

Mottu, H., *La Manifestation de l'Esprit selon Joachim de Fiore*. Paris and Neuchâtel, 1977.

Reeves, M., *The Influence of Prophecy in the Later Middle Ages*. Oxford, Clarendon, 1969.

Reeves, M., and Hirsch-Reich, B., *The 'Figurae' of Joachim of Fiore*. Oxford, Clarendon Press, 1972.

Reeves, M., *Joachim of Fiore and the Prophetic Future*. London, SPCK, 1976; New York, Harper, 1977.

Joachim of Fiore (*c.* 1135–1202), a biblical exegete of Calabrian Cistercianism, dedicated himself to the revelation of the work of the Trinity within history by the dual method of study and contemplation. In his *Expositio in Apocalypsim*, under the text 'I was in the Spirit on the Lord's Day', Joachim describes how for a year he strove against obstacles in interpreting the text, as if battering against the stone which closed the tomb, until, meditating at the hour when the Lion of the tribe of Judah rose from the dead, suddenly with the 'eyes of the mind' he saw clearly all the plenitude of the Scriptures. Again later at Pentecost, he was assailed by doubts on the Trinity. Entering the oratory, although terrified (*conterritus*), he forced himself to recite psalms and received an infusion of higher knowledge in a vision of a psaltery with ten strings. In neither experience did he receive direct intellectual answers to his problems but rather flashes of intuition which unstopped the springs of creativity and set him writing in an ecstasy of inspiration. Joachim believed that his experience was a foretaste of the *spiritualis intellectus* which would be poured out on all people in the last age. Hence he developed his doctrine of the three *status* in history: that of the Father, the age of law and of the Old Testament, that of the Son, the age of grace and of the New Testament, that of the Spirit, the age of love, freedom and of the *spiritualis intellectus* which would proceed from both the Testaments. The apostle of the third *status* was St John and at this time the *ecclesia activa* would become the *ecclesia contemplativa*. This age, though already heralded, lay in the future and was set against the backcloth of the Last Things. Refined through the tribulation of the great Antichrist, the Church would make the *transitus* to a higher level of spiritual understanding in the time left – probably brief – before the Last Judgement. Interpreting the vision of the psaltery, Joachim saw its triangularity as the three Persons, the central *Rosa* as the Unity of the Godhead and the ten strings, on one side, in ascending order, as the seven spiritual gifts and three theological virtues, and on the other, as the nine angelic hierarchies, with *Homo* at the top. Thus man would ascend the spiritual ladder to the position of *caritas*, above the angels. His two main works besides the *Expositio* were: *Liber Concordiae Novi et Veteris Testamenti* and *Psalterium decem chordarum* (see Plate 5).

To lead into the third *status* Joachim expected two new orders of spiritual men. In the following century both Mendicant Orders, but more especially certain Franciscans, claimed this prophecy. St Bonaventure used the same figure of the hierarchies to express his belief that St Francis had achieved the highest, seraphic stage, while the Order had only attained the cherubic. In later centuries various monastic and friar groups – notably some Jesuits and St Vincent de Paul – found inspiration in the eschatological role of the 'new spiritual men'.

D THE MENDICANTS

SIMON TUGWELL

BACKGROUND

Lambert, M. D., *Medieval Heresy*. London, Arnold; New York, Holmes & Meier, 1977.

Meerssemen, G. G., *Dossier de l'Ordre de la Pénitence*. Fribourg, Switz., 1961.

The twelfth century witnessed many different movements of religious reform, and not all of them fitted comfortably into the Church's official structures. In reaction against the formality and splendour of the monasteries, many people sought something more austerely evangelical. The penitential, insecure life of the hermit found a new appeal, and so did the call to wander round in drastic poverty, preaching the gospel. St Robert of Arbrissel and St Bernard of Tiron (both of whom died in 1117) are typical of this new spirit, but so also are the heretical preachers like Henry of Le Mans, Peter of Bruis and Arnold of Brescia in mid-century, who called in various ways for a radical simplification of the Church.

The widespread ignorance of Christian doctrine among the people, and the all too evident worldliness of many of the clergy, gave heretical preachers an easy target; but it is likely that many of their followers were sincere in wanting a more spiritual, more direct, religion based on the authentic gospel. Unfortunately the Church had little to offer them. Freelance religious life was usually condemned fairly indiscriminately; St Bernard, for instance, regards all the new apostolic movements as heretical (Sermon 66, *On the Canticle*), and it was probably the Cistercians who, revealingly, intervened to bully some freelance hermits near Cîteaux into adopting a rule and an abbot.[1]

The two most important movements on the fringe of the Church were the Catharists and the Waldensians. The Catharists seem to have preached a version of dualism derived from the Bogomils in Bulgaria (see p. 94), and little is known of their spirituality. It is likely that most of their ordinary followers, at least at first, were impressed more by the austerity of their lives than by their doctrine, and it has been suggested that their main attraction was their promise of safe-conduct to heaven after death (a widespread concern in this period).[2]

The Waldensians at first had no intention of separating themselves

---

[1] Pl. F. Lefèvre and A. H. Thomas, *Le Coutumier de l'Abbaye d'Oigny* (Louvain, 1976), pp. viii, 43. More generally, H. Grundmann, *Religiöse Bewegungen im Mittelalter* (repr. Darmstadt, 1970).

[2] Jean Duvernoy, *La Religion des Cathares* (Toulouse, 1976), p. 269.

from the official Church. Waldes, their founder, was a prosperous merchant in Lyons, who in 1176 abandoned his property and his home to adopt a life of mendicant itinerant preaching. He and his followers were convinced that it was incumbent on everyone to preach, if they were able to, and that those who could preach should abandon all other concerns to devote themselves entirely to this spiritual work. When the Italian Waldensians opted for a more settled life in community, with a regular income derived from manual work, Waldes excommunicated them. His vision was entirely dominated by the apostolic life, as defined by the instructions given to the preachers in Matthew 10. He and his followers fell foul of ecclesiastical authority precisely because of their insistence on preaching without an ecclesiastical mandate.[1]

Apart from these more extreme manifestations, there was also a growing movement among the laity to adopt the status of 'penitent', recognized by the Church, but requiring no formal adhesion to any organized fraternity. This was the status originally adopted by St Francis, and his friars were among the most effective propagators of it in the thirteenth century, which is why Francis is often credited with being the founder of the Third Order. In line with the general anxiety of church officials to organize people into communities with clear legal definition, in the thirteenth century penitents were progressively grouped into chapters, most of which had, by the end of the century, been more or less officially affiliated to the Mendicant Orders.

The two major Mendicant Orders, the Dominicans and the Franciscans, can both be seen to some extent as attempts to channel within the institutional Church the evangelical aspirations which had generally been driven underground in the previous century. Both involved a return to the gospel, and particularly to the apostolic life as indicated in Matthew 10; both, at first, dispensed with many of the precautions and proprieties which were traditional in religious life. Both, in particular, relied on individual commitment and enterprise, rather than on conventual supervision.

[1] For a history of the Waldensians up to the present time, see G. Tourn, (ET) *The Waldensians* (Turin, Claudiana; New York, American Waldensian Aid Society, 1980).

1 The Dominicans

SIMON TUGWELL

Brett, E. T., *Humbert of Romans: His Life and Views of Thirteenth-Century Society*. Toronto, Pontifical Institute of Mediaeval Studies, 1984.

Foster, K. ed. and trans., *The Life of Saint Thomas Aquinas*. London, Longmans, Green; Baltimore, Helicon, 1959.

Hinnebusch, W., *History of the Dominican Order*, 2 vols. Staten Island, N.Y., Alba House, 1966–73.

Koudelka, V. J., *Dominikus*. Olten and Freiburg im Breisgau, Walter, 1983. ET in preparation, New York, Philosophical Library.

Meerssemen, G. G., *Ordo Fraternitatis*. Rome, 1977.

Tugwell, S., ed., *Early Dominicans* (= *ED*), CWS 1980.

Tugwell, S., *The Way of the Preacher*. London, DLT; Springfield, Ill., Templegate, 1979.

Vicaire, M.-H., (ET) *Saint Dominic and his Times*. London, DLT; New York, McGraw-Hill, 1964.

Weisheipl, J. A., *Friar Thomas D'Aquino: His Life, Thought, and Work*. Oxford, Basil Blackwell; Garden City, N.Y., Doubleday, 1974.

The Order of Preachers (Dominicans) was founded by St Dominic Guzman (*c.* 1170–1221), with the approval of Honorius III, in 1216, but it had begun to take shape ten years earlier, when Dominic, then a canon of Osma in Spain, with his bishop, Diego of Azevedo, happened to meet the three papal legates who were in charge of the mission against the heretics in the south of France. The legates were conscious that they were making little headway and were thinking of abandoning their mission, but Diego advised them instead to change their tactics and adopt the apostolic style favoured by the heretics. He persuaded them to travel round on foot, without funds or retinue, begging their bread from door to door and preaching the gospel. Diego, after commuting between his diocese in Spain and the Midi for some eighteen months, died at the end of 1208. The Cistercian legates and other monks came and went. But Dominic continued preaching, in the way Diego had suggested, and became the effective leader of the campaign. In 1215 he was invited to move into Toulouse, and a burgher there called Peter Selhan gave him a house and, together with another burgher, attached himself to Dominic by religious profession. A small community grew up, which was given official status by the Bishop of Toulouse as a group of poor religious devoted to assisting the Bishop in his work of preaching and teaching. In 1216 the Pope gave his approval and the Order of Preachers came into existence officially in the Church as a whole.

Diego's apostolic vision was clearly founded on the same text which inspired Francis in 1208, but whereas Francis found in Matthew 10 chiefly a model for his own personal life, Diego saw it essentially as a way of responding to a public need in the Church. From the outset Dominican spirituality was dominated by a concern to be 'useful to the souls of our neighbours' (*ED*, p. 457). Dominican life is defined essentially by the Order's job (*ED*, pp. 149f), not by the spiritual needs or desires of its members.

The primacy of the apostolic job necessitated an unprecedented relativizing of the normal conventual and individual practices of piety. Whereas previously dispensations had been regarded as concessions to human weakness, the Dominicans used them widely as a concession to the superior importance of their job (*ED*, p. 457); and the fifth Master of the Order, Humbert of Romans (*c*. 1200–77), explicitly says that those who have the grace to be preachers should prefer preaching to all other spiritual exercises, including prayer, reading, liturgy and sacraments (*ED*, pp. 256ff).

Poverty was adopted from the outset as an essential ingredient in the apostolic life. Mendicancy was practised by the preachers in the campaign against heresy in the Midi, and was continued by Dominic's friars. During the early years of the Order's existence, Dominic urged his brethren to extend the principle and make their convents mendicant too. In 1220 the Order officially gave up all its revenues and possessions, retaining only the houses it lived in and their appurtenances. Dominic had a profound personal love of extreme poverty, but his Order recognized that poverty was secondary to preaching, and rigorous mendicancy was gradually abandoned, until in 1474 the Order was given permission by the Pope to become possessionate. Contrary to the Franciscan ideology of poverty, the Dominicans tended to make more practical claims. They argued that responsibility for large estates or regular paid work would interfere with their work; but so equally would destitution (Thomas Aquinas, *ST* IIa IIae q. 188 a.7). The essential point is that the Order should trust in God rather than earning its living, and it is this dependence on Providence that is the typical note of Dominican poverty, rather than rigorous austerity or total common possession.

The next observance to be introduced, which came to be the most important of all, was study. It was doctrinal preaching that was needed, so Dominic took his first followers to theology classes in Toulouse, and then started sending them to university centres such as Paris and Bologna. The first Dominicans to come to England went straight to Oxford in 1221. Increasingly it was in the universities that the Order looked for its recruits, and every house was envisaged as a house of study.

During the thirteenth century a complex educational system was established in the Order. Study replaced the traditional manual labour of the monks, and Dominic's successor, Jordan of Saxony (d. 1237), presents it as being a matter of life and death in the Order (*ED*, pp. 123f).

The unity of the Order was guaranteed by the vow of obedience which every member took to Dominic or his successors. This is the only vow taken by Dominicans, and it is personal in form. Obedience is promised to the Master of the Order, not to the Constitutions. The Dominican rite of profession lacks all the pomp of traditional rites, and is essentially a feudal gesture of submission to the Master. The Constitutions define the limits and context of this submission, but the Dominicans innovate by insisting that these laws are only human laws, with no supernatural sanctions. It is the solemn precept of the superior, not the laws, which are binding in conscience (*ED*, p. 457). And obedience is expressly meant to channel, not to eliminate, the spontaneous generosity of self-oblation which the Dominicans regard as all-important.

Instead of the elaborate legislation of the older Orders, the Dominicans provide only an outline of the daily life of their convents (*ED*, pp. 457ff). Conventual life is flexible, to allow for the different jobs being done by the friars, and a great deal of initiative is left to individual friars and to individual superiors.

Dominican life is as a result much less sheltered than that of the monks. It is a salient characteristic of Dominic himself that he trusted his friars far more than most monks thought proper (cf. *ED*, p. 91). Humbert of Romans accepts fully that there is a risk involved in being a preacher; he talks of the 'sins which will unavoidably occur' and says that they should not deter the preacher (*ED*, p. 242). The meritoriousness of preaching outweighs the faults which the preacher must expect to incur in his active life (*ED*, p. 195).

The life of preaching, with all its risks, is seen as a genuinely supernatural life, because it is only with the 'grace of preaching' that it is possible to be a preacher (*ED*, p. 204). Preaching is a sharing in the activity of God himself (*ED*, p. 184).

The Dominicans were characterized by a pragmatic attitude to piety. Unlike most people, they were unexcited about 'states of perfection', of which their greatest theologian, St Thomas Aquinas (*c*. 1225–74), gave a polemically cool account. Poverty, chastity and obedience are means to an end, not values in their own right; the end is the universal Christian goal, perfect charity. The 'state' consists simply in the fact that people make public profession of these three means, and their practice needs to be regulated realistically. Thomas rejects the notion that greater austerity necessarily means greater holiness (*De Perfectione*; *ST* IIa IIae qq. 184ff).

Thomas is equally pragmatic about prayer, which he interprets to mean essentially petition, which is a rational response to our total dependence on God and an expression of our readiness to subject our desires to his will (*ST* IIa IIae q. 83). Nothing is gained by forcing ourselves to pray for long periods, when we are simply getting bored (*loc. cit.*, a. 14). This remains standard Dominican teaching. And, though all prayer is 'mental prayer', in the sense that without some involvement of the mind there will be no prayer at all, Thomas and later Dominican writers regard it as indifferent whether we pray with or without bodily expression. Dominic was famous for his noisy and gymnastic prayer (*ED*, pp. 94ff). And prowess in prayer is never regarded as the touchstone of spiritual progress.

Contemplation is seen by Thomas as the goal of human life, in that our final fulfilment will be the vision of God. But in this life the most perfect occupation is not that of the pure contemplative, but that of the preacher or teacher who communicates to others what he has learned in contemplation. And this 'contemplation', in Thomas and other Dominican writers, is not a process of mystical abstraction, but ordinary human thought maturing, through mental discipline and study, into wisdom. And the study of nature and the study of philosophy are integral parts of it, as we see with particular clarity from Thomas' mentor, St Albert the Great (*c.* 1200–80), who was an outstanding philosopher and natural scientist. It is interesting that the great commentator on St Thomas, Thomas de Vio Cajetan (1469–1534), argues for the legitimacy of calling scientists 'contemplative' even if they make no express reference to God in their work (comment on *ST* IIa IIae q. 180 a. 4).[1]

St Albert and St Thomas both espouse an intellectualist view of the Christian life. Our final union with God is essentially the union of our intellect with God; charity motivates our minds to seek God and is the reason why we enjoy union with him supremely, but it is not, as it is in William of St Thierry, for instance, a mode of knowing beyond the reach of our minds.[2]

Thomas' vision rests essentially on his very strong doctrine of creation.

[1] On Dominican understanding of prayer and contemplation see S. Tugwell, 'A Dominican Theology of Prayer', *Dominican Ashram* 1 (Sept. 1982). For the widely differing senses in which contemplation is understood in different traditions, cf. Index, s.v. 'contemplation'.

[2] cf. E. H. Wéber, 'L'Interprétation par Albert le Grand de la théologie mystique de Denys Ps. Aréopagite', in G. Meyer and A. Zimmerman, ed., *Albertus Magnus, Doctor Universalis* (Mainz, 1980).

In his view, God is at work immediately in all that goes on in the world, even in our own free acts. This enables Thomas to develop an equally strong doctrine of grace, without endangering his insistence on human freedom. His doctrine was developed especially in the sixteenth and seventeenth centuries, against the doctrines of the Jesuit theologians, particularly Molina. It may be argued that the Thomist doctrine made for a more relaxed, more adventurous kind of spirituality, based on trust in the act of God (cf. John of St Thomas, q. 70 d. 18 a. 1.7).

Another highly controversial doctrine was Thomas' teaching of unicity of form, which, even if it was not directly concerned with spirituality, had consequences for spirituality. It meant that there was no room for any kind of dualism between body and spirit, and this may be connected with a general tendency among Dominicans to be suspicious of interiority divorced from external expression. Thus the Dominicans found it difficult to accept that the Franciscans did not possess anything just because they did not intend to possess anything, when they plainly did possess things for all practical purposes.[1] And they took it for granted that their useful works were meritorious, without anxious scrutiny of their motivation, because they assumed that, unless there was evidence to the contrary, charity, the ground of merit, was incarnated in their useful works (*ED*, p. 150).

In addition to the friars, St Dominic also founded monasteries of enclosed nuns. The first foundation was made by Diego at Prouille in the south of France, to accommodate converts from heresy, and Dominic took charge of this after Diego's departure. Dominic himself made foundations in Rome and Madrid. Later on a great many nunneries were founded or incorporated into the Order. The purpose of these foundations was to provide a stricter monastic life for women than was available elsewhere, and it is not clear what their relationship was to the spirituality of the friars.

There were also a number of lay confraternities, some of which were associated with the mission of the friars, but most of them were simply devotional. The most successful was the Confraternity of the Rosary, established in the late fifteenth century (the legend that the rosary was instituted by Dominic is without historical foundation).

In 1285 Munio of Zamora, the Master of the Order, created a specifically Dominican branch of the Order of Penance under his own jurisdiction; from this grew the Dominican Third Order. Its most famous member was St Catherine of Siena (see pp. 311–12).

---

[1] cf. A. G. Little, *The Grey Friars in Oxford* (Oxford, Oxford Historical Society, 1892), pp. 321ff.

2 The Franciscans

JOHN R. H. MOORMAN

ST FRANCIS

St Francis of Assisi: Writings and Early Biographies (= *Omn.*), ed. Marion Habig. 3rd rev. edn, Chicago, Franciscan Herald, 1973. Contains Thomas of Celano, *First Life of St Francis* (= 1 Cel.).

Francis and Clare, *Complete Works*, CWS 1983.

Lambert, M. D., *Franciscan Poverty*. London, SPCK, 1961.

Moorman, J. R. H., *Richest of Poor Men*. London, DLT; Huntington, Ind., Our Sunday Visitor, 1977.

Moorman, J. R. H., *Saint Francis of Assisi*. 2nd edn, London, SPCK, 1976.

ST BONAVENTURE

Cousins, E., ed. and trans., (ET) *St Bonaventure. The Soul's Journey into God and Other Works*, publ. in USA as *Bonaventure: The Soul's Journey into God; The Tree of Life; The Life of St Francis* (= *Leg. Mai.*). CWS 1979.

de Vinck, José, ed. and trans., (ET) *The Works of Bonaventure*. 5 vols. Paterson, N.J., St Anthony Guild, 1960–70.

OTHER WRITERS

Doncoeur, P., ed., *Le Livre de la Bienheureuse Angèle de Foligno*. Toulouse, 1925.

Lull, Ramón, (ET) *The Book of the Lover and the Beloved*, ed. Kenneth Leech. London, Sheldon; New York, Paulist, 1978.

Todi, Jacopone da, (ET) *The Lauds*, trans. Hughes, S. and E. CWS 1982.

Further bibliography in

Englebert, O., (ET), *St Francis of Assisi* (2nd edn, Chicago, Franciscan Herald, 1965), pp. 497–601.

The Church in the twelfth century was in great need of reform. The parish clergy were, for the most part, poor and ill-educated and did little for the people whom they were supposed to serve. The monks were busy growing rich on their estates. The people were neglected, ignorant and superstitious. In the midst of this a number of sects sprang up, which condemned the life of the Church, its sacraments and saints, its indulgences and its wealth. They had their own clergy who refused to obey the Pope. They wanted to restore the primitive character of Christendom as they saw it. They found the Church too authoritative, too powerful, too rich, too separated from the people.

Into this world Francis was born *c.* 1182, the son of a merchant in Assisi called Bernardone. Like most rich boys he grew up in the hopes of becoming a knight, though he was also good to the poor. Then came his conversion with the dreaming of dreams and the hearing of voices. Gradually he moved away from the life which he had undertaken and was drawn towards a life given up entirely to God. He got his marching orders in the church of St Mary of the Angels, near Assisi, where he heard the Gospel read in which Christ told his disciples that they were to own nothing, but were to go out as paupers, preaching the gospel to the poor. This, he said, was what he wished to do with all his heart, and he set out on a life of extreme and absolute poverty and in strict obedience to the words of Christ (1 Cel. 22). Thus he lived for about three years, until he was joined by Bernard of Quintavelle, another rich man of Assisi. Thus was brought about what came to be called the Order of Friars Minor. When they reached the number of twelve they went to Rome to see the Pope, Innocent III, who, miraculously, recognized their genuineness and gave them permission to preach repentance everywhere (1 Cel. 32f).

Thus they continued for some years, attracting more and more men to the Order, men prepared to accept the very high standards which Francis set before them. But about 1219 things began to change in the life of the community. Poverty was being overthrown in favour of simplicity, houses were being built and the friars were accumulating property of various kinds. From this point onwards, Francis retired more and more from the life of the Order. His little community of itinerant evangelists was becoming a great religious Order with plans for grafting itself into the life of the Church. So he sought out quiet places for prayer and meditation. In 1224 he spent some weeks on the top of the mountain called La Verna, where he received the stigmata, the five wounds of Christ. Two years later he died.

There were few moments when Francis was not thinking about God. He was often rapt in ecstasy, unaware of what was happening around him. But he did not retire entirely to places like La Verna where he could be alone with God. He went about the world, preaching the gospel, tending lepers, guiding his brotherhood, writing the rule by which they were to live, but always praying. Thomas of Celano tells us that, towards the end of his life, Francis appointed certain of the brothers to take charge of him, so that he might 'direct his attention more fully to God, and, in frequent ecstasy, wander about and enter the workshops of the blessed mansions of heaven and present himself with an abundance of grace on high before the most kind and serene Lord of all things' (1 Cel. 102).

Francis' devotion to Christ was completely absorbing. 'No human tongue,' wrote Bonaventura,

> could describe the passionate love with which Francis turned to Christ, his Spouse. He seemed to be completely absorbed by the fire of divine love like a glowing coal . . . The memory of Christ Jesus crucified was ever present in

the depths of his heart like a bundle of myrrh, and he longed to be wholly transformed into him by the fire of his love . . . He loved Christ so fervently, and Christ returned his love so intimately, that he seemed to have his Saviour before his eyes continually, as he once privately admitted to his companions (*Leg. Mai.* 9.1–2).

As Thomas of Celano said,

His safest haven was prayer; not prayer of a single moment or idle or presumptuous prayer, but prayer of long duration, full of devotion, serene in humility . . . Walking, sitting, eating or drinking, he was always intent upon prayer (1 Cel. 71).

To Francis the sufferings of Christ were always present, and he had a great desire to suffer with him. From the moment when the cross in the church of San Damiano in Assisi spoke to him in the early days of his conversion 'his heart was stricken and wounded with melting love and compassion for the passion of Christ; and, for the rest of his life, he carried in it the wounds of the Lord Jesus' (*Omn.* p. 904). This came to its climax on La Verna, when he prayed:

My Lord Jesus Christ, I pray you to grant me two graces before I die: the first is that during my life I may feel in my soul and in my body, as much as possible, the pain which you, dear Jesus, sustained in the hour of your most bitter passion. The second is that I may feel in my heart, as much as possible, that excessive love with which you, O Son of God, were inflamed in willingly enduring such suffering for us sinners (*Omn.* p. 1448).

At the same time he had great love for everything that God had made. He is well known for his preaching to the birds; but everything in nature that was beautiful he loved as belonging to God. Moreover he saw everything as symbols of God – rocks, lambs, trees, light. He wrote, late in life, the *Canticle of the Sun*, which shows his love of the natural world.

To sum up, Francis' spirituality was created out of four things: his total obedience to Christ, his prayer at all times, his desire to suffer with Christ, and his love of nature in all its forms.

Meanwhile there had grown up, alongside the Franciscan Order, the Poor Ladies or Poor Clares. In 1212 Clare, a young woman of Assisi, who had heard St Francis preach and had followed all his doings, left her home and presented herself at the Portiuncula asking to be received as one of the community. Francis accepted her, but being unable to make her a friar and let her wander about with the members of the Order, put her eventually into S. Damiano where she lived, together with a number of fellow-sisters, the life of a religious devoted to poverty. The friars looked after their needs, both temporal and spiritual, and the Order grew rapidly as women flocked to join them in many parts of the world, so that, by 1300, there were about four hundred houses, and many more after that.

The sisters were given up entirely to prayer and poverty, Clare having won from Gregory IX, in 1228, the 'Privilege of Poverty' which allowed the sisters to own nothing whether individually or as a community, and to rely on the friars for support. The Clares wrote very little, and not much therefore is known of their spirituality; but there is no doubt that the communities flourished, containing a number of holy women.

When Francis died, the Order was not in a very happy condition. There were some who wished to preserve its original simplicity, to go about in absolute poverty, preaching the gospel to the people, saying their simple prayers in the parish churches, living on the generosity of those whom they served. But there were others who wanted to make the Order fit into the life of the Church as a whole. The friars were so full of vigour, so devoted to their profession, so great a force for reform in many ways. All they needed was organization. They needed centres where they could be found. If they were to preach they needed books to read and chapels where they could say their prayers.

This meant that the 'Spirituals', as they came to be called, gradually retired from the scene. They included most of Francis' closest friends, Leo, Giles, Bernard and the rest. Some of them lived on in Assisi, but gradually they concentrated in the tiny monasteries and even in the rocks and caves of the Marches of Ancona, where they were joined by younger men like Conrad of Offida and John de la Verna. These men tried to keep up the high spiritual activities of Francis. Giles, living near Perugia, spent most of his life in prayer and acquired a great reputation as a mystic. Leo kept alive the stories of Francis, whom he had known and loved so well. John of Parma, elected Minister General in 1247, a good scholar who had taught at Paris and Bologna, was a man of deep spirituality who spent long hours in prayer and travelled everywhere on foot to encourage the friars. Meanwhile, in the south of France, Hugues de Digne kept the spiritual tradition alive by his strict poverty and devotion to prayer.

John of Parma was, unfortunately, known to be a Joachimist, a follower of the Calabrian monk whose writings had been condemned as heretical (see pp. 292–3). He had, therefore, to go; and the man who succeeded him was Giovanni Fidanza, known to history as St Bonaventure. Born at Bagnoregio, probably in 1217, he later wrote, 'When I was still a child I became seriously ill and my mother made a vow to St Francis, so that I was snatched from the jaws of death and restored to perfect health and strength' (*Leg. Mai.* 7.8). A scholarly young man, he went to study at Paris, where he became a pupil of Alexander of Hales who said of him that his 'innocence and dove-like simplicity were such that it seemed as though Adam had never sinned in him'.

Bonaventura joined the Franciscan Order in 1243, where he showed his great capacity for writing works of the deepest mysticism. The most important period of his life were the ten years from 1257 to 1267 when he was Minister General. These began with his writing *The Soul's Journey into God*. 'I withdrew', he wrote,

> to Mount La Verna, seeking a place of quiet and desiring to find there peace of spirit. While I was there, reflecting on various ways by which the soul ascends into God, there came to mind, among other things, the miracle which had occurred to blessed Francis in this very place, the vision of a winged Seraph in the form of the Crucified. While reflecting on this, I saw at once that that vision represented our father's rapture in contemplation and the road by which this rapture is reached (Prol. 2).

Later on he wrote *The Tree of Life*, a meditation on the Life of Christ, two lives of St Francis, and a number of mystical works such as *The Fire of Love*, *The Six Wings of the Seraph* and *The Mystical Vine*. He was made a cardinal in 1273 and died at the Council of Lyons in 1274.

'*The Soul's Journey into God* expresses the Franciscan awareness of the presence of God in creation; the physical universe and the soul of man are seen as mirrors reflecting God, and as rungs in a ladder leading to God'.[1] The first six chapters trace the stages of the journey, and the seventh the goal of ecstatic rapture. Bonaventura starts with the rational world. 'Let us place our first step in the ascent at the bottom, presenting to ourselves the whole material world as a mirror through which we may pass over to God, the supreme Craftsman' (1.9). He then describes the six stages through which we must pass. 'There are six stages in the powers of the soul, through which we ascend from the lowest to the highest, from the exterior to the interior, from the temporal to the eternal . . . We have these stages implanted in us by nature, deformed by sin and reformed by grace' (1.6). He dwells on 'the three theological virtues by which the soul is purified, illumined and perfected' (4.3), so introducing the three stages of spiritual growth generally accepted. 'Christ is the way and the door, Christ is the ladder and the vehicle, like the mercy seat placed above the ark of God and the mystery hidden from eternity' (7.1). He ends by referring to Francis and the six-winged seraph fastened to the cross, and says that, if we want these things, we must 'ask grace not instruction, desire not understanding, the groaning of prayer not diligent reading . . . not light but the fire that totally inflames and carries us into God' (7.6).

[1] Cousins, E., ed., *Bonaventure*, p. 13.

The Tree of Life is a wonderful life of Christ, 'his life, passion and glorification'. On the death of Christ Bonaventura writes:

O human heart, you are harder than any hardness of rocks, if at the recollection of such great expiation you are not struck with terror, nor moved with compassion nor shattered with compunction nor softened with devoted love (29).

Both this work and *The Mystical Vine* dwell all the time on the life of Christ, which is the basis of his mystical teaching. Here we get that tenderness, that affective spirituality, which runs all through his writings. Christ was the man who was born, lived a life of exemplary goodness, was betrayed, tried and finally crucified. His sufferings are referred to over and over again, they are to be felt by the faithful disciple in his own body. All this brings the author very near to Francis whom he greatly admired.

For many years attributed to Bonaventura, but now known to be by the Franciscan John de Caulibus of San Gemignano, was a book called *Meditationes Vitae Christi*, which was a life of Christ told in the greatest detail, the bare narrative of the evangelist being supplemented at every point by the fertile imagination of the writer. Addressed to a Poor Clare, this became one of the most widely read books of its time, being translated into English early in the fifteenth century. Christianity is presented above all things as a personal experience. As the scenes of Christ's life pass before the eyes of the reader one is asked to imagine that one is present, not as a spectator but as a participant. Similarly Ubertino da Casale, who wrote the *Arbor Vitae Crucifixae* and who, like Bonaventura, spent a year on La Verna contemplating the experiences of St Francis and producing what he called his 'little bundle of fragrant myrrh', declared that 'in a strange manner I knew that I was with Christ at his baptism, in the desert, in the course of his preaching and constantly in treacheries, desertions, insults and injuries'.[1]

Bonaventura inspired a number of Franciscan friars to compose mystical works. Among them was Jacopone da Todi who was born about 1230, shortly after the death of Francis. He grew up to be a young lawyer, much addicted to luxury and with little interest in religion. He married, however, a deeply religious girl, who died shortly after as the result of an accident. This was a great shock to the pleasure-loving Jacopone, who wandered about for some years as an itinerant evangelist and a member of the Third Order of St Francis, writing poems, some of which were exquisite lyrics of divine love. In 1278 he became a Friar Minor and lived for a time with the Spirituals in their mountain retreats. In 1298 he was

---

[1] Moorman, J. R. H., *A History of the Franciscan Order* (Oxford, Clarendon, 1968), p. 197f.

put in prison for an attack on the new Pope, Boniface VIII. Five years later he was liberated, and he died in 1306. As a Christian mystic Jacopone ranks high, passing through a stage of pure asceticism to a degree of mystical achievement. His poems, wrote Evelyn Underhill, 'are the perfect literary monument of Franciscan spirituality – its intensity of emotion, its religious realism, its paradoxical combination of austere penitence and gentle sweetness, its sudden flights into the unseen'.[1] Like all Franciscan writers his thought was dominated by an intense identific-ation with the sufferings of Christ in all his poverty, humiliation and pain. At the same time he was on fire with love.

> Love, Love, O Love, thy touch so quickens me,
> Love, Love, O Love, I am no longer I:
> Love, Love, O Love, thyself so utterly
> Thou giv'st me, Jesu, that I can but die.
> Love, O Love, I am possessed of thee,
> Love, Love, my Love, O take me in a sigh!
> Love, glad and spent I lie.
> O Love, my Bliss,
> O Lover's Kiss!
> O quench my soul in Love![2]

Apart from the friars, some members of the Third Order contributed seriously to Franciscan mysticism. One of these was Ramón Lull, who crowned a long life of service with a martyr's death. Lull, after spending years in teaching and in the study of Arabic, went to north Africa at the age of 82 in 1314, where he preached Christ openly and was duly killed by the Moslems. He wrote a number of books of a mystical nature, especially his *Art of Contemplation* and *The Book of the Lover and the Beloved*, in which the Christian soul meets its Master and the lover talks to the Beloved.

> Far above love is the Beloved; far beneath it is the Lover; and Love, which lies between these two, makes the Beloved to descend to the Lover and the Lover to rise toward the Beloved. And this ascending and descending is the being and the life of Love – of that Love which makes the Lover endure pain and which ever serves the Beloved (258).

The other great Third Order mystical writer was Angela of Foligno. Born in 1248, married, the mother of several children, she eventually retired to become an anchoress near the Franciscan church in Foligno, where she poured out her mystical experiences to her cousin, Brother

[1] Underhill, E., *The Mystics of the Church* (London, J. Clarke, 1925; New York, G. H. Doran, 1926), p. 96.

[2] Underhill, E., *Jacopone da Todi, Poet and Mystic* (London and Toronto, Dent; New York, Dutton, 1919), pp. 381–3.

Arnaldo, who wrote them all down. Her mysticism is typically Franciscan, for she based her meditations on the facts of Christ's life and death. Francis is her model. Like him she loves to speak of the passion of Christ and of the mingled joy and sorrow with which the disciple can share in his sufferings.

Many others, friars or tertiaries, wrote mystical works, some of them of considerable merit. But gradually the strain died out as the friars became more and more attached to the things of this world. But Franciscan spirituality holds a special place in the history of mysticism. The human Christ, the Word made flesh, the attachment of Christ to earthly things, the Lover and the Beloved, and, above all, the sharing in the sufferings and joys of Christ – these are the elements of Franciscan spirituality.

E ITALIAN SPIRITUAL WRITERS

1 Dante Alighieri

MAX SAINT

Bosco, U., and Reggio, G., *La Divina Commedia*. 3 vols, Florence, le Monnier, 1979.

Boyde, P., *Dante Philomythes and Philosopher, Man in the cosmos*. Cambridge and New York, CUP, 1981.

Cosmo, U., *L'ultima ascesa*. Florence, la Nuova Italia, 1968.

Foster, K., 'Dante', in *A Catholic Dictionary of Theology*, vol. ii (London, Nelson, 1967) pp. 153–154.

Foster, K., *The Two Dantes*. London, DLT; Berkeley, University of California Press, 1977.

Gardner, E. G., *Dante's Ten Heavens*. London, Constable, 1900.

Gardner, E. G., *Dante and the Mystics*. London, Dent; New York, E. P. Dutton, 1913.

Jackson, W. W. (trans.), *Dante's Convivio*. Oxford, Clarendon, 1909.

Nardi, B., 'Dante Profeta', in *Dante e la cultura medievale*. Bari, Laterza, 1942.

Padoan, G., 'Dante e la mirabile visione', in *Il pio Enea*. Ravenna, Longo Editore, 1977.

Sayers, D., *Introductory Papers on Dante*. London, Methuen; New York, Harper & Row, 1954.

Sayers, D., *Further Papers on Dante*. London, Methuen; New York, Harper & Row, 1957.

Sapegno, N., *La Divina Commedia*. 3 vols, Florence, la Nuova Italia, 1955, 1957.

Sinclair, J. D., *The Divine Comedy*, text, ET and comment. London, John Lane, 1939–1946 (now OUP Paperbacks).

Toynbee, P., *Dante Dictionary*, rev. Singleton, C. S. OUP, 1968.

Toynbee, P., *The Letters of Dante*, text, ET and notes. OUP, 1920.

For further bibliography, see *ODCC*.

Dante (1265–1321) calls his greatest work 'my Comedy' and 'the sacred poem' (*Inferno* 21.2; *Paradiso* 25.1). His son Pietro says that by means of it the author 'teaches us morally in his own person to open the eyes of our mind to see where we are, whether on the right road to our fatherland or not'. There is more than a touch of Everyman in the *Comedy* as the first words show: 'In the middle of the journey of *our* life *I* found *myself* lost in the middle of a dark wood', the wood of ignorance and sin. Writing to his patron (*Ep.* 13) Dante explained that his purpose was 'to remove those living in this life from a state of misery and to bring them to a state of happiness'. He went on to say that 'the meaning of this work is not of one kind only. It is literal and allegorical.' He gave an illustration. In Psalm 114 (113) the literal meaning of the first verse is the exodus of the Israelites from Egyptian slavery; allegorically it signifies the redemption of mankind from the bondage of sin, or the conversion of the penitent soul into the freedom of grace, or the deliverance of the sanctified soul from mortality to glory. The three sorts of secondary meaning he called allegorical, moral and anagogical – what is to be *believed*, what is to be *done*, what is to be *striven for* (see above, p. 132). Clearly Dante was deeply concerned about personal religion. 'A small spark kindles a great fire; perhaps after me prayer will be made with better voices' (*Purgatorio*, 1.34).

The poet had a social purpose also. He wrote like a prophet 'for the good of the world that lives so ill' (*Purg.* 32.103). His belief was that God intends happiness for us here and beatitude hereafter. He has provided two rulers, Emperor and Pope, the former to secure temporal justice and peace, the latter to teach by word and example the things we need to know for eternal life. When a just Emperor and a holy Pope rule together in Rome in brotherly concord, God's will will be done on earth. But the emperors had forsaken Italy; ambitious pontiffs had seized temporal power. The Church which exists to manifest apostolic simplicity had become avaricious, opportunist and corrupt. Christendom was like a vicious horse without a rider to control her with whip and spur (*Purg.* 6.96). By the time the *Comedy* was written the Popes also abandoned Rome for Avignon. The city whose very stones and soil are worthy of reverence (*Convivio*, 4.4) was now so vile that even Hannibal would pity her (*Ep.* 11.21). St Peter's burying place had become a *cloaca* of blood and filth (*Par.* 27.25).

This profound religious seriousness has no place in Dante's early writings. It is the consequence of the sorrows of exile. Unjustly doomed by hostile compatriots to be burned alive should he ever return to his beloved Florence, he was for the rest of his life 'truly a ship without sail or rudder, wafted to divers havens, inlets and shores by the parching wind which woeful poverty exhales' (*Conv.* 1.3). He chose to assert his innocence and to proclaim his faith in a poem in which imagination and autobiography were mingled. He feigns that in Holy Week 1300 he had as a living man descended into Hell to learn God's justice, climbed the mountain of Purgatory to prove God's mercy, and been carried up to the height of Heaven to see God's glory.

The fictional factor in the *Comedy*, the sophisticated *mise-en-scène*, and the poet's evident theological debt to Boethius, St Bernard, Aquinas and Bonaventura, have made commentators chary of ascribing mystical experience to the poet. But it is undeniable that as the work proceeded

Dante's genius became adult in the flame of love (cf. *Par.* 7.59). This maturity will be recognized in the great paradisal descriptions, in the passionate pity for the plight of the world, in the frequent asides to the reader, in the economy and precision in the use of such key-words as *carità, specchiare* – creatures reflecting the glory of their Creator – and in the unique felicity of devotional expressions. 'In his will is our peace' (*Par.* 3.85). Mary is the lovely flower whom Dante always invokes morning and evening in his prayers. 'Hers is the face which most resembles Christ' (*Par.* 22.88 and 32.85). 'Each leaf wherewith the garden of the eternal Gardener is leafed I love in the measure in which good has been bestowed upon it by him' (*Par.* 26.64). Of heaven he writes:

> That infinite and unspeakable good which is there above speeds to love as a sunbeam comes to a bright body. It gives so much of itself as it finds there of ardour, so that the more charity extends the more does the eternal goodness increase upon it; and the more souls are increased there above the more there are to be rightly loved, and the more love there is; like a mirror each returns to each (*Purg.* 15.67).

Dante's thought is permeated by Scripture, which is quoted above two hundred times. Characteristic and incomparable passages are the meditation on the *Pater noster* made by the souls expiating the sin of pride (*Purg.* 11), St Bernard's prayer and the Beatific Vision of the Holy Trinity (*Par.* 33). 'How scant is speech to what I saw . . . but already my desire and will, like to a wheel which spins truly balanced, were being turned by the Love that moves the sun and the other stars.'

2 Catherine of Siena

MAX SAINT

Cavallini, G., *Il dialogo della Divina Provvidenza*. Rome, Ed. Cateriniane, 1960.

Cavallini, G., *Le Orazioni*. Rome, Ed. Cateriniane, 1978.

Fawtier, R., *Sainte Catherine de Sienne*. 2 vols, Paris, E. de Boccard, 1921 and 1930.

Foster, K., and Romayne, M. J., *I Catherine* (ET of sixty letters and part of Dialogue). London, Collins, 1980.

Gardner, E. G., *St Catherine of Siena*. London, Dent, 1907.

Kerns, C., *Raymond of Capua's Life of St Catherine*, ET, intro. and notes. Dublin, Dominican Pub., 1980.

Meattini, D. U., *Epistolario di santa Caterina*. Rome, ed. Paoline, 1966.

Noffke, S., *Dialogue*, ET and ed. CWS 1980.

For further bibliography, see *ODCC*.

Catherine Benincasa (1347?–1380), a Sienese dyer's daughter who entered the Dominican Third Order, is among the greatest teachers of spirituality. The Bull of her canonization (1461) says, 'Her doctrine was infused not acquired'. She told her confessor that she never learned anything from other people about the way of salvation 'but only the sweet Bridegroom of my soul, the Lord Jesus Christ'. The unique clarity, force, sweetness and profundity of her writings arises from the immediacy of her own experience of God's love, her own nothingness apart from God, and the strong visual and auditory character of her religious experiences. Our Lord said to her, 'You are she who is not; I am he who is'. Once when she said, 'Lord where have you been all this time?' he answered, 'I was in your heart'. She always taught her followers the need for self-knowledge – your own nothingness apart from the fact that God has made you for love and that your soul is a created image of the Trinity; and she says repeatedly that one must make of this knowledge a cell, a holy solitude from which to go out in loving service and to which one must retire for recuperation. 'Match love with love', she says. At the heart of her teaching we always encounter Christ crucified and in particular the thought of his blood, the sign of his obedience to the Father's will and of his love in our salvation. God is a Trinity of Power, Wisdom and Mercy, and it is fitting that the Wisdom should take upon himself our human nature so as to remedy our disobedience, ignorance and selfishness. The cross is the sign, the blood the medium through which we find the clue to self-awareness. The Church 'holds the keys of the blood'; the blood reaches us in the Eucharist. For Catherine this was the principal function of the Church. The way God starts is here, though Catherine has much to say about the degrees of perfection. A consequence of her affective devotion and her complete self-abnegation was a courageous active charity. She became a teacher simply out of love, the imperative need to communicate her own experience to others. In the end her sanctity became so well known as to involve her in the troubled affairs of the Church. She travelled to Avignon and she died in Rome.

3 Catherine of Genoa

MAX SAINT

Debognie, P., *Sainte Catherine de Gênes*. Brussels, Desclée de Brouwer, 1960.
von Hügel, F., *The Mystical Element in Religion as studied in St Catherine of Genoa and her Friends*. 2 vols, London, Dent, 1908; New York, E. P. Dutton, 1921, 1926.
Hughes, S., ET and ed., *Catherine of Genoa: Purgation and Purgatory, The Spiritual Dialogue*. CWS 1979.
Ombres, R., *The Theology of Purgatory*. Dublin and Cork, Mercier; Butler, Wisc., Clergy Book Service, 1978.

The Fieschi were among the greatest families in Genoa. A member of that family, Catherine (1448–1510) was married at sixteen to a man who neglected and persecuted her. In 1473, at a time of loneliness, mental anguish and aversion from all the things of the world, she had a vision of Christ, bleeding with the wounds of the passion, his cross upon his shoulder. From this time she began to receive communion daily and to work as a nurse among the sick in the Pammatone. Later she lived in the hospital and became its matron and administrator. Her conversion was unexpectedly followed by that of her husband, who died in 1497. Catherine went rarely to confession, being impelled simply by interior inspiration without priestly direction. The purpose of her life was to destroy all self-love, at whatever cost, so that she might be filled by the divine love. This transformation required an ever more rigorous self-discipline. She practised extraordinary fasting and experienced extraordinary spiritual consolation, but she was neither exhausted by the one nor exalted by the other. She continued to nurse the sick with unabated zeal. Her primary motive was zeal rather than compassion. She did not use intercession, nor seek the prayers of others; she avoided public notice. Her desire was that nothing should interpose itself between God and the soul. 'I do not want what proceeds from thee, I want thee alone, O tender Love.' 'I feel myself drawn interiorly to do this or that, without any resisting, and I believe that God wills it so. He does not wish me to have any object in his way in my spirit.' Love tends to union, to identification – expressed by Catherine more boldly perhaps than by any other mystic. God is 'my being, my self, my strength, my beatitude.' She is speaking here of Love as identification to which one can attain 'only elsewhere by the annihilation of one's own being . . . not by sharing, but by true transformation into God'.

In her last years Catherine gathered a group of admirers who wrote down her teaching. The important works are *Life and Doctrine* and the

Treatise on Purgatory. She suffered a long, painful terminal illness which she accepted serenely as a foretaste of the joy of Purgatory.

> I believe no happiness can be found worthy to be compared to that of a soul in Purgatory except that of the saints in Paradise. Day by day the happiness increases as God flows into these souls, more and more as the hindrance to his coming is burned away. Sin's rust is the hindrance.

Purgatory is the final joyous cleansing of the soul from the effects of self-love. This teaching is the basis of Catherine's repute as mystic and theologian.

F   TEUTONIC MYSTICISM

1   The Rhineland Mystics

CYPRIAN SMITH AND OLIVER DAVIES

GENERAL WORKS

Clark, J. M., *The Great German Mystics*. Oxford, Blackwell, 1949 (bibliographies).
Cognet, L., *Introduction aux mystiques rhéno-flamands*. Paris, 1968.

ECKHART

Works

Die deutschen und lateinischen Werke, ed. Kohlhammer. Stuttgart, 1936–   .

Translations

Colledge, E., and McGinn, B., ed., *Meister Eckhart*, CWS 1982.
Walshe, M. O'C., trans and ed., *Meister Eckhart, Sermons and Treatises*. 2 vols. London and Dulverton, Watkins, 1979 and 1981 (bibliography).

Studies

Clark, J. M., *Meister Eckhart, an introduction to the study of his works, with an anthology of his sermons*. London and New York, Nelson, 1957.
Lossky, V., *Théologie négative et connaissance de Dieu chez Maître Eckhart*. Paris, 1960.

TAULER

Works

Predigten, ed. F. Vetter. Berlin, 1910.
Predigten, ed. A. L. Corin. Bibliothèque de la Faculté de Philosophie et Lettres de l'Université de Liège, 1924.

Translations

Colledge, E., and Sr M. Jane, *Spiritual Conferences* (Selections). St Louis and London, Herder, 1961.

Studies

Filthaut, E. ed., *Johannes Tauler: Gedenkschrift zum 600. Todestag*. Essen 1961 (complete bibliography).
Weilner, I. *Johannes Taulers Bekehrungsweg*. Regensburg 1961.

SUSO

Works

Deutsche Schriften, ed. K. Bihlmeyer, Stuttgart, 1907; Freiburg, 1961 (excellent introduction).

Translations

Clark, J. M., *The Life of the Servant*. London, J. Clarke, 1952.
Clark, J. M., *The Little Book of Eternal Wisdom and The Little Book of Truth*. London, Faber, 1953.
Ancelet-Hustache, J., *Henri Suso, oeuvres complètes*. Paris, 1977 (useful introduction).

Studies

Filthaut, E., ed. *Heinrich Seuse: Studien zum 600. Todestag*. Cologne, 1966.

MEISTER ECKHART (*Cyprian Smith*)

Eckhart was born *c.* 1260 in Hochheim – probably the one near Erfurt in Thuringia. He entered the Dominican priory at Erfurt *c.* 1275, and then went to the Studium Generale at Cologne, where Albert the Great was still alive. Until 1325 his life was divided into periods in Paris, where he became renowned for his skill as scholar, lecturer and disputator, and periods in Germany, where his Order appointed him to important administrative posts. In 1302 he received his degree from the University of Paris, and was thereafter known as 'Magister' or 'Meister'. Around 1323 he returned to the Studium Generale in Cologne.

He was by now a famous man, admired for his saintly life and his many gifts as scholar, administrator, preacher and director of souls. It was therefore all the more shocking when the Franciscan Archbishop of Cologne, Heinrich von Virneburg, instigated proceedings against him for heresy. The proliferation of heresies in Cologne at that time, the rivalry between Dominicans and Franciscans, and the bold, easily misinterpreted language which Eckhart used in his vernacular preaching, must all have contributed to the archbishop's hostility. His two Franciscan accusers compiled a list of allegedly heretical statements which he was supposed to have made at various times. He defended himself ably, and in 1327 declared solemnly that he had no heretical intent. After an appeal to the Pope, it was decreed that there should be a further trial at Avignon, where Eckhart accordingly went. The principal judge was Jacques Fournier, later Pope Benedict XII. John XXII appointed a commission which produced a new list of allegedly heretical statements by Eckhart. By 30 April, 1328, Eckhart was dead. He did not live to see the promulgation of *In Agro Dominico*, which declared fifteen of his statements heretical, and eleven 'ill-sounding and suspect'; two others from German sermons were also condemned.

Eckhart wrote in both Latin and German. The Latin works, for the most part, date from his second period in Paris (1311–13), and were intended for inclusion in the unfinished *Opus Tripartitum*, in which he hoped to give a full exposition of his theology and metaphysics. The surviving portions consist of commentaries on Genesis, Exodus, the Book of Wisdom and the Fourth Gospel, together with lectures on Ecclesiasticus 24, and an *Opus Sermonum* consisting of notes for sermons.

It is the German works which have won Eckhart most fame. They consist of a large body of sermons, of uncertain date, and a handful of tractates, written in response to particular needs. The *Talks of Instruction* (*c.* 1298) were apparently delivered after supper in the religious houses which Eckhart supervised. They are full of deep, practical spiritual counsel. The *Book of Spiritual Consolation* (*c.* 1308) was composed for Queen Agnes of Hungary, to comfort her in her many bereavements. Many of the deepest and most controversial elements of Eckhart's thought appear in this work, which was much quoted at the trial. There are two further sermons: one called *The Nobleman* and another *On Detachment*. The authenticity of this last has been questioned, but is accepted by Quint, the editor of the German writings, on firm evidence.

The appeal of the German works is immediate and powerful. Despite the depth and, sometimes, abstruseness of their thought, the language is direct and forceful, full of striking images and teasing paradoxes. Eckhart was one of the first to show that the vernacular could have the dignity and clarity of Latin. An immense energy radiates from this writing.

When we turn to the Latin works, the contrast is obvious, though it should not be exaggerated. Eckhart's Latin is scholarly, clear and technical, aiming at precise definition rather than flights of imagination. Nevertheless his authorship is unmistakable. He was well aware, in these as in the German works, that some of his views might seem *monstruosa, dubia et falsa*. It would be wrong to see the Latin works as merely a routine professional task; Eckhart clearly enjoyed writing them and intended them to be taken seriously.

Eckhart's doctrine is essentially mystical, concerned with the possible union between the human soul and God. Eckhart knew that this possibility rests upon the grace of God, freely given; but he maintained that it also rests upon something within the soul itself, its intrinsic similarity or analogical likeness to God. He sometimes stressed this likeness so much that he seemed to obliterate the distinction between creature and Creator. As God has an infinite capacity for giving, so the soul has an infinite capacity for receiving. The soul, which can be satisfied only by the transcendent God, mirrors his transcendence by never resting in any finite object, by eluding all forms or names: 'God, who has no name . . . is ineffable, and the soul in her ground is also ineffable, as he is ineffable' (Walshe, vol. i, p. 172).

Eckhart distinguishes between God, personified as Trinity, and 'Godhead', the unfathomable mystery of the divine nature, which he calls the 'Abyss' or 'Source', the 'Silent Desert' (Walshe, vol. ii, p. 105). From this darkness of Godhead comes the Trinitarian God, who pours himself out in loving communion, both within the Trinity and by creating and sustaining the world. The communion between the Persons and loving care of creation would be impossible were it not grounded upon the transcendent abyss of Godhead; but the abyss in its turn transcends itself by issuing forth as Trinity, Creator, Redeemer. The human soul has a similar 'double face': it informs the body and engages in virtuous action in the world, but it cannot do this effectively unless it discovers its own 'ground', its essence of receptivity which images the transcendent God-head: 'Elsewhere I have declared that there is a power in the soul which touches neither time nor flesh . . . In this power God is ever verdant and flowering in all the joy and all the glory that he is in himself' (Walshe, vol. i, p. 79). Without this purification, its works in the world, however virtuous in appearance, will be marred by self-seeking. Only those works are truly virtuous which spring from self-renunciation and detachment, *Abgeschiedenheit* (Colledge, p. 251, Counsel 5).

Detachment means letting go of self and of dependence on creatures, and recognizing that in one sense all aspects of life, pleasant or unpleasant, 'holy' or 'profane', express something of God, but none expresses the whole truth. It means withdrawing from creatures into the ground of the soul, seeking beyond the sacraments, beyond Christ in his humanity, beyond God himself conceived as person, to enter the abyss of Godhead. The soul thus enflamed has kindled within it a spark (*funkelīn*), which rejoices for ever in the Godhead. It is then drawn into the communion of Persons within the Trinity through the birth of God within the soul (Walshe, vol. i, pp. 15–16). It can then turn to the world again, free to love and value it truly, protected by its detachment from being ensnared in self-seeking. Having found God in its own depths, it finds him everywhere (Colledge, pp. 252–3).

Eckhart's doctrine differs from that of some later mystics in that it is based on *ontology*, expressing the relation of created being to the Uncreated. It is thus both speculative and experiential. He powerfully influenced the German mystics immediately after him, Suso and Tauler, but was then gradually forgotten. Only in more recent times has interest in him revived, and the fruits of this could be rich indeed.

JOHANNES TAULER (*Oliver Davies*)

Prominent among the successors to Eckhart was the Dominican, Johannes Tauler. He was born into a prosperous middle-class family in Strasbourg *c.* 1300. Although details of his life are scarce, we know that he held pastoral responsibilities in some of the numerous convents in the Strasbourg area. He appears to have enjoyed many contacts with the mystics and mystical literature of the day and travelled widely, his travels including a period of exile with his brethren in Basle, on account of a papal interdict. He visited Cologne and, in all probability, visited Ruysbroeck at Groenendael. It is unclear whether he met Eckhart or not, but the warmth with which he refers to the 'beloved master' suggests a personal acquaintance. Certainly he knew Eckhart's writings well, and Eckhartian spirituality breathes throughout his work. He died on 16 June, 1361.

Tauler is remembered today for his collection of eighty-four sermons, which gained great popularity in his lifetime and have remained over the centuries a highly esteemed collection of devotional writings. They have survived in the form of *reportata*, but there is reason to believe that they represent with a high degree of accuracy his authentic utterances.

Tauler's writing is characterized by a simple, graphic and direct style and a high devotional sense. The sermons were intended as homilies on set days of the liturgical year for the nuns under his spiritual supervision. He makes effective use of images from the everyday world of his hearers, including the language of hunting, viticulture and seafaring.

Tauler is most at ease with a simple didacticism and with the primary virtues of the spiritual life. Mindful of the experience of Eckhart he warns against excessive speculation although, as can be seen from the seventh and twenty-first sermons, he sometimes attempts to articulate in bold, imaginative language the process whereby a person 'becomes one with the sweetness of the Godhead, his being so penetrated with the divine Being that he loses himself, just like a drop of water in a vat of wine' (Sermon 7). He speaks particularly of the 'ground of the soul', 'the concealed abyss . . . the secret realm' of our being. 'We strive that God might gain free and vigorous possession of this our ground, in which he has implanted his divine image, and that he might dwell within it, in which lies all his striving' (Sermon 12). Tauler stresses the acceptance of suffering: 'The least and the greatest suffering that God ever sent you, he gave you on account of his inexpressible love, which is as great as the highest and best gift he has given you or ever could give you' (Sermon 3). The pursuit of humility and the ceaseless abnegation of self are also greatly to be desired: 'Truly, if you wish to speak, then God must be silent' (Sermon 1). Above all, echoing the language of his master, he advocates 'true detachment', whereby 'a person turns and parts himself from everything that is not wholly and purely God' (Sermon 23).

His emphasis upon the inner person rather than outer works was one of the factors which led the Protestant theologians of the Reformation to claim him as one of their own. The young Luther read his sermons and was inspired by their spirit of simple devotion. Later he aroused the interest of the Pietists and the Romantics. Tauler has been regarded as one of the chief mediators of Eckhartian thought to Spain and the Netherlands.

HENRY SUSO (HEINRICH SEUSE) (*Oliver Davies*)

Suso was born in or near Constance *c.* 1295. According to the *Life of Suso*, a work of disputed authenticity, Suso entered the Dominican priory in Constance at the age of thirteen. Five years later he underwent a second conversion as the result of a mystical experience and began to follow a life-style of extreme asceticism, which only ended many years later in consequence of a vision. Between 1324 and 1327 he studied in Cologne where he came under the profound influence of Meister Eckhart. After a series of personal misfortunes, he eventually settled down to pastoral work among the religious communities of southern Germany, the Rhineland and the Netherlands. Suso died in Ulm on 25 January, 1366.

In his first work, *The Little Book of Truth* (*c.* 1326), he sought to expound the teaching of Eckhart in non-controversial language and particularly to defend him against the claims of the libertarian 'Brethren of the Free Spirit'.

Between 1333 and 1340 Suso wrote *The Little Book of Wisdom* and its Latin counterpart, the *Horologium Sapientiae*. During the medieval period this became as popular as the *Imitation of Christ*. Its theme is a lyrical meditation on the passion of Christ, leading to a discussion on sin, the illusion of the world, God's love and justice, and to a meditation on 'the pure Queen of the heavenly realm and her heart's woe'. It is here that Suso's language approaches that of the *Minnesänger*, the minstrels of courtly love. The final part of the book consists of a hundred meditations on the passion, which may have already existed independently.

Two collections of Suso's letters are extant, which contain, in the varied pastoral themes which they treat, a good deal of Suso's own spiritual teaching. *The Little Book of Letters* was included with the *Life of Suso, The Little Book of Truth* and *The Little Book of Eternal Wisdom* in the compilation which Suso himself made in 1362.

Suso's immense popularity in the Middle Ages was followed by a period of neglect. He was rediscovered by the Romantics at the beginning of the nineteenth century and was beatified by Gregory XVI in 1831.

2 Ruysbroeck, à Kempis and the *Theologia Deutsch*

OLIVER DAVIES

GENERAL WORKS as in the previous section

RUYSBROECK

Works

Ruusbroec, *Opera Omnia*, ed. G. de Baere, 10 vols. Leiden, Brill, 1981– .
Werken, ed., J. B. Poukens and others, 4 vols. Tielt, 1944–8.

Translations

Dom, C. A. W., *The Adornment of the Spiritual Marriage, The Sparkling Stone and The Book of Supreme Truth*. London, Dent, 1916; Watkins, 1951.
Colledge, E., *The Spiritual Espousals*. London, Faber, 1952; New York, Harper, 1953; Westminster, Maryland, Christian Classics, 1983.
Bizet, J. A., *Ruysbroeck, oeuvres choisies*. Paris, 1946 (modern French; important introduction).

Studies

Ampe, A., *Kernproblemen uit de Leer van Ruusbroec*, 4 vols. Tielt, 1950–7.
Wautier d'Aygalliers, (ET) *Ruysbroeck the Admirable*. London, Dent; New York, Dutton, 1925.

THEOLOGIA DEUTSCH

Theologia deutsch, ed. F. Pfeiffer. Gütersloh, 1923 (= FP).
Hoffman, B., tr. and ed., *The Theologia Germanica of Martin Luther* (sic) (= ML). CWS 1980.

THOMAS À KEMPIS

Works

Opera Omnia, ed. M. J. Pohl, 7 vols. Freiburg, 1902–22.

Translations

Sherley Price, L., *The Imitation of Christ*. Harmondsworth and Baltimore, Penguin Classics, 1952.
Knott, B. I., *The Imitation of Christ*. London, Collins, 1963 (good general introduction; bibliography).

Studies

Post, R. R., *The Modern Devotion* (Leiden, Brill, 1968), pp. 521–36.

JAN VAN RUYSBROECK (RUUSBROEC)

Ruysbroeck was born in 1293 of humble origins in the village near Brussels from which he took his name. In 1304 he joined his relative Jan Hinckaert, who was a canon of Sainte-Gudule in Brussels. The extent of the education he received at this time is unclear, but it is assumed it was not great. He was ordained at the age of twenty-four and for the next twenty-five years was attached to Sainte-Gudule. In 1343, with Hinckaert and Frank van Coudenberg, Ruysbroeck left Brussels to found a model community nearby at Groenendael. They were soon joined by others and adopted the Augustinian Rule. The community became a vital spiritual centre, whose visitors included Geert Groote and, probably, Tauler. Ruysbroeck died, a venerated spiritual teacher, in 1381.

Ruysbroeck wrote entirely in Flemish. The first of his writings, which critical opinion generally holds to be his finest, date from the period in Brussels and his stand against heretics and freethinkers of the day. Ruysbroeck was uncertain of the value of *The Kingdom of the Lovers of God*, and it was only through an indiscretion that the book came into circulation. Many of the same themes are taken up again in *The Spiritual Espousals*, widely regarded as Ruysbroeck's chief and most successful work. *The Sparkling Stone*, which is a synthesis of these early writings, also dates from this time.

The works written after 1343 are concerned more with moral and pastoral problems and tend, at times, towards a certain prolixity of style. *The Mirror of Eternal Salvation*, written perhaps in 1359, includes an important treatise on the Eucharist. *The Seven Cloisters*, to judge by its emphasis on asceticism, was intended for a monastic readership, and *The Seven Steps of the Ladder of Spiritual Love* returns again to the high inspiration which characterizes Ruysbroeck's early works.

The Spiritual Tabernacle is a complex and difficult book which was begun in Brussels and completed at Groenendael. It is an exhaustive commentary on the chapters of Exodus which are concerned with the tabernacle.

Answering the charge of obscurity, in his final work, *The Book of Supreme Truth*, Ruysbroeck attempted to make the outline of his thought as accessible as possible.

The doctrine of this outstanding, original mystic is not easily summarized. In *The Spiritual Espousals* Ruysbroeck divides the spiritual path into three stages: the 'active life' of virtue and obedience to the Church, the 'life of yearning for God' and the 'life of contemplation of God'. In discussing the second stage, he says that the inward person may know God without mediation:

And out of the unity of God there shines upon him a single light, and this light reveals to him Darkness, Nakedness and Nothingness. In the Darkness he is enveloped and falls like one that is lost into waylessness. In the Nakedness he loses the discernment of things and is pervaded with a single brilliance. In the Nothingness all his works fail him, for, in the working of God's unfathomable love, he is vanquished. And in the inclination of his soul to delight, he vanquishes God and becomes one spirit with him (Book ii, Part 4, C, a.).

God, too, may be known by mediation, which is that of 'savouring Wisdom'; then for the inward person

the hunger and thirst of love will become so great that every hour he surrenders himself, his works fail him, he exhausts himself and perishes in love. For he hungers and thirsts to savour God. And in each perception of God he is seized by God and stirred afresh by love. So, living he dies and dying he lives again (Book ii, Part 4, C, b.).

Characteristically Ruysbroeck interprets the contemplative state in terms of the Trinity:

The concealed nature of the Divinity, which is eternally active in contemplation and in love in the manner of the Persons, ceaselessly delights in the embracing of the Persons in the unity of their Essence. In this embrace of the essential unity of God, all inward spirits are one with God in an outpouring of love, and are themselves that same One, which the Essence in Itself is, in blessedness (Book iii, introd.).

There has been much debate as to whether Ruysbroeck stands at the end of the Rhineland school or at the beginning of the *devotio moderna*. Linguistically and culturally he belongs to the latter, but his concern with contemplation and union with God draw him rather into the Eckhartian school.

THEOLOGIA DEUTSCH

The *Theologia deutsch* (*Theologia Germanica*) was written by an anonymous priest of the Teutonic Order in Sachsenhausen probably in the latter half of the fourteenth century. Its name dates from the important edition of 1518 by the young Luther, who found in it much that echoed his developing ideas on justification by faith (see pp. 343–6).

The book, in the 1518 edition, is divided into fifty-six chapters, and its pastoral character points to its possible origin as a collection of *collationes*, or spiritual addresses. The writer of the *Theologia deutsch* has absorbed much of the practical spirituality of the Eckhartian school, mediated probably through Tauler, and stresses a life of self-abnegation: 'When the creature or the person denies and abandons his own and his self, then God enters with his own, which is his Self' (ML ch. 22, FP ch. 24). He lacks, however, their profound scholarship and secure theoretical base. Like Thomas à Kempis he distrusts excessive learning: 'Let no one think that he can come to this true light and perfect knowledge and to the life of Christ through much questioning or hearsay, or through reading and studying . . .' (ML ch. 17, FP ch. 19).

Although the author only occasionally attains to the inspirational standard of his masters, on account of its directness and simplicity of style the *Theologia deutsch* has remained a popular, widely disseminated work of moral literature.

THOMAS À KEMPIS

Thomas à Kempis, named after his birthplace, Kempen in the Rhineland, was born *c*. 1380 of lowly origin. At thirteen years he was sent for his schooling to the monastery at Deventer, which had recently been founded by Geert Groote of the Congregation of the Common Life. In 1399 he joined the monastery of St Agnietenberg at Zwolle, where his brother was prior, and became an Augustinian Canon. Thomas kept the chronicle of the monastery, and in 1425 was elected sub-prior. He died on 1 May 1471.

Despite several theories which assert an alternative authorship, the *Imitation of Christ* is generally attributed to Thomas. It is regarded as the finest expression of the spirituality of the *devotio moderna*, an influential movement founded by Geert Groote, which spread as far abroad as Switzerland and northern Germany. Although much influenced by the Rhineland mystics, they eschewed their high concern with contemplation and speculative theology, preferring to stress the practice of simple piety and asceticism.

The four books of the *Imitation* were originally written separately and circulated independently. Book Four discusses the Eucharist and the preceding books expound in their many aspects the *via purgativa* and the *via illuminativa* of the devout soul. The precise rhythms of the author's Latin, his bold simplicity of style and his profound love of God and humanity have each contributed to the unparalleled popularity of this book. Thomas advocates an uncompromising renunciation of the world: 'Forsake all, and you shall find all. Renounce desire, and you shall find peace' (iii. 32). Even learning will not enhance us in the eyes of God: 'If you knew the whole Bible by heart and all the teachings of the philosophers, how would this help you without the grace and love of God?' (i.1) At the centre of his vision is the uplifting power of love:

> Nothing is sweeter than love, nothing stronger, nothing higher, nothing wider, nothing more pleasant, nothing fuller or better in heaven or earth; for love is born of God, and can rest only in God, above all created things (iii. 5).

3 Nicholas of Cusa (Cusanus)

EDWARD YARNOLD

Bibliography compiled by Raymond Klibansky.

Editions

Strasbourg 1488; Cortemaggiore 1502; Paris 1514; Basle 1565.
Modern critical editions: *Nicolai de Cusa Opera Omnia* (= *Opera*), E. Hoffmann
et. al., ed., Leipzig, Hamburg, 1932– . *De docta ignorantia*, ed. R. Klibansky, Latin with Germ. tr. by H. G. Senger. Hamburg, 1977.

English translations

The Vision of God, tr. E. G. Salter, introd. by E. Underhill. London, Toronto,
Dent; New York, Dutton, 1928.
De li non aliud (1979), *On Learned Ignorance* (1981), *Apologia doctae ignorantiae*,
in *Debate with John Wenck* (1981), tr. J. Hopkins. Minneapolis, the first
University of Minnesota Press, the last two Banning.
De possest, tr. J. Hopkins, in *A Concise Introduction*. See below.
Unity and Reform: Selected Writings of Nicholas de Cusa, ed. J. P.
Dolan. University of Notre Dame, 1962.

Studies

Bett, H., *Nicholas of Cusa*. London, Methuen, 1932.
Collins, J., *God in Modern Philosophy* (Chicago, Regnery, 1959), pp. 2–11.
Hopkins, J., *A Concise Introduction to the Philosophy of Nicholas of Cusa*.
Minneapolis, University of Minnesota, 1978.
Hopkins, J., *Nicholas of Cusa's Dialectical Mysticism* (Text, ET and interpre-
tation of the *De visione Dei*). Minneapolis, A. J. Banning Press, 1985.
Jacob, E. F., 'Cusanus the Theologian', in *Bulletin of the John Rylands Library*,
21 (1937), pp. 406–24, and reprint.
Klibansky, R., *The Continuity of the Platonic Tradition during the Middle Ages*.
London, Warburg Institute, 1939.
Vansteenberghe, E., *Autour de la docte ignorance: Une controverse sur la théologie
mystique au XVe siècle*. Münster, Aschendorff, 1915.
Watts, P. M., *Nicolaus Cusanus: a Fifteenth-Century Vision of Man*. Leiden,
Brill, 1982.

Nicholas Chrypffs (Krebs), was born, the son of a prosperous barge-
owner, in 1400/1 at Cues (Cusa) on the Mosel near Trier. He was
educated by the Brothers of Common Life before entering the Universities of Heidelberg, Padua (where he gained a doctorate in Canon Law)
and Cologne. Well known among humanists as a collector of manuscripts, he was one of the first to expose the False Decretals. At the ill-

fated Council of Basle he submitted a scheme for the unity and reform of the Church (*De concordantia catholica*, 1433), envisaging a general council to be superior to the Pope. Despairing however of Basle as a source of reform, he turned to Pope Eugenius IV, who sent him in 1437 to Constantinople to make final arrangements with the Greeks for a council of reunion. In 1438 he escorted the Greek Emperor and Patriarch to Ferrara, where the council began before transferring to Florence. His next years were devoted to seeking support in Germany for Eugenius against the rival pope appointed by Basle. Eugenius' successor Nicholas V made him cardinal, and Archbishop of Brixen in 1450, but at once sent him on a mission of church reform which took him to Germany, the Netherlands, Austria and Bohemia. When at last free to govern his diocese, his strenuous efforts at reform brought him into conflict with the secular ruler. In 1459 a new Pope, Pius II, needing to absent himself from Rome, entrusted the administration of the papal states to Nicholas. He died in Umbria in 1464.

The view most commonly associated with Nicholas' name is that of the incomprehensibility of God, which he first expounded in his work on learned ignorance, *De docta ignorantia* (1440: DI): we know about God what he is not rather than what he is. It can be said of God affirmatively that he is the 'concordance of opposites', containing and transcending all distinctions. But we have no standard for grasping how the distinctions apply to God: *finiti et infiniti nulla proportio*. Nicholas himself attributed this conviction to a mystical illumination he received two years earlier on the voyage from Constantinople. Such thinking was clearly within the Platonic tradition with which Nicholas was already familiar, and was later to study in depth in such authors as Proclus, Pseudo-Dionysius and the Rhineland mystics. His understanding of his own development seems therefore to have been not accurate, or at least not accurately recorded:

> At that time I had not seen Dionysius or any of the true theologians when I received my idea from on high. But I betook myself eagerly to the writings of the doctors, and found there nothing but variations on what had been revealed to me (*Apologia doctae ignorantiae: Opera* ii. 12).

Nicholas was not interested in a mere philosophical theory concerning the knowledge of God. The theme of DI is faith, by which we are taken up into 'the third heaven of most simple intellectuality' above sense and reason. 'Led in learned ignorance to the mountain that is Christ', though still in darkness, 'we come, as in a thinner cloud, to perceive him more clearly' (DI iii.11).

In expressing the creature's utter dependence on God, Nicholas allowed himself to use language which some contemporaries misinterpreted as pantheistic: e.g. God is 'the absolute quiddity of the world' (DI ii. 4).

The spiritual concern which underlies all Nicholas' philosophy is evident in his little book on the gaze of God, *De visione Dei* (VD), which he dedicated in 1453 to a Benedictine community with whom he enjoyed discussing his ideas. The book sets out 'an easy path to mystical theology' (VD, dedication); it is largely a devotional and popular presentation of the ideas of DI. The subtitle of the work, the *Icon*, refers to a represent-ation of the face of God, the eyes of which seem to follow the observer as one moves.[1] In the same way God's gaze never turns aside from his creatures. It is creative: 'with you to behold is to work' (VD 5). But to the human gaze God's face is veiled:

> It is not seen unveiled until beyond all faces one enters into a certain secret and hidden silence where there is no knowledge or concept of a face . . . That very darkness reveals your face to be there, beyond all veils (VD 6).

Few have combined a life of affairs with range of scholarship and fertility of imagination to the extent of Nicholas. He made substantial contributions to the development of physics, geography, mathematics, astronomy and the reform of the calendar; he anticipated the discovery of the circulation of the blood. He intersperses his theological writing with mathematical comparisons and vignettes drawn from ordinary life: a dog running up and down, a bear addicted to honey, a speed-reader. In his irenic attitude to the Hussites and his belief that the faith of pagans is faith in Christ he was five centuries ahead of ecumenical thought.

[1] The original of this icon is reproduced here as Plate 8.

G   THE ENGLISH MYSTICS

CLIFTON WOLTERS

RICHARD ROLLE

Selected Works, G. C. Heseltine, ed. London and New York, Longmans, 1930; Westport, Ct., Hyperion, 1980.

The Fire of Love or Melody of Love, and The Mending of Life or Rule of Living, F. M. M. Comper, ed. (in some edns with introd. by E. Underhill) [ET of the *Incendium*]. London, Methuen, 1914; New York, Benziger, 1916; London, Clarendon Press, 1931.

English Prose Treatises, G. G. Perry, ed. London, Early English Text Society, 1866, 1921.

English Writings, H. E. Allan, ed. London, Clarendon Press, 1931.

Melos Amoris, E. J. F. Arnold, ed. Oxford, Blackwell, 1957.

Selected Writings, J. G. Harrell, ET and ed. London, SPCK, 1963.

The Fire of Love, C. Wolters, ET and introd. Harmondsworth and New York, Penguin, 1972.

The Form of Perfect Living and Other Prose Treatises, G. E. Hodgson, trans. London, T. Baker, 1910.

Comper, F. M. M., *The Life of Richard Rolle, together with an Edition of his English Lyrics*. London and Toronto, Dent, 1928. New York, Barnes and Noble; London, Methuen, 1969.

Hodgson, G. E., *The Sanity of Mysticism. A Study of Richard Rolle*. London, Faith Press, 1926; Folcraft, Pa., Folcraft Library Edns, 1976.

Hodgson, P., *Three 14th Century Mystics* [R. Rolle, W. Hilton and *The Cloud*]. London, Longmans, 1967.

THE CLOUD OF UNKNOWING

*The Cloud of Unknowing, J. McCann, ed., with commentary by Augustine Baker. London, Burns Oates; Westminster, Md., Newman, 1952.

The Cloud of Unknowing, Ira Progoff, trans. and introd. New York and London, Harper, 1948; London, Rider and Sons, 1959; New York, Dell, 1973.

*The Cloud of Unknowing, P. Hodgson, ed. London, Early English Text Society, 1944; OUP, 1958.

The Cloud of Unknowing, C. Wolters, trans. and introd. Harmondsworth and New York, Penguin, 1961.

*The Cloud of Unknowing, W. Johnston, ed. New York, Doubleday, 1973.

The Cloud of Unknowing, J. Walsh, trans. and ed. CWS 1982.

A Study of Wisdom, by the anonymous author of *The Cloud*, C. Wolters, trans. and ed. Oxford, S.L.G. Press, 1980.

Dreyer, E., *The Cloud of Unknowing*, in *DCS*, pp. 89–91 (with bibl.).

Johnston, W., *The Mysticism of The Cloud of Unknowing*. New York, Harper & Row, 1967.

*These editions include *The Epistle of Privy Counsel*.

WALTER HILTON

The Scale of Perfection, E. Underhill, introd. London, J. M. Watkins, 1923.
The Scale of Perfection, G. Sitwell, trans. and introd. London, Burns Oates;
Westminster, Md., Newman, 1953.
The Ladder of Perfection, L. Sherley Price, trans. and introd. Harmondsworth,
Penguin, 1957.

Milosh, J. E., *The Scale of Perfection and the English Mystical Tradition.*
Madison, University of Wisconsin Press, 1966.

JULIAN OF NORWICH

Revelations of Divine Love, G. Warrack, ed. London, Methuen, 1901, 1950.
Revelations of Divine Love, R. Hudleston, ed. London, Burns Oates, 1927; West-
minster, Md., Newman, 1952.
Revelations of Divine Love, J. Walsh, ed. London, Burns Oates, 1961; London,
Anthony Clarke, 1973.
Revelations of Divine Love, C. Wolters, ed. Harmondsworth and New York,
Penguin, 1966.
Showings, E. Colledge and J. Walsh, trans. CWS 1979.
The Blissful Passion of Our Lord and Saviour Jesus Christ, J. Walsh, trans.
Worcester, Stanbrook Abbey Press, 1973.

Molinari, P., *Julian of Norwich: The Teaching of a 14th Century English Mystic.*
Darby, Pa., Arden Library, 1978.

From the years 1000 to 1500 a considerable amount of mystical writing
has survived, much of which is still relevant. The contribution from this
island has not been insignificant. We have works by Aelred of Rievaulx
(d. 1167), Adam of Dryburgh (d. 1212), Stephen of Sawley (d. 1252),
Edmund of Abingdon (d. 1240), William Langland (*c.* 1370), Richard
Rolle (d. 1358), 'the Monk of Farne' (*c.* 1370), William Flete (d. 1390),
the author of 'The Cloud of Unknowing' (*c.* 1370), Walter Hilton (d.
1396), and Julian of Norwich (d. 1416). It has been suggested that there
may be others, awaiting discovery in the great medieval libraries that
have escaped the ravages of the Reformation and the passing years.

MEDIEVAL¹ ENGLISH MYSTICS

Of those whose works are still treasured, four are outstanding. They are
Richard Rolle, the anonymous author of *The Cloud*, Walter Hilton, and
Mother Julian. They were all writing in the fourteenth century, but they
cannot be said to form a 'school' of English spirituality in the sense that
people speak of a 'Rhenish' or a 'Spanish' school. The writings are the
product of independent minds, and though from internal evidence it can
be seen that the author of *The Cloud* and Hilton had read Rolle – not
always approvingly – and Hilton *The Cloud*, and Julian Hilton (or Hilton

Julian – sometimes they are very close in style) there is no evidence of any conscious borrowing.

However, there are characteristics common to all four, and they can be briefly summarized: (1) They wrote as individuals for individuals. It has often been pointed out that each writer was a solitary, or writing for such. Rolle was a hermit, *The Cloud* was written for another, Hilton wrote for an anchoress, and Julian was enclosed in her cell at Carrow. But even while they were writing with particular people in view, they were aware that others were looking over their shoulders. (2) English was the language they used. Rolle and Hilton also wrote in Latin, but by now the vernacular was entirely adequate for the expression of the deepest truths, and for the many nuns who comprised the staple reading public Latin would have been a hindrance. (3) All of them wrote with directness and purpose. There is little rhetoric, but a wealth of common sense. Their intention was to help their readers, and as they were writing of basic spirituality they do so still. (4) There is not a text-book among them, but a good deal of personal testimony and experiential religion. Even Hilton, commonly regarded as the theologian of the four, writes subjectively and warmly. Together they give a sound introduction to the devout life.

The background against which they wrote was sordid enough. From 1337 to 1453 England and France were engaged in what is now called 'the Hundred Years' War', a debilitating conflict which with its repercussions throughout the land, both at the domestic and social levels, helped break up the pattern of medieval society. This calamity was heightened by the appalling devastation of the bubonic plague which swept through Europe in the mid-fourteenth century and raged through England in 1348/49 and again in 1361. It has been suggested that this 'Black Death' reduced the population by a third, or even by as much as a half. It certainly contributed to one major social change, the emancipation of the villeins, those quasi-helots upon whose labours the maintenance of the manorial estates which covered England depended. Gradually the survivors found they were a commodity in short supply, and began to realize the power of organized labour. The threatening 'Peasants' Revolt' (1381) was put down by the treachery of King and Parliament, but the new spirit of egalitarianism was not quenched, and the old order began appreciably to change. None of this turmoil is reflected in the four writers, and it is almost as though they had deliberately turned away from the chaos of their day to contemplate the unchanging, unhasting holiness of God.

RICHARD ROLLE

Of these four, Richard Rolle (1300–49) is chronologically the first, and to judge by the number of manuscripts we still possess, probably the most prolific and popular. He was a hermit living in Yorkshire, and most of our knowledge about him is drawn from the *Legenda*, a compilation made by the nuns of Hampole in preparation for his canonization, a cause which got lost in the upsets of the Reformation, but which did not prevent his being regarded as 'St Richard, hermit' up to that time.

He was born at Thornton-le-Dale about the turn of the century. Though he went up to Oxford he does not seem to have graduated, for we find him literally running away from home at nineteen in order to become a hermit. The *Legenda* has nothing of serious note to say about his ministry or his character, but from the internal evidence of his writings a fair picture of the man may be built up. He wrote poems, treatises and tracts on a variety of subjects, both in Latin and in English, and in the process shows himself to be a sincere, devout and opinionated enthusiast, confident of his own soundness and suspicious of those who did not measure up to it. In his early works he reveals a flair for invective which he did not hesitate to use against the 'Establishment', and which added nothing to his popularity; maturity brought milder manners. Maybe his attacks were justified, but the general brashness of this self-appointed scourge has even today blunted the appreciation of his spiritual teaching. This is a pity, because undoubtedly he describes experiences which would be recognized as mystical even if we hesitate to rank them with the deepest of God's gifts to human beings.

Rolle has always attracted attention because of certain quirks peculiar to himself. For example he is incorrigibly addicted to alliteration, far more than any of his contemporaries, who while they too indulged this fashion did so with much greater circumspection. His *Melos Amoris* is surely the most alliterative work ever to have been written in Latin, and is virtually untranslatable, but the vulgar tongue sometimes provided similar opportunities: 'Gastly gladnes in Jhesu, and joy in hert, with swetnes in sawle of the savor of heven in hope, is helth intil hele [salvation]; and my lyfe lendes [dwells] in luf, and lyghtsumnes unlappes [enfolds] my thoght' (Longleat ms 29). He stresses his misogyny throughout his works, and though this attitude is not unusual in a day when many medievals laid man's sins at Eve's door, with Rolle it takes on unwonted bitterness.

More important is the emphasis he puts on the physical concomitants of his mystical experiences. He knows actual warmth (*calor*) and hears celestial music (*canor*) and is aware of what he calls 'sweetness' (*dulcor*) infusing his whole being. This threefold gift was strongly criticized by his contemporaries as it has been by Western scholars since, who regard it as the mark of the beginner who might need such encouragement: it is not for the proficient, who can get on perfectly well without it. But this is to fly in the face of the evidence provided by the mystics of Orthodoxy who not only claim to know of such heat but to expect it as a normal accompaniment of prayer. To them prayer affects the whole person, and spiritual emotions do sometimes express themselves in bodily feelings. It is Western Christians who are over-cerebralized in their approach to things of the Spirit, and who need to be reminded of this simple truth. Richard Rolle needs no such prompting, though one might wish him to be less dogmatic about it. To the Eastern Christian deep mystical experience is often closely linked to the practice of the 'Jesus Prayer' (see pp. 175–84), the continued repetition of the biblical sentence 'Lord Jesus Christ, Son of God, have mercy upon me a sinner'. The sentence itself can be shortened in various ways, even down to one word, that of the Holy Name. The effect will be the same: to the devout and persevering soul there comes that immediate knowledge that Rolle was seeking to describe, and which most would call 'mystical'. Ignorant of Orthodox practice, Rolle had a special devotion to the Holy Name, and he often associates this with his heat, delight, and sound. It is a common factor in mystical experience that there is a heightened sensitivity to life generally, and it is always possible that some at least should know first-hand what Rolle never tires of telling.

But when one might be tempted to think that Rolle was exaggerating his experiences, we are reassured by the practical common sense that he shows in all his writings. For instance, there are two sorts of rapture (*Incendium*, 37), one of seizure that holds the faculties bound, and the other of love which lifts up the mind to God in contemplation, quite apart from any 'rapture out of the senses'. This, says Rolle, was the rapture Christ knew for he 'was always contemplating God, yet it never detracted from his self-possession'. It is, of course, this latter that Rolle approves, and it is on this background that he sees the 'door of heaven swing back to reveal the Face of the Beloved, so that his inner eye could contemplate the things that are above' (*Incendium*, 15). The way to such an experience is to love God. Were it possible to sum up so diffuse a writer in one sentence it would have to be, 'Love God'. In all his works he puts immense stress on our need to fulfil the first and great commandment; he is ever pleading, urging, cajoling, and even nagging to this end, so that those who read him solidly without break can feel occasional irritation at such pressure. But whatever may be one's superficial reaction, there always remains the inescapable conviction that what he preached he practised, which is why he is still so well worth reading today.

THE CLOUD OF UNKNOWING

The Cloud of Unknowing was written in the same century but about a generation later. It is almost unbelievable that it was written so close in time for the atmosphere it breathes is completely different. Gone are the passionate appeals of a consciously good man to love God; instead there is the cool recognition of the fact that God as God cannot be known, but only in so far as he reveals himself – which he has done in Jesus Christ.

Unlike Richard Rolle, *The Cloud* has been deeply affected by Pseudo-Dionysius, whose *Mystical Theology* was now influencing the Western Church. The message of Dionysius (it was not until the sixteenth century that he was recognized as 'Pseudo') is that God is so wonderful that it is better and safer to describe him in negative rather than in positive terms, because whatever is postulated of him will not be wholly true, for he, being God, by definition is so infinitely more. Human language implies human limitation and cannot be accurately used of God.

This conviction is shared by the author of *The Cloud* and its cognate works. At the very outset of the book, the original recipient (who has already embraced the religious life) is reminded that his whole life must be one of longing for God; he has to think only of God, all things else forgotten. This longing is fundamental and is expressed in prayer and love: 'Lift up thine heart unto God with a meek stirring of love; and mean himself and none of his goods' (c. 3). Yet this 'naked intent' is no guarantee that God will reveal himself; it is but the necessary preliminary, for 'if ever thou shalt feel him or see him, as it may be here, it behoveth always to be in this cloud or this darkness'. This intellectual darkness is the cloud of unknowing. Yet such is God's grace that the soul 'is made sufficient to the full to comprehend all him by love' (c. 4). To our intellect, however, he 'is evermore incomprehensible'. But not to our love: 'by love he may be gotten and holden: by thought never' (c. 6). Perhaps the most difficult of all the preliminary exercises is to put all thought, however edifying, into a 'cloud of forgetting' (c. 5). Nothing must be allowed to distract the soul's attention to God, 'for though it be good to think upon the kindness of God, and to love and praise him for it, yet is it far better to think upon the naked being of him, and to love and praise him for himself' (c. 5).

Most of the book is given over to the exposition and development of this basic premiss, and is rarely without interest and inspiration. The six cognate works apply *The Cloud*'s teaching to various situations, and one in particular (*Privy Counsel*) is outstanding for its stress on the longing, determination, and love which make the soul ready for any touch that God might choose to bestow. *Benjamin* sets out, under the analogy of Jacob and his sons, the development of those virtues which lead to contemplation, and *Hid Divinity* is a free précis of Dionysius' *Mystical Theology*. The remaining tracts all have to do with aspects of the spiritual life.

They are the *Epistle of Prayer*, the *Discernment of Stirrings*, and the *Discerning of Spirits*.

The teaching of *The Cloud* writings is neatly summed up in the *Discernment of Stirrings*:

> For silence is not God, nor speaking; fasting is not God, nor eating; solitude is not God, nor company; nor any other pair of opposites. He is hidden between them, and cannot be found by anything your soul does, but only by the love of your heart. He cannot be known by reason, he cannot be thought, caught, or sought by understanding. But he can be loved and chosen by the true, loving will of your heart . . . If God is your love and your purpose, the chief aim of your heart, it is all you need in this life, although you never see more of him with the eye of reason your whole life long. Such a blind shot with the sharp dart of longing love will never miss its mark, which is God.

To come to *The Cloud* for the first time is for most a stimulating experience. Its unemotional, matter-of-fact approach to the deeper levels of the life of prayer, and its profound sense of the greatness of God – all described in limpid and splendid language – can bring not only refreshment but also real enlargement to one's understanding of the ways in which God can deal with the soul.

WALTER HILTON

When we turn to Walter Hilton, the emphasis varies somewhat. Not that Hilton differs much from *The Cloud* author: indeed, his outlook is sufficiently close for some to have argued that he wrote *The Cloud*, but there are too many differences, stylistic and theological, to sustain this theory. *The Cloud* remains anonymous.

What little we know of Hilton is derived from occasional MS references. It is little enough: he took his degree at Cambridge, he had a spell as a hermit, he became a Canon of Thurgarton Priory, Nottinghamshire, and there he died in 1396. He wrote in Latin and English various spiritual works of popular appeal, some of which have persisted to this day. In medieval fashion more works have been attributed to him than he actually wrote. Of his undoubted writings we have *The Scale* (or *Ladder*) *of Perfection* (his best known and most loved work), an *Epistle to a Devout Man*, the *Song of Angels*, and, in Latin, expositions of the *Benedictus, Qui Habitat*, and *Bonum Est*, together with a few minor pieces. Several other books, notably the *Stimulus Amoris*, have been associated with his name, but without the unquestioning support of all scholars.

He is commonly regarded as the theologian of the four, and in *The Scale* he sets out with insight and authority the spiritual development of the soul. Unusually for his time, he relates the active life with the contemplative, and stresses that the higher reaches of prayer are not reserved for the enclosed but are available to all willing to make the necessary effort. He divides the Christian life into two parts separated by a dark night. The first part he calls 'reformation in faith' and it is the experience of us all; the second part is 'reformation in feeling'. It is the 'highest state attainable by a soul in this life'. The 'understanding is uplifted and illumined by the grace of the Holy Spirit to see God as he is more clearly and fully than can be expressed, with wondering reverence, ardent love, spiritual delight, and heavenly joy.' Few reach this stage, however, for they must first undergo the bitter purging of the dark night which detaches the soul from earthly things.

There is a charity about Hilton which most find engaging:

> I do not intend to limit the ways in which God works to any laws of my own making, nor to imply that God works in a soul in one particular way and no other. This is not my meaning: I say only that I am sure that God does work this way in some of his creatures. I am certain that he also works in other ways outside my own knowledge and experience.

In whatever way God works, 'if all tends to the same end, which is the perfect love of him, then that way is good'.

Perhaps the most memorable of all the chapters in *The Scale* is that which likens the Christian life to a pilgrimage:

> A real pilgrim going to Jerusalem leaves his house and land, wife and children; he divests himself of all that he possesses in order to travel light and without encumbrances. Similarly, if you wish to be a spiritual pilgrim, you must divest yourself of all that you possess; that is, both of good deeds and bad, and leave them all behind you. Recognize your own poverty, so that you will not place any confidence in your own work; instead, always be desiring the grace of deeper love, and seeking the spiritual presence of Jesus. If you do this, you will be setting your heart wholly on reaching Jerusalem, and on nothing else. In other words, set your heart wholly on obtaining the love of Jesus and whatever spiritual vision of himself that he is willing to grant, for it is to this end alone that you have been created and redeemed; this is your beginning and your end, your joy and your bliss. Therefore, whatever you may possess, and however fruitful your activities, regard them all as worthless without the inward certainty and experience of this love. Keep this intention constantly in mind and hold to it firmly; it will sustain you among all the perils of your pilgrimage.

MOTHER JULIAN

Very little is known about Julian of Norwich apart from the fact she was an anchoress enclosed in her cell at the church of St Julian and St Edward at Carrow. She is mentioned as a beneficiary in several wills of the early fifteenth century, and Margery Kempe enjoyed 'holy dalliance' with her at a time unspecified – possibly in 1413. For the rest it is largely conjecture. It is not known whether 'Julian' was her baptismal name, or whether she took it when she entered religion. She relates that her 'shewings' were given her on 8 May 1373 when she was in her thirty-first year. But again it is not clear whether she was a secular or a religious at the time; certainly she was seemingly dying when they came, but where did it all happen? Probably at home, as hints in the shorter version suggest. It is thought that she lived well into the fifteenth century. No one can be sure. None of these things really matters: her value lies in her wonderful book.

It seems that she wrote two accounts of the event, both of which survive. The first, the shorter version, must have been written soon after it happened, and the longer twenty years later, the fruit of many years' brooding. It is this fuller work that is mostly referred to. It is a comprehensive record of her spirituality, full of theological insights which she claimed were granted her supernaturally. The revelations came when she was desperately ill, and brought with them complete healing. There were sixteen of them given in the course of a few hours. Their purpose was: 'first, that we know our Lord God; second, that we know ourself: what we are by him in kind [i.e. nature] and grace; third, that we know meekly what ourself is anent our sin and feebleness'. They cover a wide range of doctrine and experience.

Her greatest stress is on the immense love of God for his creation in general, and for the human soul in particular. It is expressed in many ways, but supremely in the cross and passion of Christ. The first ten 'shewings' are related to the crucifixion, but her whole thought is suffused with her understanding of the atonement.

In her effort to find adequate expression for such love she constantly calls it 'homely' – its modern equivalent might be 'intimate' – and 'courteous' – a word which would speak to her of the loving condescension, loyalty and refinement which (it is conjectured) she might have known in her girlhood. Today she is almost invariably associated with her teaching about the motherhood of Christ, a concept which she handles with delicacy and insight in several chapters.

Once the love of God is accepted the effect is considerable: there is security, an awareness of heaven, a delight in prayer, a sense of joy, and much else. 'Julian', wrote Paul Molinari in a paper prepared for the Sexcentenary celebrations held in Norwich in 1973, 'helps man to look at himself with the eyes of God, and thus to experience the ultimate joy of a creature: his consciousness of being the object of his Creator's love.' Julian herself is always saying it: 'In his love he clothes us, enfolds and

embraces us; that tender love completely surrounds us, never to leave us.'
Or again:

You would know our Lord's meaning in this thing? Know it well. Love was his
meaning. Who showed it you? Love. What did he show you? Love. Why did
he show it? For love. Hold on to this and you will know and understand love
more and more. But you will not know or learn anything else – ever!

H   NORTHERN HUMANISTS BEFORE
THE REFORM

JAMES MCCONICA

Bainton, R. H., *Erasmus of Christendom*. London, Collins, 1970.

Erasmus, Desiderius, *Opera omnia Desiderii Erasmi Roterodami*. Amsterdam, 1969– .

Opus epistolarum Des. Erasmi Roterodami, ed. P. S. Allen, H. M. Allen, and H. W. Garrod. OUP, 1906–58.

Erasmi opuscula, ed. W. K. Ferguson. The Hague, 1933.

Ijsewijn, J., 'The Coming of humanism to the Low Countries', *Itinerarium Italicum*, ed. H. A. Oberman and T. A. Brady Jr. (Leiden, 1975), pp. 193–301.

Margolin, J.-C., *Douze années de bibliographie érasmienne (1950–61)*. Paris, 1963.

Margolin, J.-C., *Quatorze années de bibliographie érasmienne (1936–49)*. Paris, 1969.

Margolin, J.-C., *Neuf années de bibliographie érasmienne (1962–70)*. Paris and Toronto, 1977.

Martz, L. B., 'Thomas More: the Tower Works', in *St Thomas More: Action and Contemplation*, ed. R. S. Sylvester (New Haven, Yale University, 1972), pp. 57–83.

Massaut, J.-P. 'Note sur le "Thrésor de prières" de Jean de Ferrières', in *Revue d'histoire ecclésiastique*, 58 (1963), pp. 142–8.

McConica, J., 'The patrimony of Thomas More', *History and Imagination: Essays in honour of H. R. Trevor-Roper*, ed. H. Lloyd-Jones, Valerie Pearl and Blair Worden (London, Duckworth, 1981; New York, Holmes & Meier, 1982), pp. 56–71.

More, St Thomas, *The Yale Edition of The Complete Works of St Thomas More*. Yale University, 1963– .

Noreña, C. G., *Juan Luis Vives*. The Hague, 1970.

Screech, M. A., *Ecstasy and the Praise of Folly*. London, Duckworth, 1980.

In 1528 Erasmus put his writings in order for a future editor of his works. He placed his most widely known treatise of piety, the *Enchiridion militis Christiani*, in the volume allocated to 'works of religious instruction' (*his quae instituunt ad pietatem*). This description was retained in his revised 1530 catalogue of his works, where the *Enchiridion* shared the fifth *ordo* with (among other related works) the *De contemptu mundi*, the *Paraclesis* or exhortation to the study of Scripture, with his commentaries on the Psalms and on the two hymns of Prudentius, his paraphrase of the Lord's Prayer, the *Concio de puero Jesu*, written for Colet's school at St Paul's, his comparison of a virgin and a martyr, the *Virginis matris paean*, and his liturgy for the Virgin of Loretto. His description of these, which to many would fall naturally under the heading of spirituality, as works of instruction, reveals the difficulty we encounter in applying a conventional understanding of spirituality to most humanistic writing, with its strong pedagogical orientation.

Lack of familiarity with the humanist outlook helps to account for verdicts such as that of R. G. Villoslada (*Dict. Sp.* 4.1.931): 'Erasmus was never truly devout; he never had to undergo any severe spiritual crises' (ET). One may dispute the view that severe spiritual crises are essential to true devotion, even if this were true of Erasmus. If spirituality can be seen rather as the natural consequence of faith, in which a Christian life, informed by the Holy Spirit, is interiorly directed to the following of Christ, then the doctrine of Erasmus must be regarded as one chiefly centred on spirituality.

In his account of the coming of humanism to the Low Countries Jozef Ijsewijn has shown that the full incorporation of Italian humanism into the general culture of the Netherlands

> hardly ever led, during the fifteenth century, to a sustained practice of the study of the *humanae litterae* for their own sake or to a pursuit of a profane literature which would imitate the pagan glories in order to attain a similar immortality of fame (*Itin. Ital.* p. 223).

Rather, the Mediterranean ideal of *humanitas* and the general problem of the *vita activa* versus the *vita contemplativa* were supplanted by the ideals of Christian *pietas* and discussions of the Christian life. Erasmus, like some others, gave himself to youthful experiments in purely neo-classical literary form, but his main purpose was that of other northern humanists, to seek the restoration of Christendom through sacred letters, especially through the renewal and propagation of the text of Scripture. Ijsewijn cites Erasmus' profession of faith at the end of his *Ciceronianus*: 'Here pupils are taught, here philosophy and eloquence are learned, so that we may know Christ and may celebrate his glory. This is the whole goal of erudition and eloquence' (*ibid.* p. 224). That this goal was conceived in terms of a life well-led in the community at large and dedicated to the renewal of Christian society, rather than as a contemplative ideal, merely identifies Erasmian spirituality as part of the humanist movement as a whole. Any definition of spirituality that insists on the contemplative life as a priority will be bound to exclude such works from the canon, but it must be pointed out that the *Enchiridion* itself, with its strong Pauline and Neo-platonic elements, served as a handbook for the contemplative revival in sixteenth-century Spain, while the work of M. A. Screech points to a broad stratum of mystical theology underpinning much of the Erasmian corpus. There is something of this note, indeed, at the end of

Erasmus' famous exhortation to the study of Scripture, the *Paraclesis*, where he claims that the gospel writings 'bring you the living image of his holy mind and the speaking, healing, dying, rising Christ himself, and thus they render him so fully present that you would see less if you gazed upon him with your very eyes' (tr. J. Olin).

Erasmus' humanist friend and associate, the Spanish émigré Juan Luis Vives, was even more obviously committed than Erasmus to the reform of European society as a theorist of education, a tireless propagandist for international peace, and as a highly original thinker on such problems as the relief of poverty, social ethics, and epistemology. Nevertheless, Vives too shared the characteristic concern for the renewal of *sacrae litterae*; his devotional writings, like those of Erasmus, fed the reformed liturgy of the English church. He was even more critical than Erasmus of the secularism of much Italian humanist writing, and his considerable output of educational, philosophical, and political treatises is punctuated by the appearance of meditative and spiritual works (see the Appendix in Noreña). Among other things, Vives composed a liturgical prayer and sermon on the bloody sweat of Christ in Gethsemane and a meditation on the passion. There was also an important collection of prayers published in 1535 under the general title of *Excitationes animi in Deum*. This last work includes a treatise on preparation of the soul for prayer, daily prayers and meditations, with prayers for every occasion and a commentary on the Lord's Prayer. Earlier in his career he had published a volume of meditations on the seven penitential psalms (Louvain 1518), and in 1529, a meditation on Psalm 37 concerning the passion of Christ. Such themes show the continuity of humanist devotion with late medieval precedents, however different were the typical humanist priorities in the sphere of public policy.

The blend of medieval devotional patterns and humanist learning is nowhere more evident than in the life and work of Thomas More, who, as a third representative of the northern humanist community, also serves to illustrate the wide variety of taste and temperament that could be found among those who shared the commitment to the revival of antiquity. More's close friendship with Erasmus is too well known to need rehearsal here; even after the Lutheran controversies had brought the reproach of heterodoxy against the older man More was always prepared to defend him in the public forum. He was thoroughly at home with the canon of classical and early Christian texts, both Greek and Latin, which formed the antiquity of the humanist community, and his commitment to reform of the commonweal through education and the propagation of *sacrae litterae* was unqualified. More's zeal for the remedy of poverty and social injustice surpassed even that of Vives, and his *Utopia* is only the best-known of the writings in which he vented his anger and dismay at a moral and political order that seemed so utterly bent upon violence and injustice.

More's writings on spiritual matters, however, are much closer to the English devotion of the previous century than they are to the works of piety penned by Erasmus and Vives. The constant themes of his interior devotion are the passion of Christ, the Eucharist, and meditation on the Four Last Things. His devotional output reached its apogee in the so-called Tower Works, *A Dialogue of Comfort*, *A Treatise to Receive the Blessed Body of our Lord, Sacramentally and Virtually Both*, *A Treatise upon the Passion of Christ*, and his Latin treatise on the Passion (see Martz). The actual title of this last treatise, of which the holograph was recently discovered, is a better account of its character: *De tristia, tedio, pavore, et oratione Christi ante captionem eius* ('On the sadness, repugnance, fear and prayer of Christ before his capture') – meditations on the agony of Christ written while More was preparing to meet his own death. The present writer has argued ('More's Patrimony') that the devotional themes and interior discipline of spirit which characterize all the mature life of More, and which bore their fruit in the extraordinary flowering of his last works, can be directly linked with the late medieval tradition of spirituality in England. It was this tradition that also produced the *Orchard of Syon* and the conventual discipline of the monastery of Syon and of the Charterhouse. More's anthropology too seems to have been more purely Augustinian than was that of Erasmus, and despite More's consistent and unqualified support for the humanist educational programme, there is little in him of the Stoic optimism about the susceptibility of human nature to improvement through education and good example that pervades the writings of the Dutch humanist. If his is a striking instance among the leaders of the northern renaissance of the coexistence of late medieval with humanistic convictions, it is by no means the only one. Altogether, the student of spirituality concerned with this phase of European history must be prepared to examine each representative writer, and each text, with care and discrimination, before venturing into generalization about the allegedly secularist and pragmatic bent of humanist piety.

VIII
THE MODERN WORLD
A THE PROTESTANT REFORMATION
Introduction
D. H. TRIPP

Elton, G. R., *Reformation Europe 1517–1559*. London, Collins, 1963; Cleveland, Ohio, Meridian Books, 1964; New York, Harper & Row, 1966 (bibliography).
Gherardini, B., *La spiritualità protestante: Peccatori santi*. Rome, 1982.

The popular spirituality of the medieval Western Church, as it passed into the Reformation, may be summed up in two lines of a hymn which had had itself a large part in forming that spirituality, the twelfth-century *Dies Irae* of Thomas of Celano:

> Quaerens me, sedisti lassus,
> Redemisti, crucem passus . . .
>
> 'Exhausted by your search for me, you sat down;
> By suffering the cross, you redeemed me . . .'[1]

Factors manifest here were largely determinative of Reformation spiritualities: the view of individual salvation as the prime purpose of the Incarnation; an all-pervasive sense of personal and corporate sin; a terrible urgency in the awareness of moral responsibility, especially in association with a preoccupation with personal eschatology – all these concerns meeting in an intense interest in the humanity of Jesus, specifically in his sufferings. For example: concentration on personal eschatology, with readiness for death – 'which alone ought to be the topic of our reflection', according to St Augustine (Ep. 204) – both had its specialist literature (such as Thomas Peuntner's *Kunst des Heilsamen Sterbens*,[2] or, 'The Art of Dying in the hope of Salvation', of 1434) and its secure place in more general manuals, such as the *Imitation of Christ*. All the Reformation spiritualities meet the need for a personal eschatology with a theology of grace which is also (in Luther's phrase, recently recognized also by a sympathetic Roman Catholic[3] writer as the key to Reformation

---

[1] Author's trans.
[2] See R. Rudolf, ed., *Thomas Peuntners 'Kunst des heilsamen Sterbens'* (= *Texte des späten Mittelalters*, 2, Berlin-Bielefeld-München, 1956); on the whole genre, pp. 73–81.
[3] Gherardini, op. cit.

theology) a 'theology of the cross'. The conviction that the plight of humanity could be met by God's action in the soul had been maintained both by the *devotio moderna* and by the Dionysian tradition (Louis of Blois, Eckhart, Tauler), which otherwise the *devotio moderna* distrusted, and was continued and intensified in the Reformation schools. All these schools were at least as much schools of spirituality as of reforming policy. What G. R. Elton said of Luther – 'his theology of grace in a way represents the universalisation of the individual case history of the great mystics' (op. cit., p. 29), is true also of such 'Radical Reformation' figures as Harrison and Browne[1] in their *Book which Sheweth the Life and Manners of all True Christians* (1582), and even more true of Calvin, whose expectation of the inward working of the Holy Spirit was less limited by the *simul justus et peccator* soteriology than was Luther's (and far less so than that of most later Lutherans except Arndt).

Where the 'Radical Reformation' parted company from Luther and Calvin was in the expectations of the church on earth – in those areas of spirituality which depend on eschatology: whether God can act in this age within a compromised church and culture. The *devotio moderna* had faced this issue: only the few love the cross of Jesus, and those few must carry the defects of the lax majority. This position was preserved by Luther and Calvin, but not by the 'Radical Reformation', although the latter, like so many millenarian movements, allowed for a vast variety of spiritualities, 'from the most violent aggressiveness to the mildest pacifism and from the most ethereal spirituality (*sic*) to the most earthbound materialism'.[2]

1 Luther

D. H. TRIPP

The Theologia Germanica of Martin Luther (sic), CWS 1980 (bibliography).
Dr Martin Luthers Werke. Weimar, 1883– (= WA).
Dr Martin Luthers Werke, Briefwechsel. Weimar, 1883– (= WB).
Luther's Works. St Louis, Concordia; Philadelphia, Fortress, 1955– (= LW–USA).
'The Freedom of a Christian', in WA 7. 20–38 (German), 49–73 (Latin), LW–USA 31, pp. 343–77.

[1] A. Peel, L. H. Carlson, ed., *The Writings of Robert Harrison and Robert Browne* (= *Elizabethan Nonconformist Texts*, 2, London, Allen and Unwin, 1953), esp. pp. 221–395.
[2] N. Cohn, *The Pursuit of the Millennium*, 3rd ed. (London, Paladin, 1970), p. 14.

'A Simple Way to Pray', in WA 38. 351–73, LW–USA 43, pp. 187–211.
Die Bekenntnisschriften der evangelisch-lutherischen Kirche. 3rd edn, Göttingen, 1956 (= BELK).
The Book of Concord: The Confessions of the Evangelical Lutheran Church, ed. T. G. Tappert. Philadelphia, Fortress, 1959.
Doberstein, J. W., *The Minister's Prayer Book.* Philadelphia, Muhlenberg, 1959; London, Collins, 1964.
Rupp, E. G., *The Righteousness of God.* London, Hodder & Stoughton, 1953 (bibliography).
Rupp, E. G., and Drewery, B., ed., *Martin Luther* (in the series Documents of Modern History). London, Arnold; New York, St Martin's Press, 1970.

Martin Luther (1483–1546) came to a thoroughgoing rejection of Dionysian mysticism; it was too confident of meeting God in the apex of the soul. For Luther God is *Deus absconditus*: hidden, and yet also self-revealing through his Word. He acknowledged kinship with Tauler and *Theologia Germanica*, but in his mature position he was somewhat distanced from them.

For Luther the agonizing personal quest for knowledge of God was resolved in faith only after a costly surrender of confidence in the possibility of a direct knowledge of God's inner nature, and equally of confidence in the possibility of securing the divine favour by a meritorous quality of life. It is well known how his conscientious performance of monastic devotions, his diligent keeping of the rule, spawned scruples which tormented his conscience the more, and how at last as he

> meditated day and night . . ., God showed mercy and I turned my attention to the connection of the words, 'The *righteous* shall live by faith'; and there I began to understand that the righteousness of God is the righteousness in which a just man lives by the gift of God, in other words, by faith; and that what Paul means is this: the righteousness of God is *passive* . . . (from the 'Autobiographical Fragment' of 1545, Rupp and Drewery, p. 6; WA54. 186; LW–USA 31, p. 337).

Luther teaches a disinterested adoration of God for the sake of his being God. Only the overwhelming love of God can take away the pride that denies to God the sovereignty of his love; only God's love can awaken in the sinner the humble and grateful faith that allows God to be God. The saving power of God in Christ is present in the Church, through the word and the sacraments. To an age which took sacraments for granted, Luther stressed the ministry of the word.

He lays down no normative pattern for the course of the conversion experience, and avoids two pitfalls of later Evangelical piety: he fully recognizes the reality of the work of the Spirit in childhood religious

growth, and he does not limit the value of the sacraments to their useful-
ness in individual religious experience. The foundations of the spiritual
life are laid in the Christian family, where the Commandments, the Creed
and the Our Father (note the order) are learned and first explanations are
given of baptism and the sacrament of the altar (with confession linked
with it by way of introduction).

When the sinner despairs of himself and puts his trust in Christ, 'the
absorption of the Word makes the soul a sharer in everything that belongs
to the Word' ('The Freedom of a Christian', WA7. 24 and 53; LW–USA
31, p. 349); there is a marriage between Christ and the soul (cf. Eph.
5.30ff; WA7. 25 and 54; LW–USA 31, p. 351). The Christian life, however, is a progress in growth never completed in this life. Baptism is soon
performed, but its significance continues so long as we live (cf. 'The Holy
and Blessed Sacrament of Baptism', WA 2. 728; LW–USA 35, p. 30).

The believer in Christ is no longer a slave but a free person. How the
Christians may exercise this freedom depends on their individual
vocations, both as citizens and as church members. This may involve
suffering, but for Christians to do and to suffer are charged with triumph.

Prayer is the setting of the working day and the dedication of the hours
of sleep. Morning prayers link the priestly duty of prayer with the fulfilment of vocation in worldly business. Intercession is prayer for the
victory of the cross and so also for the enemies of the cross. Like the
Catechism, Luther's *Simple Way to Pray*, written in 1535 for his barber,
singles out the Commandments, the Creed and the Our Father as the
immediate preparation for mental prayer. The mental prayer itself selects
one or more of the texts listed and makes

> 'a garland of four twisted strands. That is, I take each commandment *First*, as
> a teaching, which is what it actually is, and reflect on what our Lord God so
> earnestly requires of me here; *Secondly*, I make of it a Thanksgiving; *Thirdly*,
> a Confession; *Fourthly*, a Prayer' (WA 38. 364f.; LW–USA 43, p. 200;
> Doberstein, p. 446).

Because prayer is the act of faith *par excellence*, it is the point where the
powers of darkness attack faith most sharply. His doctrine of *Anfechtung*,
onslaught, temptation, is a doctrine about prayer. 'Without the Word of
God the enemy is too strong for us. But he cannot endure prayer and the
Word of God' (WB 6. 323). Prayer is always set in the combat of this
world; yet it realizes more of God's will for our perfection than Luther is
usually credited with admitting. In his exposition of the *Magnificat*,
Luther notes that Mary rightly called God her Lord before calling him
her Saviour (WA 7. 556; LW–USA 21, p. 309); and in prayer even sinful
persons so far rise above themselves as to give the precedence to the

honour of God's name, the triumph of God's Kingdom, and the fulfilment of God's will over the matters of our own safety and deliverance (*The Large Catechism* III, 118; BELK, p. 690; Tappert, p. 436). Hence also the conclusion of the prayer of faith with the Amen which is the *summa vis orationis*, the certainty that our prayer is heard (ibid. III, 119–24).

2 Zwingli

C. M. DENT

Texts

Huldreich Zwinglis sämtliche Werke, in Corpus Reformatorum, vols. 88ff, ed. E. Egli *et. al.* Berlin, Leipzig, Zurich, 1905– .

Bromiley, G. W., ed., (ET) *Zwingli and Bullinger*. LCC, vol. XXIV, 1953.

Jackson, S. M. *et. al.*, ed., *The Latin Works and the Correspondence of Huldreich Zwingli, together with selections from his German Works.* 3 vols., New York, G. P. Putnam's, 1912; Philadelphia, Heidelberg, 1922, 1929.

Jackson, S. M., ed., (ET) *Selected Works of Huldreich Zwingli*. Philadelphia, University of Pennsylvania, 1901.

Potter, G. R., ed., (ET) *Huldrych Zwingli*. Documents of Modern History, London, Arnold; New York, St Martin's, 1978.

Studies

Courvoisier, J., (ET) *Zwingli. A Reformed Theologian*. Richmond, Va., John Knox; London, Epworth, 1963.

Garside, C., *Zwingli and the Arts*. New Haven, Conn., Yale University, 1966.

Locher, G. W., *Zwingli's Thought: New Perspectives*. Leiden, Brill, 1981.

Potter, G. R., *Zwingli*. Cambridge, New York, CUP, 1976.

Walton, R. C., *Zwingli's Theocracy*. Toronto, University of Toronto, 1967.

In the critical months of the late summer of 1522, when, after four years preaching the 'plain gospel' in Zurich, Zwingli found himself in conflict with the Bishop of Constance and was challenged by the City Council to make a public defence of his orthodoxy, he set down a short introduction to the study of Scripture entitled *The Clarity and Certainty of the Word of God*. It reveals his mature theology as a theology of the Spirit. God in his divine sovereignty, who created and controls the world by his power and who foreordained the destiny of humanity, communicates his purpose in the life of the human race and of the whole creation through the activity of the Spirit.

> Truly, that spirit of life which God blew or breathed into Adam's nostrils is no vain or powerless breath like the breath of man . . . For as we live physically by the inbreathing of air, so the Spirit of God is that true life in which all things live and from which they derive their life.[1]

True religion, then, is totally dependent upon this inbreathing; without it, natural man turns to idolatry. Where people trust in themselves, they can never be truly pious. If they are to be inwardly moved, the external word must be preached, but it is always absolutely dependent upon the inner word, the Spirit's activity which opens the heart of the believer. There is no conflict here between Zwingli's predominant pneumatology and the formal Reformation doctrine of the supremacy of Scripture. The Scriptures themselves must be approached through the working of the Spirit.

> How are we to come? In this way: If you want to speak on any matter or to learn of it, you must first think like this: Before I say anything or listen to the teaching of man, I will first consult the mind of the Spirit of God: 'I will hear what the Lord will speak.' Then you should reverently ask God for his grace, that he may give you his mind and Spirit, so that you will not lay hold of your own opinion but his. And have a firm trust that he will teach you a right understanding, for all wisdom is of God the Lord. And then go on to the written word of the Gospel . . . You must be *theodidacti*, that is, taught of God, not of men.[2]

For Zwingli, even though the external word is the most important mandate in Christendom, it is always dependent on the Holy Spirit in opening the heart of the believer. The process of justification also is inward and spiritual. 'Those who have God's Spirit, who know that Christ is their salvation, who rely on the word, do not sin. For the only mortal sin is unbelief.'[3] This theocentric emphasis is not only applied to the individual believer and to the community of the elect; it also animates the whole of life in society. God wills the renewal of political, social and even military life, not merely the gathering together of a small, purified congregation. Only through the Spirit and with Christ as guide, captain and head can civil relationships be restored and people be enabled to live at peace with themselves and with one another in one *corpus christianum*. Zwingli's desire that all Christendom might be renewed needed the active co-operation of the magistracy. In this, Zwingli differed from many Anabaptists who criticized the temporizing nature of the Zurich reform programme.

[1] *Zwingli and Bullinger*, ed. G. W. Bromiley, pp. 63–4.
[2] Ibid., 88–9.
[3] Zwingli, *Schlussreden*, no. 5, in *Sämtliche Werke*, II, p. 44.

The city magistracy sought to answer the increasing criticism of Zwingli's teaching in a great public debate which took place on 29 January 1523. For this disputation, Zwingli proposed sixty-seven theses, dealing with the Church, its authority, sacraments, purgatory and priesthood. Discussion of prayers to the saints and the elimination of superstition figured prominently in the deliberations. Six months later, Zwingli's *Commentary on the Sixty-Seven Theses (Auslegung und Gründe der Schlussreden)* provided an extensive explanation of his theology. The essence of his teaching on prayer appears in theses forty-four and forty-five. 'Those who call on God in spirit and truth should do so without great publicity. Those who act in order that they may be seen by men and secure praise during their lifetime are hypocrites.'[1] Zwingli had reached these convictions not only through the study of the Scriptures. He had personally experienced the omnipotent God, who had raised him up from the shadow of death to be his servant in the city of Zurich. In 1519, he had almost perished when plague struck the city and, finding himself near to death, he had prayed:

> Help, Lord God, help
> In this need.
> So let it be: Do what thou wilt.
> I nothing lack.
> Thy vessel I am: to make or break altogether.[2]

In Zwingli's experience and theology, prayer is direct and from the heart; it is the outreaching of the human spirit towards the sovereign Lord. Hence, he believed that many words were unnecessary, that much ostentation was hypocritical and that the best prayer, both for the individual and for the congregation, was silent. Private prayer is his ideal of the true worship of God, bound to no particular locality, form of words, or ceremonial. Zwingli realized, nevertheless, that Christian spiritual life could not be entirely inward and private if the worship of the visible Church was to be retained at all. To avoid the danger of display, the exterior form was to be simplified; music, including choirs and organs, eliminated and the content restricted to the exposition of the Scriptures.

> Farewell, my temple-murmurings! I am not sorry for you. I know that you are not good for me. But welcome, O pious, private prayer that is awakened in the hearts of believing men through the word of God . . . Greetings to you, too, common prayer that all Christians do together, be it in church or in their

[1] G. R. Potter, ed., *Huldrych Zwingli*, p. 24.
[2] Zwingli's Plague Hymn; ibid., p. 15.

chambers, but free and unpaid; I know that you are the sort of prayer to which God will give that which he has promised.[1]

Such prayer, in its irreducible purity, needs no intermediary. Christ alone is mediator, he who has expiated our sins. Scripture gives no indication of our need of the intercession of the Blessed Virgin Mary or of the saints.[2] Mary might be judged an example, but never a mediator since God could not be approached through any creature, but only through Christ. Zwingli may have adopted this opposition to the cult of the saints from his early mentor, Erasmus. His early humanist training also furnished support for his criticism of prayer to the saints on the grounds that it lacked scriptural foundation and deviated from the sincere and simple prayer practised by the first Christians.

Shortly before his death at the battle of Kappel in October 1531, Zwingli wrote *An Exposition of the Faith* which he sent to the French court to clear misunderstandings of his teaching. The same, fundamentally theocentric, emphasis dominates this exposition as it did his early writing.

> Only the eternal and infinite and uncreated God is the basis of faith. Hence the collapse of all that foolish confidence with which some rely upon most sacred things or the most holy sacraments. For it is in God that we must put our firm and sure trust . . . For if we are to enjoy only God, we must trust only in God; we must trust in what we are to enjoy, and not in what we are to employ . . . For true piety is the same everywhere and in all men, having its source in one and the self-same Spirit.[3]

This is the basis of Zwingli at prayer, prayer in the Spirit which, in its purity, has the power to work in city and in society to break down sinfulness, as well as in the individual to transform *homo mendax* into *homo spiritualis*.

---

[1] Zwingli, *Schlussreden*, no. 46, in *Sämtliche Werke*, II, pp. 353–4; translated by C. Garside in *Zwingli and the Arts*, p. 51.

[2] Zwingli, First Zurich Disputation (Jan. 1523), in S. M. Jackson, ed., *Selected Works*, pp. 63–5. 'Von der ewig reinen Magd Maria' (Sept. 1522), in G. R. Potter, *Zwingli*, pp. 89ff.

[3] Zwingli, '*An Exposition of the Faith*', in *Zwingli and Bullinger*, ed. G. W. Bromiley, p. 247.

3 The Anabaptists

C. M. DENT

Texts

Williams, G. H. and Mergal, A. M., ed., (ET) *Spiritual and Anabaptist Writers*. LCC, vol. XXV, 1957.

Studies

Bender, H. S., *Conrad Grebel c. 1498–1526, the Founder of the Swiss Brethren*, in Studies in Anabaptist and Mennonite History (= SAMH), 6. Scottdale, Pa., Herald, 1950.

Blanke, F., (ET) *Brothers in Christ; the History of the Oldest Anabaptist Congregation, Zollikon, near Zurich*. Scottdale, Pa., Herald, 1961.

Braght, T. J. van, (ET) *The Bloody Theatre, or, Martyrs' Mirror (1685)*. Scottdale, Pa., Herald, 1938.

Clasen, C.-P., *Anabaptism; a Social History, 1525–1618*. Ithaca, N.Y.; London, Cornell University, 1972.

Davis, K. R., *Anabaptism and Asceticism; a Study in Intellectual Origins*, in SAMH, 16. Scottdale, Pa., Herald, 1974.

Friedmann, R., *The Theology of Anabaptism*, in SAMH, 15. Scottdale, Pa., Herald, 1973.

Hershberger, G. F., ed., *The Recovery of the Anabaptist Vision*. Scottdale, Pa., Herald, 1957.

Hillerbrand, H. J., *A Bibliography of Anabaptism (1520–1630)*. Elkhart, Ind., Institute of Mennonite Studies, 1962.

Jones, R. M., *Spiritual Reformers in the Sixteenth and Seventeenth Centuries*. London, Macmillan, 1914.

Lienhard, M., ed., *The Origins and Characteristics of Anabaptism*. The Hague, M. Nijhoff, 1977.

Littell, F. H., *The Anabaptist View of the Church*. 2nd edn, rev., Boston, Starr King, 1958.

The Mennonite Encyclopaedia, 4 vols, ed. Bender, H. S., and Smith, C. H. Scottdale, Pa., Herald, 1955–9.

The Mennonite Quarterly Review, published by the Mennonite Historical Society, Goshen, Ind., since 1927, contains many important texts and studies.

Packull, W. O., *Mysticism and the early South German–Austrian Anabaptist Movement, 1525–1531*, in SAMH, 19. Scottdale, Pa., Herald, 1977.

Williams, G. H., *The Radical Reformation*. London, Weidenfeld & Nicolson; Philadelphia, Westminster, 1962.

The geographical and theological origins of the Anabaptist movements remain a matter of controversy. Their distinctive piety may have had its roots as much in the medieval ascetical, mystical and prophetical traditions as in the sixteenth-century reform emanating from Zurich or

Wittenberg. Zurich was undoubtedly one of the most important sources of the Anabaptist mainstream, but Zwingli accurately recognized that, while the followers of Manz and Grebel, later called the 'Swiss brethren', had once adhered to his reforming projects, they differed fundamentally from him in spirit. 'They went out from us, but were not of us.' A questioning of the practice of infant baptism in Wittenberg in the early 1520s and the activity of the Zwickau prophets may also have been influential, and Thomas Müntzer was often an inspiration and guide, despite the efforts of later Mennonites to discredit his extremism. Early Anabaptism overcame relatively small numbers and fierce persecution, particularly in the first decade of its existence; groups spread rapidly in south Germany, Moravia and Austria, and there was vigorous growth in Switzerland and in the Low Countries. Magistrates and reformers alike feared their charismatic power. In 1531, Bullinger admitted that 'the people were running after them as if they were living saints'. In the same year Sebastian Franck, in his *Chronica*, recognized the essence of their spirituality and the cause of their success.

> The Anabaptists spread so rapidly that their teaching soon covered, as it were, the land. They soon gained a large following, and baptized many thousands, drawing to themselves many sincere souls who had a zeal for God. For they taught nothing but love, faith, and the need of bearing the cross. They showed themselves humble, patient under much suffering; they brake the bread with one another as an evidence of unity and love. They helped each other faithfully, called each other brothers, etc. They increased so rapidly that the world feared an uprising by them, though I have learned that this fear had no justification whatsoever. They were persecuted with great tyranny, being imprisoned, branded, tortured and executed by fire, water and the sword. In a few years very many were put to death. Some have estimated the number of those who were killed to be far above two thousand. They died as martyrs, patiently, and humbly endured all persecution.[1]

The Anabaptists formed independent, voluntary congregations, which they often referred to as brotherhoods. All who belonged to them separated themselves from the territorial or magistral churches, distinguishing their membership of the church by a public profession of faith, followed by baptism. Although they soon received the title Anabaptist, (Wieder)täufer, their rejection of infant baptism was not the corner-stone of their profession, but rather a consequence of their insistence that God's will must be fulfilled absolutely, regardless of state regulations or traditional practice. On this basis also, they rejected military service, refused to take the civil oath and would not allow the magistrate any

[1] Sebastian Franck, *Chronica* . . . (1531), fo. 444v; ET by J. Horsch in *Mennonite Quarterly Review*, 12 (1938), pp. 3–4.

power over matters of religion. Their conspicuous separation from the world and their refusal of all compromise was matched by their insistence on holiness of life. The common ownership of property in some congregations, together with simplicity of dress, restraint in social life and the repudiation of luxury, sets the Anabaptists apart as a distinctive reformation piety, sharing the ideals of the early Franciscans and with affinities with the Brethren of the Common Life and Gerhard Groote. Erasmus, who also shared this tradition, sought, as they did, a vital, inward Christian faith. Although they affirmed the moral freedom of natural man, this should not render them open to charges of Pelagianism. Rather, the freedom of the will they preached was that freedom to be found in a person reborn, the freedom of those who live absolutely under divine grace. Their distinctive soteriology may also have drawn breath from the German mystical tradition of Eckhart, Tauler and the *Theologia Deutsch* (see pp. 316–24). These writings also animated Thomas Müntzer. Some of the south German Anabaptists certainly stressed that one became righteous by following Christ the exemplar and by being inwardly cleansed. For all Anabaptists, the call was to a radical discipleship (*Nachfolge*). Hans Denck maintained that 'none may truly know (Christ) unless he follow after him with his life'.[1] They saw Christ less as the Saviour and Teacher who had brought salvation and more as the Lord and Master to be followed and obeyed. Rebirth and baptism could only be truly meaningful if they were immediately followed by a determination to follow Christ on the narrow way of life. Only those who pursued this way would enter the Kingdom, which was already breaking into the world in the apocalyptic encounter of good and evil in their own age.

A distinctive Anabaptist piety was expressed less in acts of worship and devotion than in the whole of life. Wolfgang Capito, one of the Strasbourg reformers, who had shown sympathy towards visiting Anabaptists in the 1520s, characterized them thus: 'They are determined to shun the evil life of the world, the sins of gambling, drunkenness, gluttony, adultery, warring, killing, speaking evil of one's neighbour and living in the fleshly lusts, and to flee from that which is in conformity with the flesh and the world.'[2] Many reformers were not so generous in their assessment. Jacob Andreä of Tübingen cautioned: 'Do not be deceived if an old Anabaptist leader appears, wearing a shabby old coat and a felt hat with his hair sticking out of the crown and bowing as if he were almost collapsing with holiness. Underneath these fellows are proud and arrogant, condemning all people, even those they have not seen.'[3]

[1] Hans Denck, 'Whether God is the cause of evil', in *Spiritual and Anabaptist Writers*, LCC, p. 108.
[2] Cited by J. Horsch in *Mennonite Quarterly Review*, 8 (1934), p. 132.
[3] Cited by C.-P. Clasen, *Anabaptism. A Social History*, p. 144.

In general, Anabaptists lived moderately, avoiding ostentation, although sometimes the charismatic tendency in the movement led to excesses of behaviour and occasional outbursts of ecstatic utterance. It was, however, not excess, but their refusal to compromise in any way which led inevitably to persecution and this, in its turn, lent a distinctive emphasis to their piety. It gave groups of Anabaptists a solidarity of membership as they held together in brotherly love, expectantly waiting for the coming of the Kingdom in the trials of their time.

> Foremost, apply love
> Through which we overcome, while on this life's course;
> It is the bond of perfection. Love is God Himself,
> It remains in eternity.[1]

Most Anabaptist meetings were held in secret. They gathered frequently in barns or in fields, small conventicles of men and women who were always prepared to bear the cross in life. Their *Nachfolge* was not that of à Kempis' 'royal road of the holy cross', inward and spiritual only. The cross, they believed, stood over the events of this aeon, which was the age of the suffering Church. On 5 September 1524, Conrad Grebel wrote to Thomas Müntzer: 'True Christian believers are sheep among wolves . . . they must be baptized in anguish and affliction, tribulation, persecution, suffering and death.'[2] Baptism in the Spirit was followed by baptism with water and might, eventually, lead to baptism of blood. While they did not willingly seek death, they valued their uncompromised holiness more than life and livelihood. The piety of the martyr, illustrated and described in *The Bloody Theatre or Martyrs' Mirror*, a collection of documents from the sixteenth and seventeenth centuries, collected and published in 1685, came to dominate the spiritual outlook of the movement.[3] In prison, they composed hymns which were subsequently used for private and family devotion. As they faced the scaffold they invariably fell to their knees in prayer. The manner of their suffering and death encouraged the brethren to persevere.

> Some sang praises to God while they lay in grievous imprisonment, as though they were in great joy. Some did the same as they were being led to the place of execution and death, singing joyfully with uplifted voice that it rang out loud. Others stepped to the place of death with a smile on their lips, praising God that they were accounted worthy to die the death of a Christian hero . . . The

---

[1] *Aussbund*, hymn 124; cited by R. Friedmann, *The Theology of Anabaptism*, p. 74. The *Aussbund*, the Anabaptist hymn-book, the first extant copy of which dates from 1583, contains hymns from earlier periods of Anabaptist development.

[2] *Spiritual and Anabaptist Writers*, LCC, p. 80.

[3] See the illustrations in *Het Bloedig Tooneel of Martelaers Spiegel der Doops-Gesinde*, compiled by T. J. van Bragt (Amsterdam, 1685), especially vol. ii, 1, 17, 30, 47.

fire of God burned within them. They would die the bitterest death, yea they would die ten deaths rather than to forsake the divine truth which they had espoused.[1]

4 Calvin

D. H. TRIPP

Battles, F. L. and Tagg, S., ed., *The Piety of John Calvin*. Grand Rapids, Baker, 1978.

Calvin, John, (ET) *Institutes of the Christian Religion*, ed. H. Beveridge. repr. Grand Rapids, Eerdmans, 1957.

Calvin, John, (ET) *Institutes of the Christian Religion*, ed. J. T. McNeill, trans. F. L. Battles. LCC XXI, 1960.

Wallace, R. S., *Calvin's Doctrine of the Christian Life*. Edinburgh and London, Oliver & Boyd; Grand Rapids, Eerdmans, 1959.

Wendel, F., (ET) *Calvin: The Origins and Development of his Religious Thought*. London, Collins; New York, Harper & Row, 1963 (bibliography).

Calvin (1509–64) is much easier to expound than Luther because in his *Institutes of the Christian Religion*, expecially in its final form, we have a summary of his thought in his own long-pondered words. Although it has often been used as a model for dogmatic systems, its true character is that of a spiritual guide to Christian believing and living. This may be seen from its structure in the first edition of 1536; of the six chapters, the first four expounded the law, the Creed, the Lord's Prayer, and the dominical sacraments – exactly the programme of Luther's catechisms. Even in the final edition of 1559, where the structure has long since been radically altered, the purpose is practical; from the captivating brief glance at the possibility of knowing God (I. 1–3), the seeker is led through a progressive experience of seeing human pride demolished while at the same time God's renewing grace unfolds its plan (I. 4–II. 17), to the point where the seeker can become the penitent believer, with all the privileges that confers (III. 1–18); thereafter the believer lives the life of faith and prayer, going on to the complete joy of the resurrection (III. 19–25). Thus far, we have a guide for a particular kind of 'interior soul'; but the individual believers, though in the last analysis alone in confrontation with God, enjoy the divinely given support of the Church, its ministers

[1] From a Hutterite chronicle, cited by J. Horsch in *Mennonite Quarterly Review*, 12 (1938), p. 17.

and sacraments, to allure them into the life of faith and to strengthen them as they serve God in religious and secular life (IV. 1–20). This fivefold division of the material is the real plan of the work, whereas the division into four books on the pattern of the Creed (Father, Son, Spirit, Church) is a mnemonic device – but not a gratuitous one, for it reminds us that the individual spiritual life of the believer is set against the back-drop of an objectively true doctrine. Church and sacraments are not a mere appendage to individual devotion; the Church is already present in the world to call the elect to realization of their calling, and its provisions march beside their needs as they grow.

Unlike Luther, Calvin allows that the human mind can conceive of God with truth long before he is trusted by the soul. But the essential fault of fallen humanity is ignorance of God, *wilful* self-misinformation, which turns all natural religion into idolatry. God has given us the Scriptures, from which we learn the falsehood of idolatry (I. 10–12). Calvin takes a positive view of the creation narrative, by which we are led to praise. But we must turn to the terrible tragedy of human disobedience and bondage (II. 1–5). Yet God will appear as a Redeemer in the person of his Son (II. 6.1). In the light of this hope, we can endure a consider-ation of the law of God. The Commandments reveal our unrighteousness (II. 7–8); yet also lead us towards Christ (II. 9–10). Christ our mediator is prophet, priest and king and in him we too are priests, 'offer ourselves and our all to God, and freely enter the heavenly sanctuary, so that the sac-rifices of praise and prayer which we present are grateful and of sweet odour before him' (II. 15.6).

All this has been God's strategy to lead us to himself, but also the subject of meditation, which is one of his means for achieving that end. The realization of his will in the individual is possible only through the secret working of the Holy Spirit, who unites the soul with Christ in a spiritual marriage (III. 1.3). We embark on the spiritual life, at once penitent and joyful. Believers find themselves free, but freedom is dan-gerous and must be used responsibly. First, there is freedom from the accusations of the law; secondly, freedom from a sense of bondage; third-ly, a realization that there are areas in which God leaves us to do as we will – the *adiaphora*. This mature relationship with God can be sustained only by faith, which has its centre in prayer (III. 20). Prayer is the acceptance of what God has offered.

The rules of prayer are:

(*a*) 'The mind must . . . rise to a purity worthy of God' (III. 20.4). This is recollection.

(*b*) 'We are to ask only so far as God permits' (III. 20.5).

355

(*c*) We are to ask only for things really needed, and with ardent desire, whether for ourselves or not (III. 20.6–7).

(*d*) Prayer should be utterly humble, and yet confident (III. 20.11).

Yet God will not reject prayer simply because these rules are not kept. More important than any rule is the mediation of Christ, through which all prayer must be offered (III. 17–27), as it must be offered to God alone. The model prayer is the Our Father, in which the first three petitions link us to something more important than ourselves (III. 20.35).

Prayer sums up much of the believer's relationship with God, a fusion of deep humility with utter confidence. The last three chapters of Book III seem at first sight to turn away from prayer to the destiny of the elect and their final blessedness – at first sight only, for they speak of endurance, the proper setting of prayer. For the adopted child of God prayer is an anticipation of the triumph to come.

Conclusion

D. H. TRIPP

The classical Reformers were men of prayer, and the movements they led were, at least in part, movements of prayer. Like all traditions, theirs suffered change and degeneration; they also underwent improvements and revivals. In Calvinism even the rough and ready John Knox brought into the tradition which Calvin bequeathed a neglected element of thanksgiving.[1] Luther's church spent the latter part of the sixteenth century in minute theological disputes which suggest a loss of nerve in other areas, and was reminded of the heritage it was in danger of losing by John Arndt, who gathered the *disjecta membra* of Luther's insights on prayer into a synthesis as orderly as Calvin's but still distinctively Lutheran (see below, p. 450).

The inheritors of the left-wing tradition have tended to see themselves as 'the gathered church'. Sometimes this has led them to a spirituality appropriate to the 'little flock'; in other cases, they have been inspired to reach out in evangelism and mission in order to bring others in.

[1] Macgregor, J. G., *The Thundering Scot. A Portrait of John Knox*. London, Macmillan, 1958.

B THE CATHOLIC REFORMATION
I SPAIN

I Ignatius Loyola

MICHAEL IVENS

Texts

Critical editions in the series Monumenta Historica Societatis Jesu, Rome.
Corbishley, T., *The Spiritual Exercises*. London, Burns & Oates; New York, Kennedy, 1963.
Ganss, G., *The Constitutions of the Society of Jesus*. St Louis, Mo., The Institute of Jesuit Sources, 1970.
Longridge, W., *The Spiritual Exercises of Saint Ignatius of Loyola*, with a commentary and translation of the *Directorium in Exercitia*. London, Mowbray, 1919; Milwaukee, Morehouse, rev. edn 1930.
O'Callaghan, J., (ET) *The Autobiography of St Ignatius Loyola*. London and New York, Harper & Row, 1974.
Puhl, L., (ET) *The Spiritual Exercises*. Chicago, Loyola University, 1951; Westminster, Md., Newman, 1960.
Rahner, H., (ET) *Saint Ignatius Loyola: Letters to Women*. Freiburg, Herder; Edinburgh, Nelson, 1960.
Young, W., *Letters of St Ignatius of Loyola*. Chicago, Loyola University, 1959.

Biographies and studies

Brodrick, J., *The Origin of the Jesuits*. London, Longmans, Green, 1940; Westport, Conn., Greenwood, 1971.
Brodrick, J., *Saint Francis Xavier*. London, Burns & Oates; New York, Wicklow, 1952.
Brodrick, J., *Saint Ignatius Loyola: The Pilgrim Years*. London, Burns & Oates; New York, Farrar, Straus & Cudahy, 1956.
Brodrick, J., *The Progress of the Jesuits*. London and New York, Longmans, Green, 1947.
Dalmases, C., (ET) *Ignatius of Loyola, Founder of the Jesuits*. St Louis, Institute of Jesuit Sources, 1985.
de Guibert, J., (ET) *The Jesuits: Their Spiritual Doctrine and Practice*. Chicago, Institute of Jesuit Sources, 1964.
von Matt, L., and Rahner, H., (ET) *St Ignatius of Loyola: A Pictorial Biography*. London, Longmans, Green; Chicago, H. Regnery, 1956.
Rahner, H., (ET) *Ignatius the Theologian*. London and Dublin, G. Chapman; New York, Herder & Herder, 1968.
Rahner, K., and Imhof, P., (ET) *Ignatius of Loyola*. London and Cleveland, Collins, 1979.

Young, W., trans. *Finding God in All Things* (essays in Ignatian spirituality selected from the French review *Christus*). Chicago, H. Regnery, 1958.

Articles

Articles on Ignatian spirituality appear in the supplements of the English Jesuit periodical *The Way*, in *Studies* (published by the American Seminar on Jesuit Spirituality, St Louis University), and in the publications of the Centrum Ignatianum Spiritualitatis, Rome.

LIFE

On an unknown day in 1491, Ignatius Loyola was born in the castle that bears his family name in the Basque province of Guipúzcoa. In his late teens he was placed in the household of the royal treasurer, passing later into the service of the viceroy of Navarre. A true product of the Spain of Ferdinand and Isabella, he grew up strictly orthodox in religion, essentially medieval in culture and staunchly monarchist. In early adulthood he exhibited, as well as acute personal vanity, the qualities of romanticism, audacity and leadership that were to mark him as a saint; but until the year 1521 his values and aspirations were those of the courtier and gentleman-soldier. In that year, however, while convalescing from a battle wound, he underwent a profound spiritual crisis as the result of reading two books: the *Life of Christ*, by Ludolph of Saxony and the *Golden Legend*, a work of hagiology. The spiritual movement associated with his name has its source in this crisis and its aftermath.

Restored to health, he lived as a beggar in the small town of Manresa in the neighbourhood of the Benedictine monastery of Montserrat. At first his intention was to imitate as closely as possible the austerities described in the lives of the saints. But in the space of less than a year, the traits emerged that would characterize his mature religious personality. He grew into a confirmed mystic of action. He acquired the gift of spiritual discernment. He became in a true sense a 'theologian', endowed with that 'intimate understanding and relish of the truth' that he would later distinguish from merely quantitative knowledge. The key to this remarkable maturation is to be found not in external influences – these are hard to determine – but in a sequence of intense personal experiences through which 'God taught him as a schoolmaster teaches a child'. In his autobiography, he traces the main stages of this spiritual pedagogy: the initial ease and joy followed by acute suffering, the breakthrough into a period of enlightenment with attendant visions and illuminations, the final transfiguring moment on the bank of the river Cardoner when 'the eyes of his mind were opened and he received an understanding of many things, spiritual as well as matters concerning faith and theology, with such enlightenment that these things seemed altogether new'.

When Ignatius left Manresa, he believed that his vocation lay in the Holy Land, where he went in 1523 in the hope of spending the remainder of his life as a perpetual pilgrim. Sent home for his own safety by the Franciscan guardians, he turned his attention to study, an occupation which was to dominate his life for more than ten years. Having learned Latin from a Barcelona schoolmaster, he attended courses at the universities of Alcala and Salamanca. In 1528, mainly on account of harassment by the inquisition, which on two occasions put him in prison, he enrolled at the university of Paris. Here he gained the degree of Master of Arts and studied theology under the Dominicans, becoming a devoted adherent of St Thomas.

In Paris, he gathered the group of students who with him were to found the Society of Jesus. In 1534 these companions pronounced private vows of poverty and chastity, together with the vow either to join Ignatius in returning to Jerusalem or, should that prove impossible, to place themselves at the disposition of the Pope. When hopes of travelling to the Holy Land were finally destroyed by the outbreak of a Mediterranean war, the alternative project came into effect; and in 1538 the companions committed themselves by vow – as subsequently every professed Jesuit was to do – to undertake any apostolic work anywhere in the world at the behest of the Pope. The previous year, during his journey to Rome, another decisive event had occurred in Ignatius' inner life: the vision in the wayside chapel of La Storta. It seemed to him, wrote Diego Laynez, the future Jesuit general, 'as if God the Father had imprinted on his heart the words "I will be favourable to you in Rome" . . . He saw Christ with the cross on his shoulder and next to him the eternal Father. The Father said to Jesus: "I want you to take this man to be your servant"; and Jesus thus took Ignatius to himself with the words: "It is my will that you should serve us".' It is readily understandable that this experience, summarizing as it does his entire trinitarian and christocentric mysticism of service, should have affected Ignatius profoundly. But to appreciate the full significance of the La Storta vision, two details must be kept in mind: the event occurred on the threshold of his work in Rome, and the Father's promise (*'ego vobis propitius ero'*) embraced the companions as well as Ignatius himself. As the offering to the Pope was the practical prelude to the foundation of the Society of Jesus, La Storta was the mystical prelude.

From the moment of Paul III's sympathetic response to the companions' offer of service, events moved rapidly. In 1540 the bull 'Regimini' authorized the establishment of a new religious order, whose members would 'campaign (*militare*) for God, beneath the banner of the cross, and serve the Lord alone and the Church his spouse under the Roman

Pontiff, Christ's vicar on earth'. By the end of Ignatius' life, some thousand Jesuits were at work in education, theological scholarship, retreat-giving, locally-based pastoral ministries, and a wide variety of specialized fields. Jesuit missionaries were established in Africa and Brazil, and the death in 1552 of St Francis Xavier (one of the Paris companions) had closed a spectacular career of evangelization in India and Japan. Ignatius' last years were largely devoted, in the face of failing health, to the spiritual guidance and practical administration of this expanding international body. He died suddenly in the early morning of 31 July, 1556.

WORKS

Ignatius was not in the ordinary sense a 'literary' saint. The concern for accuracy and qualification which marks him as a thinker makes him heavy and tortuous as a writer. He bequeathed, however, a considerable written legacy, consisting in a voluminous correspondence, a spiritual journal, a dictated autobiography, and copious notes and instructions, in addition to his best-known works, the *Spiritual Exercises* and the Jesuit *Constitutions*. Here it will be possible to consider only these latter.

The *Spiritual Exercises*, though revised and expanded over a period of years, were composed in substance at Manresa. Derived from Ignatius' conversion, they are intended to lead others to find God, as Ignatius himself had done, in the school of experience. In making the Exercises, the retreatant is guided through an intensive spiritual education, beginning with repentance and purification and leading to the desire, rooted in a deep love and knowledge of Christ, to serve the Kingdom of God under the standard of Christ in ever-growing docility to the Holy Spirit. When undertaken in conditions of seclusion, the Exercises last about a month, considerably longer when made concurrently with everyday life. They can also be abridged and adapted to meet a wide range of situations and needs. Thus, while Ignatius tended to limit the full Exercises to 'outstanding persons or to those desiring to choose a state of life', modified forms of the Exercises, often consisting simply of the meditations of the 'first week', were part of the early Jesuits' pastoral stock-in-trade. In Ignatius' lifetime, the Exercises were generally made, even in their modified forms, under personal direction, the 'preached retreat' being a later development of Ignatius' own concept.

The *Constitutions*, while differing from the Exercises in form, are wholly in continuity with them in content and spirit. Their spiritual doctrine has its source in the Exercises. Like the Exercises, they are permeated by the qualities of humanity and practical and psychological realism. But, above all, it is the achievement of the *Constitutions* to have developed and codified the concept, implicit throughout the Exercises, of an integrally apostolic form of religious life; a concept which carried to new and radical lengths the break from monasticism pioneered by the Dominicans and Franciscans in the twelfth century. The *Constitutions* exemplify Ignatius' uncompromising subordination of means to end. The apostolic end of the Society is conceived in the widest possible terms: 'to labour for the defence and propagation of the Christian faith and the progress of souls', not only through preaching and the sacraments, but by 'any ministry of the word' and 'any work of charity', and this throughout the world even among the Turks or in the Indies. To this apostolic end the entire Jesuit way of life is aligned. The *Constitutions* insist, therefore, upon a high degree of mobility and an 'ordinary' external life-style. They do away with office in choir, statutory fasting and the monastic habit. They contain few rules, preferring that rules be local, variable and accommodated to times, persons and places. Their approach to poverty and obedience is worked out in terms of the order's corporate commitment to a diversified, international apostolate. Numerous other instances could be cited to illustrate specific ways in which Ignatius discards or rewrites the traditions of monasticism. But it is not only in particular themes but in their overall tenor that the *Constitutions* communicate a vision of religious life as dedicated completely to an apostolic purpose. Despite many outdated details, it is a strikingly modern vision.

SPIRITUAL DOCTRINE

Ignatius' spirituality is 'apostolic' not only in its external expression but in its underlying conceptions of God and of God's ways with mankind. Every theme of spiritual theology is perceived and lived with reference to the service of God in the world. Ignatius' outlook, while dominated by the divine transcendence, does not see the sense of transcendence as leading to the oblivion of creatures but always as illuminating them in a new way. The Trinity for Ignatius is emphatically the creator and redeemer God, continually at work in 'all things'. Union is union-in-service, the involvement of the human person in the redemptive work of the Trinity in the world. Asceticism consists in the striving for interior freedom and right intention, the qualities needed for ordering all things to the glory of God. The discernment of spirits, one of the major themes of Ignatius' spiritual doctrine, is brought to bear on the concrete decisions that arise from the life of action. And it is precisely in and through the exigencies of apostolic service that the apostle lives the mystery of the cross. As Ignatius' companion Jerome Nadal wrote in connection with La

Storta: 'Jesus Christ still carries his cross in the Church militant; him we follow with our own cross because the eternal Father has made us his servants.'

As a teacher of prayer and contemplation, Ignatius is widely associated with an emphasis on methods. Undoubtedly, the methods expounded in the *Exercises*, especially the method by which the retreatant is initiated into the tradition of imaginative contemplation, have proved a significant contribution to post-Reformation spirituality. But the distinctive characteristic of his doctrine on prayer is not a concern with methods (which he regarded as important at the early stages of growth, but as constrictive later on), but a concern that prayer be integrated with service.

The implications of this extend both to prayer in the strict sense and to the wider reach of prayer. Even when he withdraws from action in order to pray, the apostle remains a person called to and gifted for service. Thus, whatever the forms of his prayer and whatever his unitive gifts, the graces of prayer are conferred on him for service; and Ignatius is vigorous in his censure of any ways of prayer that spoil the apostle's appetite for 'helping one's neighbour'. Moreover, Ignatius' apostolic doctrine lays heavy emphasis on the prayer which belongs to action itself, the prayer of 'finding God in all things'. Certainly, the growth of such prayer is a gradual and usually uneven process, and conditional upon the conscientious search for God's will in everything; nor will every follower of Ignatius experience the world with Ignatius' own strictly mystical perception. Nevertheless, finding God in all things is not in itself an extraordinary gift but a grace linked with the apostolic calling, a possibility offered to the apostle in some degree at every stage of his developing commitment to the life of service. The apostle does not consign his action, with its necessary involvement in the world, to the status of a distraction. Rather, in and through his action, he grows towards the contemplative versatility which makes it possible to 'find God in all things, actions and conversations', to 'enjoy the Lord in many places and duties rather than in one only', so to live that every action is itself a prayer. In his life of action, in his commerce with immediate realities, the apostle comes progressively to live out the vision set before the retreatant at the close of the *Exercises* in which all things are contemplated in the light of the 'above', and the world is seen as a divine milieu where 'in all creatures on the face of the earth God works and labours for me'.

2 Teresa of Jesus and John of the Cross

E. W. TRUEMAN DICKEN

Works and biographies

St Teresa of Jesus, *Obras Completas*, Efrén de la Madre de Dios and Otilio del Niño Jesús, ed., 3 vols. BAC, 1951.

St John of the Cross, *Vida y Obras Completas*, Lucinio del SS Sacramento and Matías del Niño Jesús, ed. BAC, 1955.

St Teresa of Jesus, (ET) *Complete Works*, E. Allison Peers, ed. and trans., 3 vols. London and New York, Sheed & Ward, 1946.

St Teresa of Avila, (ET) *The Interior Castle*, K. Kavanaugh, trans. and introd. CWS 1980.

St John of the Cross, (ET) *Complete Works*, E. Allison Peers, ed. and trans. 3 vols. London, Burns, Oates & Washbourne, 1934–5; Westminster, Md., Newman, 1945.

Peers, E. Allison, *Handbook to the Life and Times of St Teresa and St John of the Cross*. London, Burns, Oates & Washbourne; Westminster, Md., Newman, 1954.

Efrén de la Madre de Dios and Otger Steggink, *Tiempo y Vida de Santa Teresa*. BAC, 1968.

General

Arintero, J. G., (ET) *Stages in (Mental) Prayer*. London, Blackfriars; St Louis, Herder, 1957.

Barrientos, A., ed., *Introducción a la Lectura de Santa Teresa*. Madrid, 1978.

Dicken, E. W. Trueman, *The Crucible of Love*. London, DLT; New York, Sheed & Ward, 1963.

Gabriele di Santa Maria Maddalena, (ET) *St Teresa of Jesus, Mistress of the Spiritual Life*. Cork, Mercier; Westminster, Md., Newman, 1949.

Gicovate, B., *San Juan de la Cruz*. New York, Twayne, 1971 (written in English).

Hatzfeld, H. A., *Santa Teresa de Avila*. New York, Twayne, 1969 (written in English).

Marie-Eugène de l'Enfant-Jésus, (ET) *I Want to See God*. Chicago, Fides, 1953.

Marie-Eugène de l'Enfant-Jésus, (ET) *I Am a Daughter of the Church*. Chicago, Fides, 1955.

Pablo Maroto, D. de, *Dinámica de la Oración*. Madrid, 1973.

Ruiz Salvador, F., *Introducción a San Juan de la Cruz*. BAC, 1968.

Steggink, O., *Experiencia y Realismo en S. Teresa y S. Juan de la Cruz*. Madrid, 1974.

Teresa de Jesús Doctora de la Iglesia (special number of *La Revista de Espiritualidad*). Madrid, 1970.

Frs Thomas and Gabriel ODC, ed., *St Teresa of Avila*. Dublin, Clonmore & Reynolds; Westminster, Md., Newman, 1963.

The Catholic Reformation

Specific topics

Duvivier, R., *La genèse du Cantique Spirituel de St Jean de la Croix*. Paris, 1971.
Eulogio de la Virgen, *El Cántico Espiritual*. Rome, 1967.
Juan de Jesús María, 'Le amará tanto como es amada', in *Ephemerides Carmeliticae*, 6 (1955), pp. 3–103.
Moriones, I., *Ana de Jesús y la Herencia Teresiana*. Rome, 1968.
Rodríguez, I., *Santa Teresa de Jesús y la espiritualidad española*. Madrid, 1972.
Rodríguez, O., (ET) *The Teresian Gospel: an Introduction to a fruitful reading of The Way of Perfection*. Darlington, Carmel, 1974.
Sanson, H., *L'esprit humain selon St Jean de la Croix*. Paris, 1953.

Among internationally acknowledged specialists in the theology of the spiritual life over the past hundred years there has been a clear consensus that in this vital area of study St Teresa of Jesus and St John of the Cross are the pre-eminent authorities of the Western Church.[1] Regrettably, barely a handcount of important contributions to the immense literature concerned with their life and work has emanated from English-speaking scholars, and the cogency and relevance of their achievement for our own day goes almost unrecognized in the Anglo-Saxon world.

The generations after the Renaissance lived, like ourselves, amidst an explosion of knowledge, with all its consequential social, economic and political upheavals and an often intemperate questioning of fundamental moral and religious standards; and it was against this background that the two great Carmelites struggled, as do many of our contemporaries, to restate and re-establish the spiritual values which alone give meaning to life. It was a significant tribute to their current relevance that as recently as 1926 Rome recognized St John of the Cross as a Doctor of the Universal Church, according a like recognition to St Teresa, the first woman ever to receive it, only in 1970. Typically the practical pastor, Pope John Paul II, as a young man chose to write his doctoral thesis on 'Faith according to St John of the Cross'.[2]

Undeniably these are not easy authors to read: they wrote as experts, in their different ways, for readers well versed in the traditions of Christian spirituality.[3] Yet they were not isolated from the affairs of the world. When they could, they withdrew into the cloister, much as scientists must withdraw into their laboratory for the purpose of their research; but

[1] cf. e.g. Andrew Louth, *The Origins of the Christian Mystical Tradition* (OUP, 1981), pp. 18off.
[2] Now published in ET, San Francisco, Ignatius Press, 1981.
[3] *The Ascent of Mount Carmel*, III.ii.1. All references to chapters, paragraphs etc. in the works of Teresa and John of the Cross follow the numberings in the authoritative editions of their *Obras Completas* in the BAC. Numbering in current English translations is not entirely uniform, but differs only rarely from that of the BAC editions.

it was in the face of bitter hardship and continual struggle against almost inconceivable pressures of ecclesiastical and political intrigue that they attained to a height of sanctity seldom paralleled in Christian history. Their dedication, their endurance and their unremitting love are their credentials as guides to Christians in all walks of life.

LIFE AND WORKS

Teresa de Cepeda y Ahumada was born of a wealthy family in Avila, in Old Castile, in 1515, and entered the local Carmelite convent in 1536 at a time when the rule of the Order was far from demanding. In 1562 she founded the first convent of 'discalced' (i.e. unshod) Carmelites under a stricter reformed rule, and added twenty more before her death in 1582.

Juan de Yepes, the future St John of the Cross, came of a very different background. Born in 1542 and brought up in poverty by a widowed mother, he was fortunate to receive his early education from the Jesuits in Medina del Campo, and later to be sent as a calced Carmelite novice to the University of Salamanca. When, in 1568, the Teresan reform was extended to men of the Order, he became one of the first two discalced friars, subsequently holding important offices in the Order but dying in neglect in 1591.

The writings of the two saints are as sharply contrasted as their family backgrounds. A poet of the highest order, John of the Cross is also a consummate theologian, whose prose treatises (*The Ascent of Mount Carmel, The Dark Night, The Spiritual Canticle* and *The Living Flame of Love*) lack nothing of objectivity and scholarly precision, although, like the short collections of his *Counsels* and *Sayings*, they are shot through with a consuming love of God and a deep pastoral concern for his readers. Teresa of Jesus, on the other hand, innocent as she was of any formal theological training, writes always from her own personal experience – which, remarkably, included the friendship of three other subsequently canonized saints[1] as well as a number of eminent theologians. She writes with great charm and verve, but with a disregard for orderliness which often gives rise to serious problems of interpretation. Unfortunately the best known of her works, her autobiography, *The Life*, is also the most puzzling. Her *Way of Perfection* is both simpler and more assimilable, but for her definitive teaching one must refer to *The Mansions of the Interior Castle*.

Nevertheless, one can never fully penetrate the works of either Teresa or John of the Cross in isolation of the one from the other. Teresa was incapable of the precise theological and psychological analyses which came easily to the younger saint, whilst he purposely refrains from re-

[1] St Peter of Alcántara, St Francis Borgia and St John of the Cross.

working topics which she had already covered before he embarked on his own major works.[1]

Certainly there are occasional marked differences of emphasis between the two writers,[2] but detailed comparative study of their works has increasingly underscored the essential compatibility and complementarity of their findings, doubtless the result of their particularly close collaboration in Avila from 1572 to 1577.[3] Together they present us with an overall perspective view of the theology and practice of the spiritual life which, for Christians of the Western Church, constitutes the almost indispensable key to all serious study of the subject in both earlier and later writers.

THE HUMAN BEING AS A UNITY

Fundamental to the whole outlook of the two saints is their understanding that the human being is essentially a unity (*Night*, II.i.1), a single entity in whom body and soul are inextricably interdependent. 'We aren't angels: we've got bodies', writes Teresa, and goes on to warn us of the folly of forgetting this (*Life*, xxii.10). The body does indeed give rise to all kinds of conflicting and disturbing impulses, the 'natural passions' of scholastic psychology; and the inner peace and equilibrium without which one cannot respond freely to the love of God is to be found only by bringing these impulses under control.[4] But the body is also an integral part of the human make-up by which God may be loved and served and glorified.

It is this consideration which underlies an otherwise perhaps surprising feature of the writings of the two Carmelites, namely that there is less specific guidance on methods of prayer than on the Christian way of life in general. We are shown a wide variety of approaches to prayer, and are warned against those which are bound to prove sterile, but our authors firmly decline to formulate any structured methods at all. 'Pray as you can,'[5] advises Teresa, 'for prayer doesn't consist of thinking a great deal, but of loving a great deal' (*Mansions*, IV.i.7), and God can lead to the heights of contemplation one who uses no other words than those of the Lord's Prayer (*Way* T, xxv.1; xxx.7). The one irrefragable rule is that we must 'Never, for any reason whatever, neglect to pray' (*Counsels*, 184, 188, etc.).

---

[1] *The Spiritual Canticle* B (= 2nd recension), xiii.7.

[2] In particular, Teresa was apparently less convinced of the unreliability of visions than was John of the Cross.

[3] E. W. Trueman Dicken, 'The Imagery of the Interior Castle and its Implications', in *Ephemerides Carmeliticae*, 21 (1970), pp. 198ff.

[4] *Ascent*, II.i.4; *Conceptions of the Love of God*, ii–iii etc.

[5] *The Way of Perfection* T (= Toledo version), xxiv.5.

Greater prominence is given to guidance on living the Christian life and to the importance of growth in Christian virtue. Teresa indicates in particular three prerequisites which, she says,

> are necessary for those who aim to follow the way of prayer – so necessary that, even if one isn't much of a contemplative, they will help one forward greatly in the service of the Lord; and it isn't possible to be much of a contemplative without them. Those who think they are, are badly deceived. The first is love for one another; the second is [emotional] detachment from all created things; the third is true humility (*Way* T, iv.3–4).

The quality of one's life and the quality of one's prayer, in short, interact mutually the one on the other. Both must be steadfastly oriented towards God.

The root of the matter, as John of the Cross explains, is that the more one is concerned for the things of this world, the things of the created order, the less capacity one inevitably has for relationship with God. 'Love of God and love of created things are contrary the one to the other', he says, and 'two contraries cannot coexist in one and the same person' (*Ascent*, I. vi.1; cf. I.iv.2). Hence the crucial necessity for detachment from all that is not God if one is to become united to him at the inmost point of one's being (*Living Flame*, i.10–12). Only through voluntary or involuntary privation of those things on which we rely for our comfort, for our self-esteem and for our personal security in this world can we become free of them and capable of unstinted love for God.[1]

In this lies the clue to the interpretation of the much-misunderstood phrase 'the dark night' in the writings of John of the Cross. A passage from M. L. Haskins strikingly illustrates the saint's thought:

> I said to the man who stood at the gate of the year: 'Give me a light that I may tread safely into the unknown.' And he replied: 'Go out into the darkness and put your hand into the hand of God. That shall be to you better than light and safer than a known way.'[2]

One is, in truth, ultimately secure only in the darkness, as John of the Cross so confidently affirms (Poem, 'On a dark night', stanza 2).

The words 'night' and 'darkness' in his works thus come to include 'privation' in all its forms, privation not only of satisfactions which are sinful by their very nature, but of any satisfaction other than that perfect loving relationship with God which, like Teresa, John of the Cross speaks of as *union* with God. In the last analysis all such satisfactions militate against that ultimate satisfaction. Hence the counsel:

[1] *Way* E(= El Escorial version), xxiv.2.
[2] M. L. Haskins, *God Knows*, quoted by King George VI in his Christmas radio broadcast, 1939.

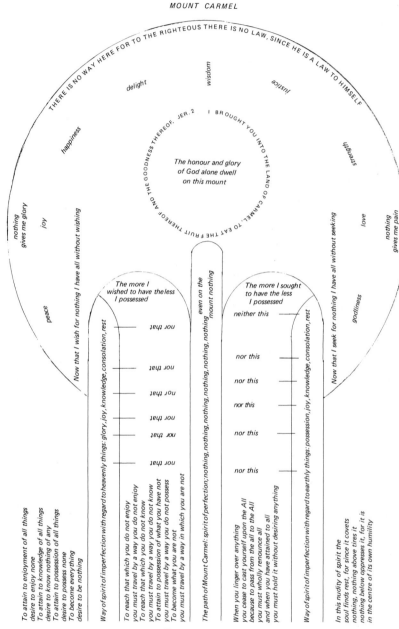

MOUNT CARMEL

THERE IS NO WAY HERE FOR TO THE RIGHTEOUS THERE IS NO LAW, SINCE HE IS A LAW TO HIMSELF

delight

wisdom

justice

happiness

AND THE GOODNESS THEREOF. JER.2   I BROUGHT YOU INTO THE LAND OF CARMEL, TO EAT THE FRUIT THEREOF

The honour and glory
of God alone dwell
on this mount

strength

nothing
gives me glory

joy

love

nothing
gives me pain

peace

godliness

Now that I wish for nothing I have all without wishing

Now that I seek for nothing I have all without seeking

The more I
wished to have the less
I possessed

even on the
mount nothing

The more I sought
to have the less
I possessed

nor that

nor this

neither this

nor that

nor this

nor that

nor this

nor that

nor this

nor that

nor this

To attain to enjoyment of all things
desire to enjoy none
To attain to knowledge of all things
desire to know nothing of any
To attain to possession of all things
desire to possess none
To become everything
desire to be nothing

Way of spirit of imperfection with regard to heavenly things: glory, joy, knowledge, consolation, rest

To reach that which you do not enjoy
you must travel by a way you do not enjoy
To reach that which you do not know
you must travel by a way you do not know
To attain to possession of what you have not
you must travel by a way you do not possess
To become what you are not
you must travel by a way in which you are not

The path of Mount Carmel: spirit of perfection: nothing, nothing, nothing, nothing, nothing, nothing, nothing

When you linger over anything
you cease to cast yourself upon the All
because to pass from the all to the All
you must wholly renounce all
and when you have attained to all
you must hold it without desiring anything

Way of spirit of imperfection with regard to earthly things: possession, joy, knowledge, consolation, rest

In this nudity of spirit the
soul finds rest, for since it covets
nothing, nothing above tires it
nothing below oppresses it, for it is
in the centre of its own humility

For my daughter Magdalen

Reproduction of the original sketch of Mount Carmel by St John of the Cross,
unaltered apart from regularization of the lines and translation of the Spanish and Latin words

368

> In order to attain to the enjoyment of all,
>> wish to enjoy nothing;
> In order to attain to the possession of all things,
>> desire to possess nothing whatever (*Ascent*, I.xiii.11).

The saint's doctrine of '*nada, nada, nada*' (nothing, nothing, nothing)[1] is therefore in no sense a doctrine of *nirvana* or of extinction of human personality. On the contrary, filled out with his wise and sympathetic guidance for safe passage through the nights of privation, it has in view the one totally positive human aim of all, true self-fulfilment in accordance with the all-loving purpose of the creator.

THE NATURE OF MYSTICISM

It has been objected by contemporary critics that the demands made by our authors are severe to the point of irrelevance for twentieth-century people, who find such austerity alien and unacceptable. In fact the teaching of the great Carmelites is at all points rock-rooted in holy writ, and a comfortable determination to water down the wine of the gospel is as common, and no less enervating, today as in the sixteenth or the first century of the Christian era.

Admittedly we are offered no easy road; but the saying of John of the Cross, that 'One who does not seek the cross of Christ isn't seeking the glory of Christ' (*Sayings*, 99), does but echo the dominical warning that, 'No one can be my disciple who does not take up his own cross and follow after me' (Luke 14.27). John of the Cross does not conceal the fact that, for those who single-mindedly embrace their Christian calling,

> the darkness and the trials, both spiritual and temporal, through which these blessed souls normally pass in order to arrive at this exalted state of perfection [of union with God] are so great and profound that human comprehension cannot grasp them nor experience relate them; only the person who passes through them will feel them, and even such a one will not be able to tell of them (*Ascent*, prol. 1).

Yet, 'the blessing and the glory to which they lead, and the delicate love of God for the soul, are such that I do not even wish to speak of them, for I see very plainly that I cannot possibly do so, and should mislead if I tried' (*Living Flame*, iv.17).

At the same time, and again entirely in line with scriptural doctrine, the two Spanish mystics agree that the self-renunciation required of those who follow Christ cannot be asked of babes in Christ (cf. 1 Cor. 3.2), beginners in the spiritual life. The indispensable fortitude and faith are built up only over years, and the constant concern of our authors is to

---

[1] See his sketch of the 'Mount of Perfection' (Plate 10).

lead the Christian safely through an apprenticeship in these virtues.

It must be emphasized, however, that the way set before us by Teresa and John of the Cross entails no esoteric or arcane lore, nor do they countenance any immoderate or extravagant asceticism. The application to their doctrine of that currently ill-defined and much abused word 'mysticism' has been a fertile source of misunderstanding.[1] Both saints themselves experienced, and have much to say about, the para-mystical phenomena frequently associated with exceptionally holy people – the trances, raptures, visions and clairvoyance well attested in the lives of many Christian saints. Nevertheless, the vast majority of such occurrences, especially the more dramatic among them, are by no means reliable indications of the sanctity of those who experience them (*Ascent*, II.xxii.19). They are paralleled in the lives of both charlatans and hypocrites, and even in the truly saintly Christian they are usually to be attributed, according to John of the Cross, to residual spiritual weakness rather than to saintliness (*Night*, II.i.2).

Similarly the daunting asceticism practised by many earlier Christians in the pursuit of self-discipline meets with unambiguous disapproval from the two Carmelites. It is not privation as such which liberates, but the willingness for God's sake to endure privation (*Ascent*, I.iii.4) so that one may overcome one's stultifying incapacity to resist self-indulgence.

The essence of mysticism, then, lies neither in ascetic practices nor in supernatural or preternatural manifestations, but in a union with God which, as Teresa writes, consists in

> making my will one with the will of God. This is the union which I myself desire and should like to see in everyone, and not just a few of those raptures, however delightful, which go by the name of union (*Foundations*, v.13).

Evidently the process of Christian maturation which may lead to this union is not the work of a few days (*Night*, II.i.1), and although, in Teresa's characteristically energetic phrase, it calls for 'very determined determination' (*Way* T, xxi.2) on our part, it cannot be brought about through either spiritual ambition or self-domination, but only by an unselfregarding response to the love of God. We have to come to share something of the overwhelming consciousness of God's infinite providence and love which permeates the whole outlook of all the great Christian spiritual masters. God orders all circumstances for our good, and through them guides us, as John of the Cross says, much as a mother brings up a child (*Ascent*, II.xvii.2–3). The tiny infant must be cosseted, suckled and carried everywhere, but as it begins to grow it must be

---

[1] See, e.g., Louis Bouyer's criticism of F. Heiler and A. Nygren in his (ET) *Introduction to Spirituality* (London, DLT; New York, Desclee, 1961), pp. 288ff.

weaned from the cosy breast to take solid food, and put down to walk on its own feet.[1]

Like the infant, Christians often clamour to walk when they are, in a manner of speaking, being carried by God, and to be carried when they are made to walk. We are poor judges both of our needs and of our own strength; and it is the implicit purpose of all spiritual writing from the New Testament onwards to help us to 'read off' the divine purpose in the actual situations in which God places us. More particularly, as John of the Cross reminds us, since 'it is well known that in the spiritual life not to make gains is to lose what one has' (*Ascent*, I.xi.5), Christians need experienced guidance especially at those times when they are gaining ground and mistakenly fear that they are losing it, or are losing ground and remain convinced that they are gaining.

THE DARK NIGHT OF THE SOUL

Properly speaking, the 'dark night of the soul' in John of the Cross is a generic term denoting the whole discipline of privation which starts from the very beginning of the spiritual life, when the Christian first becomes seriously committed, and continues throughout his or her life. It has two distinguishable aspects: the active night of voluntary self-discipline, and the passive night into which God himself leads the Christian, whether directly or through external circumstances. Each of these aspects itself has two phases, one in which it affects the senses (including the 'interior sense' or imagination) and a second in which it affects the spirit with its three 'faculties' of understanding, memory and will. The Christian enters these nights as his or her spiritual stamina allows, but they are not strictly successive in so far as they overlap and interlock, and the most rudimentary of disciplines can never be neglected even at the highest level of sanctity. 'No one is ever such a giant in this matter as not to need often to return like an infant to the breast', observes Teresa (*Life*, xiii.15).

It is a truism that the initiative in human affairs lies always with God, and the first conscious response of the newly awakened Christian commonly takes the form of a joyous though immature fervour for the service of God in the faith that all things are possible to one who loves God (*Night*, I.i.2–3). It is a shallow-rooted conviction which will hardly persist (*Night*, I.i.3ff; *Mansions*, I.ii.14) unless one voluntarily renounces self-indulgences one has previously taken for granted, so entering the 'active night of the senses' characteristic of the purgative way. This is not merely a question of avoiding deliberate sin, but of learning detachment from worldly satisfactions and, still more, from what John of the Cross calls 'spiritual vices' (*Night*, I.i–viii): self-regarding desire for the ex-

[1] *Night*, I.i.2; cf. *Ascent*, II.xvii.6; *Way* T, xxxi.9, etc.

ternals of worship and for those consolations of religion which feed the human ego. There must also be a serious effort to pray, accompanied by continual reflection on the truths of the Christian faith, without which love for God would be lacking in substance and, indeed, illusory.

Yet such reflections can never achieve more than an understanding of God 'by analogy'.[1] The divine nature is in essence infinite and un-knowable, definable only in negative terms; and it is this which accounts for what John of the Cross speaks of as the 'passive night of the senses'. It arises when Christians who have faithfully persevered in the purgative way for many years find that the way of prayer to which they have been accustomed is no longer possible for them, when, as John of the Cross puts it, 'the soul has, in a manner, received all the spiritual benefit which it was to find in the things of God by way of meditation' and when, without further mental effort in prayer, it is given by God the prayer of passive contemplation (*Ascent*, II.xiv.1–2).

God is now communicating himself directly to the Christian without the medium of intelligible or imaginable thought, as John of the Cross explains; but the sheer glory of God's self-communication is such that it fogs the understanding just as brilliant sunlight blinds the eyes. Passive contemplation, in the evocative phrase borrowed by John of the Cross from Pseudo-Dionysius, is a 'ray of darkness' (*Ascent*, II.viii.6). The knowledge of God which the Christian thought he possessed has deserted him, and has been replaced by a 'knowledge' which is not knowledge in any sense which can be verbalized or even imagined. Such a Christian is entering the illuminative way, and now, as John of the Cross says, 'must grow in knowledge of God by learning what he is not rather than what he is, and in order to come to him must reject all that can be rejected of what he can grasp, whether natural or supernatural' (*Ascent*, III.ii.3).

What must be stressed is that the passive contemplation characteristic of this 'night' has nothing in common, except at the most superficial level, with the kinds of prayer most commonly spoken of as 'contemplation' at the present day. John of the Cross is speaking neither of the contemplation achieved by the techniques of Yoga, Zen or Transcendental Meditation, nor of the very different type of contemplation envisaged, for example, in the *Spiritual Exercises* of St Ignatius Loyola (see pp. 361–2).

The distinction here is crucial. Entry into the passive night of the senses necessitates a radical change in the Christian's mode of prayer (*Ascent*, II.xiii.1), a change which would be meaningless to those who experience contemplation as defined in oriental religions, even in chris-

---

[1] cf. Aquinas, *Summa Theologiae*, I q. 13, art. 5, etc.

tianized forms, and damaging to those who know of contemplation only in the popular sense of the term.

The distinctive characteristics of the early stages of passive contemplation are both bewildering and distressing to the Christian to whom God grants this prayer. One is possessed by a powerful love of God and an urgent desire for him, yet one's prayers seem utterly sterile and the world around devoid of all attraction.[1] So far from bringing any immediate illumination, still less any elation, passive contemplation at first leaves the recipient confused and frustrated, and it will hardly be recognized for what it is without the guidance of someone who has passed that way himself.[2] There is a very real danger that the Christian in this situation may in all good faith resist the prayer he is being given in a vain attempt to return to the way of prayer he has now lost (*Flame*, iii.33).

For Christians who now humbly place themselves unconditionally in the hands of God, however, this phase of their spiritual growth may be the prelude to unlimited progress – a progress at times almost unbearably · glorious, at times overwhelmingly painful, whose alternations are traced in detail by Teresa and John of the Cross up to those heights of sanctity to which they themselves were raised.

A point established beyond doubt, however, in the writings of all the great spiritual masters, is that this passive contemplation can neither be self-induced nor acquired by any kind of technique or discipline, or indeed by any effort which the Christian can make. It is actually fairly rare; and although it comes only to those who have over a period of many years lived and prayed with more than usual dedication (*Mansions*, IV.i.2; ii.9), it is an uncovenanted gift which, as Teresa asserts, 'God gives when he will, as he will, and to whom he will' (*Mansions*, IV.i.2). Equally, as John of the Cross observes, the fact that a Christian has entered the passive night of the senses gives no guarantee that he or she will advance further. Most, he says, do not (*Night*, I.ix.9).

THE ILLUMINATIVE AND UNITIVE WAYS

As such Christians begin to acclimatize to their new and bewildering experience of God, so they find themselves receiving the 'prayer of quiet', an effortless prayer of immense delight and serenity described at length in the fourth of Teresa's spiritual mansions (*Mansions*, IV.ii.2). It is, in her vivid analogy, as if the ornamental basin in a Moorish garden is now being filled by God himself, no longer by leading water through a pipe but rather, as it were, by the spring itself welling up directly into the bowl (*Mansions*, IV.ii.4).

[1] *Ascent*, II.xiii; *Night*, I.ix; *Flame*, iii.32.
[2] *Flame*, iii.43; cf. *Way* T, xxx.7; *Relations*, V.14, etc.

Although this prayer is characteristic of the illuminative way, it is by no means a continuous feature of it. It is a manifestation of God's love inviting the Christian to enter what John of the Cross designates the 'active night of the spirit'. This is not to say that the disciplines of the active night of the senses may now be disregarded, or that meditation on the truths of the faith becomes superfluous, since 'that which previously the soul was acquiring gradually by reflection on particular truths has now through usage become habit, and is essentially a generalized loving knowledge.'[1] Yet just as the active night of the senses aims at detachment from things perceptible to the senses, so the active night of the spirit has as its goal detachment from all that is apprehended by the understanding, the memory and the will. Those who depend upon human understanding cannot know the unknowable God who makes himself known to faith alone; those who cling to the memory of what has been known in the past cannot have perfect hope in God for the future;[2] those whose will is directed to anything that is not God necessarily fall short of perfect love for him.

As the Christian progresses through the illuminative way, from time to time he or she begins to experience touches of the passive night of the spirit (*Night*, II.i.1), by which God effects supremely what human effort cannot achieve for itself, until with the onset of this night in its full force the Christian is lifted into the unitive way. As in the case of the earlier passive night which led into the illuminative way, the immediate experience of the passive night of the spirit is one of unspeakable distress (*Night*, II.v.4ff). There comes a sense of appalling dereliction (*Night*, II.vi.2–4), said by John of the Cross to be inexpressibly more painful than the severity of the passive night of the senses (*Night*, I.viii.2), which only gradually gives way to a second period of the prayer of quiet (*Night*, II.xxiv.2–3) and to that state of conformity to the will of God which is traditionally spoken of as 'perfect' holiness (*Night*, prol.). Necessarily this perfection is never more than a human and therefore comparative perfection,[3] and there is no inconsistency in the observation that it becomes both more stable and more continuous (*Mansions*, VII.ii.3–4) in the state known to Teresa and John of the Cross as the 'spiritual betrothal',[4] finally to be consummated in the indescribable bliss of the

---

[1] *Ascent*, II.xiv.2. The importance of this point is axiomatic for Orthodox spiritual theology: apophatic theology is possible only if there is an infra-structure of cataphatic theology. See p.188.

[2] cf. Romans 8.24: 'Hope that is seen is not hope'.

[3] Perfection, that is to say, is not an absolute category. The 'very perfect knight' is no more than a knight, and is perfect only *as* a knight; cf. *Ascent*, II.v.11.

[4] *Mansions*, V.iv.2; VI.i.2; *Canticle* A (= 1st recension), xxvii.3.

'spiritual marriage'.[1] In this state, says John of the Cross, the soul is so strengthened and purified by God that it can love him with the self-same love with which he loves it (*Canticle* B, xxxviii.2–3); but of the unitive way as a whole, only the saints themselves can speak with authority.

A PATTERN OF INFINITE VARIETY

The outlines of this 'normal' pattern of Christian spiritual growth, from the lowest to the highest reaches, had already been established well over a thousand years before the sixteenth-century Carmelites began their work, but it was their crowning theological achievement to have filled in systematically the salient detail over the whole area of spiritual progress. Ironically, the very precision of their findings has caused them to be called in question by recent writers on spirituality, on the grounds that they impose a straitjacket on a sphere of human life where essentially the spirit blows where it will.

The objection rests upon a serious misconception. Nothing could be further from the mind of the two saints than to lay down a rigid programme of exercises which must be followed. They simply describe the observable (though not easily observed) course of healthy spiritual development, and on that basis offer incomparably wise counsel to help the Christian to overcome both the perplexities which are inevitable and the adventitious problems which may or may not arise in individual cases. In the course of biological life a child is born, attains to puberty and adolescence and reaches a physical prime before reaching the height of its intellectual and critical powers; and although within this pattern infinite variation is possible, healthy development follows a predictable sequence.[2] Hence the hormonal imbalances of puberty will seldom be thought to require medical intervention, whereas an attack of diphtheria invariably must.

By the same token, those who are responsible for guiding and advising their fellow Christians in the spiritual life must be able to distinguish what is predictable and beneficial from supervening disturbances which are deleterious. The criteria are far from self-evident, and a sure grasp of the course of spiritual maturation described by Teresa and John of the Cross, allowing as it does for the fact that God leads Christians to himself

---

[1] *Mansions*, VII.ii.1; *Canticle* A, xxvii.2. The 'three ways' are represented by Teresa's 'mansions' as follows:

Purgative way: Mansions I–III
Illuminative way: Mansions IV
Unitive way: Mansions V (union), VI (spiritual betrothal) and VII (spiritual marriage).

[2] Teresa points out that in the spiritual life, unlike biological life, it is possible to fall back (*Life*, xv.12).

by an infinite variety of paths,[1] is an indispensable tool for the physician of souls, i.e. the spiritual director or 'soul friend'. To suggest, as some recent writers have done,[2] that modern people may well find it suitable to pray contemplatively from the first, and only much later to move on to the self-discipline and mental effort appropriate to the purgative way, is gravely to misunderstand the entire situation.

It is often overlooked that the findings of the great Carmelites, so far from being speculative and doctrinaire, are essentially based on empirical data. They observed with perspicacity amounting to genius the spiritual development of a great number of Christians of the most diverse kinds and of every degree of holiness and waywardness. They collated their observations, formulated hypotheses and tested their hypotheses by further observation. Only then did they find it possible to link them to the theological structures explored over the centuries by the great saints and theologians of the past. Teresa was the pioneer, whose findings reached definitive form only towards the end of her life; and it is only in the works of John of the Cross, almost entirely written after Teresa's death, that the theological implications of the empirical data are fully worked out.

Yet to say this is to indicate no more than the bare bones of the incalculable contribution made by the two saints to the theology and practice of Christian spirituality, and to touch but the fringe of the possibilities which they have to show us of the intimacy of relationship between the Christian and the triune God, Father, Son and Holy Spirit. Their deepest conviction is that God himself is the one ultimate teacher of prayer (*Flame*, iii.46), who will most certainly provide all that is needful to those who humbly, patiently and generously place themselves unconditionally in his hands. As Teresa says, we cannot safely dispense with human assistance in this vitally important matter, and, given the choice, we should seek the guidance of a learned director (*Way*, T, v.2); but, significantly, it is the academic theologian, John of the Cross, who reminds us that no one will be saved by intellectual prowess (*Ascent*, I.iv.5), for 'at the end of the day, the subject of examination will be love'. (*Sayings*, 57).

---

[1] *Conceptions*, ii.5; *Way* T, xxiv.2; *Flame* B, iii.59.
[2] cf. J. B. Coburn, 'The New Mood in Spirituality', in *Spirituality for Today*, ed. Eric James (London, SCM, 1968).

3 Other Spanish Spiritual Writers

E. W. TRUEMAN DICKEN

General

Márquez, A., *Los Alumbrados*. Madrid, Taurus, 1972.
Peers, E. Allison, *Studies of the Spanish Mystics*. 3 vols. London, SPCK; New York, Macmillan, 1951–1960.

Selected Texts

Cisneros, García J. de, *Obras Completas*. Montserrat, Abadía, 1965.
Laredo, Bernardino de, *The Ascent of Mount Sion*, ET and ed. E. Allison Peers. London, Faber, 1952.
León, Luis de, (ET) *The Names of Christ*. CWS 1984.
Osuna, Francisco de, (ET) *The Third Spiritual Alphabet*. London, Burns Oates & Washbourne; New York, Benziger, 1931.

Ramón Lull apart (see p. 307), medieval Spain produced no outstanding spiritual writing. Then, in that same dramatic upsurge which brought the Spain of Ferdinand and Isabella into the top rank of European powers politically, commercially and culturally, there came an access of spiritual vigour in which, in the course of the sixteenth century, her spiritual theologians achieved almost unparalleled pre-eminence.

First, the *Devotio Moderna* (see p. 324) found a brilliant autumn flowering in the *Ejercitatorio de la Vida Espiritual* of García de Cisneros, published in 1500 and destined to become a primary source for the *Spiritual Exercises* of Ignatius Loyola. Then, as Charles V drew Spain into ever closer contact with the Netherlands, her scholarly friars seized avidly upon the newly published Latin (and in some cases Spanish) editions of the works of the Rhineland mystics, notably those of Eckhart, Tauler, Ruysbroeck, Herp (Harphius) and the *Divine Institutions* mistakenly attributed to Tauler (see pp. 319–20). Francisco de Osuna and Bernardino de Laredo especially laid these Rhenish sources under contribution; and in her turn Teresa was indebted to Osuna's *Spiritual Alphabets*, and was stimulated by Laredo's *Ascent of Mount Sion* to investigate for herself the course of spiritual progress.

By the middle of the sixteenth century Spanish spiritual guides had already a rich tradition of their own on which to draw, and such authorities as St Peter of Alcántara, Luis de Granada, St Francis Borgia, Luis de León and Baltasar Alvarez became widely known outside the peninsula. The profound influence of Spanish spirituality in the following century nevertheless owed even more to personal contacts than to written works. The Jesuits carried the teaching of their founder far and wide, whilst

Carmelite spirituality was disseminated outside Spain primarily through one remarkable woman, Ana de Jesús. A close friend of both Teresa and John of the Cross, as prioress of the discalced convent in Brussels and foundress of houses in Paris and Dijon she became friend and mentor of both Mme Acarie and St Jeanne de Chantal (see pp. 387 and 382), who similarly diffused her understanding of the spiritual life to ever widening circles.

The one early development in Spanish spirituality which apparently owed little or nothing to foreign sources was the rise of the *Alumbrados* (Illuminists), a lay movement originating in the first quarter of the sixteenth century, teaching an anti-sacramental, anti-intellectual, quietistic form of spirituality. Given theological expression by Juan de Valdés, the movement was publicly condemned in 1529, but persisted and in due course spread into Italy, France and beyond. Its most momentous consequence was that it aroused in the Inquisitorial mind, through its apparent affinity with Protestantism, so deep a mistrust of all contemporary spirituality that almost every spiritual writer from the middle of the century onwards sooner or later came under suspicion of bearing the illuminist taint. Illuminism nevertheless survived, and attained its widest influence and fullest development in the Quietism of Miguel de Molinos (1640–97) and his contemporary French disciples Mme Guyon and F. Lacombe and their fellow-traveller Archbishop Fénelon (see pp. 408–15).

II FRANCE

1 François de Sales

ELISABETH STOPP

Works

Oeuvres de Saint François de Sales, 27 vols. Annecy, 1892–1932 and 1964.
Saint François de Sales: Oeuvres, André Ravier and Roger Devos, ed. Paris,
1969. Contains authoritative texts of the three main works and a full
bibliography.
(ET) *Introduction to the Devout Life*. London, Burns & Oates; Westminster,
Md., Newman, 1956.
(ET) *On the Love of God*. London, Burns & Oates, 1962; New York, Doubleday
(Image Books), 1963.
(ET) *Spiritual Conferences of St Francis de Sales*. London, Burns & Oates; New
York, Benziger, 1906; Westminster, Md., Newman, 1943 (Library of St Fran-
cis de Sales, vol. 5).
(ET) *St Francis de Sales, Selected Letters*, Elisabeth Stopp, trans. and introd.
London, Faber; New York, Harper, 1960.
Ste Jeanne-Françoise Frémyot de Chantal: sa Vie et ses Oeuvres, 8 vols. Paris,
1874–9. (The correspondence is now being re-edited at the Annecy
Visitation.)
(ET) *St Francis de Sales: A Testimony by St Chantal*, Elisabeth Stopp, trans.,
ed., and introd. London, Faber, 1967; Hyattsville, Md., Institute of Salesian
Studies, 1967.

General

Bedoyère, M. de la, *François de Sales*. London, Collins; New York, Harper,
1960.
Camus, J. P., (ET) *The Spirit of St François de Sales*, C. F. Kelley, ed. and trans.
New York, Harper, 1952; London, Longman Green, 1953.
Charmot, F., (ET) *Ignatius Loyola and François de Sales: Two Masters, One
Spirituality*. St Louis, Herder, 1966.
Kelley, C. F., *The Spirit of Love*. New York, Harper; London, Longman Green,
1951.
Lajeunie, E., *Saint François de Sales: l'Homme, la Pensée, l'Action*, 2 vols. Paris,
1962.
Liuima, A., *Aux Sources du traité de l'Amour de Dieu de S. François de Sales*. 2
vols. Rome, 1959–60.
Sérouet, P., *De la Vie dévote à la Vie mystique: de Ste Thérèse d'Avila à S
François de Sales*. Paris, 1958 (see full bibliography).
Stopp, E., *Madame de Chantal, Portrait of a Saint*. London, Faber, 1962;
Westminster, Md., Newman, 1963.

François de Sales (1567–1622), Prince Bishop of Geneva in exile at Annecy, was the author of an immensely popular, much translated handbook of ascetical spirituality, *The Introduction to the Devout Life*, which, together with the mystical *Treatise on the Love of God* (1616), his posthumously published letters and his talks, the *Conferences* (1629), represents the main body of his written work. He was also an influential preacher in his time: 'We should speak candidly and trustfully,' he said,

> really be in love with the doctrine we're trying to teach and get people to accept; the great art is to be art-less. The kindling power of our words must not come from outward show but from within, not from oratory but straight from the heart. Try as hard as you like, but in the end only the language of the heart can ever reach another heart while mere words, as they slip from your tongue, don't get past your listener's ear.

John Henry Newman quoted from this letter in his *Idea of a University* (1852) and later took from it his motto, *Cor ad cor loquitur*.

François' great impact was as a person and as a writer of personal letters of direction; his whole spirituality is indissolubly linked, not so much with a body of argued doctrine, as with the wholly individual manner and method of his direction and his writing. While his rather more official emblem as a saint is a quill pen – he is shown seated at a desk, writing and looking heavenward for inspiration – the more popular imagery of his mountain homeland shows him holding out a heart on fire with love for God and for his neighbour. In an essentially personal synthesis, he combined holiness with shrewd psychological insight and the capacity to impart spiritual teaching creatively: he was declared a Doctor of the Church in 1877, and this set the official seal on his outstanding influence as someone able to teach. He explained 'devotion', that is, real holiness, not as something reserved for a spiritual élite, but as attainable by all who were willing to put their heart and mind to it. He wrote and spoke, said St Jeanne de Chantal, the most important and articulate witness to his special kind of sanctity,

> in such a way as to be understood by the unlearned and yet not despised by the learned. He used such precise and easily understood terms that he made people grasp very readily the most delicate and subtle truths of the spiritual life (*Testimony*).

He himself said in the preface to the *Introduction*,

> I want to teach people who live in crowded cities within their families, in the middle of domestic cares at home or in the press of public affairs in their professional life . . . It's a mistake, even a heresy, to want to banish the devout life from the soldier's camp, the manual worker's workshop, the court of princes, the homes of married people.

Though the emphasis was new, the message itself was a return to the Gospels: a call to universal holiness.

By his education in France and in Italy, François was a humanist and he succeeded in humanizing the idea of absolute Christian commitment. He was the saint of 'devout' humanism as distinct from that other and more worldly form of it in the earlier Renaissance which glorified human nature. For François, humankind was glorious in spite of its fallen nature, Christ having undertaken its redemption. François knew as much about the gloom of original sin as did Calvin, or the Jansenists later on, but after a severe crisis of despair on the subject during his student days in Paris (1583) he elected to concentrate on the *felix culpa* aspect of sin and predestination, and so to help people to live by the joyful and consoling truths of the Christian revelation. This is the side of his teaching which has been most emphasized, the serene confidence, the general *douceur* (untranslatable!) of his approach. Too often, later generations have seen only this flowery, gentle path to holiness along which he directed souls; people have not really understood the steely determination beneath the sweetness, the uncompromising sternness of his own self-sacrifice and his insistence on unconditional surrender to God for those he directed to sanctity.

As the eldest son in a family of the Savoyard nobility that had managed to remain Catholic in a region by then largely Calvinist, François was educated at the Jesuit college of Clermont (later Lycée Louis-le-Grand) in Paris, and then at the University of Padua, where he took doctorates in law, to please his father, and in theology, to follow his own bent. Against considerable family opposition, he was ordained, and after a hard but in the end successful mission in the Calvinist territory south of Lake Geneva, he became coadjutor to his ageing bishop and then in 1602 himself Bishop of Geneva with his residence in nearby Annecy. The rest of his life was devoted to the complex pastoral and administrative affairs of his divided mountain diocese, to his apostolic work as a preacher and director in Paris and other great cities in France, to his writing work and spiritual correspondence, both of which arose directly out of his contacts while preaching, as did, too, his own contemplative religious foundation in Annecy in 1610, the Visitation of Holy Mary. He died twelve years later at the age of 55.

François' life and all his varied apostolic work formed an unbroken unity. He gave himself completely to the work of converting souls in the spirit of the reforms within his own Church as laid down by the Council of Trent. He lived under Jesuit direction from his school days onwards, he made the Spiritual Exercises annually at a private retreat and he took as his apostolic model the life and work of St Charles Borromeo, the

Counter-Reformation bishop saint of his own era. Like Teresa of Avila, whose example as a founder and mystic was of much significance to François, he completely assimilated influences of this kind and integrated them into his own life and spirituality. His paramount aim was to restore unity of faith in his diocese and beyond; for him, this meant the Catholic faith, and he therefore devoted his entire effort as a pastor and director to the spiritual formation and reformation of his flock – laity, religious and priests. The order of the Visitation of Holy Mary which he founded together with Madame de Chantal (1572–1641) played an important and successful part in his pastoral programme, providing a pattern of the contemplative life lived without undue austerity but with exacting demands on the simple, hidden virtues.

François' writings, like his life, form a close-knit unity in themselves and in relation to his apostolate. His three main works, together with the letters as a background, should not be seen as representing successive stages or simply as the evolution of his own thought but as the varied facets of a central and unified spiritual doctrine. This may be described as mysticism in action, explained in accordance with the varying needs of those he directed as the love of God increased and developed in their souls. He was no theoretical theologian but one whose sound and expert theology was addressed in dialogue form, or colloquy, to known and loved people and also to his own soul in practical application. His main works have closely interrelated points of view, one being incomplete without the other. Chronologically, too, his books overlap. The *Treatise on the Love of God*, not published till 1616, was planned and well begun before the *Introduction to the Devout Life* of 1609; this, in turn, was based on earlier letters, then carefully revised, restructured and enlarged for a second edition in 1619. The *Conferences* began with the Visitation in 1610 and went on until virtually the last day of his life. He did not himself write down these talks, which were his informal answers to questions put to him by the sisters, some of whom took notes which were then collated and are characterized by what appears to have been astonishing faithfulness to his actual words and speech rhythms.

His teaching – one hesitates to use the more formal word 'doctrine' – was simple and yet totally comprehensive: holiness, that is, 'devotion', is for all; love holds absolute primacy and is the way; Jesus Christ, meek and humble of heart, is the model and the way. All that François ever wrote, however carefully structured, and however complex it may at times seem, as in the *Treatise*, can without undue simplification be reduced to this basic programme of spirituality.

In the *Introduction*, Philothea, the soul that longs to love God, is told what 'devotion' is: 'the spiritual alertness which makes us respond wholeheartedly and promptly to what love asks of us', that is, you don't only *do* the right and so often hard thing, but you jump to it. Philothea is then shown how to make a willed choice for devotion, how to make a beginning and then confirm her decision to belong completely to God. To this end, she is taught how to meditate on our Lord's life and death, how to pray, how best to respond to God's grace in the sacraments. The third and fourth sections of the work are primarily psychological in their analysis of virtues to be aimed at and pitfalls to be avoided in everyday living. As a psychologist, François first of all defines and explains right and wrong attitudes while bracing the will to salutary effort. He wants to help people to accept themselves and their circumstances and so make them independent of both, that is, abandoned to God's providence and his will. 'What's the use of building castles in Spain', he said, 'when we've clearly got to go on living in this house here in France?' In a final section, Philothea is helped to renew her resolutions in an annual retreat and review. All is clear, orderly and put across in the most heartening way. Important points are reinforced by parallels and images drawn from nature, from family life, but also with deliberate naivety from the medieval world of bestiary and fable. This rather luxuriant imagery, which may prove a stumbling-block in an age when such parallels are less familiar, was in its time an important aid to understanding, making abstract concepts plain and memorable.

The *Treatise* was originally also addressed to Philothea but in the end François decided that this colloquy was to be with Theotimus, a man in love with God, and who had also read and lived the *Introduction*. As the title implies, this treatise is a systematic and, in fact, Thomistically based inquiry into the way the love of God arises, grows and develops in the soul, what practical effects this growing love has on prayer, on human relationships, on day-to-day living. In spite of its length and complexity, it has the same firmness and clarity of logical structure as the *Introduction* to draw it together. The four opening Books show the origins of the mystical life of the soul's love of God and the laws that govern it; the central section (Books 5–9) describes the state of union towards which love tends, the nature of mystical prayer; the final part (Books 10–12), as is reasonable while the soul is still on earth, goes right back to the beginning, to the simple practice of humble virtues from which no ecstasy can dispense the lover. François sees the love of God as 'ec-stasy' in the primary Greek sense of the word, not as visions in a remote cloister, but simply as standing outside self. The measure in which you lose yourself in the love of your neighbour, that is, of Christ our Lord, in your neighbour, is the measure in which you will find God. Jesus in his life and death is the pattern of the soul standing outside self and lost in God. The style of the

Treatise to some extent reflects the more intensive nature of the subject-matter: discursive argument is more frequent, the imagery less exuberant but giving place to parables of great beauty to make plain and readily understandable what lies beyond the conscious realm. 'God had flooded the centre of his soul with such brilliant light', said Jeanne de Chantal in a letter of 1623, 'that he had the power to survey the truths of faith at a single glance and also to explain them.'

The absolute love of François' 'ecstasy' is a free gift of grace but it also demands a continuous response of the will on the part of the soul. Though a number of the *Conferences* are of rather more domestic Visitan-dine interest, these talks are a kind of *vade-mecum* for the everyday life of the contemplative, for attitudes, choices or special contingencies facing the emotions and the will. François' most illuminating achievement as a director and teacher is perhaps precisely this: to have made a clear and convincing distinction between the role of the feelings and that of the will in our love of God and of our neighbour, to have taught people how to distinguish between God and their awareness (or non-awareness) of him. On the one hand, there is the basic set of the will towards God, on the other, the surface sensation of revolt, doubt, misery, fear, all like hungry dogs barking outside in the dark while the house – and you're inside it – is safely locked. The soul, he says, is like this house, or like a temple; we know what's going on outside and in various other rooms but we must identify ourselves only with 'the inner sanctuary where we are alone with God and nothing else may enter in'. This, as Jeanne de Chantal says, 'was his retreat and his usual dwelling-place. He kept his spirit within this inner solitude, living in the topmost point of the spirit, without depend-ing on any feelings or on any light save that of a bare and simple faith.'

Characteristically, François did not use the term the 'ground' of the soul for this familiar mystical concept, but 'la cime', the mountain-top. The utmost summit of a mountain is a vanishing point, as it were linking earth and heaven; it is a no-place which is yet a place, where we find ourselves at the same time most deeply within the real self and yet most completely outside it because our abode is in God and we dwell in him alone. We can only reach this dwelling place by a movement of love towards the 'summit' where self ends and God begins, for our love comes from him and must return, unselfed, to him. Then we learn to live, as François did, in this sphere of unchanging reality, the point of unknow-ing known only to faith, where prayer is unceasing but wordless.

Insight into this distinction between the feelings and the will, and the determination to live by it, release positive energies for Christian action in a spirit of faith; it uncovers an unfailing well-spring of serenity of the kind that François himself radiated in his lifetime and can still convey now in his writings. It is the characteristic mark of his particular form of spirituality and of his sanctity. His teaching releases and expands psychological possibilities. We can make an effective reality of this inner sanctuary, of the 'fine point of the soul', first of all by becoming fully aware that such a place actually exists, by recognising and accepting it, as François teaches, as a true experience. It will then become, increasingly, the secret place where we 'spin our thread of prayer', to use another of his images, the place of encounter with God, our own true place in the world we live in.

The *Introduction*, a best-seller in its author's life-time, has continued to exert influence as a classic of French spirituality. Sound theology, presented with conversational ease and seeming casualness, is François' particular contribution to French spiritual writing and has had particular appeal among Catholics and Anglicans alike in English-speaking countries. James I, Thomas Ken and Jeremy Taylor were readers of the *Introduction*; Richard Challoner gave it a new translation at the end of the eighteenth century, and Nicholas Grou, the Jesuit chaplain to an English recusant family at the time of the French Revolution, based his *Manual of the Interior Life* on the teaching and approach of François de Sales. This also applies to a large extent to Jean-Pierre de Caussade's *Abandonment to Divine Providence*. (The whole subject of François de Sales' influence, particularly on Anglicans, has been analysed by the present writer in 'Healing Differences', *Salesian Studies*, Hyattsville, 1966, and also in *The Month* (58, 1–2), 1967.)

The new edition of the writings of Jeanne de Chantal now in progress at Annecy will serve to make her more fully understood as the great mystic she was, perfectly exemplifying the road to sanctity along which François directed her. Her life and her spiritual development are his doctrine in action and essentially complete it. She has also contributed directly to our knowledge of his spirituality by the *Testimony* she gave on him for the first canonization process at Annecy in 1628.

In conclusion it may be said that it is the mystical rather than the ascetical aspect of François de Sales' spirituality that now tends to be the focal centre of interest. This is part of a general climate of opinion after Vatican II, but it applies also to scholarly writing on the saint, for instance the work of Pierre Sérouet and Antanas Liuima (see pp. 379, 525).

2 Bérulle and the 'French School'

JOHN SAWARD

Works of Bérulle

Bourgoing, P., ed. and preface, *Oeuvres*, 1644, and 1657.
Migne, J. P., ed., *Oeuvres*. Paris, 1856 and 1960.
Harang, J., ed., *La spiritualité bérullienne*. Chambray-lès-Tours, 1983.
Rotureau, P. Gaston, ed., *Opuscules de Piété*. Paris, 1943.
Dagens, J., ed., *Correspondance*. 3 vols. Paris and Louvain, 1937–9.
There appears to be no ET of a complete work by Bérulle.

Studies

von Balthasar, H. Urs, *Herrlichkeit: Eine theologische Aesthetik, 3/1, Im Raum der Metaphysik* (Einsiedeln, 1965), pp. 471–9.
Bremond, H., *Histoire littéraire du sentiment religieux en France*. Vol. III. Paris, 1923.
Dagens, J., *Bérulle et les origines de la restauration catholique (1575–1611)*. Paris, 1952.
Mersch, E., (ET) *The Whole Christ* (London, Dobson; Milwaukee, Bruce, 1938), pp. 531–55.
Orcibal, J., *Le cardinal de Bérulle: Évolution d'une spiritualité*. Paris, 1965.
Preckler, F. G., *'État' chez le Cardinal de Bérulle: Théologie et spiritualité des 'états' bérulliens*. Rome, 1974.
Preckler, F. G., *Bérulle aujourd'hui. Pour une spiritualité de l'humanité du Christ*. Paris, 1978.

The masters of the French School of post-Reformation Catholic spirituality are Cardinal Pierre de Bérulle (1575–1629), the founder of the French Oratory; Charles de Condren (1588–1641), his disciple and successor as Superior-General of the Oratory; and Jean-Jacques Olier (1608–57), the founder of the Society and seminary of Saint-Sulpice. We should also include within the French School those who developed particular aspects of its spiritual doctrine, such as St John Eudes (1601–80), the apostle of devotion to the Sacred Heart of Jesus and the Most Holy Heart of Mary, and St Louis-Marie Grignion de Montfort (1673–1716), the author of *A Treatise on True Devotion to the Blessed Virgin*.[1]

---

[1] Bremond argues that all orthodox French spirituality from Bérulle to Grignion de Montfort can be classified as 'the French School' because of its remarkable cohesion and unanimity. See his *Histoire littéraire du sentiment religieux en France* III, (Paris, 1923), p. 10. Henceforth, the *Histoire littéraire* will be referred to as 'Bremond' with the numbers of volume and part.

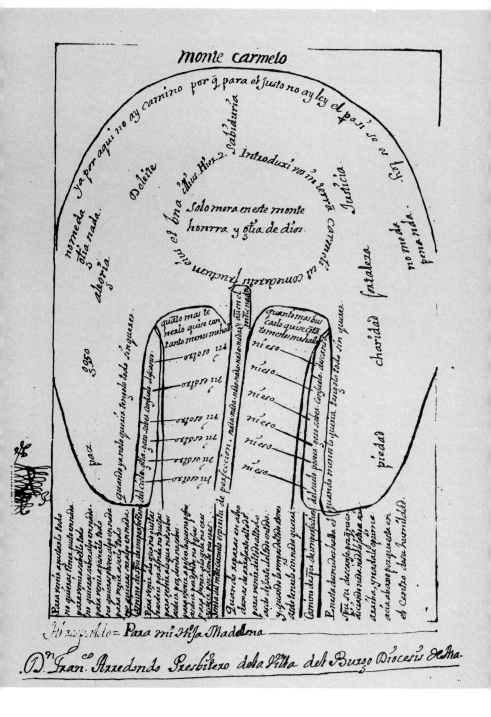

10   The original sketch of *Mount Carmel* by St John of the Cross (*see p. 369*)

100   La vie Symbolique

EMBLEME XXVI.

Son esprit de conduite & de direction.

MEDIVM TENVERE BEATI.

Parmy tous les perils que l'on voit en ce lieu;
Les plus heureux sont ceux qui tiennent le milieu.

172   La vie Symbolique

EMBLEME XLIV.

Sa parfaite conformité à la volonté de Dieu.

TE QVOCVMQVE SEQVAR.

Je cherche son aspect, & par tout ie le veux suivre;
Et s'il me luit sur moy, ie dois cesser de vivre.

11   Emblems of François de Sales (see p. 379)

The New
Whole Duty of Man,

Containing

The *Faith* as well as *Practice*

OF

A Christian;

Made Easy

For the *Practice* of the *Present Age*,
As the Old *Whole Duty of Man* was design'd
for those *unhappy* Times in which it was written;

AND

Supplying the *Articles*

OF

The Christian *Faith*,

Which are wanting in that Book,

THO'

Essentially necessary to Salvation.

Necessary for All Families,
AND
Authorised by the King's most Excellent Majesty.

With Devotions *proper for several Occasions*

The Third Edition.

Without Faith it is impossible to please God. Heb. xi. 6.
This is his Commandment, that we should Believe on the Name
of his Son Jesus Christ, and Love one another. 1 John iii. 23.

LONDON:

Printed Only for Edward Wicksteed at the Black-Swan in New-gate-Street, near Warwick-Lane.

Publish'd according to an Act of Parliament 31 March 1744.

Ye are not under the LAW, but under GRACE. Rom. 6. 16.

The Law was given by Moses but Grace & Truth came by
Jesus Christ __ That whosoever believeth in him should
not Perish but have eternal Life. John 1.17. and 3.16.

12   The title page of the *New Whole Duty of Man*

13 (above)   The 'Holy Club',
led by John Wesley (*see p. 456*)

14 (left)   'Primitive Methodism'
(*see p. 458*)

15 Søren Kierkegaard (see p. 469)

16 (above)   Paul Couturier
(*see p. 541*)

17 (left)   Josef Höfer
(*see p. 545*)

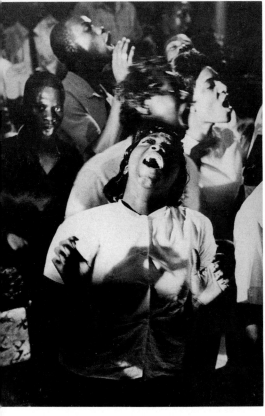

18 (above)   The Monastery
of Simon Peter, Mount Athos

19 (left)   Members of the Pentecostal
Church in Chile

20 The body at prayer

In what follows we shall concentrate on the spirituality of Bérulle, the chief founder of the School.

BÉRULLE: LIFE

Pierre de Bérulle was born on 4 February 1575 in the château of Sérilly, near Troyes, into an ancient and distinguished family. Having been educated by the Jesuits and at the Sorbonne, he was ordained priest in 1599 and became honorary chaplain to the king. Even before his ordination he had published a *Bref discours de l'abnégation intérieure*, an adaptation of a work by Isabella Bellinzaga, and worked indefatigably for the conversion of Protestants. Cardinal du Perron said of him: 'If it is a question of convincing the heretics, bring them to me; if it is a question of converting them, introduce them to M. de Genève (St François de Sales). But if it is a question of both convincing them and converting them, direct them to M. de Bérulle.'[1]

Bérulle worked with Mme Acarie (Blessed Marie de l'Incarnation, 1566–1618)[2] and others, in the face of great opposition, to introduce the reformed Carmelites of St Teresa into France. From about 1605 he also became increasingly concerned with implementing the decrees of the Council of Trent on training for the priesthood and with the renewal of the priestly life in general. With these ideals in mind Bérulle founded the Congregation of the Oratory of Jesus Christ after the pattern of the Oratory founded by St Philip Neri in Rome. This preoccupation with priestly formation was shared by Condren, whose spirituality centres on the priesthood and sacrifice of Christ, and by Olier, whose foundation at Saint-Sulpice became a model for other seminaries in the Church.

In addition to his work as a spiritual leader and writer, Bérulle was also involved in public affairs. He conducted the negotiations with Rome for Princess Henrietta Maria's dispensation to marry Charles I of England in 1625, and was a trusted adviser to members of the French royal family. In 1627 he was made Cardinal for his services to the Church.

While at the altar, on 2 October 1629, just as he was saying the words *Hanc igitur oblationem* in the Canon of the Mass, Bérulle collapsed and died.

THE SOURCES OF BÉRULLE'S SPIRITUALITY

The most obvious influences on Bérulle were personal. In his youth he came into contact, especially in the circle of Mme Acarie, with some of the great spiritual masters of the day, including Benedict of Canfield and St François de Sales. He had a profound knowledge of the Fathers, both

---

[1] Cited by A. Molien, *Dictionnaire d'histoire et de géographie ecclésiastiques* VIII, col. 1117.
[2] See Bremond II, ch. 4.

Greek and Latin, esteeming St Augustine most highly of all, not only for his teaching on grace but also for his doctrine of the Mystical Body.[1] Where Aquinas is concerned, Bérulle assures us that he follows him on the incarnation and on grace 'and, as far as we can, on everything else'.[2] Finally, we should note the undeniable influence of the spiritual writers of the Low Countries, especially Ruysbroeck and Harphius.[3]

THE MAIN SPIRITUAL DOCTRINES OF BÉRULLE

Adoration

According to Bérulle, the fundamental duty of creatures is religion, the worship and adoration of God, the acknowledgement of his infinite grandeur and majesty. In his preface to Bérulle's *Oeuvres*, P. Bourgoing, the third Superior-General of the Oratory, tells us that the great achievement of 'our most honoured Father' is to have 'renewed in the Church . . . the spirit of religion, the supreme cult of adoration and reverence due to God, to Jesus Christ our Lord, to all his states and mysteries, to his life, to his actions, and to his sufferings'.[4] We must adore one God in Trinity and the Trinity in unity, the three divine persons in their consubstantiality and eternal circumincession.[5]

Now the Second Person of the Holy Trinity, God the Son, who is eternally begotten of the Father, has taken flesh from the Virgin Mary and been born in time. The Son's eternal love of the Father is now expressed in a human nature, in a human life, with a human heart and voice. Christ as man is thus the perfect adorer; the incarnate Son offers an infinite adoration to the Father, and our adoration of God is but a participation, through grace, in his. Through the incarnation we have not only a God adored and adorable but a God adoring.[6]

Christocentrism

The most striking characteristic of Bérulle's spirituality is its Christocentrism. Pope Urban VIII called him the 'Apostle of the Word

---

[1] Bérulle describes St Augustine as 'l'aigle des docteurs, et le grand maître du prince de l'école saint Thomas' (*Grandeurs de Jésus* 10, 6; *Oeuvres complètes de Bérulle*, ed. J. P. Migne [Paris, 1856], col. 346). Henceforth, we shall refer simply to *Grandeurs*, and for all references to Bérulle's works, we shall give treatise title, chapter number etc., and then the column number in Migne.

[2] Cited by A. Molien, *Dictionnaire de spiritualité*, 4. 1543.

[3] See Dom Huijben, 'Aux sources de la spiritualité française du xviie siècle', *Vie spirituelle*, supp. December 1930, pp. 134ff.

[4] *Oeuvres*, 102f.

[5] cf. *Opuscules de piété* (henceforth OP) 154; 1197.

[6] cf. *Grandeurs* 2, 13; 183; cf. St Thomas, ST, 3a, 9,20.

Incarnate', and P. Bourgoing claimed that he was sent 'as a new St John to point out Jesus Christ . . . That . . . was his apostolate and mission.'[1] By placing the incarnate Son of God at the centre of all his reflections, Bérulle effected, so to speak, a 'Copernican revolution' in spirituality. In contrast to the more 'abstract' tendency of the Flemish and Rhineland schools, it is Jesus, the Word incarnate, the Jesus of Bethlehem and Calvary, the crucified and risen Lord, who is the 'sun' at the centre of the universe. Bérulle himself suggests this image:

> One of the outstanding intellects of this age [sc. Copernicus] has tried to maintain that the sun, and not the earth, is at the centre of the universe . . . This novel opinion, little followed in the science of the stars, is useful and must be followed in the science of salvation. For Jesus is the sun, immobile in his grandeur and moving all things . . . Jesus is the true centre of the world, and the world must be in a continual movement towards him. Jesus is the sun of our souls, from whom they receive all graces, lights and influences.[2]

The 'States' of Christ

> The central idea of the spirituality of Bérulle is that by the incarnation all human actions, all human states, which had been corrupted and debased in the person of the first man, have been deified in the person of Jesus.[3]

The key word there is 'state' (*état*).[4] His most characteristic use of the word is to describe the divers ontological situations of the Son of God: 'Jesus is living in three different and wonderful states, that is, in the heart of the Father, in our humanity, in his Eucharist'.[5] The first of these *états* is eternal, the second is permanent (from the incarnation onwards and forever), while the third (the sacramental state) lasts only until the end of the world.

The first state of Christ is his state as the Second Person of the Holy Trinity. The Trinitarian persons are subsistent relations, their being is an *esse ad*, and so Bérulle can speak of the 'relation that (the Son) has to the Father by the wonderful state of his divine and eternal filiation'.[6] Now in his human nature, which is united hypostatically to himself, he is in this same relation to the Father. In his two natures, what Bérulle calls 'the eternal and the new',[7] the Son refers all that he is to the Father. The

[1] Preface, *Oeuvres*, 98.
[2] *Grandeurs* 2, 2; 161.
[3] J. Dagens, *Bérulle et les origines de la restauration catholique 1575–1611* (Bruges, 1952), p. 302.
[4] See F. G. Preckler, '*État*'.
[5] *Grandeurs* 7,3; 263.
[6] ibid., 5,9; 240.
[7] OP 87, 2; 1071.

personal property of being a 'substantial relation' to the Father is communicated to the assumed human nature, and it is this which constitutes the hypostatic union, the grace of union.

> The same Word, who is necessarily begotten within eternity, wanted to be begotten a second time in the fulness of time; and by this second birth he wanted to imprint on this humanity the adorable character of his divine and eternal filiation, which it receives and bears for eternity. For he possesses this humanity not just as God, but as Son of God, and in this quality he imprints on it his proper and personal subsistence.[1]

The human nature of the Son of God, all his human life and activity, above all his human obedience, have a filial character. In the love of the blessed Trinity and in the fulfilment of his mission on earth the Son makes the same filial response to the Father.

Not only the eternal generation of the Son but also the incarnation of the Son can be called an *état*: the hypostatic union of human nature to the person of the Word is a permanent 'state'. God has become human and remains human for ever. So, within the context of the incarnation, the word *état* can be used in a further sense, in the plural, to describe the various stages of Christ's life on earth: 'all Jesus' states of life (*status vitae Jesu*) and all the actions and all the parts and all the moments of that life'.[2] Human beings are historical and go through various stages of development – fetal life, infancy, adolescence, maturity, joy and sorrow, living and dying. All of these states and moments of life have been appropriated by the Son of God, who assumed a complete and concrete (and therefore, so to speak, graduated) human nature. He could have assumed human nature in a glorious state, but in fact he voluntarily assumed a passible human nature, a human nature in the *status viatoris*, and thus he entered into and made his own all human experience (sin alone excepted) from the weakness and dependence of life in the womb to the ultimate poverty of death. And not only did he appropriate all our human states, he also sanctified and deified them.[3]

Bérulle's great insight is that, while the exterior circumstances of these various states and mysteries of Christ's life are past, the interior state or living disposition within Christ's human soul remains, and it is this disposition which can have an effect, as *vertu* or *mérite*, on us. The 'interior states' of the mysteries of our Lord's life produce correlative 'states' in chosen souls. 'They are past with regard to execution, but they are present with regard to their efficacy (*vertu*)'.[4] To explain himself, Bérulle

[1] *Grandeurs* 6,11; 259f.
[2] *Collationes* 1615; cited in Preckler, p. 71.
[3] See OP 17–18; 940f.
[4] OP 77, 1; 1052.

takes the primordial example of our Lord's wounds: if Jesus could take the scars on his body into glory, 'why will he not be able to preserve something in his soul, in the definitive state of his glory? . . . What remains in him of these mysteries forms on earth a kind of grace, which pertains to those souls chosen to receive it'.[1] All the mysteries of Christ's life, because of the interior dispositions and sentiments in his soul corresponding to them, affect and vivify us.

But how can we be said to 'reap fruit'[2] from the interior states of Christ? Bérulle's answer to this question depends on two central doctrines in the Christology of St Thomas: (1) that the individual grace of Christ, the habitual grace with which his soul is endowed, is really identical with 'capital grace', the grace that makes Christ Head of the Church;[3] (2) that the humanity of Christ is an active, living 'instrument' united to his divinity.[4] Because Christ's individual grace is really identical with his grace as Head, 'every action of the Son of God, his every mystery and state, infuses a certain special grace into the soul'.[5]

> It pleases him to imprint on souls his states and effects, his mysteries and his sufferings, and one day it will please him to imprint on us his grandeurs and his glory.[6]

Bérulle's thought is clearly dependent on that of St Thomas, but he is also recapitulating the classical doctrine of the Fathers, who, in both East and West, see the redemptive incarnation as an *admirabile commercium*.[7]

According to the Cardinal, there are two ways in which we can participate in the mysteries and states of Christ – the universal and the particular. As the Preface in the Roman Missal puts it, 'By his birth we are reborn. In his suffering we are freed from sin. By his rising from the dead we rise to everlasting life . . .' But, in addition to this universal share, there is also a particular or singular share: certain souls are called in a special way to share in individual mysteries. One is called specially to be with him in his infancy, another shares in the contemplation of the desert, the agony in the garden or the dereliction.[8]

The State of Infancy

The state of Christ which Bérulle contemplated more than any other is

[1] OP 77, 2; 1053.
[2] cf. ibid., 1; 1053.
[3] ST, 3a, 8, 5; also *in 3 Sent.*, d. 18, a. 6, sol. 1, ad 2.
[4] ST, 3a, 2, 6, ad 4; 7, 1, ad 3; 48, 6; 49, 3, ad 1.
[5] *Collationes* 1614; Preckler, p. 240.
[6] OP 78; 1054.
[7] e.g. Irenaeus, *Adversus Haereses*, book V, prologue; cf. also J. M. Garrigues, *Maxime le Confesseur. La charité, avenir divin de l'homme* (Paris, 1976), p. 149.
[8] OP 17, 2; 940f.

his sacred infancy, not only the infancy of the new-born Christ-child but also the life of Jesus in the womb of Mary: Jesus living in Mary. Human life in the womb, fetal life, has been assumed, appropriated, by God the Son and is thus divinized in him.

> The infancy of the Son of God is a passing state, the circumstances of this infancy have passed, and he is no longer a child, but there is something divine in this mystery, which continues in heaven, and which effects a similar kind of grace in the souls which are on earth, whom it pleases Jesus Christ to affect and to dedicate to this humble and first state of his person.[1]

Here we have the theological foundation for devotion to the holy Child, and for the mystical encounter with him experienced by such saints as St Catherine of Siena. Bérulle inspired a fervent cultus of the sacred infancy. Marguerite du Saint-Sacrement (1619–48) of the Carmel at Beaune believed herself to be chosen by our Lord 'to honour his infancy and his manger' and formed a society of 'domestics and associates of the family of the Child Jesus', which, among other practices, celebrated the twenty-fifth day of every month in honour of the annunciation and nativity.[2]

Spiritual Infancy

The state of Christ's infancy has an efficiency and exemplarity in relation to us. The childhood of Christ perpetually confers childlike obedience and docility on souls. Among Bérulle's spiritual heirs is J. Blanlo (1617–57), who came under the influence of M. Olier at Saint-Sulpice:

> This infancy . . . is but a consequence of baptism . . . After baptism, which is a supernatural birth, follows spiritual infancy, by which the baptized person, inspired by a new spirit, begins to lead a new life, which has a certain proportion and resemblance to natural infancy.[3]

The holy Child Jesus is, then, the cause of, and model for, our spiritual rejuvenation, our becoming like little children (cf. Matt. 18.3f).

Spiritual infancy is one of the major themes of the French School in the seventeenth century and constantly re-emerges in French Catholic spirituality, finally achieving its supreme expression in the 'Little Way' of St Thérèse of the Holy Child Jesus (1873–97). It is also a preoccupation of the poet Charles Péguy (1873–1914) and the novelist Georges Bernanos (1888–1948).

The Sacred Heart of Jesus

The so-called 'author of the liturgical cult of the most Sacred Hearts of

[1] OP 77, 2; 1053.
[2] See Bremond III/2, pp. 218ff.
[3] *L'enfance chrétienne* . . . (Paris, 1665), p. 9.

Jesus and Mary' is St John Eudes. It must not be forgotten, however, that Bérulle was St John's spiritual father for six years at the Oratory, and in his own writings we find many anticipations of the doctrine of his disciple.

> Let us note that the living heart of Jesus is deeply enough wounded by love. That is why this wound of the lance is reserved for his dead heart. It is as if before death this steel could inflict no deeper wound, so great was the wound of love. His heart is eternally open, eternally wounded; his glory does not take this wound away, for it is a wound of love; this wound of the lance is only the outward sign of the true and interior wound of his heart.[1]

The Eucharistic State of Christ

Bérulle devotes much of his writing, both spiritual and controversial, to the subject of the eucharistic 'state' of Christ, which lasts, he says, until the end of the world.

> There is a divine and inviolable chain of unity and charity, of the charity of the Father and of the Son towards men, and of the unity of the Father with the Son in the Trinity, of the unity of the Son with human nature in the incarnation, and of the unity of the body of Jesus Christ with us . . .[2]

But, of course, the 'chain' is not simply an external connection. It is through the 'substantial and corporeal residence of the living and glorious body of the Son of God' in our mortal bodies through Holy Communion that we share in his holy and divine life, the life he shares with the Father (cf. John 6.57), and so we enter an 'excellent communion with the divinity', a participation in the triune life of God.[3]

The most developed eucharistic piety in the French School is that of Condren, whose devotion centres on Christ as Priest and Sacrifice, perpetual victim before the Father:

> You must remember that the sacrifice you offer is not only the sacrifice of the Son of God, but of the Head and of the members, of the whole Christ (*Jésus Christ accompli*), who contains his Church, to whom he communicates his priesthood, and she offers it with him, and he offers himself with her.[4]

Throughout we see eucharistic theology grounded in the doctrines of the Trinity, the incarnation and the mystical Body.

Marian Spirituality

Bérulle contributed to a great renewal of devotion to our Lady in

[1] OP 69; 1046.
[2] *Grandeurs* 6, 4; 248.
[3] ibid., 247.
[4] Cited in Bremond III/2, p. 114.

393

seventeenth-century France and inspired later apostles of Marian devotion such as St John Eudes and St Louis-Marie. Here, as always, we find a profound Christocentrism. He never separates the Son from his Blessed Mother; he contemplates Jesus in Mary and Mary in Jesus. 'Speaking of you, Mary, we speak of Jesus; speaking of your grandeurs, we speak of the grandeurs of Jesus.'[1] The Son of God took flesh from the Virgin Mary; it was in her womb that he united human nature to himself. But not only that, it was God's will that Mary should give her free consent to the incarnation on behalf of the whole human race. Mary's humble *fiat* is 'much more powerful in its consequence and effect than that which God pronounced in the creation of the world'.[2]

> It is the portion of the Virgin at this sacred time to be in silence. That is her state, her way, her life. Her life is a life of silence, which adores the eternal Word. In seeing before her eyes, at her breast, in her arms, that same Word, the substantial Word of the Father, mute and reduced to silence by the state of his infancy, she enters into a new silence and is there transformed in the example of the incarnate Word who is her Son, her God and her only love.[3]

ASSESSMENT OF THE FRENCH SCHOOL

The strengths of the French School of spirituality are obvious: its Christocentrism, its firm dogmatic base, its synthesis of the wisdom of other schools of Catholic spirituality. Above all, it produced saints, including some of the greatest heroes of apostolic endeavour of the period, such as St Vincent de Paul, St John Eudes, and St Louis-Marie. But it also has its limitations. Some of the writings of a Bérulle or a Condren betray a certain grim pessimism about human nature, an undue severity, an almost inhuman sternness. The constant emphasis on abnegation, 'annihilation', adherence, dependence in the spiritual life makes it hard for us to see sometimes what place there is for free and full human cooperation with grace. Our authors, in their understanding of sin and grace, remain firmly within orthodoxy and never manifest that open contempt for human nature and that excessive passivity which are the hallmarks of those other schools of spirituality in the seventeenth century, Jansenism and Quietism (see pp. 396–415). Nonetheless, there are certain unfortunate resemblances between the French School and these other traditions, and it is not surprising that certain tenets of Bérulle were exaggerated and exploited by the Jansenists, for example, the 'particular' participation by individual souls in the various states of Christ, which was

---

[1] *Opuscules de piété* 117, 2; ed. G. Rotureau (Paris, 1943), p. 361.
[2] *Grandeurs* 11, 10; 576.
[3] OP 39, 3; 988.

interpreted literally by the Jansenists. The Oratorian spiritual directors at Port-Royal attributed all differences between souls to God's designs, as evidence of the variety of ways God wanted to sanctify them. The attitude of both directors and clients was one of complete passivity before the 'states' of their souls, which were so many ways of appropriating the 'states' of Christ. How different is this approach from that of the saints of the Church! The saints may have a special devotion to one of the states of Christ, but it is never an exclusive attachment, for they worship not so much the state itself as the *person* of the Son of God who has appropriated it, and they worship him in the wholeness of his economy: as Babe of Bethlehem, yes, but also as the crucified Son of Man, as the suffering Servant but also as the risen and ascended Lord. St Thérèse of Lisieux, for example, is not only Thérèse of the Holy Child Jesus, she is also (to give her full name) Thérèse of the Child Jesus *and the Holy Face*. Her Little Way is a purified and perfected form of the spiritual infancy of the French School. To the somewhat sombre tones of Bérulle's depiction of childhood (uselessness, dependence, poverty) Thérèse adds the light and colour of a cheerful intimacy in the presence of the Father and the enjoyment of play with 'our little brother Jesus'. There is the childlike heart of God's adopted children.[1]

Our final word should not be negative. Perhaps the most practical contribution of the French School to Catholic spirituality was its firmly christocentric approach to prayer, exemplified most clearly in the so-called 'Sulpician Method', in which there is adoration (Jesus before my eyes), communion (Jesus drawn into my heart), and finally co-operation (Jesus in my hands).[2] This last stage, in which, relying on God's grace, I make a practical resolve to bring my life into conformity with him whom I have adored and who has come into my heart, shows how far removed we are from the destructive world of Jansenism and Quietism, in which the

---

[1] See, for example, the playful letter of Christmas Eve 1896 (as) from 'your little Brother Jesus' to 'my dearest little bride, skittles-player on Mount Carmel' (St Thérèse of Lisieux, [ET] *Collected Letters*, [London, 1949], p. 266f). For a profound theological discussion of the notion of play in St Thérèse's spirituality, see Hans Urs von Balthasar, (ET) *Thérèse of Lisieux, The Story of a Mission* (London and New York, Sheed & Ward, 1953), pp. 215f.

[2] For a useful summary of the Sulpician Method, see L. Bouyer, (ET) *Introduction to Spirituality* (London, DLT; New York, Desclée, 1961), pp. 84f. We find it taught by Evelyn Underhill in her later period (Christopher J. R. Armstrong, *Evelyn Underhill (1875–1941)* [London, Mowbrays; Grand Rapids, Eerdmans, 1975], pp. 268–272).

Bérulle's Christocentrism also underlies the teaching of Columba Marmion, OSB (1858–1923), whose works (ET) *Christ the Life of the Soul* (London and Edinburgh, Sands; St Louis, Herder, 1922), (ET) *Christ in His Mysteries* (London and Edinburgh, Sands; St Louis, Herder, 1924), and others, were deeply influential in the middle of this century.

divine overwhelms the human and abolishes freedom. Let us conclude with M. Olier's great prayer, which beautifully sums up the teaching of Bérulle and his school.

> O Jesus living in Mary,
> Come and live in thy servants,
> In the spirit of thy sanctity,
> In the fulness of thy strength,
> In the reality of thy virtues,
> In the perfection of thy ways,
> In the communion of thy mysteries,
> Be Lord over every opposing power,
> In thine own Spirit, to the glory of the Father. Amen.

3 Jansenism

ELFRIEDA DUBOIS

Abercrombie, N., *The Origins of Jansenism*. Oxford, Clarendon, 1936.
Adam, A., *Du mysticisme à la révolte: Les Jansénistes du XVIIe siècle*. Paris, 1968.
Cognet, L., *Les origines de la spiritualité française au XVIIe siècle*. Paris, 1949.
Cognet, L., *De la dévotion moderne à la spiritualité française*. Paris, 1958.
Cognet, L., *Le Jansénisme*. Que sais-je?, Paris, 1961.
Davidson, H. M., *The Origins of Certainty: Means and Meanings in Pascal's Pensées*. University of Chicago, 1979.
Delforge, F., *Les petites écoles de Port-Royal 1637–1660*. Paris, Cerf, 1985.
Duchêne, R., *L'Imposture littéraire dans les Provinciales de Pascal*. Marseille, Université de Provence, 1984.
Knox, R. A., *Enthusiasm* (Oxford, Clarendon; New York, OUP, 1950; Westminster, Maryland, Christian Classics, 1983), chaps 9 and 10.
Orcibal, J., *La Correspondance de Jansénius* in *Les origines du jansénisme*, vol. i. Louvain, 1947.
Orcibal, J., *Jean Duvergier de Hauranne, Abbé de Saint-Cyran et son temps*. Louvain, 1947; Paris, 1948.
Orcibal, J., *La spiritualité de Saint-Cyran*. Paris, 1947–62.
'Le Siècle de Saint Augustin', in *Revue XVIIe Siècle* 135/2 (1982) (a special number).
Sedgwick, A., *Jansenism in Seventeenth-Century France: Voices from the Wilderness*. Charlottesville, Va., University Press of Virginia, 1977.

The movement rightly or wrongly known as Jansenism, a collective term with somewhat blurred outlines,[1] derives from different sources. It

[1] J. Orcibal, 'Le jansénisme, Saint-Cyran et Barcos', in *Les deux abbés de Saint-Cyran*,

originated in the University of Louvain, then migrated to Paris through the meeting of two students, Cornelius Jansen (or Jansenius) and Jean Duvergier de Hauranne, later Abbot of Saint-Cyran. The latter provides the link with Port-Royal, as spiritual director of both the Cistercian nuns and the *Solitaires*, a group of men who, in a spirit of prayer and penance, lived nearby at the *Granges*. From being initially a matter of theology, the interpretation of the Augustinian teaching on grace and free will, Jansenism became a public controversy with the publication of Pascal's *Provincial Letters*. It took on a marked political bias in the writings of Arnauld, Nicole, and particularly Quesnel, towards the end of the seventeenth century; and this aspect came to predominate in the eighteenth.

In the second half of the sixteenth century Michel de Bay, or Baius, attempted to renew the theological teaching in the University of Louvain; he turned away from scholasticism and went back to the Fathers of the Church and St Augustine in particular. In his *Opuscula* (1564–6) he claimed that since the fall man's nature is so corrupt that he is no longer in possession of his free will. The list of errors extracted from the *Opuscula* was somewhat ambiguously condemned by Pius V in 1567. However, the impetus given to Augustinian studies continued with a new edition of the writings of the 'Doctor of Grace' in 1577, *Opera per theologos Lovanienses*.[1] Controversial exchanges among theologians arose frequently, particularly with the members of the newly established Jesuit college.[2] Some twenty years after Baius, the Jesuit Luis de Molina (1536–1600) proposed in his *De concordia liberi arbitrii cum divinae gratiae donis* (Lisbon, 1588) the notion of sufficient grace, given to everyone, so as to enable all to follow God's way; but it depended on the co-operation of human free will.[3] The then popes, Clement VIII and Paul IV, did not care for Molina's teaching, but did not condemn him. The whole question was examined at the sessions of the Congregation *De auxiliis* (1598–1607). Molina's teaching had its repercussion in France and moreover the Society of Jesus was useful to the papacy. The Council of Trent, at its sixth session in January 1547, had reasserted free will as a human prerogative together with the necessity of grace to attain good works, but without tackling the difficult theological problem of their interrelation. It thus left the field open to discussion until Rome,

---

Chroniques de Port-Royal, 1977–9, no. 26–9; for the 'Prétendus Jansénistes', called so by their enemies, see Letter of Arnauld d'Andilly to Claude Auvry, 18 February 1656.

[1] It served as a basis for the Maurist edition of 1679–1700.

[2] The most eminent of their theologians, L. Leys or Lessius, 1554–1623.

[3] Molina also introduced the idea of a *scientia media*, a middle knowledge, between God's knowledge of all things possible and the knowledge of actual future events. God knows, *post praevisa merita*, how beings would behave freely under certain conditions and gives them sufficient grace accordingly.

in 1625, put and end to the increasingly embittered exchange of views.

Augustine's extensive works could be and were used as an authoritative source for a variety of arguments. He developed his views on grace, predestination and free will in his polemical writings against the Pelagian heresy (condemned at the Council of Carthage in 418), according to which man's free will without divine grace suffices in attaining good works. Molinists were accused of being semi-Pelagians, since they took a favourable view of human nature. Augustine's pessimistic view of fallen human nature was also held, in their different ways, by Luther and Calvin.

Jansen followed up the study of St Augustine, first as a student in Louvain (1600–4), then in Paris where he met up with Duvergier. Their common interest in St Augustine brought them together for several years of private study at Camp-de-Prats, near Bayonne, Duvergier's home town (1611–16). Jansen then returned to a university career at Louvain; but the two friends continued to share their interests by correspondence,[1] using a cipher over the vexed question of grace and free will and their attack on the Jesuits. Duvergier, after his ordination in 1618, experienced an inner conversion largely under the influence of Bérulle and his brand of Augustinian spirituality. He collaborated on Bérulle's *Grandeurs de Jésus*, and under the pseudonym of Petrus Aurelius engaged in controversies with Father Garasse[2] and other Jesuits. He followed Bérulle as a leading figure of the *parti dévot*, opposed to Richelieu's policy of securing French supremacy in Europe at the price of his alliance with Protestant powers. His relations with Richelieu became strained, leading to his arrest in 1638; he was released from the prison in Vincennes only after Richelieu's death, and died soon after in 1643.

In Paris, Duvergier, since 1620 Abbot of Saint-Cyran, met the Arnauld family,[3] many of whom had or were to have links with Port-Royal. Founded in 1204, the Cistercian nunnery of Port-Royal, like most other religious houses under the impact of the Counter-Reformation, had undertaken its reform in 1609, under their abbess Angélique Arnauld who had held the position since 1602, when she was eleven years old. The Cistercian community put itself under episcopal authority in 1627 and

---

[1] J. Orcibal, *La Correspondance de Jansénius*.

[2] *La Doctrine curieuse*, 1623; Saint-Cyran, *La Somme des fautes et faussetés principales contenues dans la Somme théologique du P. Garasse*, 1626.

[3] Antoine Arnauld belonged to the *noblesse de robe*; he had with his wife Catherine twenty children; the eldest Robert Arnauld d'Andilly and the youngest Antoine Arnauld ('le Grand') were both involved in Jansenism and their sisters were nuns at Port-Royal, the best known of whom are Angélique, Agnès, also their widowed mother, Catherine de Sainte Félicité and her six grand-daughters, among whom was Angélique de Saint Jean.

became the Institute of the Blessed Sacrament in 1633.[1] From the valley of the Chevreuse the nuns moved to Paris and acquired a house in the rue St Jacques; subsequently both houses were used. After several spiritual directors, including St François de Sales, the Abbot of Saint-Cyran took over and began to impose his spirituality.

Under his guidance also some men withdrew from their position in the world and settled around Port-Royal des Champs, the *Solitaires*, or *Messieurs de Port-Royal*, in an informal group, specifying that they had

> no rules, no vows, no constitution, no community, no society, no cells, nor anything remotely like it . . . and there are no assemblies.[2]

What united them was their loyalty to Port-Royal and the Jansenist cause, as well as bonds of family (Arnauld) and friendship, strengthened at times of persecution and sometimes dispersal. They pursued manual and intellectual work, always immersed in a life of prayer. The first *Solitaire* was Antoine Le Maistre who gave up a brilliant legal career in 1637, followed by his brothers Isaac Le Maistre de Sacy[3] and Simon Le Maistre de Séricourt. Later came Claude Lancelot, the distinguished Hellenist,[4] Abbé Singlin, confessor of the nuns, and Robert Arnauld d'Andilly, eldest son of the Arnauld family, who settled in 1644 at the *Granges*. He kept his Court connections and pleaded on behalf of his Jansenist friends with Mazarin through the mediation of the Bishop of Coutances (Claude Auvry).[5] Among the intellectual work undertaken by the *Solitaires* were translations, such as the *Confessions* of St Augustine (Robert Arnauld d'Andilly), the New Testament ('de Mons', as it was known, by Le Maistre de Sacy), but also original work, *La Logique ou l'Art de Penser*, by Arnauld and Nicole, in various versions, 1660–83.[6] Some of the *Solitaires*, Fontaine, Du Fossé and Lancelot, recorded the events in which they and their friends were involved. Intermittently they kept a small boarding-school ('Petites Ecoles'); the small number of pupils benefited from the teaching of their devoted and cultured masters. Racine was one of their pupils (1649–53). The nuns also had a boarding-school, like most women's orders. According to Racine (*Abrégé de*

---

[1] F. E. Weaver, *The Evolution of the Reform of Port-Royal from the Rule of Cîteaux to Jansenism*. Paris, 1978.
[2] Robert Arnauld d'Andilly to Mazarin, 10 January 1654.
[3] G. Delassault, *Le Maistre de Sacy et son temps*. Paris, 1957.
[4] L. Cognet, *Claude Lancelot, Solitaire de Port-Royal*. Paris, 1950.
[5] *Arnauld d'Andilly Défenseur de Port-Royal (1654–59). Sa correspondance inédite avec la Cour, conservée dans les Archives du Ministère des Affaires Etrangères*, ed. P. Jansen. Paris, 1973.
[6] Ed. P. Clair and F. Girbal, Paris, 1965; ed. L. Marin, Paris, 1970.

l'histoire de Port-Royal) the girls were educated to be 'either perfect nuns or excellent mothers'.

Saint-Cyran's idea of 'renewal' (*'renouvellement'*) was based on a withdrawal from the world, to become dead to it, in fact quite unlike St François de Sales who guided people living in the world to attain a fully Christian life. This renewal also entailed rigorous penance; after confession absolution was often withheld for a prolonged period of penance and the penitent deprived of the Eucharist. In view of the utterly corrupt human nature, when was one worthy to receive communion? To abstain was sometimes a self-imposed act of humility.

An occasion arose in 1640 when Saint-Cyran's directives to Mme de Guémenée clashed with those of the Jesuit Father Sesmaisons to Mme de Sablé with regard to receiving communion after having been to a ball; the Jesuit allowed it and Saint-Cyran did not. Arnauld defended Saint-Cyran's rigorism and, in this spirit, wrote *De la fréquente communion*, 1643 (with a preface by Barcos, Saint-Cyran's nephew). To the psychological perspective of Saint-Cyran's 'renewal' as a kind of second conversion Arnauld adds his own historical, indeed antiquarian viewpoint, recalling the practice of the primitive Church, as he saw it. The book was something of a publisher's success, but it also raised a certain hostility on doctrinal grounds, mainly from the Jesuit theologians, Fathers Petau and Sirmond.[1]

Jansen's magnum opus, the *Augustinus*, a folio of some 1,300 pages, was posthumously published in 1640. Bishop of Ypres since 1636, Jansen died in 1638. The work was claimed to be a systematic study of Augustinian theology, but is in fact Jansen's personal interpretation of the doctrine of the fall, of free will, predestination and grace. Jansen's aim was to persuade theologians to accept Augustinian teaching on grace, in his interpretation. In a first part Jansen examines Pelagianism and semi-Pelagianism,[2] tacitly including Molinism. A comparative appended text, *Statera*, shows the parallels between the two. It is from the rigid position St Augustine adopted in his controversy with the heretical Pelagians that Jansen develops his. Augustine distinguishes between man before the fall who, endowed with free will, turned to God, and man after the fall who turned towards evil. He had lost the capacity of free will and is now enslaved by concupiscence. There is a fundamental difference between the grace given to Adam, sufficient for him to persevere, and which involves man's free co-operation, and, on the other hand, the remedial

---

[1] D. Petau, *De la pénitence publique et de la préparation à la communion*, 1644; J. Sirmond, *Historia poenitentiae publicae*, 1651.

[2] A heretical movement, condemned by the Council of Carthage in 418; free will alone was considered sufficient to attain good works without grace.

grace of Christ. The latter acts indelibly and overrides free will. Indeed this efficacious grace gives back to man the freedom lost in original sin, in turning him towards God. According to Jansen, sufficient grace is no longer a possibility in view of the corrupt nature of man; it is a mere '*chimère*'. He thus rejects the Molinist position according to which sufficient grace is given to everyone subject to man's free consent. Human beings move between two poles of happiness, earthly and heavenly (*delectatio*), as they do between love of self (concupiscence) and love of God (charity), evil and good. Christ's irresistible grace always achieves its end in leading people to their true happiness in God, without needing their free consent; it is a *delectatio victrix*. Jansen's position on the question of free will is thus brought close to the Reformers'. Basing himself on the most rigorous conceptions of St Augustine, he did not take into account the fluctuations and development in Augustine's thought. One other particularly controversial point in the *Augustinus* is the assertion that Christ died only for the elect and not for all.[1]

The immediate reception of the *Augustinus* seemed favourable among some religious orders and some members of the Sorbonne, always excepting the Jesuits. Father Jacques Sirmond, in *Historia Praedestiniana* (1643), corrected points of history; his pupil Father Denis Petau, in *De Concilii Tridentini interpretatione et S. Augustini doctrina dissertatio* (1649), queried Jansen's restrictive theological position, confined to one author and bypassing all subsequent teaching of church councils. Richelieu, who inclined towards Molinism and moreover disliked the author of *Mars Gallicus*, instigated the attack. Controversial writings together with the *Augustinus* were condemned by the Bull *In eminenti* of March 1642 (published in 1643), on lines similar to the condemnation of Baius. The University of Louvain tried unsuccessfully to intervene in Rome on behalf of one of its eminent theologians.

The implied and often open criticism of the Jesuit positions, qualified as Molinist or semi-Pelagian, became suspect, as did the central issue of the *Augustinus*: how far is the work representative of Augustinian teaching? And is the Bull directed against St Augustine as much as against Jansen? Attitudes on both sides hardened among laity and clerics. The Sorbonne, through the services of Nicolas Cornet, examined the *Augustinus* and presented initially Seven, then Five Propositions which were deemed to summarize the main points of the book:

1. Some of God's commandments are impossible to just men.
2. In the state of fallen nature no resistance is ever made to interior grace.

[1] R. Armogathe, 'Jansénisme', in *Dict. Sp.*, 8.102–128.

3. For merit and demerit man does not need freedom from necessity, but only freedom from compulsion.

4. Semi-Pelagians were heretical because they held that the human will could resist grace or correspond to it.

5. It is semi-Pelagian to say that Christ died for all.

The fifth Proposition obviously contradicts the orthodox position of the Church. The response of the Sorbonne to the Five Propositions was equivocal; were they or were they not a true résumé of a large work? The matter was once again submitted to papal judgement by both parties.[1] Rome condemned the Five Propositions and with it Jansen's work; Urban VIII in 1643 and Innocent X in 1653 with the Bull *Cum occasione* would seem to have defeated the Jansenist cause. While the opponents triumphed rather too readily,[2] the Jansenists, in the person of the 'Grand Arnauld', brought in a distinction between the *fait*, that only the first proposition is really contained in the *Augustinus*, the others being inaccurate summaries, and the *droit*, that the Pope had therefore rightly condemned the Five Propositions. To the Pope's condemnation he and his fellow Jansenists fully subscribed, but the Propositions did not represent Jansen's book. The point was again submitted to Rome by Mazarin, and Innocent X explicitly stated that with the Five Propositions he had condemned Jansen's work, but not Augustinian teaching.[3] Arnauld continued to cling to the orthodoxy of the *Augustinus* and its betrayal in the Five Propositions, and was excluded from the Sorbonne in January 1656. He took refuge at the *Granges* and enlisted the help, in his controversial pamphlets, of a young theologian, Pierre Nicole.[4] The rather dry theological writings, composed in the solitude of Port-Royal and distributed among bishops, proved fruitless. It was at this point that the Jansenist party thought of enlisting public opinion in its favour. It so happened that Pascal (see pp. 406–8) was staying at Port-Royal des Champs at the time; Arnauld and the other *Solitaires* asked him to write a first defensive letter. He composed it there and then, dated 23 January

---

[1] Habert for the Sorbonne and a letter from the Augustinian bishops, handed over by Saint-Amour, in Rome, 1651.

[2] Father Annat's *Cavilli jansenianorum* and 'La déroute et confusion des jansénistes', a caricature in an Almanach, both in 1654.

[3] Bossuet considered the Five Propositions were at the very centre of Jansen's book; they represented the whole book and the whole book was contained in the propositions (Letter to maréchal de Bellefond, 30 September 1677). Cf. Y. Poutet, 'Les docteurs de Sorbonne et leurs options théologiques au XVIIe siècle', in *Divus Thomas*, 81 (1974), pp. 213–348.

[4] E. D. James, *Pierre Nicole, Jansenist and Humanist. A Study of his Thought*. The Hague, Nijhoff, 1972.

1656. Printed copies were circulated widely and the immediate success encouraged further letters in defence of Arnauld and on the matter of grace. With the fifth letter Pascal undertook a direct attack on the laxist moral teaching of the Jesuits. Letters V to X, written in the form of imaginary conversations between the narrator and a fictitious Jesuit of unusual naivety, take up a number of moral issues: mental restriction, probabilism, casuistry (which is in fact the method, employed in manuals for the use of confessors, of applying the moral law to specific cases), the direction of one's intentions. From the eleventh letter onwards Pascal answered directly to attacks by a number of Jesuits, Fathers Brisacier, Annat, Pinthereau, Lemoyne and others, raising further moral issues on almsgiving, homicide, attrition and contrition (from fear or love of God), calumny. Replies and counter-replies followed until the eighteenth and last letter, May 1657 (a nineteenth letter remained unfinished). The *Provincial Letters* are a collective work; Pascal used material provided by Arnauld (from the *Théologie morale des jésuites*, 1643) and Nicole. He is said to have read Escobar's *Liber theologiae moralis*, 1644, but he admitted himself that he mainly rearranged material provided by theologians. However, he quoted out of context, interpreted texts to support his line of argument, marked as quotations what was in fact a tendentious résumé of some Jesuit document. The *Lettres Provinciales* proved a remarkable and lasting literary success.[1] Several editions of the letters came out in 1657 and in the same year an English translation, under the title *Mystery of Jesuitisme* (by J. Davies).

A Formulary had been introduced and confirmed by Alexander VII which had to be signed, submitting to all papal pronouncements on the *Augustinus* and the Five Propositions.[2] Arnauld would have been ready to sign with the proviso of the distinction between *droit* and *fait*. The nuns, mostly incapable of understanding the theological issues, except perhaps Angélique de Saint-Jean, stuck to the same distinction in their pious loyalty to the memory of Saint-Cyran. However, the Archbishop of Paris, Hardouin de Péréfixe, in 1644 intervened personally and sent the leading rebellious nuns to the Visitation in the rue St Antoine (under their Superior, Louise-Eugénie de Fontaine) and put the rest under

---

[1] *Lettres Provinciales*, ed. L. Cognet. Paris, 1965. ET by A. Krailsheimer, Harmondsworth, Penguin, 1967.

[2] Gerberon, *Histoire du Formulaire qu'on a fait signer en France*, 1668: 'I, the undersigned, submit to the Apostolic Constitution of Innocent X, given on 31 May 1653, and of Alexander VII, given on 16 October 1656 and I reject and sincerely condemn the Five Propositions, taken from the book by Cornelius Jansen, entitled *Augustinus*, as in the proper meaning of the author, as the Apostolic See has condemned them by these Constitutions, this I swear: so may God help me and his holy Gospels.'

guard.[1] Those who had signed under duress were sent to the Paris convent.

The turning point in the continuing controversy came with Clement IX, who worked out a compromise solution, signed in 1669: the Clementine Peace. It did not satisfy the extremists, but gave Port-Royal and the Jansenist party some ten years of quiet expansion. Port-Royal enjoyed the friendship of some women of high society, some of whom came to live in semi-retirement near the monastery. This brought considerable prestige and support to the party.[2] Certain publications also underpinned their position: a first edition of Pascal's *Pensées* in 1670, and earlier, in 1667, the *Nouveau Testament de Mons*. The next archbishop of Paris, Harlay de Champvallon, in 1671 proceeded with renewed severity against the nuns, and removed the pupils, novices and confessors from the monastery. With the death of Mme de Longueville in 1679 the Jansenists lost one of their most vigorous supporters.

In the meantime the conflict of the *Régale*[3] had arisen, opposing Louis XIV and Innocent XI (favourable to the Jansenists). Arnauld, at the time, defended the papal prerogative and thought it wise to go into exile in Brussels (1680). He was joined there, temporarily or permanently, by Nicole, Quesnel and Du Guet. In Louvain the strict Jansenist positions were still defended by the Maurist Gabriel Gerberon who, in exile in Holland, composed a very partial *Histoire abrégée du jansénisme* (1697).

Controversy revived around the *Cas de conscience*, printed in 1702 by Ellies du Pin: could someone unwilling to sign the Formulary be admitted to the sacraments? The Jansenists' affirmative answer was rejected and Fénelon's compromise intervention was unsuccessful; by his views he stood on the side of the Jesuits. The main figure of the Jansenist party was now Quesnel, author of the *Réflexions morales*, 1699, who had all the makings of a leader. Afraid of renewed Jansenist activity Louis XIV turned again to Rome and Clement XI in the Bull *Vineam Domini*, 1705, repeated the condemnation of the Jansenist positions. It was reluctantly accepted in France, least of all by the few remaining nuns at Port-Royal. They were dispersed by order of Louis XIV and the monastery des Champs razed to the ground in 1711. Clement XI's Bull *Unigenitus* of 1713, directed against Quesnel's *Réflexions morales*, was the last important papal intervention in the history of Jansenism. It did not prevent appeals against it. The religious side of Jansenism was disintegrating but

---

[1] cf. Montherlant's play, *Port-Royal*, 1953/4, covering the days 21–6 August 1664.

[2] C. Gazier, *Les Belles amies de Port-Royal*. Paris, 1930.

[3] 1673–93, the conflict between Louis XIV and the 'Gallican' clergy over the rights to the nomination of bishops. The assembly of the clergy in 1682 gave support to the King's prerogative, but a break with Rome was avoided when both sides compromised.

for some popular phenomena of miracles around the person of the deacon Pâris in the churchyard of St Médard, ending in hysterical convulsions. But it took on a political turn, standing against the 'Establishment', for a kind of bourgeois individualism; it readily joined with the parliamentary opposition and the Gallican cause. The political dimension had existed almost from the beginning, in the resistance against Richelieu, later in the alliance with the Fronde; it predominated in the eighteenth century.[1] Publications did not cease: memoirs of Port-Royal were published around the mid-century and the *Nouvelles ecclésiastiques*, a largely clandestine journal, kept a certain cohesion between the group (1728–1803).

With the publication of Sainte-Beuve's *Port-Royal*, 1840–59, Jansenism re-entered the literary and academic scene and has since been firmly established in the world of scholarship. A. Gazier's *Histoire générale du mouvement janséniste* of 1922 was perhaps the last major work written in the spirit of Port-Royal. There remains the *Bibliothèque de Port-Royal* in the rue St Jacques and the *Société des Amis de Port-Royal* and their publications.[2] Since around the middle of our century there has been a scholarly renewal in studies on Port-Royal and Jansenism with the publications by L. Cognet, J. Orcibal and L. Ceyssens, to which one must add the critical work done on Pascal's *Pensées*.

In seventeenth-century studies Port-Royal and Jansenism seem to have predominated over the far more considerable religious renewal, prompted by the Counter-Reformation. In its anti-humanistic attitude Jansenism was a backward-looking, antiquarian movement, seeking to recapture the spirit of the primitive Church, as it saw it. The more rigorous writing of St Augustine was a germane source, as it was for the Reformers. The severe, almost repressive moral teaching could only lead to an élitist movement with something of a clannish outlook where spiritual pride was perhaps never far away. It also had its modern side, in its defence of the individual conscience against authority, Church and state. The unbending spirit of controversy over fine points of theology turned into legalistic quarrels. While one can only admire the moral stature and religious fervour of many Jansenists and the nuns of Port-Royal in particular, one must acknowledge that their teaching did not provide for the majority who wanted to fulfil their *devoirs d'état* in a Christian spirit in the world. In modern usage the term 'janséniste' is akin to 'puritanical'.

[1] R. Taveneaux, *Jansénisme et Politique*. Paris, 1965.
[2] C. Gazier, *Histoire de la Société et de la Bibliothèque de Port-Royal*. Paris, 1966.

4 Pascal

ELFRIEDA DUBOIS

Davidson, H. M., *Blaise Pascal*. Boston, Mass., Twayne, 1983.
Davidson, H. M., *The Origins of Certainty, Means and Meanings in Pascal's Pensées*. Chicago, University of Chicago Press, 1979.
Krailsheimer, A., *Pascal* (Past Masters). OUP, 1980.
Mesnard, J., *Pascal* (Les écrivains devant Dieu). Paris, 1965.

To his contemporaries Blaise Pascal (1623–62) was known as an eminent mathematician and scientist, for his work on the so-called probability theory, his experiments with the vacuum and atmospheric pressure, the invention of a calculating machine and his introduction of a public bus service, the 'carosse à cinq sous'. The *Lettres Provinciales* provided him with the anonymous reputation of a brilliant and witty prose writer. That he is now acknowledged as an important spiritual writer is due to the posthumous reputation of what he intended to be an Apology for the Christian Religion, his *Pensées*, written after his second inner conversion, the 'nuit de feu' of 23 November 1654, recorded in the *Mémorial*. He had come under the influence of Port-Royal spirituality and become an ally to the Jansenist cause (see pp. 402–3). At the end, he chose church discipline with regard to the Five Propositions, without breaking his friendship with Port-Royal. The *Pensées* were left unfinished, mainly in two bundles of papers, one classified and one unclassified. Many editions, in various orders of arrangement, have appeared since the first, partial, one of 1670 (by his nephew Etienne Périer); the one mostly used today is Lafuma's of 1952 (paperback, Livre de vie, 1962), on which the English translation by A. Krailsheimer is based (Penguin, 1968).

Pascal's analysis of the human condition runs between two poles:

Wretchedness of man without God, happiness of man with God (6).

Man's life is one of 'inconstancy, boredom, anxiety' (24). He therefore seeks diversion ('divertissement', 132–9), that is ceaseless activity, in his profession or for his entertainment, so as not to face himself as he really is, if he stayed 'quietly in his room'. After the brief spell of his life (68) he is confronted with the inevitability of death:

The last act is bloody, however fine the rest of the play. They throw earth over your head and it is finished for ever (165).

The French 'existentialist' writers of the forties and fifties propounded similar ideas. Man is placed between two extremes:

A nothing compared to the infinite, a whole compared to the nothing (un néant à l'égard de l'infini, un tout à l'égard du néant, 199),

and he is overawed by

the eternal silence of these infinite spaces (le silence éternel de ces espaces infinis m'effraie, 201).

But Pascal also concedes him greatness as a 'thinking reed' ('un roseau pensant', 200); he is thus superior to the unthinking universe.

The Apology is an *argumentum ad hominem*, addressed to the cultured gentleman of the day, the *honnête homme*, the intelligent agnostic, following Montaigne, who is addicted to gambling (418). In this dialogue with the sceptical unbeliever Pascal introduces the first step towards belief in God, in terms of a wager, 'heads or tails': if you win you gain everything by choosing God, if you lose you lose nothing but this finite life. A choice is unavoidable, since we are committed ('nous sommes embarqués'). Reason alone cannot prove the existence of God; Pascal brushes aside the rational, scholastic proofs for God's existence. For

it is the heart which perceives (*sent*) God and not the reason (424),

and the two facets of human nature are unrelated to each other:

The heart has its reasons of which reason knows nothing (Le coeur a des raisons que la raison ne connaît pas, 423).

Just as we accept the concept of mathematical infinity (which we do not see), so we can accept the hidden God; Pascal transfers a mathematical argument into a metaphysical one. The unbeliever's hesitations come from his passions which have to be kept under control; by following custom, he must acquire the habit of belief and with it a virtuous life.

The central point of the Apology is the person of Jesus, the Redeemer who heals man's corrupt nature:

Jesus Christ is the object of all things . . . whosoever knows him knows the reason for everything (449).

The deep gulf between man's corrupt nature and the redeeming power of Christ belongs to the Augustinian and Jansenist position. The part of the *Pensées* where Pascal demonstrates the close connection between the Old and the New Testaments, 'Christ foretold in the Prophecies as the Messiah', is often belittled today, partly because his biblical scholarship is now outdated, but it completes the Apology in favour of the unique validity of Christianity, in the Catholic Church, over all other religions. Human happiness lies in possessing God and he who truly seeks will find him:

You would not seek me if you did not possess me (929).

If Pascal has met the libertine of his day on his own ground, gambling, and relying on his work on probability, he reveals at the end of the wager argument his own personal way of interceding for the unbeliever so that he should turn to God:

> If my words please you and seem cogent, you must know that they come from a man who went down on his knees before and after to pray the infinite and indivisible being, to whom he submits his own, that he might bring your being also to submit to him . . .

5 Fénelon and Quietism

ELFRIEDA DUBOIS

Armogathe, J. R., *Le Quiétisme*. Que Sais-je? Paris, 1973.

Bedoyere, M. de la, *The Archbishop and the Lady, The Story of Fénelon and Madame Guyon*. London, Collins; New York, Pantheon, 1956.

Carcassonne, E., *Fénelon, l'homme et l'oeuvre*. Paris, 1946.

Cognet, L., *Crépuscule des mystiques*. Tournai, 1958.

Fénelon, F. de Salignac de la Mothe, *Correspondance*, ed. J. Orcibal. Paris, 1972–6.

'Fénelon et le Tricentenaire de sa naissance', in *Bulletin de la Société du XVIIe Siècle*, Nos 12, 13, 14 (1951–2).

Gouhier, H. G., *Fénelon philosophe*. Paris, 1977.

Knox, R. A., *Enthusiasm* (Oxford, Clarendon; New York, OUP, 1950; Westminster, Maryland, Christian Classics, 1983), chaps. 11, 12, 13.

Raymond, M., *Fénelon* (Les Écrivains devant Dieu, 13). Paris, 1967 (bibliography).

Varillon, F., *Fénelon et le pur amour* (Maîtres spirituels, 11). Paris, 1957 (bibliography).

Seventeenth-century spirituality was dominated by the problem of grace. Where the Augustinian Jansenists insisted on humanity's fallen nature and proposed a rigorous moral code, what became known as Quietism (since 1682) opened the way to contemplative union with God. Both agree on man's nothingness (see Pascal) and his total dependence on God.

The history of the Quietist controversy must be inserted into the currents of sixteenth- and seventeenth century mysticism, even if the form it took in the teaching of Molinos[1] and Madame Guyon deviated from the

---

[1] The Spanish theologian (1640–97); *Guida spirituale*, 1675, condemned by the Bull *Coelestis Pastor*, 1687. John Shorthouse, in *John Inglesant* (1853), shows Molinos in a favourable light.

orthodoxy of the Spanish mystics and those of the early seventeenth century in France. In his book on St John of the Cross (1931) J. Baruzi claimed that Fénelon and Madame Guyon 'have given the doctrine of St John of the Cross a continuation with a metaphysical character'.

The anecdotal history of the adventurous life of Jeanne-Marie Bouvier de la Mothe Guyon (1648–1717) interests us here only in so far as it throws light on her surprising friendship with François de Salignac Fénelon, the Archbishop of Cambrai.[1] Left a young and wealthy widow she explored the ways of mental prayer, having as a girl read the writings of Saint Chantal. Her meeting with a Barnabite priest, Father La Combe, who had similar spiritual experiences, led to mutual spiritual direction with Madame Guyon as the leading partner. Together they travelled and spread their teaching of complete abandonment into the hands of God through the practice of mental prayer. Mutual exaltation rather than any dubious moral behaviour (in spite of accusations) was their failing. They appeared to be close to the recently condemned teaching of Molinos and as such suspect. Father La Combe was imprisoned and died in a state of mental derangement. Madame Guyon was sent to the Visitation nuns in the Faubourg St Antoine (where some of the Port-Royal nuns had been under the same Superior, Mother Louise-Eugénie de Fontaine). Having just been released, in October 1688, Madame Guyon met Fénelon.[2] Saint-Simon somewhat dramatized the encounter:

> He saw her, their minds sympathized, and their sublime natures amalgamated.

Fénelon was never blind to Madame Guyon's weaknesses, her sentimentality, childishness, her spiritual *bavardage*, her gushing style. Fénelon was for her 'another self' (*un autre moi-même*), as she wrote later to the Duc de Chevreuse. But she also realized that it was onesided:

> I had the feeling . . . that he did not care for me: but something prompted me to pour out my heart into his (*La Vie par elle-même*).

In her books on spirituality[3] she taught detachment from any sense images in prayer so as to feel the presence of God. Death to the world and to

---

[1] *La Vie de Madame J. M. B. de la Mothe-Guyon écrite par ellé-même qui contient toutes les expériences de la vie intérieure*, completed in 1709; Thomas C. Upham, *Life, Religious Opinions and Experience of Madame Guyon* (New York, Revell, 1905; London, Allenson, 1908); Michael de la Bedoyere, *The Archbishop and the Lady*.

[2] Through the Duchesse de Béthune-Charost at the château de Beynes.

[3] In 1699 a collective volume was published in Cologne, containing *Le Moyen Court* and *L'Explication du Cantique des Cantiques*, together with the (orthodox) *Maximes spirituelles* and letters of Brother Lawrence of the Resurrection, as documents of the Quietist controversy.

the self are the preliminary stages for the union with God in an attitude of saintly indifference. The soul is then possessed by God and intimately united with him. This union of the soul with God is common to mystics, however inadequately it may be expressed. Madame Guyon wrapped it in some kind of spiritual gratification (*volupté*) without any thought of sin (with Molinos it went as far as disregard for morality). The prayer of quietude could be in danger of leading to the neglect of Christian duty and morals. Madame Guyon's writings are more effusions of her heart than any systematic teaching. Fénelon introduced her to spiritual litera-ture, but he discovered in her a living example of detachment, an inner opening up to God that he wanted to attain, but in which he was defeated by his scrupulous intellectualism: 'Our trouble is simply our passion for reasoning.' One could say that Fénelon's personal dilemma lay between the Cartesian *cogito*, leading to universal knowledge, and the Augustinian *cogito* leading to God. Fénelon does not share Descartes' ready conviction that he exists, but explains: 'I am not what is . . . I am almost what is not' (*Traité de l'existence de Dieu*). For Madame Guyon and in Quietist spiri-tuality the soul abandons itself to God once and for all and is thus dis-pensed from any further effort. Fénelon could not go along with this:

> The passive state, whether during the limited time of pure and direct con-templation, or in the intervals when one does not contemplate, does not exclude the real action or successive acts of the will, nor the drawing of a specific distinction between virtues in relation to their proper objects, but only the simple activity or interested restlessness; it is a peaceful practice of prayer and virtues in pure love.[1]

Through Fénelon Madame Guyon was invited by Madame de Main-tenon, the wife of Louis XIV, to explain her prayer of quietude at St Cyr. However, Madame de Maintenon was warned by the Bishop of Chartres, Godet des Marais, against these dangerous spiritual effusions. They also seemed to be beyond her understanding and she put an end to Madame Guyon's visits at St Cyr. Bossuet, the Bishop of Meaux, cautioned Fénelon against the false prophetess. Madame Guyon asked for her writ-ings to be formally examined and judged. The committee appointed consisted of Bossuet, Tronson (Superior of St Sulpice) and de Noailles, then Bishop of Châlons, later Archbishop of Paris. She sent all her writ-ings and papers to Bossuet and awaited the outcome at the Visitation Convent in Meaux. Fénelon, who had been a close friend of Bossuet and who readily deferred to his authority, knew that any adverse judgement would also fall on him. Although not a member of the Issy committee he provided a good deal of material in support of Madame Guyon. This was

[1] Conclusion of the *Maximes des saints*.

to serve him for the future *Maximes des saints*; it consisted of extracts from orthodox mystics on mental prayer and contemplative union with God. In the meantime he was appointed to the see of Cambrai in 1695; for two years he added to this his position of tutor to the Duc de Bourgogne. But Cambrai became his exile. When in March 1695 Fénelon was asked to put his signature to the articles worked out at Issy, he gained cause over Bossuet in the matter of disinterested love and passive mental prayer. But the compromise solution proved unsatisfactory, and both prelates had second thoughts which they formulated in a regular sequence of controversial writings. Bossuet sent Fénelon the manuscript of his *Instruction sur les états d'oraison* in the summer of 1696, concerning Madame Guyon's *Moyen Court*. Fénelon's view was[1] that she was being misinterpreted and that she would accept as errors any points made if they corresponded to her intended meaning. He was himself ready to submit to any church decision (without following the Jansenists in distinguishing between *droit* and *fait*; see p. 403). The *Explication des Maximes des saints sur la vie intérieure* was published in January 1697, a few weeks before Bossuet's *Instruction sur les états d'oraison*. This enraged Bossuet and broke their friendship. Bossuet set about composing his *Relation sur le quiétisme*, an aggressive pamphlet in which he indiscreetly used Fénelon's personal letters and Madame Guyon's confessions. He was moreover in a position to bring pressure to bear on the King and the matter was submitted to Rome.[2] Both prelates had representatives there. Innocent XII, who esteemed Fénelon, was reluctant to condemn the *Maximes*; would he not also condemn the teaching of St Teresa? But he also wanted to please Louis XIV. Political pressure triumphed and twenty-three Propositions were condemned (March 1699). Fénelon, with dignified humility and obedience, accepted this publicly in his cathedral. Over the two years that the Curia had been examining the *Maximes*, Fénelon and Bossuet publicly exchanged their views by way of venomous pamphlets.[3] Fénelon was supported by the Jesuits in Rome, but had other Orders against him, as well as the Jansenists pleading in Rome. Bossuet had political and clerical support. Soon after the condemnation Innocent XII wrote Fénelon a letter of personal sympathy and appreciation. He was even on the point of being made a cardinal by Clement XI when he died in January 1715.

The *Maximes des saints* is a study of the notion of *pur amour*, pure love, in an historical but not chronological perspective. Each of the articles is

---

[1] Letter to Mme de Chevreuse, 24 July 1696.
[2] R. Schmittlein, *L'Aspect politique du différend Bossuet – Fénelon*. Baden, 1954.
[3] To Bossuet's malicious *Relation sur le quiétisme* Fénelon replied in *Réponse de l'archevêque de Cambrai á l'évêque de Meaux* and several letters.

treated from a positive and a negative point of view (true and false). In the *Avertissement* to the work Fénelon states that

> . . . my doctrine must not be my own, but that of Christ who sends his priests. It would be regrettable if I said anything of my own.

Fénelon deliberately leaned on recognized spiritual writers and mystics to give his arguments authority: Clement of Alexandria, Cassian, John Chrysostom, Gregory Nazianzen, Anselm and Augustine.[1] He had read St Teresa, St John of the Cross and some of the Rheno–Flemish mystics.[2] He frequently quotes from St François de Sales' *Treatise of the Love of God*, in particular for the notion of indifference and abandonment of self-will to the will of God. According to Fénelon there are five stages in the love of God:

1. carnal love, that is purely servile love, for the gifts God may bestow, as seen in the Old Testament;
2. concupiscence, the love of God as our supreme good, the means of our happiness;
3. love with hope, love of self mingled with an incipient love of God for his sake;
4. still a combination of self-love with a stronger love of God and an emphasis on hope;
5. pure love when the soul loves God for his sake, disinterested charity not motivated by the hope of reward or happiness.

For Fénelon the important point is the difference between the fourth and the fifth stages of love. In the fourth stage love is already close to perfection, since there is no immediate thought of happiness, but merely the desire of salvation. At the next stage the self is entirely excluded and the love of God pure. The soul is now totally indifferent; it only wants to please God and is ready to sacrifice eternal life if such were God's will. If in its trial the soul believes, wrongly, that it is damned, it would consent to this damnation. The soul has become passive in the hands of God; it is in a state of contemplation and perfect quietude. As Fénelon explained to Madame Guyon in a letter (11 August 1689): 'The soul is transformed, for the life and the will of God have been substituted for its own.' There is

---

[1] Fénelon also used a collection of mystical writers: *L'Eclaircissement théologique* de Nicolas de Jésus-Maria, and *Notes et remarques en trois discours* de Jacques de Jésus, published in French by Cyprien de la Nativité, 1641.

[2] Dom Beaucousin edited *La Perle évangélique* (1602), and Ruysbroeck's *Ornement des Noces* (1606). Saint Teresa was translated into French in 1601 by J. Quintanadoine de Brétigny and later by Arnauld d'Andilly, Saint John of the Cross in 1621–2 by R. Gaultier.

a parallel with a passage in St François de Sales' *Treatise of the Love of God* (IX/13, 15):

> It would seem to me that the soul which is in this state of indifference . . . wills nothing, thus lets God will what he pleases . . .

Madame Guyon coined the term non-will (*involonté*) for it. In *Maxime* XXXV Fénelon considers it erroneous to call this transformation of the soul a deification, in an hypostatical union as Madame Guyon would have it. Fénelon sticks to the term transformation which can also be found in Benet of Canfield's *Rule of Perfection* (1/2):

> . . . yet not that this union of wills is hypostatical . . . but is made by the links of love and light of grace.[1]

The passive state belongs to contemplation. Fénelon defines it in *Maxime* XXXIV, in accordance with other mystics:

> a state of suspension or binding of the powers when the soul remains incapable of producing any discursive or other acts pleasing to God during the time of prayer.

The passive state of contemplation is one of pure love. One moves from meditation with its discursive and methodical acts to the directness and simplicity of contemplation as self-love becomes disinterested love.[2] Contemplation in pure love becomes habitual, but it can only be actual at limited times. St John of the Cross and St Teresa restrict the state of pure contemplation to half an hour. Molinos, on the other hand, speaks of a state of uninterrupted contemplation, 'unconstraint in the pilgrimage of this life' (*laisser-aller dans le pèlerinage de cette vie*). In reality, and at a conscious level, it cannot be one continuous act, but a series of acts. Since there are no images included in the state of pure contemplation, where does the humanity of Christ come in? It would appear to be an entirely abstract notion of God. In *Maxime* XXVII Fénelon explains that in this pure contemplation the soul no longer considers the mysteries of Christ either systematically or in pure images. The soul sees Christ in a simple and loving glance and in pure faith. There is a very similar notion in Benet of Canfield's *Rule of Perfection*: faith transcends the imagination. In Part III Benet describes a similar abstract way of contemplation into which he has inserted, perhaps to prove its orthodoxy, a few chapters on the passion of Christ. Indeed Christ is always present in contemplation

---

[1] *The Rule of Perfection* (1608), *La Règle de perfection* (1609). Modern bilingual edition by J. Orcibal, 1982. The Italian version of Part III was condemned in 1689 at the same time as the *Moyen Court*.

[2] Letter of 11 March 1696 to Sr Charlotte de St Cyprien, Carmelite; see also *Maxime* XXIII.

even if his presence is not linked to any concepts or images. Between actual contemplation and meditation Fénelon introduces an intermediary notion, the *oraison perpétuelle*, continuous prayer. Pure love does not need any illumination or elation (*transport*), nor enquiring reason; wisdom and feeling are both silenced as well as will power. It is a complete renunciation of the will so as to comply with the will of God, be it merciful or severe. It means renouncing personal happiness and also personal perfection. For Fénelon what he calls *retour sur soi-même*, looking into onself so as to watch and measure one's spiritual progress, is the mark of self-love. The soul is conscious of its imperfection and thus glorifies the power of God in his perfection.

There remains the notion of hope. The Bull *Coelestis Pater* accused Molinos of denying hope and Bossuet took up this point in his *Ordonnance* (III/6) as the central point of accusation against the 'nouveaux mystiques', i.e. the Quietists. Fénelon was aware of the problem and wanted to redefine hope, as disinterested hope, rather on the lines of the distinction St François de Sales made between servile and filial fear. In the *Explication des articles d'Issy*, Fénelon asserts that hope could not be a reason for loving God, but to love God must be a reason for hope. In the state of perfect love hope is strongest.

The notion of indifference, that is love indifferent to any self-interest, but only complying with the will of God, belongs to a state of passivity. One could liken it to Pascal's *oubli du monde et de tout hormis Dieu*, 'to forget the world and everything except God' (*Mémorial*). For Fénelon indifference means to be free from all satisfaction, even the most subtle spiritual one.

For Bossuet, on the other hand, loving God as the sovereign good means that he is *the* as well as *my* sovereign good (*l'aimer en tant que le et* mon *souverain bien*). Each of these sentiments is part of the other. Bossuet does not distinguish love of self from love of God; mystical concepts were alien to him. There were others besides Bossuet who could not accept the idea of pure love. Malebranche, in a letter to Lamy of June 1698, said that pure love, independent of any motivation of happiness, seemed to him fanciful (*chimérique*). The perfectly disinterested love as a justification for everything one wants to transcend and leave behind seemed to Bossuet an individualistic tendency which could (and did) endanger the clerical and social system he firmly supported. These considerations were uppermost in his mind during the prolonged and embittered controversy.

Fénelon's concepts, forward-looking as they were, made their impact. His very sensitivity appealed to the eighteenth century. His reputation went beyond his country. *The Maxims of the Saints Explained* appeared in English in February 1698 with a laudatory introduction. The main link with Britain was through the chevalier Ramsay, who, converted by Fénelon, wrote a life, *Vie de Fénelon*, 1723. The archbishop was esteemed as a victim of an odious absolutism and his spiritual teaching appealed to various groups with mystical tendencies: the Quakers; an episcopalian group in Aberdeen in the early part of the eighteenth century (where Fénelon came second to Madame Guyon); Wesley, who was acquainted with Ramsay's life of Fénelon.[1]

Looking back on the long and bitter controversy between two eminent theologians one could leave the judgement to a contemporary who knew them both, Innocent XII:

Cambrai loved God too much; Meaux loved man too little.

Erravit Cameracensis excessu amoris Dei; peccavit Meldensis defectu amoris proximi.

❧

6 Jean-Pierre de Caussade

MARK GIBBARD

Works

L'Abandon à la Providence divine. Paris, Desclée de Brouwer, 1966.

Lettres spirituelles. Paris, Desclée de Brouwer, t. I., 1961; t. II., 1964.

Traité sur l'oraison du coeur, et Instructions spirituelles en forme de dialogues sur les divers états d'oraison suivant la doctrine de M. Bossuet. Paris, Desclée de Brouwer, 1981. (The former of these treatises is a previously unpublished, anonymous writing by de Caussade; the latter is the second book of a work published anonymously by de Caussade in 1741 with the editorial help of a fellow-Jesuit, Père Antoine.) ET by Algar Thorold, *On Prayer*, London, Burns, Oates & Washbourne, 1931; Springfield, Ill., Templegate, 1949.

Spiritual Letters, ET by Algar Thorold. London, Burns, Oates & Washbourne, 1934.

Self-Abandonment to the Divine Providence, ET by Algar Thorold. London, Burns, Oates & Washbourne, 1933.

Abandonment, ET by E. McMahon. New York, Benziger, 1945.

The Sacrament of the Present Moment, ET of M. Olphe-Galliard's text of *L'Abandon* by Kitty Muggeridge. London, Fount, 1981.

Bremond, H., *Bossuet, Maître d' Oraison*. Paris, Bloud et Gay, 1931. (This book contains both parts of de Caussade's *Instructions spirituelles*.)

[1] Gilbert Burnet, *Three letters . . . written in 1687* (London, 1688); H. C. Foxcroft, ed., *A Supplement to Burnet's History* (Oxford, Clarendon, 1902); G. H. Henderson, *Mystics of the North-East* (Aberdeen, Third Spalding Club, 1934); on Fénelon and Wesley, J. Orcibal, 'Les spirituels français et espagnols chez John Wesley et ses contemporains', in *Revue d'Histoire des Religions*, 139 (1951), pp. 50–109.

Studies

Olphe-Galliard, M., 'Le Père Jean-Pierre de Caussade et Mme Guyon', in *Bulletin de littérature ecclésiastique de l'Institut Catholique de Toulouse*, 82 (1981), pp. 25–56 (the most recent evaluation of *L'Abandon*).

Olphe-Galliard, M., 'Caussade', in *Dict. Sp.*, 2. 354–71.

Olphe-Galliard, M., 'L'Abandon à la Providence divine et la tradition salésienne', in *RAM*, 38 (1962), pp. 324–53.

Olphe-Galliard, M., 'Le Père Jean-Pierre de Caussade, directeur d'âmes', in *RAM*, 19 (1938), pp. 393–417; 20 (1939), pp. 50–82.

Dom David Knowles placed de Caussade on the same spiritual level as St Teresa, St John of the Cross and St François de Sales and discovered in him 'a steady friend' to whom one could turn in crises and in the ordinary run of life. Abbot John Chapman spoke equally highly of him.

LIFE

Yet de Caussade lived as an obscure Jesuit. Little more is known of him than the dates of main events of his life. He was born in 1675 at du Quercy, near Toulouse; he studied the humanities at the university of Cahors, where Fénelon had been a student twenty years before; he entered at the age of eighteen the Jesuit noviciate at Toulouse; he lived in several of their houses in that province and taught a wide range of subjects in their schools. In 1704 he was ordained priest, became doctor of theology in 1705 and the next year was professed. About 1720 he seems to have been assigned to preaching missions. About 1728 he was sent to Nancy in Lorraine and found congenial work in directing a house of Visitation Nuns, an order founded by François de Sales and Jeanne de Chantal. In 1731 he was withdrawn from Nancy and lived for two years in semi-disgrace in the diocesan seminary of Albi. He wrote rather sadly to one of the sisters that he had let slip some 'indiscreet words'. And his known sympathy with Fénelon probably increased the suspicion that he was teaching Quietism.

This Quietist controversy, which had reached its climax in the confrontation between Bossuet and Fénelon, still caused acute tension and suspicions throughout France. De Caussade himself taught a simple contemplative praying, long established in the orthodox mystical tradition of the Church. His teaching had some similarities to the prayer of these seventeenth- and eighteenth-century Quietists; but he clearly repudiated their excessively passive attitude, which sometimes led them to neglect both the sacraments and offices of the Church as well as personal active concern for salvation.

He was allowed to return in 1733 to Nancy, to the delight of the

Visitation nuns. Yet in 1739 he had to leave Nancy again, to become superior in turn of two Jesuit houses at Perpignan and Albi. Finally he was recalled to the mother-house at Toulouse to become spiritual director to students there until he died in 1751. He suffered from increasing blindness, which he bore heroically.

WRITINGS

The only book he produced himself was *Spiritual Instructions in the Form of Dialogues on the Various States of Prayer according to the teaching of M. Bossuet*. This he published in 1741 when he was at Perpignan. It is rather a prosaic book of questions and answers. He claims – perhaps with a little special pleading – that Bossuet never condemned true mysticism but only the extravagant excesses of the Quietists.

De Caussade, out of modesty and to avoid painful controversy, published this book anonymously. He himself was so little known, that for a time this book was attributed to a better-known colleague.

His second work, published long after his death, is a collection of his letters, sent chiefly to the sisters of the Nancy convent. They throw valuable light on his character and sensitivity, and also on the spiritual condition of those whom he advises in the third collection of his material.

The first critical edition of his third work, *L'Abandon à la Providence divine*, was published by Michel Olphe-Galliard in 1966. The MS of this book has been touched up and indeed probably interpolated by other hands. But the earlier part of it, which is almost certainly in de Caussade's own words, comes from his letters and instructions given to the Visitation nuns at Nancy. It is there that we find teaching particularly valuable for us in the present age with all its pressures and tensions.

DISTINCTIVE TEACHING

Through the years of his ministry he discovered he had a distinctive vocation within his vocation, as he put it in a letter to one of the sisters at Nancy – he was *investi d'une mission*: that is, God had entrusted to him a distinctive insight into praying, loving and a way of living. This he felt inwardly impelled to proclaim, like Paul, 'through ill repute and good repute'.

In every Christian life, 'the sure and solid foundation is', he maintained, 'to give ourselves to God and to put ourselves entirely in his hands, body and soul'. This total giving of ourselves to God in gratitude and love, worked out in every detail of personal and corporate life, is, as Paul again says, our genuine *latreia* (worship: Rom. 12.1).

What is distinctive in de Caussade's insight is, first, that all this springs from and is rooted in a particular kind of *abandon*, and, secondly, that it issues into a particular kind of living, which is enshrined in his ever-pregnant phrase, *'the sacrament of the present moment'*.

This true *abandon* is quite different from the Quietists' passivity. It is a moment-by-moment active self-offering through every kind of climate and circumstance. He sees its prototype in Mary's words at the Annunciation: 'Behold the handmaid of the Lord; be it unto me according to thy word.' No nervous fear is here nor any narrowing down of her life; on the contrary, it was 'something very glorious', running like a thread of gold through all 'occupations, commonplace or lofty' of her life.

Such an *abandon* can only be sustained through our own assurance of God's unalterable love. In spite of the suffering and evil which we see around us, we are sure that God's love ever streams to us, like, as de Caussade says, 'that sublime sun, which from dawn to dusk – however dark and heavy the clouds which hide it – illuminates, warms and inspires us'. 'Did the Lord not prove that he loved us more than life itself, since he laid down his life for us?' And so, de Caussade urges, 'Can we not be assured that, having done so much, he will never forget us?'

So God intends that his love should reach us through the duty of the *present* moment. We cannot live in yesterday's solar heat nor in tomorrow's, but only in its present warmth. In the very same way we can receive God's love through each of today's events, not yesterday's or tomorrow's. So de Caussade teaches, 'God makes of *all* things mysteries and sacraments of love', and so he asks, 'Why should not every moment of our lives be a sort of communion with the divine love?'

The practical problem is to train ourselves to approach each present task or suffering as a sacrament in the same loving concentration with which we receive the blessed sacrament. So he counsels us, 'We must cut off all more distant views, we must confine ourselves to the duty of the present moment, without thinking of what preceded it or what will follow it'; and similarly in one of his letters he writes, 'Try not to let apprehension about the future or regret about the past flood over into your present living and make you miserable.'

The priceless value, specially in our hurrying, tightly-packed days, of his teaching on this sacrament of the present moment is clear. But he reminds us that it demands long, persistent, loving practice. In touching humility in a letter to a nun he explains how he himself succeeded only after failure. So he tells her frankly how he tried to get out of being appointed superior of the Jesuit house at Perpignan. He, who had so advocated *abandon*, grumbled and said he would do anything rather than become a superior; he complained he had no aptitude for the post. And when he arrived at Perpignan, it was far worse, he told this sister, than he anticipated. He hated ceremonial visits; yet the bishop, the steward, the

King's lieutenant, the sheriff, the chief of the garrison, all called on him officially. Yet afterwards – to his own surprise – he could write, 'I remain calm and in peace in the midst of a thousand worries and complications in which I should have expected to be overwhelmed.' We feel that de Caussade is very human. There is no hardness or aloofness, particularly in his letters. 'Little falls are', he writes, 'permitted in order to help us practise humility and patience and to accept ourselves.' Our falls, when seen like this, he adds, are 'far more useful to us than victories that are spoiled by vain complacency'. Such words are part of his charm.

7 Charles de Foucauld

MARK GIBBARD

Life

Bazin, R., (ET) *Charles de Foucauld, Hermit and Explorer*. London, Burns, Oates & Washbourne; New York, Benziger, 1923.
Hamilton, E., *The Desert My Dwelling Place: A Study of Charles de Foucauld*. London, Hodder & Stoughton, 1968.

Writings

Les Ecrits Spirituels. Paris, n.d.
Père de Foucauld – Abbé Huvelin – Correspondance inédite. Paris, 1957.
Charles de Foucauld, D. and R. Barrat, ed. Paris, 1958 (contains selected passages).
Lettres à Mme de Bondy. Paris, 1966.
(ET) *Spiritual Autobiography of Charles de Foucauld*, ed. J. F. Six. London, A. Clarke; New York, Kennedy, 1964 (contains selected passages).
(ET) *Meditations of a Hermit*. London, Burns, Oates & Washbourne; New York, Benziger, 1930.

Spirituality of his Fraternities

Voillaume, R., *Au Coeur des Masses*. Paris, 1952; (ET) *Seeds of the Desert*, London, Burns & Oates; Chicago, Fides, 1955 (contains selected translations).
Voillaume, R., *Lettres aux Fraternités*. Paris, vol. i, 1960; vol. ii, 1960; vol. iii, 1966; (ET) *Brothers of Men*. London, DLT, 1971; Baltimore, Md., Helicon, 1966 (contains selected translations).
Magdaleine de Jésus, Sr., *Du Sahara au Monde Entier*. Paris, 1981.

LIFE

The young Charles de Foucauld was a 'dandy' *de la belle époque*. He was born into a devout, aristocratic family at Strasbourg in 1858. Both of his parents died before he was six. He was brought up and spoilt by his grandfather. He entered the military academy of St Cyr. He lost his faith. He squandered a fortune. He passed out eighty-seventh in a class of eighty-seven.

He became a soldier, but he was never a military man. He was posted to Algeria. He sent his mistress ahead of him with her first-class ticket made out as his wife, Mme la Vicomtesse de Foucauld. She charmed everyone. Then trouble began. His commanding officer said, 'Either this woman goes or you go.' 'Then', he replied, 'we shall go', and threw up his commission.

The affair did not last long. Then an immensely strong will and courage emerged, which marked the rest of his life. Off he went into Morocco disguised as a rabbi and was lost to the world for eighteen months, exploring that then closed country. He had several close shaves with death.

Back in Paris he produced a detailed report and was awarded the gold medal of the Geographical Society. Restored to his family, he began to have second thoughts about religion. He often went into churches and prayed, 'My God, if you exist, show yourself to me.' His cousin, Marie de Bondy, introduced him to a priest, Abbé Huvelin, urbane and discerning. After a sleepless night Charles went to the church, where the Abbé was an assistant priest, near the Opéra. Charles de Foucauld himself tells us what happened. 'I was asking him for instruction in religion. He told me to kneel and confess, and then straightaway to receive Holy Communion.' His doubts dispersed. Jesus became real for him. Love for Jesus became – and remained – literally the passion of his life. For him there were no half measures.

He became a Trappist, but he was no monk. Life there was not hard enough for him. He dreamt of founding a more extreme order and even sent its proposed rule to the Abbé Huvelin, who replied, 'This rule is impossible, it contains everything except discretion. Do not think of gathering others around you, I beg of you. You need to be protected against this striving towards the infinite, which takes away peace of heart.'

After four years with the Trappists, he was summoned to Rome to study. His Father-General saw what was happening, released him from his vows and as a parting present gave him his own cross. Now he was free to discover his unique vocation. He lived for two years as an odd-job man in a tiny hut by the convent of the Poor Clares at Nazareth. In this obscurity he was supremely happy. There it was revealed to him that austerity was not the heart of the matter. Love was. A burning human and supernatural love had broken through into his life.

This led him to Beni-Abbès in Algeria and eventually to Tamanrasset on an island of mountains deep in the Sahara, four hundred miles from the nearest Europeans. He found he could live the life of Nazareth there – *Nazareth est partout*: Nazareth is everywhere. He built himself a long, narrow hermitage; at one end was his altar, at the other end his table and chair with an ever-open door. At that table he compiled the first Tuareg grammar and dictionary; he translated the Gospels and transcribed Tuareg proverbs and love-songs.

Through a tragic misunderstanding he was shot during the First World War by anti-French tribesmen. The grain of wheat that then fell into the ground has borne much fruit. The man of such prayer has become Frère Charles de Jésus, *le frère universel*.

SPIRITUALITY

'More than fifteen hours with nothing else to do but to gaze on you, Lord, and tell you that I love you', wrote Charles de Foucauld in his spiritual journal at Nazareth. He knelt motionless lost in contemplation with his eyes fixed upon the tabernacle on the altar usually for seven hours on weekdays and nearly all day on Sundays and feasts.

The genuineness of his *contemplative prayer* was proved by his cease-less love, which flowed from it, to all his neighbours, even the most abject. Indeed he lived for months without Mass or tabernacle, so infinitely precious to him, in order to minister to desert tribesmen.

His prayer was focused almost exclusively on the eucharistic presence of Jesus. He did not write much about the sacrifice of the Mass, still less about the Eucharist as a communal feast. Nor does he seem to have had an adequate understanding of the indwelling of the triune God within us, as expressed, for example, in the Fourth Gospel: 'My Father will love him and we will come to him and make our home in him' (John 14.23), and 'The Spirit dwells with you and will be in you' (John 14.16). But this lack of doctrinal balance, which is typical of much of the fervent Catholicism of his day, did not lessen the depth of his contemplative life. He found in it his joy: 'I am in peace full to overflowing.' Yet he had to pass through many inner trials: 'God sometimes permits such darkness without any star coming to shine in our sky.'

For many Christians *systematic meditation* is a preliminary stage on the road to contemplation. But in Charles de Foucauld they run *side by side*. He wrote to a friend,

> You must find time to read a few lines of the holy Gospels every day. You must steep yourself in the mind and spirit of Jesus by reading and re-reading, meditating and re-meditating constantly on his words and example; they must

work on our souls like a drop of water which falls again and again on a slab of stone, always in the same place.

On his knees before the altar he wrote out thousands of meditations intended for no eyes except his own. These meditations are always alive with a freshness and direct simplicity. Many would find this kind of practice constricting, but he did not. It was of one piece with his love of Jesus in the sacrament. The tabernacle and the Bible open beside it on his altar *together* enabled him to see Jesus in everyone he met, as Mother Teresa of Calcutta does in our days.

Besides his contemplative praying and his systematic meditation Charles de Foucauld was convinced that he was also called to *vocal prayer*, both the liturgical offices of the Church and also to ever-faithful intercession. 'Praying for those I love', he wrote to his cousin Marie, 'is the chief business of my life.' 'What must come first in all prayers, however varied they may be, and what gives them real value', he maintained, 'is the love with which they are made.'

Nearly all Charles de Foucauld's writing on prayer was personal and spontaneous. He never set himself up as a spiritual director. And yet his words as well as his life have now inspired thousands within his fraternities and far, far beyond them.

THE FRATERNITIES

After the First World War his writings, mimeographed, began to circulate. Little groups began to try out his ideas. René Voillaume and four other young priests followed a Trappist-like rule in a simple desert monastery at El Abiodh in Algeria, where Charles de Foucauld had once lived. In 1927 Charles de Foucauld's body was moved from distant Tamanrasset to El Goléa, a Christian village in Algeria. At the re-burial Père Voillaume and Sister Magdaleine, who had already founded the Little Sisters of Jesus, met for the first time. They had been leading the same kind of life, though quite unaware of each other. Soon after the Second World War the Little Brothers and Sisters of Jesus moved into the dechristianized slums of the West and into the poorest parts of the third world.

The Brothers live in small fraternities of three or four or five. However poor their housing, they keep one room as a chapel where the holy sacrament is reserved. They dress like their fellow-workers. When they return from work, they spend a silent hour in prayer together. They keep open house. They do not engage in any specifically Christian works. They are, like their inspirer, simply men of prayer; and they live the gospel in prayer and friendship.

For this they need an exacting noviciate and training. They begin in a tough, working fraternity. Next they spend part of their noviciate in the Sahara. They go off on trek in the immensity of the desert. They have weeks of solitude in a cave with iron rations. They acquire the mark of the desert. Then they all go, laymen as well as priests, to a house of study for a firmer foundation for their life of prayer and love.

By 1981 there were some 270 Brothers, working in forty-five countries, and 1,300 Sisters of sixty-one nationalities. There is a much smaller company of a hundred Little Brothers of the Gospel, who live in the same spirit but engage in a teaching apostolate.

They all treasure the word 'little' in their title. It speaks both of their utter dependence on God in prayer and also of their complete equality with the poor among whom they live in a warm, open friendship – without trace, as Charles de Foucauld used to say, *de cette charité froide et distante.*

III ENGLISH ROMAN CATHOLICS IN THE EIGHTEENTH AND NINETEENTH CENTURIES

JOHN COULSON

NEWMAN (see also below, pp. 463–8).

Newman, J. H., *Apologia pro Vita Sua*. London, Longman, 1864, OUP, 1913; New York, Macmillan, 1931; Oxford, Clarendon, 1967.

Newman, J. H., *Parochial and Plain Sermons*. London, Pickering, 1958; Westminster, Md., Christian Classics, 1966– (= *PPS*).

Newman, J. H., *Meditations and Devotions*. London, Burns & Oates; Springfield, Ill., Templegate, 1964.

Newman, J. H., *Essay on the Development of Christian Doctrine*. London and New York, Longmans, Green, 1909; Harmondsworth, Penguin, 1974.

Newman, J. H., *Letters and Diaries*, ed. C. S. Dessain and others. London and New York, T. Nelson, 1961– .

Newman, J. H., *Sermons Preached on Various Occasions*. London and New York, Longmans, Green, 1908.

Blehl, V. H., ed., *Realizations – Newman's own Selection of his Sermons*. London, DLT, 1964.

Coupet, A. J., ed., *A Newman Companion to the Gospels*. London, Burns Oates, 1966.

VON HÜGEL

von Hügel, Baron Friedrich, *Essays and Addresses* (= *E*). 2 vols., London, Dent; New York, Dutton, 1921, 1926.

von Hügel, Baron Friedrich, *The Mystical Element of Religion* (= *ME*). 2 vols., London, Dent, 1908; New York, Dutton, 1923.

Thorold, A., ed., *Friedrich von Hügel*. London, Ontario, Dent, 1928.

STUDIES

Bouyer, L., (ET) *Newman, His Life and Spirituality*. London, Burns Oates, 1958.

Burton, E. H., *The Life and Times of Bishop Challoner*. 2 vols., London, Longmans, 1909.

Chapman R., *Father Faber*. London, Burns Oates, 1961.

de la Bedoyere, M., *Baron Friedrich von Hügel, Life*. London, Dent, 1951.

Dessain C. S., *John Henry Newman*. London, Nelson, 1966.

Nédoncelle, M., (ET), *Baron Friedrich von Hügel, His Life and Thought*. London, Longmans, 1937.

Norman, E., *The English Catholic Church in the Nineteenth Century*. OUP, 1984.

Trevor, M., *Newman's Journey*. London, Fontana, 1974.

With the overthrow of James II English Roman Catholics became politically powerless and socially isolated; but the subsequent collapse of the movement to restore the Stuarts and the Catholic unwillingness to support it meant that the penal laws, although still existing, were seldom enforced. It is against this background of growing indifference that the achievement of Richard Challoner must be measured.

Born at Lewes on 29 September 1691 of Presbyterian parents, he spent part of his boyhood at the house of his mother's employer, George Holman of Warkworth, whose chaplain supervised Challoner's education and conversion to the Roman faith. Only fourteen years old, Challoner left England for the English College at Douay, where he spent his next twenty-five years as student, priest, professor and vice-president. He returned to England in 1730 with the reputation of being 'one of the brightest men that was ever bred in Douay College'.

Although there were twenty thousand Catholics in London, in social terms they constituted, throughout the country, an upper-class sect centred upon large country-house communities to which the mission priests acted as chaplains. From about thirty to forty thousand in the beginning of the seventeenth century, they were to grow to about seventy thousand by the end of the eighteenth century. The problem was how to provide Catholics with a distinctive spiritual identity during a time of declining persecution and growing indifference. The dilemma was resolved by Challoner's publication of *The Garden of the Soul* in 1740. Its sub-title shows the wide scope of its intention: 'A Manual of spiritual exercises and instructions for Christians who, living in the world, aspire to Devotion'. It begins with a summary of Christian doctrine, and provides forms of devotion for each part of the day, including guidance for 'the ordinary actions of the day', to which is added a warning against idleness. With each edition the manual was enlarged to include such information as a manner of serving Mass, instructions and devotions for confirmation, and miscellaneous invocations. Challoner brought to this compilation his talents as abridger, and adapter, rather than an innovative genius. His most obvious debt was to St François de Sales who, after the Bible, was the chief formative factor in Challoner's own spiritual life. Following St François, Challoner aimed to bring devotion out of the cloister into the world.

A less popular but still influential factor in forming the spirituality of eighteenth-century Catholics was provided by *The Lives of the Saints*, first published in London between 1756 and 1759 by Alban Butler (1710–73). This both forms and expresses the ethos of contemporary Catholic spirituality which has been described as strong, earnest and undemonstrative; and Butler's approach to the saints is equally sober.

Far from being exuberantly credulous, it is, within the limitations of the time, critical. His aim is stated thus:

> In the lives of the saints we see the most perfect maxims of the gospel reduced to practice, and the most heroic virtue made the object of our senses, clothed as it were with a body, and exhibited to view in its most attractive dress.

Butler goes on to claim that the lives of the saints, in their variety, show that the 'practice of perfection' is possible to all, and that we need 'only sanctify our employments by a perfect spirit, and the fervent exercises of religion, to become saints ourselves, without quitting our state in the world.'

The first Catholic Relief Act was passed three years before Challoner's death in 1781. Although this had been followed by the Gordon riots, by the end of the century Catholic worship and schooling had become officially recognized. The nature of the Catholic population was itself changing. As the nineteenth century developed, the Catholic Church centred less on the gentry and their country-houses, and more on the growing influx of Irish immigrants. A further factor was to be the arrival of converts from the Established Church which reached a climax in 1845 with the reception of the leader of the Oxford Movement, John Henry Newman. The Church Newman joined had, by then, grown to about 750,000.

The spirituality of John Henry Newman (1801–90) is most fully expressed in the eight volumes of the *Parochial and Plain Sermons* preached from 1834 to 1843 while Newman was Vicar of the University Church of St Mary's, Oxford, until his resignation in 1843. They have much in common with the spirituality of the old English Catholics; but where Challoner's spirituality was essentially defensive, Newman's exudes a confidence derived, not only from a Church nationally established, but from a movement of reform within that Church which had affected not only the entire nation, but even 'the backwoodsmen of America'.[1]

Newman is, for example, as much opposed to worldliness and to the acceptance of indifference as Challoner. In fact, Newman goes further, being particularly suspicious of the high-minded man who, although he possesses an enlightened sense of duty, is 'yet on the side of God's enemies':

> The aim of most men esteemed conscientious and religious, or who are what is called honourable and upright men, is, to all appearance, not how to please God, but how to please themselves without displeasing him. I say confidently . . . that they make this world the first object of their minds, and use religion as a corrective, a restraint upon too much attachment to the world.

[1] *Apologia* (1913), p. 175.

To conceive religion 'as a negative thing' is to commit the sin of Balaam who prayed, not to know God's will, but to change it.[1]

This warning, directed as it is to the lay person, reflects a further factor in common with Challoner and Alban Butler – that our spiritual life should be developed within the world and by means of our daily life. The spirituality which Newman requires is one which unites 'conceptions the most lofty concerning God's majesty and bounty towards us, with the most lowly, minute and unostentatious service to him'.[2] So spoke Newman the Anglican. As a Roman Catholic Newman fleshes out this proposal, when in 1856 he describes his short road to perfection[3] (printed in full in the last part of *Meditations and Devotions*): 'If we wish to be perfect, we have nothing more to do than to perform the ordinary duties of the day well.' The road to perfection is short, 'not because easy, but because pertinent and intelligible'. It is easy 'to have ideas what perfection is, which serve well enough to talk about, when we do not intend to aim at it'. Perfection does not mean any extraordinary service or heroic acts, it means what the word usually means: what is complete, consistent and sound: 'He, then, is perfect who does the work of the day perfectly, and we need not go beyond this to seek for perfection. You need not go out of the *round* of the day.' Newman concludes with practical advice which includes such admonitions as: 'Do not lie in bed beyond the due time of rising; give your first thoughts to God; eat and drink to God's glory; be recollected; examine yourself daily; go to bed in good time, and you are already perfect.'

These are the everyday, humdrum methods which bring about a true inwardness. This, the essential purpose of the spiritual life, is the divine indwelling, which 'pervades us as light pervades a building, or as a sweet perfume the folds of some honourable robe'.[4] This divine indwelling is encountered in the smallest details of daily life, not outside them, or in spite of them, or in addition to them. Instead, as Newman remarks in his sermon 'Doing Glory to God in pursuits of the World', the believer 'will see Christ revealed to his soul amid the ordinary actions of the day, as by a sort of sacrament'.[5]

Where Newman differs from those who preceded him and where his innovative genius is most apparent is in the importance he attaches to an adequate and substantial theological basis for an effective spirituality. If his thought has a master-principle it is that put forward in his *Essay on the*

[1] *PPS*, IV, pp. 26–9.
[2] *PPS*, III, 270.
[3] *Meditations and Devotions* (1964), p. 261.
[4] *PPS*, II, 224.
[5] *PPS*, VIII, 165.

Development of Christian Doctrine, when he speaks of Christianity as a whole circle of doctrines of which our Lord is the subject; and since the incarnation is the announcement of a divine gift, 'it establishes in the very idea of Christianity the *sacramental* principle as its characteristic.'[1] It follows, therefore, that the spiritual life is like that of the Church itself, 'dogmatical, devotional, practical all at once',[2] qualities which a healthy spirituality is able to keep in balance.

Since Christ is encountered in a sacramental form, he is uniquely present to each Christian in 'that special mode of approaching him', the eucharistic assembly:

> He has shown us, that to come to him for life is a literal bodily action; not a mere figure, not a mere movement of the heart towards him, but an action of the visible limbs; not a mere secret faith, but a coming to church, a passing along the aisle to his holy table . . . If then a man does not seek him where he is, there is no profit in seeking him where he is not. What is the good of sitting at home seeking him, when his presence is in the holy Eucharist?[3]

Newman's spirituality found its ideal in St Philip Neri, but it is significant that what he has to say of St Philip, the Roman, repeats what he had to say of John Keble, the Anglican:

> This great saint reminds me in so many ways of Keble that I can fancy what Keble would have been had he been born in another place and age: he was formed in the same type of extreme hatred of humbug, playfulness, nay oddity, tender love for others, and severity, which are the lineaments of Keble.

For Newman, holiness consists in bringing many things into a unity, and it is Keble again whom he chooses as his exemplar. He speaks of being unable to separate Keble the writer from Keble the man, or to view him as poet, critic, scholar or divine, except as these aspects of him are gathered up in one in his own proper personality.[4]

This conception of the unifying nature of an effective spirituality is not confined to the clerical as distinct from the lay; being as it is the conception of the whole person, so it applies equally to the lay person as to the priest, as we can see when we compare it to the portrait of James Robert Hope-Scott which Newman drew in his funeral oration of May 1873. For him Hope-Scott was the pattern layman, possessing as he did that refinement of heart, that courtesy and grace, which Newman believed to be especially the characteristic of St Paul, so that 'when a religious question came up suddenly in conversation, he had no longer the manner and the

---

[1] *Development of Christian Doctrine*, VII, i, 4.
[2] *ibid.*, I.i.3.
[3] *PPS*, VII, 149.
[4] *Letters and Diaries*, vols. XII (p. 25) and XXVII (p. 373).

voice of a man of the world. There was a simplicity, earnestness, gravity in his look and in his words, which one could not forget.'[1]

'No one has ever touched the Gospels with so much innate kinship of spirit as he', wrote the eminent Anglican scholar, William Sanday, of Newman;[2] and it has been the intensely scriptural basis of his spirituality which has made Newman so attractive to members of all Christian confessions. He learned his way of praying from Lancelot Andrewes in particular, and he used Andrewes' *Preces Privatae* all his life (see p. 433). His desire to promote 'mutual sympathy between estranged communions and alienated hearts' witnesses to his ecumenical intentions; and in teaching us common forms of spirituality, Newman teaches us how to pray together and thus how to grow together.

No greater contrast to Newman's spirituality can be found than in that of his fellow convert and erstwhile disciple, Frederick Faber (1814–63), since Faber desired above all to stress whatever elements of Catholic spirituality were most opposed to the sober piety of Protestantism. Yet, in so doing, he was remaining true to one of the fundamental impulses of the Oxford Movement which, in common with the revivalism of John Wesley, had encouraged Englishmen not to be ashamed of their religious feelings. It was in poetry that the Oxford Movement began. Keble described poetry as possessing the power to 'guide the mind to worship and prayer'. This was the basis of Newman's appreciation of Wordsworth, in particular, as it was Faber's, whose friendship with the poet encouraged his writing of hymns. Faber is also noted for the eight books on the spiritual life of which the first, *All for Jesus* (1853), is the best known. His dominant theme is that of the experience of the love of God:

> We cannot look at him as simply external to ourselves. Things have passed between us; secret relationships are established, fond ties are knitted; thrilling endearments have been exchanged, there are memories of forgiveness full of tenderness.

If Faber's tone now appears as over-exuberant – he usually refers to the Blessed Virgin as 'Mamma' – he is nevertheless just as much opposed to a cold-hearted worldliness as Newman: 'Better far to flutter like a moth round the candles of a gay Benediction, than to live without love in the proprieties of sensual ease and worldly comfort.' And he defends his deliberately exuberant and aggressive style with the 'bold words of St Mary Magdalene of Pazzi: "Oh Jesus! Thou hast made a fool of thyself – through love!"'

---

[1] *Sermons on Various Occasions*, p. 275.
[2] Cited by Archbishop Michael Ramsey in *The Rediscovery of Newman*, ed. J. Coulson and A. M. Allchin (London, Sheed & Ward and SPCK, 1967), p. 8.

In his emphasis upon private prayer, Faber was not untypical, since from the Reformation until the nineteenth century the trend of spirituality was away from the public worship of the Church towards individual prayer, so much so that people were instructed in the art of praying privately while the public prayer of the Church at Mass was taking place simultaneously. To this habit Newman is an outstanding exception; but his views were not given general currency until the writings of Baron Friedrich von Hügel (1852–1925), who, although born in the middle years of the nineteenth century, did not publish his chief works until the early years of the twentieth.

'It was Newman', writes von Hügel, 'who first taught me to glory in my appurtenance to the Catholic and Roman Church' (*ME* i. p. xv). By 'appurtenance' von Hügel means the dependence of the spiritual life – however intense or 'mystical' – upon the life of the institution: 'Behind every saint stands another saint. In vain do all mystics, as such, vividly feel their experience to be utterly without human antecedent connection. Behind St Paul stands the Jewish synagogue and the earthly Jesus; and behind George Fox stands the entire New Testament. Here is the abiding right and need of the Church, as the fellowship and training school of believers' (*E* i.293).

Newman's legacy – that Christianity is dogmatical, devotional, practical all at once, and that the three offices of Christ are expressed in prayer, theology and institutional form – is expressed by von Hügel in general terms., viz., the spiritual life is compound of three elements, the emotional, the intellectual, and the institutional; and it is the third element – so easily overlooked, because so obvious – which prevents religion from evaporating into mere emotion, or freezing into a negative worldliness. But the institution, for von Hügel as for Newman, is not a mere legal entity. It is 'where the good and the true are to be found mixed up with error and with evil'; but it aspires to become 'the greatest possible multiplicity in the deepest possible unity' (*ME* i.67). This ideal, anticipating as it does the ecclesiology of the second Vatican Council, manifests a foundation for the spiritual life which, authentically Catholic and Roman, has already proved itself to be ecumenical in its possibilities.

C LATER PROTESTANT SPIRITUALITY

1 The Caroline Divines and the Cambridge Platonists

MARTIN THORNTON

More, P. E. and Cross, F. L., ed., *Anglicanism*. London, SPCK; Milwaukee, Morehouse, 1935. (Contains 362 extracts from 104 sources, indexed and annotated, and provides by far the most exhaustive bibliography of the period available.)

Smaller bibliographies

McAdoo, H. R., *The Spirit of Anglicanism*. London, Black; New York, Scribner, 1965.

Thornton, M., *English Spirituality*. London, SPCK, 1963.

Wand, J. W. C., *Anglicanism in History and Today*. London, Weidenfeld & Nicholson, 1961; New York, T. Nelson, 1962.

THE COMPLETE WORKS of the major Caroline Divines were published during the nineteenth century by the LACT, the Surtees Society, the University Presses, and occasionally by private printers.

For introductory commentary

Cuming, G. J., *The Anglicanism of John Cosin*. Durham, Dean and Chapter of Durham, 1975.

McAdoo, H. R., *The Structure of Caroline Moral Theology*. London and New York, Longmans, Green, 1949.

Stranks, C. J., *Anglican Devotion*. London, SPCK; Greenwich, Conn., Seabury, 1961.

Wood, T., *English Casuistical Divinity*. London, SPCK, 1952.

For more general historical background

Babbage, S., *Puritanism and Richard Bancroft*. London, SPCK, 1962.

Clark, G. N., *The Later Stuarts, 1660–1714*. Oxford, Clarendon, 1934; New York, OUP, 1976.

Curtis, M. H., *Oxford and Cambridge in Transition, 1558–1642*. Oxford, Clarendon, 1959.

Hill, C., *The Century of Revolution, 1603–1714*. London, Nelson; New York, W. W. Norton, 1961.

Soden, G., *Godfrey Goodman, Bishop of Gloucester, 1583–1656*. London, SPCK, 1953.

I

The Caroline Age[1] forms the foundation and first flowering of the Anglican tradition, while its overall principle remains in an appeal to antiquity. Anglicanism firmly rejects any suggestion that it is a seventeenth-century invention, and if this period sees the evolution of a new variety of spiritual flower its root-stock is traceable to the New Testament and the Fathers. So in order to understand and evaluate the spirituality of the Caroline age it must be seen as a strand in a continuing tradition. It is necessary to glance at its antecedents and follow its historical development.

At first sight Caroline devotional writing looks somewhat removed from its fourteenth-century English ancestor, but deep down a continuing development is discernible, even if the direct Caroline appeal was to a more primitive age. Walter Hilton's *Scale of Perfection* was possibly the most influential spiritual guide during the fourteenth century, and it was reprinted five times between 1494 and 1679, the last three editions within twenty years. The strong suggestion is that it continued to be the English clergy's *Vade Mecum* throughout and beyond the Reformation period.

The Reformation imposed legislation upon liturgy, ritual and ecclesiastical polity, all under the influences of social and political upheaval. But it is less easy to legislate for personal devotion. On the Sunday after Ascension, 2 June 1549, English Christians would have worshipped according to the medieval Latin Mass; seven days later they were introduced to Cranmer's first Prayer Book. What happened to the private piety of ordinary people? We can only guess that it went on much as before, and that the influence of Hilton survived. Deep-seated devotional habit does not change radically in a week. Some acquaintance with the English fourteenth-century writers is an essential prologue to Caroline studies.

II

Both ages share common characteristics, but with a slowly evolving shift in emphasis. These may be briefly stated.

1. Christian spirituality in general is apt to veer towards either a cold and formal intellectualism on the one hand or to an undisciplined emotionalism on the other; towards a theological straitjacket for the spirit or towards sentimentality divorced from doctrine. The fourteenth century

---

[1] An ambiguous and strictly inaccurate phrase, variously interpreted. This article assumes the period 1594 to 1728, that is from the initial publication of Hooker's *On the Laws of Ecclesiastical Polity* to William Law's *A Serious Call to a Devout and Holy Life*. Law himself, however, is treated on pp. 453–4.

achieved a sublime balance between the two extremes while the Carolines aimed at the same ideal: 'true piety with sound learning'. Some of the more pastorally-minded representatives, such as Horneck, Sherlock, Taylor, Ken, Andrewes, Traherne, Donne and Herbert, can be as affectively drawn to the humanity of Jesus as was St Bernard or Julian of Norwich.[1] But the gradual movement is towards the opposite side; sound learning tends to rule and restrict the freedom of the affections. The best of medieval devotion was not jettisoned but the direct appeal was to the Fathers, the pre-Bernardine age of theology.

2. Throughout the period, affective prayer never dies out, much spirituality is expressed as poetry,[2] religious emotion is properly disciplined but not suppressed. Yet the ascendant keynote of the age is *order*. As foundation to the good life, prayer is predominantly a series of regulated acts. Monasticism has vanished from the English scene but its ordered spirit lives on and its essential aspiration remains: alternating periods of prayer and work issuing in an habitual sense of the presence of God. Several Caroline writers advise daily prayer according to the canonical hours[3] while others compose prayers for everyday occasions: on waking, dressing, grace before meals, on starting a journey.[4]

The result is Christian life, solid and serious with not a little scrupulous tension. There are rules about what may, or may not, be prayed for,[5] which seems a little superfluous since all prayer is reduced to authorized set forms. Extempore prayer remains the Puritan hall-mark and the Anglican sin of sins. Meditations on Scripture are also carefully composed, vetted for error and printed for private use.[6] But there is little sense of any ongoing relation with the living Lord, and no rein given for personal imaginative freedom: beware the extempore!

3. If the monastic ethos lives on, the monasteries are gone. The patristic doctrine of priesthood is also maintained but not the professional and

---

[1] e.g. Beveridge, *Collected Works* (LACT), vol. i, sermon xviii on 1 Cor. 2.2; sermon xix on 2 Cor. 5.17; vol. iii, sermon cxvi on Matt. 11.28. Joseph Hall, *Contemplation on the Passion*, in *Collected Works* (Oxford, 1827), vol. iv, pp. 25–32; *Practical Meditation on the Love of Christ*, Works, vol. viii.

[2] e.g. George Herbert, *The Temple*; John Donne, *Poems*; Richard Crashaw, *The Poems, English, Latin and Greek*; Thomas Traherne, *Poems, Centuries of Meditations*; et al.

[3] e.g. John Cosin, *Private Devotions in the Practice of the Ancient Church called the Hours of Prayer*, Works (LACT), vol. ii, pp. 83–217; Susanna Hopton, *Devotions in the way of Offices*.

[4] e.g. John Cosin, *Works* (LACT), vol. ii, pp. 133–5. Oxford, 1845.

[5] e.g. Jeremy Taylor, *Holy Living*, chap. iv, sec. 10; Thomas Wilson, *Sacra Privata*, Works (LACT), vol. v. *The Whole Duty of Man*, part iv.

[6] e.g. Jeremy Taylor, *The Life of Our Blessed Lord and Saviour*, Part ii, sections, 10–12, *Works*, Wm. Ball, 1837, vol. I, pp. 140–99; William Sherlock, *Meditations and Prayers*.

sacerdotal clericalism of the Middle Ages. The emphasis is upon the *unity of the Church* with the lay intelligentsia playing a leading part.[1] The Prayer Book is neither Missal, Breviary nor lay-manual but *Common Prayer* for the whole Church.

4. There follows a pronounced *domestic* emphasis and setting, the 'homeliness' of the fourteenth century. Home, farm and workshop provide the setting for Christian living, with the parish church replacing convent and seminary. Despite a seemingly artificial gravity, a restrictive tension, the whole becomes pervaded with a subdued optimism; a domestic gentleness of which Little Gidding is perhaps the most enlightening symbol.[2]

5. From this emerges a *moral theology* of much originality, which stamps the spirituality of the age more decisively than any other single factor. The majority of Caroline moralists advocated auricular confession[3] but the emphasis changed from the application of juristic rules to the training of the individual conscience. Their characteristic phrase 'casuistical divinitie' means an interrelation of faith, prayer and conscience, all pointing to the ideal of moral maturity and responsibility. Caroline Anglicanism is Christianity for adults. The confessional was encouraged for practical purposes, but it was not the source of a moral theology calculated by priestly confessors in the universities. Moral teaching, rather, was hammered out from the pulpit and frequently presented in sermon form; a consensus of the whole Church.[4]

6. The study of fourteenth-century religion and the study of Middle English literature are almost the same thing: language and piety are inseparable. The same applies to the Caroline age. At the heart of this religio-literary link is the English Bible from Wycliffe to King James. Amongst other, more obvious things, this points to an evolving spirituality framed in an idiom built for the purpose. Apart from its religious significance, the English Bible did more than anything to encourage

---

[1] The Caroline age produced an impressive list of lay theologians and spiritual directors, e.g. Robert Boyle, Sir Thomas Browne, John Evelyn, Robert Nelson, Isaac Newton, Izaac Walton, Henry Dodwell, Mary Astell, Susanna Hopton, Margaret Godolphin, and Hester Gibbon.

[2] A. L. Maycock, *Nicholas Ferrar*. London, SPCK; New York, Macmillan, 1938; Grand Rapids, Eerdemans, 1980. Maycock, *Chronicles of Little Gidding*. London, SPCK, 1954. *The Story Books of Little Gidding*. London, Seeley, 1899.

[3] e.g. *The Whole Duty of Man*, Sunday III, 21–3; Francis White, *A Reply*; Jeremy Taylor, *A Dissuasive from Popery*, Pt. 1.

[4] *See* H. R. McAdoo, *The Structure of Caroline Moral Theology*; Thomas Wood, *English Casuistical Divinity*.

literacy among the seventeenth-century populace: Anglicanism is for adults.

III

Today, when liturgical lawlessness is followed by legalized chaos, it is difficult to appreciate the weight of authority given to the Book of Common Prayer from 1549 onwards. 'Bible and Prayer Book' were the twin pillars of Caroline spirituality, with the latter given almost equal status, and subjected to the same kind of systematic study as the former. John Cosin spent the better part of his life writing commentary and annotation on the Prayer Book, with not a rubric, colon or comma regarded as insignificant. Other considerable studies were made by Claggett, Sanderson, Patrick, Sparrow and Durel; while all without exception assumed it as familiar background to devotional instruction.

It is again necessary to look at its antecedents, for the Book of Common Prayer is derived from a long line of ancestors, ultimately from St Benedict's *Regula*, with which it has more in common than at first meets the eye.[1] The vital principle, so tragically missed by both modern liturgists and their critics, is that, like the *Regula*, the Prayer Book is not a list of church services but a foundation for Christian living in all of its minutiae. To the seventeenth-century layman the Prayer Book was not a shiny volume to be borrowed from a shelf on entering the church and carefully replaced on leaving. It was a beloved and battered personal possession, a lifelong companion and guide, to be carried from church to kitchen, to living room, to bedside table. It was a symbol of the domestic emphasis, providing spiritual stimulus, moral guidance, meditative material and family prayer.

The Prayer Book was also guide to theology, 'true piety with sound learning' objectified. The common collect form which begins 'O God who . . .' followed by a theological statement and then a petition, may irritate modern people, but it fulfils the Caroline purpose and is not so far removed from the structure of St Paul's Epistles: first expound the doctrine, then its practical application. Pray from the heart but only once the head is clear.[2]

Study of the Prayer Book, as ascetical system as well as liturgical composition, is central to the study of Caroline spirituality. The two are indissociable.

[1] *See* Martin Thornton, *English Spirituality*, pp. 256–9.
[2] See, for example, the Collects for Lent I, Lent II, Sunday Next before Easter, Trinity XII, XIX, XXIII, etc.

IV

If 'true piety with sound learning' is the Caroline ideal, with the Book of Common Prayer as its foundation and focus, then its method or process might be summed up in the significant phrase *via media*. This points to a subtle process, unformulated and almost sub-conscious, by which a unique spirituality has evolved, and which has little or nothing to do with compromise or moderation. It is true that, at first sight, the Prayer Book Prefaces point to compromise, yet the unfolding result is more like an Hegelian triad: not red mixed with white equals pink but oxygen plus hydrogen equals water, a remarkable new substance that looks nothing like its original constituents.[1]

Caroline spirituality, in other words, has evolved by disciplined response to the leading of the Spirit. Drawing upon a wide variety of sources and influences, cross-fertilization has eventually developed into a pure new breed. So initially, the only way to appreciate this spirituality is to follow the Psalmist's injunction: 'Taste and see'. The student might well start with practising the prayer offered by some of the devotional manuals of the age,[2] to be followed up by the weightier theologies[3] and moral treatises.[4] All such studies should always be seen against the social and historical background, and with recognition that familiarity with Bible and Prayer Book is always assumed.

It is likely that modern students will experience both inspiration and disappointment. There is, perhaps, a certain deficiency of depth and feeling, a deadly serious tension, a tendency towards moralism. But in our age of subjectivism, of over-stress on the divine immanence, of a quest for quasi-mystical feeling, of a glib palliness with God, the seventeenth century could well provide a healthy counterbalance of solid discipline and commonsense devotion.

V

Christian history teaches that, in a sinful world, perfect ascetical balance does not usually last very long. Golden periods soon give way to distortion of one kind or another. 'True piety with sound learning' could have led into a deepening of personal devotion, to a less prejudiced attitude to a sane mysticism; or it could have moved to more and more sound learning and ultimately to rationalism.

[1] *See* E. L. Mascall, *Via Media* (London, Longmans, 1956; Greenwich, Conn., Seabury, 1957).

[2] e.g. *The Whole Duty of Man*; Baily, *The Practice of Piety*; Horneck, *The Happy Ascetic*; Sherlock, *The Practical Christian*; Patrick, *The Pilgrim*; Andrewes, *Preces Privatae*; Doddridge, *Rise and Progress of Religion in the Soul*; Ken, *Winchester Manual*; *et al.*

[3] Particularly Hooker's *Ecclesiastical Polity*, Book V.

[4] Particularly, Taylor, *The Great Exemplar*; Sanderson, *Cases of Conscience*.

It is here that the *Cambridge Platonists*,[1] notably Cudworth, Whichcote, More and John Smith, come into the picture. This little group within the seventeenth-century ethos is both attractive and bewildering. They upheld sound learning, but not the rarefied hair-splitting that had become fashionable. They upheld the scholastic principle of synthesis between faith, reason and revelation, but they did not like scholasticism as such. They felt, with some justification, that divine transcendence was exaggerated in Caroline prayer, and countered this tendency with a kind of Neoplatonic mysticism. God dwelt in the human soul so that faith–reason–revelation combined into something like biblical 'wisdom', divine illumination subjectively experienced.

God also dwelt in the material world of nature, and was thereby manifested to reason, but still in the mystical sense of illuminating wisdom. The result is an inspiring muddle between learning, philosophy, and personal piety. For some unaccountable reason, the *via media* process had not quite come off.

The remarkable figure of William Law marks the end of the age;[2] Caroline as an earnest moral and spiritual guide, disciplined and dutiful, with some leaning towards the Cambridge Platonists, and a dangerous flirtation with the heretical Boehme. Once again the true *via media* has collapsed.

How was Anglican spirituality to develop out of this melting pot? It moved towards learning against piety, reason against affective feeling, transcendence against immanence, and landed in Deism.

2 The Puritans

GORDON S. WAKEFIELD

Caldwell, P., *The Puritan Conversion Narrative*. CUP, 1983.

Collinson, P., *The Elizabethan Puritan Movement*. London, Cape; Berkeley, Calif., University of California, 1967.

Cragg, G. R., *Puritanism in the Period of the Great Persecution, 1660–88*. CUP, 1957.

Davie, D., *A Gathered Church: the Literature of the English Dissenting Interest, 1700–1930*. London, Routledge & Kegan Paul; New York, OUP, 1978.

Davie, D., *Dissentient Voice*. Notre Dame, Ind., University of Notre Dame, 1982.

Davies, H., *The Worship of the English Puritans*. London, Dacre, 1941.

---

[1] *See* H. R. McAdoo, *The Spirit of Anglicanism*, pp. 81–155; *HCS*, vol. iii, pp. 148–54.
[2] See pp. 455–9 (Wesley) and 453–4 (Law).

Davies, H., *Worship and Theology in England: from Andrewes to Baxter and Fox 1603–1690*. Princeton, Princeton University, 1975.

Haller, W., *The Rise of Puritanism*. New York, Columbia University, 1938.

Keeble, N. H., *Richard Baxter, Puritan Man of Letters*. Oxford, Clarendon; New York, OUP, 1982.

Miller, P., *The New England Mind: the Seventeenth Century*. New York, Macmillan, 1939.

Nuttall, G. F., *The Holy Spirit in Puritan Faith and Experience*. Oxford, Blackwell, 1946.

Nuttall, G. F., *Visible Saints: The Congregational Way 1640–1660*. Oxford, Blackwell, 1957.

Nuttall, G. F., *The Puritan Spirit*. London, Epworth, 1967.

Wakefield, G. S., *Puritan Devotion*. London, Epworth, 1957.

Watkins, O. C., *The Puritan Experience*. London, Routledge & Kegan Paul, 1972.

Watts, M. R., *The Dissenters: From the Reformation to the French Revolution*, vol. i. Oxford, Clarendon, 1978.

Ziff, L., *Puritanism in America*. New York, Viking; London, OUP, 1973.

The name 'Puritan' is fraught with difficulties. It is commonly used, even by scholars in their off-moments, to describe a kill-joy Christianity, with a glint of fanaticism, indifferent to humanity and the beauties of the world, the antithesis of 'Catholic', which, by contrast, implies sacramental awareness, rich culture, and, by union of nature and grace, dances to the music of the morning stars. The Puritans abolished Christmas and promoted witch hunts.

The name was first applied in the 1560s to those who did not think that the Elizabethan Settlement had gone far enough to reform the English Church. Its sting lay in its being a translation of 'cathari' (from the Greek *katharos*, pure), a name given to some of the harshest medieval heretics (see p. 294). It best describes those from the reign of Elizabeth I onwards, who found themselves in conflict with the ruling party in the established Church, but were not separatists. They were not 'root and branch' reformers, though they were divided into Presbyterians, Independents, and even moderate Prayer Book men. Richard Baxter (1615–91) could even say of himself, 'You could not (except a Catholick Christian) have trulier called me than an *Episcopal-Presbyterian-Independent*'.[1] He was more ecumenical (or eclectic?) than most, yet the only term which fits his spirituality is Puritan.

It is usual to call the Puritans' opponents within the Church 'Anglicans', or, after the death of Elizabeth and especially in the reign of Charles I and under the Commonwealth, 'Carolines'. They wished to see

[1] *Richard Baxter's Penitent Confession* (London, 1691), p. 23.

no reform beyond the Elizabethan Settlement, were strong for the rights of the Church under the Crown, and contended for 'the beauty of holiness', with a use of Prayer Book ceremonial, which presupposed the ecclesiology of the early Fathers, rather than what the Puritans claimed to find in the Bible alone. They came to think of the English Church as the *via media* between Rome and the more extreme reformers. But the name 'Anglican' was first used in the nineteenth century, and, from 1625 to 1662, 'Laudian' might be a better term, since the Puritans, being originally concerned with the re-modelling and renewal of the state Church, and having no desire to destroy it or leave it, might have some claim to be called Anglican themselves. Disheartened, some of the Puritans emigrated to America under James I and in the years when his son governed without a Parliament. Some, indeed, deserted the moderation of their party and became more extreme as time went on, which is a further source of confusion. This caused great embarrassment when the Puritans in consequence of the Civil Wars gained control of the government and the fissiparous nature of reforming movements was manifest. After the failure of the Commonwealth and the Savoy Conference, the Puritans were driven into dissent.

Most Puritans were deeply influenced by Calvinism, though of an English form, which to a Dutchman to this day would seem 'soft'.[1] Some were Arminian. Generalizations are dangerous, even when made by such fine scholars and stylists as William Haller, who is not wholly justified in asserting either that the passion and nativity came to mean little to the Puritan saints, or that, for them, the diary was the substitute for the confessional.[2]

The heart of Puritan piety was personal religion. Such a trite statement could, of course, be made of Lancelot Andrewes, Jeremy Taylor, or any serious Christian. But for the Puritans personal religion was not first a matter of human resolve, but had its origin in the divine initiative and the awesome and overwhelming call of God. Conversion was a necessity – a recognition of the call, its sovereignty and precedence over the whole of life, which thereafter became an unceasing effort to make one's calling and election sure, to seek total and unwavering confidence in what, for many Puritans, was the unalterable decree of God. Conversion was neither achieved nor followed without agony or struggle, often intense, to which, for instance, Bunyan's *Grace Abounding* bears classic witness. Macaulay is guilty of much gross caricature of the Puritans, but his eloquence was never more appropriately employed than when he wrote of the Puritan individual:

[1] See A. Eckhot, *De Theologische Faculteit de Leiden in de 17de Eeuw* (Leiden, 1921).
[2] William Haller, *The Rise of Puritanism*, pp. 151, 38.

He had been wrested by no common deliverer from the grasp of no common foe. He had been ransomed by the sweat of no vulgar agony, by the blood of no earthly sacrifice. It was for him that the sun had been darkened, that the rocks had been rent, that the dead had risen, that all nature had shuddered at the agonies of her expiring God.[1]

All this was often described in terms of 'covenant', an Old Testament notion very prominent in the New. The Methodist Covenant Service of the next century was derived from the Puritans Richard and Joseph Alleine. God in Christ had pledged himself for ever to the redeemed; their whole spirituality was to be total response, entire dedication, left not simply to feelings, but often set down in rules like a business contract.

This was not a theology invented by English and Scottish Puritans but 'derived from the theological tradition of the Zwinglian reformation in Zurich, transmitted in part to the whole family of the Reformed churches in the doctrinal *consensus* of the mid-sixteenth century'.[2] It was no mere individualism. As in Scripture, God's covenant is with the Church; with Israel as a person, yes, but also with Israel as a people. Puritanism knows nothing of solitary religion. Christian, in *Pilgrim's Progress*, is never without the Church for one moment; Evangelist points the way to the Interpreter's House where there are tremendous resources from the tradition; he has Faithful and Hopeful as his companions, while in the sequel, Christiana and her family travel as a caravan, led by Greatheart, type of the Puritan pastor. But the Church is the covenant-people of God, the fellowship of believers, and it is constituted by God's act in Christ, not by a mystical hierarchy of supposed succession from the first apostles. The ministry is, none the less, vital, but it is a leadership of the called and the learned, pastors, preachers, spiritual guides, a clear order to prevent confusion and guard the tradition, not a caste of those who keep the keys and know the spells, but who otherwise may be ignorant, lewd, worldly.

Contrary to popular belief, sacraments, the seals of the covenant, are essential to Puritan spirituality. There are but two – those believed to have been instituted by Christ himself – though the others may, according to Richard Baxter, who did not relish disputes about things indifferent, be reckoned as sacramental ordinances. The majority of Puritans were not Anabaptists. On infant baptism they took the position of the Book of Common Prayer and of Luther and Calvin. And this because, as William Ames said,

[1] Lord Macaulay, *Critical and Historical Essays*, ed. F. C. Montague (London, Methuen; New York, G. P. Putnam's, 1903), vol. i, p. 50.
[2] Patrick Collinson, *Studies in Church History*, ed. C. W. Dugmore and Charles Duggan (London, Nelson, 1964), vol. i, p. 211.

Faith and repentance doe no more make the Covenant of God now than in the time of Abraham (who was the Father of the Faithfull), therefore the want of those acts ought no more to hinder baptism from infants now, than it did circumcision then.[1]

The adult Christian life was 'an improvement of baptism'. The sacrament should be administered in the presence of the whole congregation and the individual member is exhorted:

Repay thy debts in praying for the infant which is to be baptised (as other Christians did in the like case for thee) that God would give him the inward effects of baptism by his blood and spirit . . . assist the Church in praising God for grafting another member into his Mystical Bodie . . . prove whether the effects of Christ's death killeth sin in thee, and whether thou be raised to newness of life by the virtue of his Resurrection . . . show thyself to be a free man of Christ's corporation, having a voice or consent into the admission of others into that holy society.[2]

The Lord's Supper, the scriptural name which the Puritans preferred, is of perpetual obligation. They would have no patience with those who, in more modern language, would contend that what mattered was 'practical Christianity', rather than going to communion. 'The truth is, we have been apt to content ourselves with a profession of moral obedience; but it is a profession of Christ's institution by which alone we glorify him in this world.'[3] Communion should be frequent, since Christ is to be remembered continually. The Prayer Book minimum obligations of attendance at the great festivals were scorned. Every Lord's Day was by most Puritans believed to be the scriptural norm; a Christian should live in a state of constant preparation, and meditations were prescribed, very much in the Western medieval tradition. There are indications in Puritan sacramental theology of the eschatological dimension of the Lord's Supper of which the Reformers were aware, which is part of the Eastern Orthodox understanding and which modern theologians are seeking to recover. Arguments about the nature of Christ's presence in the sacrament and the use of the term 'real presence' have darkened counsel. Of the reality of the union between Christ and the believer, for which the New Testament uses such graphic metaphors and to which the sacrament bears such close relation, the Puritans had no doubt. But they were conscious of what T. F. Torrance, interpreting Calvin, once called 'eschatological distance'.[4]

---

[1] William Ames, *The Marrow of Sacred Divinity* (London, 1642), p. 50.
[2] Lewis Bayly, *The Practice of Piety* (London, 1669), pp. 215–16.
[3] John Owen, *Works*, ed. Witt. Goold (Edinburgh and New York, R. Carter, 1851–3), vol. ix, p. 527.
[4] T. F. Torrance, *Kingdom and Church* (Edinburgh, Oliver & Boyd; Fair Lawn, NJ, Essential Books, 1956), p. 130.

Christ, the glorified Saviour, is at the right hand of God. He is no longer incarnate on earth, as he was, subject to mortality. 'He is not here; he is risen.' His coming means the end of the world. In the sacrament, we 'lift up our hearts' to enter the heavenly glory, and then, strengthened by the pilgrim fare we have received, resume our journey through this world, to the eternal habitations of the Kingdom of God.

Central to the Puritan liturgy of time is the Lord's Day. The Puritans in the 1590s became exponents of the continental theology which maintained that the Sabbath was no mere institution of the Jewish law, transformed under the New Covenant, but that it antedated the fall, being an ordinance of the first creation (Genesis 1) long before Moses, and was reaffirmed at the new creation in Christ. More than on the continent was sabbatarian theology translated into practice. The whole day was to be devoted to the exercises of religion, and play as well as work was unlawful. Sabbath observance loomed large in the covenant.

Some recent historians have argued that this ordering of time, with six days for labour, and the seventh a spiritual feast day, delivered from the orgies and excesses of the holy days which Catholicism and the Laudians countenanced, admirably suited the economic interests of the new industrial middle class. The 'Protestant work-ethic' which is so much a cant phrase of twentieth-century intelligentsia, found its apogee in the Sabbath and established the prosperity of the grocer and the later industrialist alike. This thesis has been challenged, notably by M. Walzer in *The Revolution of the Saints* (New York, Atheneum, 1968); he would see Puritans as the innovators of the ideological party, which in ages since has been 'the most successful (not to say catastrophic) agent of revolution the world has ever seen'. They sprang from the new social groups, the professional intellectuals, and the educated laity, who emerged from the ruins of the pre-Reformation order.[1]

Such scholarly arguments take us from spirituality to socio-politics; they show that Puritanism was much more than a religious movement, which after losing control over the establishment became a dun thread in the pattern of English life until the twentieth century went far to tearing it out. But whatever its wider causes or consequences, the Puritan liturgy of time made possible a worldly asceticism, founded, not on the canonical hours, which the Puritans thought ridiculous, and the alternation of fasts and feasts, but on the Lord's Day, private and family prayers each morning and evening, and honest toil from Monday to Saturday. The Christian week rather than the Christian year, with the whole of redemption commemorated every Sunday, was for them the 'sanctification of time'.

[1] For a summary of the debate, see Lawrence Stone, *The Past and the Present* (Boston and London, Routledge & Kegan Paul, 1981), pp. 145–53.

Puritan spirituality was 'true to the kindred points of heaven and home'. The latter was regarded as a church, 'and what the preacher is in the pulpit, the same the householder is in the house'. Twice a day must the whole household be assembled for worship. Children had their place in the centre of the home and were a parental responsibility. Wet-nursing was condemned. But there was fear of inordinate affection both between husband and wife and parents and children, which may sometimes have led, if not to repression, to a detachment which would be deemed somewhat unnatural in much modern family life.

Puritan spirituality was supremely of the word, and fed on preaching. Visual aids were deplored, though there was much musical appreciation.[1] The pulpit was a means of propaganda, but also of moral guidance and inspiration. In the latter, the Puritans and the Laudian divines were at one.

In terms of spirituality, this means that meditation was central to Puritan prayer. A sermon, after all, is a meditation and often follows one of the classic forms. With Augustine, the Puritans regarded the sacraments as visible words and a supreme medium of meditation. Contemplation, seen as a stage beyond meditation, was suspect. Mystical states were not encouraged, as tending to a kind of Purgatory in devotion. Irrationalism was dreaded; the mind was a gateway to God.

Yet there were transports and ecstasies, and, if a word so ethereal and imprecise is allowed, it is appropriate to speak of a Puritan mysticism.[2] John Owen, in one of his long sentences, writes of 'the *spiritual intense fixation of the mind*, by contemplation on God in Christ, until the soul be as it were swallowed up in admiration and delight'. This state, which is the subject of many subordinate clauses, which describe the adoring soul always conscious of the infinite distance between itself and God, will be enjoyed 'in seasons beautiful and rare', and 'in mental or vocal prayer indifferently'.[3] G. F. Nuttall understands mysticism to be

> a sense of being carried out beyond the things of time and space into unity with the infinite and eternal, in which the soul is filled with a deep consciousness of love and peace, a unity so intimate as to make erotic terms the most natural on which to draw.[4]

John Preston (1587–1628), 'Prince Charles's Puritan Chaplain', com-

---

[1] See Percy A. Scholes, *The Puritans and Music* (London, OUP, 1934; New York, Russell & Russell, 1962).
[2] See G. S. Wakefield, 'Mysticism and its Puritan Types', in *London Quarterly and Holborn Review*, 191 (1966), pp. 34–45; G. F. Nuttall, 'Puritan and Quaker Mysticism', *Theology*, 78 (1975), pp. 518–31.
[3] John Owen, *Works*, vol. iv, pp. 328ff.
[4] G. F. Nuttall, *The Holy Spirit in Puritan Faith and Experience*, p. 146.

posed *The Soliloquy of the Devout Soul panting after the Love of the Lord Jesus*, which longs for Christ not in the story but the heart. Even Richard Baxter, more prosaic than some, can burst out, 'Thy presence makes a croud, a Church; thy converse maketh a closet, or solitary wood or field, to be kin to the Angelical Chore'.[1]

The Puritans were prolific in their commentaries on *The Song of Songs*. Erotic language came naturally to them to describe the intensity of union with Christ, for they knew not Anders Nygren, and the *Song* was there in the canon of Scripture, with a long tradition of allegorical exegesis, supremely that of St Bernard of Clairvaux, whom they much revered. Walter Marshal, in *The Gospel Mystery of Sanctification*, writes of the 'mystical union' between Christ and believers (1692). Scripture 'shadows out' this union 'by many earthly patterns'; consequently to refer to the realistic metaphors of vine and branches, bread and eater, head and members, is to draw from a stock held in common by Puritan writers. But sexual intercourse is one of these, and the Puritans are not afraid to talk of rapes, ravishments and ecstasies.[2]

'Affectionate' or 'affective' piety is strong in the Puritans, and there is a tradition of English dissent which extends from Preston through Baxter into the next century, where Watts and Doddridge are the best known names. This tradition has none of the hardness often associated with Puritanism in its extremer Calvinist forms; it breathes a spirit of gentleness and tolerance, despite its essential *gravitas* and godly sobriety.

Spiritual guidance was not provided only in sermons. Ministers are to be spiritual fathers, tutors, physicians and 'soul friends'. Baxter in Kidderminster followed up the Sunday sermon with a Thursday evening group at his house. ' . . . there one of them repeated the Sermon; and afterwards they proposed what Doubts any of them had about the Sermon, or any other Case of Conscience, and I resolved their Doubts'.[3] And there was much private counselling also. Puritan casuistry did not hesitate to follow the scholastic tradition. It is not very different from that of the Carolines, and is best studied with it simply as English. To do so destroys many of the familiar anti-Puritan jibes. William Perkins (d. 1605), for instance, *pace* Macaulay, objects to bear-baiting and cock-fighting because they are cruel. Where we begin to see divergences between Puritan and Laudian moral theology is in a view of marriage, such as Milton came to hold, in which what was essential was not a sacramental bond made indissoluble by priestly mediation, but 'the marriage of true

---

[1] Richard Baxter, *The Reasons of the Christian Religion* (London, 1667), p. 458.
[2] cf. Edward Polhill, cited at length in Nuttall, *Theology*, 78 (1975), pp. 521ff.
[3] *Reliquiae Baxterianae* (London, 1696), I.83.

minds'. 'Any other union is sin, and any law which could counsel men to sin is not law but tyranny'.[1]

An important part of Puritan casuistry, which may differentiate it from that of the more Catholic teachers of the English Church, but which is continued in Evangelical and Methodist spirituality, concerns the question: How may I know that I am saved? William Perkins stated it in the title of a treatise: *A Case of Conscience, the greatest that ever was; how a man may know whether he be the child of God or no.* Here again there is an appeal to reason, faith in God's love, whether we have immediate apprehension of it or not, and a syllogism of assurance, the logic of God's mercy and the good works that apart from self-consciousness testify that we are in Christ. This is not, in fact, very different from Richard Hooker: '"That we have passed from death to life, we know it" saith St John "because we love our brethren".'[2]

3 The Quakers

GORDON S. WAKEFIELD

Braithwaite, W. C., *The Beginnings of Quakerism*. London, Macmillan, 1912; 2nd edn, 1970.

Braithwaite, W. C., *The Second Period of Quakerism*. CUP, 1961.

Davies, H., *Laudian Worship and Theology in England from Andrewes to Baxter and Fox*. Princeton, Univ. Press, 1975.

Fox, George, *Journal*, ed. J. L. Nickalls (CUP, 1952); ed. R. M. Jones (Richmond, Ind., Friends United, 1976).

Haller, W., *The Rise of Puritanism*. New York, Columbia Univ. Press, 1938.

Miller, P., *The New England Mind: the Seventeenth Century*. New York, Macmillan, 1939.

Nuttall, G. F., *The Holy Spirit in Puritan Faith and Experience*. Oxford, Blackwell, 1946.

Nuttall, G. F., *The Congregational Way*. Oxford, Blackwell, 1957.

Nuttall, G. F., *The Puritan Spirit*. London, Epworth, 1967.

Steere, D., ed., *Quaker Spirituality*. CWS 1984.

Watkins, O. C., *The Puritan Experience*. London, Routledge & Kegan Paul, 1972.

Watts, M. R., *The Dissenters: From the Reformation to the French Revolution*. Oxford, Clarendon Press, 1978.

---

[1] John Milton, summarized by William Haller, *Liberty and Reformation in the Puritan Revolution* (New York, Columbia University, 1955).

[2] See Richard Hooker, 'Sermon I on St Jude', in *Works* (London, John Walthoe, 1723), p. 508.

The Puritans proper, as we have seen, were not radical revolutionaries. They wished neither to overthrow the parliamentary system of government, nor the 'godly discipline' of the Church, based firmly on Scripture and guided by the authentic tradition. They regarded themselves as the true 'Catholics'.[1] But in the ferment of the Civil Wars, when the foundations of Church and state alike were shaken by the clash of armed men and the clamour of endless theological disputes, there arose a multiplicity of sects. The removal of the restraints of traditional government, when the King was at war with some of his most influential people and, later, imprisoned and beheaded, seemed to let loose a babel of tongues, but also many new Pentecosts, groups of men and women who claimed a more direct inspiration than that which came from the reading of ancient texts or the recalling of past events, and who stood for the rights of the common people, the liberty of the submerged and exploited, and the priesthood of all believers. These movements did not spring up without father or mother. They were, in England, manifestations of tendencies discernible on the Continent from the dawn of the Reformation, and, indeed, the heirs of the subterranean, persecuted sects of the Middle Ages. The Puritans, no longer in opposition, grave with the responsibilities of government, abominated them cordially, though we may be more aware of similarities than differences, and it has been contended that the sects are logical developments from Puritanism itself, a Puritanism which in part had grown stiff and cold. They do indeed represent the more rapturous and enthusiastic strain of Puritanism, and some people moved from the more orthodox to the more radical position in the course of their spiritual journey.

Most notable among the sects were the Quakers, who emerged around 1647 and grew astonishingly in a very few years. The name was first given them by Justice Bennett of Derby in 1650 because 'we bid them tremble at the word of God'.[2] They had several leaders of notable charisma, but they were founded by one man of outstanding religious genius, George Fox. He was a large man and loud, self-educated, courageous, obstinate, and withal a gentle spirit, who conquered men and women by his ironclad forbearance and made them long for his friendship. Cromwell once said to him on parting, with tears in his eyes: 'Come again to my house; for if thou and I were but an hour in a day together, we should be nearer one to the other.'[3]

---

[1] See the works of e.g. Richard Greenham, Thomas Adams, John Owen, Richard Baxter. Greenham writes: 'The Papists will say we forsake them, and not they us. We forsake them in the wall, they us in the foundation' (*Workes*, London 1601, p. 273).

[2] George Fox, *Journal*, p. 58.

[3] ibid., p. 199.

For Fox, the whole of church history was to be condemned as 'the Apostasy since the Apostles' days'. Nor was he satisfied with a return to scriptural foundations. He preached immediacy and realism in Christian experience. Christ was no figure of the past, of whom we read in a book, nor was his real presence conveyed in outward sacramental forms, which might make no apparent difference to people's lives. It is 'a nearer and a further state' to be in fellowship with Christ in his death, than to take bread and wine in remembrance of his death. Fox uses the Pauline and Johannine language which has been the material of sacramental theology to describe the reality of spiritual communion, 'which makes perfect'. 'The word is nigh thee, in thy mouth and in thy heart.' 'Christ within thee, the hope of glory.' 'You will say, Christ saith this, and the apostles say that; but what canst thou say?'

Quakerism was perfectionist. It took the promises of God in Christ seriously. Sinlessness was possible because Christ had taken away sin and given us his Spirit. The Spirit is also the light within, 'the light that lightens everyman', antedating Scripture, shining through all creation, bringing believers out of darkness, but condemning those who reject it. This inner light exposes evil, but the soul must not look to that but always to the light itself so that it be not helplessly obsessed with corruption and sin.

The inner light of Fox and the Quakers must not slickly be confused with the teaching of the Cambridge Platonists and their key text, 'The Spirit of man is the candle of the Lord' (Prov. 20.27; see p. 437). The Platonists were scholars and rational theologians who had no *point d'appui* with the Quaker enthusiasts whom they found rough, crude and embarrassing. John Norris, indeed, attacked Robert Barclay, the theologically trained Scot, who was the Quaker apologist of the second generation, in *The Grossness of the Quakers' Principle of the Light Within.*

There were dangers in the Quaker teaching, which Fox's contemporaries were not slow to recognize – hence the severe persecutions which Quakers endured before the Toleration Act of 1687, and the many criticisms by those like Richard Baxter, who were not persecutors. The identification of the inner light with Jesus of Nazareth is not always clear. Karl Holl pointed out that there is no mention of 'grace' throughout Fox's journal. James Nayler, one of the movement's most gifted early leaders, rode into Bristol as Messiah in 1656; a literal and dramatic imitation of Christ which met with terrible punishment. What is not so well remembered is Nayler's penitence and restoration to a deeper faith and to true understanding of Christlikeness.[1]

[1] See G. F. Nuttall, *James Nayler: a Fresh Approach* (London, Friends Historical Society, 1954).

The Quakers were opposed to nominal Christianity and believed that the Christian is to be as Christ in the world, having no part in its violence, always 'turning the other cheek'. Suffering would be inevitable for them as for their Lord. In William Penn's phrase, 'No cross, no crown'.

By and large, Quakers claimed the liberty of the Spirit, but were no antinomians, rather those for whom freedom gave power to live according to Christ's laws. They were enjoined to 'think soberly according as God hath dealt to every man the measure of faith' (Rom. 12.3). The notion of 'measure' may have been the Quaker equivalent of the Catholic's 'canonical obedience'. They may have become more sober as time went on. By the end of the seventeenth century, a uniform plain dress was required of them, under the protest of George Fox's wife, Margaret Fell; and Geoffrey Nuttall has sadly contrasted Elizabeth Fry's fearing to hum to her baby lest it instil into him a love of music with Fox's singing in prison fit to drown his jailer.[1]

The Quakers flourished on both sides of the Atlantic. William Penn founded the colony of Pennsylvania in 1685. Sobriety brought wealth. From the late eighteenth century they became known as the Society of Friends and their form of Christianity became ever more sedate with silence characterizing their meetings in contrast to earlier, more charismatic enthusiasm, with prayer in danger of falling into desuetude on the grounds that all life should be prayer, just as all life is sacramental. But it was not the silence of mystic absorption so much as of waiting upon the word in order to speak with prophetic inspiration. Organized without benefit of clergy, they have maintained a consistent testimony against war, and a considerable philanthropy. They have produced some fine spiritual teachers, such as two Americans, John Woolman (1720–72), campaigner against slavery and author of a famous *Journal* (see pp. 476–8), and Thomas R. Kelly (1893–1941), philosopher, whose *A Testament of Devotion* (1941) is an outstanding spiritual writing of our century.

4 Continental Pietism

DAVID W. LOTZ

Brown, D. W., *Understanding Pietism*. Grand Rapids, Eerdmans, 1976.
McNeill, J. T., *Modern Christian Movements* (New York, Harper & Row, 1968), chap. 2.
Schmidt, M., *Pietismus*. Stuttgart, Kohlhammer, 1972.

[1] G. F. Nuttall, *The Puritan Spirit*, p. 172.

Schmidt, M., *Wiedergeburt und neuer Mensch: gesammelte Studien zur Geschichte des Pietismus.* Witten, Luther-Verlag, 1969.
Stoeffler, F. E., *The Rise of Evangelical Pietism.* Leiden, Brill, 1965.
Stoeffler, F. E., ed., *Continental Piety and Early American Christianity.* Grand Rapids, Eerdmans, 1976.

The most important development within Continental Protestantism between the Reformation and the Enlightenment was the great religious revitalization movement known as Pietism. It profoundly stirred and renewed Protestant church life, both Lutheran and Reformed, during the later seventeenth and the eighteenth centuries, first in Germany and the Netherlands, and soon in France, Switzerland, Scandinavia, and, not least, the United States.

The movement's leading figures were Philipp Jacob Spener (1635–1705), August Hermann Francke (1663–1727), Gottfried Arnold (1666–1714), Johann Albrecht Bengel (1687–1752), Count Nicholas Ludwig von Zinzendorf (1700–60), and Friedrich Christoph Oetinger (1702–82).[1]

Pietism was, in part, the creative response of earnest Christians to the religious and moral lassitude found among all social classes in Germany in the aftermath of the devastating Thirty Years War (1618–48). The pietists blamed the system of government-controlled territorial churches for this condition, and regularly called for the separation of church and state. They also exhorted believers to exercise their own spiritual priesthood rather than to tolerate a clergy-dominated church.

Pietism was also a reaction against the arid intellectualism that characterized much of Lutheran and Reformed orthodoxy. Hence the pietists opposed 'pure life' to 'pure doctrine', elevated 'doing' over 'knowing', and advocated a complete reform of ministerial training, to the end that pastors should have an experiential knowledge of God and thus be able to awaken a 'living faith' in their hearers.

The pietists also sought to check, if not eliminate, confessional intolerance and polemic. Hence one finds among them a new ecumenical openness directed to the goal of uniting all Christians, at least all 'reborn' Christians, in one universal fellowship.

Pietism claimed, above all, to be a completion of that 'unfinished' Reformation of the sixteenth century which had been 'stunted' in its growth, and emptied of its epoch-making significance, by the rapid development of Protestant dogmatism and intolerance, and thus by the

---

[1] Selections by Spener, Francke, Arnold, and Zinzendorf in *The Pietists* (CWS 1984).

egregious failure of orthodoxy to effect a moral transformation of church and society.

In Pietism, therefore, everything came to focus on the 'new birth' (regeneration, conversion), understood as a one-time decision to accept God's offer of grace and thus to experience a 'breakthrough' from the lostness of sin to the new life of 'Christian perfection', which many pietists identified with becoming 'partakers of the divine nature' (2 Pet. 1.4), though not with sinlessness. No less central was the goal or end-result of conversion, namely, the 'new man', understood as the believer's real moral transformation evidenced in works of love.

Most of Pietism's distinguishing marks are already displayed in P. J. Spener's *Pia Desideria* ('Pious Longings'), published in 1675 at Frankfurt am Main, where Spener was head pastor of the Lutheran clergy.[1] He is justly considered the founder of Pietism (certainly of German Pietism), and his *Pia Desideria* the movement's manifesto. To Spener (acting on a suggestion made over a century earlier by Martin Bucer) is also due the institution, in 1670, of the so-called *collegia pietatis*, or 'conventicles' (the *ecclesiolae in ecclesia*): small gatherings of the faithful for purposes of nurturing 'true Christianity' through prayerful Bible study and devotions.

As regards its antecedents, Pietism owed much to English Puritanism, whose leading writers (Lewis Bayly, William Perkins, Richard Baxter, John Bunyan) were avidly read by Spener and his fellow pietists. There were also lines of connection between Pietism and Dutch Puritanism or 'precisianism', the so-called Dutch pre-Pietism of the early seventeenth century (associated primarily with William Ames, Gisbert Voetius, and Willem Teelinck). Pietism's chief debt, however, was to native Lutheran traditions of spirituality, above all to Luther himself and, after him, to Johann Arndt (1555–1621), whose devotional classic, *True Christianity* (1605), soon became *the* handbook of the mainline pietists.[2] Following in Arndt's train, the pietists also went back of the Reformation – and, as they believed, *through* Luther – to the Christ-centred 'bridal mysticism' of the Middle Ages (Bernard of Clairvaux, Thomas à Kempis, Johann Tauler, and the anonymous *Theologia Deutsch*).[3] Some of the more radical pietists also reappropriated the themes of Jakob Boehme (1575–1624), the leading Lutheran representative of a mystical spiritual-

---

[1] *Pia Desideria*, ed. and trans. Theodore G. Tappert. Philadelphia, Fortress, 1964. See Johannes Wallmann, *Philipp Jakob Spener und die Anfänge des Pietismus* (Tübingen, Mohr, 1970).

[2] See Arndt, *True Christianity* (CWS 1979). See pp. 342–6.

[3] See *Theologia Germanica* (CWS 1980) and LI (Bernard, *Homilies on the Song of Songs*).

ism deriving from Caspar Schwenckfeld (1490–1561) and Valentin Weigel (1533–88).[1]

Pietism's second great leader, after Spener, was A. H. Francke, who made the University of Halle (where he was a professor of Greek and Oriental languages) the movement's headquarters. Here he established the world-famous 'Halle Foundations' – educational, eleemosynary, and missionary institutions – that proved Pietism to be socially concerned, educationally innovative, and global in its vision. For Francke, who had undergone an intense conversion experience as a young man, the 'new birth' was the *sine qua non* of Christian existence.

The later history of Pietism was largely determined by the opposition between its Halle form and that represented by Count N. L. von Zinzendorf, who fashioned the Moravian Church out of the remnants of the Bohemian Brethren (*Unitas Fratrum*) that had settled on his estate at Herrnhut, in Saxony, in 1722. Zinzendorf proclaimed a 'religion of the heart' based on intimate fellowship with the Saviour: a theme that was later sounded in a new key by the 'father' of modern Protestant theology, F. D. E. Schleiermacher (1768–1834), who called himself 'a Moravian of a higher order'. Moravians also exercised a profound influence on John Wesley. One may even say that in Wesleyan Methodism Pietism found its own 'new birth' as a worldwide spiritual movement.

Pietism in southwestern Germany (Württemberg) was decisively shaped by J. A. Bengel and F. C. Oetinger. The saintly Bengel was the foremost Bible scholar among the pietists, the originator of their classical principles of biblical interpretation, and a founder of modern textual criticism. Oetinger, deeply indebted to Boehme, was the architect of a theosophical system that purported to harmonize heavenly and earthly knowledge, science and faith, in a unified 'sacred philosophy' (*philosophia sacra*): a system that subsequently influenced the development of the Idealist philosophers, and one-time theological students at Tübingen, Friedrich Schelling (1775–1854) and G. W. F. Hegel (1770–1831).

The German tradition of mystical spiritualism also shaped the thought of the Lutheran pastor and church historian, Gottfried Arnold, best known for his *Impartial History of the Church and Heresy* (1699–1700). This work sought to win a fair hearing for all the heretics, especially the mystics, on the ground that they, rather than their persecutors, were invariably the bearers of authentic piety.

Pietism also powerfully affected Reformed territories (Holland, the Lower Rhine, France, Switzerland) and had important Reformed representatives, among them Theodor Untereyck (1635–93), who made the

---

[1] See Boehme, *The Way to Christ* (CWS 1979).

451

city of Mühlheim on the Ruhr a pietist citadel. It was here that Gerhard Tersteegen (1697–1769) later worked (from 1727), writing his influential hymns and biographies of selected Catholic mystics. In this Tersteegen continued the keen study of mysticism and of spiritual diaries and auto-biographies undertaken by Pierre Poiret (1646–1719), once a French Protestant minister and afterward the companion of the visionary Antoinette Bourignon (1616–80) and editor of the works of Madame Guyon (1648–1717: see pp. 409–11). In the case of Tersteegen and Poiret (and of most of the radical pietists) mystical spiritualism entailed separatism, i.e., indifference if not hostility to the institutional church in favour of cultivating the 'inner man.'

While Pietism often encouraged and sometimes ended in subjectivism, separatism, legalism, anti-intellectualism, and mystical-ascetic flight from the world, it must be given credit on the whole, and in its mainline representatives, for the rise of Protestant ecumenicity and mission-mindedness; for significant impulses to philanthropic and educational work; for renewal of the pastoral ministry and preaching office, as well as for a remarkable efflorescence of hymnody and devotional literature; and, not least, for restoring the emphasis on *personal* Christianity (faith as decision) in opposition to 'nominal' and 'notional' Christianity, and for saving the institutional church (the *community* of the faithful) from disso-lution by a radical religious individualism that might otherwise have won the day.

5 The Nonjurors and William Law

W. JARDINE GRISBROOKE

ON THE NONJURORS

The existing works on the Nonjurors are all outdated by recent research; until the results of the latter can be published, probably the least misleading book for the reader to use is J. H. Overton, *The Nonjurors: their Lives, Principles and Writings* (London, Smith, Elder, 1902; New York, Whittaker, 1903).

ON WILLIAM LAW

William Law, *A Serious Call to a Devout and Holy Life*, and *The Spirit of Love*, ed. P. G. Stanwood, CWS 1979 (bibliography).

William Law, *Complete Works* (London, 1762); reprinted by 'G. Moreton' (G. B. Morgan), 9 vols. Brockenhurst; Canterbury, 1892–3.

Hobhouse, S. H., *Selected Mystical Writings of William Law* (with notes and

valuable 'studies'). London, Daniel, 1938; 2nd edn, New York, Harper, 1948.
Hopkinson, A. W., *About William Law*. London, SPCK, 1948.
Overton, J. H., *William Law, Nonjuror and Mystic*. London, Longmans, 1881; Ann Arbor, University Microfilms International, 1975.
Walker, A. K., *William Law: His Life and Thought*. London, SPCK, 1973.

The Nonjurors (the basic historical facts about whom can be found in the article *Nonjurors* in *ODCC*) regarded themselves as the true Church of England, and were the inheritors in the eighteenth century of the tradition of the Carolines in the seventeenth. The sacramental and liturgical element in the spirituality of the Carolines was further developed and emphasized by the Nonjurors, among whom such practices as frequent communion became common, while the more 'advanced' Nonjurors departed largely from the Anglicanism they had inherited, and revived many primitive and supposedly primitive practices, notably infant confirmation and communion.

As might be expected among a group whose very existence was due to the abandonment of all worldly prospects for conscience' sake, the ethical and devotional standards taught by the Nonjuring divines were high, and their application rigorous. In some of them, indeed, the rigour becomes rigorist, and in none more so than in William Law.

Born in 1686 at King's Cliffe, Northamptonshire, Law entered Emmanuel College, Cambridge, in 1705, took his B.A. in 1708, and his M.A. in 1712. He was ordained deacon and elected Fellow of his college in 1711, but resigned his fellowship and was reconciled with the Nonjuring Church in 1715 after the accession of George I. He was ordained priest in 1728. From 1727 to 1737 he resided in the household of a Mr Gibbon at Putney, as tutor to his host's son Edward, afterwards father of the historian. In 1740 he retired to King's Cliffe, where he set up a semi-monastic household with a widow, Mrs Hutcheson, and the sister of his former pupil, Miss Hester Gibbon. He died in 1761.

Law's writings fall into two distinct groups, coinciding with the periods before and after his retirement to King's Cliffe. As a spiritual guide, Law has been aptly described as 'a master of Christian seriousness': he will tolerate no compromise, no equivocation, and no double standards: there are no degrees of Christian commitment – the counsels of perfection are addressed not to a few, but to all who would profess and call themselves Christians. This 'seriousness' is already evident in a set of 'Rules for my Future Conduct' which he drew up before going up to Cambridge in 1705, and is the outstanding characteristic of his most famous work, *A Serious Call to a Devout and Holy Life*, first published in 1728. Law's teaching has to be seen against its background: he is reacting against the eighteenth century's distaste for 'enthusiasm' and 'fanaticism', and its easy-going Christianity, too often too ready to compromise with 'the world' to almost any extent. It is typical of Law, and reflects his environment, that he taught that 'the world' was far more dangerous a foe of the Christian than 'the flesh' or 'the devil'.

But Law's fear of 'the world' is taken to extremes: he appears to despise *all* human reason, learning and culture. Moreover, there is not much that is *specifically* Christian about the 'devout and holy life': he seems less concerned with the salvation wrought by Jesus than with his ethical teaching, and much that Law says could as well be based on the teaching of many another great spiritual master.

About 1734 Law started to read the works of Jakob Boehme (see pp. 450–1). He had already a wide acquaintance with the spiritual and mystical writers, and had been particularly influenced by Tauler, Ruysbroeck, and à Kempis; but he now became increasingly obsessed – no other word will do – with Boehme. Why? On the one hand, the very fact that Boehme was, supposedly, 'semi-illiterate' attracted the anti-humanist in Law; on the other, Boehme led him into realms in which the speculative side of his mind, hitherto suppressed, could indulge its revenge. From about 1740 Law's spiritual teaching becomes more and more fanciful and wayward. He is now impatient of the kind of advice he had given in the *Serious Call*, he has no time for any such 'aids to devotion', his teaching is based less and less on the Scriptures than on Boehme, whom he regards as 'illuminated' and 'inspired' (equally with the Scriptures? and did he come to regard himself in the same light?); and he appears to sit very loose to orthodox Christian doctrine. The most significant works of this period are *The Spirit of Prayer* (1749, 1750) and *The Spirit of Love* (1752, 1754).

The later eccentric developments in Law's thought alienated many of his contemporaries – e.g. Wesley (see pp. 455–9) and Johnson – who had hitherto held his work in high regard, and one can but agree with Louis Bouyer's verdict on his later books: while admitting that they 'contain passages of high spirituality', he says that 'Boehme's bizarre genius here turns into a very British kind of mild dottiness'. But the *Serious Call* is undoubtedly one of the classics of English spiritual literature. It has influenced many in the two and a half centuries since it was first published, and, whatever its failings, it has an abiding value in the emphasis it places on the single-mindedness which is essential to real progress in the spiritual life.

6 John Wesley and the Methodist Movement

A. RAYMOND GEORGE

The literature on John Wesley and Methodism is very large; so we refer simply to three standard works with their bibliographies.

Davies, R. and Rupp, G., ed., *A History of the Methodist Church in Great Britain*, vol. i. London, Epworth, 1965.
Schmidt, M., (ET) *John Wesley, A Theological Biography*. London, Epworth; New York and Nashville, Abingdon, vol. i, 1962; vol. ii, Part 1, 1971; Part 2, 1973.
Whaling, F., ed., *John and Charles Wesley*. CWS 1982.

In these will be found bibliographical details about John Wesley's *Works*, the *Poetical Works* of John and Charles Wesley, the standard editions of John Wesley's *Sermons*, *Letters*, and *Journal*, and the *Lives of the Early Methodist Preachers*. The new edition of *The Works of John Wesley*, of which the earlier volumes were published by Oxford under the title 'The Oxford Edition' while later volumes are being published by Abingdon under the title 'The Bicentennial Edition', will eventually replace most of these. It already includes some Sermons and Letters, as shown in the footnotes.

John Wesley (1703–91) was the leading figure of the eighteenth-century evangelical revival. Both his grandfathers were Dissenting ministers; both his parents had joined the Church of England; his father was Rector of Epworth; his mother had been guided in his education by an account of the mission of A. H. Francke. Thus Dissenting, Anglican and pietist influences were combined in his background. At the time of his ordination as deacon in 1725 he underwent a kind of moral and indeed spiritual conversion to a more disciplined and ascetic mode of life; he was ordained priest in 1728. In 1726 he was elected Fellow of Lincoln College, Oxford, but had frequent leaves of absence to assist his father at Wroot, near Epworth. Though he once described himself as a man of one book, the Bible, he read widely.[1] He read chiefly the Fathers, the Anglican divines such as John Norris, the Scottish Henry Scougal, some of the post-Tridentine Roman Catholic writers such as François de Sales, and biographers such as de Renty. But he was most influenced, though he was not uncritical of them, by Thomas à Kempis, Jeremy Taylor, and above all by the *Christian Perfection* and *Serious Call* of William Law, whom he also visited. His own views were in general typical of the high-church Anglicanism of his day.

[1] V. H. H. Green, *The Young Mr Wesley* (London, Arnold; New York, St Martin's, 1961), pp. 305–19 gives lists of some of the books which he read from 1725 to 1734.

In 1729 he joined and rapidly became the leader of a group of men in the University of Oxford who held regular meetings to study the Greek New Testament and were so methodical both in their religious practices, such as attendance at Holy Communion, and in good works, that they were nicknamed Methodists or the Holy Club (see Plate 13). In this period he realized that religion was of the heart and sought inward holiness, but becoming dissatisfied with his religious state travelled to America to convert the Indians. Among the books which he took with him were A. H. Francke's *Nicodemus* and the life of Gregory Lopez, representing respectively the German pietism of Halle and the mysticism of the peoples who speak the Romance languages. The two were indeed linked for French and Spanish mysticism had been introduced to Germany and the Netherlands by the work of Pierre Poiret. Wesley was also much influenced by the views on perfection and on repentance in the writings of 'Macarius the Egyptian'[1] and of Ephrem Syrus. He had been greatly impressed by a party of Moravians who were with him on the voyage, and in Georgia he had several conversations with their local leader A. G. Spangenberg, who was also interested in mysticism. Soon Wesley was translating the hymns of German Pietism from the Moravian hymnbook. His mission to the Indians came to nothing and his ministry to the English Colony was unsuccessful; he returned to England disillusioned. He had tried asceticism, solitude (while helping his father at Wroot), works of charity with the Holy Club and mysticism. None had brought to him the assurance which he sought.[2] He regarded the mystics as the most dangerous, for he thought that they encouraged neglect of the means of grace and trust in one's own righteousness.[3]

After the return to England he was persuaded by the Moravian Peter Böhler to renounce all dependence on his own works and by the use of the means of grace to seek true faith in Christ, which would be attended by dominion over sin and a sense of forgiveness. Even before he found the faith of which Böhler spoke he wrote harshly to William Law, using 'mystical' pejoratively and blaming Law for not pressing upon him the need for faith.[4]

At last, as he recorded in his *Journal*, on 24 May 1738 he found the object of his quest at a meeting of a society in a room in Aldersgate Street,

---

[1] On the authorship and provenance of 'Macarius' see A. C. Outler, ed., *John Wesley* (OUP, 1964), p. 9, n. 26. See above pp. 173–5.

[2] cf. R. G. Tuttle Jr, *John Wesley, His Life and Theology* (Grand Rapids, Zondervan, 1978), especially p. 143.

[3] *Letter* of 23 November 1736 in F. Baker, ed., *The Works of John Wesley*, vol. 25, *Letters I, 1721–1739* (OUP, 1980), pp. 487–90. cf. *Journal*, 24 January and 24 May 1738.

[4] *Letters* of 14 and 20 May 1738, and Law's replies in F. Baker, op. cit., pp. 540–50.

London, where one was reading Luther's preface to the Epistle to the Romans.

> About a quarter before nine, while he was describing the change which God works in the heart through faith in Christ, I felt my heart strangely warmed. I felt I did trust in Christ, Christ alone for salvation; and an assurance was given me that he had taken away *my* sins, even *mine*, and saved *me* from the law of sin and death.

This experience, usually described as his conversion, coupled with other experiences in the same period, such as the adoption of open-air preaching, was a decisive turning-point in his ministry. Thereafter he preached with a new conviction the common doctrines of evangelical religion, especially those which concern the work of the Holy Spirit, such as salvation by faith and the new birth. He laid special emphasis on certain distinctive points, such as the Arminian doctrine of God's universal love, the prevenient free grace which mitigates total depravity, present assurance through the Spirit bearing witness with our spirits that we are children of God (Rom. 8.16) and entire sanctification, scriptural holiness, perfect love, attainable in this life. His own sense of assurance, however, was not continuous, nor did he ever claim perfection; and his formulation of these doctrines underwent some changes in the last part of his life.

His warm relationship with the Moravians soon cooled, chiefly because of the emphasis which the Moravian P. H. Molther laid on stillness, i.e. quietism, neglect of the means of grace. Wesley laid great emphasis on 'the means of grace', as is shown by his sermon with that title, and in the *Minutes of Conference* of 1744 he listed them for the preachers. The instituted means are prayer (private, family, public), searching the Scripture (reading, meditating, hearing), the Lord's Supper, fasting, and Christian conference. The prudential means are the Society, Class and Band meetings of the Methodist system which he had founded, and watchnight and love-feasts, to which might be added the Covenant Service, derived from Puritanism. He published collections of prayers for daily use and in later years *The Sunday Service of the Methodists*, an abridgement of *The Book of Common Prayer*, 1662.

We may further judge the type of spirituality which Wesley encouraged from the books which he recommended to his preachers and people. For them he began in 1749 to publish *The Christian Library* (a kind of forerunner of *The Classics of Western Spirituality*), which ran to fifty volumes of 'practical divinity'. It reflected his own wide reading, and there was now a much greater emphasis on the Puritans. By abbreviating, i.e. expurgating, his authors he was able to retain the 'gold', as he once put it, of the mystics; indeed he sometimes retained more than might have been expected. On 6 January 1756, however, he sent an open letter to William Law, whose later writings he greatly disapproved, because Law had fallen under the influence of the writings of Jakob Boehme.[1] In later years Wesley, though speaking kindly of Law personally, still wrote against mysticism.[2]

What he enjoined, he practised. He observed regular times of prayer, and though he abandoned some of his high-church practices, he retained his devotion to the Holy Communion, which he received constantly. Justification by faith did not mislead him into either stillness or antinomianism.

While utterly remote from Pelagianism, he largely avoided the forensic soteriology characteristic of Continental Protestantism. Though deeply influenced first by mysticism and then by Pietism he was neither a mystic nor a typical pietist. Not for him that ascetic striving which A. Nygren classes as Eros and F. Heiler as mystical piety. The phrase 'means of grace' has a different tone from 'spiritual exercises'. Though like a pietist he in effect established *ecclesiolae*, he never lost sight of the *ecclesia*. He was led by Eastern writers to lay great emphasis on the Spirit, but his spirituality was not of a pentecostalist or enthusiastic type. Though he avoided the sentimentality of the Moravians, it has been well described as affectionate.

John Wesley was important not only in his own right, but as the founder of 'the people called Methodists', who gradually formed a fresh denomination. His brother Charles (1707–88) was their hymn-writer. His hymns are a clear expression of evangelical doctrine, with occasional touches of mysticism, and a deep vein of eucharistic devotion. The influence of the Wesleys can be seen in the spiritual biographies of the preachers which John delighted to publish in *The Arminian Magazine*. In England, as elsewhere, the Methodists split into various branches, of which the Primitive Methodists showed a more enthusiastic type of piety. Various holiness movements have their roots in Methodism, as has the Salvation Army.

Wesley had Anglican helpers who stayed in their parishes, precursors of the Anglican evangelicals of the following century. There was also a Calvinistic wing of the revival. Others not closely associated with the revival made important contributions to spirituality. Isaac Watts (1674–1748), Independent minister, wrote on prayer, but his permanent influence comes through his hymns. The spirituality of the Dissenting Academies is represented by the hymns of Philip Doddridge (1702–51) of

[1] cf. E. W. Baker, *A Herald of the Evangelical Revival* (London, Epworth, 1948); J. B. Green, *John Wesley and William Law* (London, Epworth, 1945).
[2] e.g. *Letter* of 26 February 1783.

the Northampton Academy. A. M. Toplady (1740–78), bitter opponent of John Wesley, yet expressed the heart of evangelical religion in a hymn:

> Nothing in my hand I bring,
> Simply to thy Cross I cling.

7 The Evangelical Revival in the Church of England

MICHAEL HENNELL

Bradley, I., *The Call to Seriousness*. London, Cape, 1976.
Carus, W., *Memoirs of the Life of the Rev. Charles Simeon*. London, Hatchard, 1847.
Coupland, R., *Wilberforce*. 2nd edn, London, Collins, 1945.
Forster, E. M., *Marianne Thornton*. London, Arnold, 1956.
Hennell, M. M., *John Venn and the Clapham Sect*. London, Lutterworth, 1958.
Hennell, M. M., *Sons of the Prophets*. London, SPCK, 1979.
Hopkins, H. E., *Charles Simeon of Cambridge*. London, Hodder, 1977.
Jones, M. G., *Hannah More*. CUP, 1952.
Pollard, A., and Hennell, M. M., ed. *Charles Simeon 1759–1836; Essays written in commemoration of his Bi-centenary*. London, SPCK, 1959.
Pollock, J. C., *Wilberforce*. London, Constable, 1977.
Russell, G. W. E., *A Short History of the Evangelical Movement*. London, Mowbrays, 1915.
Russell, G. W. E., *The Household of Faith*. London, Mowbrays, 1906.
Smyth, C., *Simeon and Church Order*. CUP, 1940.
Wilberforce, R. I. and S., *Life of William Wilberforce*. London, Murray, 1838.

'I hope you read your Bible with much prayer', Henry Venn (1724–97) writes to a member of his congregation at Huddersfield.[1] To his daughter Catherine he goes into greater detail.

> Rise always by seven. Be sure that you do not omit prayer; and strive to pray in earnest, that you may be of a meek and humble spirit . . . Prayer in secret statedly and prayer frequently in our mind, is to keep us from yielding to our natural temper, and to bring us to imitate the meek, humble, patient, and loving, Jesus, our Saviour, and our God . . . I assure you, my dear Kitty, the watching, the prayer, the pains, it costs me to get the better of myself, and behave in any degree becoming my profession, are much indeed.[2]

[1] H. Venn, *Life of H. Venn* (London, Hatchard, 1834), p. 103.
[2] ibid., pp. 280–1.

This letter written by Henry Venn to a sixteen-year old daughter says a great deal about the Anglican Evangelical attitude to prayer and meditation. Early rising was considered essential; some were up at five each morning. Prayer could be verbal or silent. Its object was to control and guide the Christian mind and form the Christian character through an imitation of Christ. 'It is a glorious end to live for, that we may be like God in our temper, glorify him for a few years on earth, and then dwell in his presence for ever.'[1]

John Newton (1725–1807) also stressed prayer and Bible reading. 'Let your backwardness to prayer and reading the Scripture be ever so great, you must strive against it.'[2] In prayer there was, for Newton, particular stress on thanksgiving, confession and petition. Newton believed that petition should be bold:

> Thou art coming to a King:
> Large petitions with thee bring;
> For his grace and power are such
> None can ever ask too much.[3]

His *Cardiphonia* is full of wise words on prayer: 'Secret prayer, and the good word, are the chief *wells* from whence we draw the water of salvation. These will keep the soul alive when creature streams are cut off.'[4]

Newton also wrote about family prayer and social prayer. By his day both practices were within the Evangelical tradition. He congratulates a father about to worship God with all his house. Family prayers became almost the hall-mark of Victorian Evangelicalism. Henry Thornton (1760–1815) provided a book of *Family Prayers*[5] which was in regular use in Victorian Evangelical households. Social prayer, i.e. prayer meetings, was also advocated by Newton.

William Wilberforce (1759–1833), soon after his conversion, introduced 'constant family prayer, and resolved to have it every morning and evening, and to read a chapter when time.'[6] He also began to rise at six for two hours of prayer and Bible study; later he talks of the benefit of early rising, though 'it sadly wears my frame.'[7] He is often critical of his

[1] ibid., p. 281.
[2] J. Newton, *Works* (London, 1822), vol. iii, pp. 61–2.
[3] 'Come my soul, thy suit prepare'. *Hymns Ancient and Modern Revised*, no. 319.
[4] J. Newton, *Works*, vol. iii, p. 213.
[5] H. Thornton, *Family Prayers*, London, 1834.
[6] R. I. and S. Wilberforce, *Life*, i p. 91.
[7] Coupland, op. cit., p. 187.

shortcomings which makes him ask: 'Is it that my devotions are too hurried, that I do not read the Scripture enough, or how is it, that I leave with reluctance the mere chit-chat of Boswell's Johnson, for what ought to be the grateful offices of prayer and praise?'[1] Wilberforce used to put a pebble in his shoe to remind him of eternal things. He practised fasting during a day of secret prayer that he arranged for himself. Sundays always included a time for church and a time for retirement when Wilberforce left his guests for an hour and a half during the afternoon to study Baxter's *Works* or some other spiritual classic. 'Often on my visits to Holwood', he wrote in old age, 'when I heard one or another speak of this man's place or that man's peerage, I felt a rising inclination to pursue the same objects, but a Sunday in solitude never failed to restore me to myself.'[2] Coupland attributes Wilberforce's indomitable perseverance in the slave trade campaign to his strong devotional life.[3]

John Venn (1789–1813) articulated for the Clapham Sect their sense of accountability to God in both their public and private lives.[4] He also gave them a vision of heaven, 'where all things are as substantial as here they are vain; where all things are as momentous as here they are frivolous; where all things are as great as here they are little; where all things are as durable as here they are transitory; where all things are as fixed as here they are mutable.'[5] In heaven opportunity is subject, he says, neither to frustration nor to limitation. 'In heaven there is scope for infinite enlargement and perfection; for boundless good and immeasurable glory.'[6]

Charles Simeon (1759–1836) rose at four a.m. and gave four hours to prayer and Bible study. If he overslept he fined himself a guinea which he threw in the Cam; this he had to do only once. His influence over ordinands and other Christian students was immense, as it was over local clergy and their wives, both of whom attended his clerical society. In his teaching Simeon distinguished between prayer and meditation. He always encouraged his pupils to wait on God in quietness, and not always to frame their prayers in words. Simeon was a spiritual director of rare insight. He urged moderation in devotion; he asked a friend to tell his son 'from me, that I thought an hour in the morning, and the same in the

---

[1] *Life* iii, p. 63.
[2] ibid., i, p. 316.
[3] Coupland, op. cit., p. 187.
[4] M. M. Hennell, *John Venn*, p. 207.
[5] J. Venn, *Sermons* (London, 1822), i, p. 85; also Hennell, op. cit., pp. 209–10.
[6] ibid., iii, p. 177.

evening, was sufficient for religious exercises, and better than a longer time.'[1]

Simeon's attitude to the world was very positive – God was to be enjoyed in everything. His attitude to other people is revealed in the entry in his diary for Saturday, 14 March 1807.

> When reading 1 Corinthians xiii this morning, I asked myself, How should I act towards Mr and Mrs Edwards[2] and Mr and Mrs Thomason,[3] and regretted that the same spirit did not animate me towards every other person. I began to pray for our Provost, and Mr Flower, and Mr Twiss, the grocer. I apprehend that the best mode of understanding Christian love, is to consider what dispositions we show towards the dearest objects of our affections, and put every human being in their place.[4]

Henry Martyn (1781–1812), when Simeon's curate, read his Bible three times a day. Following the example of William Law, he rose at 'half after five' each morning: Prayer and the holy Scriptures were 'those wells of salvation whence he drew daily the living water' when a missionary in India and Persia. He practised fasting.

Hannah More (1745–1833) wrote in *Practical Piety* (1814),

> In prayer ... the perfections of God, and especially his mercies in our redemption, should occupy our thoughts as much as our sins; our obligation to him as much as our departures from him. We should keep up in our hearts a constant sense of our own weakness, not with a design to discourage the mind and depress the spirits; but with a view to drive us out of ourselves, in search of the Divine assistance (p. 109).

Edward Bickersteth (1786–1850) continued within the Victorian church the devotional tradition of the Evangelical Revival. He was, for a time, Secretary of the Church Missionary Society and later vicar of Watton. He wrote a number of theological and devotional works of which the most important are: *A Treatise on Prayer* (1817) and *A Treatise on the Lord's Supper* (1822); he also compiled a hymn book, *Christian Psalmody* (1832) which was widely used by Victorian Evangelical congregations. *A Treatise on Prayer* is designed to help Christians to pray and to provide them

[1] Carus, op. cit., p. 578.
[2] Edward Edwards, Lecturer at St Nicholas Chapel, King's Lynn, a convert of Simeon and a great friend of both Simeon and John Venn.
[3] Thomas Thomason was for many years Simeon's curate; subsequently he became Chaplain to the East India Company. Most of Simeon's letters are to the Thomasons.
[4] Carus, ibid., p. 219.

with forms of prayer. It includes a consideration of the theology of prayer, public worship and private prayer. It also faces problems caused by distraction and lack of feeling. Following on an analysis drawn up by Bishop Wilkins (1614–72), Bickersteth allows his reader to look in considerable detail at the different components of prayer; confession, petition and thanksgiving. A chapter on 'Family Worship' has a footnote, 'The greatest part of this chapter may perhaps be read with advantage by the master of a family, when first beginning to attend to this duty.'[1] The final chapter gives forms of prayer which can be used in private and in the family. Concerning *A Treatise on the Lord's Supper*, Bickersteth's biographer writes: 'Communion seasons had been so blessed to his soul, and he had been in the habit of so carefully preparing for them, that he was eminently qualified to guide the devotions of others.'[2]

Soon after Bickersteth's death there was a considerable change in Evangelical spirituality. With the Revival Movements and the Keswick Convention the approach became more pietistic and world-denying.

8 The Catholic Revival in the Church of England

R. D. TOWNSEND

Battiscombe, E. G., *John Keble, a Study in Limitations*. London, Constable, 1963; New York, Knopf, 1964.
Butler, P., ed., *Pusey Rediscovered*. London, SPCK, 1983.
Chadwick, W. O., *The Victorian Church*, Part 1 (2nd edn, London, A. & C. Black, 1971), ch. 4.
Chadwick, W. O., *Newman*. OUP, 1983.
Church, R. W., *The Oxford Movement: Twelve Years, 1833–1845*. London, Macmillan, 1892; New York, Macmillan, 1891; Lousville, Ky., Lost Cause, 1978.
Dessain, C. S., *John Henry Newman*. OUP, 1980.
Dessain, C. S., *Newman's Spiritual Themes*. Dublin, Veritas, 1977; Minneapolis, Winston, 1980.
Faber, G. C., *Oxford Apostles: a Character Study of the Oxford Movement*. London, Faber, 1933; New York, Scribner, 1934.
Jones, O. W., *Isaac Williams and his Circle*. London, SPCK, 1971.
Liddon, H. P., *Life of Edward Bouverie Pusey*. 4 vols, London and New York, Longmans, 1893–7.

[1] E. Bickersteth, *A Treatise on Prayer* (10th ed, 1825), p. 145.
[2] T. R. Birks, *Memoir of Edward Bickersteth* (1852), vol. i, p. 351.

Lough, A. G., *The Influence of John Mason Neale*. London, SPCK, 1962.

Lough, A. G., *John Mason Neale – Priest Extraordinary*. Newton Abbot, privately printed, 1976.

Rowell, G., *The Vision Glorious*. OUP, 1983.

Ward, W., *Life of Cardinal Newman*. 2 vols, London and New York, Longmans, 1913.

The twelve years between 1833 and 1845 embraced an event in the Church of England known as the Oxford Movement, or popularly the Tractarian Movement, which sought a revival of the Christian religion in its fulness. It distinguished itself from two schools in English religious life: the rationalism of liberal Anglican theology, which was largely lacking in a spiritual dimension; and the emotional and narrow approach to the Bible and Christian piety which characterized the Evangelicals. This chapter limits itself to this first period (the *Oxford* phase) of the Catholic revival, because it was here that the significant themes in spirituality were formulated. The concern of the later Ritualist movement was essentially pastoral and ceremonial: between 1833 and 1845 we find that the dominant themes are moral, doctrinal and ecclesial.

The event which can conveniently be said to mark the beginning of the Movement was a sermon preached by John Keble (1792–1866) in Oxford in July 1833, entitled 'National Apostasy'.[1] With John Henry Newman (1801–90) and Edward Bouverie Pusey (1800–82), Keble preached a revival of spirituality which has had a profound influence on the whole character of Anglicanism (see pp. 537–40).

The occasion of the Oxford Movement was partly political change. The withdrawal of the Anglican monopoly of government in England forced the Church to reconsider its character and identity.[2] The *Tracts for the Times* were the official means of enunciating the aims and beliefs of the Movement. They were begun by Newman in 1833 and continued until January 1841, contributions having been made by J. W. Bowden (1798–1844), A. P. Perceval (1799–1853), R. H. Froude (1803–36), Charles Marriot (1811–58) and Isaac Williams (1802–65), in addition to Keble and Pusey. In some ways the Movement reflects the general change in sensibility we call Romanticism, and it is an example of a conservative reaction to the threat of revolutionary change in society.[3] The Oxford Movement also relates to the wider movement of the Gothic Revival and medievalism, as a result of which it has often been character-

---

[1] See R. W. Church, *The Oxford Movement 1833–1845*, ch. 6.

[2] See W. O. Chadwick, *The Victorian Church*, Part I, chaps. 1 and 2.

[3] See Stephen Prickett, *Romanticism and Religion: the Tradition of Coleridge and Wordsworth in the Victorian Church* (CUP, 1976).

ized as merely nostalgic or aesthetic. A notable progenitor of the positive spiritual aspects of the Gothic Revival associated with the Oxford Movement was John Mason Neale (1818–66), one of the founders of the Cambridge Camden Society, and the author and translator of many hymns through which the spiritual revival of Tractarianism was transmitted.

At the heart of the preaching and writing of Keble and Newman (Fellows of Oriel College) and Pusey (Regius Professor of Hebrew and Canon of Christ Church), and of those who grouped themselves around them, was a concern for holiness, a call to a renewal of spirituality. The Oxford sermons of this period, many of them preached in the University Church, presented Christianity not (as it had become frequently understood) as a comfortable religion which made no demands, but as a quest for 'holiness rather than peace'.[1] This concern for holiness was one which, particularly in Newman's case, referred to Evangelical ideals: religious faith was of the heart as well as the mind.[2] Newman's *Parochial and Plain Sermons* were of enormous influence in attacking latitudinarianism in doctrine, and in broadening and deepening the Evangelical interpretation of the Pauline doctrine of justification by faith. They stressed the theme of personal responsibility in Christian living. Keble was the inheritor of the Catholic tradition of High Church Anglicanism, a tradition of ordered devotion, the regular saying of the daily offices of Morning and Evening Prayer, a sense of reserve and reverence deeply aware of the mystery of God, a sacramental and eucharistic spirituality.[3] Pusey became aware, through his study of the German biblical critics of his time, of the negative character of much of their work, and observed the dead orthodoxy of Protestantism lacking in spiritual vitality.[4] On the other hand, his study of Hebrew, Arabic, and other Semitic languages both at Oxford and in Germany took him into intimacy with the roots of Christian spirituality.

The Oxford men stressed the mystical unity of the biblical corpus and affirmed the primacy of the Gospels in Christian culture. A principal means by which this spiritual culture was communicated was the calendar of the Christian year. By using the Church's seasons as the framework for worship and preaching week by week, the Tractarians were able to stress versatility as opposed to narrowness in the present-

---

[1] J. H. Newman, *Apologia pro vita sua* (London, Longman, 1864, p. 61.).
[2] See C. S. Dessain, *John Henry Newman*, chaps. 1 and 2. For further treatment of Newman, see pp. 426–30.
[3] See Church, op. cit., ch. 2.
[4] See L. Frappell, '"Science" in the Service of Orthodoxy: The Early Intellectual Development of E. B. Pusey', in P. Butler, ed., *Pusey Rediscovered*.

ation and interpretation of the Bible, and to explore the richness of the liturgical tradition of Christian spirituality. As the Christian year began at Advent, Keble spoke of the round of the Church's year as a structure by which spiritual growth and seriousness could be measured and tested:

> This is the great question for us all, now at this solemn time, when our services for the year are going to begin again, and our Lord's glorious kingdom is nearer by one whole round of holy memorial days. Let each person consider first, whether he has yet applied himself in earnest to the plain simple duty of praising Christ in His Church . . . Our very Prayer books seem to ask us . . . how we used them during the year that is past.[1]

The Oxford sermons and Keble's poems *The Christian Year* (1827), which were the most popular manifestation of the character of the movement, were frequently concerned with the place of image and symbol in the expression of theological truth, and with the imaginative expression of experience. The leaders of the Movement found in the Fathers of antiquity, and the Fathers as taken up in the work of the great Anglican divines of the seventeenth century, that deep in the Christian tradition there had been this stress on the imagination in theological writing. In Keble's Tract *On the Mysticism attributed to the Fathers of the Church* (Tract LXXXIX) the distinction is made between the symbolic understanding of Christian antiquity and the speculation of natural philosophy. In a letter of 1835 Newman wrote of the way in which 'Christians receive the Gospel literally on their knees, and in a temper altogether different from the critical and argumentative spirit which sitting and listening engender'.[2] The sermons of the Christian year, and the worship within which they were preached, aimed at balancing the effects of 'sitting and listening'.

The deference of the Tractarians to the Book of Common Prayer as giving order to the spiritual life in its forms of public worship and seasonal and festal observances, appealed to the patristic tradition which understood forms of common prayer as the matrix of theology. The framework of the Church's calendar enabled them to focus the core theological idea of their spirituality, the principle of the indwelling of Christ. Theology was for them, as for the Greek Fathers, an engagement and ultimately a participation in the mystery of God. Newman wrote in his *Lectures on Justification* that

> faith . . . [is] the beginning of that which is eternal, the operation of the

---

[1] John Keble, 'The Solemn Procession', in *Sermons for the Christian Year*, vol. 1 (London, Walter Smith, 1887; Louisville, Lost Cause, 1979), pp. 10–11.

[2] Q. R. C. Selby, *The Principle of Reserve in the Writings of John Henry Cardinal Newman* (OUP, 1975), p. 25.

Indwelling Power which acts from within outwards and round about . . . pours itself out into our whole mind, runs over into our thoughts, desires, feelings, purposes, attempts, and works, combines them all together into one, makes the whole man its one instrument . . . one embodied act of faith.[1]

The indwelling of the Holy Spirit, who makes Christ present to the believer, is the heart of the Christian life. Christianity is a 'presence of Persons'.[2]

Implicit in the principle of the indwelling of Christ was what the Tractarians called a doctrine of reserve, a secrecy in which God reveals himself to men and women. God will reveal himself to those who seek him and do his will, and not to the world. Isaac Williams wrote of this in Tract LXXX:

> That Jesus Christ is now, and has been at all times, hiding Himself from us, but at the same time exceedingly desirous to communicate Himself, and that exactly in proportion as we show ourselves worthy He will disclose Himself to us; that if we constrain Him He will come in and abide with us; that unsatisfactory as human knowledge is, and the increase of which is the increase of care, and knowledge which puffeth up; yet there is a knowledge which humbleth, which is infinite in its nature, and is nothing else than deeper, and higher, and broader views of the mystery which is hid in Christ.
>
> That although the Scripture does not set before us any sensible joy or satisfaction to be sought for, as the end of holiness, yet it does this knowledge; which is attainable by nothing else but by making the study of Divinity to consist in a Divine life.[3]

The principle of indwelling led the Tractarians to emphasize the growth of the spiritual life through the sacraments, received in faith, and to stress God's inward presence in them. By the indwelling of Christ the Christian is called to live in obedience to Christ's will in a 'real participation of the Son by His presence within us, a participation so intimate that in one sense He can be worshipped in us as being His temple or shrine'.[4] By becoming man Jesus found a way to sanctify human nature, of which his own manhood is the pattern. As Newman put it, 'He inhabits us personally, and this inhabitation is effected by the channel of the Sacraments.'[5] The core idea of Tractarian spirituality is that we may become by grace what Christ is by nature: we are transfigured by the divine indwelling. Pusey spoke of this mystery metaphorically:

[1] J. H. Newman, *Lectures on Justification* (2nd edn, London, Rivington, 1840), pp. 343–4.

[2] Dessain, *John Henry Newman*, p. 22.

[3] Isaac Williams, *On Reserve in Communicating Religious Knowledge* (Tract LXXX) (1839 ed.), p. 82.

[4] J. H. Newman, *Select Treatises of St Athanasius in Controversy with the Arians* (2nd edn, London, Pickering, 1881), p. 88.

[5] ibid. p. 193.

He Himself hath likened to leaven the workings of His Grace, His kingdom within us. Ye know how leaven works. Small it is at first; hidden out of sight; but it spreads silently and slowly, until it has reached every part; and the heavy lump is lightened, and it expands and unfolds itself and rises upwards. So mostly is it with the grace of God. God lodges it in the soul. He places in Baptism a principle of life within us, which, if we allow it to work, as we grow on, will fill our every power, penetrate our whole souls, transform this heavy mass of our earthliness into its own divine nature . . . Let it work on peacefully, and, like the leaven, it will transform the whole self into itself, the whole soul into its own perfection, the perfection of Christ.[1]

By their teaching of the divine indwelling as that which is at the heart of Christian living, the Tractarians conveyed their conviction that theology is rooted in spirituality and worship. We are not simply reasoning animals, but beings who see, feel, contemplate and act:

We cannot picture to ourselves the Presence of God, because we have no faculties to imagine what a spirit is. We are conscious that we have souls. Let materialists say what they will, our consciousness is a witness to us. The blindness of the blind is no evidence against our sight. But in vain we should set ourselves to imagine the Presence of God, who cannot imagine our own souls, which we know that we have. We cannot picture to ourselves spirit, so God speaks to us of Himself in Holy Scripture under images, taken from what we do know, ourselves, whom He, in some degree, made in His own likeness. But the facts we know. We know that God is close to us, closer to us than any of His creatures which He has made. He surrounds us and penetrates us: He is within us, without us.[2]

In 1845 Newman left the Church of England for Rome. He hoped that Keble and Pusey would follow him, but they shrank from the Ultramontane authoritarianism of contemporary Catholicism. More positively, Keble and Pusey continued to believe that the deep experience of the grace of God that they knew within the Church of England witnessed to its true continuity with the Church of the Fathers and its identity as part of the Catholic Church.

[1] E. B. Pusey, *Parochial Sermons*, vol. ii (London, Walter Smith, 1869), pp. 350–1.
[2] E. B. Pusey, *Parochial and Cathedral Sermons* (London, Walter Smith, 1883), pp. 509–10.

9 Kierkegaard

D. A. HART

Primary Sources

Edifying Discourses, I–IV, tr. David F. Swenson and Lillian Swenson. Minneapolis, Augsburg, 1943–6.

Repetition (1843), tr. Walter Lowrie. Princeton University Press, 1941.

Philosophical Fragments (1844), tr. David Swenson, rev. Howard V. Hong. Princeton University Press, 1967.

The Concept of Dread (1844), tr. Walter Lowrie. Princeton University Press, 1944.

Stages on Life's Way (1845), tr. Walter Lowrie. New York, Schocken Books, 1967.

Thoughts on Crucial Situations in Human Life (1845), tr. David Swenson. Minneapolis, Augsburg, 1948.

Concluding Unscientific Postscript (1846), tr. David Swenson and Walter Lowrie. Princeton University Press, 1941.

Purity of Heart is To will One Thing (1847), tr. Douglas V. Steere. New York and London, Harper, 1938.

Purify your Hearts! (1847), tr. A. S. Aldworth and C. W. Daniel. London, W. S. Ferrie, 1937.

Works of Love (1847), tr. David Swenson and Lillian Swenson. Princeton University Press, 1946.

Christian Discourses (1848) including also *The Lilies of the Field and the Birds of the Air* and *Three Discourses at the Communion on Fridays*, tr. Walter Lowrie. OUP, 1939; Princeton University Press, 1971.

For Self-Examination and *Judge for Yourselves!* and *Three Discourses* (1851), tr. Walter Lowrie. OUP, 1941.

The Journals of Søren Kierkegaard: A Selection, tr. Alexander Dru. OUP, 1938.

Søren Kierkegaard's Journals and Papers, tr. Howard and Edna Hong. Bloomington, Ind., and London, Indiana University Press, I (1967), II (1970), III (1975), IV (1975), V (1978).

The Prayers of Kierkegaard, ed. Perry D. LeFevre. University of Chicago Press, 1956.

Parables of Kierkegaard, ed. Thomas C. Oden. Princeton University Press, 1978.

Selected Secondary Sources

Collins, J., *The Mind of Kierkegaard*. Chicago, Henry Regnery, 1965.

Geismar, E., *Lectures on the Religious Thought of Søren Kierkegaard*. Minneapolis, Augsburg, 1937.

Heinecken, M., *The Moment Before God*. Philadelphia, Muhlenberg, 1956.

Patrick, G. M., *Pascal and Kierkegaard*, 2 vols. London, Lutterworth, 1947.

Sponheim, P., *Kierkegaard on Christ and Christian Coherence*. London, SCM; New York, Harper & Row, 1968; Westport, Conn., Greenwood, 1975.

Swenson, D. F., *Something About Kierkegaard*. Minneapolis, Augsburg, 1945.
Walker, J., *To Will One Thing*. Montreal, McGill-Queen's University, 1972.

Søren Aabye Kierkegaard (1813–55) lived and wrote in Protestant Copenhagen in a time of great social change. Introduced into Lutheran doctrine by an intensely intellectual yet guilt-ridden merchant-father (who believed he had once cursed God), he became rather overtowered by his elder brother Peter, who was to become a bishop in that church. Kierkegaard was slightly deformed in an early accident. In accounts by contemporaries of his formative years at school, the term *fremmed* keeps recurring, meaning 'strange' in the sense of having odd or peculiar tastes, as well as of being an alien or a foreigner. His sense of a significant isolation was enhanced by the fact that while he and Peter survived childhood, five brothers and sisters died in their youth. And at the death (during childbirth) of the fifth, his youngest sister, Petrea, Søren noted in his diary that he 'felt the silence of death gathering around me.'[1] This was the predominant mood of his life and writings, and may explain something of the partiality of his appeal.

Feeling life to be fragile and frequently despairing of his purpose in it, Kierkegaard believed himself unable to take the acceptable path of a career which his family willed for him. Rejecting both the established comfort of the Lutheranism of his day and the systematic verbosity of the dominant Hegelian philosophy in the universities, he turned his attention to the ambiguities of his own life as an 'existing individual' (*den Enkelte*), and this became the dominant category of his philosophy. If Hegel was indeed correct in his diagnosis of the nineteenth-century malaise as 'spiritlessness' (*das Geistlose*), then the correct prescription for that was not an immersion of the self into the unfolding of the Absolute Spirit but rather the vocation to a spiritual journey of the self before God. The spiritual longing of the self to escape from the social swamp was for him 'the umbilical cord of the higher life'.[2] And the biblical precursors of that path of salvation had been the lonesome knights of faith, who had wrested themselves from the comfort of their fellows – Abraham, whom Hegel could only interpret as a stranger to the social life, and the suffering Job, 'who does not cut a figure in a universal chair and with reassuring gestures vouch for the truth of this thesis, but sits among the ashes and scrapes himself with a potsherd, and without interrupting his manual labour lets fall casual hints and remarks'.[3] Hence the modesty of some of Kierkegaard's titles – 'Philosophical Fragments', 'Concluding Unscien-

[1] *Journals*, II A 805.
[2] ibid., 4409 (Dru).
[3] *Repetition*, p. 90.

tific Postscript'; and his sermons, of which he wrote over twenty, he preferred to style as 'edifying discourses of varied tenor'. Since he had not been ordained by any denomination and had moreover grave doubts as to whether Christendom still represented in any sense the original gospel of Jesus Christ, he did not believe that his words held any intrinsic authority. The homilies he wrote – largely on the occasion of Christian festivals in the Church's year – he wished to have read aloud by individuals, and if his words became for them the word of God this was not because they were passive recipients of some universal message of salvation but 'it will be because of your own activity that you will be the one to whom the intimate "thou" is spoken'.[1] The success of his words depended not on his own eloquence (though eloquent they certainly are) but on the free response of the believer who had learned to make the proverb his own, 'Drink waters from thine own well'.[2] Experience of God and the self in divine relation are the key to Kierkegaard's spiritual direction and in that stress his doctrine remains essentially Lutheran. Accepting the Johannine teaching that only God is Spirit[3] he holds firmly to the *finitum capax infiniti* in his view that man or woman is 'derived spirit'.[4] But one is only that in the sense that one is created with the possibility of becoming spirit, and so must traverse several 'Stages on Life's Way' in order to become a spiritual being, or a mature self.[5]

A brief synopsis of one of Kierkegaard's homilies must here suffice. *Purity of Heart is to Will One Thing* (1847) is typically an extended meditation on Scripture – in fact a composite of Luke 10.42 and James 4.8. The occasion for the address is revealed in the subtitle, *Spiritual Preparation for the Feast of Confession*. Although at first sight the sacramental context might seem surprising, we are reminded that Penance is the most private of the sacraments and it is yet 'to that solitary individual this little work is dedicated'.[6] Characteristic of his spiritual writings is the opening prayer:

> Father in Heaven! What is a man without thee! What is all that he knows, vast accumulation though it be, but a chipped fragment if he knows not thee! Thee the One, who art one thing and art all! So mayest thou give to the intellect, wisdom to comprehend that one thing; to the heart, sincerity to receive this understanding; to the will purity that wills only one thing.'[7]

[1] *Purity of Heart is To Will One Thing*, p. 163.
[2] Prov. 5.15.
[3] John 4.24.
[4] *Concluding Unscientific Postscript*, p. 218.
[5] The work cited and *The Concept of Dread* are his best maps to this spiritual development.
[6] *Purity of Heart*, p. 200, and title-page.
[7] ibid., p. 1.

Karl Jaspers has argued that such piety in Kierkegaard is simple and straightforward while his philosophy is contorted and complex.[1] Yet there is still a high degree of intensity in these prayers, and there is still the central paradox of creature in communion with Creator. The possibility of such intercourse, though implanted by the Creator, requires the free initiative of the individual who must come to see, often by bitter experience, that his or her life is totally inadequate without the spiritual element. Hence individual faith is a vital appropriation of the gospel, not a rarefied intellectual assent but a resolution of the whole self in the face of the anxiety of differing choices. As Luther expressed it, 'the two, faith and God, hold close together. Whatever thy heart clings to and relies upon, that is properly thy God'[2] and this has been adapted here by Kierkegaard, 'Wherever a man may be in the world, whichever road he travels, when he wills one thing, he is on the road that leads him to thee!'[3]

If the will to the one thing needful is the Christian's spiritual goal, then the corresponding temptation or 'spiritual trial' (*Anfaegtelse*) is 'double-mindedness' – a wavering of the will between the good and the evil or even between two goods, which makes for a divided self. For it was a basic indecision which was at the root of the despair Kierkegaard had faced before his decisive turn to Christian faith, and it was ever the fatal accomplice to disbelief. This 'double-mindedness' could hazard many disguises, among which was the weakness of one 'who only wills the Good up to a certain degree' and the wiliness of the other who considers it prudent to diversify his interest, or hedge his spiritual bets. Both of these temptations had to be countered with the knowledge that one could not trifle with one's eternal destiny. And this depended upon one's present choices.

Now Kierkegaard touches upon a perceptive and recurrent theme, that those who resolved aright their crisis of faith then had to wear the badge of faith, the cross, to face the greatest test of undeserved suffering. 'If a man in truth wills the Good then he must be willing to suffer for the Good . . .'[4] And the prescription is: the continuation of one's resolution in the face of adversity, the courage to be what one has chosen and to remain patient in the knowledge of the eternal consequences of that decision. Here we reach the heart of the discourse which is at the same time the realization of the limitations of any external prescription:

[1] See K. Jaspers, (ET) 'The Importance of Kierkegaard', in *Cross Currents*, II/3 (1952), pp. 5–16.
[2] Luther, *The Large Catechism*; cf. Kierkegaard's comment, 'O, Luther is still the master of us all' (*Journals*, VIII A 642).
[3] *Purity of Heart*, p. 26.
[4] ibid., p. 128.

As it is a comfort to seafarers to know that no matter on what strange water they may venture there are always pilots within call, so the edifying contemplation stands near the breakers and reefs of this life prepared by daily sight of terrible sufferings swiftly to render what little aid it can. Yet it cannot help in the way that a pilot helps a ship. The sufferer must help himself.[1]

Only by taking the helm and steering one's own individual course through choices and tribulations can one reach the firm ground of eternity, and this task of 'living as an individual' is one in which *any* external guidance must inevitably be modified to be adapted to the salvific needs of the resolving self.

Kierkegaard's lasting contribution to spiritual thought lies in his exploration of the relationship between each individual and the realm of the Eternal. This necessary relation had to be established in the area of 'inwardness' where the human soul in liberty discovered the one true source of its being and its goal. The means to nurture this inward life were provided through prayer, which he described as a person's 'greatest earthly happiness'.[2] Through the experience of his own short life, which had more than a fair share of pain and disappointments, Kierkegaard forged the foundations of an existential theology in which the exigencies of the self were to become the focus of the search for God. Although his situation might have seemed desperate to an outsider, Kierkegaard himself had no doubt that 'I have absolutely lived with God as one lives with a father'.[3] And it is this strong spiritual conviction which is the anchor of his thought for his many twentieth-century interlocutors.

10 Some Patterns in American Protestantism

ROBERT HANDY

Clebsch, W. A., *American Religious Thought: A History*. Chicago, University of Chicago, 1973.

Kates, F. W., *Things That Matter: The Best of the Writings of Bishop Brent*. New York, Harper, 1949.

Miller, P., *Jonathan Edwards*. Amherst, Mass., University of Massachusetts, 1981 (orig. pub. 1949).

Moulton, P. P., ed., *The Journal and Major Essays of John Woolman*. New York, OUP, 1971.

[1] ibid., p. 139.
[2] *Journals*, VIII A 532.
[3] ibid., IX A 65.

The various types of Protestant spirituality in America have generally been grounded in particular denominational traditions that were brought to the western hemisphere, chiefly from Europe, or that arose indigenously. Here three of these types will be discussed by treating three notable persons who exemplified a way of spirituality consistent with their traditions and thereby enriched the spiritual treasury of Christianity.

1   EDWARDS

Among the churches of European background that grew on American soil in the colonial period, those related to the Reformed or Calvinist tradition formed a sizable majority. The intensity of the spiritual life that could be encouraged by that branch of Christianity found distinctive embodiment in Jonathan Edwards (1703–58), pastor, preacher, revivalist, theologian, author, controversialist, educator. It was his deep piety and fervent devotional life that gave coherence to the life of this talented, many-sided man. In a letter written in 1830 to his son George at Yale, Lyman Beecher exclaimed that Edwards's

> vigor of intellect, compass of thought, patience of investigation, accuracy of discrimination, power of argument, knowledge of the Bible, and strength of holiness, stand unrivalled. But for his piety, he might have been a sceptic more dangerous than Hume or Voltaire; and but for the command of his religion over all his powers, he might have been one of the most dangerous, as he certainly was one of the most original and fearless of speculators. But the attractions of his heart to God kept him in his orbit . . .[1]

A contemporary scholar has entitled a finely wrought essay on this intellectual giant 'The Sensible Spirituality of Jonathan Edwards', stressing his genius for consistency between theory and practice and his insistence on practising the piety and purity he taught.[2]

The son of a Connecticut Congregational minister, Edwards remained at Yale after graduation to study theology. Probably during this period he had the experience later recorded in his spiritual autobiography, the *Personal Narrative* or *Narrative of his Conversion*. It came while he was reading a passage from the Bible, 1 Timothy 1.17:

> As I read the words, there came into my soul, and was as it were diffused through it, a sense of the glory of the Divine Being; a new sense, quite different

---

[1] Charles Beecher, ed., *Autobiography . . . of Lyman Beecher* (New York, Harper, 1865), II. 237–8.
[2] William A. Clebsch, *American Religious Thought: A History* (Chicago, University of Chicago Press, 1973), pp. 11–56.

from any thing I ever experienced before. Never any words of scripture seemed to me as these words did. I thought with myself, how excellent a Being that was, and how happy I should be, if I might enjoy that God, and be rapt up to him in heaven, and be as it were swallowed up in him for ever![1]

Such experiences became even more lively and intense during his first short pastorate in New York; early in 1723 he added these to a list of 'Resolutions' to guide his life: 'frequently to renew the dedication of myself to God', never to act 'as if I were any way my own, but entirely and altogether God's', and 'that no other end but religion shall have any influence at all on any of my actions' (ibid. pp. 41–2). Those experiences faded somewhat when he returned to Yale to teach, but reawoke when he went to the Congregational Church at Northampton, Massachusetts, in 1727, first as associate and then as successor to his grandfather, Solomon Stoddard. In 1727 also he married Sarah Pierrepont, whose intense mystical piety deepened her husband's interpretation of the spiritual life.[2]

That interpretation came to mature expression in a sermon delivered in 1733, 'A Divine and Supernatural Light, immediately imparted to the soul by the spirit of God, shown to be a spiritual and rational doctrine'. Many find that this is the most important single statement of Edwards' fundamental position; Perry Miller declared that 'the whole of Edwards' system is contained in miniature within some ten or twelve of the pages of this work.'[3] Edwards described the spiritual and divine light as 'a true sense of the divine excellency of the things revealed in the word of God, and a conviction of the truth and reality of them thence arising', and taught that it was bestowed by grace on the elect. Only this spiritual light will 'bring the soul to a saving close with Christ', and only it, he declared, 'has its fruit in a universal holiness of life'.[4]

Such preaching helped to prepare the way for the Great Awakening in New England, in which Edwards played a major role as leader and defender of what he understood to be true revivals, but critic of those not based on what he regarded as sound principles.[5] He perceived the revivals as forerunners of a greater outpouring of the Spirit that would

---

[1] Clarence H. Faust and Thomas H. Johnson, ed., *Jonathan Edwards: Representative Selections* (New York, Hill & Wang, 1962 [1935]), p. 59.

[2] Elisabeth D. Dodds, *Marriage to a Difficult Man: The 'Uncommon Union' of Jonathan and Sarah Edwards*. Philadelphia, Westminster Press, 1971.

[3] *Jonathan Edwards* (Amherst, University of Massachusetts Press, 1981 [originally published, 1949]), p. 44.

[4] The sermon is reprinted in Faust and Johnson, ed., *Edwards*, pp. 102–11.

[5] Definitive editions of Edwards' writings are in process of publication by Yale University Press, see esp. vol. ii, *Religious Affections*, ed. John E. Smith (1959), and vol. iv, *The Greak Awakening*, ed. C. C. Goen (1972).

bring in the great day of the Lord; he was an exponent of postmillennial eschatology.[1]

His later career was stormy; his emphasis on the purity of the Church brought him into conflict with his congregation, from which he was deposed in 1750; he settled in Stockbridge, preaching to both Indian and English congregations, and producing some of his most famous works. In 1758 he journeyed to Princeton to become president of the Presbyterian college there, but soon died of an inoculation for smallpox. To the end of his life, he followed the vision of Christian spirituality that had guided him since his youth. His influence gave Calvinism in America a new lease on life, and his ideas were reflected in the work of such followers as Joseph Bellamy, Samuel Hopkins, Nathaniel Emmons, and Jonathan Edwards Jr.

2   WOOLMAN

The Religious Society of Friends (Quakers), which first appeared in North America in 1656, had become by the eighteenth century one of the major Protestant denominations of the time. With its teaching on the inner light, its simple patterns of worship with much time given to silence, its concern for justice, and its pacifism, it provided a distinctive context for the spiritual life. One of its most remarkable figures was John Woolman (1720–72), author of a distinctive, widely read *Journal*.

Brought up in a devout Quaker farm family in western New Jersey, Woolman's formal education was not extensive. A likeable and gregarious youth, he quite deliberately chose a somewhat secluded life in his search for God. As he later remembered this period in his life,

> I kept steady to meetings, spent First Days after noon chiefly in reading the Scriptures and other good books, and was early convinced in my mind that true religion consisted in an inward life, wherein the heart doth love and reverence God the Creator and learn to exercise true justice and goodness, not only toward all men but also toward the brute creatures; that as the mind was moved on an inward principle to love God as an invisible, incomprehensible being, on the same principle it was moved to love him in all his manifestations in the visible world; that as by his breath the flame of life was kindled in all animal and sensitive creatures, to say we love God as unseen and at the same time exercise cruelty toward the least creature moving by his life, or by life derived from him, was a contradiction in itself.[2]

He slowly learned the art of speaking lucidly and concisely in Quaker meetings, rising only when he was convinced he was responding to a

[1] Goen, ed., op. cit., esp. pp. 353–8.
[2] Phillips P. Moulton, ed., *The Journal and Major Essays of John Woolman* (New York, OUP, 1971), p. 28.

divine 'opening'. In time he became well known among Quakers, and was 'minuted' thirty-eight times for a ministry among Friends.

Leaving the family farm at twenty-one to go into business in nearby Mt Holly, shopkeeping with sidelines in preparing legal documents and tailoring, he soon discovered that his talents could lead to wealth. He resolved to live a simple life, but as one of his most perceptive biographers put it, 'success dogged his footsteps.'[1] He persisted:

> My mind through the power of Truth was in a good degree weaned from the desire of outward greatness, and I was learning to be content with real conveniences that were not costly, so that a way of life free from much entanglements appeared best for me, though the income was small. I had several offers of business that appeared profitable, but did not see my way clear to accept of them, as believing the business proposed would be attended with more outward care and cumber than was required of me to engage in. I saw that a humble man with the blessing of the Lord might live on a little, and satisfy the craving, but that in common with an increase of wealth the desire of wealth increased. There was a care on my mind to so pass my time as to things outward that nothing might hinder me from the most steady attention to the voice of the True Shepherd.[2]

He was comfortable with a simple pattern of life; he later bought a small farm where he lived with his wife and surviving child.

His ability to prepare legal documents brought him into direct contact with slavery. When his employer directed him to write a bill of sale for a slave, he became acutely aware of the hideousness of the practice. He did it under protest, but then resolved never to do it again, but to fight the evil. With patient deliberation he worked out three main anti-slavery strategies. He took long journeys, south and north, some of them on foot, first to learn the facts of slavery for himself, then to witness against it among Quakers in direct personal encounter. He used his skill at writing, especially in his *Essay on Some Considerations on the Keeping of Negroes* (1753–4), which was duly approved by the Quaker Overseers of the Press and circulated widely but focused on the spiritual harm done to both slaves and masters. Thirdly, he undertook in 1758 a public ministry to induce Quaker meetings to forbid slaveholding among Friends. In time the strategies which Woolman and others used had their effect; meetings did disown slavekeepers and the Quaker influence helped northern states to limit and eventually outlaw slavery.

Woolman drew on his spiritual resources for inner strength and guidance in his crusading. He was acquainted with the mystical tradition, having read *The Imitation of Christ*, probably some Fénelon, and possibly

[1] Janet Whitney, *John Woolman: American Quaker* (Boston, Little, Brown, 1942), p. 170.
[2] Moulton, ed., *Journal*, p. 35.

Molinos. In his *Journal* he recorded but left uninterpreted a vivid spiritual experience that occurred when he awoke early one day in 1757:

> It was yet dark and no appearance of day nor moonshine, and as I opened my eyes I saw a light in my chamber at the apparent distance of five feet, about nine inches diameter, of a clear, easy brightness and near the center the most radiant. As I lay still without any surprise looking upon it, words were spoken to my inward ear which filled my whole inward man. They were not the effect of thought nor any conclusion in relation to the appearance, but as the language of the Holy One spoken in my mind. The words were, 'Certain Evidence of Divine Truth', and were again repeated exactly in the same manner, whereupon the light disappeared (*Journal*, p. 58).

His last journey was to England, to urge friends there to be more active in their opposition to slavery, but soon after arriving he died of smallpox. His *Journal* and other writings have remained a source of inspiration to many since; Paul Rosenblatt's summary is eloquent: 'To know the life and writings of John Woolman is to be haunted forever by the mystery of the endless dimensions of love'.[1]

3 BRENT

The Episcopal Church has been influenced by several distinctive streams of spirituality. One who drew on several of these currents in a creative way reached the peak of his influence in the twentieth century – Charles Henry Brent (1862–1929). His life was marked by a remarkable tension between external activity and internal spirituality. Outwardly he was a vigorous, driving, confident leader, but inwardly he lived an intense spiritual life with its heights and depths.

Born in a country rectory in Ontario, Brent was educated at Trinity College, Toronto, but when he sought ordination there were no openings in Canada, so he migrated to Buffalo, New York, and was ordained priest in 1887 (and later became an American citizen). He came under the influence of an Anglican monastic movement, the Society of St John the Evangelist, or Cowley Fathers (see p. 573), serving in Boston for three years as priest-in-charge of a mission for blacks. He was about to take monastic vows, when a sharp disagreement with the authorities in England intervened. Yet he remained grateful for those three years under monastic discipline; years later he wrote, 'It may be that there are artificial features in conventual life but I experienced it in its best form, and can never have aught but affectionate and grateful memories of it.'[2] He then served for some ten years in a team ministry in a depressed and

---

[1] P. Rosenblatt, *John Woolman* (New York, Twayne Publishers, 1969), p. 11.
[2] *The Churchman*, 31 Jan. 1914.

deteriorating section of Boston. The external demands of such a social ministry were often heavy; to keep from being overwhelmed he developed an intense devotional life. He set aside a regular time daily, and often prayed with his pen as well as on his knees. Hence much of Brent's writing was done while he was in the mood of worship, giving an unusual quality and texture to his prose.

His major decisions were made in the context of prayer, as when early in the century he received several calls to wider fields of service. Though his health was not well suited to life in the tropics, he was finally convinced that it was God's will that he become Missionary Bishop to the Philippines, and was consecrated in 1901. Here he led by action and inspiration; he was not at his best in administrative detail, yet devoted much attention to the founding of churches, schools, and hospitals. He also became a crusader against the spreading evil of opium, and was elected president of the First International Opium Conference at Shanghai in 1909. His duties required much travel; the long voyages gave him respite from administrative burdens and provided him time for meditation, study, and writing. He produced fourteen books in those years, many on devotional themes. Characteristic of his work is the following passage:

> Active or dormant, the instinct of prayer abides, a faithful tenant, in every soul. The instinct to pray may be undeveloped, or paralyzed by violence, or it may lie bedridden in the soul through long neglect; but even so, no benumbed faculty is more readily roused to life and nerved to action than that of prayer . . .
>
> Prayer is man's side of converse with God; it is speech Godward. Yes, prayer is speech Godward, and worship is man's whole life of friendship with God, the flowing out, as it were, of all that tide of emotion and service which is love's best speech.
>
> The essence of prayer is desire, forming itself into hope and aspiration, and mounting up into effort, in the direction of the unattained. Prayer is the address made by human personality to that with which it is desired to establish affiliations . . .
>
> Prayer is the committal of our way unto the Lord, just as a deed of trust is the committal of our possessions to those who can handle them better than we. By living one day with God, preparation is made for living all days with God.[1]

When invitations to serve elsewhere came to him, as they often did, he made his decisions in the context of prayer.

---

[1] As quoted by Frederick W. Kates, *Things That Matter: The Best of the Writings of Bishop Brent* (New York, Harper, 1949), pp. 44–5.

Finally, knowing that his health would no longer stand the Philippine climate, he accepted election as Bishop of Western New York, but first ministered to troops in World War I, becoming Senior Headquarters Chaplain of the American Expeditionary Force, effectively chief of chaplains abroad. Then when he took up his new post in 1919, it was said that his 'coming into the diocese was like a strong, fresh breeze stirring up a heavy atmosphere . . . In his greatness he swept the diocese along with him'.[1]

Much of his energy in the last decade of his life was given to the ecumenical movement. In 1910 he had gone rather reluctantly to the World Missionary Conference at Edinburgh, but there was converted to ecumenism, convinced that 'the Spirit of God . . . was preparing for a new era in the history of Christianity'.[2] There too the vision of a World Conference on Faith and Order came to him, for he believed that true Christian unity could come only when there was a full and sincere facing of the most basic and controversial theological issues. His dream was of a great society of God's children, rising above nations and cultures, a peaceable society based on faith in the ultimate reality of omnipotent love as revealed by Jesus Christ and rooted in devotion to him. It took years of labour, but finally the First World Conference on Faith and Order met at Lausanne in 1927, over which he presided. It proved to be an important event in ecumenical history, for the deepest issues of faith had been faced, and it was determined to move ahead. During the conference Brent's heart was troubling him, but his habits of self-discipline kept him serene, patient, and firm. Two years later, when he happened to be in Lausanne again, he died.

The secret of his life was prayer; as his leading biographer observed:

> Brent's powerful energizing influence was the radiance of an inward light. That light was the result of his direct relation to God, to whose cleansing and invigorating influence he continuously exposed himself through meditation and prayer (Zabriskie, *Brent*, p. 142).

His influence has lived on, not only in his own communion, but through the ecumenical movement to which so much of his spiritual energies were directed.

---

[1] As quoted by Alexander C. Zabriskie, *Bishop Brent: Crusader for Christian Unity* (Philadelphia, Westminster Press, 1948), p. 135.

[2] Bishop Brent, *The Inspiration of Responsibility* (New York and London, Longmans, Green, 1915), p. 80.

11 Black Worship

JAMES CONE

Alho, O., *The Religion of the Slaves*. Helsinki, Suomalainen Tiedeakatemia, 1976.

Carter, H., *The Prayer Tradition of Black People*. Vally Forge, Pa., Judson Press, 1976.

Cone, J. H., *The Spirituals and the Blues*. New York, Seabury, 1972.

Cone, J. H., *God of the Oppressed*. New York, Seabury, 1975.

Johnson, C. H., ed., *God Struck Me Dead*. Philadelphia, Pilgrim Press, 1969.

Johnson, J. W., and J. R., *The Books of American Negro Spirituals*. New York, Viking Press, 1969.

Mays, B., *The Negro's God*. New York, Atheneum, 1968.

Pipes, W. H., *Say Amen, Brother! Old-Time Negro Preaching*. Westport, Conn., Negro Universities Press, 1970.

Raboteau, A. J., *Slave Religion: The 'Invisible Institution' in the Antebellum South*. New York, OUP, 1978.

Rivers, C. J., *Soulful Worship*. Washington, D.C., National Office for Black Catholics, 1974.

Rivers, C. J., *The Spirit in Worship*. Cincinnati, distributed by Stimuli, 1978.

This Far By Faith: American Black Worship and its African Roots. Washington, D.C., National Office for Black Catholics, 1973.

Thurman, H., *The Negro Spiritual Speaks of Life and Death*. New York, Harper, 1947.

Thurman, H., *Deep River*. Port Washington, N.Y., Kennikat Press, 1955 and 1969.

Wilmore, G. S., *Black Religion and Black Radicalism*. Garden City, N.Y., Doubleday, 1972.

Black worship is connected with black life, and it is characterized by a religious sense inseparable from the suffering that determined it. Whether Catholic or Protestant, black worship is not derived primarily from these theological and historical traditions. To be sure, there are elements of Catholic and Protestant doctrine and rituals (mostly Protestant) in black worship. But to use John Wesley's theology or the Westminster Confession as the point of entry for the meaning of a black congregation that has adopted the Methodist or Presbyterian denominational structure is to misunderstand black worship and thus to distort its meaning. When black people gather together for worship and praise to the Lord, it is not because they have made a decision about the theological merits of Luther's ninety-five theses or of Calvin's *Institutes*. These are not our traditions. At most, they are secondary structures in which God has placed us so that we might 'work out our salvation in fear and trembling'.

Since we did not create the various Catholic and Protestant structures, we cannot use these labels as the primary definition of our religious experience. Indeed, these white religious structures are the reason for the black necessity to create a style of worship that did not deny our essential humanity. A black congregation may be Methodist, Baptist, or even Catholic, but always with a difference. And this difference is far more important in the assessment of the meaning of black worship than the white traditions from which the black church often derives its name.

Black worship has been wrought out of the experience of slavery and lynching, ghettoes and police brutality. We have 'been buked and scorned' and 'talked about sho's you borned'. In worship, we try to say something about ourselves other than what has been said about us in the white church and the society it justifies. Through sermon, prayer and song, we transcend societal humiliation and degradation and explore heavenly mysteries about starry crowns and gospel shoes. Our church is the only place we can go with tears in our eyes without anyone asking, 'What are you crying about?' We can preach, shout, and sing the songs of Zion according to the rhythm of the pain and joy of life, without being subjected to the dehumanizing observations of white intellectuals – sociologists, psychologists and theologians. In worship we can be who we are as defined by our struggle to be something other than the society says we are. Accordingly our gathering for worship is dictated by an *historical* and *theological* necessity that is related to the dialectic of oppression and liberation. Apart from the historical reality of oppression and our attempt to liberate ourselves from it, we should have no reason to sing, 'My soul looks back and wonders how I got over'. To understand the interplay of the past, present, and future as these are expressed in black worship, it is necessary to examine the historical context that created its unique style.

Black worship was born in slavery. What else could the word 'black' mean in relation to worship except a description of the historical origin of those assembled? Most black worshippers do not know the details of our historical beginnings. What they know and feel is that they are *black* and therefore connected with Africa, slavery, and the struggle of freedom. Black worship was born on the slave ships and nurtured in the cotton fields of Alabama, Arkansas and Mississippi. What we believe and how we express it in worship cannot be separated from our African heritage, on the one hand, and American slavery and Christianity, on the other. African life and culture was the bedrock of the African personality. It was that element in the black slaves' being that structured their response to American slavery and the Christian gospel. Black worship was born in the meeting of the West African High God with the God of Moses and Jesus. Black worship was created and formed in the context of American slavery as African slaves sought to create meaning in an oppressive environment. In order to keep a measure of sanity in a completely alien and oppressive environment, African slaves had to fashion a theological system of beliefs and create a worship style which did not destroy them physically or mentally.

Initially black worship was largely determined by our African heritage, with an emphasis on the rhythm of our dance and music. There was no separation of the secular and sacred. Reality was viewed as a single system. In some sense, everything one did should be service to the divine. Worship consisted in giving appropriate adoration to the High God, lesser divinities, and ancestors in the expectation that African slaves in the Americas would soon return to their African homeland. Many Africans believed that death would be the gateway for their reincarnation in Africa. These beliefs and ideas gave structure and meaning to the African world and they served as the theological starting point for African captives in the Americas. In Latin America and the Caribbean, African theology and ritual were visibly present in the content and styles of black worship. Even to this present day one finds *Candomblé* in Brazil, *Santeria* in Cuba, *Shango* in Trinidad, *Obeah* in Jamaica and *Voodoo* in Haiti. Few scholars deny that the African diaspora in Latin America and the Caribbean carried to the New World African styles of worship, African patterns of religious music and dance, African magical and folk beliefs, and most importantly for cultural continuity African religious institutions and sacred offices.[1]

In North America, however, white slaveholders did not permit Africans to practise their religion openly. White slaveholders readily perceived the connection between African worship and slave insurrections. The intensity and success with which whites attempted to destroy African life and culture led many scholars to conclude that Africanisms were completely eliminated in the life of the American slaves. The studies of Melville Herskovits changed the course of scholarly debate on this issue. With the publication of his *Myth of the Negro Past*,[2] it was no longer possible to take for granted that everything black slaves did was derived from their oppressors. Although Herskovits was seriously challenged by E. Franklin Frazier[3] and others, it is safe to say that he showed

---

[1] For a fuller discussion of the influence of Africanism in the Americas, see Albert J. Raboteau, *Slave Religion*.

[2] Boston, Beacon Press, 1958; originally published 1941.

[3] See E. Franklin Frazier, *The Negro Church in America* (New York, Schocken Books, 1964); *The Negro Family in the United States* (New York, Macmillan, 1957).

483

that Africans in North America did preserve some African cultural forms. Beliefs and customs were transmitted by slaves to their descendants, and they are found in our music, speech, and thought patterns. Africanisms are also found in the rhythm of our dance and the emotional structure of our being. When Christianity was introduced to slaves, Africans converted it to their religious heritage, by refusing to accept any version of the gospel that did not harmonize with the African spirit of freedom.

This conversion of Christianity by Africans to their life-situation accounts for the radically different views of the gospel between white slaveholders and African slaves. Initially, white masters did not permit their slaves to be Christianized. Christian baptism implied manumission, according to some; and there were too many biblical references to freedom. But white missionaries and preachers convinced many slave masters that Christianity made blacks 'better' slaves, that is, obedient and docile. As one slave-holder put it: 'The deeper the piety of the slave, the more valuable he is in every respect.'[1] However, it is important to point out that before the First and Second Great Awakening and the emergence of the Methodists and Baptists, most African slaves remained outside the belief systems of Christianity. Later, when Africans did 'convert' to it, their conversion was not identical with the religious conversion of the whites who held them as slaves. That was why the independent black churches were founded in the North and the so-called 'invisible institution' flourished in the South.

If worship is inseparably connected with life, then we must assume that slaves' and slaveholders' worship services did not have the same meaning, because they did not share the same life. They may have used the same words in prayer, songs and testimony or even preached similar sermons. But slaves and slaveholders could not mean the same thing in their verbal and rhythmic expressions, because their social and political realities were radically different. That was why black slaves organized the first Baptist Church in Silver Bluff, South Carolina, between 1773 and 1775, and also why Richard Allen and Absalom Jones walked out of St George Methodist Church of Philadelphia in 1787. Similar events happened in New York, Baltimore and other places among black Methodists and Baptists. This same black version of the gospel produced such prophetic persons as Henry Highland Garnet, David Walker and Nathaniel Paul – all of whom recognized the radical incompatibility of Christianity

[1] Cited in Vincent Harding, 'Religion and Resistance Among Ante-Bellum Negroes 1800–1860', in *The Making of Black America*, vol. i, ed. A. Meier and E. Rudwick (New York, Atheneum, 1969), p. 181.

and slavery. No one exposed this point any more clearly than Garnet's famous address to slaves in 1843:

> If . . . a band of Christians should attempt to enslave a race of heathen men . . . the God of heaven would smile upon every effort which the injured might make to disenthrall themselves. Brethren, it is as wrong for your lordly oppressors to keep you in slavery as it was for the manthief to steal our ancestors from the coast of Africa. You should therefore use the same manner of resistance as would have been just in our ancestors when the bloody foot-prints of the first remorseless soul-thief were placed upon the shores of our fatherland . . . Liberty is a spirit sent from God and, like its great Author, is no respecter of persons.[1]

However, even before Garnet made his famous address and prior to the rise of the independent black Baptist and Methodist churches, there was already present an 'invisible institution' in the South with its emphasis on the overturned pot, the prayin' ground, and the 'hush harbor'. An ex-slave preacher described those secret meetings in this manner:

> Meetings back there meant more than they do now. Then everybody's heart was in tune and when they called on God they made heaven ring. It was more than just Sunday meeting and then no more Godliness for a week. They would steal off to the fields and in the thickets and there, with heads together around a kettle to deaden the sound, they called on God out of heavy hearts.[2]

The slaves were searching for a private place where they could sing and shout and there would be nobody to turn them out. In these secret meetings were born not only the major slave insurrections, but also a black version of Christianity that was consistent with their African search for freedom.

African slaves refused to accept Christianity as a given datum or as a deposit of fixed doctrines from white missionaries and preachers. Christianity as a rigidly defined system of beliefs about God, Jesus and the Holy Spirit was inconsistent with the African personality where rhythm, passion, and feeling defined the structures of one's being in the world. Therefore, when white Baptists and Methodists arrived on the North American scene in a significant manner during the late eighteenth and early nineteenth centuries, Africans, for the first time during their presence, responded with enthusiasm. This response, contrary to popular scholarly opinion, was not due to the system of beliefs in either denomination or to a religious consciousness traceable merely to white evangelical

---

[1] Henry H. Garnet, *An Address to the Slaves of the United States of America* (New York, Arno Press, 1969), p. 93.

[2] Cited in George P. Rawick, *From Sundown to Sunup* (Westport, Conn., Greenwood, 1972), p. 40.

Protestantism. African slaves' response to Baptists and Methodists was due to a certain flexibility within these denominations, thereby enabling black people to create a *new* version of Christianity more consistent with its biblical origins. In contrast to Anglicans, Presbyterians and Quakers, there were less rigid structures among Methodists and Baptists, which partly permitted blacks to 'do their thing' as defined by their aspiration of freedom.

Black worship is not white worship, no matter how close the similarities might be in appearance. Black people have always known that. It does not matter that white people sometimes copy our preaching style. Whites may pray, sing, or clap their hands with a rhythm that makes it difficult for even blacks to make the distinction. Conversely, no one can deny that evangelical Protestantism of the Second Great Awakening, particularly the revival hymns, did influence the content and style of black worship. One only needs to point to the popularity of the hymns of Isaac Watts among black congregations in order to demonstrate that point. Nevertheless there is a radical difference between black and white worship services. Both white and black people know this, and that is why even today one seldom finds them worshipping together.

The source of the difference between black and white worship services is found at the point of a difference in life. Even when slaves worshipped with their masters, it was usually out of necessity to put on a 'good front' so that the master would think of them as pious and religious. The 'real meetin'' and 'real preachin'' was held in the swamp, out of the reach of the patrols. An ex-slave, Litt Young, tells of a black preacher who preached 'obey your master' as long as her mistress was present. When the mistress was absent, she said, 'he came out with straight preachin' from the Bible.'[1]

The need for secret meetings was created by the legal restrictions against African slaves' assembling without the presence of whites and also by black people's dissatisfaction with the worship and preaching of white churches. Although slaves knew they were risking a terrible beating or perhaps death, they nonetheless found it necessary to 'steal away' into the woods at night in order to sing, preach and pray for their liberation from slavery. Adeline Cunningham, an ex-slave from Texas, reported:

> No suh, we never goes to church. Times we sneaks in de woods and prays de Lawd to make us free and times one of de slaves got happy and made a noise dat dey heerd at de big house and den de overseer come and whip us 'cause we prayed de Lawd to set us free.[2]

[1] Cited in Norman R. Yetman, *Life Under the 'Peculiar Institution': Selections From the Slave Narrative Collection* (New York, Holt, Rinehart & Winston, 1970), p. 337.
[2] Cited in Rawick, *From Sundown to Sunup*, p. 35.

Black slaves had to create their own style of worship. They shouted and prayed for the time they would 'most be done toilin' here'.

Because black people were victims, they could not accept white people's interpretation of the gospel. Apostle Paul's 'slaves, be obedient to your masters' was a favourite text of white missionaries and preachers. Hannah Scott of Arkansas expressed her reaction to one such preacher in this way: 'But all he say is 'bedience to the white folks, and we hears 'nough of dat without him tellin' us.'[1]

In order to hear another word and to sing another song, they held secret worship services in the slave-cabin or in the woods at night. As one ex-slave put it: 'Dey law us out of church, but dey couldn't law 'way Christ.'[2] These worship services included singing, preaching, shouting and conversion. Black slaves used the 'overturned pot' in order to keep from being heard by their masters or the patrollers. Carey Davenport, a former slave, remembered those meetings: 'Sometimes the cullud folks go down in dugouts and hollows and hold they own service and they used to sing songs what come a-gushing up from the heart.'[3] In this worship context was born their encounter with the Lord, the One they believed would bring them through. The preacher often spoke about 'dark clouds hanging over their heads' and of the 'rocky roads they have to travel'. At other times, he told them about 'deep valleys' and 'high mountains', but he assured them that they had a future not made with human hands. The element of faith in the righteousness of God prevented black slaves from accepting despair as the logical consequence of their servitude.

Immediately following the legal abolition of slavery, the 'invisible' institution became visible as newly freed blacks joined independent black churches. What was once done in secret could now be done in the open. Like the secret meetings during slavery, black worship after the Civil War was defined by the sermon, song, shout, and the experience of conversion. Each of these elements in black worship was defined by the freedom of the Spirit who moved into the lives of the people, giving them courage in an extreme situation of oppression.

An important moment in the history of black worship happened during World War I when many blacks migrated to the cities in search of a measure of freedom in employment and other aspects of black life. Needless to say, most did not find what they had hoped for, and once again they found it necessary to 'take their burdens to the Lord and leave them there'. This they did by creating storefront churches and other praise-

---

[1] Cited in Eugene Genovese, *Roll, Jordan, Roll* (New York, Pantheon Books, 1972), p. 207.
[2] ibid., p. 213.
[3] Cited in Rawick, *From Sundown to Sunup*, p. 34.

houses of the Lord. This was also the period of the rise of black sects and cults with such figures as Father Divine and Daddy Grace. But more important for black Christian churches was the rise of gospel music with Thomas Dorsey and Mahalia Jackson as dominant personalities. This music put life into the church by emphasizing the presence of the Spirit. It was the presence of the Spirit as defined by gospel music which gave the old and young alike the faith that 'we shall overcome'.

Black worship today is very similar to what it was in the past. The names of the denominations may be new but the style and content of our worship is very much like that of our grandparents. Instead of singing and preaching in those small southern church houses, we are now proclaiming the word in storefront churches in New York, Detroit and Chicago. We sometimes call the places the 'United House of Prayer For All People' or 'the Church of What's Happening Now'. Sometimes black worship takes on a more 'secular' form with no obvious reference to the God of Christian theism. The theatre and poetry workshops become the replacement of the church. An example is the National Black Theatre in Harlem founded by Barbara Ann Teer. Some black churches had become too middle-class to accommodate the spirit and aspirations of the Black Power movement of the late 1960s. A new form of black ritual was developed wherein the poet became the preacher with a message for the people.

It was in this context that Black Theology was born. Black Theology is an attempt to show liberation as the central message of the Christian gospel and thereby bring the black church back to its liberating heritage. Our worship service must be free and liberating because we believe 'the Lord will make a way somehow'. Therefore, we must fight until freedom comes.

When analysing worship in black history, however, it is important to note that black worship is more than an expression of our historical strivings to be free. Because it is more than what we do, a mere historical analysis of the context of its origin is simply not adequate. We can talk about certain sociological conditions, and how they affected the style and content of our songs and sermons. We can mention slavery, the great migrations, the Civil Rights Movement, and their effect on black worship. But we have not really touched the heart of black worship from the perspective of the people until we deal with the *theological* claim affirmed in prayer, song, and story.

In the black slaves' struggle to define their humanity according to freedom and not slavery, they believed that there was present in their strivings the divine Power who was greater than the white structures that enslaved them. When black slaves were tempted to give up in despair, this Power gave them hope that slavery would soon come to an end.

The source which black people used for explaining this Power was the Scripture. Black worship is biblical. One of the most amazing facts of history is that many black slaves did not accept the white interpretation of the gospel, even though they could not read or write. While white people contended that Scripture endorsed slavery, black slaves argued differently. They contended that God willed their freedom and not their slavery. Their hermeneutics was not derived from an intellectual encounter with the text, but from a gift of the Spirit. A white preacher in 1832 noted: 'Many of the blacks look upon white people as merely taught by the Book; they consider themselves instructed by the inspiration of the Spirit.'[1]

Because slaves were able to make a distinction between the gospel of God and the religion of whites, they also came to different theological conclusions about God. When African slaves heard about the Old Testament story of Israel in Egypt, they identified themselves with Hebrew slaves and identified white slaveholders with the Egyptians, and no amount of clever white exegesis could change their thinking on this matter. 'As Israel was in Egyptland, oppressed so hard they could not stand,' so black people were in American slavery, working under the whip and pistol. As Israel was liberated from Egypt across the Red Sea, so black people would also be set free. It is this theological certainty that characterizes black worship, enabling blacks to sing with assurance:

> Oh Mary, don't you weep, don't you moan,
> Oh Mary, don't you weep, don't you moan,
> Pharaoh's army got drownded,
> Oh Mary, don't you weep.

The certainty about God's immediate presence with the weak is the heart of the black worship service. Black worship is a series of recitals of what God has done to bring the people out of 'hurt, harm, and danger'. Through sermon, song, prayer and testimony, the people tell their story of 'how they got over'. God is that divine miracle who enables the people to survive amid wretched conditions. God is holy, personal and all-powerful. God is everything the people need in order to triumph over terrible circumstances.

It is important to note that there are no metaphysical distinctions between God and Jesus in black worship. The distinction between the Father and the Son is defined according to the rhythm of the people's language as they seek to communicate with the divine. Jesus is their constant companion, the one who walks with the people and tells them he

---

[1] Cited in Genovese, *Roll, Jordan, Roll*, p. 214.

489

is their own. He is the Oppressed One, the Black Messiah, who experiences the brokenness of humanity. He is God's Son who was born of 'Sister Mary' in Bethelehem, and 'everytime the baby cried, she's a-rocked him in the weary land'.

The importance of Jesus and God in the black church service is perhaps best explained when one considers the preponderance of suffering in black life. When we consider slavery, lynching and ghettoes, how can we explain black people's mental and physical survival? How was it possible for black slaves to hope for freedom when a mere empirical analysis would elicit despair? How is it possible for blacks today to keep their sanity in the struggle for freedom when one considers the continued existence of black suffering? The answer is found in Jesus and God. Jesus heals wounded spirits and broken hearts. No matter what trials and tribulations the people encounter, they refuse to let despair define their humanity. They simply believe that 'God can make a way out of no way'. Black people do not deny that trouble is present in their life; they merely contend that trouble does not have the last word, and that 'we'll understand it better by and by'. In the words of Charles Tindley:

> Trials dark on every hand, and we cannot understand
> All the ways that God would lead us to that Blessed Promise Land.
> But he guides us with his eye and we'll follow till we die.
> For we'll understand it better by and by.
>
> > By and by, when the morning comes,
> > All the saints of God are gathered home.
> > We'll tell the story how we overcome.
> > For we'll understand it better by and by.[1]

Black religion, while accepting history, does not limit salvation to history. Our fight for justice is God's fight, too, and Jesus' resurrection already defines what the ultimate outcome will be.

---

[1] Cited in *Songs of Zion: Supplemental Worship Resources 12*, ed. J. J. Cleveland and V. Nix (Nashville, Abingdon, 1981), hymn no. 55.

IX
OTHER RELIGIONS

1 Judaism

LOUIS JACOBS

CLASSICAL WORKS IN HEBREW

Alexander Süsskind of Grondo, *Yesod ve-Shoresh ha-Avodah*. Jerusalem, 1965.
Bahya Ibn Pakudah, *Hovot ha-Levavot*; (ET) Moses Hyamson, *Duties of the Heart*. New York and Jerusalem, Feldheim, 1970.
Cordovero, Moses, *Tomer Devorah*; (ET) Louis Jacobs, *Palm Tree of Deborah*. London, Valentine Mitchell, 1960; New York, Hermon, 1974.
Dobh Baer of Lubavitch, *Kunteros ha-Hitpaalut*; (ET) Louis Jacobs, *Tract on Ecstasy*. London, Valentine Mitchell, 1963.
Keter Shem Tov (Crown of Good Name), ed. Aaron of Zelichov. Jerusalem, 1968.
Kook, A. I., *Orot ha-Kodesh* (*Sacred Lights*). Jerusalem, 1961.
Kook, A. I., *Writings*, (ET) Ben Zion Bokser. CWS 1979.
Luzzatto, M. H., *Mesillat Yesharim*; (ET) M. Kaplan, *Path of the Upright*. Philadelphia, Jewish Publication Society, 1936.
Maimonides, Moses, *Mishneh Torah* (*Second to the Torah*), various edns.
Maimonides, Moses, *Moreh Nevukhim*; (ET) S. Pines, *Guide of the Perplexed*. Chicago University Press, 1963.
Otzar ha-Geonim (*Treasury of the Geonim*), ed. B. M. Lewin. vol. iv, *Hagigah*. Jerusalem, 1931.
Zohar (*Illumination*) [the 'Bible' of the Kabbalists, attributed to Rabbi Simeon ben Yohai but probably compiled by Moses De Leon], (ET) Harry Sperling and Maurice Simon. London, Soncino Press, 1949; New York, Rebecca Bennet, 1958.

WORKS ON THE KABBALAH

Bension, A., *The Zohar in Moslem and Christian Spain*. London, Routledge, 1932; New York, Hermon, 1974.
Scholem, Gershom G., *Kabbalah*. Jerusalem, Keter; New York, Quadrangle, 1974 (the best work by far in English by the greatest contemporary exponent of Jewish mysticism).
Tishby, I., *Mishnat ha-Zohar* (The Teaching of the Zohar). Jerusalem, 1951–61.

WORKS ON HASIDISM

Buber, Martin, (ET) *Tales of the Hasidim*. New York, Schocken, 1947–8.
Dressner, Samuel H., *The Zaddik*. New York and London, Abelard-Schuman, 1960.
Jacobs, Louis, *Seeker of Unity*. London, Valentine Mitchell; New York, Basic Books, 1966.

Other Religions

Jacobs, Louis, *Hasidic Prayer*. New York, Schocken, 1973.
Langer, J., (ET) *Nine Gates*. London, J. Clarke; New York, D. McKay, 1961.
Nahman of Bratzlav, *The Tales*; (ET) Arnold J. Band. CWS 1979.
Newman, Louis I., *The Hasidic Anthology*. New York, Bloch, 1944; Schocken, 1963.
Schatz, Rivka, 'Contemplative Prayer in Hasidism', in *Studies in Mysticism and Religion presented to Gershom G. Scholem* (Jerusalem, Magnes & Hebrew University, 1967), pp. 209–26.
Schatz Uffenheimer, Rivka, *ha-Hasidut ke-Mistika* (Quietistic Elements in 18th Century Hasidic Thought, with English summary). Jerusalem, 1968.
Weiss, J. G., 'The Kavvanoth of Prayer in Early Hasidism', in *Journal of Jewish Studies*, 9 (1958), pp. 163–92.
Wiesel, Elie, (ET) *Souls on Fire*. New York, Random House; London, Weidenfeld & Nicolson, 1972.
Ysander, T., *Studien zum Beschten Hasidismus*. Uppsala, 1933.

Other classical Jewish texts are contained in Menahem Nahum of Chernobyl (CWS 1983) and *Safed Spirituality* (CWS 1985).

GENERAL WORKS

Altmann, A., *Studies in Religious Philosophy and Mysticism*. London, Routledge & Kegan Paul, 1967; Ithaca, Cornell University, 1969.
Dan, Joseph, *The Esoteric Philsophy of Hasidey Ashkenaz* (Hebrew). Jerusalem, 1968.
Enelow, H. G., 'Kawwanah: the Struggle for Inwardness in Judaism', in *Studies in Jewish Literature in honor of Kaufmann Kohler* (Berlin, G. Reimer, 1913), pp. 82–107.
Günzig, J., *Die 'Wundermänner' im jüdischen Volke*. Antwerp, 1921.
Heschel, A. J., 'Did Maimonides Believe that he had Attained to Prophecy?' (Hebrew), in the Louis Ginzberg Jubilee Volume (New York, 1945), pp. 159–88.
Heschel, A. J., *God in Search of Man*. New York, Harper, 1955.
Jacobs, Louis, *A Jewish Theology*. New York, Behram House; London, DLT, 1973.
Jacobs, Louis, *Jewish Mystical Testimonies*. New York, Schocken, 1977.
Neher, A., 'Le voyage mystique des quatre', in *Revue de l'Histoire des Religions*, 140 (1951), pp. 59–82.
Schechter, Solomon, 'Safed in the Sixteenth Century', in his *Studies in Judaism*, Second Series (Philadelphia, Jewish Publication Society of America, 1945), pp. 202–306.
Scholem, Gershom G., *Major Trends in Jewish Mysticism*. 3rd edn, London, Thames & Hudson; New York, Schocken, 1955.
Scholem, Gershom G., *Jewish Gnosticism, Merkavah Mysticism and the Talmudic Tradition*. New York, Jewish Theological Seminary of America, 1960.
Scholem, Gershom G., *The Messianic Idea in Judaism*. New York, Schocken, 1971.

Vajda, G., *L'Amour de Dieu dans la théologie juive du moyen âge*. Paris, 1957.
Weiner, H., *9½ Mystics*. New York, Holt, Rinehart & Winston, 1969.
Werblowsky, R. J. Z., *Joseph Karo: Lawyer and Mystic*. Oxford, Clarendon, 1962.
Zangwill, Israel, *Dreamers of the Ghetto*. Philadelphia, Jewish Publication Society of America, 1945.

The study of Jewish spirituality of the mystical kind is made difficult by the unwillingness on the part of the Jewish mystics to share with others their more intimate, personal experiences. Yet, while there is a paucity of Jewish mystical testimonies, the few that are available, together with the evidence to be gleaned from the vast theosophical literature (though presented in a detached, objective manner, this itself is obviously the fruit of mystical contemplation), provide students with sufficient material for their investigations. In the following brief survey only a few of the major tendencies can be noted and these should be supplemented by the works recorded in the bibliography.

From the period of the Talmudic Rabbis (the first and second centuries) for roughly a thousand years, the Jewish mystical tradition was centred on contemplation on the vision of the *Merkavah*, the heavenly chariot described in the first chapter of the book of Ezekiel. The contemplatives of this lengthy period were known as the 'Riders of the Chariot', that is, those who engaged in soul ascents to the heavenly halls where they saw God and his holy angels. It is interesting to observe that the majority of these 'Riders' were scholars well-versed in the Law. Jewish mysticism, on the whole, far from being antinomian, generally seeks to infuse new life into the practical observances of the Torah. For instance, in the *Responsa* of Hai Gaon, head of the College at Pumbedita in the tenth century, the Babylonian head of world Jewry at the time, there is found this vivid description of the techniques used by the 'Riders of the Chariot' (Lewin, *Otzar ha-Geonim*, pp. 13–15):

> You may perhaps know that many of the Sages hold that when a man is worthy and blessed with certain qualities and he wishes to gaze at the Heavenly Chariot and the halls of the angels on high, he must follow certain exercises. He must fast for a specified number of days, he must place his head between his knees, whispering softly to himself the while certain praises of God with his face towards the ground. As a result he will gaze in the innermost recesses of his heart and it will seem as if he saw the seven halls with his own eyes, moving from hall to hall to observe that which is therein to be found.

What might have been considerable tension between the demands of inwardness and obedience to the Law was avoided by the medieval teachers through extending and deepening the ancient Rabbinic concept of *kavvanah*. This word means 'direction' (of heart and mind) and in the earlier Rabbinic sources denotes concentration, before the performance of the precepts, on the idea that these are divine ordinances. In prayer, *kavvanah* denotes reflection on the meaning of the words. The medieval teachers stressed *kavvanah* over external practice, not, of course, as a substitute for action but as a means of endowing the active life of religion with spiritual vitality. A saying in this connection, frequently attributed to Bahya's *Duties of the Heart* but not found in that work, is: 'Prayer without *kavvanah* is like a body without a soul.' It is not surprising, therefore, that the most outstanding of the medieval rationalist philosophers and codifiers of the Law, Maimonides (1135–1204), should see the intellectual love of God as the ultimate aim of practical observance. It appears that Maimonides believed he had attained, at least, to the lower stages of prophecy, despite the conventional view that prophecy had ceased after the biblical period. In his *Guide of the Perplexed* (III.51) Maimonides speaks of the saint whose mind is always with God. In its most perfect form this elevated stage is possible only for the select few, like Moses, who is said to have died by a divine kiss; the soul, while in the body, is so attached to God that it departs with the utmost ease. Such a man can walk through fire and water without suffering harm! Even in his far less esoteric Code of the Law (*Mishneh Torah, Teshuvah* 10.3), intended for the average Jew, Maimonides can write:

> What is the fitting love of God? It is that man should love God with an extraordinary love to the extent that his soul becomes attached to God's love so that he pines for it constantly. It should be as if he were lovesick, unable to get the woman he loves out of his mind, pining for her constantly when he is at rest and in motion, when he eats and drinks. Even more than this should be the love of God in the heart of those who love him and yearn constantly for him, as he commanded us: 'with all your heart and with all your soul' (Deut. 6.5). Solomon expresses it in the form of a parable: 'For I am lovesick' (Cant. 2.5). The whole of the Song of Songs is a parable to illustrate this theme.

For Maimonides (*Mishneh Torah, Yesodey ha-Torah*, 2.2) the way to attain to this love of God is by deep reflection on man's lowliness in the presence of God's creation. For this reason, Maimonides, unlike the 'Riders', identifies the 'Chariot' with Aristotelean metaphysics, i.e. with the profound discourses of the religious philosophers on the glory of God as revealed through the wonders of the *physical* universe.

With the rise of the Kabbalah in Spain and Provence in the twelfth century, culminating in the *Zohar* at the end of the thirteenth century, the object of contemplation shifted from the heavenly halls of the 'Chariot Riders' and the wonders of the physical universe of the philosophers to the divine nature as conceived of in the Kabbalistic doctrine of the *Sefirot*

('Numbers'), the powers or potencies in the Godhead. In the Kabbalistic scheme, man, created in God's image, mirrors forth in his being the realm of the *Sefirot*. Every human deed has cosmic significance in that it exerts an influence on the *Sefirot*. There is a saying found frequently in the *Zohar*: 'The impulse from below awakens the impulse from on high'. When man is virtuous he sends on high beneficent impulses to promote harmony in that realm, with the result that the divine grace can flow unimpeded throughout all creation. Man's vicious acts produce discord and disharmony on high and the flow of the divine grace is arrested. Thus every human deed produces in the Sefirotic realm either a *pegam* ('flaw') or a *tikkun* ('rectification'). The Kabbalist has this in mind in every deed he performs and in those he avoids for the greater glory of God. In the light of the Kabbalistic doctrine, Moses Cordovero (1522–70) in Safed composed his *Palm Tree of Deborah*, in which the doctrine of *Imitatio Dei* is given a Kabbalistic turn. For instance, man should resemble in his life the *Sefirah* which represents the divine wisdom by his concern for every one of God's creatures. Cordovero, and the mystics who thought like him, never intentionally killed a mosquito or even plucked a blade of grass. In his prayers, the Kabbalist surveys in his mind the whole map of the *Sefirot*, dwelling not on the plain meaning of the words but on the relationships among the *Sefirot* hinted at by these words. In the school of Isaac Luria (1534–72), also of Safed, this map receives a further series of the most complicated associations to form the object of mystical contemplation. Basic to the Lurianic Kabbalah is the idea of the 'breaking of the vessels'. At one stage in the divine creative processes, the doctrine runs, as *Deus absconditus* emerged from concealment to become *Deus revelatus*, the illuminations pouring into the vessels of the *Sefirot* became too powerful for the vessels to contain and these were shattered and later reconstituted. The result is that there are 'holy sparks' scattered throughout all creation, man's task being to restore these, by holy living, to their Source. When all the 'sparks' have been reclaimed for the holy, the Messiah will come to redeem Israel and through Israel the whole of humanity. The Lurianic Kabbalists were ascetics, with a strong messianic thrust to their activities. It should be noted, however, that ascetics though these mystics were, they were not celibates, not only because, as Orthodox Jews, they held the duty to procreate to be a divine command, but also because the union of husband and wife on earth was the counterpart of the 'sacred marriage', the union of the male and female principles in the Sefirotic realm. For all that, the marital act was to be carried out, they taught, as a purely devotional act, without either pleasure or passion.

The Hasidic movement, founded in Eastern Europe by Israel Baal

Shem Tov (1698–1760), spread rapidly, as a mystical mass movement, throughout the Jewish communities and still has hundreds of thousands of adherents. At the centre of Hasidic philosophy is the doctrine of *devekut* ('attachment'), the perpetual being with God, as Maimonides taught, but now as an ideal possible of realization for others than the select few. Since this ideal is still thought of as extremely difficult to realize, the movement developed the institution of the Zaddik, the Guru-like master and miracle worker, who is with God at all times and who can inspire his followers, the Hasidim ('saints'), to come closer to the ideal. Eventually, dynasties of Zaddikim were to be found, each of whom had his own spiritual way and his own special form of Hasidic devotion.

Another idea prominent in Hasidism is that of *bittul ha-yesh*, 'self-annihilation', the loss of selfhood in God, the nearest thing one finds in Judaism to the *unio mystica* in which the individual soul is absorbed in God. The physical universe is seen as God's garment which, though concealing him, also reveals his glory. Indeed, in the more far-reaching idea of many Hasidic teachers, there is no physical universe at all from the point of view of God. This idea is sometimes described as pantheistic. A more correct term is panentheistic, that is, all is *in* God. The Hasidim were not ascetics. On the contrary, for them man has to be involved in the things of the world. But his involvement must be in a spirit of devotion in order to reclaim the 'holy sparks'. For example, the Hasidim taught that the beauty of women is but a very pale reflection of the divine, spiritual beauty on high. If a Hasid happens inadvertently to see a pretty girl, he should elevate the thought of beauty to its Source. Similarly, when the Hasid eats or drinks he should think of the taste in the food and drink as the 'spiritual aspect', which should turn his thoughts to God. Especially during his prayers, the aim of the Hasid is to transcend his grasping ego to gaze on the sublime. An early Hasidic text (*Keter Shem Tov*, p. 24b) states:

> It is necessary for man, as he begins to pray, to have the sensation of being in the *world of action*. Afterwards, he should have the sensation of being in the *world of formation*, the world of the Ophanim and holy angels. Afterwards, he should be in the *world of creation* until he has the sensation that his thought has soared so high that it has reached the *world of emanation*. Just as a man strolls from room to room so should his thoughts stroll through the upper worlds. He should take care not to fall from his elevated state in the upper worlds but should strengthen himself with all the powers at his disposal so as to remain there on high, his thoughts exceedingly elevated in the upper worlds. He should do this by having a bit and a rein on his thoughts so that he makes a kind of vow not to descend. If he wishes to do this in order to achieve *devekut* at times other than those of prayer, it is essential that no other person be

present in the house. For even the chirping of birds can distract him and so, too, the thoughts of another person can be a distraction.

To achieve the aim of self-annihilation, the Hasidim were fond of unrestrained gestures in prayer. The Baal Shem Tov is reported as saying that a drowning man is not ashamed to gesticulate wildly in order to call attention to his plight. By the same token, gestures, even of the wildest kind, were in order during prayer, and sweet melodies were a further aid to the worshipper who wishes to abandon himself to God.

An ideal akin to that of self-annihilation, practised by the Hasidim as well as by other Jewish mystics, one that goes back to the Talmud and the *Zohar*, is that of symbolic martyrdom. Especially when reciting the *Shema* ('Hear O Israel, the Lord our God, the Lord is One') twice daily, but also at other times, the mystic depicts to himself that he is being offered the choice of apostasy or death. He steadfastly refuses to abandon his faith, joyfully accepting torture and death, which he depicts to himself in all its gruesome details. The warning is always added by the masters who advocate this practice: 'But he must really mean it and not delude himself.'

The mystical tradition received a fresh impetus in the writings of A. I. Kook (1865–1935), Chief Rabbi of Palestine. Kook believed that the advance of modern science and technology has to be recognized as the means provided by God in order to bring the world to greater perfection. In Kook's view the Jewish people had become too spiritualized in its long divorce from the land and from practical life as a people and so, paradoxically, incapable of fulfilling its true aim, that of spiritualizing the material. Kook's maxim: 'Let the old be renewed and the new sanctified', enabled him to see no incongruity in his befriending the non-religious pioneers in the Holy Land, because they, without knowing it, were doing God's work. Unlike many Orthodox rabbis of his day, Kook also embraced the theory of evolution, holding that the view of creation progressing to ever greater heights is typical of the Kabbalah, in which he was a believer. New though the idea is that spirituality must be wedded to material existence if it is to be effective, it is not entirely without precedent in Jewish thought. A Hasidic tale tells of a master who would place his watch on the stand at which he prayed as a reminder to him not to allow himself to become lost in eternity but to return to the world of time.

497

2 Islam

F. W. ZIMMERMANN

Arberry, A. J., *Sufism*. London, Allen & Unwin; New York, Macmillan, 1950.

Austin, R. W. J., (ET and introd.) *Ibn al-'Arabi, The Bezels of Wisdom*. CWS 1981.

Goldziher, I., (ET) *Introduction to Islamic Theology and Law*. Princeton University, 1981.

McCarthy, R. J., (ET of Ghazali) *Freedom and Fulfilment*. Boston, Twayne, 1980 (contains bibliography).

Nicholson, R. A., *Studies in Islamic Mysticism* (CUP, 1921), ch. 3.

Trimingham, J. S., *The Sufi Orders in Islam*. Oxford, Clarendon, 1971; OUP, 1973 (contains bibliography).

All Koranic quotations are taken from the translation of A. J. Arberry, *The Koran Interpreted*, The World's Classics 596 (OUP, 1964; New York, Macmillan, 1969). Additional Islamic texts in the CWS series are: XVIII (Maneri); XXXI (Ibn Iraqi); XLIV (Attar); L (Rumi); LVIII (Ali-Alawi/Al Yashrutiyyah).

> God is the light of the heavens and the earth; the likeness of His light is as a niche wherein is a lamp, the lamp in a glass, the glass as it were a glittering star, kindled from a blessed tree, an olive that is neither of the east nor of the west whose oil wellnigh would shine, even if no fire touched it; light upon light – God guides to His light whom He will, and God strikes similitudes for men, and God has knowledge of everything – in temples God has allowed to be raised up, and His name to be commemorated therein; therein glorifying Him, in the mornings and the evenings, are men whom neither commerce nor trafficking diverts from the remembrance of God and to perform the prayer, and to pay the alms, fearing a day when hearts and eyes shall be turned about, that God may recompense them for their fairest works and give them increase of His bounty; and God provides whomsoever He will, without reckoning (Koran 24.35–8).

The spirituality of classical Islam is undoubtedly found in sufism, i.e. Islamic mysticism. But mysticism did not complete its conquest of the spirit of Islam until the twelfth century. And a good way of exploring Muslim spirituality is to follow the progress of sufism during the first five or six centuries of Islam.[1]

[1] *The Encyclopaedia of Islam* (= *EI*) (Leiden and Leipzig 1913–38; new edn., Leiden and London, Luzac, 1960–   ), s.v. 'taṣawwuf'; R. A. Nicholson, *The Mystics of Islam*. London, Bell, 1914; London and Boston, Routledge & Kegan Paul, 1974. R. A. Nicholson, (ET) *The Kashf al-Mahjúb . . . by . . . Hujwírí*. London, Luzac, 1934, 1974. A. J. Arberry, *Sufism*. A. J. Arberry, 'Mysticism', in *The Cambridge History of Islam*

The story of sufism is about two major events: the development of primitive Muslim piety into mysticism, and the rise of the sufi to sainthood. Like other facets of classical Islam, sufism can be traced back to the living traditions of the regions, from the Mediterranean to India, conquered by the Arabs in the seventh and eighth centuries. Many of these were alive with monks of various descriptions. Asceticism was rife, and mysticism on the increase.[1] The Koran itself is not without a mystical dimension. There are passages – one is quoted at the head of this chapter – of plainly mystical inspiration. Others, obscure and suggestive, invite or lend themselves to mystical interpretation. This side of the Koran was discovered in due course by the mystics, as was the mystic in Muhammad.[2] But for centuries the Arabs held out against the spirituality of the solitary life. Their mission was to rule the world, not to renounce it. 'No monkery in Islam', goes a slogan of the period preserved as a saying of the Prophet. 'The monasticism of this community is the Holy War.'

The religion of the conquest society was organized around the concepts of *umma* (community) and *imām* (leader). As changing circumstances robbed these concepts of their basis in reality, the prospect of individual salvation held out by the solitary life gained in attraction. Yet the communal spirit of the first period lived on in tradition, the anecdotal lore accorded quasi-scriptural authority at a time when sufism was still hovering on the fringes of Islam.[3] The solitary life was to remain extracanonical. The heroism of the hermit and the mendicant was no doubt impressive.[4] But by Islamic standards it was spiritually no less than socially unhinged. Asceticism in Islam primarily means spiritual discipline, not renunciation of the world.[5] Sufism never went wholly monastic.

(CUP, 1970, 1978), vol. 2, pt. viii, ch. 6. A. J. Arberry, (ET) *The Doctrine of the Ṣūfīs.* CUP, 1935, 1977. L. Massignon, *Essai sur les origines du lexique technique de la mystique musulmane.* Paris, 1968. H. Ritter, *Das Meer der Seele.* Leiden, 1955 (bibliography). The best historical introduction remains I. Goldziher, *Introduction to Islamic Theology and Law,* ch. 4.

[1] For the Christian background see especially the article by S. P. Brock in this volume, pp. 199–215.

[2] I. Goldziher, *Die Richtungen der islamischen Koranauslegung* (Leiden, 1920), pp. 180ff; T. Andrae, *Die Person Muhammeds in Lehre und Glauben seiner Gemeinde.* Stockholm, 1918.

[3] *EI,* s.v. 'ḥadīth'; I. Goldziher, 'On the Development of the ḥadīth' in his (ET) *Muslim Studies* (London, Allen & Unwin, 1967; Chicago, Aldine, 1973), vol. 2.

[4] *EI,* s.v. 'darwīsh', 'faḳīr', 'ḳalandar'.

[5] *EI,* s.v. 'zuhd'. The spirituality of the conquest society is exemplified by Ibn al-Mubarak (d. 797), merchant, campaigner, scholar, ascetic, who compiled traditions on both Holy War (*jihād*) and Spiritual Discipline (*zuhd*).

An early centre of ascetic piety was Basra. Hasan of Basra (d. 728) made the Koran the sole standard of right and wrong. He preached the Koranic virtues of remembrance of God, fear of God, repentance, rectitude, sincerity, patience, trust in God. We must live every moment of our lives as though it were the last. We must purify our hearts and examine our conduct in the light of the Koran.[1] These are the beginnings to which sufism traces its asceticism. It is on the Koranic derivation of this asceticism that its claim to Islamic authenticity chiefly rests. The Koranic element is of course most apparent in the *language* of sufism, but to some extent also in its basic conceptions. For example, the Koran is innocent of the Christian contrast between flesh and spirit. The word 'spirit' does occur; and it is possible in Arabic to speak of 'spirituality' without sounding altogether Greek or Christian.[2] More typically, however, religion resides in the *heart*.[3] The constant foe of the heart in sufism is the nagging, petulant *soul* of Koran 12.53 ('Surely the soul of man incites to evil'). The human soul is the seat of self-seeking aspirations, the wilful self.[4] The paradigm sin of the Christian flesh is lust; the Muslim soul sins by wanting at all. 'But will you shall not, unless God wills, the Lord of all being' (Koran 81.29).

The heart is the seat also of love. Hasan's *fear* of God was soon overtaken in sufism by *love* of God. Erotic passion eventually became the prime metaphor of ecstatic ('intoxicated') mysticism.[5] Sexuality is not intrinsically sinful, celibacy not necessarily beneficial (Muhammad had been a man of many marriages). Material poverty is good if it purges the love of 'the dirham and the dinar'. But what matters is the 'poverty of the heart': the knowledge that we utterly depend on God. The progress of the heart requires constant self-examination. Systematic elaboration of this spiritual discipline led to the 'way' of sufism with its many 'stations' of repentance, fear, etc. – and, ultimately, mystical union.

Preoccupation with the life of the heart engendered a movement of introversion. In the ninth century, sufis began to uncover the 'inner' meaning of the Law (Koran and tradition). For example, the Koranic 'struggle in the path of God', i.e. the Holy War of Islam, became the sufi's struggle with his self-assertive soul. The most momentous of these reinterpretations was that administered to the theological concept of monotheism. The Arabic word for monotheism – *tawḥīd*, 'declaring to be

[1] H. Ritter, 'Studien zur Geschichte der islamischen Frömmigkeit (I)', in *Der Islam*, 21 (1933), and *EI*, s.v. 'Ḥasan al-Baṣrī'.
[2] For *rūḥ*, 'spirit', see *EI*, s.v. 'nafs'.
[3] *EI*, s.v. 'kalb'.
[4] *EI*, s.v. 'nafs'.
[5] R. A. Nicholson, *Studies in Islamic Mysticism*, ch. 3.

one' – literally means 'unification'. For Junayd (d. 910), later acclaimed as a pillar of moderate ('sober') sufism, *tawḥīd* most intimately means mystical union: the disappearance (*fanā'*) of self-consciousness in the enveloping presence of God; the ultimate triumph over the 'nagging soul', the self.[1] *Fanā'* henceforth remains the keynote of sufism. (The word could relate to Koran 55.26: 'All that dwells upon the earth is perishing (*fānin*), yet still abides the face of thy Lord, majestic, splendid.') Junayd's theory of *tawḥīd* marks the beginning of what has aptly been described as a shift from monotheism to theomonism. This was completed by Ibn al-'Arabi (d. 1240) in his theosophy of the 'unity of being'.[2] Earlier sufis understood that, most profoundly, we fall short of monotheism in fancying that beside God there is anything at all. According to Abu Sa'id (d. 1049), even sufism was guilty of 'assigning partners to God' (*shirk*, the Koranic term for polytheism): 'for sufism guards the heart from what is other than God; and there is nothing other than God'.[3]

The arrival of mysticism in their midst alarmed the guardians of the faith. Jurists were scandalized by antinomian tendencies, theologians by the violence done to their concept of divine transcendence. When the mystic Hallaj (d. 922) proclaimed that God had come to dwell in him, he was tried for blasphemy and executed.[4] His death came as a sobering shock for many. On the sufi side there were calls for moderation. Antinomianism was deplored; extravagant talk of union with God eschewed; and sufi orthodoxy written up in ways appealing to traditional and traditionist scholarship. Sufism put its house in order, and a century later was ready to welcome the rest of Islam.

In the meantime orthodoxy had come to be troubled by worse than the enthusiasm of the mystics. The caliphate was crumbling, and with it the idea of Islamic theocracy. With *imām* and *umma* in decline, Muslims turned for guidance to those most palpably inspired: the sufi sheikhs, the 'friends of God'. The surge of allegiance led, in the twelfth century, to the formation and proliferation of sufi orders, convents, shrines.[5] The holy

[1] A. H. Abdel-Kader, *The Life, Personality and Writings of al-Junayd* (London, Luzac, 1962), pp. 176f; *EI*, s.v. '(al-) Djunayd (Abu l-Ḳāsim)'.

[2] *EI*, s.v. 'Ibn al-'Arabī (Muḥyi l-Dīn)'; R. W. J. Austin, *Ibn al-'Arabi, The Bezels of Wisdom*, pp. 25ff.

[3] Nicholson, *Studies*, ch. 1, pp. 49f; *EI*, s.v. 'Abū Sa'īd b. Abi l-Khayr'; F. Meier, *Abū Sa'īd-i Abū l-Ḥayr* (Leiden, 1976, bibliography).

[4] L. Massignon, (ET) *The Passion of al-Hallāj*. Princeton University, 1982; *EI*, s.v. '(al-) Ḥallādj'.

[5] *EI*, s.v. 'ṭarīḳa', 'khānḳāh', 'ribāṭ', 'zāwiya'; 'ḳubba' J. S. Trimingham, *The Sufi Orders in Islam*; R. Gramlich, *Die schiitischen Derwischorden Persiens* (Wiesbaden, 1965–81), Abhandlungen für die Kunde des Morgenlandes, XXXVI, 1–4; XLV, 2 (bibliographies).

man of late antiquity was celebrating his comeback in Islam.[1] According to the claim of al-Hakim al-Tirmidhi (d. c. 900), now widely accepted, the leaders of 'the friends of God' are the true heirs of the prophets.[2] The expression is Koranic, the conception ancient.[3] The friends of God are carriers of divine grace.[4] 'They are the pillars of the earth, through whose blessings God's mercy descends upon its people – as tradition has the Prophet say: It is on their account that you are given rain and sustenance'.[5]

The dramatic change which took place in this period is illustrated by the contrasting ideals of Farabi (d. 950) and Ibn Tufayl (d. 1185). The philosopher Farabi, for all his reliance on Neoplatonic tradition, admits no possibility of individual happiness or perfection outside society. Society, indeed, is the vehicle of salvation. Farabi's ideal state is an idealised *umma* headed by an idealized *imām*, his perfect man. By contrast, Ibn Tufayl's perfect man – the hero of his philosophical romance *Hayy ibn Yaqzan* – is a solitary whose intellectual progress culminates in the discovery, through mystical union, of the transcendent truth of divine unity.[6] Hayy is the perfect man of Islamic mysticism.[7]

The turning point is marked by the life and work of Ghazali (d. 1111), a religious scholar of exceptional powers of perception and persuasion.[8] His cardinal work, *The Religious Sciences Revived*, integrates sufi ethics into Islamic law and ritual. He insists on the ineffability of mystical experience; expounds the difference between lawful and unlawful sufism; and throws the weight of his example behind his endorsement of lawful sufism by retiring from his professorship at Baghdad to a life of spiritual discipline. Conceptually, his endorsement of sufism takes the form of a neat extension of the received (Aristotelian) theory of perception. There

[1] *EI*, s.v. 'walī'; *Shorter Encyclopaedia of Islam*, ed. H. Gibb and J. Kramers (Leiden, Brill; Ithaca, Cornell, 1953), s.v. 'marabout'. Goldziher, 'Veneration of Saints in Islam', in *Muslim Studies*; R. Kriss and H. Kriss-Heinrich, *Volksglaube im Bereich des Islam* (Wiesbaden 1960–2, bibliography); C. E. Padwick, *Muslim Devotions* (London, SPCK, 1961), pp. 235ff.

[2] J. A. Williams, *Themes of Islamic Civilisation* (Berkeley; London, University of California, 1971), ch. 6, 'The Friends of God' (anthology), pp. 318–23; B. Radtke, 'Der Mystiker al-Ḥakīm at-Tirmidī', *Der Islam*, 57 (1980), pp. 237–45.

[3] P. Brown, *The Making of Late Antiquity*. Cambridge, Mass., Harvard University; London, Faber, 1978; P. Brown, *The Cult of the Saints*. Chicago University; London, Faber, 1981.

[4] *EI*, s.v. 'baraka', 'karāma'.

[5] From Ghazali's autobiography; cf. McCarthy, *Freedom and Fulfilment*, pp. 77f. An early example of a sufi saint is Abu Sa'id (cf. note 3, p. 501).

[6] L. E. Goodman, (ET) *Ibn Tufayl's Hayy Ibn Yaqzān*. New York, Twayne, 1972.

[7] *EI*, s.v. '(al-) insān al-kāmil'; Nicholson, *Studies*, ch. 2; 'The Perfect Man'.

[8] R. J. McCarthy, (ET) *Freedom and Fulfilment* (Ghazali's autobiography and other texts).

is no justice, he argues, in the notion that reason is the highest faculty of perception. There may well be, and in fact there clearly is, a faculty transcending reason just as reason transcends sensation. The workings of this faculty are witnessed, albeit not experienced by all, in all manner of inspiration, in mysticism, and above all in prophecy. Mysticism, then, is of the nature of prophecy; Muhammad started out as a sufi.

> If you are not granted a taste of sufi experience, you cannot grasp the nature of prophecy, only the word. The marvels of the friends of God are truly the beginnings of prophecy, the stages through which the Prophet passed when he first went to Mount Hira to be alone with his Lord and worship; so that the bedouin would say: Muhammad does love his Lord passionately.[1]

Sufism could not wish for better credentials.

Ghazali's conviction was not shared in all quarters. Traditionists, led by the Hanbalite school of law,[2] looked askance at the rash of extracanonical holiness. Theirs was the letter of the Law, which knew nothing of saintly dispensations or the unity of being. It is a measure of the sheer irresistibility of sufism that it succeeded in making notable recruits among Hanbalites.[3] But there is also a community of spirit. The creed of traditionism is characterized by fideism, its scholarship by unquestioning transmission. This ethos of intellectual self-abnegation has much in common with sufi asceticism. Where the sufi combats the self-seeking aspirations of the soul, the traditionist combats the self-seeking aspirations of the intellect. Both practise the Koranic virtues of self-surrender: patience, contentment, acquiescence in God's will (*tawakkul*).[4] *Islam*, after all, means 'submission'.[5]

---

[1] From Ghazali's autobiography; cf. McCarthy, *Freedom and Fulfilment*, p. 95.
[2] *EI*, s.v. 'Aḥmad b. Ḥanbal', 'Ḥanābila'.
[3] G. Makdisi, 'The Hanbali School and Sufism', *Actas del iv Congresso de Estudos Árabes e Islâmicos* (Coimbra – Lisbon 1968; (Leiden, 1971), pp. 71–84. For an early Hanbalite sufi, see W. M. Thackston (ET and introd.), *Khwaja 'Abudullah Ansari, Intimate Conversations*. CWS VIII.
[4] B. Reinert, *Die Lehre vom tawakkul in der klassischen Sufik*. Berlin, 1968 (bibliography).
[5] *EI*, s.v. 'islām'. For the continuity of sufism in the modern world, see A. Hourani, 'Rashid Rida and the Sufi Orders', in *Bulletin d'études orientales de l'Institut Français de Damas*, 29 (1977), pp. 231–41.

3 Hinduism

J. DUNCAN M. DERRETT

Sources

Alston, A. J., ed. and (ET), *The Devotional Poems of Mīrābāī.* Delhi, Motilal Banarsidass, 1980.

Babineau, E. J., *Love of God and Social Duty in the Rāmcaritmānas.* Delhi, Motilal Banarsidass, 1979.

Happold, F. C., *Mysticism: a Study and an Anthology* (Harmondsworth and New York, Penguin, 1963), pp. 143–8; 154–8.

O'Flaherty, W. D., *The Rig Veda: an Anthology.* Harmondsworth and New York, Penguin, 1981.

Pope, G. U., ed. and (ET), *The Tiruvāçagam; or, 'Sacred Utterances' of . . . Mānikkvāçagar.* Oxford, Clarendon, 1900.

Ramanujan, A. K., (ET) *Speaking of Śiva.* Harmondsworth and Baltimore, Md., Penguin, 1973.

Zaehner, R. C., ed. and (ET), *Hindu Scriptures.* London, Dent; New York, Dutton, 1966.

Studies

Babb, L. A., *The Divine Hierarchy: Popular Hinduism in Central India.* New York, Columbia University, 1975.

Bose, Shib Chunder, *The Hindoos as They Are.* Calcutta, Thacker, Spink; London, W. Thacker, 1883.

Brent, P. L., *Godmen of India.* London, Allen Lane; Chicago, Quadrangle Books, 1972.

Coudhary, K. P. S., *Modern Indian Mysticism.* Delhi, Motilal Banarsidass, 1981.

Clothey, F. W., *The Many Faces of Murukan: the History and Meaning of a South Indian God.* The Hague and New York, Mouton, 1978.

Das, Bhagavan, *The Essential Unity of All Religions.* Benares, Ananda, 1947; Wheaton, Ill., Theosophical, 1966.

Dhavamony, M., *Love of God according to Śaiva Siddhānta.* Oxford, Clarendon, 1971.

Farquhar, J. N., *Modern Religious Movements in India.* London and New York, Macmillan, 1915.

Gonda, J., *Viśhnuism and Sivaism: a Comparison.* London, University of London, 1970; New Delhi, Munshiram Manoharlal, 1976.

Hopkins, E. W., *The Religions of India.* Boston, Ginn, 1895.

Klostermaier, K., (ET) *Hindu and Christian in Vrindaban.* London, SCM, 1969.

Lele, Jayant, ed., *Tradition and Modernity in Bhakti Movements.* Leiden, Brill, 1981.

Lott, E. J., *Vedantic Approaches to God.* London, Macmillan; New York, Barnes & Noble, 1980.

Parrinder, E. G., *Avatar and Incarnation*. London, Faber; New York, Barnes & Noble, 1970.

Pocock, D. F., *Mind, Body and Wealth; a Study of Belief and Practice in an Indian Village*. Oxford, Blackwell; Totowa, N. J., Rowman & Littlefield, 1973.

Radhakrishnan, S., *Indian Philosophy*. London, Allen & Unwin; New York, Humanities, 1940.

Radhakrishnan, S., ed. and (ET), *The Brahma Sūtra. The Philosophy of Spiritual Life*. London, Allen & Unwin; New York, Harper, 1960.

Rajagopalachari, C., *Hinduism: Doctrine and Way of Life*. Bombay, Bharatiya Vidya Bhavan, 1970.

Stutley, M. and J., *A Dictionary of Hinduism*. London, Routledge; Bombay, Allied Publishers, 1977.

Zolla, E., 'Mystical Love in Hinduism', in *Studies in Mystical Literature* (Taichung), 1 (1984), pp. 8–25 (bibliographies).

The religious amalgam, 'Hinduism', derives in part from the culture ('Brahminism') of the composers of and specialists in the Vedic scriptures (*c.* 1500–1000 BC) and partly from Indian cults of greater age. Hindus now accept converts to Hinduism (membership of an endogamic hereditary caste no longer being essential), but query conversions *from* Hinduism, which includes, in their estimation, all religions (cf. BhG 9.23). Two ideas dominate: firstly that there is a transcendental order, englobing innumerable social norms – and yet individuals may aspire to a supersubstantial status independent of the performance of their prescribed duty; and secondly that apprehensions of truth arise in personalities subject to multiple limitations: no vision (*darśana*) therefore is exclusively true; correspondingly all *darśanas*, whether intellectually systematized or not, are co-valid without harmonization. Society which upholds specific *dharmas* (norms) as manifestations of an abstract *dharma* (righteousness) will nonetheless reprehend manifestations of religiosity repugnant to the moral sense. The interaction of these two fundamental notions will be explored below.

Hindus, exulting in 'spirituality', rightly cherish their tolerance. The spirituality of the seventeenth-century sufi, exponent of mystical Islam, met that of the *sannyāsī*, the Hindu renouncer; earlier cults of devotion arising in non-brahminical societies had tallied with, and supplemented, the 'great tradition' mediated by north Indian Brahminism. Hinduism however (excepting the Brahmo-Samaj) finds no value in *monotheism*. Rather, amongst many gods, that is praised of which a vision has transformed life, whether of an historical person, of his sect, a sub-caste, or, latterly, some multi-caste cult-association. Pantheism, henotheism, and the cult of the *ishta-devatā* (see below) concurrently verify spirituality.

Syncretism has characterized Hinduism, as indeed it has assisted social and political change. Cults include that of the *axis mundi* merged in a phallic representation of Śiva as the power of generation; or of guardian-spirits, deceased heroes; or the trinity of gods of the great tradition: *Śiva*; the creator *Brahma*; and the Vindicator of the Three Worlds, *Vishnu*, with his major incarnations, the model king and husband, Rāma, and the embodiment of divine love, Krishna. Knowledge of the supersubstantial worlds is imputed to Brahmins in the Vedic tradition, and that caste both provides priests of the classical pantheon (while lower castes minister to older deities in various guises) and has interpreted and purveyed a Sanskritic 'Hinduism' in the subcontinent.

Devatā (deity) implies a god worshipped in some shrine; *deva* ('god'?) has not the monotheistic potential of the Greek *theos*, for it comprehends superhuman powers, especially of nature, and may extend to charismatics and kings. One may honour *deva*s indiscriminately; yet one may have a favourite deity (*ishta-devatā*) to whom one devotes oneself in abject adoration upon the principle that he (or she) who accepts humble offerings will reciprocate, and can almost be compelled to receive the suit of the prostrate devotee. This adoration requires forgetfulness of self.

> I honour those who supplicate me to the measure of their supplication; there-fore let him worship me, the Supreme Lord, with the sacrifice which is concentration of knowledge (*jñāna-yoga*) (*Īśvara-gītā*, 11.72; cf. BhG 4.11; 18.65).

Such devotion is called *bhakti*, a word with overtones of communion with the deity. Krishna is the favourite incarnation of Vishnu, offering ecstatic union: yet Śiva, combining sexuality and asceticism, receives comparable adoration.

> Without *bhakti* the self is subject to fetters which obscure the real nature of its fundamental union with God. With the dawn of grace the self melts with love of God and consequently fetters give way and the false identification of the self with the products of *karma* [action] and *māyā* [deceptive appearance] disappears (Dhavamony, p. 375).

> Nor friends, nor kin I seek; no city I desire; no name I crave;
> No learned ones I seek; and henceforth lessons to be conned suffice.
> Thou dancer, in Kutralam dwelling blissful, thy resounding feet
> I'll seek, that as the cow yearns for its calf, my longing soul may melt
> (*Tiruvāsagam*, 39.3).

Cults of Vishnu accept moreover that one may reach the deity through the preceptor (*guru*), who has an often heritable charisma, and can demand absolute obedience from his disciples. Sincerity requires the abandonment of 'I-ness' and of 'my-ness'.

From Vedic times offerings were made to deities for protection and material aid. The deity became a destination for material sacrifices. Later the *devatās*' powers became abstract. Writers of Upanishads lifted *devatā* from a passive entity to a screen for the indwelling Self, both creator and created.

> The Self pervades. Bright, without body, free from harm, unmuscular, pure, exempt from evil, wise, equipped with Mind, encompassing, Self-existent, appropriately he assigned values throughout eternity (*Īśā-upanishad*, 8).

Renunciation of desire, *knowledge* (of truth), and concentration (*yoga*): in combination these co-meritorious paths could lead even to superiority over *devas*. The most celebrated combination of Hindu principles, the *Bhagavadgītā* [BhG] (a homily placed in the mouth of Krishna, transfigured as the universal spirit, composed in the early centuries of our era), explains this:

> He whose consciousness is without attachment, whose self conquers in all directions, who has left desire behind, he, by his renunciation, achieves the highest success, transcending all action.
> To those who are constantly concentrated and worship full of love I give that consciousness-attachment by which they reach me (BhG 18.49; 10.10).

Already in a composite late *upanishad*, the personal deity, immanent and transcendent, was adored:

> Now one should know Nature (*prakriti*) as illusion (*māyā*)
> And that the Mighty Lord is the Maker of illusion.
> This whole world is pervaded with beings that are his parts.
> The One who rules every source, in whom the world unites and dissolves,
> The Lord, boon-giver, *deva* we adore – one goes to peace (*śānti*) by revering him
>
> (*Śvetāśvatara-upanishad*, 4.10-11).

Vedic sacrifices are obsolete, but *darśana*s survive based on study of the Vedas and Upanishads. Meditation on the Self, and worship of invisible powers or of idols coexist with gifts to ascetics. Village and household shrines, and the shrine of the heart, receive attention. Attendances at pilgrimages flag, but worship of the sage flourishes. Many seers, and even philosophers, have attained renown, some, as Sundar Singh half a century ago, attract serious Western students. The sage who radiates compassion and universal benevolence virtually compels a vast adherence. Satya Sai Baba (who performs distant cures) is worshipped as a saviour by persons of all classes, and temples are erected to him in his lifetime.

Devotional literature is loquacious on the *ishta-devatā*, of manifest psychological value. In contrast with the rituals of temple-worship, resembling the ceremonial of a court, the worship of the patron deity is internal, the goal and material of meditation. The hundred-verse hymn of praise to the *devatā* (listing its titles), sung to greet it in the morning, can be a medium of private worship; its archaic incantation lifts the mind from mundane reality. Women, whose frustrations are obvious, are given to cults, but men do not lag behind. Devotees offer their surrender to the deity, and though corporate worship is known (including hymn-singing, especially if 'non-denominational'), visible signs of religiosity are unnecessary. Access to the deity is direct; it selects for itself who shall come to it (cf. BhG 11.48). No intermediary is needed in such worship, and the legalism of observances and the ministrations of specialists can be avoided (the latter with more confidence than the former). Equanimity, and renunciation of all low *motive*, are essential.

> By devotion he comes to know me, how great I am, and who in reality; then knowing me in reality he enters forthwith. He should do all actions taking entirely refuge with me; through my grace he will attain the eternal, imperishable state (BhG 18.55–6).

Whereas the deity can obtain no benefit from the worshipper, its sovereign compassion is shown by acceptance of offerings (implying the corresponding obligation to protect), and approval of renunciation of self. One form of protection is relief from the burden of destiny (see below).

Devotees of a *devatā*, human or mythical, may enter trance states, and controlled hysteria. Local deities will possess priestly mediums at known places and times: the possessed speaks in the deity's name. It may show its presence and power by the possessed's insensibility to pain. The possessor–saviour verifiably lifts the devotee above mundane awareness. The devotee obtains *darśana* of the deity after years of repeated prayer: it then alters his or her personality and confers charisma. It incidentally authenticates the claim of Vedānta, the popular school based upon the Upanishads, that *devatā* and worshipper are one.

> That Being is the seed: all else has him as its self. He is truth. He is Self. Shwetaketu! Thou art That! (*Chāndogya-upanishad*, 14.3; cf. BhG 2.12, 20).

But there is no creed supporting a hierarchy, or admitting of heresies. Are the *devatā* and devotee always identical? The immortal self (*ātma*), the 'soul' in Hinduism, is denied by Buddhism. Non-atheistical *darśanas* assert that (i) the *ātma* is one with the *paramātma*, the Supreme Soul (pantheistic Entity); or (ii) the *ātma* is distinct from the *paramātma* (how else could they be joined?); or (iii) it is identical in some respects and in others non-identical. If the deity saves, it rescues as the mother monkey carries her baby, who hangs on; or, some prefer, as the cat grabs her kittens in the mouth. Observances are generally deprecated and depreciated in a faith that asks for salvation. They can never be enough, and *dharma* is, as it were, buried in a cave. The message of the *Bhagavadgītā* is primarily that one should do one's caste-duty without attachment to reward ('fruit'), thus becoming free to attain the Ultimate (cf. BhG 2.47–8; 3.25; 4.20; 5.11; 17.25; 18.6).

Hindus fear rebirth, in hells, or in inauspicious births. The saviour can defeat the inexorable, protean law of *karma*.

> The disciple (*yogi*) who participates in me who am present in all creatures, and who, established in Unity, is yet engaged in [any or] all kinds of occupations, abides in me.
>
> Those who are great of soul (*mahātmas*), seeking nearness to me, never suffer rebirth, the abode of suffering, [the equivalent of] impermanence; they achieve the highest attainment (BhG 6.31; 8.15; cf. 4.9; 12.7).

No doubt a perfect performance of *dharma* would in theory mitigate *karma*: one might be reborn so endowed as to achieve thereby emancipation from *samsāra*, the cycle of rebirth and woe. *Punya* (merit) can be earned, and *pāpa* (sin, defilement) avoided. But the saviour is urged to *condone* the devotee's shortcomings. At death (cf. BhG 7.30, 8.5ff) measures seek to secure the deity's compassion, and purity is attained. The round of observances has not been decisively reprehended, though it ties the performer to desire and to rebirth (cf. BhG 2.49; 3.4, etc.; 18.66; but cf. 16.24): but some teach that the devotee who has danced in the guise of *prakriti* (feminine) with *purusha*, the creative force (masculine), transcends *samsāra*; a theory coalescing with the role of the *ishta-devatā*. Moral achievement can thus be bypassed, ecstasy retains a value, and both rectitude and want of rectitude become, at the last, insignificant (cf. BhG 9.30). At this point of discovery non-theistic *darśana*s, and such as ignore a personal deity, prepare the mind for Buddhism.

4 Buddhism

J. DUNCAN M. DERRETT

Sources

Chalmers, Lord, *Buddha's Teaching... Sutta-nipāta*. Harvard Oriental Series, vol. 37. Cambridge, Mass., Harvard University; London, OUP, 1932.
Conze, E., *et al.*, ed. and (ET), *Buddhist Texts Through the Ages*. New York, Harper, 1964.
Cowell, E. B., *et al.*, (ET) *Buddhist Mahāyāna Texts*. Sacred Books of the East, vol. 49. Oxford, Clarendon, 1894; repr. Delhi, Motilal Banarsidass, 1972.
Radhakrishnan, S., ed. and (ET), *Dhammapada*. Madras and Delhi, OUP, 1980.
The Teaching of Buddha. 91st rev. (bilingual) edn, Tokyo, Bukkyo Dendo Kyokai, 1979.
Warren, H. C., *Buddhism in Translations*. Cambridge, Mass., Harvard Oriental Series, vol. 3, Harvard University, 1896; New York, Atheneum, 1977.

Studies

Blofeld, J. E. C., *Gateway to Wisdom*. London, Allen & Unwin; New York, Random House, 1980.
Collins, S., *Selfless Persons: Imagery and Thought in Theravāda Buddhism*. CUP, 1982.
Dayal, Har, *The Bodhisattva Doctrine in Buddhist Sanskrit Literature*. London, Kegan Paul; Delhi, Motilal Banarsidass, 1932.
Dutt, Nalinaksha, *Early Monastic Buddhism*. 2nd edn, Calcutta, Firma KLM Private, 1981.
Gard, R. A., ed., *Buddhism*. Englewood Cliffs, N.J.; London, Prentice-Hall, 1961.
Robinson, R. H., *The Buddhist Religion: a Historical Introduction*. Belmont, Calif., Dickens, 1970.
Sangharakshita, Bhikshu, 'Buddhism', in Basham, A. L., ed., *A Cultural History of India* (Oxford, Clarendon, 1975), ch. 8.
Suzuki, D. T., *Mysticism, Christian and Buddhist*. London and Boston, Unwin Paperbacks, 1979.
Thomas, E. J., *The History of Buddhist Thought*. London, Kegan Paul; New York, Knopf, 1933.

Buddhist mysticism, though belonging to the Mahāyāna (the Great Vehicle), is prepared for by implicit faith in the Theravāda, called 'Hīnayāna' (Lesser Vehicle), i.e. primitive Buddhism as developed within two centuries after Gotama, the Śākyamuni Buddha (died *c*. 543 or 373 BC). Those who have learned the Four Noble Truths about Suffering and its Cessation, have destroyed the cravings and exterminated the afflictions of impurity and the fetters binding the person to rebirth, will know that reality is not confined within the opposites (e.g. good and bad, black and white), and is Void, the 'emptiness' of characterlessness. All composite things are transient, sorrow-full, ego-less; realizing this is the path to purity, and the realizer is a conqueror:

> He whose conquest nobody can conquer, into whose conquest none can enter – by what track can you trace him, the awakened, whose limits are in-finite, the trackless? (*Dhammapada*, 179).

The mind released from all its binding conditions is no longer a slave to the 'builder of its house'. Origination is continuously dependent: in turn each of the following leads to the remainder in series: ignorance conditions volitional acts, and these in turn consciousness, phenomena, the faculties, contact, sensation, craving, clinging, becoming, birth, and finally decay and death.

> The calm one, beyond merit and sin, without stain, knowing this world and the other(s), vanquishing birth and death, he is truly called 'monk' (*Sutta-nipāta*, 3.6.11 [520]).

Sri Lanka, Burma and Thailand have developed the Theravāda, based upon the supposed teachings of Gotama as recognized in the India of the emperor Aśoka (3rd cent. BC). The pursuit of wisdom as propounded in the *Dhammapada* and the *Suttanipāta* (authentic ancient works) may not derive word for word from the Blessed One himself; and it is significant that in each land his supposed teachings coexist with older cults. Buddhism is tolerant of faiths apparently incompatible with it; converts to Buddhism need not apostatize. Buddhas preceded Gotama, and will succeed him until the Buddha Maitreya will convert the last generation of disciples. Successful adherents to and promoters of Buddhism may claim to be Bodhisattvas, committed to seeking Buddhahood, attaining *nirvāna*. This is the tranquillity of full enlightenment, the extinction of all attachments. Bodhisattvas renounce the achievement of that Goal, while they assist others to achieve it with them. Buddhism is a thinking religion (one 'comes and sees'), but the role of the Bodhisattva presupposes the transformation of craving into compassion, a sharing of wisdom by enlightened ones, hampered as they are by the limitations of language and logicality. The saviour's compassion operates through his distinctive combination of loving 'resolves'. For example the wisdom of the imagined Bodhisattva Mañjuśrī, and the compassion of the mythical Avalokiteśvara may meet in any historical personage, recognizable as a Bodhisattva. Buddhism recognizes no Creator as it rejects permanence. The *devas* are no more than highly enlightened beings inferior to the Fully Enlightened Buddha, whose only desire is to save the whole universe.

In devotion to Gotama, representing all Buddhas, one venerates his icon, as formerly symbols of his Birth and Enlightenment, and his relics encapsulated in the *stūpa* (a symbolic mound appropriated from earlier cults). Such veneration reinforces faith in the *dhamma* (Sanskrit: *dharma*, here = world-view), which commenced as a wisdom hostile to observances and to caste, but progressed because the public venerated renouncers. Gotama founded a *sangha* or association of ascetics choosing a midway path between extremes of belief and practice. His 'monks' chose 'homelessness' and earned *punya* thereby, which those who kept them at subsistence level shared. The discipline of the monks (*vinaya*), and their meditations, enabled them to attain the status of *arhat* (perfected, saint) or *nirvāna*; the laity could hardly expect to attain these states, but the monks' discipline served as a standard of perfection. There also exist nuns, who live in obedience to a *vinaya* of their own and to the monks as well but they are not found now in all parts of the Buddhist world.

The public were invited to 'take refuge' with the Three Jewels, viz. the Buddha, the Dhamma, and the Sangha. The centre of Buddhism is the realization of 'is-ness', the true character of everything in its 'such-ness': this is incomprehensible apart from the Three Jewels, in which ideology and institution are merged. Laymen were expected to observe the Noble Eightfold Path, which eschewed all forms of injury, viz. right vision, conception, speech, action, livelihood, effort, mindfulness, concentration (or meditation). 'Not to do evil, to cultivate good, to purify one's mind, this is the teaching of the Buddhas' (*Dhammapada*, 183). Gradually Hindu mystical notions and cults penetrated Buddhism in India, producing eclectic schools obscuring the primitive faith, blurring the distinction between it and Hinduism, and, except in further Asia and Tibet, prejudicing its survival. The development of the personal deity within Vedānta undermined the Bodhisattva image which had no link with ancient cults. The religion whose founder scouted irrational actions and offered liberation from fear degenerated in many places into a magical cult. Meanwhile, freed from Indian cultural presuppositions, Buddhism developed intuitive and psychological refinements in China and Japan.

The *dhamma* was ever hard to comprehend and practice; with its function understood, both meditation and moral attainment could be seen as means to an end, inferior in themselves to Wisdom. This does not imply antinomian features, but rather that the goal of understanding the Void is reached with the aid of helpers who are themselves short of it. The Bodhisattva Amitābha can save those who put their trust in him: one melts into him pronouncing the formula, 'I worship Amitābha.'

Amida Buddha (Amitābha) is not far from anyone. His Land of Purity is described as being far away to the West, but it is, also, within the minds of those who earnestly wish to be born there.

Those who are born in that Pure Land share in Buddha's boundless life; their hearts are immediately filled with sympathy for all sufferers and go forward to manifest the Buddha's method of salvation.

Lay followers (of the *sangha*) should follow the five precepts: not to kill, not to steal, not to commit adultery, not to lie or deceive, and not to use intoxicants. They should not only believe in the Three Jewels and keep the precepts themselves, but also . . . make others observe them, especially their relations and friends, trying to awaken in them an unshakeable faith in the Buddha, the Dhamma and the Sangha, so that they too may share in Buddha's compassion (*Teaching of Buddha*, pp. 212, 210, 396–8).

Separate from this faith is that known in Theravāda lands particularly, where the monks unilaterally transfer their merit to deceased lay followers. Whether in this life or afterwards, the Deceiver, Māra, cannot command those whom Gotama freed from the fetters of time, place, creed and conformity, but most schools of Buddhism insist that moral scrupulousness is material to attainment whether of *arhat*-ness or of *nirvāna*, or of the Pure Lands presided over by the Buddhas and Bodhisattvas. Those who are not scrupulous have evidently not been liberated from craving, and their devotion to Amitābha, for example, is imperfect.

5 African Religion

JOHN S. MBITI

Gaba. C., ed., *Scriptures of an African People: the Sacred Utterances of the Anlo.* New York, NOK Publishers, 1973.
Mbiti, J. S., *The Prayers of African Religion.* London, SPCK, 1975; Maryknoll, N.Y., 1976.
Shorter, A., *Prayer in the Religious Traditions of Africa.* OUP, 1975.

We use 'African Religion' here to refer collectively to the religious systems of African peoples which have evolved through the centuries without founding figures and written scriptures. While we speak of it in the singular, it is to be borne in mind that each African people (the word 'tribe' is now tainted with less good connotations) has its own religious ideas, activities, beliefs, leaders and so on. There is a sufficiently large number of common or similar elements in most of Africa to enable us to speak of African religion in a collective singular.

Spirituality is used here to refer to those religious elements dealing with the direct relationship between human beings and the spiritual realm. Africans are very much aware of the spiritual realities, including God, divinities, spirits and spiritual forces. Spirituality is expressed and exercised through prayers, rituals, symbols, dance and other art forms or representations. We shall take prayers as the best 'hunting-ground' for African spirituality, and isolate a few elements for our further observations.

The prayers of African religion are handed down orally. Those which have reached us today must have been deemed important and valuable, otherwise they would have been forgotten and lost. Through prayers we see man standing 'naked' before the spiritual realities in which God is the most prominent. God is named and acknowledged in all African societies.

Thousands of these traditional prayers continue to be used all over Africa. But since they are not written down, scholars are not sufficiently exposed to them to be able to analyse and evaluate more than a tiny proportion of them. So we are still very much in the dark concerning the wealth of African prayers, and so far only a few books have published collections of the prayers (see bibliography).

The prayers of African religion address themselves to every aspect of personal and community life. This includes life's journey from pregnancy to long after death, the environment in which humans exist, and expressions of joy and praise, blessing and cursing, rain and health. The spirituality which comes out of these prayers is an all-embracing spirituality; that is, the physical world is embraced in the arms of the spiritual, the physical is lifted up into the spiritual. A few items will suffice to be mentioned here.

Human beings approach God and the spiritual realm in prayer. They take the attitude that God is pure and clean, without fault. So on their part, people also have to be spiritually clean. They perform rituals to help create this state of spiritual purity. Cleansing ceremonies are commonly performed, involving blood, water, the stomach contents of animals and mixtures of other purification ingredients. Prayers are offered for the purification of life, for example of marriage, new home, new fields, new working season and tools (for planting, hunting and fishing), the start of new fires, and firstfruits of the harvest before the new crop is eaten. People feel that they are constantly exposed to God who has no impurity, so they have to relate to him at a level of spiritual purity.

Humility is a great spiritual element. Man prays because he needs or looks for a happy relationship with the spiritual realm. So, people call upon God as Father, Creator or Giver, and regard themselves as his children. With humility are also the elements of love, honour, respect, admiration and adoration towards God and sometimes towards departed members of the family (or their representatives).

Faith, trust and confidence are more or less assumed in the praying tradition. People invest trust in the spiritual realm, otherwise they would not pray. Praying drives out fear and cultivates confidence which in turn generates spiritual health and wellbeing.

Praise, thanksgiving and joy come out strongly in African prayers. The soul gives itself back to God through praise, and joy before him. These elements are often accompanied by singing, dancing, clapping and communal celebration since most of the religious exercises are done on a community basis. They express the feeling that people's requests before God and the spiritual realm have been rewarded. There are many things for which to praise and thank God. In general, African people approach life in a celebrating attitude, in spite of the many adversities and sufferings which they experience. They are ever ready to celebrate life, to dance life, to sing. The sound of joy is often heard in the village at night, smiling faces are often seen in the morning on the paths between the villages or in the streets of the towns.

Blessings are highly valued in African societies. So people offer many invocations of blessings. They are uttered by persons of older or higher (social and functional) status to those of lower status or younger, for example by priests to the people, the ruler to the ruled, the parents to the children, and so on.

There is also the spiritual realm in which human beings wrestle with evil. Many prayers deal with this area. They speak to the questions relating to moral evil, suffering, sickness, misfortunes, death, broken relationships, witchcraft, infertility and so on. Some of these wrestlings are addressed to God, but others to other spiritual realities.

We complete these observations by including two examples of prayers from African religion. In passing, it needs to be mentioned that in the course of this century the Christian faith has spread rapidly to the southern two thirds of Africa, reaching in varying degrees every African society. Islam has also made its inroads in certain parts of the continent. Spirituality from these two great religions is interplaying with spirituality from African religion, and indications are that the traditional African spirituality still carries great weight among converts who embrace the newer religions but often retain their traditional spirituality.

The following prayer comes from the Baluba of Zaïre:

> I shall sing a song of praise to God:
> Strike the chords upon the drum.
> God who gives us all good things –
> Strike the chords upon the drum –

Wives, and wealth and wisdom.
Strike the chords upon the drum.

In this prayer everything is summoned to offer praise to God. The drum represents the arts, wives represent human society, wealth represents material things, and wisdom represents human knowledge and learning.

The second prayer comes from the peoples of Rwanda and Burundi. In it we see the agonies of a childless wife being aired before God:

> I don't know for what Imana (God) is punishing me. If I could meet with him, I would kill him. Imana, why are you punishing me? . . . Couldn't you even give me one little child, Yo-oh-o! I am dying in anguish! If only I could meet you and pay you out! Come on, let me kill you! . . . O Imana, you have deserted me! Yo-o-o!

6 Amerindian Spirituality

D. STOVER

Brown, J. E., *The Sacred Pipe: Black Elk's Account of the Seven Rites of the Oglala Sioux*. Norman, University of Oklahoma, 1975.

Goldman, I., *The Mouth of Heaven: An Introduction to Kwakiutl Religious Thought*. New York, John Wiley, 1975.

Hallowell, A. I., *The Role of Conjuring in Saulteaux Society*. Philadelphia, University of Pennsylvania, 1942.

Neihardt, J. G., *Black Elk Speaks*. New York, Pocket Books, 1972.

Ortiz, A., *The Tewa World*. University of Chicago, 1969.

Radin, P., *The Road of Life and Death*. New York, Pantheon Books, 1945.

Storm, Hyemeyohsts, *Seven Arrows*. New York, Harper & Row, 1972.

Storm, Hyemeyohsts, *Song of Heyoehkah*. New York, Harper & Row, 1981.

Tedlock, B. and D. ed., *Teachings from the American Earth*. New York, Liveright, 1975.

The CWS series contains several volumes of Amerindian texts.

Amerindian spirituality is characterized by a holistic world-view according to which the natural, social and spiritual dimensions are understood to be profoundly integrated. Despite the cultural variety represented by Amerindian traditions, there are common patterns which are evident. Three such patterns describe the holistic scope of Amerindian spirituality: (1) the solidarity of human beings with the natural world, (2) the centering of individual human existence in the social community, and (3) the reciprocity of human spirit with spirit transcending the human. Each of these three holds together elements of reality which have undergone systematic alienation in Western culture.

The first pattern of Amerindian spirituality is apparent in the role of medicine, which is a spiritual power concretely and personally existing in the various animal and plant forms of the natural world as well as in cosmic expressions of nature such as earth, clouds, storms, sun, moon and stars. As Black Elk, the Oglala visionary, expressed it, 'We regard all created beings as sacred and important, for everything has a *wochangi* or influence which can be given to us.'[1] Access to medicine is at once sensory and spiritual, so that by dancing and feasting and the use of masks and music and numerous other sacramental modes the sacred powers of plants and animals and cosmic elements are beneficially appropriated by human beings.

The second pattern is typified by the Amerindian emphasis on healing and hunting (or farming) as intrinsically spiritual activities. Healing and hunting involve highly existential acts inasmuch as they are both critical life-and-death transactions.[2] However, in Amerindian tradition they are not so much expressions of an autonomously existing self as the performance of fundamental cultural functions. Healing and hunting, like other essential life-acts in Amerindian culture, are not so much personal acquisition of goods, status, or salvation as the participation in exchanges of spiritual power which centre the individual in a communal fabric, while nourishing and uniting all the dimensions of reality.

The third pattern in Amerindian spirituality is seen in the centrality of visions, which are not self-generated psychic phenomena, but are crucial moments of relation between humans and other-than-human persons.[3] Human beings may seek visions in a spiritual quest, employing fasting and ritual traditions. A vision is given by the grace of a spirit whose being transcends the human, and it is a communication of spiritual power which has pragmatic virtue and produces experiential verifications. The receipt of a vision is a transforming event for the human spirit, modifying identity and requiring responsible use and communication of the power received. The vision establishes a highly personalized spirit-relation with reciprocal obligations.

Medicine, healing-hunting, and visions symbolize common patterns in extensive and diversified traditions of spirituality among Amerindian cultures. Amerindian religion is no simple animism, but a theism which

---

[1] Black Elk's account in *The Sacred Pipe*, p. 59.
[2] cf. Goldman, *The Mouth of Heaven*, p. 100.
[3] cf. A. Irving Hallowell, 'Ojibwa Ontology, Behavior, and World View', in *Teachings from the American Earth*, ed. B. and D. Tedlock, p. 143.

possesses a holistic spirituality that is a challenging alternative for a highly rationalized Western religious consciousness.[1] Whereas a common view of spirituality may perceive it in opposition to ordinary experience in the secular, empirical world, Amerindian tradition understands spirituality as the depth dimension of this present social and natural world and at the same time as the transcendent source which binds the whole into a living unity.

[1] cf. Dale Stover, 'The Amerindian Liberation of European Religious Consciousness', in *The Council on the Study of Religion Bulletin*, 12.3 (June 1981), pp. 66–8.

X
CURRENT SPIRITUALITY

1 Orthodoxy

ALEXANDER SCHMEMANN

Bloom, A., *Living Prayer*. London, DLT, 1967.
Bloom, A., *School for Prayer*. London, DLT, 1970.
Hopko, T., *All the Fulness of God*. Crestwood, N.Y., St Vladimir's, 1982.
Meyendorff, J., *The Byzantine Legacy in the Orthodox Church*. Crestwood, N.Y., St Vladimir's, 1982.
A Monk of the Eastern Church (L. Gillet), *Orthodox Spirituality*, 2nd edn, SPCK, 1978.
Schmemann, A., *For the Life of the World*. Rev. edn, Crestwood, N.Y., St Vladimir's, 1973.
Schmemann, A., *Great Lent*. Rev. edn, Crestwood, N.Y., St Vladimir's, 1974.
Staniloae, D., (ET) *Theology and the Church*. Crestwood, N.Y., St Vladimir's, 1980.
Vasileios of Stavronikita, Archimandrite, (ET) *Hymn of Entry: Liturgy and Life in the Orthodox Church*. Crestwood, N.Y., St Vladimir's, 1984.
Ware, K., *The Orthodox Way*. London, Mowbray; Crestwood, N.Y., St Vladimir's, 1979.
Yannaras, C., (ET) *The Freedom of Morality*. Crestwood, N.Y., St Vladimir's, 1984.

To speak of contemporary trends in Orthodox spirituality is to speak, first of all, about the place and the meaning in today's Orthodoxy of that Byzantine 'canon' of spirituality which, during the Byzantine millennium, integrated into one vision: the writings of the Fathers, the monastic doctrine and experience of prayer, and the ascetical way of life whose *summa* is the *Philokalia* (see pp. 257–8).

To begin with, this 'canon' is necessary not only because as *the* Orthodox spiritual tradition it constitutes the self-evident criterion for the evaluation of all other 'spiritualities'. We must begin with it because, of all contemporary trends, the most important and, therefore, the most 'contemporary' one, is precisely that of a *return* to it. Indeed, if there exists today, within the Orthodox Church, a 'trend' transcending all national, cultural, ethnic and even ecclesiastical tensions so obvious on the surface of the Church's life, it is without any doubt this revival, theoretical as well as practical, of the spiritual vision inherited from Byzantium.

This trend has no particular centre, geographical or personal, no unique *starets*, no institutional form of its own. We see it growing on Mount Athos, in the religious 'catacombs' in Russia, in the traditionally Orthodox countries: Greece, Serbia, Romania, yet also in Western Europe, America and in other centres of the Orthodox diaspora. Nor is it limited to monasteries and monastic communities. That the quest for a more authentic personal spiritual life is spreading also among Orthodox laity is evidenced by the astonishing success of books and publications devoted to the classical spiritual tradition of Orthodoxy.

It is, therefore, the very fact of this return, of its emergence now, in this particular situation, at this particular time, that we must try to elucidate first. For a movement whose professed goal is a return to the *past* is of necessity generated by a particular experience of the *present*, by a desire to come to terms with it. It may be an escape from the present, a total rejection of it. It may, on the contrary, be understood and experienced as a way of acting upon the present. In both cases it is a certain perception of the present that determines the perception of the past or, to put it differently, *selects* in the past that to which one wishes to return.

Hence our first question: what in the present situation of Orthodoxy did strengthen and amplify, if not create, this renewed interest in and return to the Byzantine spirituality? It is, I submit, the double shock administered to the Orthodox Church as a whole by the collapse of the historical 'Orthodox world', or worlds, and by Orthodoxy's ensuing encounter with secularism.

There is no need to explain what is meant here by 'Orthodox world'. In the last decades several competent historians have supplied us with excellent analyses of that world's initial 'incarnation' in Byzantium and of its subsequent 'expressions' in Orthodox states and nations whose historical roots, whose very 'entrance' into history, were shaped by the religious cultural and political heritage of the Byzantine commonwealth. In that world, where the term Orthodoxy meant not faith alone but also a culture, a way of life, an all-embracing world-view, inspired and generated by faith, the Orthodox Church lived for centuries in such total and organic union with it that, in the Byzantine texts, it has been usually defined as comparable to the union of soul and body.

It is the organic character of that union which makes the collapse of the 'Orthodox world' in the twentieth century into a major event, and not just another tragedy in the tragical history of the Orthodox East. For it deprived the Orthodox Church not only of the support and protection of Orthodox states – to this the Orthodox Church has been accustomed during the long, and still lasting, period of Turkish dominion – but above all, of that *milieu*, of that world, whose existence and organic connection with the Church is postulated by, and implied in, every word of the Church's liturgy, and constitutes an essential dimension of her world-view, of her very faith. The disappearance of that world radically changed the situation of the Church in the world, and its relation to it.

What, however, made that event even more decisive, is the nature of the world, of the culture into which the Orthodox Church was 'exiled' after the collapse of her 'earthly homes'; the world and the culture whose *content* and world-view were essentially shaped by *secularism*: an equally all-embracing world-view proclaiming the self-sufficiency of the world, whose meaning can and must be found in itself, independently from any reference to the 'transcendent'.

In the Christian West the emergence and the ultimate victory of secularism were the result of a long transition, of a slow decomposition of the medieval *Christianitas*. In this sense secularism is a specifically West-ern phenomenon, a western 'heresy', with roots in the Western spiritual and intellecual development. But to Orthodoxy, to its entire doctrinal and spiritual tradition, it was, and still is, totally *alien*. Yet it is this secularistic world that the Orthodox Church *entered*; to its world-view that she became exposed; and it is above all the heresy contained in it, which is *the* heresy of our time, that she is called to oppose and to fight.

Such is the present situation which, I am convinced, reveals the true meaning of the *return*, within Orthodoxy, to the Byzantine spiritual 'canon'. This return must be seen as *the first significant Orthodox reaction to secularism*, to the secularistic culture spreading today over the whole world. I call it the *first* reaction because, strange as it may appear, the Orthodox Church at large and more especially the Orthodox hierarchical and clerical 'establishment', seem to have not even noticed the radical changes that occurred in the situation of Orthodoxy during the twentieth century, least of all the formidable challenge to the Orthodox vision and experience of the world implied in secularism. Protected from the mod-ern world by the absence of any common language or 'terms of reference', the Orthodox bishops continue to live in an illusory 'Orthodox world', zealously preserving its triumphalistic rhetorics and protocol, defending their 'rights' and 'privileges' with a power-structure inherited from a vanished Orthodox *oikoumenē*. This continuity of *form* prevents them from seeing the rapid and alarming alteration of the *content*, the pro-gressive surrender of Orthodoxy to secularism, surrender consisting primarily in the *adjustment* of Orthodoxy, of its faith, liturgy and even spirituality, to the values, thought-forms and categories of the secular-istic world-view.

It is to this surrender to the 'present', to the pervasive secularism of our culture, that the movement of *return* is both a reaction and a response.

And it is the first *significant* response because, while being indeed a return to the past, it is emphatically *not* one more 'escape' into the past, and is not moved by that nostalgia of the past which, as a matter of fact, peacefully coexists with secularism in today's Orthodoxy. The return here is the return not to the past *as past*, but to that in the past which transcends the very fragmentation of time into past, present and future, to that which must shape the Church's 'today' as it shaped the 'yesterday' and, hopefully, shall shape its 'tomorrow'. And since the world's *today* is primarily determined by secularism, which in its essence is a *heresy* about the world, the Church's response to this heresy must of necessity be the *confession* by her of the Christian vision of the world. In the judgement of the present writer, this vision is nowhere better expressed, not only theoretically, doctrinally, but truly *existentially*, than in the vision and experience that stand at the very centre of the traditional Orthodox spirituality.

To a 'modern' man, even to a 'modern' Orthodox, this may sound paradoxical. Is not this traditional spirituality essentially *monastic*? Therefore does it not require, as its very foundation, a withdrawal and separation from the world, a radical *denial* of it? And if it is so, what help can it be in fighting secularism?

What, however, the 'modern' man and even the 'modern' Christian seems no longer to understand, is that the meaning of this, indeed essential, denial of the world depends entirely on what in this monastic spirituality is meant by 'world'. And it suffices to read the 'classical' texts, in which this spirituality was described and codified, it suffices to *hear* the innumerable hymns of the Byzantine liturgy, written almost without exception by monks and in monasteries, to realize that the vision of the world revealed by these texts and hymns is not only different from, but radically opposed to, any and all dualistic, Manichean, and 'world-hating' identification of the world with *evil*.

It is time to understand that, in its essence, the Byzantine monastic spirituality is first of all in direct continuity with the *eschatological* world-view of the early Church; it is above all an *eschatological* spirituality. This means that it is equally alien to the cosmic pessimism of all 'dualisms', as it is to the cosmic optimism of secularist 'monism'. Here the ultimate horizon of the world, its true goal, is the Kingdom of God in which 'God shall be all in all' (1 Cor. 15, 28). This Kingdom, however, was revealed, 'bestowed upon us', by Christ and it is in the light of its presence 'in the midst of us' and 'inside' us that the world is perceived and experienced as the *good* world created by God, given to man as life and communion with God; as the world stolen from God by sin and death, enslaved to the prince of 'this world'; and finally as the new creation, as the presence, the foretaste, of the world to come, of the Kingdom. There is nothing 'exclusively' monastic about that eschatological spirituality because every Christian and the entire Church have their true life 'hidden with Christ in God' (Col. 3.3). For each Christian the world is crucified and he is crucified unto the world (Gal. 6.14). The particular calling and function of the monk in the Church (for monasticism was and is a 'movement', a vocation within and not outside the Church) is to bear *witness* to the eschatological nature of the Christian faith and of Christian life, of the impossibility of reducing the Church to anything in 'this world'.

This explains why monasticism not only 'returned' to the world, but in a sense became the spiritual centre of that 'Christian world', whose historical origin is to be found in the 'conversion' of Constantine. Ultimately it was neither a juridical agreement between the 'Imperium' and the 'Sacerdotium', nor the status of Christianity as the Empire's official religion, that constituted the true foundation of that Orthodox world, but the acceptance by it of the Church's eschatological world-view, its 'openness' to the 'one thing needful', the Kingdom of God. Monasticism, as the 'guardian' of that vision, as a living *martyria* of its *reality*, became thus an essential dimension, one can truly say, the heart of that Orthodox world, as long as it lasted.

Today the 'Orthodox world' is gone and no nostalgia, no attachment to its external forms can resurrect it. For even before its historical collapse it was, in fact, already dead, having rejected its only real foundation, the *eschatological* world-view, and replaced it with an unconditional surrender to its own 'worldly' pride, self-centredness and self-sufficiency. It made the Church into its obedient servant, the religious bearer of its very 'worldliness'. And now, if not the whole Church, if not her 'establishment', then at least more and more of her members, are beginning to react to that both historical and spiritual defeat, by returning to that alone in the Church against which the gates of hell shall not prevail and which no secularism shall ever destroy. It is the *living reality of a new life*, the possibility in this world, and in spite of all its 'secularist' reductions, of *transfiguration*, of the joy which no one can take away. This movement has not begun overnight; it is not the result of an instant charismatic 'revival'. In Russia, to limit myself to one example, it began in the eighteenth century and certainly as the reaction to the first 'secularization' of Russia by the cultural revolution of Peter the Great. It was initiated by the Moldavian *starets* Paissy Velichkovskii, the restorer of monasticism in the Russian Empire; it bloomed in the shining, paschal holiness of St Serafim of Sarov and in the ministry, to the people and, indeed, to the Russian culture itself, of the *elders* of Optino monastery (see pp. 270–1). It is in that monastery that began the 'Russian' rediscovery of the Fathers and of the *Philokalia*; it is there that Dostoevskii nourished his prophecy concerning the demonic nature of secularism. Then came a new awareness of the Church's liturgy, of the sacramental life, of the Eucharist as the sacrament of the Church, of her eschatological fulfilment at the table of the Lord, in his Kingdom.

No doubt the dangers and the obstacles encountered by this movement of return are many. There are those, on the one hand, whose understanding of that return is *apocalyptic*, rather than eschatological, and is moved primarily by fear and hatred for anything 'modern', for the world as such. There are those, on the other hand, who try to 'reinterpret' the Orthodox spiritual tradition in typically secularist terms of 'help' and 'therapeutics'.

There are enough signs, however, indicating that the genuine *return* will overcome these obstacles, so that Orthodoxy will again become fully aware of its mission: not only to oppose the pseudo-eschatology of secularism, but to fight it with the only eternal weapon – personal *martyria*. The pagan Roman Empire was overcome, not by Christian 'ideas', not by books and dialogues, but above all by the blood of martyrs. The 'Christian world', its culture and way of life, was preserved by the world-denying monk. In our own secularist world the Church has nothing to offer but the certitude living in her that whatever else man 'needs', his first and essential need is for God. It is to that certitude that the movement of return to the genuine Orthodox spirituality bears witness.

2 Roman Catholicism

EDWARD MALATESTA

Allchin, A. M., ed., *Solitude and Communion*. Oxford, SLG, 1977.

Bernard, C., 'Courants spirituels dans l'Eglise d'aujourd'hui', in *Seminarium*, 17 (1977), pp. 116–29.

Buckley, M. J., 'Atheism and Contemplation', in *Theological Studies*, 40 (1979), pp. 680–99.

Chicago Studies, 15 (1976), 'A Spiritual Life Handbook'.

Christian Spirituality. Essays in Honour of Gordon Rupp, ed. P. Brooks. London, SCM, 1975.

McBrien, R. P., *Catholicism* (Minneapolis, Winston; London, G. Chapman, 1980), vol. ii, ch. 28, 'Christian Spirituality', pp. 1057–99.

Megyer, E., 'Theological Trends: Spiritual Theology Today', in *The Way*, 21 (1981), pp. 55–67.

Pennington, M. B., 'Spirituality, Contemporary', in *New Catholic Encyclopaedia, Supplement*, vol. 17 (1979), pp. 621–3.

Rossetti, S., 'Psychology and Spirituality: Distinction Without Separation', in *Review for Religious*, 40 (1981), pp. 503–27.

Urbina, F., 'Models of Priestly Holiness. A Bibliographical Review', in *Concilium*, 129 (1979), pp. 88–97.

Wojtyla, K., (ET) *Sources of Renewal*. London, Collins; San Francisco, Harper, 1980.

THE COUNCIL

The Second Vatican Council (1962–5) is a convenient reference point for surveying twentieth-century Roman Catholic spirituality. The Council canonized the positive developments of the preceding years, honestly faced many contemporary challenges, and provided an impetus for what has followed since. It is likely that the implementation of the Council will be a high priority for decades to come.[1] The Council's aim was to make the entire Church community a more authentic and more comprehensible sign to the modern world of God's saving design for the human race. The Council Fathers clearly proclaimed that God calls all his people, not just priests and religious, to the perfection of love taught by Jesus in the Gospels,[2] and they strongly encouraged all the faithful to minister to others since all share responsibility for the life and mission of the Church at every level.[3] Although the challenge raised by the Council has been met in varying degrees according to persons, communities, places and circumstances, the following points would seem to characterize contemporary RC spirituality almost everywhere.

SOURCES OF SPIRITUAL LIFE[4]

Even before the Council, increasing numbers of Catholics found in the liturgy, the Bible and retreats their principal spiritual nourishment. Since 1965 devotional expressions such as stations of the cross, novenas, holy hours, and special practices in honour of the Eucharist, the Heart of Jesus, and the Blessed Virgin have sharply declined in many places, not without serious loss, when they have not been replaced by something better. But liturgical renewal, *Cursillos de Cristiandad*, more personalized retreats (see pp. 578–81), Bible and theology courses and study groups, the charismatic renewal (see pp. 549–54), Focolarini, Marriage Encounter, Christian Family Life, Young Christian Workers, Christian

---

[1] See Karol Wojtyla, *Sources of Renewal*. Pope John Paul II has made it very clear that the main objective of his pontificate is the implementation of the Council.

[2] *Lumen Gentium*, ch. 5.

[3] *Decree on the Apostolate of the Laity*.

[4] See above, pp. 3–9 and 39–44.

Life Communities, social action groups, base communities, and other movements have supplied new insights, fresh fervour and creative action (see p. 580). Regular spiritual direction is sought after by increasing numbers of persons and excellent training programmes have been created to prepare qualified spiritual guides (see pp. 568–70). Catholics of the Roman rite are gradually discovering the riches contained in the liturgy, spiritual writings and iconography of Eastern Christians.[1]

HUMAN DEVELOPMENT

The progress made in the sciences of psychology and psychiatry and their influence in contemporary society have awakened and refined the psychological awareness of several generations. Psychological counselling and psychotherapy, when used well, offer greater understanding of the developmental nature of human life, remove obstacles to spiritual growth, facilitate responsible decisions and thus favour Christian maturity. At the same time, misuse of these disciplines, or lack of a complementary faith dimension, can lead to spiritual regression and at times to a total loss of religious commitment. But sound science immensely benefits spirituality and will continue to do so.[2]

THE FAITH THAT DOES JUSTICE[3]

The Council's document on *The Church in the Modern World*, the 1971 bishops' synod on justice, and the social teaching which continues to come from Rome, episcopal conferences, and a growing number of authors, joined to an increasing conscientization of all peoples regarding the serious social problems of our times, have brought it about that contemporary Catholic spirituality is characterized by an active concern for the promotion of justice and peace.[4] Dorothy Day, Mother Teresa,

---

[1] cf. Thomas Špidlík, *La spiritualité de l'Orient chrétien. Manuel systématique.* Orientalia Christiana Analecta, 206. Rome, Pontificium Institutum Orientalium Studiorum, 1978. See also the many excellent spiritual books of George A. Maloney, such as *Inward Stillness* (1976); *Bright Darkness* (1977); *Jesus, Set Me Free!* (1977); *Inscape* (1978); *Invaded by God* (1979); *The Everlasting Now* (1980); *Prayer of the Heart* (1981); and his translations of St Symeon the New Theologian, *Hymns of Divine Love* (1976), and of Pseudo-Macarius, *Intoxicated with God* (1978).

[2] See pp. 24–33, 588–91 and the journal *Human Development* (1980–   ).

[3] cf. John C. Haughey, ed., *The Faith that Does Justice*, Woodstock Studies, 2. New York, Paulist Press, 1977; Joseph Gremillion, *The Gospel of Peace and Justice.* Maryknoll, N.Y., Orbis Books, 1976.

[4] cf. C. M. Magsam, *The Experience of God.* Outlines for a Contemporary Spirituality (Maryknoll, N.Y., Orbis Books, 1977), pp. 9–65.

Dom Helder Camera, and more recently Lech Walesa exemplify various approaches in very different circumstances. From Medillin (1968) to Puebla (1980) the Latin American Church has been strongly committed to the total liberation of the poor. These efforts, which have issued in the founding of base communities, new theological reflection and the heroic witness of thousands of martyrs, are moving the rest of the Church to reflection and imitation.[1] The constant challenge is to join together faith and efforts for justice in such a way as to realize the often quoted words of the 1971 synod: 'Action on behalf of justice and participation in the transformation of the world fully appear to us as a constitutive dimension of the preaching of the Gospel . . .' ('*Justice in the World*', no. 6; Latin text in *AAS* 63 [1971]).

CONTEMPLATION[2]

At the same time as it strives to reach out to the world in ever more effective forms of presence and service, the Catholic Church is experiencing a thirst for union with God in contemplative prayer as an indispensable source for perseverance in a life of deep faith, generous love, and unshakeable hope in an age characterized by atheism, consumerism, hedonism, selfishness, violence and despair. Contemplative religious communities are attracting young people. One of the most positive effects of the charismatic renewal is the desire for and growth in more personal, contemplative prayer experienced by many adherents. One of the good results of encounter with non-Christian religions, especially Buddhism and Hinduism, has been the learning of ways of contemplation which can favour Christian prayer (see pp. 504–13). But it is regrettable that some Western Christians, ignorant of their own spiritual traditions, have totally abandoned Christianity to join other religions or sects.

VARIETY OF GIFTS[3]

The 'ministry explosion' continues among Catholics almost everywhere as increasing numbers of lay persons share more actively in the witness and ministry of the Church to its own members and to others. To the officially recognized permanent deacons, extraordinary ministers of the

---

[1] cf. Rosino Gibellini, *Frontiers of Theology in Latin America*, London, SCM, 1980; Jon Sobrino, 'The Christ of the Ignatian Exercises', in his *Christology at the Crossroads* (Maryknoll, N.Y., Orbis Books; London, SCM, 1978), pp. 396–424.

[2] See pp. 15–24; 25–9. On this subject the writings of Thomas Merton have been influential. See p. 574.

[3] cf. Sandra Schneiders, 'Ministry and Ordination', in *The Way* 20 (1980), pp. 290–9, and 21 (1981), pp. 137–49.

Eucharist, readers and acolytes, must be added religious women named as administrators of parishes which have no resident priest; lay women and men who, in the absence of priests or deacons, lead their communities in the celebration of baptism, marriage, the receiving of the Eucharist, and other prayers; the leaders of base communities, and the growing numbers of laity who work together with their clergy in a great variety of ways. The experience of exercising such ministries, as so many gifts of the Holy Spirit, has opened to the Catholic laity new dimensions of spirituality. One of the outstanding gifts of the Spirit to the twentieth century is the life and ministry of the secular institutes.[1]

RELIGIOUS LIFE[2]

Religious communities have expended enormous energy in attempting to follow conciliar and post-conciliar directives regarding the renewal of religious life. Unfortunately, during the past twenty years of adaptation and experimentation there has been much confusion and uncertainty about goals and lifestyles. Great numbers have left religious life and many communities have few or no new candidates. However, during this trying time, many religious have continued their role of building up the Church through witness and service according to a great variety of charisms. As religious families rediscover their roots, a certain clarity of vision and renewed stability are emerging. But these are not to be confused with the reactionary stance adopted by some communities, an attitude which calls for sensitive modification if such communities are to be effective witnesses in the long run. New religious communities continue to appear as encouraging signs of the Spirit's activity and as fresh sources of vitality and inspiration for the entire Church.

MINISTERIAL PRIESTS[3]

The ordained priest continues to exercise the predominant role in the guidance of the majority of Catholic communities. The past twenty years have seen many departures from the ranks of the clergy, a fact which has

---

[1] cf. Jean Beyer, ed., *Études sur les instituts séculiers*. 3 vols. Bruges, Desclée De Brouwer, 1963–6; M. P. Irwin, 'Secular Institutes', *New Catholic Encyclopaedia*, vol. 17, 601–2.

[2] See below, pp. 574–5, Cecilio de Lora, 'The Latin American Religious Life Challenged by History', in *Lumen Vitae*, 35 (1980), pp. 35–51; Philippe Bacq, 'The Religious Life in the Heart of the Western Society', ibid., pp. 53–72; J. M. R. Tillard, (ET) *A Gospel Path: the Religious Life*, Brussels, Lumen Vitae, 1975; Tillard, *There are Charisms and Charisms: the Religious Life*. Brussels, Lumen Vitae, 1977.

[3] cf. Fernando Urbina, 'Models of Priestly Holiness. A Bibliographical Review', in *Concilium*, 129 (1979), pp. 88–97.

been traumatic for clergy and laity alike. But there has also been a serious intellectual, spiritual and pastoral renewal among many priests who serve their people well, often amid great difficulties and to the point of heroism. In spite of such renewal and the impressive number of seminarians in a few parts of the world (e.g. Korea, Indonesia, Poland), many basic problems of the life and ministry of diocesan priests remain unresolved. An increasing number of responsible voices in the Church call for a total re-examination of ministry. Of special concern is the limiting to celibate men of the presidency at the sacrament of reconciliation and the celebration of the Eucharist. The spiritual good of the laity and of priests themselves requires that these questions be studied frankly, serenely, and without delay.

CHURCH OF SILENCE AND SILENT MAJORITY

Among the most eloquent witnesses to Catholic spirituality in our century figure those countless men and women who speak to us by their silence. There are those who because of repressive political regimes keep the faith and grow in love while enjoying few or no public expressions of religion, with little or no access to religious ministers, teachers, books and devotional objects. There are those who because of their faith and concern for the poor are isolated, harassed and even tortured or killed in jails, labour camps, and prisons. Finally there are those millions who have no forum and who would not know what to say if they were invited to speak about 'spirituality'. From day to day, all of these in a confused and trying age love the Lord Jesus whom they have not seen (1 Pet. 1.6–9).

THE WAY

Before and during the Council, Roman Catholics prayed for a 'new Pentecost'. The Holy Spirit did indeed come and continues to come in new ways. As Karl Rahner has pointed out,[1] at the Second Vatican Council the world Church began to act as such. In the subsequent years the Catholic Church has been attempting to give its faith and prayer, and therefore its spirituality, expressions in harmony with the genius of each culture. In some parts of the world, such as India, progress is evident. In other places, like China, the work has scarcely begun. But everywhere seeds are being sown which promise a spiritual harvest we can await with hope and joy.

[1] K. Rahner, 'Towards a Fundamental Theological Interpretation of Vatican II', in *Theological Studies*, 40 (1979), pp. 716–27. See also Walbert Bühlmann, *The Coming of the Third Church*. Maryknoll, N.Y., Orbis Books, 1977.

3 Protestantism

GORDON S. WAKEFIELD

WESLEYAN AND OTHER HYMNS

Flew, R. N., *The Hymns of Charles Wesley: a Study of their Structure*. London, Epworth, 1953.

Hodges, H. A., and Allchin, A. M., ed., *A Rapture of Praise: Hymns of John and Charles Wesley*. London, Hodder & Stoughton, 1966.

Manning, B. L., *The Hymns of Wesley and Watts*. London, Epworth, 1942.

Rattenbury, J. E., *The Evangelical Doctrines of Charles Wesley's Hymns*. London, Epworth, 1941.

Rattenbury, J. E., *The Eucharistic Hymns of John and Charles Wesley*. London, Epworth, 1948.

Routley, E., *Hymns and Human Life*. London, John Murray, 1952.

BONHOEFFER

Bonhoeffer, D., (ET) *Letters and Papers from Prison*. London, Fontana, 1959; enlarged edn, London, SCM, 1971; New York, Macmillan, 1972.

Bethge, E., (ET) *Dietrich Bonhoeffer: Theologian, Christian, Contemporary*. London, Collins; New York, Harper & Row, 1970 (American title: *Dietrich Bonhoeffer: Man of Vision, Man of Courage*).

Bosanquet, M., *The Life and Death of Dietrich Bonhoeffer*. London, Hodder & Stoughton, 1968; New York, Harper & Row, 1969.

HAMMARSKJÖLD

Hammarskjöld, D., (ET) *Markings*. London, Faber; New York, Knopf, 1964.

Aulen, G., (ET) *Dag Hammarskjöld's White Book*. SPCK, 1970.

van Dusen, H. P., *Dag Hammarskjöld: the Statesman and his Faith*. London, Faber; New York, Harper & Row, 1967.

TAIZÉ

González-Balado, J., (ET) *The Story of Taizé*. London, Mowbray, 1980.

Schutz, Brother Roger, (ET) *The Rule of Taizé*. Presses de Taizé, 1965.

Thurian, Max, (ET) *Confession*. London, SCM, 1958; 2nd edn, Mowbray, 1985.

MISCELLANEOUS

Baillie, J., *A Diary of Private Prayer*. London, OUP, 1936; New York, Scribner, 1952.

Baillie, J., *The Sense of the Presence of God*. London, OUP; New York, Scribner, 1962.

Baillie, J., *Christian Devotion*. London, OUP; New York, Scribner, 1962.

Barth, K., trans. E. C. Hoskyns, *The Epistle to the Romans*. OUP, 1933.

Bennett, A., *The Valley of Vision: A Collection of Puritan Prayers*. Edinburgh, Banner of Truth Trust, 1975.

Ecclestone, A., *Yes to God*. London, DLT; St Meinrad, Ind., Abbey Press, 1975.

Kelly, T. R., *A Testament of Devotion*. New York, Harper, 1941; London, Hodder & Stoughton, 1943.

Lockley, A., *Christian Communes*. London, SCM, 1976.

Macleod, G., *We Shall Rebuild*. Glasgow, Iona Community, 1945.

Macleod, G., *Only One Way Left*. Glasgow, Iona Community, 1956.

Micklem, N., ed., *A Book of Personal Religion*. London, Independent Press, 1938.

Micklem, N., ed., *Prayers and Praises*. London, Hodder & Stoughton, 1941.

Nygren, A., (ET) *Agape and Eros*. 3 vols. London, SPCK; New York, Macmillan, 1932–9.

Oman, J., *Honest Religion*. CUP, 1941.

Pannenberg, W., *Christian Spirituality*. Philadelphia, Westminster, 1983 = *Christian Spirituality and Sacramental Community*, London, DLT, 1984.

Phillips, D. Z., *The Concept of Prayer*. London, Routledge & Kegan Paul, 1965; 2nd edn, Oxford, Blackwell, 1981.

Robinson, J. A. T., *Honest to God*. London, SCM; Philadelphia, Westminster Press, 1963.

Rupp, E. G., *Principalities and Powers*. London, Epworth, 1952.

Wakefield, G. S., *The Life of the Spirit in the World Today*. London, Epworth; New York, Macmillan, 1969.

Ward, J. N., *The Use of Praying*. London, Epworth, 1967.

Weil, S., (ET) *Waiting on God*. London, Routledge & Kegan Paul; New York, Putnam, 1951. (American title: *Waiting for God*).

Wyon, O., *The School of Prayer*. London, SCM, 1943.

Wyon, O., *The Altar Fire*. London, SCM; Philadelphia, Westminster Press, 1954.

Wyon, O., *Living Springs*. London, SCM, 1963; Philadelphia, Westminster Press, 1962.

There was a renewed interest in classic Protestant spirituality in the years 1935–55. The so-called 'Biblical Theology' school gave Protestants a new confidence. A teacher such as Edwyn Clement Hoskyns of Cambridge (1884–1937), brought up an Anglo–Catholic and in some sense remaining one, believed, none the less, that mystical and scholastic piety led one into self-indulgent preciosity; confrontation by the Word is the only hope. As we stand helpless in the ruins of our world, especially our Christian world, we receive our confidence in 'Forgiveness, resurrection, life – God' (E. C. Hoskyns, *We are the Pharisees* [SPCK 1960], p. 7). He expounded the Anglican homilies in the chapel of Corpus Christi College, and became an exponent of the theology of the Book of Common Prayer. Wrestling with the word, rather than the making of retreats, characterized his spirituality.

531

Mysticism was also assailed by Reinhold Niebuhr (1892–1971) as denying the second commandment; by Anders Nygren (1890–1975) as confusing Agape and Eros, the love of divine grace towards sinners, with human desire; and by John Oman (1860–1939), whose analysis was philosophic and sought to expose the self-deception of the fictitious abandonment of the intellect. 'The mind does not become empty when discursive understanding is dismissed – it is left with what has been most meditated.' 'Asceticism and austere morality are only justified if required for our tasks in life . . . As an arranged scheme of self-deliverance from evil, self-sacrifice is apt to be only an arranged scheme of self-exaltation' (John Oman, *The Natural and the Supernatural* [CUP 1931], pp. 494f.).

There was also a return to confessionalism, which was prompted both by the need to dig for foundations in the world crisis and by the increasing ecumenical encounter. The pamphlet *Catholicity* (1947), produced by a team of Anglo–Catholic scholars, was met in England by a Free Church rejoinder, *The Catholicity of Protestantism* (ed. R. Newton Flew and Philip S. Watson, 1950), and along with such works of ecclesiology – the polemics before the peace of the churches – was an attempt to republish the Protestant and Puritan ascetic, often with a view to demonstrating its place in the 'coming great Church' and its essentially Catholic principles. Nathaniel Micklem's *A Book of Personal Religion* (1938 and 1954) consisted of extracts from Puritan divines to be used in family prayers, while in 1941 the same author published *Prayers and Praises*, a book of offices for Free Churchmen, which both in its prefaces and contents sought to unite Catholic and Protestant ways of prayer, discerning the possibility of mutual enrichment, stressing the evangelical notes of Catholic piety, while reaffirming some of the essentials of Protestantism. There were many studies of Puritanism at this time, the majority, as was to be expected, from the United States. One of the most important, however, was from England, G. F. Nuttall's *The Holy Spirit in Puritan Faith and Experience* (Oxford, Blackwell, 1946), which dealt chiefly with the Puritans of the Independent type, some of whom went through the 'whole gamut' from Presbyterianism to Quakerism.

All this effort of scholarship and church leadership has not resulted in a revival of classic Protestant spirituality commensurate with the renewed interest in mysticism instanced in the discovery of Julian of Norwich. Books interpreting and applying Catholic mystical theology have poured from the presses, but such teachers of prayer from Protestant churches as have had much influence have adopted a fundamentally Catholic approach. There is, for instance, J. Neville Ward's *The Use of Praying* (1967), though philosophically he follows D. Z. Phillips, *The Concept of Prayer* (1965 and 1981), 'perhaps the first extended essay in the philosophy of religion, influenced by Wittgenstein's philosophy'.

The Wesley hymns had their revival in the 1940s and beyond. The works of the Congregationalist Bernard Lord Manning, *The Hymns of Wesley and Watts* (1942), and the Methodist J. E. Rattenbury, *The Evangelical Doctrines of Charles Wesley's Hymns* (1941), and *The Eucharistic Hymns of John and Charles Wesley* (1948), were outstanding contributions, as were R. Newton Flew, *The Hymns of Charles Wesley: A Study of their Structure* (1954) and H. A. Hodges and A. M. Allchin's *A Rapture of Praise* (1968), an exposition and anthology of the Wesleys with a particular attempt to commend them to Anglicans at a time of hope for Anglican–Methodist union. But it is doubtful whether the Wesley hymns have a prime place in Methodist devotion today. Some Anglicans, who are deep into Eastern Orthodoxy, honour them more. They have been replaced in popular usage by more recent compositions, some good, some bad, some appallingly indifferent, and by a flood of banal choruses which seem to be more the vogue in our candyfloss culture, than those amazing theological and scriptural verses which converted boozers made their own in the eighteenth and nineteenth centuries. But the 'Methodist and ecumenical' hymn book *Hymns and Psalms* (1983) has a fair proportion of Charles Wesley, and brings better scholarship to bear than that of 1933 in its skilful selection and knitting together of verses from Wesley's vast and unequal output. Whether modern Methodists will use this book for private devotion in the manner of their predecessors is not certain.

Biblical theology has survived neither advancing scholarship, nor the need for a wider perspective for our communion with the God of this vast universe; classic Puritan spirituality has not recaptured the Christian imagination in our world, though Calvinism may be awaiting revival; but the Protestant tradition has not been without its representatives, and two works, both from a Lutheran background, will always remain high on the list of decisive 'spiritual' works of the last decades – Dietrich Bonhoeffer's *Letters and Papers from Prison* (first published 1954), and Dag Hammarskjöld's *Markings* (1964).

Bonhoeffer (1906–45) was steeped in Lutheranism and Pietism. The Bible, Thomas à Kempis' *The Imitation of Christ*, and Paul Gerhardt's hymns were never out of his mind, nor far from his hand. But he had to relate his traditional spirituality both to the need to destroy Hitler, and to human life in a world in which man could be said to have 'come of age', not because he had grown into moral perfection but because God had given him the key of the house and resigned to him a mastery over nature, formerly believed to be the divine prerogative alone.

Bonhoeffer was reacting against an ineffective Protestant scholasticism and pietism, which had been blind to the evil of Hitler and indifferent to the world in which most people live, which had gone on with its prayers and its assertion that we are justified by faith alone, and ignored hideous crimes and a world in ferment. For him, 'religion' was the enemy. He had been a pupil of Karl Barth, who had written in his early years: 'Religion is not a thing to be extolled; it is a misfortune which takes fatal hold upon some men and is by them passed on to others' (Karl Barth, *Romans*, p. 258). Bonhoeffer had little faith in the prayers of the natural unregenerate person, crying for God in extremity. This is very much the type of target envisaged by Kierkegaard in his *Attack Upon Christendom* and the nineteenth-century Anglican theologian F. D. Maurice, who declared: 'We have been dosing our people with religion when what they want is not that but the living God'; and again: 'God must be sought and honoured in every pursuit and not merely in something technically called religion.' Hence Bonhoeffer's inchoate efforts for 'a non-religious interpretation of the gospel', 'a religionless Christianity'.

He was critical of 'religion', because it so often preaches a 'God of the gaps', calls in God as a hypothesis to explain the residue of scientific bewilderment, while removing him from the centre of life. This is very unbiblical. An ugly consequence is that the Church may be always trying to manipulate the world into a position favourable to itself, using natural disasters and personal tragedies and sorrows to 'corner' man for Christ, and welcoming an end to prosperity, economic growth, scientific advance and our fragile security, because this may drive men and women back to religion. Bonhoeffer was opposed to strident evangelism, counting heads, claiming success. He was aware that it is often easier to weep with those who weep than to rejoice with those who rejoice, but it is imperfectly Christian to be capable of one and not the other. There should be discipline, a rule of life for Christians banded together, not very different from Catholic and Protestant tradition, but arcane as in the early Church, secret, unadvertised.

Bonhoeffer's is the Christ of Gethsemane and Golgotha, like Simone Weil (1904–43), the Jewish philosopher, 'almost Christian', another influential modern guide. She declared: 'If the Gospels omitted all mention of Christ's resurrection, faith would be easier for me. The cross by itself suffices me'. Bonhoeffer did not so testify, but he did write that 'belief in the resurrection is not the solution of the problem of death'. Heinrich Ott of Basel, cited by Donald MacKinnon, has contrasted the Christologies of Bonhoeffer and the Jesuit Teilhard de Chardin (d. 1955), who has had considerable vogue, particularly in the 1960s. At the core of the spirituality of both is an overwhelming sense of the presence of God in Christ at the centre of the ordinary ways of the world. Teilhard learned this in his researches in the deserts of Central Asia, Bonhoeffer in his prison cell; but Teilhard's was the Christ of Easter Day, on which he hoped to die and did; Bonhoeffer's Christ in the midst of the world was the Christ of Good Friday, calling on men to share God's own sufferings in the midst of creation (cf. Donald MacKinnon, *Explorations in Theology* 5 [London, SCM, 1979], pp. 8f).

Bonhoeffer has been much exploited and abused by those who have disregarded his deep faith and sanctity and made his Christianity entirely activist and political and himself the patron saint of protest marches over against prayer. Even more dangerous is a tendency towards a practical atheism, which Alasdair McIntyre exposed and castigated. This clothes 'ordinary liberal forms of life with the romantic unreality of a catacombic vocabulary' (Alasdair McIntyre, 'God and the Theologians', *Encounter*, September 1963).

Dag Hammarskjöld (1905–61) was Secretary General of the United Nations, and seemed to have abandoned the Swedish Lutheranism of his upbringing and to have become a humanitarian agnostic. But after his mysterious death in a plane crash, a kind of spiritual journal was found among his papers, called *Markings*, or 'Signposts'. Here is the record of a pilgrimage of one who passed through deep desolation to a true faith, a journeying trust, not dogmatic affirmation, nourished by his own Lutheran tradition, by the Psalmists and the Book of Common Prayer, à Kempis' *The Imitation of Christ* (shared with Bonhoeffer), by medieval and Carmelite mystics, and by a moving awareness of the communion of saints. Hammarskjöld remains an enigma, but his spiritual legacy, wrought in solitude out of his preoccupied life, has sustained many in their oscillation between faith and doubt amid the agonies and perplexities of the last half of the twentieth century. Some of his words will long be enshrined: 'The longest journey is the journey inwards'; 'In our era, the road to holiness necessarily passes through the world of action'; 'For all that has been, thanks – to all that will be, yes'; 'The Communion of Saints – and – within it – an eternal life'.

One incalculable development of widespread influence, which began just before and during the Second World War, has been the founding of two Protestant communities – those of Iona and Taizé. Both sprang from Calvinist soil but have sought to revive something of the monastic ideal, with liturgy and offices as central, though the former, in the Church of Scotland, has not included celibacy or habit in its rules, or tried so openly to reconcile Protestantism and Catholicism. It has, however, sought to recover some of the emphases of the old Celtic spirituality, as well as to achieve a Benedictine balance between prayer and work, the work being in the world and the parish as well as in the rebuilding of Iona Abbey. Taizé has become an even larger centre for pilgrimages and tourist parties, with greater liturgical influence. There are brothers in every continent, and the ministry of reconciliation, like that of Iona, reaches beyond the desire to heal the wounds of the Reformation to the search for the unity of all mankind. Iona and Taizé are but the best-known examples of a yearning among Protestants for life together under rule, which has included Baptists and Evangelicals as well as the Reformed tradition in a proliferation of communities.

More recent Protestant spirituality has divided into two types. There is the radical, which believes strongly with Hammarskjöld that 'the road to holiness passes through the world of action', i.e. political action. Opposition to apartheid is an incarnational witness in the real world, in contrast to the escapism of much that passes for spiritual and soul-converting religion. 'Liberation Theology', an alliance of biblical religion and Marxism, may be seen as belonging to this development. There is also a desire to seek accommodation with other faiths, though there are some differences as to whether anti-imperialism as a world-view and a political position assails the finality of Christ in theology. There seems no recovery of Evangelical Arminianism, the theology and spirituality of the Wesleys, even among Methodists. This might save us from 'the awful guilt-ridden "frantic philanthropy",' which for many anti-racialists and others seems to be a substitute for the gospel. 'Our concern for others should stem not from our guilt about the supposed crimes of our imperialist grandfathers but from "the wonder why such love to me"' (J. M. Turner, *Conflict and Reconciliation: Studies in Methodism and Ecumenism in England 1740–1982* [Epworth Press 1985], p. 48).

The other type is an evangelicalism, often unsophisticatedly scriptural, ignoring historical criticism to a large extent, though inclined to be based on translations of the Bible which in places are paraphrases in the interests of a certain school of theology. The extreme radicals do not disdain to anathematize the extreme manifestation of this as 'Christo-Fascism'. There is something of a revival of 'the language of Canaan', talk of 'putting out a fleece' (Judg. 6.36ff) and so on. Also there is great interest in healing, and in many parts of the world something of a revival of those phenomena which feature in the longer ending of St Mark's Gospel. Nor is social concern everywhere lacking.

The Charismatic Movement must be mentioned here, though there is fuller treatment below (pp. 549–54). W. H. Auden thought it more of Babel than Pentecost (W. H. Auden, *Secondary Worlds* [London, Faber, 1968], p. 139). It has undoubtedly brought release into 'the liberty of the Spirit' for many souls, and may be seen as a reaction against the hyper-intellectual and cerebral. It has crossed confessional boundaries, though it has been better contained within Catholicism and has there been less harmful and divisive. It will be interesting to see if this modern form of Montanism is but a temporary recurrence. Will its wider effects have passed by the end of the century?

4 Anglicanism

A. M. ALLCHIN

Coggan, D., *The Prayers of the New Testament*. London, Hodder, 1967.
Cragg, K., *The Call of the Minaret*. London and New York, OUP, 1956.
Dix, G., *The Shape of the Liturgy*. London, Dacre, 1945.
Ecclestone, A., *Yes to God*. London, DLT; St Meinrad, Ind., Abbey Press, 1975.
Ecclestone, A., *A Staircase for Silence*. London, DLT, 1977.
Farrer, A. M., *Said or Sung*. London, Faith; New York, World, 1960 (American title: *A Faith of Our Own*).
Farrer, A. M., *A Celebration of Faith*. London, Hodder, 1970.
Furlong, M., *Travelling In*. London, Hodder, 1971.
Harton, F. P., *Elements of the Spiritual Life*. London, SPCK, 1932; New York, Macmillan, 1943.
Hebert, G., *Liturgy and Society*. London, Faber, 1935.
Hebert, G., ed., *The Parish Communion*. London, SPCK, 1937.
Hoskyns, E. C., and Davey, F. N., *Crucifixion/Resurrection*. London SPCK, 1981.
Kirk, K., *The Vision of God*. London and New York, Longmans, 1931.
Leech, K., *True Prayer*. London, Sheldon; New York, Harper & Row, 1980.
Lewis, C. S., *Mere Christianity*. London, Bles, 1952; New York, Macmillan, 1956.
Lewis, C. S., *Letters to Malcolm on Prayer*. London, Bles; New York, Harcourt, Brace, 1964.
Llewelyn, R., *With Pity not with Blame*. London, DLT, 1982.
Louth, A., *Origins of the Christian Mystical Tradition*. Oxford, Clarendon; New York, OUP, 1981.
Macquarrie, J., *Paths in Spirituality*. London, SCM; New York, Harper & Row, 1972.
Mary Clare, Mother, *Encountering the Depths*. London, DLT, 1981.
Ramsey, A. M., *The Glory of God and the Transfiguration of Christ*. London and New York, Longmans, 1949.
Ramsey, A. M., *The Christian Priest Today*. London, SPCK; New York, Morehouse-Barlow, 1972.
Robinson, J. A. T., *Exploration into God*. London, SCM; Stanford, Stanford University Press, 1967.
Smith, M., ed., *Benson of Cowley*. London, OUP, 1980; Cambridge, Mass., Cowley Publications, 1983.

Taylor, J., *The Primal Vision*. London, SCM, 1963.
Temple, W., *Readings in St John's Gospel*. London, Macmillan, 1939.
Thornton, M., *English Spirituality*. London, SPCK, 1963.
Toynbee, P., *Part of a Journey*. London, Collins, 1981.
Underhill, E., *Mysticism*. London, Methuen; New York, E. P. Dutton, 1911.
Underhill, E., *Worship*. London, Nisbet, 1935; New York, Harper & Row, 1937.
Vanstone, W. H., *Love's Endeavour, Love's Expense*. London, DLT; New York, OUP, 1977 (American title: *The Risk of Love*).
de Waal, E., *Seeking God*. London, Collins, 1984.
Williams, C., *He Came down from Heaven*. London, Faber, 1950.
Williams, H. A., *True Resurrection*. London, Beazley; New York, Holt, Rinehart and Winston, 1972.
Williams, R., *The Wound of Knowledge*. London, DLT, 1977.

It is difficult to find any one characteristic which marks Anglican spirituality as a whole during the twentieth century. During this time the Anglican spiritual tradition has been open to influences from many quarters and has shown a remarkable capacity to assimilate material of varied kinds. Perhaps it is this very openness to others which should be seen as the dominant feature of this period.

Since the Reformation Anglicans have been in general reluctant to separate spirituality from theology. In more recent times they have resisted any tendency to divorce man's inner life from his social and political existence. Here again are reasons which make it difficult to delimit a field of spirituality, clearly distinguished from other forms of Christian reflection. It is typical that one of the most widely read spiritual books in this century, Archbishop William Temple's *Readings in St John's Gospel*, should be an informal commentary on Scripture, and that the most popular author of this period, C. S. Lewis, should have produced books in which the statement of Christian faith is always linked with the summons to prayer and discipleship.

However, some developments over the past eighty years seem to be clear. One is the much greater attention paid to the classical texts of the Christian mystical tradition. The pioneering work of Evelyn Underhill, *Mysticism*, is of decisive importance here. More recently this tendency has given rise to a very general interest in the fourteenth-century English mystics, particularly Julian of Norwich and *The Cloud of Unknowing*. It has found new strength in the work of writers like Rowan Williams and Andrew Louth, whose scholarly presentations of the subject have attracted readers whose concern is practical and devotional as well as academic. Notable too has been the growing influence of monastic spirituality, seen in a book like Mother Mary Clare's *Encountering the*

Depths, or Esther de Waal's lay commentary on the Rule of St Benedict, *Seeking God*.

But this interest in the development of tradition has not led to a neglect of the biblical basis of Christian spirituality. The work of one Archbishop of Canterbury has already been mentioned. No less significant is that of two of his successors. Archbishop Michael Ramsey's writing has consistently spanned the gulf between biblical theology and spirituality (e.g. *The Glory of God and the Transfiguration of Christ*), while Archbishop Donald Coggan's book, *The Prayers of the New Testament*, has continued the tradition of sound but popular New Testament exegesis.

Another development in Anglicanism which has had a marked effect on spiritual life during this period has been the renewal and deepening of eucharistic life and practice. Evelyn Underhill's second major work, *Worship*, bears witness to this. But the two writers who had the greatest influence in this growth of liturgical spirituality were Father Gabriel Hebert, in *Liturgy and Society* and *The Parish Communion*, and Dom Gregory Dix, in *The Shape of the Liturgy*. The genuinely sacramental nature of Christian spirituality and the centrality of the Eucharist have come to be generally accepted in more recent Anglican writing.

In the growing interchange between Christianity and the other religious traditions, Anglicans have played a part. One might instance the work of Kenneth Cragg in relation to Islam (e.g. *The Call of the Minaret*), and John Taylor's remarkable study of his meeting with African religion, *The Primal Vision*. But this is an area where often Anglicans have accepted guidance from Roman Catholic writers such as Thomas Merton, Bede Griffiths and William Johnston.

On the other hand, in the field of poetry the twentieth century has been surprisingly rich. Lines from T. S. Eliot (especially from *Four Quartets*) or from the spare but incisive lyrics of R. S. Thomas have found their way into many books of spirituality and have become part of the prayer and meditation of Christian people who might be surprised if they were told that they were lovers of poetry. The frontier between literature and spirituality has been unexpectedly open. Here the example of Charles Williams was undoubtedly important.

This literary quality of Anglican spiritual writing has been particularly evident in the last twenty years. During the sixties Anglican spirituality passed through a considerable crisis. Much that had been written in the previous fifty years seemed unbearably ecclesiastical and narrowly pious. Was prayer possible at all any longer? If it was, must it not be much more deeply involved with the inner and outer currents of life in our time? In response to this challenge a number of remarkable writers have appeared, notable among them Alan Ecclestone, W. H. Vanstone and H. A. Williams. Together with that most Anglican of Methodists, Neville Ward, they may be said to have found a new language for spirituality, more appropriate to our own day. Indeed the last fifteen years has seen an unexpected multiplication of books on spirituality, many of a high quality.

Even at times when Christian divisions were at their sharpest, a kind of underground ecumenical movement continued in the field of spirituality. In the twentieth century, which has been everywhere a time of convergence and reconcilation, it has become increasingly difficult to keep the different traditions apart from one another. In this situation Anglicans who have been delighted to learn from a Cistercian, Thomas Merton, a Lutheran, Dietrich Bonhoeffer, and a Russian Orthodox, Anthony Bloom, find themselves very much at home. In the future the different spiritual traditions will surely not lose their own identities. But they will be greatly enriched by a closer and freer collaboration and interchange.[1]

5 Ecumenical Spirituality

GEOFFREY WAINWRIGHT

To avoid magpie eclecticism, a would-be ecumenical spirituality must be grounded in a spiritual ecumenism: we have no right to borrow treasures from other Christian traditions unless we have a commitment to pray and work, in penitence and faith, for the full visible unity of Christ's Church. From the other direction, unity schemes would be so much ecclesiastical joinery unless they too were rooted in spiritual ecumenism and the desire that each church should share fully in the spiritual riches of others.

> Change of heart and holiness of life, together with public and private prayer for the unity of Christians, should be regarded as the soul of the whole ecumenical movement. This is what merits the name 'spiritual ecumenism' (Vatican II, *Decree on Ecumenism*, n. 8).

Ruth Rouse says that prayer for unity has in fact been 'the mainspring of ecumenical advance'.[2] From earlier times, the Roman prayer at the *pax*

---

[1] *Editors' Note:* A. M. Allchin has himself made notable contributions to Anglican spirituality, particularly in his mediation of Marian and Eastern Orthodox perspectives. See, for example, *The Joy of All Creation: An Anglican Meditation on the Place of Mary* (London, DLT, 1984).

[2] In R. Rouse and S. C. Neill, ed., *A History of the Ecumenical Movement*, vol. i (2nd edn, London, SPCK; Philadelphia, Westminster Press, 1968), pp. 345–9. This and the

has asked the Lord to grant his Church that peace and unity which is according to his will; the litanies of the Orthodox pray for 'the stability of the holy churches of God and the union of all'; the Anglican prayer for the Church militant beseeches God 'to inspire continually the universal Church with the spirit of truth, unity, and concord'. The origins of special prayer for unity in the sense of the modern 'multilateral' ecumenical movement may lie in the work of the Methodist minister and entrepreneur Henry Lunn, who, in the 1890s, called a number of British church leaders together in the Grindelwald conferences to discuss 'home reunion'; their call for prayer at Pentecost was taken up by Anglicans and Free Churchpeople, and (in the terms of Pope Leo XIII's directive of 1895 on prayer for unity) by Roman Catholics as well. The worldwide Faith and Order movement, right from its preparatory conference at Geneva in 1920, encouraged an annual Week of Prayer for the Unity of the Church, ending on Whitsunday.

Meanwhile there had developed a more 'bilateral' exercise, though aimed at a 'return' to Roman obedience, on the initiative of some Anglican papalists. Against the background of the nineteenth-century Association for the Promotion of the Unity of Christendom (which included some Greeks as well as Anglicans and Latins), Spencer Jones (1857–1943), an Anglican clergyman in Gloucestershire, joined forces with the American founder of the Graymoor community, Paul Wattson (1863–1940), to launch an Octave of Prayer for Unity from the feast of St Peter's Chair at Rome to that of the Conversion of St Paul (January 18–25). First observed in 1908, the year in which Wattson and his Friars of the Atonement were to make their corporate conversion to Rome, the Octave received the blessing of Pope Pius X in December 1909; and in 1916 Benedict XV extended its observance throughout the Roman Catholic church.

It was this Octave which Abbé Paul Couturier, about whom more will be said in a moment, was able in the 'thirties and 'forties to 'decentralize' (his word) by use of a more open formula: 'that God will grant the visible unity of his kingdom such as Christ wishes and through whatever means he wishes'. This recognition on the Catholic side that Christ will give the unity of the Church in the form and time that he wills helped Faith and Order to shift its own date for the Week of Universal Prayer for Christian

---

second volume (edited by H. E. Fey, 1970) contain much material of at least indirect interest for our theme. The story is told predominantly from a perspective of the World Council of Churches in which first the Faith and Order and the Life and Work movements were integrated (1948) and then the International Missionary Council (1961). Vatican II marked the official entry of the Roman Catholic Church into the ecumenical movement. Thereafter the institutional histories are intertwined, though the Roman Catholic Church is still not a member of the WCC.

Unity to January 18–25; and, after a period of what Couturier would have called *parallélaboration* and then co-operation, in 1966 complete agreement was reached between the World Council of Churches and the Vatican Secretariat for Promoting Christian Unity concerning preparations for the Week of January 18–25, so that the introductory leaflets are now composed by a mixed group.[1] The WCC has extended the fellowship of mutual intercession through an 'ecumenical prayer cycle', *For All God's People* (1978 and revisions), whereby the churches throughout the world are prayed for week by week on a geographical basis; the underlying theology is finely expounded in Lukas Vischer's little book, *Intercession* (Geneva, WCC, 1980).

At varying paces, the churches have been able to proceed from simultaneous to *joint* prayer for unity. The spirituality of the modern ecumenical movement has been, perhaps above all, a spirituality of meeting. The idea finds classical expression in the 'testament' of Cardinal Mercier (1851–1926), Archbishop of Malines, which was probably drafted by Dom Lambert Beauduin (1873–1960), pioneer of the liturgical movement and founder of the Catholic monastery at Amay, later Chevetogne, devoted to relations with the Orthodox churches:

> In order to unite with one another, we must love one another; in order to love one another, we must know one another; in order to know one another, we must go and meet one another.

Friendship through meeting has characterized ecumenical endeavours at all levels, including united services for prayer in local congregations,[2] the activities of the Student Christian Movement (where many future leaders of the churches first became acquainted), the practice and pastoral care of mixed marriages, and the formation of 'bilateral' or 'multilateral' associations of private Christians (such as the Fellowship of Saint Alban and Saint Sergius, between Anglicans and Orthodox, or the International League for Apostolic Faith and Order, later called the International Ecumenical Fellowship).

Many of these occasions and associations have engaged in common study of the Bible, and bible study has been a conspicuous feature of life in the more formal ecumenical institutions, such as the Ecumenical Institute at Bossey, near Geneva. Prominent here were Suzanne de

---

[1] The report of the agreement is contained in *One in Christ* 3/3 (1967), where one may also find articles by Y. Congar and B. Bobrinskoy on the theology of prayer for unity.

[2] Interesting remarks about the local level are found in R. E. Davies, 'The spirituality of ecumenism', in P. Brooks, ed., *Christian Spirituality: Essays in honour of Gordon Rupp* (London, SCM, 1975), pp. 307–28.

Diétrich[1] and then Hans-Ruedi Weber. A seminal early writing by Weber, based on his missionary experience in Indonesia, was *The Communication of the Gospel to Illiterates* (London, SCM, 1957). His more recent *The Cross: Tradition and Interpretation*[2] should be read in conjunction with his splendid picture-book *On a Friday Noon: Meditations under the Cross.*[3] Weber continues to direct the bible study department at the WCC.[4]

The possibilities and problems of *communicatio in sacris* come to a head in the so-called intercommunion question. Throughout the modern ecumenical movement there has been a tension between the view that still-divided Christians may already practise eucharistic sharing as an aid to growth in an as yet imperfect communion and the view that unity at the Lord's Table must wait to seal the achievement of full consensus among the churches in doctrine and life. The pain of sacramental separation and the anticipated joy of reconciliation are in any case the experience of all ecumenically committed Christians.

That some measure and form of doctrinal and structural agreement belong to Christian unity is accepted by all: that was the thrust of the Faith and Order movement from the beginning. Its realization underlay a second remarkable initiative by 'the apostle of unity', Paul Couturier (1881–1953): the dialogue between French-speaking Catholics and Protestants associated particularly with the Trappist monastery at Les Dombes, though using also various Protestant locations.[5] Before the time came for the theologians and the hierarchies to set to work, however, an urgent need already existed, Couturier held, for 'the work of psychological purification (*assainissement*) by prayer, by goodness, by reciprocal

---

[1] Important books by Suzanne de Diétrich were *Le renouveau biblique: principes, méthodes, applications pratiques* (2nd edn, Neuchâtel, Delachaux et Niestlé, 1949), and *Le dessein de Dieu: itinéraire biblique* (Neuchâtel, Delachaux et Niestlé, 1945; ET *God's Unfolding Purpose: A Guide to the Study of the Bible*. Philadelphia, Westminster Press, 1960).

[2] (ET) *The Cross: Tradition and Interpretation* (Grand Rapids, Eerdmans, 1978; London, SPCK, 1979). This is a regrettably truncated version of the original German *Kreuz und Kultur* (Geneva, WCC, 1975).

[3] H. R. Weber, *On a Friday Noon: Meditations under the Cross*. Geneva, WCC; London, SPCK, 1979. See also his *Immanuel: The Coming of Jesus in Art and the Bible* (Geneva, WCC; Grand Rapids, Eerdmans, 1984).

[4] See R. C. Rowe, *Bible Study in the World Council of Churches* (Geneva, WCC, 1969), and, more technically, E. Flesseman-van Leer, ed., *The Bible: its Authority and Interpretation in the Ecumenical Movement* (Geneva, WCC, 1980).

[5] M. Villain, *L'abbé Paul Couturier, apôtre de l'unité chrétienne* (Tournai and Paris, Casterman, 1957); G. Curtis, *Paul Couturier and Unity in Christ* (London, SCM, 1964). Couturier's writings have been gathered by M. Villain under the title *Oecuménisme spirituel* (Casterman, 1963).

appreciation on the part of individuals – all the tender fruits of charity'. Seeing charity as the herald of truth, Couturier looked for the 'interior conversion' of countless Christ-bearers (*christophoroi*) to bring before the eyes of all a shining manifestation of Christ (*christophaneia*).[1] All Christians were called to embark on a mutual 'brotherly emulation, in humble penitent prayer and the deepening of the spiritual life'.[2] Radiating from Lyons, the 'invisible monastery' of prayer for unity constructed by the schoolmaster-priest embraced not only Catholics but Orthodox (Couturier had helped the Russian émigrés in the 'twenties), Anglicans (he developed links particularly with the religious communities at Nashdom, Mirfield, Kelham and Wantage), Lutherans and Reformed. In the French context, his sensitivity concerning the massacre of the Huguenots on St Bartholomew's Day 1572 is particularly touching; and in 1946, for instance, he wrote in a circular letter:

> If you are a priest, I beg of you to offer the most holy Sacrifice on the day of the coming feast of St Bartholomew, 24 August, asking God's pardon for the acts of violence committed by our fathers, entreating him to change the atoning Blood once shed into a spring of living waters wherein the Lamb-Redeemer will enable us to find once more our profound brotherhood in him.

Begun in 1937 and then resumed on an annual basis after some wartime interruption, the Dombes meetings brought Catholics into touch particularly with the Reformed. Their increasingly detailed theological work[3] continues to be 'bathed in prayer', as Couturier used to put it. At difficult points he would call a halt for prayer, though sometimes even his glance would suffice to calm a discussion. An early participant, the Dominican ecumenist Yves Congar, writes thus:

> One only really knew the others when one had seen and heard them praying, for it is only in God's presence and in living relationship with him that a Christian can fully express himself and be himself. We realized already then that theology needs a doxological soil, a climate of prayer and praise, if it is to

[1] Using the characteristic ecumenical imagery of the road and the movement, another Lyonese ecumenist later put it this way: 'Ecumenicity is this unanimous movement, prompted by the Spirit, of Christians towards their fountain-head, where they may receive not only Christ, through the life and hands of the Church, but also, in some way, may receive the Church herself from the very heart of Christ' (G. Martelet).

[2] The Orthodox theologian Paul Evdokimov said, 'the recognition of the real, therefore saving, presence of Christ in our partner is the condition of all true ecumenical encounter'. *Verbum caro* 55 (1960) contains articles by Evdokimov, Dom O. Rousseau and M. Thurian on prayer for unity.

[3] An account of the years up to 1962 can be found in *Ecumenical Dialogue in Europe*, introduced by P. C. Rodger (London, Lutterworth; Richmond, Va., John Knox, 1966). In more recent years English versions of documents from Les Dombes have sometimes been published in the periodical *One in Christ*.

unfold, blossom and bear fruit . . . A level is attained at which the spirit of self-justification and rivalry disappears . . . As we dispose ourselves humbly in God's presence and before others, we prepare ourselves to receive the illumination and secret anointing of one and the same Holy Spirit.[1]

Although Couturier had sometimes had to endure accusations of 'false irenism' ('Those who suffer for the Church must also suffer by the Church', he recognized), the 'hierarchies' eventually followed his way. The Evanston Assembly of the WCC in 1954 declared that

> The measure of our concern for unity is the degree to which we pray for it. We cannot expect God to give us unity unless we prepare ourselves to receive his gift by costly and purifying prayer. To pray *together* is to be drawn together. We urge, wherever possible, the observance of the Week of Prayer for Christian Unity, 18–25 January (or some other period suited to local conditions) as a public testimony to prayer as the road to unity.

The Anglican bishops at the Lambeth Conference of 1958 commended 'to all Anglicans the observance of the Week of Prayer for Christian Unity in the spirit of the late Abbé Paul Couturier'. The Catholic bishops of Vatican II proclaimed that

> there can be no ecumenism worthy of the name without interior conversion . . . The faithful should remember that they promote union among Christians better, that indeed they live it better, when they try to live holier lives according to the gospel. For the closer their union with the Father, the Word and the Spirit, the more deeply and easily will they be able to grow in mutual brotherly love (*Decree on Ecumenism*, 7).

Meanwhile an equivalent to the Dombes group had sprung up on German soil. Starting in 1946 at the instigation of the Catholic Provost of Paderborn, Paul Simon, Catholic and Protestant theologians met, first separately and then together, to tackle controversial questions between the confessions. Known as the Jäger-Stählin circle, after the Catholic Archbishop of Paderborn and the Lutheran Bishop of Oldenburg, this group worked in an atmosphere of 'prayer, trust and cordiality'. For long its academic leaders were Edmund Schlink of Heidelberg and, on the Catholic side, Josef Höfer and Hermann Volk; and they have now been replaced by Wolfhart Pannenberg and Karl Lehmann. The circle's influence was felt among the advisers at Vatican II and in the setting up of the Secretariat for Promoting Christian Unity under Cardinal Bea. The meetings of the early years are reflected in a celebratory volume presented

---

[1] See N. Ehrenström, ed., *Confessions in Dialogue* (3rd edn, Geneva, WCC, 1975), pp. 212–29, where several other writers also bear testimony to their experience of prayer in ecumenism.

to the circle's episcopal founders under the title *Pro Veritate* (Münster and Kassel, 1963), while its more recent work has been published more regularly.

Another connection linked Couturier with Taizé, the most remarkable of the religious communities arising within Protestantism as ecumenical signs of renewal.[1] Starting in the Second World War and the humanitarian activities it called forth, the Taizé community was formally constituted in 1949 when the first seven brothers made their '*engagement*' to a life of shared work and property, of chaste celibacy, and of obedience to 'decisions taken in community and expressed by the prior'. Under the leadership of Roger Schutz and Max Thurian, founding prior and subprior,[2] the community gives priority to worship (a thrice-daily office), interior silence, meditation on the Beatitudes, and intercession for Church and world. It has had close links, not always uncritical, with successive Popes; and its brotherhood now includes Catholics and Anglicans as well as Protestants. The vocation to hospitality has marked the community from the beginning, and Taizé has attracted many visitors to its Burgundian site, dominated since 1962 by the Church of the Reconciliation built by the German organization *Aktion Sühnezeichen*, which also contributed to the building of the new Coventry cathedral. In the 1970s Roger Schutz launched a 'Council of Youth' which continues to bring thousands of young people to Taizé but which also takes the mobile form of visits by young people, sometimes accompanied by the prior and always respecting parish structures, to many parts of the world. Many Taizé brothers have themselves since 1951 spent time living in small 'fraternities' across the continents, as 'signs of the presence of Christ amid humanity, and bearers of joy'. With help from young

[1] See Olive Wyon, *Living Springs: New Religious Movements in Western Europe* (London, SCM; Philadelphia, Westminster Press, 1963); and Annie Perchenet, *Renouveau communautaire et unité chrétienne: regards sur les communautés anglicanes et protestantes* (Paris, Mame, 1967). On Taizé in particular see J. Heijke, *An Ecumenical Light on the Renewal of Religious Community Life: Taizé* (Pittsburgh, Duquesne University Press, 1967); P. C. Moore, *Tomorrow is too Late* (London, Mowbray, 1970); J. L. G. Balado, (ET) *The Story of Taizé* (London, Mowbray, 1980; New York, Seabury, 1981). The *Rule of Taizé* was published in French and in English by the Presses de Taizé in 1961. The quarterly theological review of Taizé long appeared under the name *Verbum caro* but later became *Communio*.

[2] Both men have written widely. Thurian specializes in sacramental theology and practice. Some of Schutz's writings have appeared in English translation also: *Living Today for God* (Baltimore, Helicon Press, 1962); *Unity, Man's Tomorrow* (London, Faith Press, 1962); *Unanimity in Pluralism* (Chicago, Franciscan Herald Press, 1967); *The Power of the Provisional* (Philadelphia, Pilgrim Press, 1969); *Violent for Peace* (London, DLT, 1970); *Festival* (New York, Seabury, 1973); *Struggle and Contemplation* (New York, Seabury, 1974).

Russian Orthodox Christians, the Council of Youth has developed the celebration of a 'weekly Easter' to orient life upon the paschal mystery:

> Friday evening, pray alone or with others around the Cross, in communion particularly with persecuted Christians and prisoners of conscience throughout the world. On the wood of the Cross, laid flat on the floor, you can place your forehead as a sign that you commit all that weighs you down to Christ, who is in agony with humankind until the end of time.

> Saturday evening, anticipate the Resurrection by a festival of the Light of Christ, with the reading of the Gospel of the Resurrection and a prayer vigil, which may last until the following morning.

> On Sunday, celebrate in a spirit of festival the Risen Lord recognized in Scripture and in the breaking of the bread, the Eucharist.

Mission and service to the world have been themes integral to modern ecumenism, represented on the WCC side by the International Missionary Council (founded in 1921) and the Life and Work movement (dating from 1920). United prayer in favour of evangelism belongs to ecumenism, and a line of ancestry can be traced from Jonathan Edwards' *Humble Attempt*[1] to the New Year Week of Prayer begun by the Evangelical Alliance from its founding in 1846 and still continuing. The World Student Christian Federation, founded in 1895, aimed to 'win the world for Christ'; and the Lord's high-priestly prayer of John 17 not only grounds the *ut omnes unum sint* of the Student Christian Movement's motto in trinitarian relations, but also opens up the cosmic goal 'that the world may believe'. It was pressure from overseas mission fields – voiced at the conference of Edinburgh 1910 from which the ecumenical movement is conventionally dated – that resulted in some of the most significant achievements of organic unity to date, notably on the Indian subcontinent (Church of South India, Church of North India, etc.).[2] As yet there has been relatively little collaboration across the lines of Orthodoxy, Catholicism and Protestantism in evangelistic enterprise; but it is when response is made to the gospel of reconciliation that the fact of disunity appears at its most absurd: into which church shall the converts be baptized?

Allowing that St Paul's collection for the saints at Jerusalem also helps

---

[1] Jonathan Edwards (1705–58), *An Humble Attempt to Promote Explicit Agreement and Visible Union of God's People in Extraordinary Prayer, for the Revival of Religion and the Advancement of Christ's Kingdom on Earth, Pursuant to Scripture Promises and Prophecies concerning the Last Time* (Boston, 1747). See above, pp. 474–6.

[2] See Lesslie Newbigin's *South India Diary* (London, SCM, 1951 = *That all may be one*, New York, Association Press, 1952), and his autobiography, *Unfinished Agenda* (Grand Rapids, Eerdmans; London, SPCK, 1985).

to set the pattern of Christian spirituality, we must note the part played by 'inter-church aid' in such diverse phases as the reconstruction of Europe after the Second World War, the various projects of material development in the so-called Third World, and the WCC programme to combat racism, which aroused controversy on account of its gifts for humanitarian purposes to organizations advocating or using military force. In more general ways, the Church and Society side of the WCC collaborated with the Pontifical Commission on Justice and Peace through the instrumentality of SODEPAX. A kind of secular ecumenism, often unofficial, is created by co-operation between Protestants, Catholics and Orthodox on social and political issues. The Christian Peace Conference, founded in 1958 and based in Prague, provides an example. In Latin America, the solidarity of the oppressed and their separation from the oppressors are raising questions about the lines of unity and division in matters of sacramental communion.

On account of our sin and the limitations of our earthly existence, it is unlikely that a single, richly comprehensive ecumenical spirituality will be achieved before the return of Christ. But many ecumenical spiritualities are growing as progress is made, often with pain and risk, towards that free circulation of the Spirit which will become possible as the vision of the New Delhi Assembly (1961) of the WCC is realized:

> We believe that the unity which is both God's will and his gift to his Church is being made visible as all in each place who are baptized into Jesus Christ and confess him as Lord and Saviour are brought by the Holy Spirit into one fully committed fellowship, holding the one apostolic faith, preaching the one Gospel, breaking the one bread, joining in common prayer, and having a corporate life reaching out in witness and service to all and who at the same time are united with the whole Christian fellowship in all places and all ages in such wise that ministry and members are accepted by all, and that all can act and speak together as occasion requires for the tasks to which God calls his people.[1]

Meanwhile we are helped by the united prayer of the saints before the face of God, for 'the walls of separation do not reach up to heaven'.[2]

---

[1] Deliberate attention to spirituality on the part of the WCC is shown in *A Spirituality for our Times: Report of a Consultation at Annecy, France, December 1984* (Geneva, WCC, 1985) and in the attendant little book by Jean Puls, *Every Bush is Burning* (Geneva, WCC, 1985).

[2] Of Russian origin, this expression was a favourite of the Abbé Couturier and it figures on his 1946 'Tract' for the Week of Prayer with a drawing by 'Rib' (Abbé Ribes, then a seminarian).

6 Pentecostals and the Charismatic Movement

Becken, H. J., *Theologie der Heilung: Das Heilen in den Afrikanischen Unabhängigen Kirchen in Südafrika.* Hermannsburg, 1972.

Bittlinger, A., *Papst und Pfingstler: Der römisch katholisch – pfingstliche Dialog und seine ökumenische Relevanz,* Studies in the Intercultural History of Christianity (= SIHC) 16. Frankfurt, Bern, Cirencester, 1978.

Bittlinger, A., ed., *The Church is Charismatic.* Geneva, WCC, 1981.

Bloch-Hoell, N., (ET) *The Pentecostal Movement: Its Origin, Development, and Distinctive Character.* London, Allen & Unwin; Oslo, Universitetsforlaget, 1964.

Fasholé-Luke, E., *et al.*, ed., *Christianity in Independent Africa.* London, Rex Collings; Bloomington, Ind., Indiana University, 1978.

Hocken, P., *et al., New Heaven? New Earth?: an Encounter with Pentecostalism.* London, DLT, 1976; Springfield, Ill., Templegate, 1977.

Hoerschelmann, W., *Christliche Gurus: Darstellung von Selbstverständnis und Funktion indigenen Christseins durch unabhängige, charismatisch geführte Gruppen in Sudindien,* SIHC 12. Frankfurt, Bern, Cirencester, 1977.

Hollenweger, W. J., (ET) *The Pentecostals,* London, SCM; Minneapolis, Augsburg, 1972, 1976.

Hollenweger, W. J., (ET) *Pentecost Between Black and White: Five Case Studies on Pentecost and Politics.* Belfast, Christian Journals, 1974.

Hollenweger, W. J., *Interkulturelle Theologie I/II.* Munich, 1979/1982.

Hollenweger, W. J., (ET) *Conflict in Corinth.* New York, Paulist, 1982.

McDonnell, K., ed., *Presence, Power, Praise: Documents on the Charismatic Renewal.* 3 vols. Collegeville, Minn., Liturgical Press, 1980.

Nelson, D., *For Such a Time as This: The Story of Bishop William J. Seymour and the Azusa Street Revival.* Ph.D. Diss., University of Birmingham, UK, 1981.

Nichol, J. T., *Pentecostalism.* New York, Harper & Row, 1966.

Samarin, W. J., *Tongues of Men and Angels: The Religious Language of Pentecostalism.* New York, Macmillan, 1972.

Sundkler, B. G. M., *Zulu Zion and some Swazi Zionists.* London and New York, OUP, 1976.

Synan, V., *The Holiness/Pentecostal Movement in the United States.* Grand Rapids, Eerdmans, 1971.

Turner, H. W., *History of an African Independent Church: The Church of the Lord (Aladura).* 2 vols. Oxford, Clarendon, 1967.

Ustorf, W., *Afrikanische Initiative: Das aktive Leiden des Propheten Simon Kimbangu,* SIHC 5. Bern, Frankfurt, Cirencester, 1975.

Williams, C. G., *Tongues of the Spirit: a Study of Pentecostal Glossolalia and Related Phenomena.* Cardiff, University of Wales, 1981.

ORIGINS

According to D. Nelson, the majority of pentecostal historians find the main root of their movement in a revival in Los Angeles (1906) under the leadership of one of the most remarkable saints of this century, black ecumenist William J. Seymour (1870–1922). Seymour lived during a time of enormous racial tensions. During his adult lifetime, 3,436 persons were known to have been lynched, averaging two per week. Innumerable brutalities took place around him, many of them instigated by Christians. In 1917 the US entered World War I 'to make the world safe for democracy'. The first man drafted was Leo Pinckney, a black man, and the first two soldiers awarded the Croix de Guerre were black Americans attached to the French army, in spite of instructions from the US government that these black soldiers were not to be treated as equals.

Such was the context of Seymour's pentecostal and ecumenical ministry. Seymour himself was a descendant of slaves. In Parham's Bible school he was allowed to follow the lectures only by sitting outside the classroom and listening through the half-open door. Nevertheless he learned very fast. He taught himself to read and write, educated himself in Scripture and theology, and became the instrument of the revival in Los Angeles which is at the root of the ever-growing pentecostal movement.

What was so extraordinary about W. J. Seymour? It is his spirituality which enabled him to prevent his heart from becoming bitter in spite of constant humiliation, both from Christians, non-Christians and later from white fellow-pentecostals. He affirmed his black heritage by introducing negro spirituals into his liturgy at a time when this music was considered inferior and unfit for Christian worship. At the same time he steadfastly lived out his understanding of Pentecost. For him Pentecost meant more than speaking in tongues. It meant to love in the face of hate, to overcome the hatred of a whole nation by demonstrating that Pentecost is something very different from the American way of life. The source of this ecumenical ministry is to be found in his prayer, both private and public.

In the revival in Los Angeles white bishops and black workers, men and women, Asians and Mexicans, white professors and black laundry women were equals (1906!). No wonder that the religious and secular press reported the extraordinary events in detail. Such things had never been witnessed before in America. As people could not understand the revolutionary nature of this pentecostal spirituality, they took refuge in ridicule and scoffed: 'What good can come from a self-appointed negro prophet?' Under the crushing weight of public opinion, which despised the developing pentecostal spirituality because of its lowly black origins, the emerging pentecostal church bureaucracy soon tamed the revival of Los Angeles. Pentecostal churches segregated into black and white organizations just as most of the other churches had done, and many of the original ingredients of black spirituality were lost.

William J. Seymour died of a broken heart. The new pentecostal organizations preferred the power of influence and money to the power of the Holy Spirit and shamefully ignored their founder and his reconciling but costly spirituality.

The charismatic movement in the Protestant, Roman Catholic and Eastern Orthodox churches came into being under the influence of a pentecostal movement which had already 'come of age', that is to say, when it was successful in its ambition for social and ecclesiastical recognition and therefore had dropped much of its original revolutionary impetus. Thus the charismatic movement is mostly an American/European prayer spirituality which tries to interpret its new experiences within the theological traditions of the respective churches in which it operates (see the work of P. Hocken and K. McDonnell).

The alternative which is certainly going to emerge in the near future is a breakaway from traditional churches (possibly in the form of so-called house churches) in the belief that the new 'charismatic "non-organizational" organizations' can and should return to what is seen as New Testament spirituality. Seymour's pioneering ministry remains an unfulfilled challenge both for the charismatics who remain in the traditional churches and for those who organize themselves into new organizations.

CHARACTERISTIC FEATURES

How one characterizes pentecostal spirituality depends on whether one considers the first five to ten years of its history as an expression of a *not yet fully developed infant spirituality* or as the *heart of* pentecostal spirituality. One is faced with a similar hermeneutical problem as students of Marxism have to tackle when they have to decide how much weight to give to Marx's early writings, or students of early church history when they have to decide whether to interpret the New Testament mainly on the basis of the understanding of the early church Fathers or rather to interpret the church Fathers using the New Testament documents as the normative basis.

In this article I take the early pentecostal spirituality as the norm by which I measure its subsequent history. Seen from this viewpoint, the characteristic features of pentecostal and charismatic spirituality are:

1. an emphasis on the oral aspect of liturgy;

2. theology and witness cast in narrative form;

3. maximum participation at the levels of reflection, prayer and decision-making, and therefore a form of community which is reconciling;

4. inclusion of dream and vision into personal and public forms of spirituality, so that the dreams function as kinds of icons of the individual and collective;

5. an understanding of the body/mind relationship which is informed by experiences of correspondence between body and mind.

If one measures by this list the experience of present-day American/European pentecostal and charismatic groups, one still discovers a fair amount of the original elements. However, they are limited by the fact that in certain instances the authority which is based on speech, narrative and communication, enters into conflict with the authority which is based on status, education, money and juridical power. A liturgy for the fair interplay of these two types of spiritual authority (for I consider status, education, money and juridical power not *eo ipso* as unspiritual) is something which we have not yet solved. Participation, vision and dreams are welcome as long as they do not jeopardize established theological and ecclesiastical values, which is of course a normal behavioural pattern in any organization, secular or religious. The field where the churches at large will probably be most eager to incorporate elements of the pentecostal/charismatic spirituality is the body/mind relationship. They might rediscover the healing power of prayer and liturgy, in particular the healing power of the Eucharist. This is also, as H. J. Becken shows, a meeting-point for the pentecostal/charismatic spirituality and the spirituality of traditional and independent churches in the Third World.

THIRD WORLD

There is no space here to trace the largely unexplored complex relationships between Western pentecostals/charismatics and the different independent churches in the Third World, e.g. the Zionists in South Africa (B. Sundkler), the Aladura churches in West Africa (H. W. Turner), the Kimbanguists in Zaire (W. Ustorf), or the Christian gurus in India (W. Hoerschelmann). In many cases there are historical links between the two. In other cases links have been established through the World Council of Churches, in particular through its study programme on the significance of the charismatic renewal (A. Bittlinger).

The impact of this spirituality on theology and development-theory and -practice has yet to be recognized. Concerning theology, it means that it is impossible for Christians submerged in this spirituality (at any rate in the Third World) to speak about God without speaking to God, thus reintroducing or reinforcing a Catholic and Eastern Orthodox principle into the theological discourse. It means furthermore for oral people that their sacred dance functions as archive and documentation, thus fulfilling similar functions as libraries and computers fulfil in the Western world.

As to development-theory and -practice, this spirituality (because of its emphasis on the relationship between body and mind) makes the separation between sacred and profane in the Western sense extremely difficult. Dance, speaking in tongues and healing of the sick liberate forces for the development of an intermediate technology, because they awaken confidence, make people feel accepted and loved by God; they strengthen the trust in the inborn inventive gifts of the people bestowed on them by the Creator Spirit and encourage them to recognize the organizational gifts of their pre-Christian existence as gifts of the Holy Spirit.

Speaking in tongues, dreams and visions help in the conscientization of the people of God. If used under the conditions laid down by Paul in 1. Cor. 12–14, they liberate the people of God and free them from dehumanizing cultural, economic and social forces. They create room for an oral theological and social debate. Thus they unfreeze liturgical, theological and socio-political formulae and replace imported ideologies (whether of a progressive or a conservative kind does not really matter) by the political literacy of the whole people of God, practised and learned within the framework of an oral liturgy for which the whole congregation is responsible.

THE ECUMENICAL DIMENSION

Superficially this spirituality has made possible a dialogue between Evangelicals and Catholics (cf. Bittlinger's study). At a deeper level there is a wider potential in this spirituality. It is, however, difficult to introduce this kind of spirituality into the ecumenical discussion because – if reduced to concepts and propositions – it loses its very essence. That is why theological papers by adherents of charismatic prayer groups, pentecostal or independent churches generally produce no great excitement. Their strength does not lie in what they conceptualize but in what happens to the participants in their liturgies. Their contribution is strongest on the level of spirituality and lived liturgy and not on the level of interpreting spirituality, liturgy and theology. To try to understand pente-costal/charismatic/independent spirituality through the books they write is as futile as trying to understand Eastern Orthodox spirituality without ever participating in their services, lighting candles in their churches, seeing the people worshipping, meditating before their icons, hearing and seeing the priest sing the liturgy, and staying for some time in one of their monasteries. We therefore have to invent new forms of ecumenical encounter if we want to learn from this spirituality and if we want to contribute with our own spiritual gifts to their spirituality. Beginnings of such new styles of encounter have been introduced: at the Assembly of the World Council of Churches at Nairobi (1975); through the continuing ecumenical study programme on charismatic and independent African spirituality (see Bittlinger again); and in the theological and historical research programme carried out by Africans, Europeans/Americans, Catholics, Protestants and Independents, which resulted in one of the most revealing studies on Christianity in Independent Africa, edited by E. Fasholé-Luke and his collaborators.

7 Interplay with Other Religions

KOSUKE KOYAMA

Boyd, R., *An Introduction to Indian Christian Theology*. Madras, Christian Literature Society, 1969, rev. edn 1975.

Elwood, D. J., ed., *What Asian Christians are Thinking*. Quezon City, Philippines, New Day Publishers, 1976.

Elwood, D. J., *Asian Christian Theology, Emerging Themes*. Philadelphia, Westminster, 1980.

Fabella, V., ed., *Asia's Struggle for Full Humanity*. Maryknoll, N.Y., Orbis, 1980.

Koyama, K., *Mount Fuji and Mount Sinai*. London, SCM, 1984; New York, Orbis, 1985.

Paton, D. M., ed., *Breaking Barriers: Nairobi 1975. The Official Report of the Fifth Assembly of the World Council of Churches*. London, SPCK; Grand Rapids, Eerdmans, 1976.

Yong-Bock, K., ed., *Minjung Theology: People as the Subjects of History*. Singapore, Christian Conference of Asia, 1981.

This section is presented in the following manner: (1) an introduction indicating that 'interplay' belongs to the essential nature of religious spirituality, including Christianity; (2) cases demonstrating contemporary religious spirituality and the interaction of Christian spirituality with that of other religious traditions; and (3) remarks on the future of interplay between Christian spirituality and other religions.

1 INTERPLAY AS ESSENTIAL TO RELIGIOUS SPIRITUALITY

'You shall receive power when the Holy Spirit has come upon you; and you shall be my witnesses in Jerusalem and in all Judea and Samaria and to the end of the earth' (Acts 1.8). This promise, studied from our perspective near the end of the twentieth century, presents us with an overwhelming history of the interplay of Christian spirituality (or spiritualities) with other historical religious and cultural spiritualities. Raimundo Panikkar writes:

> Christianity is, sociologically speaking, certainly one religion; it is the ancient paganism or, to be more precise, the complex Hebrew-Hellenic-Greco-Latin-Celtic-Gothic-Modern religion converted to Christ more or less successfully.[1]

Heinz R. Schlette speaks about the character of historical complexity relating to Christian spirituality in this way:

> There cannot be any such thing as the *ecclesia pura*, the non-mediated Church, the non-translated truth and doctrine – a Christianity chemically pure, so to speak, and in a non-adapted form.[2]

History of spirituality shares the nature of the history of the propagation of the Christian truth. 'Bearing witness' to the truth takes place within the busy context of religions and cultures to which Panikkar makes reference. There is then no 'chemically pure spirituality' which is called Christian. All spirituality is formed within the context of the historical interplay of cultural and religious situations. Interplay can be that of encounter, accommodation and even rejection. A spirituality is stimulated and developed by encounter with a different type of spirituality, as is happening today between the spiritualities of the Christian tradition and Zen Buddhism, between the spirituality of indignation against social injustice (the 'spirituality' of Marxism) and Latin American Catholic Christianity, between Islamic theocratic spirituality and American Christianity in Mindanao, Philippines, and Dutch Christianity in Indonesia.[3] Such interplay is fundamental to the life of spirituality, and it

[1] *What Asian Christians are Thinking*, ed. Douglas J. Elwood, p. 361.
[2] H. R. Schlette, 'Missions' in (ET) *Sacramentum Mundi*, ed. K. Rahner *et al.* (New York, Herder & Herder; London, Burns Oates, 1969), vol. iv, p. 81.
[3] See, for instance, the article by Abe Masao, the Japanese Zen scholar, 'The End of World Religion', in *The Eastern Buddhist* 13/1 (1980), pp. 31–45; William Johnston, *The Still Point* (New York, Fordham University Press, 1970); Daisetz T. Suzuki, *Zen and Japanese Culture* (New York, Pantheon Books, 1959).

is not a matter of peripheral importance. Even in 'a-historical' religions (both nature-religions and Indian religions, for instance) spirituality is engaged in some kind of dialogue with what is happening in the historical world. The Theravada Buddhist spirituality in Thailand is deeply concerned about this world to the extent that the monks struggle *historically* to get release from it! While the monks work hard to emancipate themselves from the world, they are deeply involved in interplay with the values, ideology and spirituality of their surroundings, including a strongly history-oriented spirituality of Christianity. It seems that, compared to the spirituality of struggle to be free from the grasp of this world to be found among these 200,000 Thai Buddhist monks, the Christian ministers in Buddhist Thailand are far less 'history'-involved.

Jerusalem is the holy city for three great faiths of the world: Judaism, Christianity and Islam. Hosea's words 'For I desire steadfast love and not sacrifice, the knowledge of God rather than burnt offerings' (Hos. 6.6), speak to humanity through these three spiritual histories. The Koranic formula, 'in the name of God, the Merciful, the Compassionate', expresses the common spiritual ground of these traditions. Seen from Eastern spiritual perception of the Buddhists, these three faiths present a spirituality informed by profound devotion to the monotheistic God. There has been a substantial theological and devotional interplay among these three traditions, the study of which has remained and will remain one of the most demanding and rewarding subjects of the history of human spirituality. The monotheistic history-oriented spirituality of these faiths has come into contact with the world of Indian religions (Hinduism, Buddhism, Jainism), the Chinese religion of Taoism, and the religious perceptions of world and life of the nature-religions which are found among the vast population of this world. Monotheistic spirituality also came into contact with the spirituality expressed by what Tillich called a quasi-religion, namely Marxism. The World Council of Churches commends dialogue to be carried on with 'people of other living faiths and ideologies'.

2   CASES OF INTERPLAY

(a) *The World Conference on Religion and Peace*

Significant occasions in which Christian spirituality has been in interplay with other spiritualities in recent years were the meetings of the World Conference on Religion and Peace (New Delhi in 1968, Kyoto in 1970, Louvain in 1974, Princeton in 1980). There Christians (Catholic, Orthodox and Protestant) worked with Buddhists, Confucianists, Hindus, Jains, Jews, Muslims, Shintoists, Sikhs and Zoroastrians on the subjects of disarmament, economic development, human rights and environment. These are deeply human issues. The Kyoto Declaration has this sentence:

> . . . love, compassion, selflessness, and force of inner truthfulness and of the spirit have ultimately greater power than hate, enmity and self-interest.[1]

The particular significance of this lies in the historical context in which it was said. It was said in a world perilously close to a nuclear holocaust, and also it was said together with people of other major faiths about which Christians know far more today than at any time in the past. What I perceive here is a spiritual movement towards the 'larger Christ' (Stanley Samartha) or the 'wider ecumenism' of the welfare of humanity breaking through the welfare of the Christian humanity.[2] The concept of a 'larger divinity' – for instance, 'the infinitely larger Buddha' that appears profusely in the scriptures of Mahayana Buddhism – had been familiar to the cosmological (divine mercy embraces cosmos) and pantheistic (divine presence is found in all things) minds of the peoples of nature-religions. Asians and Africans are deeply cosmological and pantheistic people. But now Christians with these cultural, religious and spiritual backgrounds are achieving some kind of creative spiritual formation combining the religious perception of 'cosmological pantheistic largeness' with such a strongly theological view expressed by Paul in Romans 8.25. In the world of 'many peoples, many faiths' (Robert S. Ellwood) one of the spiritual developments taking place is this dialogue between the cosmological piety of nature-religions and the eschatological devotion to the God of historical events, between the religious emotion about a nature that repeats itself and the events that do not repeat themselves. All this is going on, as the General Assembly of the World Council of Churches at Nairobi in 1975 said, under the sign of the *skandalon* of Jesus Christ.

> We are all agreed that the *skandalon* (stumbling block) of the gospel will always be with us. While we do seek wider community with people of other faiths, cultures, and ideologies, we do not think there will ever be a time in history when the tension will be resolved between belief in Jesus Christ and unbelief. It is a tension which also goes through each Christian disciple, as each is unable to say that his or her faith in Jesus Christ is perfect.[3]

---

[1] *Findings of the World Conference on Religion and Peace* (Tokyo, Japan Committee for the World Conference on Religion and Peace Publication, 1973), p. 173.

[2] Dr Samartha's words 'larger Christ' appear in the article entitled 'The Unbound Christ: toward a Christology in India Today', in *What Asian Christians are Thinking*, p. 236. 'Wider ecumenism': see *Breaking Barriers, Nairobi 1975: The Official Report of the Fifth Assembly of the World Council of Churches* (London, SPCK; Grand Rapids, Eerdmans, 1976), p. 75.

[3] *Breaking Barriers*, p. 73.

Spiritual encounter going on between the two deeply religious outlooks, cosmological piety and eschatological spirituality, has some depth or aspect which is delicately different from the words said by the Indian Christian mystic Sadhu Sundar Singh (1889–1929):

> Christianity is the fulfilment of Hinduism. Hinduism has been digging channels. Christ is the water to flow through these channels.[1]

(b) *The Ecumenical Dialogue of Third World Theologians*

The interplay of Christian spirituality with other religions is taking place in a world which is faced by the possibility of nuclear annihilation. The whole of humanity is enslaved by the destructive power that humanity has produced. This tragic enslavement is not unrelated to the human condition of which Manas Buthelezi of South Africa speaks when he writes about himself and the blacks as 'colonized humanity'.[2] The evil that colonizes humanity is like that which produces the global nuclear threat. While the white political regime claims Christian theological justification for the race policy and execution of apartheid, black people discover the 'spirituality for combat' (M. M. Thomas) against it,[3] a spirituality expressing itself in the 'cry because of their taskmasters' (Exod. 3.7). People 'eat up my people as they eat bread' (Ps. 14.4). It is the spirituality that fights against the eaters of the people (militarism, racism, sexism, hunger, poverty). A spirituality of colonized humanity becomes a spirituality of combat in the discipleship of Jesus Christ. The character of such spirituality is well expressed in the title of the book, *The Emergent Gospel, Theology from the Underside of History*, which is the report of the First Ecumenical Dialogue of Third World Theologians which met at Dar es Salaam, August 1976. (The second took place in Wennappuwa, Sri Lanka, January 1979, the third in Sao Paolo, Brazil in February 1980).[4]

It is important to note that in these conferences of 'theology from the underside of history', interplay with other religions has played an important role. The world of Africa and Asia lives extensively and deeply in the world of great religious traditions. No spirituality for combat in the Third World is possible apart from the interplay of Christian spirituality

---

[1] Robin Boyd, *An Introduction to Indian Christian Theology*, p. 107.
[2] *The Emergent Gospel, Theology from the Underside of History*, ed. Sergio Torres and Virginia Fabella (Maryknoll, N.Y., Orbis, 1978), p. 85.
[3] *Breaking Barriers*, p. 237.
[4] The reports of the second and third conferences have been published under the titles, *Asia's Struggle for Full Humanity*, ed. V. Fabella and *The Challenge of Basic Christian Communities*, ed. S. Torres and J. Eagleson (Maryknoll, N.Y., Orbis Books, 1980 and 1981).

with those of other religions. The Sri Lankan theologian Father Aloysius Pieris commends 'voluntary poverty' in these words:

> ... voluntary poverty is not merely a spiritual antidote against Mammon (as in traditional Christianity and in Asian Religions in general) but also a political strategy against the Principalities and Powers that serve Mammon.[1]

May I add here the venerable name of Mahatma Gandhi. The interplay between his spiritual principle of *satyagraha* and the Christian gospel was an event of great importance in the history of Christian spirituality. It is well known that the Gandhian Hindu ideal of *satyagraha* displayed its power in the United States through Martin Luther King.

Korean theology has been much in dialogue with the general cultural atmosphere of shamanism. The *Minjung* Theology (theology of the 'underdog' people) recently developed in Korea is keenly aware of the Korean religious spirituality. The Korean theologian Suh Nam Dong introduces the theology of Kim Chi-ha in terms of the concept of the shamanistic spirit world of Korea:

> Kim Chi-ha's theology is the theology of *han*. He decides to act as 'the messenger of *han*, the medium of murmuring grievances, because this peninsula is full of the *han* of aggrieved and weeping ghosts.'[2]

In the Philippines, liberation theology begins with a spiritual movement towards reconciliation between Christians and Muslims in Mindanao. In a letter written by Christians and addressed to Muslims in July 1978, these words occur:

> We ask of you, our Muslim brothers, that our presence among you will be welcomed. We are humbled by much that has marked our past history and we ask your forgiveness for our large share of the blame for the tragic past ... Christians need to take seriously and treat respectfully the Islamic religion and culture of Filipino Muslims.[3]

(c) *Personal Manifestations*

Thomas Merton, the American Trappist monk and writer (1915–68) who was killed in an accident while in Bangkok after his visit to the Dalai Lama, lived a life of monastic contemplation. His spiritual pilgrimage involved him deeply in the interplay of different spiritual traditions. In

[1] A. Pieries, 'Western Christianity and Asian Buddhism, a theological reading of Historical Encounters', in *Dialogue* (Colombo, Ecumenical Institute for Study and Dialogue), new series 7/2 (1980), p. 79.
[2] *Minjung Theology: People as the Subject of History*, ed. Kim Yong-Bock, p. 180.
[3] *Asian Christian Theology, Emerging Themes*, ed. Douglas J. Elwood, pp. 334–5.

him the spirituality of the West met that of the East.[1] The British Benedictine monk Bede Griffiths, author of *Christian Ashram, Essays towards a Hindu and Christian Dialogue* (Darton, Longman & Todd, 1966), has achieved a moving spiritual dialogue with the mystical tradition of Hinduism, Buddhism, Taoism and the Sufis of Islam. In this book, he writes:

> I had long been familiar with the mystical tradition of the West, but I felt the need of something more which the East alone could give; above all the sense of the presence of God in nature and the soul, a kind of natural mysticism which is the basis of all Indian spirituality (p. 17).

A Frenchman by birth, but later a naturalized Indian, Swami Abhishiktananda, who is a Roman Catholic monk, is devoted to the search for saving truth in interreligious spirituality. His book *The Church in India* (1969) discusses renewal of the Church in the perspective of the interreligious experience. In *The Still Point* (New York, Fordham University, 1970), dedicated to Thomas Merton, the Jesuit William Johnston reflects upon Zen and Christian mysticism.

These recent names remind us of the great Jesuits of the sixteenth century: Matthew Ricci (1552–1610), who spent a decade in the capital of China, and Robert de Nobili (1577–1656), who worked in south India for fifty years. Both demonstrated remarkable understanding of the culture and religion of the peoples and were deeply engaged, linguistically and spiritually, in the interreligious context.

3   COMING CHALLENGES

The interplay between the religions of the world and the spirit of the Western civilization (modernization) in our time presents an agonizing ambiguity of destructive and creative implications. Christian spirituality which has been historically a constitutive element of Western civilization is bound to go through re-formation not in terms of the Christian humanity of the West, but in the name of all humanity. This cannot be done without Christian spirituality interacting with the teaching and spiritualities of other religious traditions.

The spirituality of dominance will be challenged. A spirituality of interdependence informed by Christian theology and ministry must appear. Christianity has theological and devotional resources to move to-

[1] T. Merton, *Seven Storey Mountain* (New York, Harcourt, Brace, Jovanowich, 1948; London, Sheldon, 1975); *Asian Journal* (New York, New Directions, 1973; London, Sheldon, 1975); *Mystics and Zen Masters* (New York, Dell, 1969); *Zen and the Birds of Appetite* (New York, New Directions, 1968); *Thomas Merton on Zen* (London, Sheldon, 1976).

wards such a possibility. The gospel proclaims the centrality of Jesus Christ, who constantly goes out towards the periphery of humanity. A spirituality of the periphery of humanity is able to inspire *Christian* inter-religious spirituality, and such spirituality will speak to the needs of humanity.

PART THREE

Pastoral Spirituality

I

PASTORAL APPLICATIONS OF SPIRITUALITY

1 The Nature of Spiritual Development

CHRISTOPHER BRYANT

Bovet, T., (ET) *That they may have Life*. London, DLT, 1964.

Bryant, C., *The River Within*. London, DLT, 1978.

Cummings, C., *Spirituality and the Desert Experience*. Denville, N.J., Dimension Books, 1980.

Evdokimov, P., *The Struggle with God*. New York, Paulist, 1966.

Foster, R. J., *Celebration of Discipline: The Path to Spiritual Growth*. San Francisco, Harper & Row, 1978.

Fowler, J. W., et al., *Life Maps: Conversations on the Journey of Faith*. Waco, Tex., Word Books, 1978.

Fowler, J. W., *Stages of Faith: the Psychology of Human Development and the Quest for Meaning*. San Francisco, Harper & Row, 1981.

Guibert, J. de, (ET) *The Theology of the Spiritual Life*. New York, Sheed & Ward, 1952; London, Sheed & Ward, 1954.

Harton, F. P., *The Elements of the Spiritual Life*. London, SPCK; New York, Macmillan, 1932.

Leech, K., *True Prayer*. London, Sheldon; New York, Harper & Row, 1980.

Loder, J., *The Transforming Moment: Understanding Convictional Experience*. San Francisco, Harper & Row, 1981.

Merton, T., *Contemplative Prayer*. New York, Herder & Herder, 1969; London, DLT, 1973.

Nouwen, H. M., *Reaching Out*. Garden City, N.Y., Doubleday, 1975; London, Collins, 1976.

Sacramentum Mundi, (ET) Rahner, K., et al., ed. (London, Burns & Oates, 1970; New York, Herder, 1968–70), vol. vi, s.v. 'Spirituality', pp. 146–67.

Willis, D., *Daring Prayer*. Atlanta, John Knox, 1977.

An individual's spiritual development means growth towards a fuller union with God through prayer and a growing conformity to God's will in life. This growth in oneness with God will tend to bring about a growth in good will towards one's fellows and in personal integration. This development is possible only through the action of God's grace but it demands the individual's deliberate co-operation. It thus resembles both the growth of a tree and the journey of a pilgrim. Like a tree spiritual life grows downwards and upwards. Its roots draw nourishment from the earth of God-created nature and its branches through prayer reach out to the air of communion with God. But it is also like a voyage in search of Eldorado. Indeed a decisive spiritual advance is made when one seriously resolves to seek a closer walk with God and to put God and his Reign in the forefront of one's aims. The nature of people's spiritual development will be profoundly influenced both by their inborn temperament and childhood experience as also by the society in which they grow up. Articles in this volume on the psychology and on the sociology of prayer (pp. 24–38) deal with these factors.

Three movements of the soul, those of repentance, faith and love, characterize the Godward journey. They are inner attitudes which express themselves in aspiration and action. They are all present and operative throughout the pilgrimage but at different stages one or other will tend to predominate. It is normal in the early stages of the pilgrim's journey for repentance to be of especial importance. Later the deepening and enlarging of faith commonly becomes a major concern. Later still the progress of the spiritual pilgrim is measured chiefly by growth in love for God and one's fellows. But spiritual development is no steady, regular advance, but is punctuated by crises in which growth appears to have come to a stop for a time; old battles have to be refought and old experiences relived at a deeper level.

The movement of repentance involves the determination to make God and his will the guiding principle of life and the struggle to renounce idolatries, the undue attachment to relative goods, such as pleasure, popularity and success, which interfere with the Godward journey. It will mean the battle with selfish inclinations and habits and the endeavour to build up Christlike habits and attitudes. The cardinal virtues of prudence, justice, temperance and fortitude give an outline of the human qualities which are needed to provide a firm foundation for the specifically Christian virtues of faith, hope and love. But Christlike habits and actions will be impossible without a transformation of desires and emotions which no effort can bring about. Only reliance on the cleansing and renewing power of the Holy Spirit can bring about the inner revolution that is necessary. The pilgrim seeks to assist this inner change partly by contemplating the figure of Christ, partly by a self-examination which seeks to uncover the disordered emotions and desires which need to be cleansed and redirected. This area of excessive fear and anxiety, of anger and depression, of disordered sex-desire and morbid guilt, which is the seed-bed of actual sins, needs to be opened up to the healing and renewing of the Holy Spirit.

From the outset of the spiritual journey faith is inseparable from the movement of repentance, but it becomes increasingly important as the journey progresses. Faith involves more than just belief but must include an element of commitment to and trust in God, which should progressively influence more and more of the believer's life. The growth of faith is fostered by spiritual reading. This is not the rapid reading with which a person usually reads a newspaper or a novel, but the slow, reflective, prayerful reading of Scripture or some spiritual writer ancient or modern. It is a reading designed to awaken Godward aspirations and to lead on to prayer. Modern believers subject to the influence of secularism will have to face questions as to the truth of what they believe. Both reason and imagination have a part to play in answering contemporary doubts; reason because faith and love of truth must walk hand in hand; imagination because truths which can be in some way pictured or represented in picturable symbol make a much profounder impression on heart and mind than when stated abstractly. For this reason literature addressed to both reason and imagination can greatly help the development of faith.

Faith expresses itself especially in prayer which should be understood as an attitude, God-oriented and God-relying, which colours all the day's activities. The time given specifically to praying should be seen as focusing, intensifying and redirecting this daylong attitude. In various places in this book an account is given of particular methods of prayer and meditation. Here it will be enough to say that prayer may be divided into expressive and contemplative prayer. In expressive prayer individuals voice their faith and desires either in their own words or in those of the liturgy or in prayers composed by others. The four main types of expressive prayer are adoration, confession, thanksgiving and petition. Contemplative prayer[1] is a prayer in which the individual waits in an open and receptive attitude, looking to the Lord. It has been called a prayer of loving attention to God. For an account of contemplative prayer see especially the articles on Teutonic mysticism (pp. 315–27), the English mystics (pp. 328–37), St Teresa of Avila and St John of the Cross (pp. 363–76).

As individuals persevere in their search for oneness with God, the Holy Spirit brings about a transformation of their outlook. Through spiritual struggle and testing, the emotional and instinctive roots of their being are cleansed and redirected. Their prayer and their whole attitude to life and to other people tend to become simpler. Increasingly they will come to see all as the occasion of loving God, doing and accepting God's will and loving their fellows wholeheartedly. With this growth in simplicity they will tend to find themselves freer, more themselves, more wholehearted in all that they do than ever before.

---

[1] The word 'contemplation' is given different meanings in different traditions; cf. Index s.v.

2 The Nature of Spiritual Direction: Sacramental Confession

CHRISTOPHER BRYANT

'Author of the Way' (Ward, R. S.), *A Guide for Spiritual Directors*. London, Mowbray, 1957.

Bryant, C., *The Heart in Pilgrimage*. London, DLT; New York, Seabury, 1980.

Gratton, C., *Guidelines for Spiritual Direction* (Studies in Formation Spirituality, vol. iii). Denville, N. J., Dimension Books, 1980.

Häring, B., *Shalom*. Garden City, N.Y., Doubleday (Image Books), 1969; New York, Farrar, Straus & Giroux, 1968.

Laplace, J., (ET) *The Direction of Conscience*. London, Chapman; New York, Herder & Herder, 1967.

Leech, K., *Soul Friend*. London, Sheldon, 1977; San Francisco, Harper & Row, 1980.

Merton, T., *Spiritual Direction and Meditation*. London, A. Clarke, 1975.

Ross, K., *Hearing Confessions*. London, SPCK, 1974.

Scanlon, M., *The Power in Penance*. Notre Dame, Ind., Ave Maria, 1972.

Squire, A., *Summer in the Seed*. London, SPCK, 1979; New York, Paulist, 1980, ch. 8.

No man is a good judge in his own case. From time immemorial people who were strongly set on deepening their commitment to God have sought the guidance of someone wiser and more experienced in the spiritual life. Traditionally this guidance has been known as spiritual direction, but the term direction suggests a more authoritative pattern of guidance than is considered appropriate today. For the true guide of the soul is the Holy Spirit, and the function of the human director is to help individuals to recognize where the Spirit is leading. For this reason the director should spend much time listening to each individual who comes, drawing them to speak frankly about their life as well as their spiritual problems, but being sparing of giving advice. Often what is most needed is not advice but a sympathetic hearing and encouragement. Spiritual direction is as a rule ongoing, and the individual normally sees the director regularly. But direction is also sought and given occasionally, as in a retreat.

Spiritual direction should be closely related to the course of spiritual development (see the previous chapter). The director's task may be roughly summarized under four headings: prayer, self-knowledge, vocation and the ordering of daily life. Many for whom prayer is an important priority are hampered through ignorance and may be greatly helped by quite elementary instruction on such matters as realizing God's presence, the importance of the body as the soul's ally in prayer, the devotional use of the Bible, and the use of the imagination as a help to prayer. The many today who are drawn to contemplative prayer often need both warning and encouragement. For the attitude of waiting on God in contemplation leaves the person open not only to the Spirit of God but to the uprush of disordered impulses and emotions from the unconscious.

Modern psychology has underlined the importance traditionally given to self-knowledge in spiritual development. The director by judicious questions can help individuals to probe the unconscious motives that sustain their egocentric aims and to uncover the hidden roots of their conscious failures, and so can lead them to a more genuine repentance. But the director will not unless specially trained for it attempt psychotherapy; but where this seems needed the individual should be encouraged to seek professional psychotherapeutic treatment.

By vocation is meant not only the special vocation to the religious life or to the ordained or to some other form of Christian ministry. For God has a purpose for each individual and this purpose constitutes a call to seek salvation by following a particular path in life. The director has the task of helping the individuals who seek counsel to discern where God is calling them, whether to remain in the situation in which they are or to embrace something new.

This leads on to the question of a rule of life. Many follow an unwritten rule of Sunday worship, private prayer and Bible reading, together with some practice of almsgiving, without any thought that they are observing a rule of life. The director can often help individuals to strengthen their Christian practice by framing and writing out a set of rules or guidelines. Some are most helped by an ideal of practice which they often fail to achieve but which serves as a light beckoning them on; others need a minimum rule which they can and do keep, except perhaps in exceptional circumstances.

In the endeavour to bring the whole of life into conformity with the will of God and the following of Christ, sacramental confession is a powerful resource. Its power to heal and liberate springs partly from the fact that it links the individual penitents with their fellows in the Church. It is also due in part to its symbolic resonance, which enables it to touch and heal areas of their being not subject to their conscious control. The child within the adult, subject to moods of anxiety, resentment, bitterness and despair, is impervious to reason but is open to the power of symbols, and rejoices to hear the voice of one who speaks with the authority of Christ and brings the assurance of forgiveness. Sacramental confession expresses and so strengthens each individual in their turning away from sin to God. It expresses too their sense of responsibility for their actions and failures to act and their will to make amends.

The sacrament of confession is intended primarily for the reconciliation of those who have sinned gravely, though it is widely used by those whose sins would not be considered grave. Further it has been seen as the sacrament of absolution from actual sins. But there is a whole underworld of mood and emotion, such as excessive fear and anxiety, bitterness and resentment, depression and morbid guilt. These sick emotions which an individual does not want but cannot help are not strictly matter for confession; they need to be healed rather than forgiven. Yet though involuntary and so not blameworthy they have something of the quality of sin about them. The custom has, I think rightly, grown up of bringing these inner troubles to confession. The sacrament is then seen not only as a means of remitting actual sin but as a sacrament of healing and deliverance for the emotional sicknesses which hamper and weaken Christians in their discipleship.[1]

3 Group Prayer

JOHN GUNSTONE

ON ORGANIZING PRAYER GROUPS

Cavnar, J., *Participating in Prayer Meetings*. Ann Arbor, Mich., Word of Life, 1974.

Grigor, J. C., *Grow to Love: Developing Caring Relationships: a Resource Book for Groups*. Edinburgh, St Andrew, 1977.

Gunstone, J., *The Charismatic Prayer Group: a Handbook for Pastors, Leaders and Members*. London, Hodder & Stoughton, 1975; Minneapolis, Bethany Fellowship, 1976.

ON THE HISTORY OF PRAYER GROUPS IN CHURCH RENEWAL

Lovelace, R. F., *Dynamics of Spiritual Life*. Downers Grove, Ill., InterVarsity; Exeter, Paternoster, 1979.

Snyder, H. A., *The Radical Wesley and Patterns for Church Renewal*. Downers Grove, Ill., InterVarsity, 1980.

Where two or three Christians are gathered together, there is the opportunity for group prayer. When they turn their attention to God as well as to one another, the dynamics of relationships between them are trans-

---

[1] For the actual method of hearing confessions consult the bibliography, especially the books by Ross and Scanlon.

figured by the Holy Spirit into the dynamics of corporate prayer. But they remain sensitive to one another as well as sensitive to God. Through group prayer they become more conscious of their unity in Jesus Christ as they look to the Father.

Group prayer can happen anywhere and at any time. A family sitting down for a meal, a meeting of students in a college, a gathering of Christians at lunchtime in a business establishment, a committee called together to initiate a project in the local church – all these are occasions when believers might pray together.

Nowadays most group prayer is experienced where up to a dozen or so Christians meet regularly each week or fortnight. Usually they meet in one another's homes. Freed from the restraints imposed by church buildings and liturgical books, prayer in these groups is more informal and spontaneous than in church worship.

Individuals open themselves to God and to one another as mutual trust develops. Ideas and hopes, needs and fears, can be expressed, to be taken up by the rest of the group in petitions, words of encouragement and praise. The experience of this kind of free-wheeling group prayer can be extraordinarily supportive. In many groups like these Christians frequently experience for the first time what it means to belong to a body where, 'If one member suffers, all suffer together; if one member is honoured, all rejoice together' (1 Cor. 12.26).

Yet, for all their spontaneity, prayer groups do in fact create their own structures in what they do and say; and if these structures are analysed, they are found to contain the same elements that make up a formal act of liturgical worship.

For example, all groups need leadership or presidency. This is usually recognized in one or two of their members – perhaps the couple in whose house the group is meeting. It has to be an unobtrusive leadership: suggestions about beginning and ending the time of prayer, attention to the needs of others, responsibility for the practical arrangements. Now and then the leader has to be firm if differences of opinion arise, or when an important decision has to be made.

The most gifted leadership is hardly noticed. The members of the group claim they are 'led only by the Holy Spirit'. That may be true, but it feels like that only because the Spirit has anointed one or more of their number with charisms for the task.

Then, as the meeting proceeds, different elements emerge. There is a *preparation*. The members exchange greetings and news, make plans for the evening, and settle down when the leader says, 'Let's begin, shall we?' Bibles are opened, a preliminary prayer is said, a sense of expectancy rises among them.

There is a *ministry of the word of God*. A passage of Scripture is read, silence is kept, a few questions are asked, and individuals add their own reflections. The intention is not to wrestle with exegetical or theological points (as in, say, a Bible study group) but to try and discern what God is saying to the group through that passage at that time. Sometimes this ministry is reinforced by readings from other books, or by testimonies by members recounting experiences of God's grace in their lives.

In charismatic prayer groups there may also be simple prophecies or words of wisdom (as understood in classical pentecostal spirituality); these, of course, must be tested against the teaching of the Bible, the tradition of the Church, and enlightened commonsense.

Then there is a *response to the word of God*. Individuals are given confidence to experiment (in the best sense of that word) in all kinds of prayer. Texts from the scripture reading are woven into intercessions and thanksgivings. Members learn to listen to God so that they pray in the Spirit rather than from their own promptings. Petitions are offered in a leisurely, discerning manner. Minutes of deep, contemplative silence are followed by bursts of praise, sometimes with psalms, canticles, hymns and acclamations, sometimes with the choruses and songs that abound today in Christian worship.

Groups can also minister to the needs of individual members. Personal concerns are explained and made the subject of sustained prayer. In charismatic groups, prayer is offered with the laying on of hands for healing, for deliverance from evil influences, for guidance, and so on. Praying in tongues and gifts of interpretation are also manifested; when authentic, they convey a vivid sense of God's presence and power.

Finally, there is what corresponds to the *dismissal* in the liturgy. A final prayer is said, the last chorus sung, the peace is given, and the members depart.

At their worst, prayer groups can be cliquy, inward-looking and divisive. They need the oversight of parish priests or pastors to help them discern God's purposes for them within the congregation and wider Church. At their best, though, they can be launchpads for all kinds of Christian mission and service. They are a notable feature of church life today. Drawing their members from different denominations, they can be a significant factor in the ecumenical movement in a neighbourhood. Some pastoral theologians see them as a foreshadowing of the basic Christian communities of the future.

4 Communities Old and New

ANTHONY PRIDDIS

Brico, R., *Taizé*. London, Collins, 1978.
Clark, D., *Basic Communities*. London, SPCK, 1977.
Contemporary Monasticism, Fairacres Publication 80. Oxford, SLG Press, 1981.
Fracchia, C. A., *Living Together Alone*. New York, Harper & Row, 1979.
Harrison, A., *Bound for Life*. Oxford, Mowbray, 1983.
Moorhouse, G., *Against all Reason*. London, Weidenfeld & Nicolson; New York, Stein & Day, 1969.
Perchenet, A., (ET) *The Revival of the Religious Life and Christian Unity*. Oxford, Mowbray, 1969.
Rees, D., et al., *Consider Your Call*. London, SPCK, 1978; Kalamazoo, Cistercian, 1980.
Religious Communities in the World of Today. London, SPCK, 1970.
The Rule of Taizé. Les Presses de Taizé, 1968 (French and English).

Periodicals
Community, sponsored by One for Christian Renewal.
Encounter and Exchange. Journal of the Communities Consultative Council.
Sojourners, published by the Sojourners Community of Washington, D.C.

One of the many consequences of the Second World War for the Christian churches in the West was the emergence among churches of the Reformation of new forms of religious communities. These had blossomed in the Anglican Church a century earlier, while at the same time deaconess communities had formed on the continent. The post-war desire to find a deeper commitment to Christ in the light of the horrors of the war was a crucial influence. When this was coupled with an overwhelming sense of the need to work for peace and reconciliation, or to seek new ways of serving God within the world, or to heal the divisions among mankind (especially those within the Church), then it provided exactly the sort of soil in which the new seeds of community life could grow. Not surprisingly, these forces were felt most strongly in Germany where a number of communities developed in the post-war years. In the case of the Kommunität Imshausen, the foundation was built upon work begun before the war, as was also the case with two communities in other countries which grew out of retreat house work, Pomeyrol in France and Grandchamp in Switzerland.

Among these new communities, 'that little springtime'[1] of Taizé in France was to mushroom in a very remarkable way (see p. 546). Young

---

[1] Pope John XXIII's description.

people from all over the world have journeyed to that south Burgundian hill, drawn by the readiness of the founder, Roger Schutz, to listen to their intuitions and hopes. They witness the brothers of this ecumenical community living out a unification of work, prayer and community life, and their spiritual awareness is deepened by the offices which contain rich silence and chanting. Taizé's influence has not just been upon its visitors, but, through its *Letter*[1] and pilgrimages, has reached countless others, and affected the spirituality of traditional and older religious communities.

If the spirituality of Taizé has had a bearing on the spiritual renewal of older religious communities of the Western churches, other forces have been felt even more strongly, most notably Vatican II, calling for 'a continuous return to the sources of all Christian life and to the original inspiration behind a given community, and an adjustment of the community to the changed conditions of the times'.[2] This appeal was echoed in the Lambeth Conference 1968.[3] A further influence upon the spirituality of the religious communities, no less than the whole Church, has been the development of psychology and an increased awareness of the individual's growth. Eastern religions and the charismatic renewal have also been instrumental in leading to considerable changes in some communities. One particular monk, Thomas Merton,[4] of the Cistercian Abbey of Gethsemani, was able, through his writings, to act as a 'mouthpiece' for many religious, articulating his monastic journey and, thereby, giving confidence and inspiration to others.

These forces have led to vast changes in many religious communities, particularly in ways of greater openness and flexibility, not only in their worship. Everywhere barriers have been removed and bridges built, whether it was barriers between clerical and lay, religious and visitors, one community and another, men and women: in all areas there has been a new wind of renewal. Such changes have been costly for many communities, involving considerable pain and sacrifice, as they have scrutinized their life together. 'A community is not created once and for all at its beginning. The only thing that can prevent a community from becoming static or regressive is its daily renewed re-creation', wrote Roger Schutz[5] and this 're-creation' has been widely in evidence. It has led to

---

[1] Published monthly.
[2] *Decree on the Renewal of the Religious Life*, n. 2.
[3] Resolution 5.
[4] See for an introduction to his work, his collection of essays, *The Monastic Journey* (London, Sheldon Press; Mission, Kan., Sheed Andrews & McMeel, 1977).
[5] *L'Unanimité dans le pluralisme* (Taizé, 1966); (ET) *Unanimity in Pluralism* (Chicago, Francisan Herald, 1967), p. 34.

the monks and nuns of many communities discovering a new freedom for their individual growth. No longer are corporate patterns imposed as inflexibly as was sometimes the case. The different contributions of each individual are able to be expressed more fully in other ways, too, particularly through far greater community involvement in self-governing and decision-making: increased freedom has carried increased responsibility. The creative talents, dormant among some, have flourished in many places in this new mood.

In the Eastern churches, the wind of renewal has also been blowing powerfully, most notably on Mount Athos itself. The monastic revival that is taking place all over Greece is centred here with the old monasteries being repopulated and new monasteries beginning. The influence of the spiritual father, Father Paissios, and the spiritual sons of Father Joseph the Hesychast has been at the centre of much of this new growth. The new foundations and the old renewed ones, while full of young blood, have returned to old and traditional monasticism, following the cenobitic way of life. In Egypt, too, the monastic life has seen considerable growth, particularly with the Monastery of St Macarius, which is playing a major role in the spiritual awakening of the Coptic Church. The spiritual renewal of this fourth century monastery came about through Father Matta el Meskin moving there with a dozen monks in obedience to the Patriarch in 1969. As in Greece, so here, too, the renewal has deepened the traditional monasticism. In the East and in the West the renewal has also led to a strengthening of the eremitical life.

In addition to the new religious communities, the post-war years have seen an enormous increase in what David Clark has called 'basic communities'.[1] These have come into being where a group has gathered around some compelling concern, be it working for peace and reconciliation, self-sufficiency, a therapeutic community, charismatic renewal or one of many other possibilities. Links between these newer communities and the traditional ones have been developing. They have revealed the similarity of a number of issues facing both kinds of community, though sometimes from opposite positions, such as the tension between freedom and structure, the nature of commitment and a suitable model of community life. It is as communities are struggling to live out a resolution of issues such as these that they are finding themselves fulfilling part of what is spoken of as their 'prophetic role', and continuing their own exciting renewal and growth.

[1] See D. Clark, *Basic Communities.*

5 The Adaptation of Historic Spirituality for Today

MARK GIBBARD

I A DISCERNING CARE FOR EACH INDIVIDUAL

Baron von Hügel wrote, 'Souls are never dittos.' All persons, whether they realize it or not, are on a journey to discover and mature into the true self God has designed and called them to become.

It is easy for people to be swept along unreflectingly by some contemporary fashion. And in the life of prayer especially, as the liberal Dean Inge of St Paul's himself wrote, he who marries modern thought will find himself a widower tomorrow. This is why a knowledge of the spiritual classics and their tested wisdom is so necessary. Yet we can see how this study has sometimes misled people into modelling themselves artifically on some admired figure of the past. There has been only one Francis of Assisi; God never meant there to be two.

Not even Jesus was given to us to imitate literally. He was unavoidably a man of his own setting and culture, different from ours. So the New Testament Christ does not say, 'Imitate me', but 'In the way I have loved you, love one another' (John 13.34); and Paul puts it, 'Walk in love, as Christ loved us' (Eph. 5.2). As Jung rightly said, to imitate Christ means to live out our own individual destiny as authentically and wholeheartedly as he lived out his.

To be realistic about this and so to use the spiritual classics with discernment we need, in the words of Alexander Pope, 'a guide, philosopher, and friend'. Teresa of Avila stressed how essential it is to have a guide – prudent, learned and also experienced in prayer himself (*Life*, xiii); she suffered much needless trouble through inadequate guides. Beginners, she said, have a special need of a guide. All who are on this journey towards maturity – not a small élite – need this help. Paul saw it as his call and responsibility to 'present every person mature in Christ' (Col. 1.28: *teleios en Christō*). In every age the guide's task 'is not to teach his own way', as Augustine Baker wrote, 'but to enable others through the Spirit to discern the way proper for them'. So the guide must have a wide and perceptive knowledge of spiritual paths – particularly today – of other traditions. And the modern interest in oriental spirituality recalls us to the advice of Jung, that it is generally wiser for Westerners to keep their roots in their own deep, though often forgotten, contemplative tradition. 'How do you expect to arrive at the end of your journey', Thomas Merton asked, 'if you take the road to another man's city?'

2 THE NEED OF THE WIDER COMMUNITY

The journey must be really our own; but we mature into our true selves only by actually living *with* others. Our growing together in prayer and love is an integral part of God's purpose 'in the fullness of time to gather together all things into one in Christ' (Eph. 1.10). It is fundamentally our growing 'into mature human being, to the measure of the stature of the fullness of Christ' (Eph. 4.13).

This truth is increasingly recognized by ordinary men and women of prayer and love in these days of wide ecumenism. It is significant that the *Classics of Western Spirituality* are now being published in sixty volumes by SPCK and Paulist Press. *Only* 'with all the faithful' can we comprehend 'what is the breadth and length and height and depth and to know the love of Christ which surpasses knowledge' (Eph. 3.18–19). It is through this reading that we are deepened and encouraged in our praying and living in a rich communion of saints. 'Never pray without realizing', Baron von Hügel said, 'you are but one of a countless number of stars.'

3 A DISCRIMINATING USE OF THE SPIRITUAL CLASSICS

There are many dangers in the way, and notably dilettantism and hybrid spiritualities. But many people have been helped to find their own genuine way, as the years go by, through discovering one particular author always congenial and nourishing. Dom David Knowles found in Père de Caussade and his *Abandonment to the Divine Providence* 'a steady friendship not only at a period of crisis but during the ordinary flow of life'.

Guides also have to help us to distinguish between the heart of an author's teaching and the superficial conditioning of his or her own era. We need to read even Paul with discrimination; his advice on living and praying presupposes an expectancy, at least in his early letters, of the end of the world, and an acceptance of slavery which we today cannot share.

The Desert Fathers can still speak to us today, as Henri Nouwen has shown in his *Way of the Heart*, but only if we discard their excessive otherworldliness and their crude demonology. Von Hügel calls *The Imitation of Christ*, even while acclaiming it one of the greatest classics, too world-fleeing and insufficiently world-affirming. *The Cloud of Unknowing*, read now more than ever before, and Mother Julian's inspiring *Revelations of the Divine Love* both imply that anyone who is going to be deep in prayer must turn from the world.

This escapism is corrected for us by François de Sales in his *Introduction to the Devout Life*. 'It is an error, nay rather a heresy', he wrote, 'to wish to banish the life of prayer from the army, the workshop, from courts of princes, from married households.' But even he is not writing for us, but for the aristocracy or for the *haute bourgeoisie*; and his theological stance is that of the Council of Trent, not of Vatican II.

Whenever we read these spiritual classics, we need to remember that even from New Testament times there are at least distorting traces of Manicheism; in which matter, the human body and its feelings are regarded as second-rate. Ruth Burrows, a modern Carmelite nun and an authority on Teresa of Avila, rightly denounces escape from the material and the slighting of the needs of the body, as non-Christian. 'A Christian joyfully accepts his bodiliness, knowing he can go to God only through the body and that God comes to him through his body' (*To Believe in Jesus* [London, Sheed & Ward, 1978], p. 69). This of course is not to negate the genuine ascetic discipline, which runs like a thread of gold from Jesus to today.

A last and necessary caveat. We cannot grow in prayer by reading books on prayer. We learn to pray by praying and loving. 'You learn to study', said François de Sales, 'by studying, to play the lute by playing, to dance by dancing, to swim by swimming; and just so you learn to love God and man by loving. All those who think to learn in any other way deceive themselves. Start as a mere beginner, and by dint of loving you will become a master in the art.'

6 Retreat

JOHN TOWNROE

Texts

Goodacre, N., *Experiment in Retreats*. London, Mowbray, 1969.
Brother Hugh, SSF, *Making and Taking Retreats*. Leighton Buzzard, Faith, 1963.
Longridge, W., *Ignatian Retreats; Three Retreats for Lay People*. London, Mowbray; Milwaukee, Wis., Morehouse, 1926.
Schofield, R., ed., *Retreats, their Value, Method and Organization*. London, SPCK, 1927.
Stone, D., 'Retreats', in *Encyclopaedia of Religion and Ethics*, ed. J. Hastings. Edinburgh, T. & T. Clark; New York, C. Scribner, 1910–34.
Wareham, J., *The Conducting of Retreats*. London, Mowbrays; New York, Morehouse-Gorham, 1950.

Periodicals

The Vision: Journal of the Association for Promoting Retreats (APR) in association with the Roman Catholic National Retreat Movement; an annual publication containing articles and information.

Retreats Today, collected addresses by A. M. Ramsey et al., APR, 1962.

Retreats – Our Common Concern, papers given at an ecumenical conference. APR, 1969.

To make a retreat, in the Christian sense, is to seek God and to rest in his presence in a time set apart for prayer and reflection. Solitude, silence and stillness, in varying degrees, are normally regarded as necessary conditions. But the essence of the experience is not a matter of having special surroundings. It can be discovered in the midst of the city, and in the course of everyday life. For retreat is a kind of spiritual journey, paradoxically accompanying the stillness, and it is a journey inwards to know God at the centre of all things. Formal retreat is but a planned and more prolonged way of entering what is always accessible everywhere.

> As the birds have nests on the trees that they may have a retreat when they need it . . . so our hearts ought to seek out and choose some place each day . . . near to our Lord, that they may make their retreat on all occasions.[1]

Retreat appears to have been part of Jesus' own practice,[2] and its inner meaning can be discerned in the gospel passage which has shaped the Christian custom of making a retreat. 'The apostles now rejoined Jesus and reported to him all that they had done and taught. He said to them, "Come with me, by yourselves, to some lonely place where you can rest quietly"' (Mark 6.30–1). As for the first apostles, so for the modern Christian, the call comes to drop everything, and attend to the 'one thing necessary' (Luke 10.42). In the course of retreat, if the focus is on Christ, true priorities are restored in the retreatant's life, and a sense of direction renewed. 'To go into retreat is to withdraw to a vantage-point where we can not only see the present and the emerging pattern of our lives, but where we are also exposed to and bathed in the Spirit of the Lord.'[3]

Behind the practice of retreat, and influencing its development in the past and in the present, lies the idea of the desert. The desert in Christian tradition has symbolized the setting in which the traveller, stripped of non-essentials, comes face to face with God. It means a stark spiritual landscape with few landmarks, not to be crossed safely except by the highway called the way of holiness: 'those whom the Lord has rescued will travel home by that road' (Isa. 35.9). It stands for a place of pilgrimage and passage from captivity to freedom. It represents a place of

---

[1] St François de Sales, (ET) *Introduction to the Devout Life*, II.12.

[2] e.g. Mark 1.12,35; Luke 5.16.

[3] *The Franciscan* (Sept. 1970), p. 157.

spiritual combat, where the powers of evil are likely to be discovered, without and within. In Christian eyes, it signifies the scene of temptation, and of Christ's triumph after trial: 'where Israel fell, Jesus shows the way to victory'.[1] Some or all of these features of the symbolism are likely to reappear in the making of a retreat. For the purpose of retreat is to dispel illusion, to set aside distraction, and to penetrate the crust of superficiality in personal existence, which can deaden sensitivity to the reality of God.

Properly understood, therefore, retreat is not an escape into unreality, but the very opposite. It is a time for facing the truth and for coming to grips with the real situation in the retreatant's life. It can be a time for conversion. Consequently, a period of struggle may be necessary before the retreatant can enter into the peace of God, and experience inner 'rest' in harmony with God's will. For fantasies are slow to let go of their prisoners.

> Solitude allows man to discover, and so to face, all the obscure forces that he bears within himself . . . It is not only the depths of our own soul that we discover, but the obscure powers that are as it were lurking there, whose slaves we must inevitably remain so long as we are not aware of them . . . Only Christ can open out to us with impunity 'the mystery of iniquity', because he alone, *in* us today as *for* us in the past, can confront it successfully.[2]

Retreat can be seen in this light as the work of Christ in the retreatant overcoming the opposition, and setting the disciple free.

Organized retreats began under the influence of the Counter-Reformation, particularly of St Ignatius Loyola and his *Spiritual Exercises*.[3] The Jesuits were the first Order to make it a matter of rule to go into retreat regularly, and the laity was encouraged to do so by leaders like St François de Sales, St Vincent de Paul, Bérulle, J. J. Olier, and others. Retreat houses were opened in the seventeenth century where 'conductors' were available to guide those who came. The habit of making an annual retreat became widespread in the Roman Catholic Church in the nineteenth century. The Oxford Movement fostered the growth of the practice in the Church of England: the first retreats were held in 1856 at Chislehurst in Kent and in Christ Church, Oxford.

The twentieth century has seen a rapid increase in the number of retreat centres of many kinds, and hunger for what they can provide. 'It

---

[1] I. H. Marshall, *The Gospel of Luke* (Exeter, Paternoster Press; Grand Rapids, Eerdmans, 1978), p. 166.
[2] Louis Bouyer, (ET) *The Spirituality of the New Testament and the Fathers* (Burns & Oates, 1963), p. 313.
[3] See pp. 360–2.

seems strange to say so, but what can help modern man find answers to his own mystery and the mystery of him in whose image he is created, is silence, solitude – in a word, the desert'.[1] But there is more variety in the types of retreat being offered than ever before. Different needs call for different methods. The well-tried 'preached' (Roman Catholic) or 'conducted' (Anglican) retreats continue, at which addresses are given by a conductor to a group of retreatants, who maintain silence all or some of the time. 'Directed' or 'One-to-one' retreats are widely available to meet the needs of individuals who desire to go into silence and solitude, and yet wish to have the help of a daily meeting with a director.

At the same time, in an age when many live, through no choice of their own, in acutely lonely circumstances, and in a period when the churches are emphasizing the corporate nature of the Christian life, new styles of 'Christian Community Retreat' are being developed by several organizations. The general aim is a living experience of Christian community through worship together, dialogue, shared prayer and shared reflection on fundamental themes of the gospel and the mission of the Church in the world. The Movement for a Better World, founded in 1952 by Father Riccardo Lombardi, is instrumental in promoting retreats of this kind in many parts of the world. The purpose is as much for parochial as it is for individual renewal, in the spirit of Vatican II. Ecumenical retreats along similar lines are held in some places. The Focolare Movement, originating in Italy after the Second World War, works also through such shared experiences of prayer and rekindling of the fire of the Spirit, in the setting of life together. The Cursillo Movement from Spain presents another type, also with an emphasis on community and sharing, with a course of study centred upon the Christian apostolate, the sacraments and the renewal of the Church.

The variety of retreats seems certain to multiply, as the rigidity of former moulds is broken. Examples of a more specialized kind of retreat can be indicated by their titles: Marriage Encounter, Marriage Enrichment, Engagement Encounter, Monica Retreats for Widows, Prayer Workshops, At Home Retreats, Walk into Silence or Drop In Days, Spiritual Growth through Journalling, Retreat through Drama, Zen-Christian Retreat, Prayer and Painting, Celebration of Pentecost, Christian Yoga, and Desert Experience.

Viewed as a whole, the modern retreat movement shows marvellous vitality. If it continues to draw upon its original sources, while venturing forward in liberty of spirit, many creative developments are sure to follow.

[1] C. de H. Doherty, *Poustinia* (Notre Dame, Ind., Ave Maria Press, 1975), p. 20.

7 Spirituality and Social Justice

KENNETH LEECH

SPIRITUAL DISCERNMENT

Leech, K. *True Prayer*. London, Sheldon Press; New York, Harper & Row, 1980.

Leech, K., *True God*. London, Sheldon, 1985 = *Experiencing God*, New York, Harper & Row, 1985.

SPIRITUAL RESOURCES FOR SOCIAL AND POLITICAL STRUGGLE

Ambler, R., and Haslam, D., ed., *Agenda for Prophets: towards a political theology for Britain*. London, Bowerdean Press, 1980.

Kee, A., ed., *Seeds of Liberation*. London, SCM, 1973.

Kee, A., ed., *A Reader in Political Theology*. London, SCM, 1974; Philadelphia, Westminster, 1975.

Kee, A., ed., *The Scope of Political Theology*. London, SCM, 1978.

Leech, K., *The Social God*. London, Sheldon, 1981.

THOMAS MERTON

His writings are too numerous even to summarize, as are studies of his life and thought. Of particular importance in this context are the following:

Contemplative Prayer. New York, Herder & Herder, 1969; London, DLT, 1973.

The New Man. New York, Mentor Books, 1963.

Faith and Violence. University of Notre Dame Press, 1968.

EVANGELICAL SOCIAL THOUGHT

Wallis, J., *Agenda for Biblical People*. New York, Harper & Row, 1973.

Wallis, J., *The Call to Conversion*. New York, Harper & Row, 1981; Tring, Lion Books, 1982.

Webber, R. E., *The Secular Saint: a case for evangelical social responsibility*. Zondervan, Grand Rapids, 1979.

LATIN AMERICAN THEOLOGY

Brown, R. McA., *Theology in a New Key*. Philadelphia, Westminster Press, 1978.

Galilea, S. 'Liberation as an encounter with politics and contemplation', in *The Mystical and Political Dimension of the Christian Faith* (*Concilium*, 89, Nov. 1973); also reprinted in Richard Woods, ed., *Understanding Mysticism* (Garden City, N.Y., Doubleday [Image Books], 1980; London, Athlone Press, 1981), pp. 529–40.

Gutierrez, G., (ET) *A Theology of Liberation*. Maryknoll, N.Y., Orbis, 1973; London, SCM, 1974.

Runyon, T., ed., *Sanctification and Liberation*. Nashville, Abingdon Press, 1981.

CREATION-CENTRED AND INCARNATIONAL SPIRITUALITY

Fox, M., ed., *Western Spirituality: historical roots, ecumenical routes.* Notre Dame, Ind., Fides/Claretian, 1979.
Fox, M., *A Spirituality Named Compassion: The healing of the global village, Humpty Dumpty and us.* Minneapolis, Winston, 1979.

THE BIBLE, JESUS, AND THE KINGDOM OF GOD

Boerma, C., (ET) *Rich Man, Poor Man and the Bible.* London, SCM; Philadelphia, Westminster, 1979.
Cassidy, R. J., *Jesus, Politics and Society.* Maryknoll, Orbis, 1978.
Miranda, J. P., *Marx and the Bible.* Maryknoll, Orbis, 1974; London, SCM, 1977.
Pixley, G. V., *God's Kingdom.* London, SCM; Maryknoll, Orbis, 1981.
Yoder, J. H., *The Politics of Jesus.* Grand Rapids, Eerdmans, 1972.

PATRISTIC WRITINGS

Evans, S. G., *The Social Hope of the Christian Church.* London, Hodder, 1965.
Marson, C., 'The social teaching of the early Fathers', in *Vox Clamantium*, ed. Andrew Reid (A. D. Innes, 1894), pp. 198–224.

LITURGY AND SOCIAL JUSTICE

Balasuriya, T., *The Eucharist and Human Liberation.* Maryknoll, Orbis, 1977; London, SCM, 1979.
Robinson, J. A. T., 'Matter, power and liturgy', in *On Being the Church in the World* (London, SCM, 1964 edn), pp. 30–71.
Searle, M., ed., *Liturgy and Social Justice.* Collegeville, Minnesota, Liturgical Press, 1980.

In recent years the necessary link between spirituality and social justice has been increasingly asserted. On the one hand, the revival of gnostic and 'privatized' styles of spirituality has led to the need for discernment and discrimination between true and false, healthy and pathological, spiritual trends. Since the 1960s there has been a growing concern to provide spiritual resources and nourishment for the work of social and political struggle. The late Thomas Merton, in many books and articles, emphasized the interconnection of contemplation and justice. There is now a strong renewal of social concern and social theology among many evangelicals, and a recovery of the biblical sources of social action. Latin American theologians, contrary to much popular Western misinterpretation, are deeply concerned with 'liberation spirituality', the incarnational nature of the Christian spiritual tradition, and the prophetic dimension in prayer.

The biblical foundations for a theology which unites holiness and justice, the contemplative/mystical and the prophetic/political dimensions, are well established. The Law and the prophets link the knowledge of God with the pursuit of justice and the defence of the poor. The consensus among New Testament scholars that the Kingdom of God is central to the preaching of Jesus, and that this Kingdom is not a purely personal, inward or otherworldly hope, has undermined ideas of the ministry of Jesus as 'apolitical'. There is considerable patristic writing which relates prayer and social action. The notion that Christianity is primarily a religion of personal salvation is in fact a modern one, though it is sometimes mistaken for Christian orthodoxy. But the orthodox tradition has always rejected the false dichotomy between personal and social, rooting its concern with the inward in a materialistic and socially-based theology. Hence the stress throughout the tradition on the social dimensions of the liturgy.

It is misleading therefore to think of piety as essentially world-avoiding and reflective, while 'radical' Christians are characterized by involvement and activism. There are harmful forms of piety, and superficial forms of social radicalism. But authentic piety must have major social consequences for it demands a radical *metanoia*. Mystics and prophets are in fact remarkably akin. Those who are engaged in struggles for justice need to be more, not less, concerned with inner ascetic disciplines and spiritual direction. For, in conflicts with evil, undernourished and inadequately armed combatants are unreliable and ineffective. Prophecy is always a by-product of vision, action arising out of contemplation and enriched insight. The deepening of such contemplative vision and insight is therefore of central importance in the critique of oppression, in the unmasking of illusion, and in the struggle for the new age of God's *Shalom*.

8 Prayer and Theological Reflection

JOHN MACQUARRIE

In the Western Church today there is some tension between theology and spirituality. The faithful say their prayers and aspire to holiness, but sometimes what they are doing seems threatened by the theologian, who may be reaching conclusions that seem hard to square with the faith that finds expression in prayer and worship. Though the separation of theology and spirituality is in part due to the pressure on theologians to defend the academic status of their subject in the universities, it is equally due to the indifference and even contempt shown for theology by some clergy and laypeople.

Theology claims to be a science, while prayer is a desire and longing. The sciences seek to describe things as they are, and this means that the scientific mind must be as far as possible dispassionate. Does this mean that theologians must exclude prayer from their reflections? Tillich once warned theologians not to 'fill in logical gaps with devotional material'.[1] That would destroy theology's claim to be a science.

But what do we mean when we say that theology is a science? Sciences are of many kinds, and theology is clearly not a natural science, as, say, geology is. Theology is a science in the sense that it is an intellectual discipline with its rules of orderly procedure and its standards of intellectual integrity. Each science, however, has to formulate its own methods in accordance with its particular subject-matter. If one considers theological method as set out by Lonergan in *Method in Theology*, I think that the whole procedure he describes, beginning with the establishment of texts and ending with the communication of the content of faith, can be justly called 'scientific'. Many elements in it, e.g. methods of textual criticism and of historical investigation, are shared with other disciplines that claim to follow scientific procedures. But Lonergan also claims that a precondition of theological study is what he calls 'orientation to transcendental mystery'.[2] This distinguishes theology from all other sciences, but it does not take away its scientific character. On the contrary, such a unique and exalted subject-matter demands to be pursued with the utmost intellectual endeavour and the most stringent honesty.

Deeper reflection shows that the science of theology and the practice of prayer are closer than we ordinarily think. The scientific frame of mind (not only in theology, but in any intellectual discipline) is not far from some of the characteristics of prayer. The truly scientific mind knows humility and docility. The man or woman who pursues a science is humble, submitting himself or herself to the truth; the same person is docile, open and ready to be taught.

Humility and docility are the beginning, the first steps in the formation of a certain kind of mentality. It is not surprising that theology and other sciences are called 'intellectual disciplines'. We call them disciplines because those who engage in them voluntarily accept certain rules, principles and procedures by which they mean to abide. True scientists (in-

[1] Paul Tillich, *Systematic Theology*, I (University of Chicago Press, 1951; London, SCM, 1978), p. 118.
[2] Bernard Lonergan, *Method in Theology* (New York, Herder, 1971; London, DLT, 1972), p. 341.

cluding theologians) internalize these ways of pursuing their subject so that it becomes part of them, and that is why I spoke of the 'formation' of a certain type of mentality. Again, the parallel with prayer and spirituality is obvious.

The Greek word for training is *askēsis*, and spirituality has its 'ascetical' side. But the pursuit of an intellectual discipline has also its ascetic characteristics. These are clear in the very vocabulary that we use. We talk of scholars being 'devoted' to their subject and of the 'rigour' and 'strictness' of their pursuit of truth. Thinkers in all subjects have also to learn the meaning of *metanoia* as change of mind and repentance, when their studies lead them to set aside long cherished theories and opinions in the light of fuller truth. Perhaps this is especially painful in theology, which is in fact inseparable from a kind of mortification. Everything in one's mind, no matter how long or how tenaciously one has clung to it, must be brought into the light, tested and scrutinized, and, if it stands in the way of fuller truth, be allowed to die. This is painful, for something of oneself dies with it. I doubt if there is anyone who has studied theology with a sincere and open mind, and has not found it to be sometimes a painful pursuit. So the Bible is not, after all, an inerrant book? So the existence of God is not, after all, demonstrable by reason? So the great dogmas of the Church are not, after all, free in their formulation from cultural relativisms and even ideological influences? Theology is an uncomfortable study, even a mortification, and if one has never experienced the discomfort, then perhaps one has never been in earnest with theology. Mortification and shattering, together with rising and rebuilding, belong to the work of the theologian, and is not this very like the pathway of spirituality?

Most of the above would apply to any science or intellectual discipline. Let me now be more specific and mention some peculiarities of theology, linking it inescapably with prayer.

The first point is that theology goes on within the community of the Church. The theologian is not merely an individual investigator, but a member of the Body of Christ with the special function of expounding, interpreting and sometimes criticizing the faith of the Church in a given situation. The business of theology, even in its critical function, is to bring to expression the faith of the people of God, not merely the opinions of the individual theologian, though, of course, the theologian's individuality will not be entirely lost in the process. But theologians can perform their work only as they participate in the community, especially its liturgical life.

The second point is that the kind of thinking which is required in theology has at its heart an act of meditation. In most sciences, thinking has an active investigative character – there is inquiry, calculation, argumentation and so on. These also have their place in theology. But the heart of theology is deep meditation on the great central themes of Christian faith. This kind of thinking has a passive rather than an active character. The mind has to be open and receptive to the themes which it entertains. We speak of revelation, and we use this word because Christian truth is not something that we make up but something that is given to us in the acts of God in Israel, in Christ and in the Church. The theologian meditates and ponders deeply upon the given of God's revelation, though he or she has also the *task* of interpreting and applying it. Again, this pattern is close to that of prayer and the action to which it leads.

A last point is all-important, and marks off theology from every other science. The subject-matter of theology is God, the Holy and Ultimate Reality. This is not a subject-matter that can be subjected to scrutiny, manipulated, made the matter for an experiment, or anything of the sort. We can know God only in the way that we know other personal beings, that is to say, by communion or communication at a personal level. Indeed, we could say that we know God only to the extent that he knows us, through his gracious self-communication and revelation. But what is this communion with God if it is not prayer and worship?

Thus theology includes prayer and is even, in some respects, a kind of prayer itself. It is not surprising that such great theologians as Augustine and Anselm slip naturally from speaking *about* God to speaking *to* him, and we experience no awkwardness in this transition.

We have seen that theology needs spirituality. But the converse is also true – spirituality needs theology. From the days of the church at Corinth, there have been instances of spirituality that has gone astray through its very exuberance. Spirituality needs understanding, and it is such understanding that theology supplies. A theology without spirituality would be a sterile academic exercise. A spirituality without theology can become superstition or fanaticism or the quest for excitement. Theology and spirituality need one another within the unity of the Christian life.

9 Christian Spirituality and Healing

JOHN TOWNROE

Bryant, C., *The River Within*. London, DLT, 1978.
Dearmer, P., *Body and Soul*. London, Pitman; New York, E. P. Dutton, 1909.
East, R., *Heal the Sick*. London, Hodder & Stoughton; Minneapolis, Bethany Fellowship, 1977.
Faricy, R., *Praying for Inner Healing*. London, SCM; New York, Paulist, 1979.
Frost, E., *Christian Healing*. London, Mowbrays, 1940.
Häring, B., (ET) *Healing and Revealing*. Slough, St Paul Publications, 1984.
Harper, M., *Spiritual Warfare*. London, Hodder & Stoughton; Plainfield, N.J., Logos International, 1970.
Harris, C., 'Visitation of the Sick', in *Liturgy and Worship*, ed. W. K. L. Clarke. London, SPCK; New York, Macmillan, 1932, reprint 1981.
Jackson, E. J., *The Role of Faith in the Process of Healing*. London, SCM; Minneapolis, Winston, 1981.
Jung, C., (ET) *Memories, Dreams and Reflections*. London, Collins; New York, Pantheon Books, 1963.
Kelsey, M., *Healing and Christianity*. New York, Harper & Row, 1973.
Lambourne, R., *Community, Church and Healing*. London, DLT, 1973.
MacNutt, F., *Healing*. Notre Dame, Ind., Ave Maria, 1974.
MacNutt, F., *The Power to Heal*. Notre Dame, Ind., Ave Maria, 1974.
Maddocks, M., *The Christian Healing Ministry*. SPCK, 1981.
Melinsky, M. A. H., *Healing Miracles*. London, Mowbray, 1968.
Richards, J., *But Deliver Us From Evil*. London, DLT; New York, Seabury, 1974.
Sanford, A., *The Healing Gifts of the Spirit*. Evesham, James; Philadelphia, Lippincott, 1966.
Scanlan, M., *Inner Healing*. New York, Paulist, 1974.
Taylor, J. V., *The Go-Between God*. London, SCM, 1972; Philadelphia, Fortress, 1973.
Tournier, P. (ET) *The Meaning of Persons*. London, SCM; New York, Harper, 1957.
Weatherhead, L., *Psychology, Religion and Healing*. London, Hodder & Stoughton; New York, Abingdon–Cokesbury, 1951.
Wilson, J., *Go; Preach the Kingdom, Heal the Sick*. London, Clarke, 1962.
Wilson, M., *Health is for People*. London, DLT, 1975.

For the love of God, beware of illness as much as you can, so that as far as possible your self is not the cause of any weakness . . . For the love of God, control your body and soul with great care, and keep as fit as you can.[1]

Here speaks the positive, life-affirming voice of Christian spirituality, in

---

[1] *The Cloud of Unknowing* (Harmondsworth and New York, Penguin; 1961), p. 41.

this case from plague-ridden England of the fourteenth century. The voice is also realistic: 'should illness come in spite of everything, have patience and wait humbly for God's mercy.' Between the twin poles of the passive acceptance of unavoidable suffering and the active care of health and work for healing, Christian spirituality moves with varying emphases, first in one direction, then in the other.

In the twentieth century, Christian spirituality in its literature and practice has moved in the second direction, showing a more challenging attitude towards disease, and a wider concern for human development, personal and social. Wholeness in body, mind and spirit is presented as a goal to which ascetics need not run counter, and should indeed subserve. Wholeness and holiness, if not precisely synonymous, are regarded as related. 'Properly understood, prayer is a mature act which is essential for the complete development of the personality . . . It is only in prayer that we can achieve the complete and harmonious union of body, mind and spirit'.[1] (Compare the illustrations of the body at prayer, Plate 20.) The incarnation is seen to have implications for the redemption of every aspect of the world's activity.[2] At the same time, in society generally, a larger concept of health has begun to take hold, as meaning not merely the absence of sickness, but the realization of human potential. Advances in clinical medicine, pharmacology and psychiatry have helped to create a new climate of expectation. Partly through the growth of nuclear physics and a changed scientific and philosophical outlook, some writers have questioned the very distinction between the physical and the spiritual, as hitherto understood.

It is in this changing atmosphere that the Christian ministry of healing, as distinct from forms of 'faith-healing' which deny the value of scientific medicine, has been renewed in the churches.[3] But misunderstandings and hesitations persist, and the belief expressed by the Lambeth Conference of 1978 has still to be carried fully into effect: 'The healing of the sick in his name is as much part of the proclamation of the Kingdom as the preaching of the Good News of Jesus Christ'.[4]

A fruitful meeting-point between spirituality and medicine lies in the fact that it is the *vis medicatrix naturae*, the recreative power of nature, which brings healing. Physicians and surgeons do not directly heal anybody: they seek by their skills to remove obstacles to nature's healing

---

[1] Dr Alexis Carrel, quoted in H. Caffarel, *The Body at Prayer* (London, SPCK, 1978), p. 20.

[2] e.g. P. Teilhard de Chardin, (ET) *Le Milieu Divin*, London, Collins; New York, Harper, 1960.

[3] See M. Maddocks, *The Christian Healing Ministry* (London, SPCK, 1981).

[4] *Lambeth Report* (London, Church Information Office, 1978), p. 40, resolution 8.

energies, as when they correct chemical imbalances in the body, or take away diseased tissue. Means which touch the human spirit, such as are employed in the ministry of healing by prayer and sacrament, may equally be seen as seeking to liberate and quicken by grace the God-given forces within human nature.

Three aspects of the subject attract attention, and developments in each can be expected.

1   INNER HEALING, OR THE HEALING OF THE MEMORIES

Faith in God's power to heal has to reckon with the fact that there appear to be 'blocks' in a disordered world and within human personality to receiving God's healing energies. Such obstacles may be moral, in the form of unrepented sin. They may also be due to emotional disturbances caused by past 'wounds' to the spirit. Inner healing is concerned to bring to light the causes of the inner pain; to help the sufferer to interpret them correctly; and to release the person from the emotional grip of the past. Prayer and meditation play a crucial part in this exodus from captivity. Deeper levels of the mind are reached in contemplative prayer, when the focus is upon God alone, and the soul waits upon him. Inner healing comes also in corporate worship, when the gaze is Godward and the worshipper is lifted by the Spirit out of self-centredness or narrowness of vision.[1] Closer union with God in the depth of the spirit thus brings an integration of the whole person around the new Centre, and it is quite usual for physical health to be improved.

2   HEALING AND COMMUNITY

Diseases are caught in a diseased society. Environment counts, for better or for worse. 'It is cruel and false to brand every sufferer as a sinner: much suffering and sickness is due to the sin either of other persons, or of society in general.'[2] Conversely, communities have sprung up, such as that of Taizé in France, which embody in their life an element of protest and prophetic witness to the world, while being in themselves centres of support and prayer, where the healthy effects of true community may be experienced in microcosm (see pp. 573–4).

3   VARIETIES OF HEALING MINISTRIES

There is in some churches a growth of less formal kinds of reaching out to minister to the sick in the name of Christ, alongside the sacramental ministries of Eucharist, anointing,[3] laying on of hands, reconciliation of

---

[1] See *SL*, pp. 530–1.
[2] *Lambeth Conference Report* (London, SPCK, 1958), 2.92.
[3] A change in the attitude of the Roman Catholic Church, following the Second Vatican

penitents, and occasionally exorcism. The dedicated use by every member of Christ of his or her personal gift of the Spirit enables the local church to become an actively healing community. Where some have a physical gift of healing through the hands (a phenomenon still little understood, though real), they may use it as members of a parish team, and are sometimes licensed by a bishop for a wider ministry.

Healing seems to be restored as a normal part of the Church's ministry and of the Christian experience, wherever the Church is alive with faith in Christ. But, as with the mission to evangelize the world, so with the healing work of Christ in his Church, opposition abounds and the story is one of failure as well as success. God reigns, and the word is preached 'with signs following'. But the end is not yet, and in Christian perspective the total healing of people and nations waits for the consummation of all things, when God shall be all in all.

Council, is reflected in its new rite of Anointing (January 1974) which is for the express purpose of the healing of the whole person, and no longer primarily a preparation for death (*Constitution on the Liturgy*, n. 73).

II

TYPES OF SPIRITUALITY

GEOFFREY WAINWRIGHT

In establishing a typology of the relations between Christ and culture, H. Richard Niebuhr was particularly concerned with social ethics.[1] Niebuhr's typology has more recently been applied to the Church's liturgy.[2] It can also be used to illuminate the combination of praying and living which is spirituality. Not only did Niebuhr refine Troeltsch's three types into five, he also passed beyond sociological description to theological discrimination: he adopted a 'theocentric' criterion in the belief that 'all this relative history of men and movements is under the governance of the absolute God'. The criterion can be made more acute by sharpening providential talk of divine government into eschatological language about God's Kingdom. The eschatological vision and teaching of the Scriptures, particularly of the New Testament, will set our standard, though exegesis and hermeneutics are always interrelated, and nowhere more so than in questions of eschatology.

I CHRIST AGAINST CULTURE

In this first of Niebuhr's five types, the world is 'a naughty world'. The Synoptic Gospels present the ministry of Jesus as a conflict between the Kingdom of God and the Kingdom of Beelzebub; but even after the death and resurrection of Christ, I John 5.19 can still say that 'the whole world lieth in the evil one'. Here eschatology is of the most discontinuous kind: the world to come and this world are direct opposites; the one will simply replace the other. In the corresponding spirituality, this world is merely a place to be 'out of'. The form taken by such a spirituality varies with the historical circumstances.

In the earliest centuries of the Church, it was embodied in a spirituality of martyrdom. The Lord himself warned his followers that they would have to testify before governors and kings (Mark 13.9). New Testament writings such as I Peter and Revelation directly reflect a stituation in which Christians are persecuted. The hostile world has no place for Christians, and itself sees to their dispatch. The world imposes on Chris-

---

[1] H. Richard Niebuhr, *Christ and Culture*. New York, Harper & Row, 1951.
[2] Geoffrey Wainwright, *Doxology: The Praise of God in Worship, Doctrine and Life* (London, Epworth; New York, OUP, 1980), ch. 11.

tians a conformity to the suffering Christ. It is not simply a matter of following the example of Christ under suffering, as 1 Pet. 2.21 might suggest. Rather, to suffer 'for the name of Christ', to suffer 'as a Christian', is to *share* the sufferings of Christ, and to have the prospect of a share in his glory (1 Pet. 4.12—5.11); indeed the spirit of glory already rests upon you (4.14). The same combination of themes occurs in Rom. 8.15–39. The story of the martyrs of Lyons and Vienne, from the year 177, exemplifies the martyrs' conformity to Christ.[1] Blandina is there said to have been 'clothed with Christ'. As she was tied to the stake in prayer, her fellow-Christians saw in their sister the crucified Lord. And when she was at last thrown to the wild beasts, she went 'like one bidden to a marriage supper'. The 'baptism of blood' was in fact popularly held to give immediate access to the heavenly feast. There were indeed Christians who could hardly wait for martyrdom. The best-known example, from his own letters, is Ignatius of Antioch, already at the beginning of the second century. Had not the apostle himself, writing from prison, said that he would rather 'depart and be with Christ' (Phil. 1.23)? It may be asked whether there is not something pathological about the search for martyrdom. Is it not already sufficient, and difficult enough, to be prepared for martyrdom, if the world imposes it? If we were to take more seriously our task of 'witness' (the broader sense of martyrdom), might not martyrdom in its sharpest sense in any case occur more frequently?

As a matter of fact, the intermittent persecution of Christians practically came to a halt with the so-called conversion of the Empire, begun by Constantine and established under Theodosius. The spirituality of martyrdom was transformed: bloody martyrdom gave way to the 'white martyrdom' of monasticism (see p. 221). Persecuted or not, pre-Constantinian Christians had been well aware that their earthly attachments were relativized by their heavenly citizenship (cf. Phil. 3.20; Heb. 13.14). Ascetic practices were of a piece with what Christians perceived as their own extraterritorial status: the Epistle to Diognetus expressed that status of Christians by saying that, for them, every foreign land was fatherland, and every fatherland foreign; Origen declared that Christians had 'another system of fatherland' (*Contra Celsum*, VIII.75). Tertullian, who could say of himself '*secessi de populo*', prejudged the political side of the fourth-century problematic when he asserted the mutual incompatibility of being Caesar and being a Christian.[2] When the Roman emperor did turn Christian, numbers of lay Christians showed themselves sufficiently uneasy with the implications and consequences of his conversion to embark upon a movement of 'withdrawal' (anchoritism) (see pp.

[1] See Eusebius, *Church History*, V, 1, 3ff.
[2] Tertullian, *De Pallio*, 5 (*PL* 2.1102); and *Apol.*, 21.24 (*PL* 1.461). See above, pp. 109–11.

158–60). Apart from the theoretic problem of the secular ruler's relation to the divine Kingdom (which Eusebius of Caesarea settled *in bonam partem*), there was the practical inevitability of the qualitative decline of the Church as more and more people were first allowed, then encouraged, and finally required to become members of it. Some would say that the seeds of the Church's accommodation to the world were already present in Luke–Acts where, according to H. Conzelmann's thesis in *Die Mitte der Zeit*, eschatology takes on a *heilsgeschichtlich* (salvation-history) cast which will eventually allow the Church to settle down in human history. In any case, the growth of monasticism in the fourth century appears as a protest, or at least a warning, against the compromising of heavenly citizenship through earthly entanglements (see pp. 128–30). Alexander Schmemann insists that monasticism is not substantially new but is the continuation, in the form made necessary by the events of the fourth century, of 'the ethical and spiritual maximalism of the pre-Nicene epoch'.[1]

The monks went first to the desert. In terms of our eschatological typology, George Florovsky proposed the proportion: the Desert is to the Empire as Apocalypse is to History.[2] In its coenobitic form, monasticism essayed an alternative society, a new community that now stood out, not simply against the pagan world as it had done from the beginning, but even against imperial Christianity. From its first moment of detachment monasticism in its communal form quickly returned to the midst of the world, impelled by an obligation to bear witness. It played its part in the effort to construct a Christian empire; and for this reason I will return to monasticism under our fifth type: Christ the transformer of culture.

But let us stay a little longer with the world-renouncing moment of Christianity. This thrust has persisted throughout monastic history and comes to its most pronounced form in the strictly eremitical life. Protestantism has never had much room for monasticism in any form, seeing it as connected, whether by abuse or by its very nature, with works-righteousness. But even the classical Lutheran vision of the world as the place in which all Christians exercise their 'vocation' carries with it a certain world-renouncing moment, in so far as the exercise of *Beruf*, in virtue of the radical doctrine of justification through faith alone, is non-salvific. Lutheranism itself is not without its occasional version of the hermit. I think of Søren Kierkegaard in his reaction to Danish Christendom:

[1] Alexander Schmemann, *Introduction to Liturgical Theology*, 2nd edn (Crestwood, N.Y., St Vladimir's Seminary Press; Leighton Buzzard, Faith Press, 1975), p. 101.
[2] George Florovsky, *Christianity and Culture = Collected Works*, vol. ii (Belmont, Mass., Nordland, 1974), p. 128. The first five chapters are all relevant to our theme.

The spiritual man differs from us men in being able to endure isolation. His rank as a spiritual man is proportionate to his strength for enduring isolation, whereas we men are constantly in need of 'the others', the herd . . . But the Christianity of the New Testament is precisely reckoned upon and related to this isolation of the spiritual man. Christianity in the New Testament consists in loving God, in hatred to man, in hatred of oneself, and thereby of other men, hating father, mother, one's own child, wife, etc., the strongest expression for the most agonizing isolation.[1]

The irony is complex, but the message is plain.

Another non-monastic example of world-renouncing spirituality is provided by pentecostalism. That line stretches, perhaps with interruptions, from the ancient Montanists, who attracted Tertullian from the catholic Church (see pp. 109–11), to the twentieth-century pentecostal movement which arose in North America and Great Britain but is also significantly present in southern Europe and Latin America (see pp. 549–54). *Glossolalia* can be understood as a counter-cultural protest against the rationalistic and materialistic language of late Western Christendom.

Now in one sense this eschatology of discontinuity is an eschatology of the 'not yet', perhaps even an eschatology of the 'never', for the world may appear as beyond redemption in this perspective. Yet a spirituality of world-renunciation may also come full circle and imply a kind of 'over-realized' eschatology. The world may never be saved, but extracted believers are already fully in the Kingdom of God. The apostle needed to remind the drunken Corinthians that the Lord's *death* had to be proclaimed *until he come*. Those monks, the so-called 'sleepless ones', who were dedicated to perpetual psalmody, were attempting to anticipate the ceaseless praise envisioned in the Book of Revelation (though in actual practice they could only manage it by alternating shifts). The classical Reformers tried to cool the 'enthusiasts'. Those who speak with the tongues of angels need reminding that our knowledge is still partial. The churches of the word have, however, reserved their gravest suspicion for the mystics, who 'presumptuously' claim present union with God; though in fairness it should be noted that the greatest Christian mystics recognize the incompleteness of their present experience, both on account of its intermittency and on account of the unfathomability of God.[2]

Granted that a cruel world may impose suffering on Christians, the

---

[1] Kierkegaard's *Attack upon 'Christendom'*, quoted by Niebuhr, *Christ and Culture*, p. 180.

[2] A sympathetic account of mysticism is given in Andrew Louth, *The Origins of the Christian Mystical Tradition: From Plato to Denys* (Oxford, Clarendon; New York, OUP, 1981).

trouble with a world-renouncing spirituality in its simplistic forms is that it underestimates the world – either in its stubbornness (how much 'world' remains even in the converted!) or in its destiny as the object of God's love (John 3.16). That is why other types of spirituality have emerged.

2   THE CHRIST OF CULTURE

Here the pendulum swings to the other end of its track, to simplistic world-affirmation. This is the type of which Niebuhr rightly had least good to say.

The Church was in duty bound to take advantage of the evangelistic opportunities provided by the Emperor's conversion. In the ancient world, however, it was probably a political and sociological inevitability that the shift in the Emperor's own allegiance should bring about the institutionalization of Christianity into the official religion. And that institutionalization brought with it the practical danger of the absorption of the faith by the political and social reality of the Empire, whether Byzantine or Carolingian. It was natural that emperors should seek to make the Church subserve political ends. It is understandable that a conveniently widespread episcopate and a learned clergy should have been put to administrative tasks which necessitated compromises. It was a moral certainty that the propagation and maintenance of Christianity by political pressure and social conformism would diminish the spiritual quality of a religion whose origins lay in deliberate personal response to the preaching of a gospel and the call to discipleship. At its worst, Constantinian Christendom reduces Christ to a culture-hero, the sanction for a value-system whose deepest roots may be sunk in soil quite alien and perhaps hostile to the character, teaching, work and destiny of Jesus.

A post-imperial example of the Christ-of-culture type may perhaps be found, however unlikely this may appear (precisely) on the surface, in Puritan theocracy. Legal constraints may be necessary to hold the anti-social effects of sin in check (as will be admitted later in the argument), but legislation cannot bring forth virtue, let alone the fruits of the Spirit. The temptation to merely external observance of Christian rites and codes can of course produce hypocritical individuals: it can also render the spirituality of an entire community hollow. The problems are illustrated by the process centring on 'the half-way covenant' in seventeenth- and eighteenth-century New England.

A more modern instance of his second type is adduced by Niebuhr: it is the *Kulturprotestantismus* whose theological representative he takes Albrecht Ritschl to be. For Ritschl, culture marked man's moral victory over nature – a post-Kantian translation of the Kingdom of God. Ritschl himself held that 'the Person of the Founder . . . is the key to the Christian view of the world, and the standard of Christians' self-judgement and moral effort', as well as the standard which shows how such specifically religious acts as prayer should be carried on.[1] But the ease with which any *soi-disant* culture can be legitimated when talk of 'the brotherhood of man' takes over, as it did in Ritschl, from the Kingdom of God, is shown by the degeneration of Ritschlian and Harnackian Protestantism into *deutsches Christentum*. How little distant culture may be removed from (fallen) nature is demonstrated by the slogans of *Blut und Boden! Ein Volk, ein Reich, ein Führer!* (Blood and soil! One people, one nation, one leader!).

Anachronistically, we can view the earlier examples so far given of the Christ-of-culture type as 'conservative' in character. But contemporary liberalism (in its day, of course, Ritschlianism appeared liberal) succumbs to the same temptation. In the early 'sixties Harvey Cox was celebrating *The Secular City*. By the early 'seventies he was into the touchy-feely spirituality of California, in *The Seduction of the Spirit*. In the early 'eighties Cox rediscovered *Religion in the Secular City*. It is possible to regress from Christianity through civil religion to natural religion. This danger is perhaps particularly in evidence in a country which, since the beginning of its independent existence, has been dedicated to the 'self-evident truth', understood in an Enlightenment sense, that 'all men . . . are endowed . . . with certain inalienable rights', and among them 'life, liberty, and the pursuit of happiness'. In any case, liberalism seems always to align itself with worldly fashions and, entering into matrimony with the spirit of the age, risks being widowed in the next.

The fatal flaw of the Christ-of-culture position is its secularization of eschatology; but that is in fact a contradiction in terms, for there can be no eschatology which sets its own constitutive realization entirely within the present *saeculum*. The Christ-of-culture position has no eschatology because, as is particularly clear in its liberal forms, it has no 'fall'; and since it has no fall, it has no redemption. It remains at the stage of protology, i.e. at the level of the 'ordinances of creation', without an awareness that the order of creation has always to be modified – on account of sin – into an order of preservation, waiting for the order of redemption which is the beginning of eschatology. Curiously, by its predestinationism, whether of the supralapsarian or infralapsarian kind, Puritanism also swallows up eschatology in protology.

To sum up so far: the first two types – Christ against culture and the Christ of culture – are both cripplingly deficient from the eschatological

[1] See Niebuhr, *Christ and Culture*, p. 95.

point of view. Either the Kingdom of God can never be achieved or its achievement was never necessary in the first place, though its religious or secular substitutes appear to be only too readily realizable. I speak, of course, about the extreme positions. Hidden in the first two types lie certain values – the costliness of witness and discipleship; the obligation of evangelism and the reference of the gospel to every aspect of human life – that are better integrated into one or the other of the three middling attitudes which Niebuhr discerns. All the three mediating types have serious claims to originate in scriptural eschatology or eschatologies.

3   CHRIST ABOVE CULTURE

This third type, which stands on the Christ-of-culture side of centre, is more accurately designated the 'synthetic' view. It emphasizes the positive elements in human nature and culture, while recognizing that even these need to be purified and lifted. Grace comes not to destroy nature and culture but to perfect them. Apart from a protological grounding in the creative Word, this attitude finds a genuinely eschatological support in the Christ event. Particular weight is placed on the incarnation and the resurrection. These are interpreted in organic language as having a universal anthropological, almost biological effect: the whole human race has received an infusion of divine life through the birth of the Son and his incorruptibility in death. He has 'brought life and immortality to light' (2 Tim. 1.10). Even the redemptive work of Christ is viewed medically as a 'sanation' of the body of humanity. The objective happenedness of all this is used to favour the 'already now' over the 'not yet'.

The spirituality corresponding to this synthetic view often bears a strongly intellectual or aesthetic character or both. To mention the intellectual first: it is, I think, no accident that Niebuhr's two star representatives for this attitude are Clement of Alexandria and Thomas Aquinas, both academic theologians. Many of us who are professionally engaged in theology, as students or teachers, find that our whole way of being is thereby affected. Other scholars and scientists who are Christians often see their intellectual pursuits as part of their loving God with the whole mind also. Nevertheless there is here an important distinction to be drawn between *scientia* and *sapientia*.[1] Knowledge must become subservient to that wisdom whose beginning resides in the fear of the Lord. Incidentally, it is quite beside the point for theologians to seek 'academic freedom' in a secular libertarian sense, as though there could be some value-free search for truth in the abstract. As Christian theologians we

[1] See H. A. Oberman, *Contra vanam curiositatem* (Zürich, 1974).

are part of a community of faith which believes that the heart of the matter has been given to us in Christ Jesus. There can be a relative conflict of interpretations among theologians, but at the fundamental level there is simply the faith of the Church confessed in Christ who is Lord, Judge and Saviour. In his own speculation the theologian as sinner may perhaps see only the reflection of himself.

Again, our faith may rightly rejoice in the aesthetic achievements of Christianity. Icons were classically justified on a creational and incarnational basis, and that is proper; yet of the Suffering Servant of the Lord it is written that 'there is no beauty in him that we should desire him', and what we love is, in Charles Wesley's words, 'the dear *disfigured* face'. In Christian spirituality there can be no question of *l'art pour l'art*. There is something of a protological feel about Karl Barth's admiration for Mozart: Barth himself almost sees the end as a return to the beginning in this context.[1] An eschatological spirituality is more likely to be nourished by Bach. A prayer in the Armenian funeral rite reads thus: 'Bring near his spirit, which thou hast consigned and committed into the hand of thy angel, unto the throne of thy holy glory, in company with the other shining souls to rejoice and exult and *circle in the dance around thy holy throne* . . .' In the end-time, it is the *lame* who leap like a deer (Isa. 35.6). The elders and the living creatures fall down before the Lamb *who was slain* (Rev. 5.6–14). We may recall Charles Wesley's Advent hymn 'Lo, he comes with clouds descending':

> Those dear tokens of his passion
> Still his dazzling body bears,
> Cause of endless exultation
> To his ransomed worshippers.
> With what rapture
> Gaze we on those glorious scars.

Here, then, are some clues as to the criteria for an aesthetic spirituality if it is to be genuinely Christian. And this, I sense, is what the Orthodox theologians of the icon mean when they say that a transfiguration takes place in the artist, the work and the beholder.

4   CHRIST AND CULTURE IN PARADOX

Another designation Niebuhr uses for this fourth type is the dualist. It stands on the world-negating side of centre but is not so extreme as Christ against culture. Luther is one of Niebuhr's prize representatives. However they may nuance their interpretations, all Lutherans resonate

[1] K. Barth, (ET) *Church Dogmatics*, III/3 (Edinburgh, T. & T. Clark, 1961), pp. 297–9.

to the polarities of law and gospel, wrath and grace; they know the God who reveals himself in hiddenness and hides himself in revelation (the *sub contraria specie*); they are familiar with the 'two kingdoms', the rule of God's left hand (where he judges or at best preserves humanity against the ravages of sin), and the rule of God's right hand by which he redeems and saves.

The corresponding spirituality is characteristically one of conflict. Biblically, it is epitomized in Rom. 7.15–25, if one takes that passage as referring to the experience of the Christian believer rather than to the apostle's pre-conversion experience now viewed in a Christian light. The deliverance 'from this body of death' is still to come (7.24f), or as 8.23 puts it: 'We ourselves, who have the firstfruits of the Spirit, groan inwardly as we wait for adoption as sons, the redemption of our bodies.' Already now 'there is no condemnation for those who are in Christ Jesus' (8.1: the justification of the believer), but even the Holy Spirit apparently finds it hard work making us put to death the deeds of the body, our mind remaining so set on the flesh (cf. 8.13). 'The life of the Christian,' says the WCC Faith and Order text on *Baptism* at Lutheran insistence, 'is necessarily one of continuing struggle yet also continuing experience of grace'.[1] What Luther said of the theologian he would no doubt have extended to every believer: 'Oratio, meditatio et tentatio (= *Anfechtung*) theologum faciunt': prayer, meditation and temptation make the theologian.

Two evident modern examples of the fourth type of spirituality are in fact Lutherans. Think of Dietrich Bonhoeffer with his refusal of 'cheap grace', his ambiguous return from the USA to Germany in 1939, his maintenance of the 'secret discipline' of prayer amid all the secularity of a world come of age, his simultaneous service in the *Abwehr* and cultivation of ecumenical contacts across the lines of war, his hard-won conviction that the killing of Hitler would be an ethical act in which a Christian might, and perhaps should, participate. There are paradoxes galore in such a spirituality, yet withal a consistency and integrity which has impressed many since his execution (was it or was it not a martyrdom?). The second example is Dag Hammarskjöld, whose *Markings*[2] contain an undeniable mystical streak and yet also declare that 'in our age, the road to holiness necessarily passes through the world of action'. What do we make of a Secretary General of the United Nations who was a 'secret Christian' (W. H. Auden wrote of him: 'It is possible that his lack of participation in the liturgical and sacramental life of a church was a

---

[1] *Baptism, Eucharist and Ministry* (Geneva, WCC, 1982), Baptism, 9.
[2] Dag Hammarskjöld, *Markings*. New York, Knopf; London, Faber, 1964.

deliberate act of self-sacrifice on his part, that, as Secretary General, he felt any public commitment to a particular Christian body would label him as too "Western", but he gives no evidence in his diary of desiring such a commitment') – what do we make, then, of this international civil servant and very private Christian who was killed in mysterious circumstances on a peace mission to the Congo? Both Bonhoeffer and Hammarskjöld figure in the sanctorale of the North American *Lutheran Book of Worship* of 1978.

There is another and very different phenomenon in the history of Christian spirituality which can also be included in this paradoxical fourth type. It, too, rejoins Luther at least in his insistence on 1 Cor. 1.18–31 and 'the folly of the cross'. I refer to those who have seen themselves as 'fools for Christ's sake' (1 Cor. 4.10; cf. 2 Cor. 11–12). In *Perfect Fools*[1] John Saward has sketched the history of this *successio insipientium*, this *successio stultorum propter Christum*, from Syria and Egypt to Russia and Ireland. On the one hand, there have been those who feigned madness in order to show up the folly of the wise, 'Christ's troubadours, jongleurs, and bards', the exponents of holy idiocy and spiritual infancy. Saward cites the continuing tradition in modern Ireland, represented by Mary's Followers of the Cross, a new community of lay men and women who live in poverty and simplicity in the outhouse of a cottage in an Irish-speaking village of Co. Galway, praying, eating and sleeping in one small room.

> Like the holy fools of Russia, Mary's Followers wander the streets of nearby towns simulating madness, carrying bottles on the end of a string and addressing them like little dogs; going into barbers' shops and ordering a glass of Guinness; playing on children's amusements in department stores. In each case, like David, they will say: I will make merry before the Lord, I will make myself yet more contemptible than this, and I will be abased in your eyes.

On the other hand, there have been those who accepted 'real' madness as an opportunity for Christ's power to come to perfection in their weakness (cf. 2 Cor. 12.9), such as the enigmatic Jean-Joseph Surin, who for twenty years suffered a mental illness with many of the symptoms of catatonic schizophrenia and who was one of the most prolific spiritual writers of the seventeenth century.

> Folly for Christ's sake [says Saward] is always eschatological. The holy fool proclaims the conflict between this present world and the world to come . . . The folly of the cross is the wisdom of the world to come.

---

[1] John Saward, *Perfect Fools: Folly for Christ's Sake in Catholic and Orthodox Spirituality*. Oxford and New York, OUP, 1980.

Or as Christos Yannaras has written:

> The fool is the charismatic person who has direct experience of the new reality of the Kingdom of God and undertakes to demonstrate in a prophetic way the antithesis of this present world to the world of the Kingdom.[1]

The charism of folly is shared by the whole Christian community when in worship it experiences that 'sober inebriation' of which St Gregory of Nyssa spoke, when it plays the 'serious game' of which St Bernard of Clairvaux wrote.[2]

A solemn evaluation of folly being difficult, I will address my evaluative remarks in the Lutheran direction. To the *sub contraria specie* of the christological revelation corresponds the 'as though not' of Christian attitudes and conduct (cf. 1 Cor. 7). But the greatest strength of the fourth type, in my opinion, is that it strikes the apocalyptic note of conflict, which a scriptural eschatology will never lack. As Luther recognized:

> With force of arms we nothing can,
> Full soon were we down-ridden;
> But for us fights the proper Man,
> Whom God himself hath bidden.

But the victory does become *ours*. In Christ *we* are 'more than conquerors' (Rom. 8.37). One looks for active signs of victory in the lives of Christians. It is hard to take the *simul justus et peccator* as a total and unremitting paradox whose resolution will come with unprepared suddenness in the final Kingdom. It is hard to see how 'the resurrection of the body' will be a complete *creatio ex nihilo*, if the apostle Paul is correct when he says that 'we must all appear before the judgement seat of Christ, so that each one may receive good or evil, according to what he has done in the body' (2 Cor. 5.10). I find it difficult when, for fear of works-righteousness, Eberhard Jüngel can make such a sharp distinction between *Heil* and *Wohl* as this: 'Where there is the experience that God has done everything for man's salvation (*Heil*), there one cannot do enough for man's temporal well-being (*Wohl*).'[3] I speak as a Methodist; and that brings us to the fifth type. What, then, is there in the 'already now' that will be consummated in the 'not yet'?

---

[1] Quoted from the Greek by Saward, p. 27.
[2] For Gregory and Bernard, see Saward, p. 216. Harvey Cox's *best* book was *The Feast of Fools* (Cambridge, Mass., Harvard University Press, 1969).
[3] In W. Teichart, ed., *Müssen Christen Sozialisten sein?* (Hamburg, Lutherisches Verlagshaus, 1976), p. 21.

5 CHRIST THE TRANSFORMER OF CULTURE

In the fifth type, Niebuhr's heavyweight is Augustine, and some might wish to question whether that very complex saint does in fact play in this favoured team. But John Wesley does properly figure in Niebuhr's line-up here. And certainly Wesley was fond of quoting Augustine's dictum: 'He who made us without ourselves will not save us without ourselves' (*Qui fecit nos sine nobis, non salvabit nos sine nobis*: see Wesley's sermon 'On Working out our own Salvation', I. 1).

The transformationist view rests on a positive doctrine of creation and the incarnation, while yet admitting the radical corruption of humanity. Corruption is the perversion of the good, not intrinsic evil. Conversion and rebirth are needed. That is more radical than the 'purification' which the synthetist will admit, but it is not a question of 'replacement'. The pattern of death and resurrection displayed by the incarnate Christ means, when repeated in history through a dying to sin and living to God in dependence on Christ, at least the beginning of a transformation of human life and culture. The reality of this transformation makes it impossible to remain dualistically within the *simul justus et peccator* as a strict and irresolvable paradox. The still awaited consummation will eternalize the spiritual gains inaugurated in the present life.

The spirituality corresponding to the transformationist attitude is likely to be strongly sacramental in character. The first sacramental model is baptism – most clearly believer's baptism – which is no easy integration and which, if it is a purification, is so only by the radical route of death and resurrection, a conversion and rebirth. From baptism derives penance, whether formally or informally sacramental, which points to the continuing need to struggle against sin but keeps admitted lapses within the perspective of a genuine growth in holiness. As to the Eucharist, its presiding ministers in the Roman rite have been told at their ordination: 'Imitate what you handle (*imitamini quod tractatis*). In as much as you celebrate the mystery of the Lord's death and resurrection, endeavour to mortify all sin in your members and to walk in newness of life.' The propers of the Easter season include prayers for all who have received baptism and communion:

> Grant that the sacraments we have received at Easter
> may continue to live in our hearts and minds.

> Grant that we may imitate and achieve
> what we celebrate and profess.

> Grant that we who have celebrated the Easter ceremonies
> may hold to them in life and conduct.[1]

[1] Author's translation of the Latin. See my *Doxology*, p. 572, n. 1024 for references; and

Sacramental models for spirituality have the advantage of pointing us to the combination of passivity and activity which avoids the extremes of a heaven-storming pursuit of the millennium and a quietistic waiting for Godot. In Latin America, the liveliest of the socially and politically active base communities are grounded in bible study, prayer and the Mass. Gustavo Gutiérrez, the most impressive of the liberation theologians, maintains that faith and theology must be mystical as well as prophetic. He himself is put in the transformist category by his notion that there are not two histories, a sacred and a profane, but only one history, a 'Christo-finalized' history.[1]

The Wesleys' preaching of 'entire sanctification' or 'perfect love' was stimulated and supported by their early and continuing sacramentalism. The perfection[2] they believed attainable in this earthly life was limited. Negatively formulated, it was the condition in which no sinful attitude or action was deliberately entertained or committed. Positively formulated, perfection meant the pure love of God and neighbour, and here room was always left for growth. So very different from Calvin in many ways, the Wesleys agreed with him in the 'third use of the law' as continuing *paraklēsis* and *parainesis* (encouragement and exhortation) for Christians who were 'pressing on toward the goal' (cf. Phil. 3.14).

That was one way of breaking down the false distinction between evangelical precepts, which are incumbent on all, and counsels of perfection, which are for the chosen few.[3] I do not want, however, to end on a negative note against monasticism. At its best, monasticism is not distinct by way of exclusiveness: its distinctiveness is meant as an invitation to all. It does not run counter to John Wesley's saying that there is 'no holiness but social holiness'. After its initial retreat for the sake of organization, monasticism found varying ways of returning to the world for the sake of witness (see pp. 295, 574). Alexander Schmemann writes thus:

> In saving Christian maximalism from reduction, monasticism returned it to the Church in the form it had developed and elaborated. This was a transfer of the 'desert' into the world, a victory of the 'anchorite' idea of withdrawal and

---

then n. 1025 for references to the way in which personal conversion is proposed by some patristic writers as a model for understanding the transformation of the eucharistic bread and wine.

[1] G. Gutiérrez followed his *Theology of Liberation* (ET Maryknoll, N.Y., Orbis, 1973; London, SCM, 1974) with *We Drink from our own Wells: The Spiritual Journey of a People* (ET Maryknoll, N.Y., Orbis, 1984).

[2] See R. Newton Flew, *The Idea of Perfection in Christian Theology* (OUP, 1934).

[3] Florovsky, *Christianity and Culture*, p. 99, rejects the 'double standard'. For a nuanced discussion, see J. Houston, 'Precepts and counsels', in R. W. A. McKinney, ed., *Creation, Christ and Culture: Studies in honour of T. F. Torrance* (Edinburgh, T. & T. Clark, 1976).

renunciation in the very centre of the world. The monastery in the city became a kind of ideal society, a witness and summons to Christian maximalism. It was natural that this ideal society should become a centre of influence upon the world, and on the Church as a whole as well as on her individual members.[1]

Into this category of a transformative witness in the midst of Church and world fit the mendicants and the militants, the Dominicans and the Franciscans, the Jesuits and the (illogically unsacramental) Salvation Army; here, too, is the proper place of that missionary spirituality which has always taken some Christians into new lands for the gospel.

The Orthodox have taken to speaking of a 'liturgy after the Liturgy'.[2] The alternating rhythm and qualitative fusion of the monastic *orare et laborare* is nothing but the sharp focus of the individual and communal vocation to prayer and work which is addressed to all.[3] The dominical and apostolic call to incessant prayer (Luke 18.1; 1 Thess. 5.17f) has always found its predominant interpretation in the spirit of Col. 3.17: 'Do everything, in word and deed, in the name of the Lord Jesus, giving thanks to God the Father through him.'[4] Again, Schmemann says:

> In the early Christian understanding, prayer was not opposed to life or the occupations of life. Prayer penetrated life and consisted above all in a new understanding of life and its occupations, in relating them to the central object of faith – to the Kingdom of God and the Church . . . Work was controlled, enlightened and judged by prayer, it was not opposed to prayer . . . Prayer in the spirit meant above all a constant recollection of this relatedness and subordination of everything in life to the reality of the Kingdom manifested in this world.[5]

The earthly Church is called to become at least the adumbration, and perhaps even the anticipation, of the final Kingdom of God; and it is within that vocation that Christian spirituality is shaped.[6]

---

[1] Schmemann, *Introduction to Liturgical Theology*, p. 112.

[2] I. Bria, ed., *Martyria/Mission* (Geneva, WCC, 1980), pp. 27f., 66–71.

[3] For an exposition of the 'image of God' as the human calling to communion with God, earthly work, and social being, see my *Doxology* (as in note 2, p. 592), ch. 1. See also above, pp. 116–17.

[4] See Josef Gülden, 'Vom unablässigen Beten' in J. G. Plöger, ed., *Gott feiern* (Freiburg, Herder, 1980), pp. 327–36.

[5] Schmemann, *Introduction to Liturgical Theology*, pp. 105f.

[6] For a presentation of Christian spirituality according to a more intricate pattern – the combination of a fivefold credal structure (Trinity, Church, Kingdom) with a series of bipolar tensions and their mediation or resolution – see my lengthy article 'Christian spirituality' in the multi-volume *Encyclopedia of Religion*, ed. Mircea Eliade, forthcoming from Macmillan and Free Press, New York.

INDEXES

The Index of Subjects is not exhaustive, but it is quite comprehensive. It includes references not only to issues and movements, but also to particular persons. If a name appears in the Index of Subjects, the reader may expect the discussion of that figure to be somewhat more substantive than if it were listed only in the Index of Names.

The Index of Names is nearly exhaustive. Most readers will prefer to locate a name in the Index of Subjects first, and to turn to the Index of Names for a more complete listing. Names which describe a movement (e.g. Origenist, Molinism), unless the reference is quite substantive, and names which are used merely anecdotally (as in the case of the more obscure Desert Fathers, or the family quarrels within Jansenism), are not indexed.

The Index of Biblical References does not attempt to index the special sections on the Old and New Testaments; the reader will want to begin there (pp. 47–89). However, the editors felt it would be useful to see how Scripture has been *used* by various writers, both ancient and modern, in order to gain a sense of the *Wirkungsgeschichte* of the biblical text in the history of spirituality.

INDEX OF SUBJECTS

INDEX OF NAMES

INDEX OF BIBLICAL REFERENCES